Doing and Being

Doing and Being

Selected Readings in Moral Philosophy

Joram Graf Haber
Bergen Community College

Macmillan Publishing Company
New York

Maxwell Macmillan Canada
Toronto

Editor: Maggie Barbieri
Production Supervisor: George Carr
Production Manager: Muriel Underwood
Text Designer: Jill Bonar
Cover Designer: Cathleen Norz
Cover Illustration: © Super Stock, Inc., Pierre Auguste Renoir,
Dance at Bougival

This book was set in Palatino by V & M Graphics and was
printed and bound by Book Press. The cover was printed by
New England Book Components.

Macmillan Publishing Company
866 Third Avenue
New York, New York 10022

Macmillan Publishing Company is part of
the Maxwell Communication Group of Companies.

Maxwell Macmillan Canada, Inc.
1200 Eglinton Avenue East
Suite 200
Don Mills, Ontario M3C 3N1

Library of Congress Cataloging-in-Publication Data

Doing and being: selected readings in moral philosophy (compiled by)
    Joram Graf Haber.
        p.   cm.
    ISBN 0–02–348585–X
    1. Ethics.   I. Haber, Joram Graf.
    BJ1012.D55   1993
    170–dc20   91–43924
                                                CIP

Printing: 1 2 3 4 5 6 7   Year: 3 4 5 6 7 8 9

To Lina

Preface

Doing and Being: Selected Readings in Moral Philosophy is an anthology of readings paying homage to the resurgence of interest in virtue-based ethics. Combining classical with contemporary sources, it includes some of the best and most important of the virtue tradition together with its action-based counterpart. The book is designed to serve as the primary text for a one-term course in moral philosophy, but it is rich enough for a one-year course and diverse enough for courses combining theory with practice.

The text is divided into three parts. Part I, "Doing," contains readings concerning theoretical and practical approaches to action-based ethics, readings that are taken from both classical and contemporary sources. Presented here are standard theories such as relativism, egoism, utilitarianism, and Kantianism. Also included are selected readings on practical issues such as animal rights, capital punishment, world hunger, and justice. The article on justice, by John Rawls, also serves as an introduction to social contract theory.

Part III, "Being," is a mirror image of Part I in that it contains readings on theoretical and practical issues taken from both classical and contemporary sources. But its readings concern virtue-based ethics. Thus, the theoretical section offers readings from such sources as Aristotle, Aquinas, Anscombe, and MacIntyre, whereas the practical section considers virtues and vices such as generosity, forgiveness, wickedness, and cruelty.

Part II, "Doing or Being?," is a transitional section asking which of the two approaches holds the most promise for moral philosophy.

All three parts contain the following features: critical examinations of the respective traditions; brief introductions to the readings; reading summaries; questions for discussion; and selected bibliographies. The text also contains selections that have not been widely anthologized. Among these are John M. Taurek's "Should the Numbers Count?"; Christine McKinnon's "Ways of Wrongdoing: A Theory of the Vices"; Annette Baier's "Trust and Antitrust"; and Janet E. Smith's "Moral Character and Abortion."

Two pedagogical issues warrant brief mention. The first concerns the book's organization. Although the text is titled *Doing and Being,* it could as easily be titled *Being and Doing.* The decision to treat action-based before virtue-based issues is mostly arbitrary, yet there is also an instructional tendency to discuss action-based issues first—thus the book's arrangement. At right angles to this issue is the arbitrariness of the placement of readings found in Part II. Some of these selections could easily have been included in Parts I or III.

The second pedagogical issue concerns some readings' difficulty as well as their length. Some very important essays in moral philosophy are both difficult and long, and, in making my selections, I have chosen *not* to exclude a reading merely because of its difficulty or to highly edit the classical selections because of their length. Thus, some readings are complex and long but are included nevertheless because of their importance. Yet many of the readings are judiciously edited and easily accessible to the beginning student—and the introductions to each part presuppose no student background at all. In this way, the text serves well the beginning, the intermediate, and the more advanced student.

J. G. H.

Acknowledgments

I wish to thank a number of people for their suggestions, comments, and other valuable advice. First and foremost, there is Thomas J. Loughran, University of Portland, who provided precious guidance with the selection and editing of articles. I am especially grateful for his having shared with me his wealth of knowledge on the virtues in general and on Aquinas and MacIntyre in particular.

I also wish to thank several of my colleagues at Bergen Community College: Thomas Slaughter, who checked my writing for philosophical accuracy and offered editorial advice; Jean Fox, who combed my writing for comprehension and clarity and whose editorial skills made the text more readable; Michael Orlando, who helped with the writing; and Michael Redmond and Alan Kaufman, who helped me to make some trying decisions. I also wish to thank the students in my ethics classes, Yahav Shoost, in particular, who read and commented on the early drafts and assisted with the research.

In addition to the above, I want to thank William Shaw, San Jose State University, for his advice on writing textbooks in general, and this one in particular, and Dan Montaldi, Gonzaga University, for sharing with me his thoughts on "wickedness," which helped to shape some questions for discussion. I also want to thank those contributors who were especially forthcoming in responding to my inquiries.

Special thanks go to the editorial staff at Macmillan, those who are known to me and those who are not. Of those who are known to me, there is Maggie Barbieri, who was principally responsible for managing the project, and Laura Golden, who kept track of permissions and freed me to do more pleasurable tasks. I also want to thank Helen McInnis, who initially took an interest in publishing the book, and the following reviewers for their encouraging reviews: James M. Hughes, University of South Carolina; Richard T. Lambert, Carroll College; Eric Kraemer, University of Wisconsin–La Crosse; Glenn A. Hartz, The Ohio State University; and Richard A. Mester, Pennsylvania State University–Behrend.

Special thanks also go to Walter S. Wurzburger, Yeshiva University, whose course on ethics inspired in me a love for philosophy in general, and ethics in particular. In many ways, this text would not have been possible without him.

Finally, I want to thank my wife, Lina, to whom this book is dedicated, for her continued support in my philosophical endeavors, and my son, "Shuki," who, at the age of four-and-a-half, is convinced that philosophy has something to do with floss. May he one day understand why I seclude myself behind closed doors and spend endless hours in front of the "imputer."

Contents

Part I Doing

Action-Based Approaches to Moral Philosophy:
Theories and Applications

A. THEORIES

Part II   Doing or Being?

Rival Approaches to Moral Philosophy

Part III   Being

*Virtue-Based Approaches to Moral Philosophy:
Theories and Applications*

A. THEORIES

B. APPLICATIONS

PART I

Doing

Action-Based Approaches to Moral Philosophy: Theories and Applications

A. THEORIES

Action-based approaches to moral philosophy take the central question of ethics as asking, "What should we do when confronted with choices involving right and wrong conduct?" They answer this question by formulating principles of conduct that should govern our actions along with the reasons in support of these principles. Section A of Part I examines some of the more prominent of these action-based approaches or theories. Section B considers applications of the theories to particular moral problems.

Action-Based Theories of Moral Philosophy

Generally speaking, action-based theories are of two kinds—*consequentialist* and *deontological*. Consequentialist theories (or *teleological* theories, as they are sometimes called)[1] assert that the rightness or wrongness of human action is determined solely by reference to the outcome of such action. If the outcome is good, the action is right; if the outcome is bad, the action is wrong. More precisely, consequentialist theories first assert a principle for ranking overall outcomes from best to worst, then assert that the right action in any situation is the one that produces the highest-ranked outcome.

Deontological theories[2] deny what consequentialist theories affirm: that the morality of an action is determined solely by its outcome. For some deontologists, consequences play no role at all in determining right action; for others, consequences are only one of several factors considered. In either version, the morality of an action stems from the intrinsic nature of the action itself or from its conformity with principles of duty.

The disagreement between consequentialists and deontologists is one of the most basic in moral philosophy. To see this, imagine that a friend of yours has committed a crime and has secured your promise never to tell. You then learn that an innocent party has been accused of the crime and you plead with your friend to turn himself in. Your friend refuses and reminds you of your promise. What should you do?

For the consequentialist, the right thing to do in this situation is to break your promise and turn your friend in, because this action will yield the highest-ranked outcome. For the deontologist, by contrast, the right thing to do is to keep your promise, because promises should be kept as a matter of principle.

Of the consequentialist theories that have gained notoriety, the most prominent is *utilitarianism*. Utilitarianism asserts that the rightness or wrongness of human action is determined solely by the outcome of such action. Most utilitarian theories are also *hedonistic*[3] in that the criteria for ranking

---

[1] From the Greek word *telos*, meaning "purpose" or "goal."

[2] From the Greek word *deon*, meaning "that which is binding."

[3] From the Greek word *hedone*, meaning "pleasure" or "delight."

overall outcomes are the happiness or unhappiness of all those affected. Actions themselves have no moral value apart from their ability to influence happiness.

To see in practice how utilitarianism works, consider a case where a person must decide which of two drowning people she should save. One of these people is of no great importance to anyone but his own family. The other is a scientist who is on the verge of discovering a cure for AIDS. According to utilitarianism, saving the scientist is the right action because it is the one most likely to increase happiness for more people.

Utilitarians differ over a host of issues. One major difference concerns the question of whether the principle of utility should apply to acts as opposed to rules. *Act-utilitarians* argue that the principle of utility should apply to acts in particular circumstances. As they see it, certain actions (e.g., lying) may be wrong in one circumstance but right in another, because outcomes can vary. By contrast, *rule-utilitarians* insist on the centrality of rules in determining right action, of a moral code that is established by reference to the principle of utility, with individual actions construed as right insofar as they accord with this code.

In any of its forms, it is hard to deny utilitarianism's appeal. After all, the promotion of happiness and the diminution of suffering have something to do with the morality of actions. Powerful objections have been raised against it, however. One popular objection is that it can lead to the punishment of the innocent. To see this, imagine that the magistrate of a small community is faced with the threat from an uncontrollable mob who demands a culprit for a particular crime. Unless the criminal is produced, the mob promises to wreak vengeance on a vulnerable part of town, causing great damage to both life and property. The magistrate knows that the real culprit is unknown, but he also knows that there is within reach a disreputable person who, though innocent, could easily be framed and thereby quench the mob's thirst for vengeance. Since, under the terms of utilitarianism, an action is right if more people will benefit from it than would from its alternatives, the magistrate would be justified in framing this person, since the guilty party cannot be found and the framing of this person can be kept a secret. But such an action is clearly unjust and thus is a strike against the theory.

Of the deontological theories that have gained notoriety, by far the most prominent is Immanuel Kant's. Kant's theory is so prominent that deontological theories are sometimes referred to as Kantian rather than the other way around. It is not misleading, then, if his theory is treated as representative of deontological theories generally.

Perhaps the best way to understand Kantianism is to contrast it with utilitarianism. For utilitarians, as we have seen, actions are right if they increase happiness and wrong if they do not. For Kant, by contrast, happiness, or the satisfaction of desires, cannot serve as a basis for morality because desires are transient and subject to change. Thus, far from seeing morality as dependent on our whims, Kant sees it as objective and absolute. Consider, for instance, how utilitarians might censure telling a lie that resulted in a great deal of suffering. But by implication they would endorse telling the same lie if it led to an increase of happiness. In Kant's view, however, lying is wrong regardless of the happiness it brings; it is wrong as a matter of principle.[4] Indeed, for Kant, it is because our desires can conflict with our duties that the institution of morality exists at all. Otherwise put, morality would not exist if we always desired what was morally right and never desired what was morally wrong. Accordingly, Kant sees morality as grounded in reason rather than in the fleeting satisfaction of desires.

Having argued, then, that reason is the foundation of morality and that an action is right when it proceeds from principle, Kant puts forward his famous "categorical imperative" as an answer to our earlier question of what we should do when we are confronted with choices involving right and wrong conduct. In perhaps the most celebrated of its three formulations, the categorical imperative tells us: "Act as if the maxim of your action were to become through your will a universal law of nature."

There are two points to be made about this principle. First, the categorical imperative, as its name implies, is an imperative—a command, not a suggestion or bit of advice. Second, it is categorical—absolute, unqualified, not hypothetical. A hypothetical imperative is of the form, "If you want to do y, then you ought to do x"—for example, if you want to go to law school, then you ought to study logic. The categorical imperative, on the other hand, is of the form, "You ought to do x," with no conditions attached to it.

Note that where hypothetical imperatives are concerned, what you ought to do depends logically on what you desire. Should you wish not to go to law school, it would not follow that you ought to study logic. Similarly, should you wish to improve your grades but neglect to study, it would not follow that you ought not to cheat. The point being made is that moral imperatives are unconditional and absolute. "You ought not to murder" is a categorical imperative because murder is wrong without exception. For the utilitarian, by contrast, "You ought not to murder" is a principle of morality only because murder diminishes the happiness of mankind.

In its second formulation, the categorical imperative tells us: "Act in such a way that you treat humanity, whether in your own person or in the person of another, always at the same time as an end and never simply as a means." The basic idea here is that people, by virtue of their rational nature, have an inherent dignity and are entitled to respect. And what this means is that it is morally wrong to treat people as a means to an end (or *simply* as a means to an end), as when we steal from another to further our own interests. In its third and last formulation, the categorical imperative tells us that the moral community is constituted by a kingdom of ends.

The appeal of Kantianism is no doubt its emphasis on human dignity and principled conduct. Notwithstanding, it has been the target of widespread

---

[4] Contemporary deontologists would say that lying is wrong "across all possible worlds"; that is, that there is no imaginable world in which lying is permissible on any grounds.

criticism. Some have argued that its abstract nature fails to provide guidance on substantive issues. Others have argued that it does not take seriously enough the connection between morality and happiness. Perhaps the most biting criticism is that it requires irrational conduct. It is irrational, say its critics, to maintain that "you ought not to do x" when doing x results in a morally best outcome. If, for instance, many people will die unless one person is murdered, the Kantian insists that we not murder the one. But that means that we ought not to bring about the morally best outcome.

Ethical egoism is another moral theory. It asserts that the rightness or wrongness of human action is determined by whether such action satisfies an individual's interests. Although the theory is obviously consequentialist (the morality of an action is determined by its outcome), it differs from utilitarianism in an important way. For the utilitarian, the morality of an action is determined by how it affects everyone involved; for the egoist, the morality of an action is determined by how it affects the agent alone.

At first glance, it is hard to understand the appeal of this theory. For many of us, promoting self-interest is the antithesis of morality. It is in our interest, perhaps, to cheat on our taxes, but it is hard to deny that it is wrong to do so. Furthermore, even if it were not in our interest to cheat on our taxes, that is hardly the reason that it is wrong to do so. Thus, it is important to see how ethical egoists defend their theory against its many detractors.

Many ethical egoists defend their theory first by defending *psychological egoism*. Psychological egoism asserts that selfishness is the mainspring of all human activity and that altruism (love of others) is impossible. This is put forward as an empirical truth about all human beings. Thus, even when it appears that one's behavior is altruistic, the psychological egoist insists that it is but a means of satisfying one's selfish desires.

To see this more clearly, consider the story told about Thomas Hobbes (a proponent of psychological egoism), who was once observed giving money to a beggar. When asked if this kindly gesture did not disprove psychological egoism, Hobbes replied that this gesture *proved* the theory because helping beggars made him feel good.

But if it is true, as psychological egoists say, that all behavior is motivated by selfishness, then it makes no sense to require selfless, or altruistic conduct simply because it does not exist. And if altruistic conduct does not exist, then ethical egoism is the only theory that is logically coherent, however implausible it may at first seem.

Despite the ingenuity of arguments like this, ethical egoism is enormously problematic. Many philosophers are unconvinced, for instance, by the arguments in support of psychological egoism. As they see it, altruism is possible if the intent behind the action is to benefit another even if the agent also benefits. But if this is so, that is, if psychological egoism is false, then the support for ethical egoism is pulled out from under it.

Still another theory that deserves mention is *ethical relativism*. Ethical relativism asserts that the rightness or wrongness of human action is relative to the time and place in which it occurs. Otherwise put, ethical relativism denies that there is a universal moral code that can objectively determine right and wrong conduct. Rather, each society has its own moral code and one is no more valid than another.

Ethical relativists often cite *cultural relativism* in support of their theory. Cultural relativism asserts that, as a matter of empirical fact, different cultures have different moral codes. History and anthropology have documented evidence that many cultures have accepted as moral such practices as human sacrifice, polygamy, slavery, and infanticide. But if this is so, then morality must vary from culture to culture. The same action that is morally wrong in one can be morally right in another.

Ethical relativism is appealing because of our desire to be tolerant and respectful of other cultures. For this reason it has enjoyed considerable popularity, although not among philosophers who believe it does not follow that simply because a practice is accepted as moral by a particular culture it is moral. The Nazi practice of genocide was wrong, it is argued, despite Nazi beliefs to the contrary.

Other moral theories that are intrinsically interesting and deserve to be mentioned include *divine command theory*, *natural law theory*, and *social contract theory*. Briefly, divine command theory asserts that right and wrong conduct are defined in terms of God's will. Right actions are actions of which God approves, wrong actions are those of which God disapproves. Natural law theory asserts that actions are right insofar as they conform to the laws of nature, and wrong otherwise. Social contract theory asserts that right and wrong action are defined by reference to a "social contract" made among human beings before their entrance into political society. Natural law theory and social contract theory receive more extensive treatment in Section B of this part.

Summary of Readings

In the first reading of this section, "Egoism and Moral Scepticism," James Rachels distinguishes psychological egoism from ethical egoism. Psychological egoism, he says, is the view that human beings are selfish in all that they do. Ethical egoism is the view that they *ought* to be selfish in all that they do. Rachels argues against each of these views. Against psychological egoism, he argues that human beings are not always selfish even if they always do what they want to do. If, for instance, one gets pleasure out of helping others, then one is not selfish even though one does what one wants. If, however, one gets pleasure out of frustrating others, then one is selfish. Thus, what makes an act selfish is its object—not whether one wants to do it. Against ethical egoism, Rachels argues that the theory rests on a distorted view of human nature. The welfare of others is sufficient reason to sometimes engage in altruistic conduct.

In "Ethical Relativism," Paul W. Taylor considers the merits of ethical relativism—the view that moral conduct is somehow relative to the norms of a particular society. Taylor begins by noting that those who accept this theory are not always clear about what they mean. They may wish to assert that different societies have different moral codes (descriptive relativism), or that each person ought to do what is dictated by his or her society's code (normative ethical relativism). After examining in detail what these views entail, Taylor concludes that further arguments are needed before we should accept any of them.

In "Quantitative Utilitarianism," Jeremy Bentham puts forward the principle of utility, according to which actions are right when they increase happiness and diminish suffering and wrong when they do not. By "utility," he means the property of producing pleasure or happiness in sentient beings.

As Bentham sees it, deciding whether an action is right or wrong is, in theory, simple. We need only calculate the amount of pleasure it produces and determine whether, on balance, it is pleasurable for all affected. To this end, Bentham provides a "hedonistic calculus" for measuring pleasure—its intensity, duration, certainty, propinquity (nearness), fecundity (tendency to lead to other pleasures), purity (tendency not to be followed be pain), and, most important, its extent (number of persons affected).

For Bentham, the principle of utility is the sole determinant of right and wrong conduct. We need only decide whether an action's utility is more or less than that of any of its alternatives. This holds true regardless of what the action is. Thus, Bentham concludes that if two experiences contain equal amounts of pleasure, then, no matter what other differences there may be between them, neither is preferable to the other. As he put it in a famous quotation, "Quantity of pleasure being equal, pushpin is as good as poetry."

In "Qualitative Utilitarianism," John Stuart Mill, who was taught utilitarianism by his father (who in turned learned it from Bentham), takes issue with Bentham's claim that all pleasures are essentially alike and differ only in degree. As Mill sees it, there is a qualitative difference between certain pleasures. There are higher pleasures, such as one gets from reading Shakespeare, and lower pleasures, such as one gets from playing Nintendo. Thus, in answer to Bentham's famous quotation, Mill put forward his own: "It is better to be a human being dissatisfied than a pig satisfied; better to be a Socrates dissatisfied than a fool satisfied."

Mill was also interested in trying to prove the principle of utility. In a famous passage he argues that whatever is desired is desirable and that, in the final analysis, people desire happiness above all else. Therefore, happiness is the only truly desirable thing, and it should be maximized accordingly.

The next three selections form a trilogy; each criticizes a different aspect of utilitarianism. In "The Experience Machine," Robert Nozick takes issue with the hedonistic component of utilitarianism, arguing against the view that pleasure alone is what matters to us. If that were correct, he says, we would have no objection to being hooked up to a machine that would cause all our favorite sensations. Yet few of us would make this choice. The reason we would refuse, he believes, includes our desire to act in certain ways, to be certain kinds of persons, and to be in contact with reality for better or for worse. And if that is so, then things matter to us for reasons other than that they bring us pleasure.

In "Utilitarianism and Moral Character," Bernard Williams presents two cases in which individuals are required to act in ways that, on utilitarian grounds, violate their sense of integrity. In one case, a man is told that twenty people will be shot unless he himself shoots one of them, in which event the others will go free. The man is appalled by the idea of committing a murder. However, if he takes the utilitarian perspective, "he will regard these feelings just as unpleasant experiences" and thus be obliged to overcome his squeamishness. But this, argues Williams, is morally repugnant because it requires that the man abandon his sense of integrity. Williams' thesis is that utilitarianism cannot account for our deepest convictions and attitudes.

The last of the trilogy, by John M. Taurek, is provocatively titled "Should the Numbers Count?" In it, Taurek takes issue with utilitarianism's "greatest happiness" principle, which asserts that we are obliged to procure the greatest happiness for the greatest number. Otherwise put, the needs of the many outweigh the needs of the few. According to Taurek, this principle is false.

Taurek asks us to imagine six people in need of a lifesaving drug. One of the six needs a massive dose to survive, whereas the remaining five each need only one-fifth of that amount. To whom should we give the drug? For the utilitarian, the answer is obvious: we should divide it among the five because it is worse that five perish and one survive than that one perish and five survive.

Suppose, however, that one of the six (call him David) owns the drug. As Taurek sees it, it would be absurd to try to convince him that it would be worse for the others to die and that he should therefore yield the drug. David would naturally think his own death the worse outcome. Now imagine the drug is ours and that David is our friend. Since it is permissible for David to use the drug for himself, it is also permissible for us to take his perspective and give the drug to him, not to the others. But if this is so, then there is no moral requirement to save the five at the expense of one—no requirement, that is, to save the greatest number.

The next reading, "Morality and the Categorical Imperative," is taken from Immanuel Kant's *Grounding for the Metaphysics of Morals*. Here, Kant argues that the only thing that is good without qualification is a good will, by which he means a will that acts out of respect for the moral law. His point is that when we evaluate the moral worth of an action, we must consider the intention with which the act is performed. If the intention is good, if the agent is motivated by a sense of duty, then the action is good—the agent has a good will.

But how are we to know what our duty is, or what our intent should be? Kant's answer is his famous categorical imperative. The categorical imperative is the absolute rule of morality. It requires that we perform an action only if we could will that anyone else in similar circumstances would do the same thing. In other words, when thinking about doing something, we must ask ourselves, "What if everyone did this?" Kant contends that often an immoral act is an act that makes oneself the exception to a rule.

Having laid the foundation of his theory, Kant then spells out its consequences, the most important of which is that people themselves are the ultimate source of morality. Hence, all people have immeasurable value. This then leads Kant to restate the moral law in a different way: we must, he says, always treat people with respect and never as a means to some end. Finally, he tries to illuminate the moral law from still a third perspective. He suggests that we must always view ourselves as belonging to a community of persons, each of whom creates the laws governing the realm by his or her own actions.

In the final reading of this section, "Kant and the Categorical Imperative," James Rachels reconstructs Kant's central theses and discusses most of the weaknesses that critics of Kant have brought to bear on his theory.

1

Egoism and Moral Scepticism

James Rachels is dean of the School of Humanities at the University of Alabama. He is the author of *The Elements of Moral Philosophy* (1986) and the editor of several books, including *Moral Problems: A Collection of Philosophical Essays* (1979) and *Understanding Moral Philosophy* (1976).

1. Our ordinary thinking about morality is full of assumptions that we almost never question. We assume, for example, that we have an obligation to consider the welfare of other people when we decide what actions to perform or what rules to obey; we think that we must refrain from acting in ways harmful to others, and that we must respect their rights and interests as well as our own. We also assume that people are in fact capable of being motivated by such considerations, that is, that people are not wholly selfish and that they do sometimes act in the interests of others.

Both of these assumptions have come under attack by moral sceptics as long ago as by Glaucon in Book II of Plato's *Republic*. Glaucon recalls the legend of Gyges, a shepherd who was said to have found a magic ring in a fissure opened by an earthquake. The ring would make its wearer invisible and thus would enable him to go anywhere and do anything undetected. Gyges used the power of the ring to gain entry to the Royal Palace where he seduced the Queen, murdered the King, and subsequently seized the throne. Now Glaucon asks us to determine that there are two such rings, one given to a man of virtue and one given to a rogue. The rogue, of course, will use his ring unscrupulously and do anything necessary to increase his own wealth and power. He will recognize no moral constraints on his conduct, and, since the cloak of invisibility will protect him from discovery, he can do anything he pleases without fear of reprisal. So, there will be no end to the mischief he will do. But how will the so-called virtuous man behave? Glaucon suggests that he will behave no better than the rogue: "No one, it is commonly believed, would have such iron strength of mind as to stand fast in doing right or keep his hands off other men's goods, when he could go to the market-place and fearlessly help himself to anything he wanted, enter houses and sleep with any woman he chose, set prisoners free and kill men at his pleasure, and in a word go about among men with the powers of a god. He would behave no better than the other; both would take the same course."[1] Moreover, why shouldn't he? Once he is freed from the fear of reprisal, why shouldn't a man simply do what he pleases, or what he thinks is best for himself? What reason is there for him to continue being "moral" when it is clearly not to his own advantage to do so?

These sceptical views suggested by Glaucon have come to be known as *psychological egoism* and *ethical egoism* respectively. Psychological egoism is the view that all men are selfish in everything that they do, that is, that the only motive from which anyone ever acts is self-interest. On this view, even when men are acting in ways apparently calculated to benefit others, they are actually motivated by the belief that acting in this way is to their own advantage, and if they did not believe this, they would not be doing that action. Ethical egoism is, by contrast, a normative view about how men *ought* to act. It is the view that, regardless of how men do in fact behave, they have no obligation to do anything except what is in their own interests. According to the ethical egoist, a person is always justified in doing whatever is in his own interests, regardless of the effect on others.

Clearly, if either of these views is correct, then "the moral institution of life" (to use Butler's well-turned phrase) is very different than what we normally think. The majority of mankind is grossly deceived about what is, or ought to be, the case, where morals are concerned.

2. Psychological egoism seems to fly in the face of the facts. We are tempted to say: "Of course people act unselfishly all the time. For example, Smith gives up a trip to the country, which he would have enjoyed very much, in order to stay behind and help a friend with his studies, which is a miserable way to pass the time. This is a perfectly clear case of unselfish behavior, and if the psychological egoist thinks that such cases do not occur, then he is just mistaken." Given such obvious instances of "unselfish behavior," what reply can the egoist make? There are two general arguments by which he might try to show that all actions, including those such as the one just outlined, are in fact motivated by self-interest. Let us examine these in turn:

A. The first argument goes as follows. If we describe one person's action as selfish, and another person's action as unselfish, we are overlooking the crucial fact that in both cases, assuming that the action is done voluntarily, *the agent is merely doing what he most wants to do.* If Smith stays behind to help his friend, that only shows that he wanted to help his friend more than he wanted to go to the country. And why should he be praised for his "unselfishness" when he is only doing what he most wants to do? So, since Smith is only doing what he wants to do, he cannot be said to be acting unselfishly.

---

[1] *The Republic of Plato*, translated by F. M. Cornford (Oxford, 1941), p. 45.

This argument is so bad that it would not deserve to be taken seriously except for the fact that so many otherwise intelligent people have been taken in by it. First, the argument rests on the premise that people never voluntarily do anything except what they want to do. But this is patently false; there are at least two classes of actions that are exceptions to this generalization. One is the set of actions which we may not want to do, but which we do anyway as a means to an end which we want to achieve; for example, going to the dentist in order to stop a toothache, or going to work every day in order to be able to draw our pay at the end of the month. These cases may be regarded as consistent with the spirit of the egoist argument, however, since the ends mentioned are wanted by the agent. But the other set of actions are those which we do, not because we want to, nor even because there is an end which we want to achieve, but because we feel ourselves *under an obligation* to do them. For example, someone may do something because he has promised to do it, and thus feels obligated, even though he does not want to do it. It is sometimes suggested that in such cases we do the action because, after all, we want to keep our promises; so, even here, we are doing what we want. However, this dodge will not work: if I have promised to do something, and if I do not want to do it, then it is simply false to say that I want to keep my promise. In such cases we feel conflict precisely because we do *not* want to do what we feel obligated to do. It is reasonable to think that Smith's action falls roughly into this second category: he might stay behind, not because he wants to, but because he feels that his friend needs help.

But suppose we were to concede, for the sake of the argument, that all voluntary action is motivated by the agent's wants, or at least that Smith is so motivated. Even if this were granted, it would not follow that Smith is acting selfishly or from self-interest. For if Smith wants to do something that will help his friend, even when it means forgoing his own enjoyments, that is precisely what makes him *unselfish*. What else could unselfishness be, if not wanting to help others? Another way to put the same point is to say that it is the *object* of a want that determines whether it is selfish or not. The mere fact that I am acting on *my* wants does not mean that I am acting selfishly; that depends on *what it is* that I want. If I want only my own good, and care nothing for others, then I am selfish; but if I also want other people to be well-off and happy, and if I act on *that* desire, then my action is not selfish. So much for this argument.

B. The second argument for psychological egoism is this. Since so-called unselfish actions always produce a sense of self-satisfaction in the agent,[2] and since this sense of satisfaction is a pleasant state of consciousness, it follows that the point of the action is really to achieve a pleasant state of consciousness, rather than to bring about any good for others. Therefore, the action is "unselfish" only at a superficial level of analysis. Smith will feel much better with himself for having stayed to help his friend—if he had gone to the

---

[2] Or, as it is sometimes said, "It gives him a clear conscience," or "He couldn't sleep at night if he had done otherwise," or "He would have been ashamed of himself for not doing it," and so on.

country, he would have felt terrible about it—and that is the real point of the action. According to a well-known story, this argument was once expressed by Abraham Lincoln:

> Mr. Lincoln once remarked to a fellow-passenger on an old-time mud-coach that all men were prompted by selfishness in doing good. His fellow-passenger was antagonizing this position when they were passing over a corduroy bridge that spanned a slough. As they crossed this bridge they espied an old razor-backed sow on the bank making a terrible noise because her pigs had got into the slough and were in danger of drowning. As the old coach began to climb the hill, Mr. Lincoln called out, "Driver, can't you stop just a moment?" Then Mr. Lincoln jumped out, ran back, and lifted the little pigs out of the mud and water and placed them on the bank. When he returned, his companion remarked: "Now, Abe, where does selfishness come in on this little episode?" "Why, bless your soul, Ed, that was the very essence of selfishness. I should have had no peace of mind all day had I gone on and left that suffering old sow worrying over those pigs. I did it to get peace of mind, don't you see?"[3]

This argument suffers from defects similar to the previous one. Why should we think that merely because someone derives satisfaction from help-ing others this makes him selfish? Isn't the unselfish man precisely the one who *does* derive satisfaction from helping others, while the selfish man does not? If Lincoln "got peace of mind" from rescuing the piglets, does this show him to be selfish, or, on the contrary, doesn't it show him to be compassionate and good-hearted? (If a man were truly selfish, why should it bother his con-science that *others* suffer—much less pigs?) Similarly, it is nothing more than shabby sophistry to say, because Smith takes satisfaction in helping his friend, that he is behaving selfishly. If we say this rapidly, while thinking about some-thing else, perhaps it will sound all right; but if we speak slowly, and pay attention to what we are saying, it sounds plain silly.

Moreover, suppose we ask *why* Smith derives satisfaction from helping his friend. The answer will be, it is because Smith cares for him and wants him to succeed. If Smith did not have these concerns, then he would take no pleasure in assisting him; and these concerns, as we have already seen, are the marks of unselfishness, not selfishness. To put the point more generally: if we have a positive attitude toward the attainment of some goal, then we may derive sat-isfaction from attaining that goal. But the *object* of our attitude is *the attainment of that goal*; and we must want to attain the goal *before* we can find any satis-faction in it. We do not, in other words, desire some sort of "pleasurable con-sciousness" and then try to figure out how to achieve it; rather, we desire all sorts of different things—money, a new fishing-boat, to be a better chess-player, to get a promotion in our work, etc.—and because we desire these things, we derive satisfaction from attaining them. And so, if someone desires

---

[3] Frank C. Sharp, *Ethics* (New York, 1928), pp. 74–75. Quoted from the Springfield (Ill.) *Monitor* in the *Outlook*, vol. 56, p. 1059.

the welfare and happiness of another person, he will derive satisfaction from that; but this does not mean that this satisfaction is the object of his desire, or that he is in any way selfish on account of it.

It is a measure of the weakness of psychological egoism that these insupportable arguments are the ones most often advanced in its favor. Why, then, should anyone ever have thought it a true view? Perhaps because of a desire for theoretical simplicity: In thinking about human conduct, it would be nice if there were some simple formula that would unite the diverse phenomena of human behavior under a single explanatory principle, just as simple formulae in physics bring together a great many apparently different phenomena. And since it is obvious that self-regard is an overwhelmingly important factor in motivation, it is only natural to wonder whether all motivation might not be explained in these terms. But the answer is clearly No; while a great many human actions are motivated entirely or in part by self-interest, only by a deliberate distortion of the facts can we say that all conduct is so motivated. This will be clear, I think, if we correct three confusions which are commonplace. The exposure of these confusions will remove the last traces of plausibility from the psychological egoist thesis.

The first is the confusion of selfishness with self-interest. The two are clearly not the same. If I see a physician when I am feeling poorly, I am acting in my own interest but no one would think of calling me "selfish" on account of it. Similarly, brushing my teeth, working hard at my job, and obeying the law are all in my self-interest but none of these are examples of selfish conduct. This is because selfish behavior is behavior that ignores the interests of others, in circumstances in which their interests ought not to be ignored. This concept has a definite evaluative flavor; to call someone "selfish" is not just to describe his action but to condemn it. Thus, you would not call me selfish for eating a normal meal in normal circumstances (although it may surely be in my self-interest); but you would call me selfish for hoarding food while others about are starving.

The second confusion is the assumption that every action is done *either* from self-interest or from other-regarding motives. Thus, the egoist concludes that if there is no such thing as genuine altruism then all actions must be done from self-interest. But this is certainly a false dichotomy. The man who continues to smoke cigarettes, even after learning about the connection between smoking and cancer, is surely not acting from self-interest, not even by his own standards—self-interest would dictate that he quit smoking—and he is not acting altruistically either. He *is*, no doubt, smoking for the pleasure of it, but all that this shows is that undisciplined pleasure-seeking and acting from self-interest are very different. This is what led Butler to remark that "The thing to be lamented is, not that men have so great regard to their own good or interest in the present world, for they have not enough."[4]

---

[4] *The Works of Joseph Butler*, edited by W. E. Gladstone (Oxford, 1896), vol. II, p. 26. It should be noted that most of the points I am making against psychological egoism were first made by Butler. Butler made all the important points; all that is left for us is to remember them.

The last two paragraphs show (*a*) that it is false that all actions are selfish, and (*b*) that it is false that all actions are done out of self-interest. And it should be noted that these two points can be made, and were, without any appeal to putative examples of altruism.

The third confusion is the common but false assumption that a concern for one's own welfare is incompatible with any genuine concern for the welfare of others. Thus, since it is obvious that everyone (or very nearly everyone) does desire his own well-being, it might be thought that no one can really be concerned with others. But again, this is false. There is no inconsistency in desiring that everyone, including oneself *and* others, be well-off and happy. To be sure, it may happen on occasion that our own interests conflict with the interests of others, and in these cases we will have to make hard choices. But even in these cases we might sometimes opt for the interests of others, especially when the others involved are our family or friends. But more importantly, not all cases are like this: sometimes we are able to promote the welfare of others when our own interests are not involved at all. In these cases not even the strongest self-regard need prevent us from acting considerately toward others.

Once these confusions are cleared away, it seems to me obvious enough that there is no reason whatever to accept psychological egoism. On the contrary, if we simply observe people's behavior with an open mind, we may find that a great deal of it is motivated by self-regard, but by no means all of it; and that there is no reason to deny that "the moral institution of life" can include a place for the virtue of beneficence.[5]

3. The ethical egoist would say at this point, "Of course it is possible for people to act altruistically, and perhaps many people do act that way—but there is no reason why they *should* do so. A person is under no obligation to do anything except what is in his own interests."[6] This is really quite a radical doctrine. Suppose I have an urge to set fire to some public building (say, a department store) just for the fascination of watching the spectacular blaze: according to this view, the fact that several people might be burned to death provides no reason whatever why I should not do it. After all, this only concerns *their* welfare, not my own, and according to the ethical egoist the only person I need think of is myself.

Some might deny that ethical egoism has any such monstrous consequences. They would point out that it is really to my own advantage not to set the fire—for, if I do that I may be caught and put into prison (unlike Gyges, I have no magic ring for protection). Moreover, even if I could avoid being caught it is still to my advantage to respect the rights and interests of others, for it is to my advantage to live in a society in which people's rights and inter-

---

[5] The capacity for altruistic behavior is not unique to human beings. Some interesting experiments with rhesus monkeys have shown that these animals will refrain from operating a device for securing food if this causes other animals to suffer pain. See Masserman, Wechkin, and Terris, "'Altruistic' Behavior in Rhesus Monkeys," *The American Journal of Psychiatry*, vol. 121 (1964), 584–585.

[6] I take this to be the view of Ayn Rand, in so far as I understand her confusing doctrine.

ests are respected. Only in such a society can I live a happy and secure life; so, in acting kindly toward others, I would merely be doing my part to create and maintain the sort of society which it is to my advantage to have.[7] Therefore, it is said, the egoist would not be such a bad man; he would be as kindly and considerate as anyone else, because he would see that it is to his own advantage to be kindly and considerate.

This is a seductive line of thought, but it seems to me mistaken. Certainly it is to everyone's advantage (including the egoist's) to preserve a stable society where people's interests are generally protected. But there is no reason for the egoist to think that merely because *he* will not honor the rules of the social game, decent society will collapse. For the vast majority of people are not egoists, and there is no reason to think that they will be converted by his example—especially if he is discreet and does not unduly flaunt his style of life. What this line of reasoning shows is not that the egoist himself must act benevolently, but that he must encourage *others* to do so. He must take care to conceal from public view his own self-centered method of decision-making, and urge others to act on precepts very different from those on which he is willing to act.

The rational egoist, then, cannot advocate that egoism be universally adopted by everyone. For he wants a world in which his own interests are maximized; and if other people adopted the egoistic policy of pursuing their own interests to the exclusion of his interests, as he pursues his interests to the exclusion of theirs, then such a world would be impossible. So he himself will be an egoist, but he will want others to be altruists.

This brings us to what is perhaps the most popular "refutation" of ethical egoism current among philosophical writers—the argument that ethical egoism is at bottom inconsistent because it cannot be universalized.[8] The argument goes like this:

To say that any action or policy of action is *right* (or that it *ought* to be adopted) entails that it is right for *anyone* in the same sort of circumstances. I cannot, for example, say that it is right for me to lie to you, and yet object when you lie to me (provided, of course, that the circumstances are the same). I cannot hold that it is all right for me to drink your beer and then complain when you drink mine. This is just the requirement that we be consistent in our evaluations: it is a requirement of logic. Now it is said that ethical egoism cannot meet this requirement because, as we have already seen, the egoist would not want others to act in the same way that he acts. Moreover, suppose he *did* advocate the universal adoption of egoistic policies: he would be saying to Peter, "You ought to pursue your own interests even if it means destroying Paul"; and he would be saying to Paul, "You ought to pursue your own interests even if it means destroying Peter." The attitudes expressed in these two recommendations seem clearly inconsistent—he is urging the advancement of

---

[7] Cf. Thomas Hobbes, *Leviathan* (London, 1651), chap. 17.
[8] See, for example, Brian Medlin, "Ultimate Principles and Ethical Egoism," *Australasian Journal of Philosophy*, vol. 35 (1957), 111–118; and D. H. Monro, *Empiricism and Ethics* (Cambridge, 1967), chap. 16.

Peter's interest at one moment, and countenancing their defeat at the next. Therefore, the argument goes, there is no way to maintain the doctrine of ethical egoism as a consistent view about how we ought to act. We will fall into inconsistency whenever we try.

What are we to make of this argument? Are we to conclude that ethical egoism has been refuted? Such a conclusion, I think, would be unwarranted; for I think that we can show, contrary to this argument, how ethical egoism can be maintained consistently. We need only to interpret the egoist's position in a sympathetic way: we should say that he has in mind a certain kind of world which he would prefer over all others; it would be a world in which his own interests were maximized, regardless of the effects on other people. The egoist's primary policy of action, then, would be to act in such a way as to bring about, as nearly as possible, this sort of world. Regardless of however morally reprehensible we might find it, there is nothing *inconsistent* in someone's adopting this as his ideal and acting in a way calculated to bring it about. And if someone did adopt this as his ideal, then he would not advocate universal egoism; as we have already seen, he would want other people to be altruists. So, if he advocates any principles of conduct for the general public, they will be altruistic principles. This would not be inconsistent; on the contrary, it would be perfectly consistent with his goal of creating a world in which his own interests are maximized. To be sure, he would have to be deceitful; in order to secure the good will of others, and a favorable hearing for his exhortations to altruism, he would have to pretend that he was himself prepared to accept altruistic principles. But again, that would be all right; from the egoist's point of view, this would merely be a matter of adopting the necessary means to the achievement of his goal—and while we might not approve of this, there is nothing inconsistent about it. Again, it might be said: "He advocates one thing, but does another. Surely *that's* inconsistent." But it is not; for what he advocates and what he does are both calculated as means to an end (the *same* end, we might note); and as such, he is doing what is rationally required in each case. Therefore, contrary to the previous argument, there is nothing inconsistent in the ethical egoist's view. He cannot be refuted by the claim that he contradicts himself.

Is there, then, no way to refute the ethical egoist? If by "refute" we mean show that he has made some *logical* error, the answer is that there is not. However, there is something more that can be said. The egoist challenge to our ordinary moral convictions amounts to a demand for an explanation of why we should adopt certain policies of action, namely policies in which the good of others is given importance. We can give an answer to this demand, albeit an indirect one. The reason one ought not to do actions that would hurt other people is: other people would be hurt. The reason one ought to do actions that would benefit other people is: other people would be benefited. This may at first seem like a piece of philosophical sleight-of-hand, but it is not. The point is that the welfare of human beings is something that most of us value *for its own sake*, and not merely for the sake of something else. Therefore, when *further* reasons are demanded for valuing the welfare of human beings, we cannot point to anything further to satisfy this demand. It is not that we have no reason for pursuing these policies, but that our reason *is* that these policies are for the good of human beings.

So: if we are asked "Why shouldn't I set fire to this department store?" one answer would be "Because if you do, people may be burned to death." This is a complete, sufficient reason which does not require qualification or supplementation of any sort. If someone seriously wants to know why this action shouldn't be done, that's the reason. If we are pressed further and asked the sceptical question "But why shouldn't I do actions that will harm others?" we may not know what to say—but this is because the questioner has included in his question the very answer we would like to give: "Why shouldn't you do actions that will harm others? Because, doing those actions would harm others."

The egoist, no doubt, will not be happy with this. He will protest that *we* may accept this as a reason, but *he* does not. And here the argument stops: there are limits to what can be accomplished by argument, and if the egoist really doesn't care about other people—if he honestly doesn't care whether they are helped or hurt by his actions—then we have reached those limits. If we want to persuade him to act decently toward his fellow humans, we will have to make our appeal to such other attitudes as he does possess, by threats, bribes, or other cajolery. That is all that we can do.

Though some may find this situation distressing (we would like to be able to show that the egoist is just *wrong*), it holds no embarrassment for common morality. What we have come up against is simply a fundamental requirement of rational action, namely, that the existence of reasons for action always depends on the prior existence of certain attitudes in the agent. For example, the fact that a certain course of action would make the agent a lot of money is a reason for doing it only if the agent wants to make money; the fact that practicing at chess makes one a better player is a reason for practicing only if one wants to be a better player; and so on. Similarly, the fact that a certain action would help the agent is a reason for doing the action only if the agent cares about his own welfare, and the fact that an action would help others is a reason for doing it only if the agent cares about others. In this respect ethical egoism and what we might call ethical altruism are in exactly the same fix: both require that the agent *care* about himself, or about other people, before they can get started.

So a nonegoist will accept "It would harm another person" as a reason not to do an action simply because he cares about what happens to that other person. When the egoist says that he does *not* accept that as a reason, he is saying something quite extraordinary. He is saying that he has no affection for friends or family, that he never feels pity or compassion, that he is the sort of person who can look on scenes of human misery with complete indifference, so long as he is not the one suffering. Genuine egoists, people who really don't care at all about anyone other than themselves, are rare. It is important to keep this in mind when thinking about ethical egoism; it is easy to forget just how fundamental to human psychological makeup the feeling of sympathy is.

Indeed, a man without any sympathy at all would scarcely be recognizable as a man; and that is what makes ethical egoism such a disturbing doctrine in the first place.

4. There are, of course, many different ways in which the sceptic might challenge the assumptions underlying our moral practice. In this essay I have discussed only two of them, the two put forward by Glaucon in the passage that I cited from Plato's *Republic*. It is important that the assumptions underlying our moral practice should not be confused with particular judgments made within that practice. To defend one is not to defend the other. We may assume—quite properly, if my analysis has been correct—that the virtue of beneficence does, and indeed should, occupy an important place in "the moral institution of life"; and yet we may make constant and miserable errors when it comes to judging when and in what ways this virtue is to be exercised. Even worse, we may often be able to make accurate moral judgments, and know what we ought to do, but not do it. For these ills, philosophy alone is not the cure.

2

Ethical Relativism

Paul W. Taylor is a professor emeritus of philosophy, Brooklyn College, where he has taught for forty years. He is the author of *Normative Discourse* (1961), *Respect for Nature: A Theory of Environmental Ethics* (1986), and *Principles of Ethics: An Introduction* (1975). He has also edited two books of readings.

One of the most commonly held opinions in ethics is that all moral norms are *relative* to particular cultures. The rules of conduct that are applicable in one society, it is claimed, do not apply to the actions of people in another society. Each community has its own norms, and morality is entirely a matter of conforming to the standards and rules accepted in one's own culture. To put it simply: What is right is what my society approves of; what is wrong is what my society disapproves of.

This view raises doubts about the whole enterprise of normative ethics. For if right and wrong are completely determined by the given moral code of a particular time and place, and if moral codes vary from time to time and place to place, it would seem that there are no unchanging cross-cultural principles that could constitute an ideal ethical system applicable to everyone. Since the purpose of normative ethics is to construct and defend just such a universal system of principles, belief in the relativity of moral norms denies the possibility of normative ethics. It is therefore important at the outset to examine the theory of ethical relativism.

The question raised by the ethical relativist may be expressed thus: Are moral values absolute, or are they relative? We may understand this question as asking, Are there any moral standards and rules of conduct that are universal (applicable to all mankind) or are they all culture-bound (applicable only to the members of a particular society or group)? Even when the question is interpreted in this way, however, it still remains unclear. For those who answer the question by claiming that all moral values are relative or culture-bound may be expressing any one of three different ideas. They may, first, be making an empirical or factual assertion. Or secondly, they may be making a normative claim. . . . The term "ethical relativism" has been used to refer to any . . . of these . . . positions. In order to keep clear the differences among them, the following terminology will be used. We shall call the first position "descriptive relativism," the second "normative ethical relativism.". . .

Descriptive Relativism

Certain facts about the moral values of different societies and about the way an individual's values are dependent on those of his society have been taken as empirical evidence in support of the claim that all moral values are relative to the particular culture in which they are accepted. These facts are cited by the relativist as reasons for holding a general theory about moral norms, namely, that no such norms are universal. This theory is what we shall designate "descriptive relativism." It is a factual or empirical theory because it holds that, as a matter of historical and sociological fact, no moral standard or rule of conduct has been universally recognized to be the basis of moral obligation. According to the descriptive relativist there are no moral norms common to all cultures. Each society has its own view of what is morally right and wrong and these views vary from society to society because of the differences in their moral codes. Thus it is a mistake to think there are common norms that bind all mankind in one moral community.

Those who accept the position of descriptive relativism point to certain facts as supporting evidence for their theory. These facts may be conveniently summed up under the following headings:

1. The facts of cultural variability.
2. Facts about the origin of moral beliefs and moral codes.
3. The fact of ethnocentrism.

(1) The facts of cultural variability are now so familiar to everyone that they need hardly be enumerated in detail. We all know from reading anthropologists' studies of primitive cultures how extreme is the variation in the customs and taboos, the religions and moralities, the daily habits and the general outlook on life to be found in the cultures of different peoples. But we need not go beyond our own culture to recognize the facts of variability. Historians of Western civilization have long pointed out the great differences in the beliefs and values of people living in different periods. Great differences have also been discovered among the various socioeconomic classes existing within the social structure at any one time. Finally, our own contemporary world reveals a tremendous variety of ways of living. No one who dwells in a modern city can escape the impact of this spectrum of different views on work and play, on family life and education, on what constitutes personal happiness, and on what is right and wrong.

(2) When we add to these facts of cultural and historical variability the recent psychological findings about how the individual's values reflect those of his own social group and his own time, we may begin to question the universal validity of our own values. For it is now a well-established fact that no moral values or beliefs are inborn. All our moral attitudes and judgments are learned from the social environment. Even our deepest convictions about justice and the rights of man are originally nothing but the "introjected" or "internalized" views of our culture, transmitted to us through our parents and teachers. Our very conscience itself is formed by the internalizing of the sanctions used by our society to support its moral norms. When we were told in childhood what we ought and ought not to do, and when our parents expressed their approval and disapproval of us for what we did, we were being taught the standards and rules of conduct accepted in our society. The result of this learning process (sometimes called "acculturation") was to ingrain in us a set of attitudes about our own conduct, so that even when our parents were no longer around to guide us or to blame us, we would guide or blame ourselves by thinking, "This is what I ought to do"; "That would be wrong to do"; and so on. If we then did something we believed was wrong we would feel guilty about it, whether or not anyone caught us at it or punished us for it.

It is this unconscious process of internalizing the norms of one's society through early childhood training that explains the origin of an individual's moral values. If we go beyond this and ask about the origin of society's values, we find a long and gradual development of traditions and customs which have given stability to the society's way of life and whose obscure beginnings lie in ritual magic, taboos, tribal ceremonies, and practices of religious worship. Whether we are dealing with the formation of an individual's conscience or the development of a society's moral code, then, the origin of a set of values seems to have little or nothing to do with rational, controlled thought. Neither individuals nor societies originally acquire their moral beliefs by means of logical reasoning or through the use of an objective method for gaining knowledge.

(3) Finally, the descriptive relativist points out another fact about people and their moralities that must be acknowledged. This is the fact that most people are ethnocentric (group centered). They think not only that there is but one true morality for all mankind, but that the one true morality is their own. They are convinced that the moral code under which they grew up and which formed their deepest feelings about right and wrong—namely, the moral code of their own society—is the only code for anyone to live by. Indeed, they often refuse even to entertain the possibility that their own values might be false or that another society's code might be more correct, more enlightened, or more advanced than their own. Thus ethnocentrism often leads to intolerance and dogmatism. It causes people to be extremely narrow-minded in their ethical outlook, afraid to admit any doubt about a moral issue, and unable to take a detached, objective stance regarding their own moral beliefs. Being absolutely

certain that their beliefs are true, they can think only that those who disagree with them are in total error and ignorance on moral matters. Their attitude is: We are advanced, they are backward. We are civilized, they are savages.

It is but a short step from dogmatism to intolerance. Intolerance is simply dogmatism in action. Because the moral values of people directly affect their conduct, those who have divergent moral convictions will often come into active conflict with one another in the area of practical life. Each will believe he alone has the true morality and the other is living in the darkness of sin. Each will see the other as practicing moral abominations. Each will then try to force the other to accept the truth, or at least will not allow the other to live by his own values. The self-righteous person will not tolerate the presence of "shocking" acts which he views with outraged indignation. Thus it comes about that no differences of opinion on moral matters will be permitted within a society. The ethnocentric society will tend to be a closed society, as far as moral belief and practice are concerned.

The argument for descriptive relativism, then, may be summarized as follows. Since every culture varies with respect to its moral rules and standards, and since each individual's moral beliefs—including his inner conviction of their absolute truth—have been learned within the framework of his own culture's moral code, it follows that there are no universal moral norms. If a person believes there are such norms, this is to be explained by his ethnocentrism, which leads him to project his own culture's norms upon everyone else and to consider those who disagree with him either as innocent but "morally blind" people or as sinners who do not want to face the truth about their own evil ways.

In order to assess the soundness of this argument it is necessary to make a distinction between (a) specific moral standards and rules, and (b) ultimate moral principles. Both (a) and (b) can be called "norms," and it is because the descriptive relativist often overlooks this distinction that his argument is open to doubt. A specific moral standard (such as personal courage or trustworthiness) functions as a criterion for judging whether and to what degree a person's character is morally good or bad. A specific rule of conduct (such as "Help others in time of need" or "Do not tell lies for one's own advantage") is a prescription of how people ought or ought not to act. It functions as a criterion for judging whether an action is right or wrong. In contrast with specific standards and rules, an ultimate moral principle is a universal proposition or statement about the conditions that must hold if a standard or rule is to be used as a criterion for judging *any* person or action. Such a principle will be of the form: Standard S or rule R applies to a person or action if and only if condition C is fulfilled. An example of an ultimate moral principle is that of utility. . . . The principle of utility may be expressed thus: A standard or rule applies to a person or action if, and only if, the use of the standard or rule in the actual guidance of people's conduct will result in an increase in everyone's happiness or a decrease in everyone's unhappiness.

Now it is perfectly possible for an ultimate moral principle to be consistent with a variety of specific standards and rules as found in the moral codes of different societies. For if we take into account the traditions of a culture, the beliefs about reality and the attitudes toward life that are part of each culture's world-outlook, and if we also take into account the physical or geographical setting of each culture, we will find that a standard or rule which increases people's happiness in one culture will not increase, but rather decrease, people's happiness in another. In one society, for example, letting elderly people die when they can no longer contribute to economic production will be necessary for the survival of everyone else. But another society may have an abundant economy that can easily support people in their old age. Thus the principle of utility would require that in the first society the rule "Do not keep a person alive when he can no longer produce" be part of its moral code, and in the second society it would require a contrary rule. In this case the very same kind of action that is wrong in one society will be right in another. Yet there is a single principle that makes an action of that kind wrong (in one set of circumstances) and another action of that kind right (in a different set of circumstances). In other words, the reason why one action is wrong and the other is right is based on one and the same principle, namely utility.

Having in mind this distinction between specific standards and rules on the one hand and ultimate moral principles on the other, what can we say about the argument for descriptive relativism given above? It will immediately be seen that the facts pointed out by the relativist as evidence in support of his theory do not show that ultimate moral principles are relative or culture-bound. They show only that specific standards and rules are relative or culture-bound. The fact that different societies accept different norms of good and bad, right and wrong, is a fact about the standards and rules that make up the various moral codes of those societies. Such a fact does not provide evidence that there is no single ultimate principle which, explicitly or implicitly, every society appeals to as the final justifying ground for its moral code. For if there were such a common ultimate principle, the actual variation in moral codes could be explained in terms of the different world-outlooks, traditions, and physical circumstances of the different societies.

Similarly, facts about ethnocentrism and the causal dependence of an individual's moral beliefs upon his society's moral code do not count as evidence against the view that there is a universal ultimate principle which everyone would refer to in giving a final justification for his society's standards and rules, if he were challenged to do so. Whether there is such a principle and if there is, what sort of conditions it specifies for the validity of specific standards and rules, are questions still to be explored. But the facts cited by the descriptive relativist leave these questions open. We may accept those facts and still be consistent in affirming a single universal ultimate moral principle.

Normative Ethical Relativism

The statement, "What is right in one society may be wrong in another," is a popular way of explaining what is meant by the "relativity of morals." It is usually contrasted with "ethical universalism," taken as the view that "right and wrong do not vary from society to society." These statements are ambiguous, however, and it is important for us to be mindful of their ambiguity. For they may be understood either as factual claims or as normative claims, and it makes a great deal of difference which way they are understood. . . .

When it is said that what is right in one society may be wrong in another, this may be understood to mean that what is *believed* to be right in one society is *believed* to be wrong in another. And when it is said that moral right and wrong vary from society to society, this may be understood to mean that different moral norms are adopted by different societies, so that an act which fulfills the norms of one society may violate the norms of another. If this is what is meant, then we are here being told merely of the cultural variability of specific standards and rules, which we have already considered in connection with descriptive relativism.

But the statement, "What is right in one society may be wrong in another," may be interpreted in quite a different way. It may be taken as a normative claim rather than as a factual assertion. Instead of asserting the unsurprising fact that what is believed to be right in one society is believed to be wrong in another, it expresses the far more radical and seemingly paradoxical claim that what *actually is* right in one society may *actually be* wrong in another. According to this view, moral norms are to be considered valid only within the society which has adopted them as part of its way of life. Such norms are not to be considered valid outside that society. The conclusion is then drawn that it is not legitimate to judge people in other societies by applying the norms of one's own society to their conduct. This is the view we shall designate "normative ethical relativism." In order to be perfectly clear about what it claims, we shall examine two ways in which it can be stated, one focusing our attention upon moral judgments, the other on moral norms.

With regard to moral judgments, normative ethical relativism holds that two *apparently* contradictory statements can both be true. The argument runs as follows. Consider the two statements:

(1) It is wrong for unmarried women to have their faces unveiled in front of strangers.

(2) It is not wrong for . . . (as above).

Here it seems as if there is a flat contradiction between two moral judgments, so that if one is true the other must be false. But the normative ethical relativist holds that they are both true, because the statements as given in (1) and (2) are incomplete. They should read as follows:

(3) It is wrong for unmarried women *who are members of society S* to have their faces unveiled in front of strangers.

(4) It is not wrong for unmarried women *outside of society S* to have their faces unveiled in front of strangers.

Statements (3) and (4) are not contradictories. To assert one is not to deny the other. The normative ethical relativist simply translates all moral judgments of the form "Doing act X is right" into statements of the form "Doing X is right when the agent is a member of society S." The latter statement can then be seen to be consistent with statements of the form "Doing X is wrong when the agent is not a member of society S."

The normative ethical relativist's view of moral norms accounts for the foregoing theory of moral judgments. A moral norm, we have seen, is either a standard used in a judgment of good and bad character or a rule used in a judgment of right and wrong conduct. Thus a person is judged to be good insofar as he fulfills the standard, and an action is judged to be right or wrong according to whether it conforms to or violates the rule. Now when a normative ethical relativist says that moral norms vary from society to society, he does not intend merely to assert the fact that different societies have adopted different norms. He is going beyond descriptive relativism and is making a normative claim. He is denying any universal validity to moral norms. He is saying that a moral standard or rule is correctly applicable only to the members of the particular society which has adopted the standard or rule as part of its actual moral code. He therefore thinks it is illegitimate to judge the character or conduct of those outside the society by such a standard or rule. Anyone who uses the norms of one society as the basis for judging the character or conduct of persons in another society is consequently in error.

It is not that a normative ethical relativist necessarily believes in *tolerance* of other people's norms. Nor does his position imply that he grants others the *right* to live by their own norms, for he would hold a relativist view even about tolerance itself. A society whose code included a rule of tolerance would be right in tolerating others, while one that denied tolerance would be right (relative to its own norm of intolerance) in prohibiting others from living by different norms. The normative ethical relativist would simply say that *we* should not judge the tolerant society to be any better than the intolerant one, for this would be applying our own norm of tolerance to other societies. Tolerance, like any other norm, is culture-bound. Anyone who claims that every society has a *right* to live by its own norms, provided that it respects a similar right in other societies, is an ethical universalist, since he holds at least one norm valid for all societies, namely, the right to practice a way of life without interference from others. And he deems this universal norm a valid one, whether or not every society does in fact accept it.

If the normative ethical relativist is challenged to prove his position, he may do either of two things. On the one hand, he may try to argue that his position follows from, or is based on, the very same facts that are cited by the descriptive relativist as evidence for *his* position. Or, on the other hand, he may turn for support to metaethical considerations. Putting aside the second move . . . , let us look more closely at the first.

The most frequent argument given in defense of normative ethical relativism is that, if the facts pointed out by the descriptive relativist are indeed true, then we must accept normative ethical relativism as the only position consistent with those facts. For it seems that if each person's moral judgments are formed within the framework of the norms of his own culture and historical epoch, and if such norms vary among cultures and epochs, it would follow necessarily that it is unwarranted for anyone to apply his own norms to conduct in other societies and times. To do so would be ethonocentrism, which is, as the descriptive relativist shows, a kind of blind, narrow-minded dogmatism. To escape the irrationality of being ethnocentric, we need but realize that the only norms one may legitimately apply to any given group are the ones accepted by that group. Since different peoples accept different norms, there are no universal norms applicable to everyone throughout the world. Now, to say that there are no universal norms applicable worldwide is to commit oneself to normative ethical relativism. Thus, the argument concludes, normative ethical relativism follows from the facts of descriptive relativism.

Is this a valid argument? Suppose one accepts the facts pointed out by the descriptive relativist. Must he then also accept normative ethical relativism? Let us examine some of the objections that have been raised to this argument. In the first place, it is claimed that the facts of cultural variability do not, *by themselves*, entail normative ethical relativism. The reason is that it is perfectly possible for someone to accept those facts and deny normative ethical relativism without contradicting himself. No matter how great may be the differences in the moral beliefs of different cultures and in the moral norms they accept, it is still possible to hold that some of these beliefs are true and others false, or that some of the norms are more correct, justified, or enlightened than others. The fact that societies differ about what is right and wrong does not mean that one society may not have better reasons for holding its views than does another. After all, just because two people (or two groups of people) disagree about whether a disease is caused by bacteria or by evil spirits does not lead to the conclusion that there is no correct or enlightened view about the cause of the disease. So it does not follow from the fact that two societies differ about whether genocide is right that there is no correct or enlightened view about this moral matter.

A similar argument can be used with regard to the second set of facts asserted by the descriptive relativist. No contradiction is involved in affirming that all moral beliefs come from the social environment and denying normative ethical relativism. The fact that a belief is learned from one's society does not mean that it is neither true nor false, or that if it is true, its truth is "relative" to the society in which it was learned. All of our beliefs, empirical ones no less than moral ones, are learned from our society. We are not born with any innate beliefs about chemistry or physics; we learn these only in our schools. Yet this does not make us skeptical about the universal validity of these sciences. So the fact that our moral beliefs come from our society and are learned in our homes and schools has no bearing on their universal validity. The origin or cause of a person's *acquiring* a belief does not determine whether the *content* of the belief is true or false, or even whether there are good grounds for his accepting that content to be true or false.

If it is claimed that our moral beliefs are based on attitudes or feelings culturally conditioned in us from childhood, the same point can still be made. Suppose, for example, that a person who believes slavery is wrong feels disapproval, dislike, or even abhorrence towards the institution of slavery. His negative attitude, which has undoubtedly been influenced by the value system of his culture, may be contrasted with a positive stance (approval, liking, admiring) of someone brought up in an environment where slave owning was accepted. Here are positive and negative attitudes toward slavery, each being causally conditioned by the given cultural environment. It does not follow from this that the two are equally justified, or that neither can be justified. The question of whther a certain attitude toward slavery is justified or unjustified depends on whether good reason can be given *for* anyone taking the one attitude and *against* anyone taking the other. This question requires the exercise of our reasoning powers. Exactly how we can justify attitudes, or show them to be unjustified, is a complex problem. . . . But the mere fact that the attitudes which underlie moral beliefs are all learned from the social environment leaves open the question of what attitudes an intelligent, rational, and well-informed person would take toward a given action or social practice.

The same kind of argument also holds with respect to the third fact of descriptive relativism: ethnocentrism. People who are ethnocentric *believe* that the one true moral code is that of their own society. But this leaves open the question, Is their belief true or false? Two people of different cultures, both ethnocentric but with opposite moral beliefs, may each think his particular moral norms are valid for everyone; however, this has no bearing on whether either one—or neither one—is correct. We must inquire independently into the possibility of establishing the universal validity of a set of moral norms, regardless of who might or might not believe them to be universally true.

It should be noted that these various objections to the first argument for normative ethical relativism, even if sound, are not sufficient to show that normative ethical relativism is false. They only provide reasons for rejecting one argument in support of that position. To show that the position is false, it would be necessary to give a sound argument in defense of ethical universalism. . . . It is only if one or more of these arguments proves acceptable that normative ethical relativism is refuted. . . .

3

Quantitative Utilitarianism

Jeremy Bentham (1748–1832), although a distinguished philosopher, was primarily interested in social reform. A leader in a group called the Philosophical Radicals (out of which the British Liberal Party later developed), he successfully modernized Britain's political and social institutions. Shortly after the publication of his *An Introduction to the Principles of Morals and Legislation* (1789), the following verse appeared, which sums up the points on which morals and legislation are said to rest:

> *Intense, long, certain, speedy, fruitful, pure—*
> Such marks in *pleasures* and in *pains* endure.
> Such pleasures seek, if *private* be thy end:
> If it be *public*, wide let them *extend*.
> Such *pains* avoid, whichever be thy view:
> If pains *must* come, let them *extend* to few.

Nature has placed mankind under the governance of two sovereign masters, *pain* and *pleasure*. It is for them alone to point out what we ought to do, as well as to determine what we shall do. On the one hand the standard of right and wrong, on the other the chain of causes and effects, are fastened to their throne. They govern us in all we do, in all we say, in all we think: every effort we can make to throw off our subjection, will serve but to demonstrate and confirm it. In words a man may pretend to abjure their empire: but in reality he will remain subject to it all the while. The *principle of utility* recognises this subjection, and assumes it for the foundation of that system, the object of which is to rear the fabric of felicity by the hands of reason and of law. Systems which attempt to question it, deal in sounds instead of sense, in caprice instead of reason, in darkness instead of light.

But enough of metaphor and declamation: it is not by such means that moral science is to be improved.

. . . The principle of utility is the foundation of the present work: it will be proper therefore at the outset to give an explicit and determinate account of what is meant by it. By the principle of utility is meant that principle which approves or disapproves of every action whatsoever, according to the tendency which it appears to have to augment or diminish the happiness of the party whose interest is in question: or, what is the same thing in other words, to promote or to oppose that happiness. I say of every action whatsoever; and therefore not only of every action of a private individual, but of every measure of government.

. . . By utility is meant that property in any object, whereby it tends to produce benefit, advantage, pleasure, good, or happiness, (all this in the present case comes to the same thing) or (what comes again to the same thing) to prevent the happening of mischief, pain, evil, or unhappiness to the party whose interest is considered: if that party be the community in general, then the happiness of the community: if a particular individual, then the happiness of that individual.

. . . The interest of the community is one of the most general expressions that can occur in the phraseology of morals: no wonder that the meaning of it is often lost. When it has a meaning, it is this. The community is a fictitious *body*, composed of the individual persons who are considered as constituting as it were its *members*. The interest of the community then is, what?—the sum of the interests of the several members who compose it.

. . . It is in vain to talk of the interest of the community, without understanding what is the interest of the individual. A thing is said to promote the interest, or to be *for* the interest, of an individual, when it tends to add to the sum total of his pleasures: or, what comes to the same thing, to diminish the sum total of his pains.

. . . An action then may be said to be conformable to the principle of utility, or, for shortness sake, to utility, (meaning with respect to the community at large) when the tendency it has to augment the happiness of the community is greater than any it has to diminish it.

. . . A measure of government (which is but a particular kind of action, performed by a particular person or persons) may be said to be conformable to or dictated by the principle of utility, when in like manner the tendency which it has to augment the happiness of the community is greater than any which it has to diminish it.

. . . When an action, or in particular a measure of government, is supposed by a man to be conformable to the principle of utility, it may be convenient, for the purposes of discourse, to imagine a kind of law or dictate, called a law or dictate of utility: and to speak of the action in question, as being conformable to such law or dictate.

. . . A man may be said to be a partizan of the principle of utility, when the approbation or disapprobation he annexes to any action, or to any measure, is determined by and proportioned to the tendency which he conceives it to have to augment or to diminish the happiness of the community: or in other words, to its conformity or unconformity to the laws or dictates of utility.

... Of an action that is conformable to the principle of utility one may always say either that it is one that ought to be done, or at least that it is not one that ought not to be done. One may say also, that it is right it should be done; at least that it is not wrong it should be done: that it is a right action; at least that it is not a wrong action. When thus interpreted, the words *ought*, and *right* and *wrong*, and others of that stamp, have a meaning: when otherwise, they have none.

... Has the rectitude of this principle been ever formally contested? It should seem that it had, by those who have not known what they have been meaning. Is it susceptible of any direct proof? it should seem not: for that which is used to prove every thing else, cannot itself be proved: a chain of proofs must have their commencement somewhere. To give such proof is as impossible as it is needless.

... Not that there is or ever has been that human creature breathing, however stupid or perverse, who has not on many, perhaps on most occasions of his life, deferred to it. By the natural constitution of the human frame, on most occasions of their lives men in general embrace this principle, without thinking of it: if not for the ordering of their own actions, yet for the trying of their own actions, as well as of those of other men. There have been, at the same time, not many, perhaps, even of the most intelligent, who have been disposed to embrace it purely and without reserve. There are even few who have not taken some occasion or other to quarrel with it, either on account of their not understanding always how to apply it, or on account of some prejudice or other which they were afraid to examine into, or could not bear to part with. For such is the stuff that man is made of: in principle and in practice, in a right track and in a wrong one, the rarest of all human qualities is consistency.

... When a man attempts to combat the principle of utility, it is with reasons drawn, without his being aware of it, from that very principle itself. His arguments, if they prove any thing, prove not that the principle is *wrong*, but that, according to the applications he supposes to be made of it, it is *misapplied*. Is it possible for a man to move the earth? Yes; but he must first find out another earth to stand upon.

... To disprove the propriety of it by arguments is impossible; but, from the causes that have been mentioned, or from some confused or partial view of it, a man may happen to be disposed not to relish it. Where this is the case, if he thinks the settling of his opinions on such a subject worth the trouble, let him take the following steps, and at length, perhaps, he may come to reconcile himself to it.

1. Let him settle with himself, whether he would wish to discard this principle altogether; if so, let him consider what it is that all his reasonings (in matters of politics especially) can amount to?

2. If he would, let him settle with himself, whether he would judge an act without any principle, or whether there is any other he would judge an act by?

3. If there be, let him examine and satisfy himself whether the principle he thinks he has found is really any separate intelligible principle; or whether it

be not a mere principle in words, a kind of phrase, which at bottom expresses neither more nor less than the mere averment of his own unfounded sentiments; that is, what in another person he might be apt to call caprice?

4. If he is inclined to think that his own approbation or disapprobation, annexed to the idea of an act, without any regard to its consequences, is a sufficient foundation for him to judge and act upon, let him ask himself whether his sentiment is to be a standard of right and wrong, with respect to every other man, or whether every man's sentiment has the same privilege of being a standard to itself?

5. In the first case, let him ask himself whether his principle is not despotical, and hostile to all the rest of human race?

6. In the second case, whether it is not anarchial, and whether at this rate there are not as many different standards of right and wrong as there are men? and whether even to the same man, the same thing, which is right to-day, may not (without the least change in its nature) be wrong to-morrow? and whether the same thing is not right and wrong in the same place at the same time? and in either case, whether all argument is not at an end? and whether, when two men have said, "I like this," and "I don't like it," they can (upon such a principle) have any thing more to say?

7. If he should have said to himself, No: for that the sentiment which he proposes as a standard must be grounded on reflection, let him say on what particulars the reflection is to turn? if on particulars having relation to the utility of the act, then let him say whether this is not deserting his own principle, and borrowing assistance from that very one in opposition to which he sets it up: or if not on those particulars, on what other particulars?

8. If he should be for compounding the matter, and adopting his own principle in part, and the principle of utility in part, let him say how far he will adopt it?

9. When he has settled with himself where he will stop, then let him ask himself how he justifies to himself the adopting it so far? and why he will not adopt it any farther?

10. Admitting any other principle than the principle of utility to be a right principle, a principle that it is right for a man to pursue; admitting (what is not true) that the word *right* can have a meaning without reference to utility, let him say whether there is any such thing as a *motive* that a man can have to pursue the dictates of it: if there is, let him say what that motive is, and how it is to be distinguished from those which enforce the dictates of utitility: if not, then lastly let him say what it is this other principle can be good for? . . .

. . . It has been shown that the happiness of the individuals, of whom a community is composed, that is their pleasures and their security, is the end and the sole end which the legislator ought to have in view: the sole standard, in conformity to which each individual ought, as far as depends upon the legislator, to be *made* to fashion his behaviour. But whether it be this or any thing else that is to be *done*, there is nothing by which a man can ultimately be *made* to do it, but either pain or pleasure. Having taken a general view of these two grand objects (*viz.* pleasure, and what comes to the same thing, immunity from pain) in the character of *final* causes; it will be necessary to take a view of pleasure and pain itself, in the character of *efficient* causes or means.

... There are four distinguishable sources from which pleasure and pain are in use to flow: considered separately, they may be termed the *physical,* the *political,* the *moral,* and the *religious*: and inasmuch as the pleasures and pains belonging to each of them are capable of giving a binding force to any law or rule of conduct, they may all of them be termed *sanctions.*

... If it be in the present life, and from the ordinary course of nature, not purposely modified by the interposition of the will of any human being, nor by any extraordinary interposition of any superior invisible being, that the pleasure or the pain takes place or is expected, it may be said to issue from or to belong to the *physical sanction.*

... If at the hands of a *particular* person or set of persons in the community, who under names correspondent to that of *judge,* are chosen for the particular purpose of dispensing it, according to the will of the sovereign or supreme ruling power in the state, it may be said to issue from the *political sanction.*

... If at the hands of such *chance* persons in the community, as the party in question may happen in the course of his life to have concerns with, according to each man's spontaneous disposition, and not according to any settled or concerted rule, it may be said to issue from the *moral* or *popular sanction.*

... If from the immediate hand of a superior invisible being, either in the present life, or in a future, it may be said to issue from the *religious sanction.*

... Pleasures or pains which may be expected to issue from the *physical, political,* or *moral* sanctions, must all of them be expected to be experienced, if ever, in the *present* life: those which may be expected to issue from the *religious* sanction, may be expected to be experienced either in the *present* life or in a *future.* . . .

... Pleasures then, and the avoidance of pains, are the *ends* which the legislator has in view: it behoves him therefore to understand their *value.* Pleasures and pains are the *instruments* he has to work with: it behoves him therefore to understand their force, which is again, in other words, their value.

... To a person considered by *himself,* the value of a pleasure or pain considered by *itself,* will be greater or less, according to the four following circumstances:

1. Its *intensity.*
2. Its *duration.*
3. Its *certainty* or *uncertainty.*
4. Its *propinquity* or *remoteness.*

... These are the circumstances which are to be considered in estimating a pleasure or a pain considered each of them by itself. But when the value of any pleasure or pain is considered for the purpose of estimating the tendency of any *act* by which it is produced, there are two other circumstances to be taken into the account; these are,

5. Its *fecundity*, or the chance it has of being followed by sensations of the *same* kind: that is, pleasures, if it be a pleasure: pains, if it be a pain.

6. Its *purity*, or the chance it has of not being followed by sensations of the *opposite* kind: that is, pains, if it be a pleasure: pleasures, if it be a pain.

These two last, however, are in strictness scarcely to be deemed properties of the pleasure or the pain itself; they are not, therefore, in strictness to be taken into the account of the value of that pleasure or that pain. They are in strictness to be deemed properties only of the act, or other event, by which such pleasure or pain has been produced; and accordingly are only to be taken into the account of the tendency of such act or such event.

. . . To a *number* of persons, with reference to each of whom the value of a pleasure or a pain is considered, it will be greater or less, according to seven circumstances: to wit, the six preceding ones; *viz.*

1. Its *intensity*.
2. Its *duration*.
3. Its *certainty* or *uncertainty*.
4. Its *propinquity* or *remoteness*.
5. Its *fecundity*.
6. Its *purity*.

And one other; to wit:

7. Its *extent;* that is, the number of persons to whom it *extends* or (in other words) who are affected by it.

. . . To take an exact account then of the general tendency of any act, by which the interests of a community are affected, proceed as follows. Begin with any one person of those whose interests seem most immediately to be affected by it: and take an account,

1. Of the value of each distinguishable *pleasure* which appears to be produced by it in the *first* instance.

2. Of the value of each *pain* which appears to be produced by it in the *first* instance.

3. Of the value of each pleasure which appears to be produced by it *after* the first. This constitutes the *fecundity* of the first *pleasure* and the *impurity* of the first *pain*.

4. Of the value of each *pain* which appears to be produced by it after the first. This constitutes the *fecundity* of the first *pain*, and the *impurity* of the first pleasure.

5. Sum up all the values of all the *pleasures* on the one side, and those of all the pains on the other. The balance, if it be on the side of pleasure, will give the *good* tendency of the act upon the whole, with respect to the interests of that *individual* person; if on the side of pain, the *bad* tendency of it upon the whole.

6. Take an account of the *number* of persons whose interests appear to be concerned; and repeat the above process with respect to each. *Sum up* the numbers expressive of the degrees of *good* tendency, which the act has, with respect to each individual, in regard to whom the tendency of it is *good* upon the whole: do this again with respect to each individual, in regard to whom

the tendency of it is *good* upon the whole: do this again with respect to each individual, in regard to whom the tendency of it is *bad* upon the whole. Take the *balance*; which, if on the side of *pleasure*, will give the general *good tendency* of the act, with respect to the total number or community of individuals concerned; if on the side of pain, the general *evil tendency*, with respect to the same community.

... It is not to be expected that this process should be strictly pursued previously to every moral judgment, or to every legislative or judicial operation. It may, however, be always kept in view: and as near as the process actually pursued on these occasions approaches to it, so near will such process approach to the character of an exact one.

... The same process is alike applicable to pleasure and pain, in whatever shape they appear: and by whatever denomination they are distinguished: to pleasure, whether it be called *good* (which is properly the cause or instrument of pleasure) or *profit* (which is distant pleasure, or the cause or instrument of distant pleasure,) or *convenience*, or *advantage, benefit, emolument, happiness*, and so forth: to pain, whether it be called *evil*, (which corresponds to *good*) or *mischief*, or *inconvenience*, or *disadvantage*, or *loss*, or *unhappiness*, and so forth.

... Nor is this a novel and unwarranted, any more than it is a useless theory. In all this there is nothing but what the practice of mankind, wheresoever they have a clear view of their own interest, is perfectly conformable to. An article of property, an estate in land, for instance, is valuable, on what acount? On account of the pleasures of all kinds which it enables a man to produce, and what comes to the same thing the pains of all kinds which it enables him to avert. But the value of such an article of property is universally understood to rise or fall according to the length or shortness of the time which a man has in it: the certainty or uncertainty of its coming into possession: and the nearness or remoteness of the time at which, if at all, it is to come into possession. As to the *intensity* of the pleasures which a man may derive from it, this is never thought of, because it depends upon the use which each particular person may come to make of it; which cannot be estimated till the particular pleasures he may come to derive from it, or the particular pains he may come to exclude by means of it, are brought to view. For the same reason, neither does he think of the *fecundity* or *purity* of those pleasures. . . .

4

Qualitative Utilitarianism

John Stuart Mill (1806–1873) was the son of James Mill—a contemporary and colleague of Jeremy Bentham. His early education was directed exclusively by his father and included such extraordinary feats as studying Greek at age three and reading the *History* of Herodotus (as well as works of Plato, Hume, and Gibbons) before the age of eight. A philosopher in the Empiricist tradition, he published works on logic, scientific method, political philosophy, and ethics. Among his important works are *A System of Logic* (1843), *On Liberty* (1859), and *Utilitarianism* (1863), from which the following selection is taken.

The creed which accepts as the foundation of morals "utility" or the "greatest happiness principle" holds that actions are right in proportion as they tend to promote happiness; wrong as they tend to produce the reverse of happiness. By happiness is intended pleasure and the absence of pain; by unhappiness, pain and the privation of pleasure. To give a clear view of the moral standard set up by the theory, much more requires to be said; in particular, what things it includes in the ideas of pain and pleasure, and to what extent this is left an open question. But these supplementary explanations do not affect the theory of life on which this theory of morality is grounded—namely, that pleasure and freedom from pain are the only things desirable as ends; and that all desirable things (which are as numerous in the utilitarian as in any other scheme) are desirable either for pleasure inherent in themselves or as means to the promotion of pleasure and the prevention of pain.

Now such a theory of life excites in many minds, and among them in some of the most estimable in feeling and purpose, inveterate dislike. To suppose that life has (as they express it) no higher end than pleasure—no better and nobler object of desire and pursuit—they designate as utterly mean and groveling, as a doctrine worthy only of swine, to whom the followers of Epicurus were, at a very early period, contemptuously likened; and modern holders of the doctrine are occasionally made the subject of equally polite comparisons by its German, French, and English assailants.

Reprinted with permission of Macmillan Publishing Company from *Utilitarianism* by John Stuart Mill, pp. 10–15 and 44–49.

When thus attacked, the Epicureans have always answered that it is not they, but their accusers, who represent human nature in a degrading light, since the accusation supposes human beings to be capable of no pleasures except those of which swine are capable. If this supposition were true, the charge could not be gainsaid, but would then be no longer an imputation; for if the sources of pleasure were precisely the same to human beings and to swine, the rule of life which is good enough for the one would be good enough for the other. The comparison of the Epicurean life to that of beasts is felt as degrading, precisely because a beast's pleasures do not satisfy a human being's conceptions of happiness. Human beings have faculties more elevated than the animal appetites and, when once made conscious of them, do not regard anything as happiness which does not include their gratification. I do not, indeed, consider the Epicureans to have been by any means faultless in drawing out their scheme of consequences from the utilitarian principle. To do this in any sufficient manner, many Stoic, as well as Christian, elements require to be included. But there is no known Epicurean theory of life which does not assign to the pleasures of the intellect, of the feelings and imagination, and of the moral sentiments a much higher value as pleasures than to those of mere sensation. It must be admitted, however, that utilitarian writers in general have placed the superiority of mental over bodily pleasures chiefly in the greater permanency, safety, uncostliness, etc., of the former—that is, in their circumstantial advantages rather than in their intrinsic nature. And on all these points utilitarians have fully proved their case; but they might have taken the other and, as it may be called, higher ground with entire consistency. It is quite compatible with the principle of utility to recognize the fact that some kinds of pleasure are more desirable and more valuable than others. It would be absurd that, while in estimating all other things quality is considered as well as quantity, the estimation of pleasure should be supposed to depend on quantity alone.

If I am asked what I mean by difference of quality in pleasures, or what makes one pleasure more valuable than another, merely as a pleasure, except its being greater in amount, there is but one possible answer. Of two pleasures, if there be one to which all or almost all who have experience of both give a decided preference, irrespective of any feeling of moral obligation to prefer it, that is the more desirable pleasure. If one of the two is, by those who are competently acquainted with both, placed so far above the other that they prefer it, even though knowing it to be attended with a greater amount of discontent, and would not resign it for any quantity of the other pleasure which their nature is capable of, we are justified in ascribing to the preferred enjoyment a superiority in quality so far outweighing quantity as to render it, in comparison, of small account.

Now it is an unquestionable fact that those who are equally acquainted with and equally capable of appreciating and enjoying both do give a most marked preference to the manner of existence which employs their higher faculties. Few human creatures would consent to be changed into any of the lower animals for a promise of the fullest allowance of a beast's pleasures; no intelligent human being would consent to be a fool, no instructed person would be an ignoramus, no person of feeling and conscience would be selfish and base, even though they should be persuaded that the fool, the dunce, or the rascal is better satisfied with his lot than they are with theirs. They would not resign what they possess more than he for the most complete satisfaction of all the desires which they have in common with him. If they ever fancy they would, it is only in cases of unhappiness so extreme that to escape from it they would exchange their lot for almost any other, however undesirable in their own eyes. A being of higher faculties requires more to make him happy, is capable probably of more acute suffering, and certainly accessible to it at more points, than one of an inferior type; but in spite of these liabilities, he can never really wish to sink into what he feels to be a lower grade of existence. . . . Whoever supposes that this preference takes place at a sacrifice of happiness—that the superior being, in anything like equal circumstances, is not happier than the inferior—confounds the two very different ideas of happiness and content. It is indisputable that the being whose capacities of enjoyment are low has the greatest chance of having them fully satisfied; and a highly endowed being will always feel that any happiness which he can look for, as the world is constituted, is imperfect. But he can learn to bear its imperfections, if they are at all bearable; and they will not make him envy the being who is indeed unconscious of the imperfections, but only because he feels not at all the good which those imperfections qualify. It is better to be a human being dissatisfied than a pig satisfied; better to be Socrates dissatisfied than a fool satisfied. And if the fool, or the pig, are of a different opinion, it is because they only know their own side of the question. The other party to the comparison knows both sides.

. . . From this verdict of the only competent judges, I apprehend there can be no appeal. On a question which is the best worth having of two pleasures, or which of two modes of existence is the most grateful to the feelings, apart from its moral attributes and from its consequences, the judgment of those who are qualified by knowledge of both, or, if they differ, that of the majority among them, must be admitted as final. And there needs be the less hesitation to accept this judgment respecting the quality of pleasures, since there is no other tribunal to be referred to even on the question of quantity. What means are there of determining which is the acutest of two pains, or the intensest of two pleasurable sensations, except the general suffrage of those who are familiar with both? Neither pains nor pleasures are homogeneous, and pain is always heterogeneous with pleasure. What is there to decide whether a particular pleasure is worth purchasing at the cost of a particular pain, except the feelings and judgment of the experienced? When, therefore, those feelings and judgment declare the pleasures derived from the higher faculties to be preferable *in kind*, apart from the question of intensity, to those of which the animal nature, disjoined from the higher faculties, is susceptible, they are entitled on this subject to the same regard. . . .

It has already been remarked that questions of ultimate ends do not admit of proof, in the ordinary acceptation of the term. To be incapable of proof by reasoning is common to all first principles, to the first premises of our knowledge, as well as to those of our conduct. But the former, being matters of fact, may be the subject of a direct appeal to the faculties which judge of fact—namely, our senses and our internal consciousness. Can an appeal be made to the same faculties on questions of practical ends? Or by what other faculty is cognizance taken of them?

Questions about ends are, in other words, questions what things are desirable. The utilitarian doctrine is that happiness is desirable, and the only thing desirable, as an end; all other things beings only desirable as means to that end. What ought to be required of this doctrine, what conditions is it requisite that the doctrine should fulfill—to make good its claim to be believed?

The only proof capable of being given that an object is visible is that people actually see it. The only proof that a sound is audible is that people hear it; and so of the other sources of our experience. In like manner, I apprehend, the sole evidence it is possible to produce that anything is desirable is that people do actually desire it. If the end which the utilitarian doctrine proposes to itself were not, in theory and in practice, acknowledged to be an end, nothing could ever convince any person that it was so. No reason can be given why the general happiness is desirable, except that each person, so far as he believes it to be attainable, desires his own happiness. This, however, being a fact, we have not only all the proof which the case admits of, but all which it is possible to require, that happiness is a good, that each person's happiness is a good to that person, and the general happiness, therefore, a good to the aggregate of all persons. Happiness has made out its title as *one* of the ends of conduct and, consequently, one of the criteria of morality.

But it has not, by this alone, proved itself to be the sole criterion. To do that, it would seem, by the same rule, necessary to show, not only that people desire happiness, but that they never desire anything else. Now it is palpable that they do desire things which, in common language, are decidedly distinguished from happiness. They desire, for example, virtue and the absence of vice no less really than pleasure and the absence of pain. The desire of virtue is not as universal, but it is as authentic a fact as the desire of happiness. And hence the opponents of the utilitarian standard deem that they have a right to infer that there are other ends of human action besides happiness, and that happiness is not the standard of approbation and disapprobation.

But does the utilitarian doctrine deny that people desire virtue, or maintain that virtue is not a thing to be desired? The very reverse. It maintains not only that virtue is to be desired, but that it is to be desired disinterestedly, for itself. Whatever may be the opinion of utilitarian moralists as to the original conditions by which virtue is made virtue, however they may believe (as they do) that actions and dispositions are only virtuous because they promote another end than virtue, yet this being granted, and it having been decided, from considerations of this description, what *is* virtuous, they not only place virtue at the very head of the things which are good as means to the ultimate end, but they also recognize as a psychological fact the possibility of its being to the individual, a good in itself, without looking to any end beyond it; and hold that the mind is not in a right state, not in a state conformable to utility, not in the state most conducive to the general happiness, unless it does love virtue in this manner—as a thing desirable in itself, even although, in the individual instance, it should not produce those other desirable consequences which it tends to produce, and on account of which it is held to be virtue. This opinion is not, in the smallest degree, a departure from the happiness principle. The ingredients of happiness are very various, and each of them is desirable in itself, and not merely when considered as swelling an aggregate. The principle of utility does not mean that any given pleasure, as music, for instance, or any given exemption from pain, as for example health, is to be looked upon as means to a collective something termed happiness, and to be desired on that account. They are desired and desirable in and for themselves; besides being means, they are a part of the end. Virtue, according to the utilitarian doctrine, is not naturally and originally part of the end, but it is capable of becoming so; and in those who live it disinterestedly it has become so, and is desired and cherished, not as a means to happiness, but as a part of their happiness.

To illustrate this further, we may remember that virtue is not the only thing originally a means, and which if it were not a means to anything else would be and remain indifferent, but which by association with what it is a means to comes to be desired for itself, and that too with the utmost intensity. What, for example, shall we say of the love of money? There is nothing originally more desirable about money than about any heap of glittering pebbles. Its worth is solely that of the things which it will buy; the desires for other things than itself, which it is a means of gratifying. Yet the love of money is not only one of the strongest moving forces of human life, but money is, in many cases, desired in and for itself; the desire to possess it is often stronger than the desire to use it, and goes on increasing when all the desires which point to ends beyond it, to be compassed by it, are falling off. It may, then, be said truly that money is desired not for the sake of an end, but as part of the end. From being a means to happiness, it has come to be itself a principal ingredient of the individual's conception of happiness. The same may be said of the majority of the great objects of human life: power, for example, or fame, except that to each of these there is a certain amount of immediate pleasure annexed, which has at least the semblance of being naturally inherent in them—a thing which cannot be said of money. Still, however, the strongest natural attraction, both of power and of fame, is the immense aid they give to the attainment of our other wishes; and it is the strong association thus generated between them and all our objects of desire which gives to the direct desire of them the intensity it often assumes, so as in some characters to surpass in strength all other desires. In these cases the means have become a part of the end, and a more important part of it than any of the things which they are means to. What was once desired as an instrument for the attainment of happiness has come to be desired for its own sake. In being desired for its own sake it is, however, desired as *part* of happiness. The person is made, or thinks he would be made, happy by its mere possession; and is made unhappy by failure to obtain it. The desire of it is not a different thing from the desire of happiness any more than the love of music or the desire of health. They are included in happiness. They are some of the elements of which the desire of happiness is made up. Happiness is not an abstract idea but a concrete whole; and these are some of its parts. And the utilitarian standard sanctions and approves their being so. Life would be a poor thing, very ill provided with sources of happiness, if there were not this provision of nature by which things originally indifferent, but conducive to, or otherwise associated with, the satisfaction of our primitive desires, become in themselves sources of pleasure more valuable than the primitive pleasures, both in permanency, in the space of human existence that they are capable of covering, and even in intensity.

Virtue, according to the utilitarian conception, is a good of this description. There was no original desire of it, or motive to it, save its conduciveness to pleasure, and especially to protection from pain. But through the association thus formed it may be felt a good in itself, and desired as such with as great intensity as any other good; and with this difference between it and the love of money, of power, or of fame—that all of these may, and often do, render the individual noxious to the other members of the society to which he belongs, whereas there is nothing which makes him so much a blessing to them as the cultivation of the disinterested love of virtue. And consequently, the utilitarian standard, while it tolerates and approves those other acquired desires, up to the point beyond which they would be more injurious to the general happiness than promotive of it, enjoins and requires the cultivation of the love of virtue up to the greatest strength possible, as being above all things important to the general happiness.

It results from the preceding considerations that there is in reality nothing desired except happiness. Whatever is desired otherwise than as a means to some end beyond itself, and ultimately to happiness, is desired as itself a part of happiness, and is not desired for itself until it has become so. Those who desire virtue for its own sake desire it either because the consciousness of it is a pleasure, or because the consciousness of being without it is a pain, or for both reasons united; as in truth the pleasure and pain seldom exist separately, but almost always together—the same person feeling pleasure in the degree of virtue attained, and pain in not having attained more. If one of these gave him no pleasure, and the other no pain, he would not love or desire virtue, or would desire it only for the other benefits which it might produce to himself or to persons whom he cared for.

We have now, then, an answer to the question, of what sort of proof the principle of utility is susceptible. If the opinion which I have now stated is psychologically true—if human nature is so constituted as to desire nothing which is not either a part of happiness or a means of happiness—we can have no other proof, and we require no other, that these are the only things desirable. If so, happiness is the sole end of human action, and the promotion of it the test by which to judge of all human conduct; from whence it necessarily follows that it must be the criterion of morality, since a part is included in the whole.

5

The Experience Machine

Robert Nozick is professor of philosophy at Harvard University. Among his many publications are *Philosophical Explanations* (1981) and *The Examined Life: Philosophical Meditations* (1990). The following selection is from his earlier book, *Anarchy, State and Utopia* (1974).

... Suppose there were an experience machine that would give you any experience you desired. Superduper neuropsychologists could stimulate your brain so that you would think and feel you were writing a great novel, or making a friend, or reading an interesting book. All the time you would be floating in a tank, with electrodes attached to your brain. Should you plug into this machine for life, preprogramming your life's experiences? If you are worried about missing out on desirable experiences, we can suppose that business enterprises have researched thoroughly the lives of many others. You can pick and choose from their large library or smorgasbord of such experiences, selecting your life's experiences for, say, the next two years. After two years have passed, you will have ten minutes or ten hours out of the tank, to select the experiences of your *next* two years. Of course, while in the tank you won't know that you're there; you'll think it's all actually happening. Others can also plug in to have the experiences they want, so there's no need to stay unplugged to serve them. (Ignore problems such as who will service the machines if everybody plugs in.) Would you plug in? *What else can matter to us, other than how our lives feel from the inside?* Nor should you refrain because of the few moments of distress between the moment you've decided and the moment you're plugged. What's a few moments of distress compared to a lifetime of bliss (if that's what you choose), and why feel any distress at all if your decision *is* the best one?

What does matter to us in addition to our experiences? First, we want to *do* certain things, and not just have the experience of doing them. In the case of certain experiences, it is only because first we want to do the actions that we want the experiences of doing them or thinking we've done them. (But *why* do we want to do the activities rather than merely to experience them?) A second reason for not plugging in is that we want to *be* a certain way, to be a certain sort of person. Someone floating in a tank is an indeterminate blob. There is no answer to the question of what a person is like who has long been in the tank. Is he courageous, kind, intelligent, witty, loving? It's not merely that it's difficult to tell; there's no way he is. Plugging into the machine is a kind of suicide. It will seem to some, trapped by a picture, that nothing about what we are like can matter except as it gets reflected in our experiences. But should it be surprising that what *we are* is important to us? Why should we be concerned only with how our time is filled, but not with what we are?

Thirdly, plugging into an experience machine limits us to a man-made reality, to a world no deeper or more important than that which people can construct. There is no *actual* contact with any deeper reality, though the experience of it can be simulated. Many persons desire to leave themselves open to such contact and to a plumbing of deeper significance.[1] This clarifies the intensity of the conflict over psychoactive drugs, which some view as mere local experience machines, and others view as avenues to a deeper reality; what some view as equivalent to surrender to the experience machine, others view as following one of the reasons *not* to surrender!

We learn that something matters to us in addition to experience by imagining an experience machine and then realizing that we would not use it. We can continue to imagine a sequence of machines each designed to fill lacks suggested for the earlier machines. For example, since the experience machine doesn't meet our desire to *be* a certain way, imagine a transformation machine which transforms us into whatever sort of person we'd like to be (compatible with our staying us). Surely one would not use the transformation machine to become as one would wish, and thereupon plug into the experience machine![2] So something matters in addition to one's experiences *and* what one is like. Nor is the reason merely that one's experiences are unconnected with what

---

[1] Traditional religious views differ on the *point* of contact with a transcendent reality. Some say that contact yields eternal bliss or Nirvana, but they have not distinguished this sufficiently from merely a *very* long run on the experience machine. Others think it is intrinsically desirable to do the will of a higher being which created us all, though presumably no one would think this if we discovered we had been created as an object of amusement by some superpowerful child from another galaxy or dimension. Still others imagine an eventual merging with a higher reality, leaving unclear its desirability, or where that merging leaves *us*.

[2] Some wouldn't use the transformation machine at all; it seems like *cheating*. But the one-time use of the transformation machine would not remove all challenges; there would still be obstacles for the new us to overcome, a new plateau from which to strive even higher. And is this plateau any the less earned or deserved than that provided by genetic endowment and early childhood environment? But if the transformation machine could be used indefinitely often, so that we could accomplish anything by pushing a button to transform ourselves into someone who could do it easily, there would remain no limits we *need* to strain against or try to transcend. Would there by anything left *to do*? Do some theological views place God outside of time because an omniscient omnipotent being couldn't fill up his days?

one is like. For the experience machine might be limited to provide only experiences possible to the sort of person plugged in. Is it that we want to make a difference in the world? Consider then the result machine, which produces in the world any result you would produce and injects your vector input into any joint activity. We shall not pursue here the fascinating details of these or other machines. What is most disturbing about them is their living of our lives for us. Is it misguided to search for *particular* additional functions beyond the competence of machines to do for us? Perhaps what we desire is to live (an active verb) ourselves, in contact with reality. (And this, machines cannot do *for* us.) Without elaborating on the implications of this, which I believe connect surprisingly with issues about free will and causal accounts of knowledge, we need merely note the intricacy of the question of what matters *for people* other than their experiences. Until one finds a satisfactory answer, and determines that this answer does not *also* apply to animals, one cannot reasonably claim that only the felt experiences of animals limit what we may do to them.

6

Utilitarianism and Moral Character

Bernard Williams is professor of philosophy at the University of California, Berkeley and Oxford University. His books include *Morality* (1976), *Problems of the Self* (1973), *Moral Luck* (1981), and *Ethics and the Limits of Philosophy* (1985).

(1) George, who has just taken his Ph.D. in chemistry, finds it extremely difficult to get a job. He is not very robust in health, which cuts down the number of jobs he might be able to do satisfactorily. His wife has to go out to work to keep them, which itself causes a great deal of strain, since they have small children and there are severe problems about looking after them. The results of all this, especially on the children, are damaging. An older chemist, who knows about this situation, says that he can get George a decently paid job in a certain laboratory, which pursues research into chemical and biological warfare. George says that he cannot accept this, since he is opposed to chemical and biological warfare. The older man replies that he is not too keen on it himself, come to that, but after all George's refusal is not going to make the job or the laboratory go away; what is more, he happens to know that if George refuses the job, it will certainly go to a contemporary of George's who is not inhibited by any such scruples and is likely if appointed to push along the research with greater zeal than George would. Indeed, it is not merely concern for George and his family, but (to speak frankly and in confidence) some alarm about this other man's excess of zeal, which has led the older man to offer to use his influence to get George the job . . . George's wife, to whom he is deeply attached, has views (the details of which need not concern us) from which it follows that at least there is nothing particularly wrong with research into CBW. What should he do?

    (2) Jim finds himself in the central square of a small South American town. Tied up against the wall are a row of twenty Indians, most terrified, a few defiant, in front of them several armed men in uniform. A heavy man in

From J. J. C. Smart and Bernard Williams, *Utilitarianism: For and Against*, 97–104. Reprinted with the permission of Cambridge University Press.

a sweat-stained khaki shirt turns out to be the captain in charge, and, after a good deal of questioning of Jim which establishes that he got there by accident while on a botanical expedition, explains that the Indians are a random group of the inhabitants who, after recent acts of protest against the government, are just about to be killed to remind other possible protestors of the advantages of not protesting. However, since Jim is an honoured visitor from another land, the captain is happy to offer him a guest's privilege of killing one of the Indians himself. If Jim accepts, then as a special mark of the occasion, the other Indians will be let off. Of course, if Jim refuses, then there is no special occasion, and Pedro here will do what he was about to do when Jim arrived, and kill them all. Jim, with some desperate recollection of schoolboy fiction, wonders whether if he got hold of a gun, he could hold the captain, Pedro, and the rest of the soldiers to threat, but it is quite clear from the set-up that nothing of that kind is going to work: any attempt at that sort of thing will mean that all the Indians will be killed, and himself. The men against the wall, and the other villagers, understand the situation, and are obviously begging him to accept. What should he do?

To these dilemmas, it seems to me that utilitarianism replies, in the first case, that George should accept the job, and in the second, that Jim should kill the Indian. Not only does utilitarianism give these answers but, if the situations are essentially as described and there are no further special factors, it regards them, it seems to me, as *obviously* the right answers. But many of us would certainly wonder whether, in (1), that could possibly be the right answer at all; and in the case of (2), even one who came to think that perhaps that was the answer, might well wonder whether it was obviously the answer. Nor is it just a question of the rightness or obviousness of these answers. It is also a question of what sort of considerations come into finding the answer. A feature of utilitarianism is that it cuts out a kind of consideration which for some others makes a difference to what they feel about such cases: a consideration involving the idea, as we might first and very simply put it, that each of us is specially responsible for what *he* does, rather than for what other people do. This is an idea closely connected with the value of integrity. It is often suspected that utilitarianism, at least in its direct forms, makes integrity as a value more or less unintelligible. I shall try to show that this suspicion is correct. Of course, even if that is correct, it would not necessarily follow that we should reject utilitarianism; perhaps, as utilitarians sometimes suggest, we should just forget about integrity, in favour of such things as a concern for the general good. However, if I am right, we cannot merely do that, since the reason why utilitarianism cannot understand integrity is that it cannot coherently describe the relations between a man's projects and his actions.

Two Kinds of Remoter Effect

A lot of what we have to say about this question will be about the relations between my projects and other people's projects. But before we get on to that, we should first ask whether we are assuming too hastily what the utilitarian answers to the dilemmas will be. In terms of more direct effects of the possible decisions, there does not indeed seem much doubt about the answer in either case, but it might be said that in terms of more remote or less evident effects counterweights might be found to enter the utilitarian scales. Thus the effect on George of a decision to take the job might be invoked, or its effect on others who might know of his decision. The possibility of there being more beneficent labours in the future from which he might be barred or disqualified, might be mentioned; and so forth. Such effects—in particular, possible effects on the agent's character, and effects on the public at large—are often invoked by utilitarian writers dealing with problems about lying or promise-breaking, and some similar considerations might be invoked here.

There is one very general remark that is worth making about arguments of this sort. The certainty that attaches to these hypotheses about possible effects is usually pretty low; in some cases, indeed, the hypothesis invoked is so implausible that it would scarcely pass if it were not being used to deliver the respectable moral answer, as in the standard fantasy that one of the effects of one's telling a particular lie is to weaken the disposition of the world at large to tell the truth. The demands on the certainty or probability of these beliefs as beliefs about particular actions are much milder than they would be on beliefs favouring the unconventional course. It may be said that this is as it should be, since the presumption must be in favour of the conventional course: but that scarcely seems a *utilitarian* answer, unless utilitarianism has already taken off in the direction of not applying the consequences to the particular act at all.

Leaving aside that very general point, I want to consider now two types of effect that are often invoked by utilitarians, and which might be invoked in connexion with these imaginary cases. The attitude or tone involved in invoking these effects may sometimes seem peculiar; but that sort of peculiarity soon becomes familiar in utilitarian discussions, and indeed it can be something of an achievement to retain a sense of it.

First, there is the psychological effect on the agent. Our descriptions of these situations have not so far taken account of how George or Jim will be after they have taken the one course or the other; and it might be said that if they take the course which seemed at first the utilitarian one, the effects on them will be in fact bad enough and extensive enough to cancel out the initial utilitarian advantages of that course. Now there is one version of this effect in which, for a utilitarian, some confusion must be involved, namely that in which the agent feels bad, his subsequent conduct and relations are crippled and so on, *because he thinks that he has done the wrong thing*—for if the balance of outcomes was as it appeared to be *before* invoking this effect, then he has not (from the utilitarian point of view) done the wrong thing. So that version of the effect, for a rational and utilitarian agent, could not possibly make any difference to the assessment of right and wrong. However, perhaps he is not a thoroughly rational agent, and is disposed to have bad feelings, whichever he decided to do. Now such feelings, which are from a strictly utilitarian point of view irrational—nothing, a utilitarian can point out, is advanced by having them—cannot, consistently, have any great weight in a utilitarian calculation.

I shall consider in a moment an argument to suggest that they should have no weight at all in it. But short of that, the utilitarian could reasonably say that such feelings should not be encouraged, even if we accept their existence, and that to give them a lot of weight is to encourage them. Or, at the very best, even if they are straightforwardly and without any discount to be put into the calculation, their weight must be small: they are after all (and at best) one man's feelings.

That consideration might seem to have particular force in Jim's case. In George's case, his feelings represent a larger proportion of what is to be weighed, and are more commensurate in character with other items in the calculation. In Jim's case, however, his feelings might seem to be of very little weight compared with other things that are at stake. There is a powerful and recognizable appeal that can be made on this point: as that a refusal by Jim to do what he has been invited to do would be a kind of self-indulgent squeamishness. That is an appeal which can be made by other than utilitarians—indeed, there are some uses of it which cannot be consistently made by utilitarians, as when it essentially involves the idea that there is something dishonourable about such self-indulgence. But in some versions it is a familiar, and it must be said a powerful, weapon of utilitarianism. One must be clear, though, about what it can and cannot accomplish. The most it can do, so far as I can see, is to invite one to consider how seriously, and for what reasons, one feels that what one is invited to do is (in these circumstances) wrong, and in particular, to consider that question from the utilitarian point of view. When the agent is not seeing the situation from a utilitarian point of view, the appeal cannot force him to do so; and if he does come round to seeing it from a utilitarian point of view, there is virtually nothing left for the appeal to do. If he does not see it from a utilitarian point of view, he will not see his resistance to the invitation, and the unpleasant feelings he associates with accepting it, *just* as disagreeable experiences of his; they figure rather as emotional expressions of a thought that to accept would be wrong. He may be asked, as by the appeal, to consider whether he is right, and indeed whether he is fully serious, in thinking that. But the assertion of the appeal, that he is being self-indulgently squeamish, will not itself answer that question, or even help to answer it, since it essentially tells him to regard his feelings just as unpleasant experiences of his, and he cannot, by doing that answer the question they pose when they are precisely not so regarded, but are regarded as indications of what he thinks is right and wrong. If he does come round fully to the utilitarian point of view than of course he will regard these feelings just as unpleasant experiences of his. And once Jim—at least—has come to see them in that light, there is nothing left for the appeal to do, since *of course* his feelings, so regarded, are of virtually no weight at all in relation to the other things at stake. The "squeamishness" appeal is not an argument which adds in a hitherto neglected consideration. Rather, it is an invitation to consider the situation, and one's own feelings, from a utilitarian point of view.

The reason why the squeamishness appeal can be very unsettling, and one can be unnerved by the suggestion of self-indulgence in going against utilitarian considerations, is not that we are utilitarians who are uncertain what utilitarian value to attach to our moral feelings, but that we are partially at least not utilitarians, and cannot regard our moral feelings merely as objects of utilitarian value. Because our moral relation to the world is partly given by such feelings, and by a sense of what we can or cannot "live with," to come to regard those feelings from a purely utilitarian point of view, that is to say, as happenings outside one's moral self, is to lose a sense of one's moral identity; to lose, in the most literal way, one's integrity. . . .

7

Should the Numbers Count?

John M. Taurek has taught philosophy at New York University as well as at
Stanford University and the University of Southern California.

We have resources for bestowing benefits and for preventing harms. But there
are limitations. There are many people we are not in a position to help at all.
That is one kind of limitation. But there is another kind of limitation we encounter. Often we must choose between bestowing benefits on certain people,
or preventing certain harms from befalling them, and bestowing benefits on or
preventing harms from befalling certain others. We cannot do both. The general question discussed here is whether we should, in such trade-off situations, consider the relative numbers of people involved as something in itself
of significance in determining our course of action.[1] The conclusion I reach is
that we should not. I approach this general question by focusing on a particular hypothetical case in which we find ourselves in a position of being able to

---

[1] The trade-off situations that I am focusing on have relatively simple structures. They present us
with three relevant options: (1) We may aid a certain person or group of persons. (2) We may aid
an entirely different group of persons. (3) We may do nothing at all to aid anyone. (I exclude from
consideration this last option, though I do not argue that doing nothing for anyone is impermissible. Whether, why or in what sense it is, are questions best left to another occasion.) Robert
Schwartz has caused me some worries about trade-off situations that are as aptly styled as these
simpler ones, and that involve different but overlapping groups of possible beneficiaries. For example, perhaps the exercise of one option would bring aid to A but none to either B or C. A second option might bring aid to both A and B but none to C. Yet a third option might be available
that would bring aid to C but none to either A or B. It will be seen that it is not completely obvious how one holding the views I present on the simpler trade-off situations would deal with this
case and with cases of still greater complexity. After having caused me the worries, Schwartz had
the decency to think out an approach to these decision problems that would appear compatible
with my thinking about the simpler ones. But I fear that a discussion of these complications would
obscure my main argument here, so I have avoided it.

From John M. Taurek, "Should the Numbers Count?" *Philosophy & Public Affairs* 6, no. 4, pp.
293–310 (Summer 1977). Copyright © 1977 by Princeton University Press. Reprinted by permission of Princeton University Press.

prevent a certain harm from befalling one person or to prevent a like harm from befalling each of five others, but unable to spare all six from harm.

The situation is that I have a supply of some life-saving drug.[2] Six people will all certainly die if they are not treated with the drug. But one of the six requires all of the drug if he is to survive. Each of the other five requires only one-fifth of the drug. What ought I to do?

To many it seems obvious that in such cases, special considerations apart, one ought to save the greater number. . . .

Such reasoning seems appealing to many. I find it difficult to understand and even more difficult to see how it is to be reconciled with certain other convictions widely shared by these same people. Suppose this one person [who needs all of the drug to survive], call him David, is someone I know and like, and the others are strangers to me. I might well give all of my drug to him. And I am inclined to think that were I to do so, I would not be acting immorally. i suspect that many share this view with me.

Of course, some people do think that I would be acting immorally. They think it would be wrong to give all the drug to David while the five others die just because David is someone I know and like. They may allow that this could make my action excusable, but on their view it would not make it right.

For the moment, I address myself to those who, while subscribing to the general position, nevertheless share my view that it would not be wrong for me to use my drug to save a person I know and like. They must deny that the original claim, together with the thinking that lies behind it, commits them to the view that I ought to save the five strangers in this case. Perhaps they will object that, in introducing David as someone I know and like, I have introduced another of those special considerations that were meant to be excluded. . . .

But I would not think that the fact that David happens to be someone I know and like would make his death a worse thing in comparison to the deaths of these others than it would be if, by chance, I didn't know him or knew him but happened not to like him. So it is not clear to me how this fact is to make a difference in what I am *morally required* to do in this situation. It is not clear to me how it is to make a difference in the view of those who think that, apart from it, I would have a moral obligation to save the five, an obligation deriving from the fact that it is a worse thing, other things being equal, that these five innocent persons should die than it is that this one should. . . .

On the view in question, one is morally required to save the five instead of the one, other things being equal, because, other things being equal, it is a very much worse thing that these five innocent people should die than it is that this one should. But if this fact constitutes a compelling ground for a moral obligation to give the drug to these five rather than to this one, then I too shall have

---

[2] This is the case described by Phillippa Foot in her paper on "Abortion and the Doctrine of Double Effect," in *Moral Problems*, ed. James Rachels (New York, 1971).

to acknowledge its moral force. The problem, then, is to explain, especially perhaps to these five people, how it is that merely because I know and like David and am unacquainted with them I can so easily escape the moral requirement to save their lives that would fall on most anyone else in my position. The only relevant consideration here is that I happen to like David more than I like any of them. Imagine my saying to them, "Admittedly, the facts are such that I would be morally obligated to give you this drug, if it didn't happen that I prefer to give it to him." The moral force of such facts must be feeble indeed to be overridden by an appeal as feeble as this.

Contrast this situation with almost any other in which we would be prepared to acknowledge the existence of grounds for a moral requirement to give the drug to these five people. Suppose, for example, that these five had contracted with me in advance to deliver this drug to them at this time and place. It would not seem likely that anyone would think that the fact that I would prefer to give it to someone else instead would alter in any way what I was morally required to do. But of course it might make it harder, psychologically, for me to do what I ought to do. Again, suppose that these five are American soldiers and I am an army doctor with what little is left of the issue of this drug. And let us suppose that this other person is someone I know and like but is a citizen of some other country. Would anyone imagine that the fact that I would prefer to use the drug to save this one person could somehow nullify or lift my obligation to distribute the drug to the five soldiers?

The point is this. Generally, when the facts are such that any impartial person would recognize a moral obligation to do something as important to people as giving this drug to these five would be to them, then an appeal to the fact that one happens to be partial to the interests of some others would do nothing to override the moral obligation. Yet this is the position of those who maintain that in this situation any impartial person would be *morally required* to distribute his drug in fifths to the five. But because I, personally, would prefer to give it to someone else, it is permissible for me to do so.[3]

I am inclined to think, then, that we should either agree that it would be wrong for me to save David in this situation or admit that there are no grounds for a moral requirement on anyone, special obligations apart, to save the five instead of David. Now as I said earlier there are those who will take the view that I do wrong when I give preference to David in this situation. They may feel that what has been said so far only proves the point. So now I would like to say something in support of the opinion that it would be morally permissible for a person in such circumstances to save a friend rather than the five strangers.

---

[3] There are a number of possible contortions that one might go through in an attempt to reconcile these views. I cannot consider them all here. What I am chiefly interested in stressing is that there are serious difficulties involved in any attempt to reconcile these positions. My hope is that, in view of these difficulties, those who would maintain the original position might be brought to reconsider with an open mind the alleged grounds for the moral requirement to save the greater number in cases where one is in fact impartial in one's concern for those involved.

Suppose the drug belongs to your friend David. It is his drug, his required dosage. Now there are these five strangers, strangers to David as well as to you. Would you try to persuade David to give his drug to these five people? Do you think you should? Suppose you were to try. How would you begin? You are asking him to give up his life so that each of the five others, all strangers to him, might continue to live.

Imagine trying to reason with David as you would, presumably, have reasoned with yourself were the drug yours. "David, to be sure it is a bad thing, a very bad thing, that you should die. But don't you see it is a far worse thing that these five people should die? Now you are in a position to prevent either of these bad things from happening. Unfortunately you cannot prevent them both. So you ought to insure that the worst thing doesn't happen."

Don't you think that David might demur? Isn't he likely to ask: "Worse for whom?" And it seems natural and relevant that he should continue to put his case in some such way as this: "It is a far worse thing for me that I should die than that they should. I allow that for each of them it would be a worse thing were they all to die while I continue to live than it would be were I to die and they to continue to live. Indeed I wouldn't ask, nor would I expect, any one of them to give up his life so that I, a perfect stranger, might continue to live mine. But why should you, or any one of them, expect me to give up my life so that each of them might continue to live his?"

I think David's question deserves an answer. What could there be about these strangers that might induce David to think it worth giving up his life so that they might continue to live theirs? The usual sort of utilitarian reasoning would be comical if it were not so outrageous. Imagine any one of these five entreating David, "Look here David. Here I am but one person. If you give me one-fifth of your drug I will continue to live. I am confident that I will garner over the long haul a net balance of pleasure over pain, happiness over misery. Admittedly, if this were all that would be realized by your death I should not expect that you would give up your life for it. I mean, it may not be unreasonable to think that you yourself, were you to continue to live, might succeed in realizing at least as favorable a balance of happiness. But here, don't you see, is a second person. If he continues to live he too will accumulate a nice balance of pleasure over pain. And here is yet a third, a fourth, and finally a fifth person. Now, we would not ask you to die to make possible the net happiness realized in the life of any one of us five. For you might well suppose that you could realize as much in your own lifetime. But it would be most unreasonable for you to think that you could realize in your one lifetime anything like as much happiness as we get when we add together our five distinct favorable balances."

Such reasoning coming from some disinterested outside party might be a little less contemptible, but surely not a bit less foolish. But if we recognize the absurdity of trying to sell David on the idea that it would be a worse thing were these five persons to die than it would be were he to die by suggesting he focus on the large sum of their added happinesses as compared to his own, just what kind of reasoning would sound less absurd? Is it less absurd to ask him to focus on the large sum of intrinsic value possessed by five human beings, quite apart from considerations of their happiness, as compared to the value of himself alone?

I cannot imagine that I could give David any reason why *he* should think it better that these five strangers should continue to live than that he should. In using his drug to preserve his own life he acts to preserve what is, understandably, more important to him. He values his own life more than he values any of theirs. This is, of course, not to say that he thinks he is more valuable, period, than any one of them, or than all of them taken together. (Whatever could such a remark mean?) Moreover, and this I would like to stress, in not giving his drug to these five people he does not wrong any of them. He violates no one's rights. None of these five has a legitimate claim on David's drug in this situation, and so the five together have no such claim. Were they to attack David and to take his drug, they would be murderers. Both you and David would be wholly within your rights to defend against any such attempt to deprive him of his drug.

Such, in any case, is my view. I hope that most people would agree with me. But if it is morally permissible for David in this situation to give himself all of his drug, why should it be morally impermissible for me to do the same? It is my drug. It is more important to me that David should continue to live than it is that these five strangers should. I value his life more than I value theirs. None of these five has any special claim to my drug in this situation. None of them can legitimately demand of me that I give him the drug instead of giving it to David. And so the five together have no such special claim. I violate no one's rights when I use my drug to save David's life. Were these five, realizing that I was about to give my drug to David, to attempt to take it from me, I would think myself wholly justified in resisting.

Thus far I have argued that, since it would not be morally impermissible for the one person, David, to use all of his drug to save himself instead of these five others, it cannot be morally impermissible for me, were the drug mine and given that I am under no special obligations to any of these five, to use it all to save David instead of these other five. In so arguing I have committed myself to a view that may strike some as counterintuitive. . . .

[L]et me suggest what I would do in many such cases. Here are six human beings. I can empathize with each of them. I would not like to see any of them die. But I cannot save everyone. Why not give each person an equal chance to survive? Perhaps I could flip a coin. Heads, I give my drug to these five. Tails, I give it to this one. In this way I give each of the six persons a fifty-fifty chance of surviving. Where such an option is open to me it would seem to best express my equal concern and respect for each person. Who among them could complain that I have done wrong? And on what grounds?. . .

Some will be impatient with all this. . . . They will insist that I say what would be a worse (or a better) thing, period. It seems obvious to them that from the moral point of view, since there is nothing special about any of these six persons, it is a worse thing that these five should die while this one continues to live than for this one to die while these five continue to live. It is a worse thing, not necessarily for anyone in particular, or relative to anyone's particular ends, but just a worse thing in itself.

I cannot give a satisfactory account of the meaning of judgments of this kind. But there are important differences between them and those judgments which relativize the value ascribed to some particular person or group, purpose or end. When I judge of two possible outcomes that the one would be worse (or better) for this person or this group, I do not, typically, thereby express a preference between these outcomes. Typically, I do not feel constrained to admit that I or anyone *should* prefer the one outcome to the other. But when I evaluate outcomes from an impersonal perspective (perhaps we may say from a moral perspective), matters are importantly different. When I judge that it would be a worse thing, period, were this to happen than were that to happen, then I do, typically, thereby express a preference between these outcomes. Moreover, at the very least, I feel constrained to admit that I *should* have such a preference, even if I do not. It is a moral shortcoming not to prefer what is admittedly in itself a better thing to what is in itself a worse thing.

Hence, I cannot give such an impersonal evaluative judgment as the ground for a decision to give the drug to the five instead of to the one. I could not bring myself to say to this one person, "I give my drug to these five and let you die because, don't you see, it is a worse thing, a far worse thing, that they should die than that you should." I do not expect that David, or anyone in his position, should think it a better thing were he to die and these five others to survive than it would be were he to survive and they to die. I do not think him morally deficient in any way because he prefers the outcome in which he survives and the others die to the outcome in which they survive and he dies.

In a situation where the one person, David, is a friend of mine and the others strangers to me, I do have a preference for the one outcome as against the other, to me a natural and acceptable preference. But since I do not expect everyone to share such a preference I will not elevate its expression to the status of a universally binding evaluation. I do not say to the five strangers that I give all of my drug to my friend because it is a better thing in itself that he should survive than that they should. I do not believe any such thing. Rather, I simply explain that David is my friend. His survival is more important to me than theirs. I would expect them to understand this, provided they were members of a moral community acceptable to me, just as I would were our roles reversed. Further, in securing David's survival I violate no one's rights. No further justification of my action is needed, just as no further justification is needed in a situation where the drug belongs to the one person. He need not, and plainly should not, give as the ground for his decision to use his drug to secure his own survival the judgment that it is better in itself that he should survive than that they should. Who could expect any of them to accept that? He need only point out, as if this really needed remarking, that it is more important to him that he survive than it is to him that they should. Furthermore, in thus securing his own survival he violates none of their rights. What more need be said?

In the trade-off situation as presently conceived, all six persons are strangers to me. I have no special affection for any one of them, no greater concern for one than any of the others. Further, by hypothesis, my situation will be made neither worse nor better by either outcome. Any preference I might show, therefore, if it is not to be thought arbitrary, would require grounding. Of course this is precisely what an impersonal evaluative judgment of the kind discussed would do. It would provide a reason for the preference I show should I give the drug to the five. But for the reasons given, I cannot subscribe to such an evaluation of these outcomes. Hence, in this situation I have absolutely no reason for showing preference to them as against him, and no reason for showing preference to him as against them. Thus, I am inclined to treat each person equally by giving each an equal chance to survive.

Yet I can imagine it will still be said, despite everything, "But surely the numbers must count for something." I can hear the incredulous tones: "Would you flip a coin were it a question of saving fifty persons or saving one? Surely in situations where the numbers are this disproportionate you must admit that one ought to save the many rather than the few or the one."

I would flip a coin even in such a case, special considerations apart. I cannot see how or why the mere addition of numbers should change anything. It seems to me that those who, in situations of the kind in question, would have me count the relative numbers of people involved as something in itself of significance, would have me attach importance to human beings and what happens to them in merely the way I would to objects which I valued. If six objects are threatened by fire and I am in a position to retrieve the five in this room or the one in that room, but unable to get out all six, I would decide what to do in just the way I am told I should when it is human beings who are threatened. Each object will have a certain value in my eyes. If it happens that all six are of equal value, I will naturally preserve the many rather than the one. Why? Because the five objects are together five times more valuable in my eyes than the one.

But when I am moved to rescue human beings from harm in situations of the kind described, I cannot bring myself to think of them in just this way. I empathize with them. My concern for what happens to them is grounded chiefly in the realization that each of them is, as I would be in his place, terribly concerned about what happens to him. It is not my way to think of them as each having a certain *objective* value, determined however it is we determine the objective value of things, and then to make some estimate of the combined value of the five as against the one. If it were not for the fact that these objects were creatures much like me, for whom what happens to them is of great importance, I doubt that I would take much interest in their preservation. As merely intact objects they would mean very little to me, being, as such, nearly as common as toadstools. The loss of an arm of the *Pietà* means something to me not because the *Pietà* will miss it. But the loss of an arm of a creature like me means something to me only because I know he will miss it, just as I would miss mine. It is the loss *to this person* that I focus on. I lose nothing of value to me should he lose his arm. But if I have a concern for him, I shall wish he might be spared his loss.

And so it is in the original situation. I cannot but think of the situation in this way. For each of these six persons it is no doubt a terrible thing to die. Each faces the loss of something among the things he values most. His loss means something to me only, or chiefly, because of what it means to him. It is the loss to the individual that matters to me, not the loss of the individual. But should any one of these five lose his life, his loss is no greater a loss to him because, as it happens, four others (or forty-nine others) lose theirs as well. And neither he nor anyone else loses anything of greater value to him than does David, should David lose his life. Five individuals each losing his life does not add up to anyone's experiencing a loss five times greater than the loss suffered by any one of the five.

If I gave my drug to the five persons and let David die I cannot see that I would thereby have preserved anyone from suffering a loss greater than that I let David suffer. And, similarly, were I to give my drug to David and let the five die I cannot see that I would thereby have allowed anyone to suffer a loss greater than the loss I spared David. Each person's potential loss has the same significance to me, only as a loss to that person alone. Because, by hypothesis, I have an equal concern for each person involved, I am moved to give each of them an equal chance to be spared his loss.

My way of thinking about these trade-off situations consists, essentially, in seriously considering what will be lost or suffered by this one person if I do not prevent it, and in comparing the significance of that *for him* with what would be lost or suffered by anyone else if I do not prevent it. This reflects a refusal to take seriously in these situations any notion of the sum of two persons' separate losses. To me this appears a quite natural extension of the way in which most would view analogous trade-off situations involving differential losses to those involved, indeed even most of those who find my treatment of the cases thus far described paradoxical. Perhaps then, in one last effort to persuade them, it may be helpful to think about a trade-off situation of this kind.

Suppose I am told that if you, a stranger to me, agree to submit to some pain of significant intensity I will be spared a lesser one. Special circumstances apart, I can see no reason whatever why you should be willing to make such a sacrifice. It would be cowardly of me to ask it of you. Now add a second person, also a stranger to you. Again we are told that if you volunteer to undergo this same considerable pain each of us will be spared a lesser one. I feel it would be no less contemptible of me to ask you to make such a sacrifice in this situation. There is no reason you should be willing to undergo such a pain to spare me mine. There is no reason you should be willing to undergo such a pain to spare this other person his. And that is all there is to it.

Now, adding still others to our number, not one of whom will suffer as much as you are asked to bear, will not change things for me. It ought not to change things for any of us. If not one of us can give you a good reason why you should be willing to undergo a greater suffering so that he might be spared a lesser one, then there is simply no good reason why you should be asked to suffer so that the group may be spared. Suffering is not additive in this way. The discomfort of each of a large number of individuals experiencing a minor headache does not add up to anyone's experiencing a migraine. In such a trade-off situation as this we are to compare your pain or your loss, not to our collective or total pain, whatever exactly that is supposed to be, but to what will be suffered or lost by *any given single one of us.*

Perhaps it would not be unseemly for a stranger who will suffer some great agony or terrible loss unless you willingly submit to some relatively minor pain to ask you to consider this carefully, to ask you to empathize with him in what he will have to go through. But to my way of thinking it would be contemptible for any one of us in this crowd to ask you to consider carefully, "not, of course, what I personally will have to suffer. None of us is thinking of himself here! But contemplate, if you will, what *we* the group, will suffer. Think of the awful sum of pain that is in the balance here! There are so very many more of us." At best such thinking seems confused. Typically, I think, it is outrageous.

Yet, just such thinking is engaged in by those who, in situations of the kind described earlier, would be moved to a course of action by *a mere consideration* of the relative numbers of people involved. If the numbers should not be given any significance by those involved in these trade-off situations, why should they count for anyone? Suppose that I am in a position to either spare you your pain or to spare this large number of individuals each his lesser pain, but unable to spare both you and them. Why should I attach any significance to their numbers if none of those involved should? I cannot understand how I am supposed to add up their separate pains and attach significance to that alleged sum in a way that would be inappropriate were any of those involved to do it. If, by allowing you to suffer your pain, I do not see that I can thereby spare a single person any greater pain or, in this case, even as much pain, I do not see why calling my attention to the numbers should move me to spare them instead of you, any more than focusing on the numbers should move you to sacrifice for them collectively when you have no reason to sacrifice for them individually.

It is not my intention to argue that in this situation I ought to spare you rather than them just because your pain is "greater" than would be the pain of any one of them. Rather, I want to make it clear that in reaching a decision in such a case it is natural to focus on a comparison of the pain you will suffer, if I do not prevent it, with the pain that would be suffered by any given individual in this group, if I do not prevent it. I want to stress that it does not seem natural in such a case to attempt to add up their separate pains. I would like to combat the apparent tendency of some people to react to the thought of each of fifty individuals suffering a pain of some given intensity in the same way as they might to the thought of some individual suffering a pain many or fifty times more intense. I cannot but think that some such tendency is at work in the minds of those who attribute significance to the numbers in these trade-off situations.

In the original situation we were to imagine that I must choose between sparing David the loss of his life and sparing five others the loss of their lives. In making my decision I am not to compare his loss, on the one hand, to the collective or total loss to these five, on the other, whatever exactly that is supposed to be. Rather, I should compare what David stands to suffer or lose, if I do not prevent it, to what will be suffered or lost by any other person, if I do not prevent that. Calling my attention to the numbers should not move me to spare them instead of him, any more than focusing on the numbers should move him to sacrifice his life for the group when he has no reason to sacrifice for any individual in the group. The numbers, in themselves, simply do not count for me. I think they should not count for any of us.

8

Morality and the Categorical Imperative

Immanuel Kant (1724–1804), whom many consider to be the greatest philosopher of all time, was born in Konigsberg, East Prussia, where he lived his entire life. Known for his work habits and punctuality (it was said that citizens of Konigsberg could set their watches as Kant passed by their homes during his daily walks), Kant made major contributions to most of the central areas of philosophy. Concerned with asking the questions "What can I know?" "What should I do?" and "For what may I hope?" Kant went a long way toward answering them in his major works, *The Critique of Pure Reason* (1781), *The Critique of Practical Reason* (1787), and *The Critique of Judgment* (1790). The following selection is from his *Grounding for the Metaphysics of Morals*, in which he hoped to make more accessible his moral theory as developed in *The Critique of Practical Reason*.

Transition from the Ordinary Rational Knowledge of Morality to the Philosophical

There is no possibility of thinking of anything at all in the world, or even out of it, which can be regarded as good without qualification, except a *good will*. Intelligence, wit, judgment, and whatever talents of the mind one might want to name are doubtless in many respects good and desirable, as are such qualities of temperament as courage, resolution, perseverance. But they can also become extremely bad and harmful if the will, which is to make use of these gifts of nature and which in its special constitution is called character, is not good. The same holds with gifts of fortune; power, riches, honor, even health and that complete well-being and contentment with one's condition which is called happiness make for pride and often hereby even arrogance, unless there is a good will to correct their influence on the mind and herewith also to rectify the whole principle of action and make it universally conformable to its

From Immanuel Kant, *Grounding for the Metaphysics of Morals*, translated by James W. Ellington, Hackett Publishing Company, 1981, Indianapolis, IN and Cambridge, MA. With permission of the publisher.

end. The sight of a being who is not graced by any touch of a pure and good will but who yet enjoys an uninterrupted prosperity can never delight a rational and impartial spectator. Thus a good will seems to constitute the indispensable condition of being even worthy of happiness.

Some qualities are even conducive to this good will itself and can facilitate its work. Nevertheless, they have no intrinsic unconditional worth; but they always presuppose, rather, a good will, which restricts the high esteem in which they are otherwise rightly held, and does not permit them to be regarded as absolutely good. Moderation in emotions and passions, self-control, and calm deliberation are not only good in many respects but even seem to constitute part of the intrinsic worth of a person. But they are far from being rightly called good without qualification (however unconditionally they were commended by the ancients). For without the principles of a good will, they can become extremely bad; the coolness of a villain makes him not only much more dangerous but also immediately more abominable in our eyes than he would have been regarded by us without it.

A good will is good not because of what it effects or accomplishes, nor because of its fitness to attain some proposed end; it is good only through its willing, i.e., it is good in itself. When it is considered in itself, then it is to be esteemed very much higher than anything which it might ever bring about merely in order to favor some inclination, or even the sum total of all inclinations. Even if, by some especially unfortunate fate or by the niggardly provision of stepmotherly nature, this will should be wholly lacking in the power to accomplish its purpose; if with the greatest effort it should yet achieve nothing, and only the good will should remain (not, to be sure, as a mere wish but as the summoning of all the means in our power), yet would it, like a jewel, still shine by its own light as something which has its full value in itself. Its usefulness or fruitlessness can neither augment nor diminish this value. Its usefulness would be, as it were, only the setting to enable us to handle it in ordinary dealings or to attract to it the attention of those who are not yet experts, but not to recommend it to real experts or to determine its value.

But there is something so strange in this idea of the absolute value of a mere will, in which no account is taken of any useful results, that in spite of all the agreement received even from ordinary reason, yet there must arise the suspicion that such an idea may perhaps have as its hidden basis merely some high-flown fancy, and that we may have misunderstood the purpose of nature in assigning to reason the governing of our will. Therefore, this idea will be examined from this point of view.

In the natural constitution of an organized being, i.e., one suitably adapted to the purpose of life, let there be taken as a principle that in such a being no organ is to be found for any end unless it be the most fit and the best adapted to that end. Now if that being's preservation, welfare, or in a word its happiness, were the real end of nature in the case of a being having reason and will, then nature would have hit upon a very poor arrangement in having the reason of the creature carry out this purpose. For all the actions which such a creature has to perform with this purpose in view, and the whole rule of his conduct would have been prescribed much more exactly by instinct; and the purpose in question could have been attained much more certainly by instinct than it ever can be by reason. And if in addition reason had been imparted to this favored creature, then it would have had to serve him only to contemplate the happy constitution of his nature, to admire that nature, to rejoice in it, and to feel grateful to the cause that bestowed it; but reason would not have served him to subject his faculty of desire to its weak and delusive guidance nor would it have served him to meddle incompetently with the purpose of nature. In a word, nature would have taken care that reason did not strike out into a practical use nor presume, with its weak insight, to think out for itself a plan for happiness and the means for attaining it. Nature would have taken upon herself not only the choice of ends but also that of the means, and would with wise foresight have entrusted both to instinct alone.

And, in fact, we find that the more a cultivated reason devotes itself to the aim of enjoying life and happiness, the further does man get away from true contentment. Because of this there arises in many persons, if only they are candid enough to admit it, a certain amount of misology, i.e., hatred of reason. This is especially so in the case of those who are the most experienced in the use of reason, because after calculating all the advantages they derive, I say not from the invention of all the arts of common luxury, but even from the sciences (which in the end seem to them to be also a luxury of the understanding), they yet find that they have in fact only brought more trouble on their heads than they have gained in happiness. Therefore, they come to envy, rather than despise, the more common run of men who are closer to the guidance of mere natural instinct and who do not allow their reason much influence on their conduct. And we must admit that the judgment of those who would temper, or even reduce below zero, the boastful eulogies on behalf of the advantages which reason is supposed to provide as regards the happiness and contentment of life is by no means morose or ungrateful to the goodness with which the world is governed. There lies at the root of such judgments, rather, the idea that existence has another and much more worthy purpose, for which, and not for happiness, reason is quite properly intended, and which must, therefore, be regarded as the supreme condition to which the private purpose of men must, for the most part, defer.

Reason, however, is not competent enough to guide the will safely as regards its objects and the satisfaction of all our needs (which it in part even multiplies); to this end would an implanted natural instinct have led much more certainly. But inasmuch as reason has been imparted to us as a practical faculty, i.e., as one which is to have influence on the will, its true function must be to produce a will which is not merely good as a means to some further end, but is good in itself. To produce a will good in itself reason was absolutely necessary, inasmuch as nature in distributing her capacities has everywhere gone to work in a purposive manner. While such a will may not indeed be the sole and complete good, it must, nevertheless, be the highest good and the condition of all the rest, even of the desire for happiness. In this case there is nothing inconsistent with the wisdom of nature that the cultivation of reason, which is requisite for the first and unconditional purpose, may in many ways restrict, at least in this life, the attainment of the second purpose, viz., happiness, which is always conditioned. Indeed happiness can even be reduced to less than nothing, without nature's failing thereby in her purpose; for reason recognizes as its highest practical function the establishment of a good will, whereby in the attainment of this end reason is capable only of its own kind of satisfaction, viz., that of fulfilling a purpose which is in turn determined only by reason, even though such fulfillment were often to interfere with the purposes of inclination.

The concept of a will estimable in itself and good without regard to any further end must now be developed. This concept already dwells in the natural sound understanding and needs not so much to be taught as merely to be elucidated. It always holds first place in estimating the total worth of our actions and constitutes the condition of all the rest. Therefore, we shall take up the concept of *duty*, which includes that of a good will, though with certain subjective restrictions and hindrances, which far from hiding a good will or rendering it unrecognizable, rather bring it out by contrast and make it shine forth more brightly.

I here omit all actions already recognized as contrary to duty, even though they may be useful for this or that end; for in the case of these the question does not arise at all as to whether they might be done from duty, since they even conflict with duty. I also set aside those actions which are really in accordance with duty, yet to which men have no immediate inclination, but perform them because they are impelled thereto by some other inclination. For in this [second] case to decide whether the action which is in accord with duty has been done from duty or from some selfish purpose is easy. This difference is far more difficult to note in the [third] case where the action accords with duty and the subject has in addition an immediate inclination to do the action. For example, that a dealer should not overcharge an inexperienced purchaser certainly accords with duty; and where there is much commerce, the prudent merchant does not overcharge but keeps to a fixed price for everyone in general, so that a child may buy from him just as well as everyone else may. Thus customers are honestly served, but this is not nearly enough for making us believe that the merchant has acted this way from duty and from the principles of honesty; his own advantage required him to do it. He cannot, however, be assumed to have in addition [as in the third case] an immediate inclination toward his buyers, causing him, as it were, out of love to give no one as far as price is concerned any advantage over another. Hence the action was done neither from duty nor from immediate inclination, but merely for a selfish purpose.

On the other hand, to preserve one's life is a duty; and, furthermore, everyone has also an immediate inclination to do so. But on this account the often anxious care taken by most men for it has no intrinsic worth, and the maxim of their action has no moral content. They preserve their lives, to be sure, in accordance with duty, but not from duty. On the other hand, if adversity and hopeless sorrow have completely taken away the taste for life, if an unfortunate man, strong in soul and more indignant at his fate than despondent or dejected, wishes for death and yet preserves his life without loving it—not from inclination or fear, but from duty—then his maxim indeed has a moral content.

To be beneficent where one can is a duty; and besides this, there are many persons who are so sympathetically constituted that, without any further motive of vanity or self-interest, they find an inner pleasure in spreading joy around them and can rejoice in the satisfaction of others as their own work. But I maintain that in such a case an action of this kind, however dutiful and amiable it may be, has nevertheless no true moral worth. It is on a level with such actions as arise from other inclinations, e.g., the inclination for honor, which if fortunately directed to what is in fact beneficial and accords with duty and is thus honorable, deserves praise and encouragement, but no esteem; for its maxim lacks the moral content of an action done not from inclination but from duty. Suppose then the mind of this friend of mankind to be clouded over with his own sorrow so that all sympathy with the lot of others is extinguished, and suppose him still to have the power to benefit others in distress, even though he is not touched by their trouble because he is sufficiently absorbed with his own; and now suppose that, even though no inclination moves him any longer, he nevertheless tears himself from this deadly insensibility and performs the action without any inclination at all, but solely from duty—then for the first time his action has genuine moral worth. Further still, if nature has put little sympathy in this or that man's heart, if (while being an honest man in other respects) he is by temperament cold and indifferent to the sufferings of others, perhaps because as regards his own sufferings he is endowed with the special gift of patience and fortitude and expects or even requires that others should have the same; if such a man (who would truly not be nature's worst product) had not been exactly fashioned by her to be a philanthropist, would he not yet find in himself a source from which he might give himself a worth far higher than any that a good-natured temperament might have? By all means, because just here does the worth of the character come out; this worth is moral and incomparably the highest of all, viz., that he is beneficent, not from inclination, but from duty.

To secure one's own happiness is a duty (at least indirectly); for discontent with one's condition under many pressing cares and amid unsatisfied wants might easily become a great temptation to transgress one's duties. But here also do men of themselves already have, irrespective of duty, the strongest and deepest inclination toward happiness, because just in this idea are all inclinations combined into a sum total. But the precept of happiness is often so constituted as greatly to interfere with some inclinations, and yet men cannot form any definite and certain concept of the sum of satisfaction of all inclinations that is called happiness. Hence there is no wonder that a single inclination which is determinate both as to what it promises and as to the time within which it can be satisfied may outweigh a fluctuating idea; and there is no wonder that a man, e.g., a gouty patient, can choose to enjoy what he likes and to suffer what he may, since by his calculation he has here at least not sacrificed the enjoyment of the present moment to some possibly groundless expectations of the good fortune that is supposed to be found in health. But even in this case, if the universal inclination to happiness did not determine his will and if health, at least for him, did not figure as so necessary an element in his calculations; there still remains here, as in all other cases, a law, viz., that he should promote his happiness not from the inclination but from duty, and thereby for the first time does his conduct have real moral worth.

Undoubtedly in this way also are to be understood those passages of Scripture which command us to love our neighbor and even our enemy. For love as an inclination cannot be commanded; but beneficence from duty, when no inclination impels us and even when a natural and unconquerable aversion opposes such beneficence, is practical, and not pathological, love. Such love resides in the will and not in the propensities of feeling, in principals of action and not in tender sympathy; and only this practical love can be commanded.

The second proposition is this: An action done from duty has its moral worth, not in the purpose that is to be attained by it, but in the maxim according to which the action is determined. The moral worth depends, therefore, not on the realization of the object of the action, but merely on the principle of volition according to which, without regard to any objects of the faculty of desire, the action has been done. From what has gone before it is clear that the purposes which we may have in our actions, as well as their effects regarded as ends and incentives of the will, cannot give to actions any unconditioned and moral worth. Where, then, can this worth lie if it is not to be found in the will's relation to the expected effect? Nowhere but in the principle of the will, with no regard to the ends that can be brought about through such action. For the will stands, as it were, at a crossroads between its a priori principle, which is formal, and its a posteriori incentive, which is material; and since it must be determined by something, it must be determined by the formal principle of volition, if the action is done from duty—and in that case every material principle is taken away from it.

The third proposition, which follows from the other two, can be expressed thus: Duty is the necessity of an action done out of the respect for the law. I can indeed have an inclination for an object as the effect of my proposed action; but I can never have respect for such an object, just because it is merely an effect and is not an activity of the will. Similarly, I can have no respect for inclination as such, whether my own or that of another. I can at most, if my own inclination, approve it; and, if that of another, even love it, i.e., consider it to be favorable to my own advantage. An object of respect can only be what is connected with my will solely as ground and never as effect—something that does not serve my inclination but, rather, outweighs it, or at least excludes it from consideration when some choice is made—in other words, only the law itself can be an object of respect and hence can be a command. Now an action done from duty must altogether exclude the influence of inclination and therewith every object of the will. Hence there is nothing left which can determine the will except objectively the law and subjectively pure respect for this practical law, i.e., the will can be subjectively determined by the maxim that I should follow such a law even if all my inclinations are thereby thwarted.

Thus the moral worth of an action does not lie in the effect expected from it nor in any principle of action that needs to borrow its motive from this expected effect. For all these effects (agreeableness of one's condition and even furtherance of other people's happiness) could have been brought about also through other causes and would not have required the will of a rational being, in which the highest and unconditioned good can alone be found. Therefore, the pre-eminent good which is called moral can consist in nothing but the representation of the law in itself, and such a representation can admittedly be found only in a rational being insofar as this representation, and not some expected effect, is the determining ground of the will. This good is already present in the person who acts according to this representation, and such good need not be awaited merely from the effect.

But what sort of law can that be the thought of which must determine the will without reference to any expected effect, so that the will can be called absolutely good without qualification? Since I have deprived the will of every impulse that might arise for it from obeying any particular law, there is nothing left to serve the will as principle except the universal conformity of its actions to law as such, i.e., I should never act except in such a way that I can also will that my maxim should become a universal law. Here mere conformity to law as such (without having as its basis any law determining particular actions) serves the will as principle and must so serve it if duty is not to be a vain delusion and a chimerical concept. The ordinary reason of mankind in its practical judgments agrees completely with this, and always has in view the aforementioned principle.

For example, take this question. When I am in distress, may I make a promise with the intention of not keeping it? I readily distinguish here the two meanings which the question may have; whether making a false promise conforms with prudence or with duty. Doubtless the former can often be the case. Indeed I clearly see that escape from some present difficulty by means of such a promise is not enough. In addition I must carefully consider whether from this lie there may later arise far greater inconvenience for me than from what I now try to escape. Furthermore, the consequences of my false promise are not easy to foresee, even with all my supposed cunning; loss of confidence in me might prove to be far more disadvantageous than the misfortune which I now try to avoid. The more prudent way might be to act according to a universal maxim and to make it a habit not to promise anything without intending to keep it. But that such a maxim is, nevertheless, always based on nothing but a fear of consequences becomes clear to me at once. To be truthful from duty is, however, quite different from being truthful from fear of disadvantageous consequences; in the first case the concept of the action itself contains a law for me, while in the second I must first look around elsewhere to see what are the results for me that might be connected with the action. For to deviate from the principle of duty is quite certainly bad; but to abandon my maxim of prudence can often be very advantageous for me, though to abide by it is certainly safer. The most direct and infallible way, however, to answer the question as to whether a lying promise accords with duty is to ask myself whether I would really be content if my maxim (of extricating myself from difficulty by means of a false promise) were to hold as a universal law for myself as well as for others, and could I really say to myself that everyone may promise falsely when he finds himself in a difficulty from which he can find no other way to extricate himself. Then I immediately become aware that I can indeed will the lie but can not at all will a universal law to lie. For by such a law there would really be no promises at all, since in vain would my willing future actions be professed to other people who would not believe what I professed, or if they over-hastily did believe, then they would pay me back in like coin. Therefore, my maxim would necessarily destroy itself just as soon as it was made a universal law.

Therefore, I need no far-reaching acuteness to discern what I have to do in order that my will may be morally good. Inexperienced in the course of the world and incapable of being prepared for all its contingencies, I only ask myself whether I can also will that my maxim should become a universal law. If not, then the maxim must be rejected, not because of any disadvantage accruing to me or even to others, but because it cannot be fitting as a principle in a possible legislation of universal law, and reason exacts from me immediate respect for such legislation. Indeed I have as yet no insight into the grounds of such respect (which the philosopher may investigate). But I at least understand that respect is an estimation of a worth that far outweighs any worth of what is recommended by inclination, and that the necessity of acting from pure respect for the practical law is what constitutes duty, to which every other motive must give way because duty is the condition of a will good in itself, whose worth is above all else. . . .

Everything in nature works according to laws. Only a rational being has the power to act according to his conception of laws, i.e., according to principles, and thereby has he a will. Since the derivation of actions from laws requires reason, the will is nothing but practical reason. If reason infallibly determines the will, then in the case of such a being actions which are recognized to be objectively necessary are also subjectively necessary, i.e., the will is a faculty of choosing only that which reason, independently of inclination, recognizes as being practically necessary, i.e., as good. But if reason of itself does not sufficiently determine the will, and if the will submits also to subjective conditions (certain incentives) which do not always agree with objective conditions; in a word, if the will does not in itself completely accord with reason (as is actually the case with men), then actions which are recognized as objectively necessary are subjectively contingent, and the determination of such a will according to objective laws is necessitation. That is to say that the relation of objective laws to a will not thoroughly good is represented as the determination of the will of a rational being by principles of reason which the will does not necessarily follow because of its own nature.

The representation of an objective principle insofar as it necessitates the will is called a command (of reason) and the formula of the command is called an imperative.

All imperatives are expressed by an *ought* and thereby indicate the relation of an objective law of reason to a will that is not necessarily determined by this law because of its subjective constitution (the relation of necessitation). Imperatives say that something would be good to do or to refrain from doing, but they say it to a will that does not always therefore do something simply because it has been represented to the will as something good to do. That is practically good which determines the will by means of representations of reason and hence not by subjective causes, but objectively, i.e., on grounds valid for every rational being as such. It is distinguished from the pleasant as that which influences the will only by means of sensation from merely subjective causes, which hold only for this or that person's senses but do not hold as a principle of reason valid for everyone.

A perfectly good will would thus be quite as much subject to objective laws (of the good), but could not be conceived as thereby necessitated to act in conformity with law, inasmuch as it can of itself, according to its subjective constitution, be determined only by the representation of the good. Therefore no imperatives hold for the divine will, and in general for a holy will: the *ought* is here out of place, because the *would* is already of itself necessarily in agreement with the law. Consequently, imperatives are only formulas for expressing the relation of objective laws of willing in general to the subjective imperfection of the will of this or that rational being, e.g., the human will.

Now all imperatives command either hypothetically or categorically. The former represent the practical necessity of a possible action as a means for attaining something else that one wants (or may possibly want). The categorical imperative would be one which represented an action as objectively necessary in itself, without reference to another end.

Every practical law represents a possible action as good and hence as necessary for a subject who is practically determinable by reason; therefore all imperatives are formulas for determining an action which is necessary according to the principle of a will that is good in some way. Now if the action would be good merely as a means to something else, so is the imperative hypothetical. But if the action is represented as good in itself, and hence as necessary in a will which of itself conforms to reason as the principle of the will, then the imperative is categorical.

An imperative thus says what action possible by me would be good, and it presents the practical rule in relation to a will which does not forthwith perform an action simply because it is good, partly because the subject does not always know that the action is good and partly because (even if he does know it is good) his maxims might yet be opposed to the objective principles of practical reason.

A hypothetical imperative thus says only that an action is good for some purpose, either possible or actual. In the first case it is a problematic practical principle; in the second case an assertoric one. A categorical imperative, which declares an action to be of itself objectively necessary without reference to any purpose, i.e., without any other end, holds as an apodeictic practical principle. . . .

We shall, therefore, have to investigate the possibility of a categorical imperative entirely a priori, inasmuch as we do not here have the advantage of having its reality given in experience and consequently of thus being obligated merely to explain its possibility rather than to establish it. In the meantime so much can be seen for now: the categorical imperative alone purports to be a practical law, while all the others may be called principles of the will but not laws. The reason for this is that whatever is necessary merely in order to attain some arbitrary purpose can be regarded as in itself contingent, and the precept can always be ignored once the purpose is abandoned. Contrariwise, an unconditioned command does not leave the will free to choose the opposite at its own liking. Consequently, only such a command carries with it that necessity which is demanded from a law.

Secondly, in the case of this categorical imperative, or law of morality, the reason for the difficulty (of discerning its possibility) is quite serious. The categorical imperative is an a priori synthetic practical proposition; and since discerning the possibility of propositions of this sort involves so much difficulty in theoretic knowledge, there may readily be gathered that there will be no less difficulty in practical knowledge.

In solving this problem, we want first to inquire whether perhaps the mere concept of a categorical imperative may not also supply us with the formula containing the proposition that can alone be a categorical imperative. For even when we know the purport of such an absolute command, the question as to how it is possible will still require a special and difficult effort. . . .

If I think of a hypothetical imperative in general, I do not know beforehand what it will contain until its condition is given. But if I think of a categorical imperative, I know immediately what it contains. For since, besides the law, the imperative contains only the necessity that the maxim should accord with this law, while the law contains no condition to restrict it, there remains nothing but the universality of a law as such with which the maxim of the action should conform. This conformity alone is properly what is represented as necessary by the imperative.

Hence there is only one categorical imperative and it is this: Act only according to that maxim whereby you can at the same time will that it should become a universal law.

Now if all imperatives of duty can be derived from this one imperative as their principle, then there can at least be shown what is understood by the concept of duty and what it means, even though there is left undecided whether what is called duty may not be an empty concept.

The universality of law according to which effects are produced constitutes what is properly called nature in the most general sense (as to form), i.e., the existence of things as far as determined by universal laws. Accordingly, the universal imperative of duty may be expressed thus: Act as if the maxim of your action were to become through your will a universal law of nature.

We shall now enumerate some duties, following the usual division of them into duties to ourselves and to others and into perfect and imperfect duties.

1. A man reduced to despair by a series of misfortunes feels sick of life but is still so far in possession of his reason that he can ask himself whether taking his own life would not be contrary to his duty to himself. Now he asks whether the maxim of his action could become a universal law of nature. But his maxim is this: from self-love I make as my principle to shorten my life when its continued duration threatens more evil than it promises satisfaction. There only remains the question as to whether this principle of self-love can become a universal law of nature. One sees at once a contradiction in a system of nature whose law would destroy life by means of the very same feeling that acts so as to stimulate the furtherance of life, and hence there could be no existence as a system of nature. Therefore, such a maxim cannot possibly hold as a universal law of nature and is, consequently, wholly opposed to the supreme principle of all duty.

2. Another man in need finds himself forced to borrow money. He knows well that he won't be able to repay it, but he sees also that he will not get any loan unless he firmly promises to repay it within a fixed time. He wants to make such a promise, but he still has conscience enough to ask himself whether it is not permissible and is contrary to duty to get out of difficulty in this way. Suppose, however, that he decides to do so. The maxim of his action would then be expressed as follows: when I believe myself to be in need of money, I will borrow money and promise to pay it back, although I know that I can never do so. Now this principle of self-love or personal advantage may perhaps be quite compatible with one's entire future welfare, but the question is now whether it is right. I then transform the requirement of self-love into a universal law and put the question thus: how would things stand if my maxim were to become a universal law? He then sees at once that such a maxim could never hold as a universal law of nature and be consistent with itself, but must necessarily be self-contradictory. For the universality of a law which says that anyone believing himself to be in difficulty could promise whatever he pleases with the intention of not keeping it would make promising itself and the end to be attained thereby quite impossible, inasmuch as no one would believe what was promised him but would merely laugh at all such utterances as being vain pretenses.

3. A third finds in himself a talent whose cultivation could make him a man useful in many respects. But he finds himself in comfortable circumstances and prefers to indulge in pleasure rather than to bother himself about broadening and improving his fortunate natural aptitudes. But he asks himself further whether his maxim of neglecting his natural gifts, besides agreeing of itself with his propensity to indulgence, might agree also with what is called duty. He then sees that a system of nature could indeed always subsist according to such a universal law, even though every man (like South Sea Islanders) should let his talents rust and resolve to devote his life entirely to idleness, indulgence, propagation and, in a word, to enjoyment. But he cannot possibly will that this should become a universal law of nature or be im-

planted in us as such a law by a natural instinct. For as a rational being he necessarily wills that all his faculties should be developed, inasmuch as they are
given him for all sorts of possible purposes.

4. A fourth man finds things going well for himself but sees others (whom
he could help) struggling with great hardships; and he thinks: what does it
matter to me? Let everybody be as happy as Heaven wills or as he can make
himself; I shall take nothing from him nor even envy him; but I have no desire
to contribute anything to his well-being or to his assistance when in need. If
such a way of thinking were to become a universal law of nature, the human
race admittedly could very well subsist and doubtless could subsist even better than when everyone prates about sympathy and benevolence and even on
occasion exerts himself to practice them but, on the other hand, also cheats
when he can, betrays the rights of man, or otherwise violates them. But even
though it is possible that a universal law of nature could subsist in accordance
with that maxim, still it is impossible to will that such a principle should hold
everywhere as a law of nature. For a will which resolved in this way would
contradict itself, inasmuch as cases might often arise in which one would have
need of the love and sympathy of others and in which he would deprive himself, by such a law of nature springing from his own will, of all hope of the aid
he wants for himself.

These are some of the many actual duties, or at least what are taken to be
such, whose derivation from the single principle cited above is clear. We must
be able to will that a maxim of our action become a universal law; this is the
canon for morally estimating any of our actions. Some actions are so constituted that their maxims cannot without contradiction even be thought as a
universal law of nature, much less be willed as what should become one. In
the case of others this internal impossibility is indeed not found, but there is
still no possibility of willing that their maxim should be raised to the universality of a law of nature, because such a will would contradict itself. There is
no difficulty in seeing that the former kind of action conflicts with strict or
narrow [perfect] (irremissible) duty, while the second kind conflicts only with
broad [imperfect] (meritorious) duty. By means of these examples there has
thus been fully set forth how all duties depend as regards the kind of obligation (not the object of their action) upon the one principle.

If we now attend to ourselves in any transgression of a duty, we find that
we actually do not will that our maxim should become a universal law—because this is impossible for us—but rather that the opposite of this maxim
should remain a law universally. We only take the liberty of making an exception to the law for ourselves (or just for this one time) to the advantage of our
inclination. Consequently, if we weighed up everything from one and the
same standpoint, namely, that of reason, we would find a contradiction in our
own will, viz., that a certain principle be objectively necessary as a universal
law and yet subjectively not hold universally but should admit of exceptions.
But since we at one moment regard our action from the standpoint of a will

wholly in accord with reason and then at another moment regard the very same action from the standpoint of a will affected by inclination, there is really no contradiction here. Rather, there is an opposition (*antagonismus*) of inclination to the precept of reason, whereby the universality (*universalitas*) of the principle is changed into a mere generality (*generalitas*) so that the practical principle of reason may meet the maxim halfway. Although this procedure cannot be justified in our own impartial judgment, yet it does show that we actually acknowledge the validity of the categorical imperative and (with all respect for it) merely allow ourselves a few exceptions which, as they seem to us, are unimportant and forced upon us.

We have thus at least shown that if duty is a concept which is to have significance and real legislative authority for our actions, then such duty can be expressed only in categorical imperatives but not at all in hypothetical ones. We have also—and this is already a great deal—exhibited clearly and definitely for every application what is the content of the categorical imperative, which must contain the principle of all duty (if there is such a thing at all). But we have not yet advanced far enough to prove a priori that there actually is an imperative of this kind, that there is a practical law which of itself commands absolutely and without any incentives, and that following this law is duty.

In order to attain this proof there is the utmost importance in being warned that we must not take it into our mind to derive the reality of this principle from the special characteristics of human nature. For duty has to be a practical, unconditioned necessity of action; hence it must hold for all rational beings (to whom alone an imperative is at all applicable) and for this reason only can it also be a law for all human wills. On the other hand, whatever is derived from the special natural condition of humanity, from certain feelings and propensities, or even, if such were possible, from some special tendency peculiar to human reason and not holding necessarily for the will of every rational being—all of this can indeed yield a maxim valid for us, but not a law. This is to say that such can yield a subjective principle according to which we might act if we happen to have the propensity and inclination, but cannot yield an objective principle according to which we would be directed to act even though our every propensity, inclination, and natural tendency were opposed to it. In fact, the sublimity and inner worth of the command are so much the more evident in a duty, the fewer subjective causes there are for it and the more they oppose it; such causes do not in the least weaken the necessitation exerted by the law or take away anything from its validity.

Here philosophy is seen in fact to be put in a precarious position, which should be firm even though there is neither in heaven nor on earth anything upon which it depends or is based. Here philosophy must show its purity as author of its laws, and not as the herald of such laws as are whispered to it by an implanted sense or by who knows what tutelary nature. Such laws may be better than nothing at all, but they can never give us principles dictated by reason. These principles must have an origin that is completely a priori and must at the same time derive from such origin their authority to command. They expect nothing from the inclination of men but, rather, expect everything from the supremacy of the law and from the respect owed to the law. Without the latter expectation, these principles condemn man to self-contempt and inward abhorrence.

Hence everything empirical is not only quite unsuitable as a contribution to the principle of morality, but is even highly detrimental to the purity of morals. For the proper and inestimable worth of an absolutely good will consists precisely in the fact that the principle of action is free of all influences from contingent grounds, which only experience can furnish. This lax or even mean way of thinking which seeks its principle among empirical motives and laws cannot too much or too often be warned against, for human reason in its weariness is glad to rest upon this pillow. In a dream of sweet illusions (in which not Juno but a cloud is embraced) there is substituted for morality some bastard patched up from limbs of quite varied ancestry and looking like anything one wants to see in it but not looking like virtue to him who has once beheld her in her true form.

Therefore, the question is this: is it a necessary law for all rational beings always to judge their actions according to such maxims as they can themselves will that such should serve as universal laws? If there is such a law, then it must already be connected (completely a priori) with the concept of a rational being in general. But in order to discover this connection we must, however reluctantly, take a step into metaphysics, although into a region of it different from speculative philosophy, i.e., we must enter the metaphysics of morals. In practical philosophy the concern is not with accepting grounds for what happens but with accepting laws of what ought to happen, even though it never does happen—that is, the concern is with objectively practical laws. Here there is no need to inquire into the grounds as to why something pleases or displeases, how the pleasure of mere sensation differs from taste, and whether taste differs from a general satisfaction of reason, upon what does the feeling of pleasure and displeasure rest, and how from this feeling desires and inclinations arise, and how, finally, from these there arise maxims through the cooperation of reason. All of this belongs to an empirical psychology, which would constitute the second part of the doctrine of nature, if this doctrine is regarded as the philosophy of nature insofar as this philosophy is grounded on empirical laws. But here the concern is with objectively practical laws, and hence with the relation of a will to itself insofar as it is determined solely by reason. In this case everything related to what is empirical falls away of itself, because if reason entirely by itself determines conduct (and the possibility of such determination we now wish to investigate), then reason must necessarily do so a priori.

The will is thought of as a faculty of determining itself to action in accordance with the representation of certain laws, and such a faculty can be found only in rational beings. Now what serves the will as the objective ground of its self-determination is an end; and if this end is given by reason alone, then it must be equally valid for all rational beings. On the other hand, what contains merely the ground of the possibility of the action, whose effect is an end, is called the means. The subjective ground of desire is the incentive; the objective ground of volition is the motive. Hence there arises the distinction between subjective ends, which rest on incentives, and objective ends, which depend on motives valid for every rational being. Practical principles are formal when they abstract from all subjective ends; they are material, however, when they are founded upon subjective ends, and hence upon certain incentives. The ends which a rational being arbitrarily proposes to himself as effects of this action (material ends) are all merely relative, for only their relation to a specially constituted faculty of desire in the subject gives them their worth. Consequently, such worth cannot provide any universal principles, which are valid and necessary for all rational beings and, furthermore, are valid for every volition, i.e., cannot provide any practical laws. Therefore, all such relative ends can be grounds only for hypothetical imperatives.

But let us suppose that there were something whose existence has in itself an absolute worth, something which as an end in itself could be a ground of determinate laws. In it, and in it alone, would there be the ground of a possible categorical imperative, i.e., of a practical law.

Now I say that man, and in general every rational being, exists as an end in himself and not merely as a means to be arbitrarily used by this or that will. He must in all his actions, whether directed to himself or to other rational beings, always be regarded at the same time as an end. All the objects of inclinations have only a conditioned value; for if there were not these inclinations and the needs founded on them, then their object would be without value. But the inclinations themselves, being sources of needs, are so far from having an absolute value such as to render them desirable for their own sake that the universal wish of every rational being must be, rather, to be wholly free from them. Accordingly, the value of any object obtainable by our action is always conditioned. Beings whose existence depends not on our will but on nature have, nevertheless, if they are not rational beings, only a relative value as means and are therefore called things. On the other hand, rational beings are called persons inasmuch as their nature already marks them out as ends in themselves, i.e., as something which is not to be used merely as means and hence there is imposed thereby a limit on all arbitrary use of such beings, which are thus objects of respect. Persons are, therefore, not merely subjective ends, whose existence as an effect of our actions has a value for us; but such beings are objective ends, i.e., exist as ends in themselves. Such an end is one for which there can be substituted no other end to which such beings should serve merely as means, for otherwise nothing at all of absolute value would be found anywhere. But if all value were conditioned and hence contingent, then no supreme practical principle could be found for reason at all.

If then there is to be a supreme practical principle and, as far as the human will is concerned, a categorical imperative, then it must be such that from the conception of what is necessarily an end for everyone because this end is an end in itself it constitutes an objective principle of the will and can hence serve as a practical law. The ground of such a principle is this: rational nature exists as an end in itself. In this way man necessarily thinks of his own existence; thus far is it a subjective principle of human actions. But in this way also does every other rational being think of his existence on the same rational ground that holds also for me; hence it is at the same time an objective principle, from which, as a supreme practical ground, all laws of the will must be able to be derived. The practical imperative will therefore be the following: Act in such a way that you treat humanity, whether in your own person or in the person of another, always at the same time as an end and never simply as a means. We now want to see whether this can be carried out in practice.

Let us keep to our previous examples.

First, as regards the concept of necessary duty to oneself, the man who contemplates suicide will ask himself whether his action can be consistent with the idea of humanity as an end in itself. If he destroys himself in order to escape from a difficult situation, then he is making use of his person merely as a means so as to maintain a tolerable condition till the end of his life. Man, however, is not a thing and hence is not something to be used merely as a means; he must in all his actions always be regarded as an end in himself. Therefore, I cannot dispose of man in my own person by mutilating, damaging, or killing him. (A more exact determination of this principle so as to avoid all misunderstanding, e.g., regarding the amputation of the limbs in order to save oneself, or the exposure of one's life to danger in order to save it, and so on, must here be omitted; such questions belong to morals proper.)

Second, as concerns necessary or strict duty to others, the man who intends to make a false promise will immediately see that he intends to make use of another man merely as a means to an end which the latter does not likewise hold. For the man whom I want to use for my own purposes by such a promise cannot possibly concur with my way of acting toward him and hence cannot himself hold the end of this action. This conflict with the principle of duty to others becomes even clearer when instances of attacks on the freedom and property of others are considered. For then it becomes clear that a transgressor of the rights of men intends to make use of the persons of others merely as a means, without taking into consideration that, as rational beings, they should always be esteemed at the same time as ends, i.e., be esteemed only as beings who must themselves be able to hold the very same action as an end.

Third, with regard to contingent (meritorious) duty to oneself, it is not enough that the action does not conflict with humanity in our own person as an end in itself; the action must also harmonize with this end. Now there are in humanity capacities for greater perfection which belong to the end that nature has in view as regards humanity in our own person. To neglect these capacities might perhaps be consistent with the maintenance of humanity as an end in itself, but would not be consistent with the advancement of this end.

Fourth, concerning meritorious duty to others, the natural end that all men have is their own happiness. Now humanity might indeed subsist if nobody contributed anything to the happiness of others, provided he did not intentionally impair their happiness. But this, after all, would harmonize only negatively and not positively with humanity as an end in itself, if everyone does not also strive, as much as he can, to further the ends of others. For the ends of any subject who is an end in himself must as far as possible be my ends also, if that conception of an end in itself is to have its full effect in me.

This principle of humanity and of every rational nature generally as an end in itself is the supreme limiting condition of every man's freedom of action. This principle is not borrowed from experience, first, because of its universality, inasmuch as it applies to all rational beings generally, and no experience is capable of determining anything about them; and, secondly, because in experience (subjectively) humanity is not thought of as the end of men, i.e., as an object that we of ourselves actually make our end which as a law ought to constitute the supreme limiting condition of all subjective ends (whatever they may be); and hence this principle must arise from pure reason [and not from experience]. That is to say that the ground of all practical legislation lies objectively in the rule and in the form of universality, which (according to the first principle) makes the rule capable of being a law (say, for example, a law of nature). Subjectively, however, the ground of all practical legislation lies in the end; but (according to the second principle) the subject of all ends is every rational being as an end in himself. From this there now follows the third practical principle of the will as the supreme condition of the will's conformity with universal practical reason, viz., the idea of the will of every rational being as a will that legislates universal law.

According to this principle all maxims are rejected which are not consistent with the will's own legislation of universal law. The will is thus not merely subject to the law but is subject to the law in such a way that it must be regarded also as legislating for itself and only on this account as being subject to the law (of which it can regard itself as the author).

In the previous formulations of imperatives, viz., that based on the conception of actions to universal law in a way similar to a natural order and that based on the universal prerogative of rational beings as ends in themselves, these imperatives just because they were thought of as categorical excluded from their legislative authority all admixture of any interest as an incentive. They were, however, only assumed to be categorical because such an assumption had to be made if the concept of duty was to be explained. But that there were practical propositions which commanded categorically could not itself be proved. . . . But one thing could have been done, viz., to indicate that in willing from duty the renunciation of all interest is the specific mark distinguishing a categorical imperative from a hypothetical one and that such renunciation was expressed in the imperative itself by means of some determination contained in it. This is done in the present (third) formulation of the principle, namely, in the idea of the will of every rational being as a will that legislates universal law.

When such a will is thought of, then even though a will which is subject to law may be bound to this law by means of some interest, nevertheless a will that is itself a supreme lawgiver is not able as such to depend on any interest. For a will which is so dependent would itself require yet another law restricting the interest of its self-love to the condition that such interest should itself be valid as a universal law.

Thus the principle that every human will as a will that legislates universal law in all its maxims, provided it is otherwise correct, would be well suited to being a categorical imperative in the following respect: just because of the idea of legislating universal law such as an imperative is not based on any interest, and therefore it alone of all possible imperatives can be unconditional. Or still better, the proposition being converted, if there is a categorical imperative (i.e., a law for the will of every rational being), then it can only command that everything be done from the maxim of such a will as could at the same time have as its object only itself regarded as legislating universal law. For only then are the practical principle and the imperative which the will obeys unconditional, inasmuch as the will can be based on no interest at all.

When we look back upon all previous attempts that have been made to discover the principle of morality, there is no reason now to wonder why they one and all had to fail. Man was viewed as bound to laws by his duty; but it was not seen that man is subject only to his own, yet universal, legislation and that he is bound only to act in accordance with his own will, which is, however, a will purposed by nature to legislate universal laws. For when man is thought as being merely subject to a law (whatever it might be) then the law had to carry with it some interest functioning as an attracting stimulus or as a constraining force for obedience, inasmuch as the law did not arise as a law from his own will. Rather, in order that his will conform with law, it had to be necessitated by something else to act in a certain way. By this absolutely necessary conclusion, however, all the labor spent in finding a supreme ground for duty was irretrievably lost; duty was never discovered, but only the necessity of acting from a certain interest. This might be either one's own interest or another's, but either way the imperative had to be always conditional and could never possibly serve as a moral command. I want, therefore, to call my principle the principle of the autonomy of the will, in contrast with every other principle, which I accordingly count under heteronomy.

The concept of every rational being as one who must regard himself as legislating universal law by all his will's maxims, so that he may judge himself and his actions from this point of view, leads to another very fruitful concept, which depends on the aforementioned one, viz., that of a kingdom of ends.

By "kingdom" I understand a systematic union of different rational beings through common laws. Now laws determine ends as regards their universal validity; therefore, if one abstracts from the personal differences of rational beings and also from all content of their private ends, then it will be possible to think of a whole of all ends in systematic connection (a whole both of rational being as ends in themselves and also of the particular ends which each may set forth for himself); that is, one can think of a kingdom of ends that is possible on the aforesaid principles.

For all rational beings stand under the law that each of them should treat himself and all others never merely as means but always at the same time as an end in himself. Hereby arises a systematic union of rational beings through common objective laws, i.e., a kingdom that may be called a kingdom of ends (certainly only an ideal), inasmuch as these laws have in view the very relation of such beings to one another as ends and means.

A rational being belongs to the kingdom of ends as a member when he legislates in it universal laws while also being himself subject to these laws. He belongs to it as sovereign, when as legislator he is himself subject to the will of no other.

A rational being must always regard himself as legislator in a kingdom of ends rendered possible by freedom of the will, whether as member or as sovereign. The position of the latter can be maintained not merely through the maxims of his will but only if he is a completely independent being without needs and with unlimited power adequate to his will.

9

Kant and the Categorical Imperative

See page 11 for a biographical note on James Rachels.

Kant and the Categorical Imperative

Imagine that someone is fleeing from a murderer and tells you he is going home to hide. Then the murderer comes along and asks where the first man went. You believe that if you tell the truth, the murderer will find his victim and kill him. What should you do—should you tell the truth or lie?

We might call this The Case of the Inquiring Murderer. In this case, most of us would think it is obvious what we should do: we should lie. Of course, we don't think we should go about lying as a general rule, but in these specific circumstances it seems the right thing to do. After all, we might say, which is more important, telling the truth or saving someone's life? Surely in a case such as *this* lying is justified.

There is one important philosopher, however, who thought we should *never* lie, even in a case such as this. Immanuel Kant (1724–1804) was one of the seminal figures in modern philosophy. Almost alone among the great thinkers, Kant believed that morality is a matter of following *absolute rules—* rules that admit no exceptions, that must be followed come what may. He believed, for example, that lying is never right, no matter what the circumstances. It is hard to see how such a radical view could be defended, unless, perhaps, one held that such rules are God's unconditional commands. But Kant did not appeal to theological considerations; he relied only on rational arguments, holding that *reason* requires that we never lie. Let us see how he reached this remarkable conclusion. First we will look briefly at his general theory of ethics.

Kant observed that the word "ought" is often used nonmorally. For example:

1. If you want to become a better chess player, you ought to study the games of Bobby Fischer.
2. If you want to go to law school, you ought to sign up to take the entrance examination.

Much of our conduct is governed by such "oughts." The pattern is: we have a certain wish (to become a better chess player, to go to law school); we recognize that a certain course of action would help us get what we want (studying Fischer's games, signing up for the entrance examination); and so we conclude that we should follow the indicated plan.

Kant called these "hypothetical imperatives" because they tell us what to do *provided that* we have the relevant desires. A person who did not want to improve his or her chess would have no reason to study Fischer's games; someone who did not want to go to law school would have no reason to take the entrance examination. Because the binding force of the "ought" depends on our having the relevant desire, we can *escape* its force simply by renouncing the desire. Thus by saying "I no longer want to go to law school," one can get out of the obligation to take the exam.

Moral obligations, by contrast, do not depend on our having particular desires. The form of a moral obligation is not "If you want so-and-so, then you ought to do such-and-such." Instead, moral requirements are *categorical:* they have the form, "You ought to do such-and-such, *period.*" The moral rule is not, for example, that you ought to help people *if* you care for them or *if* you have some other purpose that helping them might serve. Instead, the rule is that you should be helpful to people *regardless of* your particular wants and desires. That is why, unlike hypothetical "oughts," moral requirements cannot be escaped simply by saying "But I don't care about that."

Hypothetical "oughts" are easy to understand. They merely require us to adopt the means that are necessary to attain the ends we choose to seek. Categorical "oughts," on the other hand, are rather mysterious. How can we be obligated to behave in a certain way regardless of the end we wish to achieve? Much of Kant's moral philosophy is an attempt to explain what categorical "oughts" are and how they are possible.

Kant holds that, just as hypothetical "oughts" are possible because we have desires, categorical "oughts" are possible because we have reason. Categorical "oughts" are binding on rational agents *simply because they are rational.* How can this be so? It is, Kant says, because categorical oughts are derived from a principle that every rational person must accept. He calls this principle *The Categorical Imperative.* In his *Groundwork of the Metaphysics of Morals* (1785), he expresses The Categorical Imperative like this:

> Act only according to that maxim by which you can at the same time will that it should become a universal law.

This principle summarizes a procedure for deciding whether an act is morally permissible. When you are contemplating doing a particular action, you are to ask what rule you would be following if you were to do that action. (This will be the "maxim" of the act.) Then you are to ask whether you would be willing for that rule to be followed by everyone all the time. (That would make it a "universal law" in the relevant sense.) If so, the rule may be followed, and the act is permissible. However, if you would *not* be willing for everyone to follow the rule, then you may not follow it, and the act is morally impermissible.

Kant gives several examples to explain how this works. Suppose, he says, a man needs to borrow money, and he knows that no one will lend it to him unless he promises to repay. But he also knows that he will be unable to repay. He therefore faces this question: Should he promise to repay the debt, knowing that he cannot do so, in order to persuade someone to make the loan? If he were to do that, the "maxim of the act" (the rule he would be following) would be: *Whenever you need a loan, promise to repay it, even though you know you cannot do so.* Now, could this rule become a universal law? Obviously not, because it would be self-defeating. Once this became a universal practice, no one would any longer believe such promises, and so no one would make loans because of them. As Kant himself puts it, "no one would believe what was promised to him but would only laugh at any such assertion as vain pretense."

Another of Kant's examples has to do with giving charity. Suppose, he says, someone refuses to help others in need, saying to himself "What concern of mine is it? Let each one be happy as heaven wills, or as he can make himself; I will not take anything from him or even envy him; but to his welfare or to his assistance in time of need I have no desire to contribute." This, again, is a rule that one cannot will to be a universal law. For at some time in the future this man might *himself* be in need of assistance from others, and he would not want others to be so indifferent to him.

Absolute Rules and the Duty Not to Lie

Being a moral agent, then, means guiding one's conduct by "universal laws"—moral rules that hold, without exception, in all circumstances. Kant thought that the rule against lying was one such rule. Of course, this was not the *only* absolute rule Kant defended—he thought there are many others; morality is full of them. But it will be useful to focus on the rule against lying as a convenient example. Kant devoted considerable space to discussing this rule, and it is clear that he felt especially strongly about it—he said that lying in any circumstances is "the obliteration of one's dignity as a human being."

Kant offered two main arguments for this view. Let us examine them one at a time.

1. His primary reason for thinking that lying is always wrong was that the prohibition of lying follows straightaway from The Categorical Imperative. We could not will that it be a universal law that we should lie, because it would be self-defeating; people would quickly learn that they could not rely on what other people said, and so the lies would not be believed. Surely there is something to this: in order for a lie to be successful, people must believe that

others are telling the truth; so the success of a lie depends on there *not* being a "universal law" permitting it.

There is, however, an important problem with this argument, which will become clear if we spell out Kant's line of thought more fully. Let us return to The Case of the Inquiring Murderer. Should you tell him the truth? Kant would have you reason as follows:

(1) You should do only those actions that conform to rules that you could will to be adopted universally.
(2) If you were to lie, you would be following the rule "It is permissible to lie."
(3) This rule could not be adopted universally, because it would be self-defeating: people would stop believing one another, and then it would do no good to lie.
(4) Therefore, you should not lie.

The problem with this way of reasoning was nicely summarized by the British philosopher Elizabeth Anscombe when she wrote about Kant in the academic journal *Philosophy* in 1958:

> His own rigoristic convictions on the subject of lying were so intense that it never occurred to him that a lie could be relevantly described as anything but just a lie (e.g. as "a lie in such-and-such circumstances"). His rule about universalizable maxims is useless without stipulations as to what shall count as a relevant description of an action with a view to constructing a maxim about it.

The difficulty arises in step (2) of the argument. Exactly what rule would you be following if you lied? The crucial point is that there are many ways to formulate the rule; some of them might not be "universalizable" in Kant's sense, but some would be. Suppose we said you were following *this* rule (R): "It is permissible to lie when doing so would save someone's life." We *could* will that (R) be made a "universal law," and it would not be self-defeating.

It might be replied that the universal adoption of (R) *would* be self-defeating because potential murderers would cease to believe us. But they would believe us if they thought we did not know what they were up to: and if they thought we *did* know what they were up to, they would not bother to ask us in the first place. This is no different from the situation that exists now, in the real world: murderers know that people will not willingly aid them. Thus the adoption of (R) would help save lives, at little cost, and it would not undermine general confidence in what people say in ordinary circumstances.

The problem we have identified is a difficulty for Kant's whole approach. It applies not only to the argument about lying but to any decision about what to do: for any action a person might contemplate, it is possible to specify more than one rule that he or she would be following; some of these rules will be "universalizable" and some will not; therefore, the test of "universalizability" cannot help us to establish which actions are permissible and which are not. This is equally a problem for any view that takes moral rules as absolute, regardless of whether the view takes its inspiration from Kant. For we can always get around any such rule by describing our action in such a way that it does not fall under that rule but instead comes under a different one.

2. The Case of the Inquiring Murderer is not simply an example I made up; it is Kant's own example. In an essay with the charmingly old-fashioned title "On a Supposed Right to Lie from Altruistic Motives," Kant discusses this case and gives a second argument for his view about it. He writes:

> After you have honestly answered the murderer's question as to whether his intended victim is at home, it may be that he has slipped out so that he does not come in the way of the murderer, and thus that the murder may not be committed. But if you had lied and said he was not at home when he had really gone out without your knowing it, and if the murderer had then met him as he went away and murdered him, you might justly be accused as the cause of his death. For if you had told the truth as far as you knew it, perhaps the murderer might have been apprehended by the neighbors while he searched the house and thus the deed might have been prevented. Therefore, whoever tells a lie, however well intentioned he might be, must answer for the consequences, however unforeseeable they were, and pay the penalty for them. . . .
>
> To be truthful (honest) in all deliberations, therefore, is a sacred and absolutely commanding decree of reason, limited by no expediency.

This argument may be stated in a more general form: We are tempted to make exceptions to the rule against lying because in some cases we think the consequences of truthfulness would be bad and the consequences of lying good. However, we can never be certain about what the consequences of our actions will be; we cannot *know* that good results will follow. The results of lying *might* be unexpectedly bad. Therefore, the best policy is always to avoid the known evil—lying—and let the consequences come as they will. Even if the consequences are bad, they will not be our fault, for we will have done our duty.

The problems with this argument are obvious enough—so obvious, in fact, that it is surprising a philosopher of Kant's stature was not more sensitive to them. In the first place, the argument depends on an unreasonably pessimistic view of what we can know. Sometimes we can be quite confident of what the consequences of our actions will be, and justifiably so; in which case we need not hesitate because of uncertainty. Moreover—and this is a more interesting matter, from a philosophical point of view—Kant seems to assume that although we would be morally responsible for any bad consequences of lying, we would *not* be similarly responsible for any bad consequences of telling the truth. Suppose, as a result of our telling the truth, the murderer found his victim and killed him. Kant seems to assume that we would be blameless. But can we escape responsibility so easily? After all, we aided the murderer. This argument, then, like the first one, is not very convincing.

Conflicts Between Rules

The idea that moral rules are absolute, allowing no exceptions, is implausible in light of such cases as The Case of the Inquiring Murderer, and Kant's arguments for it are unsatisfactory. But are there any convincing arguments against the idea, apart from its being implausible?

The principal argument against absolute moral rules has to do with the possibility of conflict cases. Suppose it is held to be absolutely wrong to do A in any circumstances and also wrong to do B in any circumstances. Then what about the case in which a person is faced with the choice between doing A and doing B—when he must do something and there are no other alternatives available? This kind of conflict case seems to show that it is *logically* untenable to hold that moral rules are absolute.

Is there any way this objection can be met? One way would be for the absolutist to deny that such cases ever actually occur. The British philosopher P. T. Geach takes just this view. Like Kant, Geach argues that moral rules are absolute; but his reasons are very different from Kant's. Geach holds that moral rules must be understood as absolute divine commands, and so he says simply that God will not allow conflict situations to arise. We can describe fictitious cases in which there is no way to avoid violating one of the absolute rules, but, he says, God will not permit such circumstances to exist in the real world. In his book *God and the Soul* (1969) Geach writes:

> "But suppose circumstances are such that observance of one Divine law, say the law against lying, involves breach of some other absolute Divine prohibition?"— If God is rational, he does not command the impossible; if God governs all events by his providence, he can see to it that circumstances in which a man is inculpably faced by a choice between forbidden acts do not occur. Of course such circumstances (with the clause "and there is no way out" written into their description) are consistently describable; but God's providence could ensure that they do not in fact arise. Contrary to what nonbelievers often say, belief in the existence of God does make a difference to what one expects to happen.

Do such circumstances ever actually arise? The Case of the Inquiring Murderer is, of course, a fictitious example; but it is not difficult to find real-life examples that make the same point. During the Second World War, Dutch fishermen regularly smuggled Jewish refugees to England in their boats, and the following sort of thing sometimes happened. A Dutch boat, with refugees in the hold, would be stopped by a Nazi patrol boat. The Nazi captain would call out and ask the Dutch captain where he was bound, and who was on board, and so forth. The fishermen would lie and be allowed to pass. Now it is clear that the fishermen had only two alternatives, to lie or to allow their passengers (and themselves) to be taken and shot. No third alternative was available; they could not, for example, remain silent and outrun the Nazis.

Now suppose the two rules "It is wrong to lie" and "It is wrong to permit the murder of innocent people" are both taken to be absolute. The Dutch fishermen would have to do one of these things; therefore a moral view that absolutely prohibits both is incoherent. Of course this difficulty could be avoided if one held that only *one* of these rules is absolute; that would apparently be Kant's way out. But this dodge cannot work in every such case; so long as there are at least two "absolute rules," whatever they might be, the possibility will always exist that they might come into conflict. And that makes the view of those rules as absolute impossible to maintain.

Another Look at Kant's Basic Idea

Few philosophers would dispute Paton's statement that Kant's *Groundwork* "has exercised on human thought an influence almost ludicrously disproportionate to its size." Yet at the same time, few would defend The Categorical Imperative as Kant formulated it—as we have seen, it is beset by serious, perhaps insurmountable, problems. What, then, accounts for Kant's influence? Is there some basic idea underlying The Categorical Imperative that we might accept, even if we do not accept Kant's particular way of expressing it? I believe that there is, and that the power of this idea accounts, at least in part, for Kant's vast influence.

Remember that Kant thinks The Categorical Imperative is binding on rational agents simply because they are rational—in other words, a person who did not accept this principle would be guilty not merely of being immoral but of being *irrational*. This is a fascinating idea—that there are rational as well as moral constraints on what a good person may believe and do. But what exactly does this mean? In what sense would it be irrational to reject The Categorical Imperative?

The basic idea seems to be this: A moral judgment must be backed by good reasons—if it is true that you ought (or ought not) to do such-and-such, then there must be a *reason why* you should (or should not) do it. For example, you may think that you ought not to set forest fires because property would be destroyed and people would be killed. But if you accept those as reasons in *one* case, you must also accept them as reasons in *other* cases. It is no good saying that you accept those reasons some of the time, but not all the time; or that other people must respect them, but not you. Moral reasons, if they are valid at all, are binding on all people at all times. This is a requirement of consistency; and Kant was right to think that no rational person could deny it.

This is the Kantian idea—or, I should say, one of the Kantian ideas—that has been so influential. It has a number of important implications. It implies that a person cannot regard himself as special, from a moral point of view: he cannot consistently think that *he* is permitted to act in ways that are forbidden to others, or that *his* interests are more important than other people's interests. As one commentator remarked, I cannot say that it is all right for me to drink your beer and then complain when you drink mine. Moreover, it implies that there are *rational constraints* on what we may do: we may want to do something—say, drink someone else's beer—but recognize that we cannot consis-

tently do it, because we cannot at the same time accept its implications. If Kant was not the first to recognize this, he was the first to make it the cornerstone of a fully worked-out system of morals. That was his great contribution.

But Kant went one step further and concluded that consistency requires rules that have no exceptions. It is not hard to see how his basic idea pushed him in that direction; but the extra step was not necessary, and it has caused trouble for his theory ever since. Rules, even within a Kantian framework, *need not* be regarded as absolute. All that is required by Kant's basic idea is that when we violate a rule, we do so for a reason that we would be willing for anyone to accept, were they in our position. In The Case of the Inquiring Murderer, this means that we may violate the rule against lying only if we would be willing for anyone to do so were they faced with the same situation. And *that* proposition causes little trouble. . . .

The Idea of "Human Dignity"

The great German philosopher Immanuel Kant thought that human beings occupy a special place in creation. Of course he was not alone in thinking this. It is an old idea: from ancient times, humans have considered themselves to be essentially different from all other creatures—and not just different but *better*. In fact, humans have traditionally thought themselves to be quite fabulous. Kant certainly did. On his view, human beings have an "intrinsic worth, i.e., *dignity*," which makes them valuable "above all price." Other animals, by contrast, have value insofar as they serve human purposes. In his *Lectures on Ethics* (1779), Kant said:

> But so far as animals are concerned, we have no direct duties. Animals . . . are there merely as means to an end. That end is man.

We can, therefore, use animals in any way we please. We do not even have a "direct duty" to refrain from torturing them. Kant admits that it probably is wrong to torture them, but the reason is not that *they* would be hurt; the reason is only that *we* might suffer indirectly as a result of it, because "he who is cruel to animals becomes hard also in his dealings with men." Thus on Kant's view, mere animals have no moral importance at all. Human beings are, however, another story entirely. According to Kant, humans may never be "used" as means to an end. He even went so far as to suggest that this is the ultimate law of morality.

Like many other philosophers, Kant believed that morality can be summed up in one ultimate principle, from which all our duties and obligations are derived. He called this principle *The Categorical Imperative*. In the *Groundwork of the Metaphysics of Morals* (1785) he expressed it like this:

> Act only according to that maxim by which you can at the same time will that it should become a universal law.

However, Kant also gave *another* formulation of The Categorical Imperative. Later in the same book, he said that the ultimate moral principle may be understood as saying:

Act so that you treat humanity, whether in your own person or in that of another, always as an end and never as a means only.

Scholars have wondered ever since why Kant thought these two rules were equivalent. They *seem* to express very different moral conceptions. Are they, as he apparently believed, two versions of the same basic idea, or are they really different ideas? We will not pause over this question. Instead we will concentrate here on Kant's belief that morality requires us to treat persons "always as an end and never as a means only." What exactly does this mean, and why did he think it true?

When Kant said that the value of human beings "is above all price," he did not intend this as mere rhetoric but as an objective judgment about the place of human beings in the scheme of things. There are two important facts about people that, in his view, support this judgment.

First, because people have desires and goals, other things have value *for them*, in relation to *their* projects. Mere "things" (and this includes nonhuman animals, whom Kant considered unable to have self-conscious desires and goals) have value only as means to ends, and it is human ends that *give* them value. Thus if you want to become a better chess player, a book of chess instruction will have value for you; but apart from such ends the book has no value. Or if you want to travel about, a car will have value for you; but apart from this desire the car will have no value.

Second, and even more important, humans have "an intrinsic worth, i.e., *dignity*, because they are *rational agents*—that is, free agents capable of making their own decisions, setting their own goals, and guiding their conduct by reason. Because the moral law is the law of reason, rational beings are the embodiment of the moral law itself. The only way that moral goodness can exist at all in the world is for rational creatures to apprehend what they should do and, acting from a sense of duty, do it. This, Kant thought, is the *only* thing that has "moral worth." Thus if there were no rational beings, the moral dimension of the world would simply disappear.

It makes no sense, therefore, to regard rational beings merely as one kind of valuable thing among others. They are the beings *for whom* mere "things" have value, and they are the beings whose conscientious actions have moral worth. So Kant concludes that their value must be absolute, and not comparable to the value of anything else.

If their value is "beyond all price," it follows that rational beings must be treated "always as an end, and never as a means only." This means, on the most superficial level, that we have a strict duty of beneficence toward other persons: we must strive to promote their welfare; we must respect their rights, avoid harming them, and generally "endeavor, so far as we can, to further the ends of others."

But Kant's idea also has a somewhat deeper implication. The beings we are talking about are *rational* beings, and "treating them as ends-in-themselves" means *respecting their rationality*. Thus we may never *manipulate* people, or *use* people, to achieve our purposes, no matter how good those purposes may be. Kant gives this example, which is similar to an example he uses to illustrate the first version of his categorical imperative: Suppose you need money, and so you want a "loan," but you know you will not be able to repay it. In desperation, you consider making a false promise (to repay) in order to trick a friend into giving you the money. May you do this? Perhaps you need the money for a good purpose—so good, in fact, that you might convince yourself the lie would be justified. Nevertheless, if you lied to your friend, you would merely be manipulating him and using him "as a means."

On the other hand, what would it be like to treat your friend "as an end"? Suppose you told the truth, that you need the money for a certain purpose but will not be able to repay it. Then your friend could make up his own mind about whether to let you have it. He could exercise his own powers of reason, consulting his own values and wishes, and make a free, autonomous choice. If he did decide to give the money for this purpose, he would be choosing to make that purpose *his own*. Thus you would not merely be using him as a means to achieving *your* goal. This is what Kant meant when he said, "Rational beings . . . must always be esteemed at the same time as ends, i.e., only as beings who must be able to contain in themselves the end of the very same action." . . .

Questions for Discussion

1. Why does James Rachels believe that psychological egoism is a confused theory of human behavior? Why does he believe that ethical egoism fails as a moral theory?

2. In Bernard Pomerance's play *The Elephant Man*, Dr. Frederick Treves becomes interested in the plight of David Merrick, a horribly deformed man afflicted with elephantiasis. At first, Treves's aim is to lead his patient to live as normal a life as possible. However, after he gains notoriety for helping the young Merrick, he begins to question whether he is helping his patient out of benevolent concern or whether he is motivated by his newfound fame. Might we ourselves be unaware of what motivates our conduct? Think of some cases where you were unsure of what motivated your conduct.

3. Paul W. Taylor distinguishes between descriptive relativism and normative relativism. How are these theories similar? How are they different?

4. Not many years ago the majority view in the Anglo-American world was that women were second-class moral citizens. Today the majority view is

just the opposite: that women are first-class moral citizens. Do you believe that women were second-class citizens then but are first-class citizens now, or that they were first-class citizens then and we were mistaken in thinking otherwise? Discuss this question in light of the claims of ethical relativism.

5. According to Jeremy Bentham, we need only to calculate pleasures using the hedonistic calculus to determine if an action is right or wrong. Do you think that pleasures can be quantified and compared? Why or why not?

6. Do you agree with John Stuart Mill that the pleasures of a Socrates are more valuable than those of a fool? Or is it true that "ignorance is bliss"? Discuss.

7. Robert Nozick believes that few of us would want to be attached to his "experience machine" because there are things we desire in addition to pleasure. Do you agree with Nozick? Remember that while we are connected to the machine all experiences we have are perceived as real.

8. Bernard Williams seems to think that directly killing a single person is morally worse than acting in a way that allows twenty people to be killed. Do you agree? Do you believe there is a morally relevant difference between killing and allowing to be killed?

9. Do you agree with John M. Taurek that "numbers don't count"? Is it permissible to torture one child to death if that is the only way to prevent everyone else in the world from being tortured to death?

10. Is God a utilitarian? Argue pro or con.

11. According to utilitarianism, our concern should be with increasing the sum of happiness in the world. Does this mean that a world filled with many marginally happy people is better than a world filled with fewer people who are individually happier?

12. What does Immanuel Kant mean by "good will" and why does he believe that it is an "unqualified good"?

13. Do you agree with Kant that one's greatest moral virtue is the capacity to be rational and self-governing? What is the place of one's capacity to feel sympathy for one's fellow creatures?

14. It has been argued, in the spirit of Kantianism, that it is better for all the criminally guilty to go free than for one innocent person to be wrongly imprisoned. Do you agree? Why or why not?

15. Kant tells us never to treat a person "merely as a means." What would be an example of this? What would be an example of treating a person as a means but not "merely" as such?

Selected Bibliography

Ethical Egoism

Baier, Kurt. *The Moral Point of View* (Chapter 8). Ithaca, N.Y.: Cornell University Press, 1958.

Brandt, R. B. *Ethical Theory* (Chapter 14). Englewood Cliffs, N.J.: Prentice-Hall, 1959.

Campbell, Richmond. "A Short Refutation of Ethical Egoism," *Canadian Journal of Philosophy* 2 (1972): 249-54.

Hobbes, Thomas. *Leviathan*. Edited by C. B. MacPherson. New York: Penguin Books, 1968.

Nagel, Thomas. *The Possibility of Altruism*. New York: Oxford University Press, 1970.

Plato. *The Republic* (Chapter 5). Translated by Francis Cornford. New York: Oxford University Press, 1945.

Rachels, James. "Egoism and Moral Skepticism." In *Philosophy: Paradox and Discovery*. Edited by Arthur J. Minton, 272–281. New York: McGraw-Hill, 1976.

Rand, Ayn. *The Virtue of Selfishness: A New Concept of Egoism*. New York: New American Library, 1964.

Ethical Relativism

Benedict, Ruth. "Anthropology and the Abnormal." *Journal of General Psychology* 10 (1934): 59-82.

Brandt, Richard. *Ethical Theory* (Chapters 2–5 and 7–11). Englewood Cliffs, N.J.: Prentice-Hall, 1959.

Garrett, K. Richard. *Dialogues Concerning the Foundations of Ethics*. Savage, Md.: Rowman & Littlefield, 1990.

Ladd, John. *Ethical Relativism*. Belmont, Calif.: Wadsworth, 1973.

Midgley, Mary. *Heart and Mind*. New York: St. Martin's Press, 1981.

Stace, W. T. *The Concept of Morals*. New York: Macmillan, 1937.

Taylor, Paul. "Four Types of Ethical Relativism." *Philosophical Review* 62 (1954): 500-16.

Wellman, Carl. "The Ethical Implications of Cultural Relativity." *Journal of Philosophy* 60 (1963): 169-84.

Utilitarianism

Bayles, Michael D., ed. *Contemporary Utilitarianism*. Garden City, N.Y.: Doubleday, 1968.

Bentham, Jeremy. *Introduction to the Principles of Morals and Legislation* (1789), with *A Fragment on Government*. Edited by W. Harrison. Oxford, England: Hafner Press, 1948.

Frey, R. G., ed. *Utility and Rights*. Minneapolis: University of Minnesota Press, 1984.

Glover, Jonathan, ed. *Utilitarianism and Its Critics*. New York: Macmillan, 1990.

Hare, R. M. *Moral Thinking, Its Levels, Methods and Point*. Oxford, England: Oxford University Press, 1981.

Hodgson, Dennis H. *Consequences of Utilitarianism*. Oxford, England: Clarendon Press, 1967.

Lyons, David. *Forms and Limits of Utilitarianism*. Oxford, England: Clarendon Press, 1964.

Mill, John Stuart. *Utilitarianism*. Edited by George Sher. Indianapolis, Ind.: Hackett, 1979.

Moore, G. E. *Principia Ethica*. Cambridge, England: Cambridge University Press, 1903.

Quinton, Anthony. *Utilitarian Ethics*. LaSalle, Ill.: Open Court, 1988.

Scheffler, Samuel. *Consequentialism and Its Critics*. New York: Oxford University Press, 1988.

Sen, Amartya, and Bernard Williams, eds. *Utilitarianism and Beyond*. New York: Cambridge University Press, 1982.

Sidgwick, Henry. *The Methods of Ethics*. 7th ed. Indianapolis, Ind.: Hackett, 1981.

Smart, J. J. C., and Bernard Williams. *Utilitarianism: For and Against*. New York: Cambridge University Press, 1973.

Kantianism

Aune, Bruce. *Kant's Theory of Morals*. Princeton, N.J.: Princeton University Press, 1979.

Kant, Immanuel. *Critique of Practical Reason*. Translated by Lewis White Beck. Indianapolis, Ind.: Bobbs-Merrill, 1956.

―――. *Grounding for the Metaphysics of Morals*. Translated by James W. Ellington. Indianapolis, Ind.: Hackett, 1981.

―――. *Lectures on Ethics*. Translated by Louis Infield. New York: Harper Torchbooks, 1963.

―――. *The Metaphysical Elements of Justice*. Translated by John Ladd. Indianapolis, Ind.: Bobbs-Merrill, 1965.

―――. *Ethical Philosophy*. Translated by J. W. Ellington. Indianapolis, Ind.: Hackett, 1983.

Murphy, Jeffrie. *Kant: The Philosophy of Right*. London: Macmillan, 1970.

Nell, Onora. *Acting on Principle, An Essay on Kantian Ethics*. New York: Columbia University Press, 1975.

Paton, H. J. *The Categorical Imperative*. New York: Harper & Row, 1967.

Ross, W. D. *Kant's Ethical Theory*. Oxford, England: Clarendon Press, 1954.

Wolff, Robert Paul. *The Autonomy of Reason*. Harper & Row, 1973.

B. APPLICATIONS

Action-Based Theories and Their Applications

Moral theorizing has important implications for real-life problems. By bringing theory to bear on actual problems we come to understand more fully what our theories entail. By attending to the complexities of the actual world we notice theoretical issues we might otherwise overlook. And by drawing on our theoretical findings, we gain new insight into how we should behave.

Consider the question of whether our treatment of animals is morally justified. It is undeniable that humans cause animals a great deal of suffering. Take the treatment of veal calves, for instance, in the established practice of factory farming. Veal calves are kept in unnatural conditions so as to provide humans with a more marketable product: They are quartered in narrow stalls, tethered there with chains around their necks to limit their activity and make their flesh tender and pale; they are fed a nutritionally deficient diet that promotes rapid weight gain. (Some calves lick the urine-soaked sides of their stalls to get the iron the urine contains.) Is this treatment justified? Should we condone it to satisfy our palates?

Consider, as well, the question of what our policies should be toward feeding the world's poor. It is an established fact that millions around the world are malnourished or starving, and millions more will die if population levels continue to rise. Those of us who live comfortably can influence these events by making contributions to famine relief, working toward lowering the birth rate, and supporting policies that enable the poor to purchase more food. Or, alternatively, we can do nothing and let nature run its course. What are our responsibilities? What portion of our time, energy, and wealth should we give to preventing starvation?

These, of course, are only two of many moral issues that confront us in the actual world. Among others, there are the problems of gay and lesbian rights (what rights should gays and lesbians have?), of capital punishment (is it ever justified?), and of distributive justice (what, if anything, should be done about the unequal distribution of wealth in society?). In addition, there are the problems that surround such practices as abortion, euthanasia, pornography, and war.

Theorizing about morality can help solve these problems. Take, for instance, our treatment of animals. A utilitarian would be disposed to argue that it is wrong to kill animals for food because animals can feel pain, and it is wrong to inflict pain on sentient beings. In fact, the utilitarian Jeremy Bentham drew just this conclusion. Bentham wrote:

> The day may come when the rest of the animal creation may acquire those rights which never could have been withholden from them but by the hand of tyranny. The French have already discovered that the blackness of the skin is no reason why a human being should be abandoned without redress to the caprice of a tormentor. It may one day come to be recognized that the number of the legs, the

villosity of the skin, or the termination of the os sacrum are reasons equally insufficient for abandoning a sensitive being to the same fate. What else is it that should trace the insuperable line? Is it the faculty of reason, or perhaps the faculty of discourse? But a full-grown horse or dog is beyond comparison a more rational, as well as a more conversable animal, than an infant of a day or a week or even a month old. But suppose they were otherwise, what would it avail? The question is not, can they reason? nor can they talk? but can they suffer?[1]

The contemporary utilitarian Peter Singer draws a similar conclusion in his celebrated book *Animal Liberation*.

In contrast, Kantians would be disposed to draw a different conclusion. For them, ethics is grounded in reason. Reason makes possible the capacity to act on principles of moral conduct. But since (nonhuman) animals lack this capacity, they are excluded from membership in the moral community. Hence, we show no disrespect when we use them to satisfy our palates.[2]

We see, then, that theorizing about ethics is not only interesting as a philosophical enterprise, it is also useful as a tool for living. Most of us have strong opinions on concrete moral matters (e.g., Is abortion immoral? Is capital punishment wrong? Is euthanasia permissible?). Few of us, however, are able to offer a sustained defense of the opinions we hold. The task of philosophical reflection is to unify these judgments into some consistent whole while at the same time trying to discern the underlying theory that explains them. Having ascertained the theory, we could then apply it to novel issues such as those created by biomedical technology.

Finally, the goal of unifying our judgments and justifying them with philosophical theory sometimes yields surprising results. We may find, for instance, that the implications of a theory are sufficient reason for us to reject it. So convinced might we be, for instance, that animals are members of the moral community that we might reject Kantianism on that account alone. Alternatively, we might accommodate our theory by modifying our earlier views. So convinced might we be that utilitarianism is true, for instance, that we might decide that eating meat is wrong even if we had previously believed it was permissible.

Whatever the results, theorizing about ethics benefits us by forcing us to think clearly and systematically about our moral beliefs. Many of us come to the study of ethics laden with beliefs that we have never logically scrutinized. Typically, these beliefs are formed by our cultural, religious, and parental heritage, and, as such, are accepted in childhood, automatically and uncritically. Who has not suspected, at one time or other, that a deeply held belief was nothing more than an irrational prejudice? Theorizing about ethics enables us, then, to transcend the dogmatism that typifies such views and to develop a morality that is rationally satisfying.

---

[1] *Introduction to the Principles of Morals and Legislation*, Chapter 17.

[2] Kant himself argued that we should show kindness to animals lest we show cruelty to human beings. See James Rachels, "Kant and the Categorical Imperative," p. 87.

Summary of Readings

In "Ethical Vegetarianism and Commercial Animal Farming," Tom Regan asks whether the practice of animal farming is morally justified and whether we are morally obligated to become vegetarians. In this essay, one sees clearly how theorizing about morality has important implications for real-life problems.

Regan begins his inquiry with a discussion of moral anthropocentrism, a view he attributes to Kant and others that asserts that only human interests should be considered when we decide how we should behave. In this view, the interests of animals do not matter (or do not matter very much). After demonstrating how utilitarians (such as Peter Singer) reject this view and are thus opposed to commercial animal farming, Regan nonetheless argues that we do have a duty to become vegetarians but one not grounded in considerations of utility. Among the reasons he gives is a problem he sees with utilitarianism itself; namely, that it incorrectly makes the morality of individual acts depend on how others behave. Because of this, Regan is drawn to another line of argument—one that makes deontological considerations relevant to the duty to become vegetarians.

Briefly put, Regan begins with the premise that having a right means that others have a duty to respect that right. Because persons, claims Regan, have moral rights, and some (nonhuman) animals are persons, it follows that humans have a duty to respect animal rights. And the way this is done is by abolishing commercial animal farming and becoming vegetarians.

The second reading in this section, "Famine, Affluence, and Morality" by Peter Singer, addresses the question of whether we are morally obligated to contribute part of our time and resources to alleviating hunger. After describing the famine and starvation that exist in the world, Singer argues that affluent persons are morally obligated to give to those in need. As to how much to give, Singer invokes the principle that when we can prevent something bad from happening without sacrificing something of comparable importance, then morally we ought to do so. Practically speaking, this means that those who *have* are morally obligated to give to those who *have not*, but not to the point that the haves are in danger of becoming have-nots. Otherwise put, one should not blind oneself to save another from blindness, although one could, of course, contribute financially to an operation.

In putting forward this argument, it is not hard to see Singer's utilitarianism. The principle of utility requires that we maximize happiness (or minimize suffering) for the greatest number of people. Given this principle, no one person is entitled to more than he needs for survival, provided others can benefit by what he has. Thus, the principle of utility requires that we alleviate suffering if we can.

In the next selection, "Execution," Jonathan Glover addresses the question of whether execution is a morally justified means of punishment. Traditionally there have been two lines of argument in defense of execution: retributivism and deterrence. In the retributivist theory of punishment (traditionally associated with Kantianism), a person guilty of a crime deserves punishment and the punishment must be proportionate to the crime. Murder, it is argued, is a crime for which execution is the proportionate punishment. Thus, murderers and perhaps others deserve to die.

In the deterrence theory of punishment (traditionally associated with utilitarianism), punishment of criminals is justified if the benefits outweigh the costs. Now, the particular benefits claimed for the death penalty are deterrence and prevention; it deters other potential criminals from killing, and it prevents the executed criminal from committing further crimes. Thus, murderers should be executed because of the good consequences.

Needless to say, the appeals to retribution and deterrence are both problematic. Critics of retributivism have argued, for instance, that the principle that says the punishment should fit the crime, *lex talionis*, is indefensible.[3] Others who accept this principle have argued that life imprisonment is as fitting a punishment as execution.[4] Critics of deterrence have argued that capital punishment does not deter and that the benefits do not outweigh the costs: innocent people, for instance, may be unjustly executed.

Glover begins with a discussion of Kant's retributivism and the absolutist's rejection of capital punishment on the grounds that it is never justifiable to kill a human being. For Glover, from a utilitarian perspective, both of these views are unacceptable. The utilitarian approach is that the death penalty is justified if the number of lives saved exceeds the number of executions. But because of some undesirable features of capital punishment, such as its effects on the loved ones of the person executed, Glover argues that it is not justified unless it has a substantial deterrence effect and, after considering various arguments, Glover concludes that it does not.

Thus far, the readings in this section have largely portrayed the conflict between consequentialism and deontology. However, there are other theoretical approaches to practical issues. In "Homosexuality and the 'Unnaturalness' Argument," Burton M. Leiser critiques an argument typically advanced by natural law theorists designed to show the immorality of homosexuality; namely, that homosexuality is immoral because it is unnatural.

According to Leiser, a satisfactory natural law argument against homosexuality would have to provide a definition of "unnatural" that would clearly include homosexuality. It would also have to provide a reason for thinking that this unnaturalness is linked with causing harm and is therefore a ground for moral condemnation. According to Leiser, the natural law argument against homosexuality fails to satisfy either of these criteria and must therefore be rejected.

---

[3] See, e.g., Hugo Adam Bedau, "Capital Punishment," in *Matters of Life and Death*, ed. Tom Regan (New York: Random House, 1980), 148-82.

[4] See, e.g., Justice Thurgood Marshall's opinion in *Gregg* v. *Georgia*.

In the final reading of this section, "Distributive Justice," John Rawls tackles the problem of distributive justice from the perspective of social contract theory. This essay is an answer to the question, "What, if anything, should be done about the unequal distribution of wealth in society?"

Social contract theorists take contractual fairness to be the ultimate political ideal and contend that the fundamental rights and duties in a society are those that people would agree to under fair conditions. Within this tradition, Rawls argues for certain principles of justice that free and rational people would agree to if they were in an original position of equality. As Rawls makes clear in his other writings, this original position is a hypothetical one in which persons are behind an imaginary "veil of ignorance" and do not know particular facts about themselves, such as their place in society, their talents and assets, or their intelligence and strength. Rawls's claim is that people in this position would choose the following two principles of justice: (1) the principle of equality, in which everyone has a right to equal liberty; and (2) the principle of difference, in which differences of wealth and privilege are justified only if they are open to all in fair competition and are to the benefit of the least advantaged. These principles serve as a yardstick against which to measure the justice of our present social arrangements, including, but not limited to, our present distribution of wealth.

10

Ethical Vegetarianism and Commercial Animal Farming

Tom Regan teaches philosophy at North Carolina State University. He has written numerous books and articles and has edited several textbooks. On the subject of animal rights, he has written *All That Dwell Therein: Essays on Animal Rights and Environmental Ethics* (1982) and *The Case for Animal Rights* (1983).

Introduction

Time was when a few words in passing usually were enough to exhaust the philosophical interest in the moral status of animals other than human beings. "Lawless beasts," writes Plato. "Of the order of sticks and stones," opines the nineteenth-century Jesuit W. D. Ritchie. True, there are notable exceptions, at least as far back as Pythagoras, who advocated vegetarianism on ethical grounds—Cicero, Epicurus, Herodotus, Horace, Ovid, Plutarch, Seneca, Virgil: hardly a group of "animal crazies"! By and large, however, a few words would do nicely, thank you, or, when one's corpus took on grave proportions, a few paragraphs or pages. Thus we find Kant, for example, by all accounts one of the most influential philosophers in the history of ideas, devoting almost two full pages to the question of our duties to animals, while St. Thomas Aquinas, easily the most important philosopher-theologian in the Catholic tradition, bequeaths perhaps ten pages to the topic at hand.

Times change. Today an even modest bibliography listing titles of the past decade's work on the moral status of animals would easily equal the length of Kant's and Aquinas' treatments combined, a quantitative symbol of the changes that have taken place, and continue to take place, in philosophy's attempts to rouse slumbering prejudices lodged in the anthropocentrism of western thought.

With relatively few speaking to the contrary (St. Francis always comes to mind in this context), theists and humanists, rowdy bedfellows in most quarters, have gotten along amicably when questions were raised about the moral

From Tom Regan, "Ethical Vegetarianism and Commercial Animal Farming," in *Proceedings* of the Conference on Topic of Agriculture, Change, and Human Values. Copyright 1982.

center of the terrestrial universe: *Human* interests form the center of that universe. Let the theist look hopefully beyond the harsh edge of bodily death, let the humanist denounce, in Freud's terms, this "infantile view of the world," at least the two could agree that the moral universe revolves around us humans—our desires, our needs, our goals, our preferences, our love for one another. The intense dialectic now characterizing philosophy's assaults on the traditions of humanism and theism, assaults aimed not only at the traditional account of the moral status of animals but at the foundation of our moral dealings with the natural environment, with Nature generally—these assaults should not be viewed as local skirmishes between obscure academicians each bent on occupying a deserted fortress. At issue are the validity of alternative visions of the scheme of things and our place in it. The growing philosophical debate over our treatment of animals and the environment is both a symptom and a cause of a culture's attempt to come to critical terms with its past as it attempts to shape its future.

At present there are three major challenges being raised against moral anthropocentrism. The first is the one issued by *utilitarians*; the second, by proponents of *moral rights*. . . . This essay offers brief summaries of each position with special reference to how their advocates answer two questions: (a) Is vegetarianism required on ethical grounds? and (b) Judged ethically, what should we say, and what should we do, about commercial animal agriculture? To ask whether vegetarianism is required on ethical grounds is to ask whether there are reasons other than those that relate to one's own welfare (for example, other than those that relate to one's own health or financial well-being) that call for leading a vegetarian way of life. As for the expression "commercial animal agriculture," that should be taken to apply to the practice of raising animals to be sold for food. The ethics of other practices that involve killing animals (for example, hunting, the use of animals in science, "the family farm" where the animals raised are killed and eaten by the people who raise them, etc.) will not be considered, except in passing, not because the ethics of these practices should not demand our close attention but because space and time preclude our giving them this attention here. Time and space also preclude anything approaching "complete" assessments of the three views to be discussed. None can be proven right or wrong in a few swift strokes. Even so, it will be clear where my own sympathies lie.

Traditional Moral Anthropocentrism

Aquinas and Kant speak of the anthropocentric tradition. That tradition does not issue a blank check when it comes to the treatment of animals. Morally, we are enjoined to be kind to animals and, on the other side of the coin, not to be cruel to them. But we are not enjoined to be the one and prohibited from being the other because we owe such treatment to *animals themselves*—not, that is, because we have any duties *directly* to nonhumans; rather, it is because of *human* interests that we have these duties regarding animals. "So far as animals are concerned," writes Kant, "we have no direct duties. . . . Our duties to animals are merely indirect duties to mankind." In the case of cruelty, we are not to be cruel to animals because treating them cruelly will develop a habit of cruelty, and a habit of cruelty, once it has taken up lodging in our breast, will in time include human beings among its victims. "(H)e who is cruel to animals becomes hard also in his dealings with men." And *that* is why cruelty to animals is wrong. As for kindness, "(t)ender feelings towards dumb animals develop humane feelings toward mankind."[1] And *that* is why we have a duty to be kind to animals.

So reasons Kant. Aquinas, predictably, adds theistic considerations, but the main storyline is the same, as witness the following passage from his *Summa Contra Gentiles.*

> Hereby is refuted the error of those who said it is sinful for a man to kill dumb animals: for by divine providence they are intended for man's use in the natural order. Hence it is no wrong for man to make use of them, either by killing, or in any other way whatever. . . . And if any passages of Holy Writ seem to forbid us to be cruel to dumb animals, for instance to kill a bird with its young: this is either to remove men's thoughts from being cruel to other men, and lest through being cruel to animals one becomes cruel to human beings: or because injury to an animal leads to the temporal hurt of man, either of the doer of the deed, or of another: or on account of some (religious) signification: thus the Apostle expounds the prohibition against muzzling the ox that treadeth the corn.[2]

To borrow a phrase from the twentieth-century English philosopher Sir W. D. Ross, our treatment of animals, both for Kant and Aquinas, is "a practice ground for moral virtue." The *moral game* is played between human players or, on the theistic view, human players plus God. The way we treat animals is a sort of moral warmup, character calisthenics, as it were, for the moral game in which animals themselves play no part.

The Utilitarian Challenge

The first fairly recent spark of revolt against moral anthropocentrism comes, as do other recent protests against institutionalized prejudice, from the pens of the nineteenth-century utilitarians, most notably Jeremy Bentham and John Stuart Mill. These utilitarians—who count the balance of pleasure over pain for all sentient creatures as the yardstick of moral right and wrong, and who reject out of hand Descartes' famous teaching that animals are "nature's machines," lacking any trace of conscious awareness—recognize the direct moral significance of the pleasures and pains of animals. In an oft-quoted passage, Bentham enfranchises animals within the utilitarian moral community by declaring that "(t)he question is not, Can they talk?, or Can they reason?, but, Can they suffer?"[3] And Mill stakes the credibility of utilitarianism itself on its implications for the moral status and treatment of animals, writing that "(w)e (that is, those who subscribe to utilitarianism) are perfectly willing to stake the whole question on this one issue. Granted that any practice causes more pain to animals than it gives pleasure to man: is that practice moral or immoral? And if, exactly in proportion as human beings raise their heads out of the slough of selfishness, they do not with one voice answer 'immoral' let the morality of the principle of utility be forever condemned."[4] The duties we have regarding animals, then, are duties we have *directly to them*, not indirect duties to humanity. For utilitarians, animals are themselves involved in the moral game.

Viewed against this historical backdrop, the position of the contemporary Australian moral philosopher Peter Singer can be seen to be an extension of the attack on the tradition of moral anthropocentrism initiated by his utilitarian forebears. For though this sometimes goes unnoticed by friend and foe alike, Singer, whose book *Animal Liberation* is unquestionably the most influential work published in the 1970s on the topic of the ethics of our treatment of animals, *is* a utilitarian.[5] That view requires, he believes, observance of the equality of interests principle. This principle requires that, before we decide what to do, we consider the interests (that is, the preferences) of all those who are likely to be affected by what we do *and* weigh equal interests equally. We must not, that is, refuse to consider the interests of some of those who will be affected by what we do because, say, they are Catholic, or female, or black. *Everyone's* interests must be considered. And we must not discount the importance of comparable interests because they are the interests of, say, a Catholic, woman, or black. Everyone's interests must be weighed *equitably*. Of course, to ignore or discount the importance of a woman's interests *because she is a woman* is the very paradigm of the moral prejudice we call sexism, just as to ignore or discount the importance of the interests of blacks (or Native Americans, Chicanos, etc.) are paradigmatic forms of racism. It remained for Singer to argue, which he does with great vigor, passion, and skill, that a similar moral prejudice lies at the heart of moral anthropocentrism, a prejudice that Singer, borrowing a term first coined by the English author and animal activist Richard Ryder, denominates *speciesism*.[6] Like Bentham and Mill before him, Singer, the utilitarian, *denies* that we are to treat animals well in the name of the betterment of humanity, *denies* that we are to do this because this will help us discharge our duties to our fellow humans, *denies* that acting dutifully toward animals is a moral warmup for the real moral game played between humans, or, as theists would add, between humans-and-humans-and-God. *We owe it to those animals who have interests to take their interests into account, just as we also owe it to them to count their interests equitably.* Our duties regarding animals are, in these respects, *direct* duties we have to them, not indirect duties to humanity. To think otherwise is to give sorry testimony to the prejudice of speciesism Singer is intent upon unmasking.

Farming Today

Singer believes that the utilitarian case for ethical vegetarianism is strengthened when we inform ourselves of the changes taking place in commercial animal farming today. In increasing numbers, animals are being brought in off the land and raised indoors, in unnatural, crowded conditions—raised "intensively," to use the jargon of the animal industry, in structures that look for all the world like factories. Indeed, it is now common practice to refer to such commercial ventures as *factory farms*. The inhabitants of these "farms" are kept in cages, or stalls, or pens, or closely-confined in other ways, living out their abbreviated lives in a technologically created and sustained environment: automated feeding, automated watering, automated light cycles, automated waste removal, automated what-not. And the crowding: as many as nine hens in cages that measure eighteen by twenty-four inches; veal calves confined to twenty-two inch wide stalls; hogs similarly confined, sometimes in tiers of cages—two, three, four rows high. Could any impartial, morally sensitive person view what goes on in a factory farm with benign approval? Certainly many of the basic interests of the animals are simply ignored or undervalued, Singer claims, because they do not compute economically. Their interest in physical freedom or in associating with members of their own species, these interests routinely go by the board. And for what? So that we humans can dine on steaks and chops, drumsticks and roasts, food that is simply inessential for our own physical well-being. Add to this sorry tale of speciesism on today's farm the enormous waste that characterizes animal industry, waste to the tune of six or seven pounds of vegetable protein to produce a pound of animal protein in the case of beef cattle, for example, and add to the accumulated waste of nutritious food the chronic need for just such food throughout the countries of the Third World, whose populations characteristically are malnourished at best and literally starving to death at worst—add all these factors together and we have, Singer believes, the basis for the utilitarian's answers to our two questions. In response to the question, "Is vegetarianism required on ethical grounds?" the Singer-type utilitarian replies affirmatively. For it is not for self-interested reasons that Singer calls us to vegetarianism (though such reasons, including a concern for one's health, are not irrelevant). It is for ethical reasons that we are to take up a vegetarian way of life. And as for our second question, the one that asks what we should think and do about commercial animal farming, Singer's utilitarian argument prescribes, he thinks, that we should think ill of today's factory farms and act to bring about significant humane improvements by refusing to purchase their products. Ethically considered, we ought to become vegetarians.

The Challenge to Utilitarianism

Singer, then, is the leading contemporary representative of the utilitarian critique of the anthropocentric heritage bequeathed to us by humanism and theism. How should we assess his critique? Our answer requires answering two related questions. First, How adequate is the general utilitarian position Singer advocates? Second, How adequate is Singer's application of this general position to the particular case of commercial animal agriculture and, allied with this, the case for ethical vegetarianism? A brief response to each question, beginning with the second, will have to suffice. Consider Singer's claim that each of us has a duty to become a vegetarian. How can this alleged duty be defended on *utilitarian* grounds? Well, on this view, we know, the act I *ought* to perform, the act I have a *duty* to do, is the one that will bring about the best consequences for all those affected by the outcome, which, for Singer, means the act that will bring about the optimal balance of preference satisfaction over preference frustration. But it is naive in the extreme to suppose that, were *I* individually henceforth to abstain from eating meat and assiduously lead a vegetarian existence, this will improve the lot of a single animal. Commercial animal farming simply does not work in this way. It does not, that is, fine-tune its production to such a high degree that it responds to the decisions of each individual consumer. So, no, the individual's abstention from meat will not make the slightest dent, will not effect the smallest change, in commercial animal agriculture. No one, therefore, Singer included, can ground *the individual's* ethical obligation to be vegetarian on the effects *the individual's* acts will have on the welfare of animals.

Similar remarks apply to the other presumed beneficiaries of the individual's conversion to vegetarianism. The starving, malnourished masses of the Third World will not receive the food they need if I would but stop eating animals. For it is, again, naive in the extreme to suppose that the dietary decisions and acts of any given *individual* will make the slightest difference to the quality of life for any inhabitant in the Third World. Even were it true, which it is not (and it is not true because commercial animal agriculture is not so fine-tuned in this respect either), that a given amount of protein-rich grain *would not be fed to animals* if I abstained from eating meat, it simply would not follow that this grain *would find its way to any needy human being*. To suppose otherwise is to credit one's individual acts and decisions with a kind of godlike omnipotence a robust sense of reality cannot tolerate. Thus, since the type of utilitarianism Singer advocates prescribes that we decide what our ethical duties are by asking what will be the consequences of our acts, and since there is no realistic reason to believe that the consequences of my abstaining from meat will make any difference whatever to the quality of life of commercially raised farm animals or the needy people of the Third World, the alleged duties to become a vegetarian and to oppose commercial animal agriculture lack the kind of backing a utilitarian like Singer requires.

Here one might attempt to defend Singer by arguing that it is the total or sum of the consequences of *many* people becoming vegetarians, not just the results of each individual's decisions, that will spare some animals the rigors of factory farms and save some humans from malnutrition or starvation. Two replies to this attempted defense may be briefly noted. First, this defense at most gives *a sketch of a possible* reply; it does not give a finished one. As a utilitarian, Singer must show that the consequences for everyone involved would be better if a number of people became vegetarians than if they did not. But to show this, Singer must provide a thorough rundown of what the consequences would be, or would be in all probability, if we abstained from eating meat, *or* ate less of it, *or* ate none at all. And this is no easy task. Would the grains not fed to animals even be grown if the animal industry's requirements for them were reduced or eliminated? Would there be an economically viable market for corn, oats, and other grains if we became vegetarians? Would farmers have the necessary economic incentive to produce enough grain to feed the world's hungry human beings? Who knows? In particular, does Singer know? One looks in vain to find the necessary empirical backing for an answer here. Or consider: Suppose the grain is available. From a utilitarian point of view, would it be best (that is, would we be acting to produce the best consequences) if we made this grain available to the present generation of the world's malnourished? Or would it be better in the long run to refuse to aid these people at this point in time? After all, if we assist them now, will they not simply reproduce? And won't their additional numbers make the problem of famine for the next generation even more tragic? Who knows what the correct answers to these questions are? Who knows what is even "most likely" to be true? It is not unfair to a utilitarian such as Singer to mark the depths of our ignorance in these matters. And neither is it unfair to emphasize how our ignorance stands in the way of his attempt to ground the obligatoriness of vegetarianism on utilitarian considerations. If we simply do not know what the consequences of our becoming vegetarians would be, or are most likely to be, and if we simply do not know whether the consequences that would result would be, or are most likely to be, better than those that would obtain if we did not become vegetarians, then we simply lack any semblance of a utilitarian justification for the obligation to become vegetarians or for mounting a frontal assault on commercial animal agriculture. The decision to lead a vegetarian way of life and, by doing so, to lodge a moral complaint against commercial animal agriculture, viewed from the perspective of Singer's utilitarianism, must be diagnosed as at best symbolic gestures.

Aside from these matters, what can be said about the adequacy of utilitarianism in general? That is a question raised earlier to which we must now direct our attention. There is a vast literature critical of utilitarian theory, and it will obviously not be possible to survey it here. Here let us note just one difficulty. Utilitarianism, at least as understood by Singer, implies that whether *I* am doing what I ought to do is crucially dependent on what *other* people do. For example, although the consequences of *my* abstaining from eating meat are too modest to make any difference to how animals are raised or whether grains are made available to needy people, if enough *other* people join me in a vegetarian way of life we could collectively bring about changes in the number of animals raised, how they are raised, what use is made of grain, etc. The situation, in other words, is as follows: If enough people join me so that the consequences of what we do *collectively* makes some impact, then what I do might be right, whereas if too few people join me, with the result that the consequences of what we do fails to make any difference to how animals are raised, etc., then I am *not* doing what is right.

To make the morality of an individual's acts depend on how others behave is a highly unsatisfactory consequence for any moral theory. When people refuse to support racist or sexist practices (for example, in employment or education), they do what is right, but their doing what is right does not depend on how many *other* people join them. The number of people who join them determines how many people do or support what is right, *not* what is right in the first place. Utilitarianism, because it makes *what is right* dependent in many cases on how many people act in a certain way, puts the moral cart before the horse. What we want is a theory that illuminates moral right and wrong independently of how many people act in this or that way. And that is precisely what utilitarianism, at least in the form advocated by Singer, fails to give us. For all its promise as an attack on the anthropocentric traditions of humanism and theism, for all its insistence on the direct relevance of the interests of animals, and despite the radical sounding claims made by utilitarians in criticism of current practices on the farm and in the laboratory, utilitarianism proves to be more ethical shadow than substance. If we look beyond the rhetoric and examine the arguments, utilitarianism might not change these practices as much as it would fortify them.[7]

The Rights View

An alternative to the utilitarian attack on anthropocentrism is what we shall call "the rights view."[8] Those who accept this view hold that (1) certain individuals have certain moral rights, (2) these individuals have these rights independently of considerations about the value of the consequences of treating them in one way or another, and (3) the duty the individual has to respect the rights of others does not depend on how many other people act in ways that respect these rights. The first point distinguishes proponents of the rights view from, among others, those utilitarians like Bentham and Singer who deny that individuals have moral rights; the second distinguishes advocates of the rights view from, among others, those utilitarians such as Mill who hold that individuals have moral rights if, and only if, the general welfare would be promoted by saying and acting as if they do; and the third point distinguishes those who champion the rights view from, among others, any advocate of utilitarianism who holds that my duty to act in certain ways depends on how many other people act in these ways. According to the rights view, certain individuals have moral rights, and my duty to act in ways that respect such an individual's (A's) rights is a duty I have directly to A, a duty I have to A that is not grounded in considerations about the value of consequences for all those affected by the outcome, and a duty I have to A whatever else others might do to A. *Those who advocate animal rights, understanding this idea after the fashion of the rights view, believe that some of those individuals who have moral rights, and thus some of those to whom we have duties of the type just described, are animals.*

Grounds for the Rights View

To proclaim "the moral rights of Man" sounds good but is notoriously difficult to defend. Bentham, who writes more forcefully to support what he rejects than to establish what he accepts, dismisses rights other than legal rights as "nonsense upon stilts." So we will not settle the thorny question about human rights of an essay's reading or writing. And, it goes without saying, the moral rights of animals must remain even less established. Were Bentham in his grave (in fact he remains above ground, encased in glass in an anteroom in University College, London, where he is dutifully brought to dinner each year on the occasion of his birthday) he would most certainly roll over at the mere mention of *animal* rights! Still, something needs to be said about the rational grounds for the rights view.

An important (but not the only possible) argument in this regard takes the following form: Unless we recognize that certain individuals have moral rights, we will be left holding moral principles that sanction morally reprehensible conduct. Thus, in order to avoid holding principles that allow such conduct, we must recognize that certain individuals have moral rights. The following discussion of utilitarianism is an example of this general line of argument.

Utilitarians cut from the same cloth as Bentham would have us judge moral right and wrong by appeal to the consequences of what we do. Well, suppose aged Aunt Bertha's heirs could have a lot more pleasure than she is likely to have in her declining years if she were to die. But suppose that neither nature nor Aunt Bertha will cooperate: She simply refuses to die as expeditiously as, gauged by the interest of her heirs, is desirable. Why not speed up the tempo of her demise? The reply given by Bentham-type utilitarians shows how far they are willing to twist our moral intuitions to save their theory. If we were to kill Aunt Bertha, especially if we took care to do so painlessly, then, these utilitarians submit, we would do no wrong to Aunt Bertha. However, if *other* people found out about what we did, they would quite naturally grow more anxious, more insecure about their own safety and mortality, and these mental states (anxiety, insecurity, and the like) are painful. Thus, so we are told, killing Aunt Bertha is wrong (if it is) because of the painful consequences for others!

Except for those already committed to a Bentham-style utilitarianism, few are likely to find this account satisfactory. Its shortcomings are all the more evident when we note that *if* others did not find out about our dastardly deed (and so were not made more anxious and insecure by their knowledge of what we did), and *if* we have a sufficiently undeveloped conscience not to be terribly troubled by what we did, and *if* we do not get caught, and *if* we have a jolly good time with Aunt Bertha's inheritance, a much better time, in fact, than we would have had if we had waited for nature to run its course, then Bentham-style utilitarianism implies that we did nothing wrong in killing Aunt Bertha and, indeed, acted as we morally ought to have acted. People who, in the face of this kind of objection, remain Bentham-type utilitarians, may hold a consistent position. But one pays a price for a "foolish consistency." The spectacle of people "defending their theory to the last" in spite of its grave implications must, to put it mildly, take one's moral breath away.

There are, of course, many ethical theories in addition to utilitarianism, and many versions of utilitarianism in addition to the one associated with Bentham. So even if the sketch of an argument against Bentham's utilitarianism proves successful, the rights view would not thereby "win" in its competition with other theories. But the foregoing does succeed in giving a representative sample of one argument deployed by those who accept the rights view: If you deny moral rights, as Bentham does, then the principles you put in their place, which, in Bentham's case, is the principle of utility, will sanction morally reprehensible conduct (for example, the murder of Aunt Bertha). If those who affirm and defend the rights view could show this given *any* initially plausible theory that denies moral rights, and if they could crystalize and defend the methodology on which this argument depends, then they would have a powerful reason for their position.

The Value of the Individual

The rights view aspires to satisfy our intellect, not merely our appetite for rhetoric, and so it is obliged to provide a theoretical home for moral rights. Part, but by no means not the whole, of this home is furnished by the rights views' theory of value. Unlike utilitarian theories (for example, value hedonism), the rights view recognizes *the value of individuals*, not just the value of their mental states (for example, their pleasures). Following custom, let us call these latter sorts of value "intrinsic values" and let us introduce the term "inherent value" for the type of value attributed to individuals. Then the notion of inherent value can be explained as follows. First, the inherent value of an individual who has such value is not the same as, is not reducible to, and is incommensurate with the intrinsic value of that individual's, or of any combination of individuals', mental states. The inherent value of an individual, in other words, is not equal to any sum of intrinsic values (for example, any sum of pleasures). Second, all individuals who have inherent value have it equally. Inherent value, that is, does not come in degrees; some who have it do not have it more or less than others. One either has it or one does not, and all who have it have it to the same extent. It is, one might say, a categorical concept. Third, the possession of inherent value by individuals does not depend on their utility relative to the interests of others, which, if it were true, would imply that some individuals have such value to a greater degree than do others, because some (for example, surgeons) have greater utility than do others (for example, bank thieves). Fourth, and relatedly, individuals cannot acquire or lose such value by anything they do. And fifth, and finally, the inherent value of individuals does not depend on what or how others think or feel about them. The loved and admired are neither more nor less inherently valuable than the despised and forsaken.

Now, the rights view claims that any individual who has inherent value is due treatment that respects this value (has, that is, a *moral right* to such treatment), and though not everything can be said here about what such respect comes to, at least this much should be clear. We fail to treat individuals with the respect they are due whenever we assume that how we treat them can be defended *merely* by asking about the value of the mental states such treatment produces for those affected by the outcome. This must fail to show appropriate respect since it is tantamount to treating these individuals as if they lacked inherent value—as if, that is, we treat them as we ought whenever we can justify our treatment of them *merely* on the grounds that it promotes the interests other individuals have in obtaining preferred mental states (for example, pleasure). Since individuals who have inherent value have a kind of value that is not reducible to their utility relative to the interests of others, we are not to treat them merely as a means to bringing about the best consequences. We ought not, then, kill Aunt Bertha, given the rights view, even if doing so brought about "the best" consequences. That would be to treat her with a lack of appropriate respect, something she has a moral right to. To kill her for these reasons would be to violate her rights.

Which Individuals Have Inherent Value?

Even assuming the rights view could succeed in providing a coherent, rationally persuasive theoretical framework for "the rights of Man," further argument would be necessary to illuminate and justify the rights of animals. That argument, not surprisingly, will be long and tortuous. At least we can be certain of two things, however. First, it must include considerations about the criteria of right possession; and, second, it will have to include an explanation and defense of how animals meet these criteria. A few remarks about each of these two points will have to suffice.

Persons[9] are the possessors of moral rights, and though most human beings are persons, not all are. And some persons are not human beings. Persons are individuals who have a cluster of actual (not merely potential or former) abilities. These include awareness of their environment, desires and preferences, goals and purposes, feelings and emotions, beliefs and memories, a sense of the future and of their own identity. Most adult humans have these abilities and so are persons. But some (the irreversibly comatose, for example) lack them and so are not persons. Human fetuses and infants also are not persons, given this analysis, and so have no moral rights (which is not to say that we may therefore do anything to them that we have a mind to; there are moral constraints on what we may do in addition to those constraints that involve respect for the moral rights of others—but this is a long story . . . !).

As for nonhumans who are persons, the most famous candidate is God as conceived, for example, by Christians. When believers speak of "the blessed Trinity, three persons in one," they don't mean "three human beings in one." Extraterrestrials are another obvious candidate, at least as they crop up in standard science fiction. The extraterrestrials in Ray Bradbury's *Martian Chronicles*, for example, are persons, in the sense explained, but they assuredly are not human beings. But, of course, the most important candidates for our purposes are animals. And they are successful candidates if they perceive and remember, believe and desire, have feelings and emotions, and, in general, actually possess the other abilities mentioned earlier.

Those who affirm and defend the rights of animals believe that some animals actually possess these abilities. Of course, there are some who will deny this. All animals, they will say, lack all, or most, or at least some of the abilities that make an individual a person. In a fuller discussion of the rights view, these worries would receive the respectful airing they deserve. It must suffice here to say that the case for animal rights involves the two matters mentioned and explained—first, considerations about the criteria of right possession (or, alternatively, personhood), and, second, considerations that show that some animals satisfy these criteria. Those who would squelch the undertaking before it gets started by claiming that "it's *obvious* that animals cannot be persons!" offer no serious objection; instead, they give sorry expression to the very speciesist prejudice those who affirm and defend the rights of animals seek to overcome.

Line Drawing

To concede that some animals are persons and so have moral rights is not to settle the question, *Which* animals are persons? "Where do we draw the line?" it will be asked; indeed, it must be asked. The correct answer seems to be: We do not know with certainty. Perhaps there is no exact line to be drawn in this case, any more than there is an exact line to be drawn in other cases (for example, "Exactly how tall do you have to be to be tall?" "Exactly how old must you be before you are old?"). What we must ask is where in the animal kingdom we find individuals who are *most like* paradigmatic persons—that is, most like us, both behaviorally and physiologically. The greater the similarity in these respects, the stronger the case for believing that these animals have *a mental life similar to our own* (including memory and emotion, for example), a case that is strengthened given the major thrust of evolutionary theory. So, while it remains a matter of uncertainty *exactly* where we are to draw this line, it is implausible to deny that adult mammalian animals have the abilities in question (just as, analogously, it would be implausible to deny that eighty-eight-year-old Aunt Bertha is old because we don't know exactly how old someone must be before they are old). To get this far in the argument for animal rights is not to finish the story, but it is to give a rough outline of a major chapter in it.

The Inherent Value of Animals

Moral rights, as explained earlier, need a theoretical home, and the rights view provides this by its use of the notion of inherent value. Not surprisingly, therefore, the rights view affirms this value in the case of those animals who are persons; not to do so would be to slide back into the prejudice of speciesism. Moreover, because all who possess this value possess it equally, the rights view makes no distinction between the inherent value human persons possess as distinct from that possessed by those persons who are animals. And just as *our* inherent value, as persons, does not depend on our utility relative to the interests of others, or on how much we are liked or admired, or on anything we do or fail to do, the same must be true in the case of animals who, as persons, have the same inherent value we do.

To regard animals in the way advocated by the rights view makes a truly profound difference to our understanding of what, morally speaking, we may do to them, as well as how, morally speaking, we can defend what we do. Those animals who have inherent value have a moral right to respectful treatment, a right we fail to respect whenever we attempt to justify what we do to them by appeal to "the best consequences." What these animals are due, in other words, is the same respectful treatment we are. We must never treat them in this or that way merely because, we claim, doing so is necessary to bring about "the best consequences" for all affected by the outcome.

The rights view therefore calls for the total dissolution of commercial animal agriculture as we know it. Not merely "modern" intensive rearing methods must cease. For though the harm visited upon animals raised in these circumstances is real enough and is morally to be condemned, its removal would not eliminate the basic wrong its presence compounds. The *basic* wrong is that animals raised for commercial profit are viewed and treated in ways that fail to show respect for their moral right to respectful treatment. *They* are not (though of course they may be treated as if they are) "commodities," "economic units," "investments," "a renewable resource," etc. They are, like us, persons and so, like us, are owed treatment that accords with their right to be treated with respect, a respect we fail to show when we end their life before doing so can be defended on the grounds of mercy. Since animals are routinely killed on grounds other than mercy in the course of commercial animal agriculture, that human enterprise violates the rights of animals.

Unlike the utilitarian approach to ethical vegetarianism, the rights view basis does not require that we know what the consequences of our individual or collective abstention from meat will be. The moral imperatives to treat farm animals with respect and to refuse to support those who fail to do so do not rest on calculations about consequences. And unlike a Singer-type utilitarianism, the rights view does not imply that the individual's duty to become a vegetarian depends on how many other people join the ranks. *Each individual* has the duty to treat others with the respect they are due independently of how many others do so, and each has a similar duty to refrain in principle from supporting practices that fail to show proper respect. Of course, anyone who accepts the rights view must profoundly wish that others *will* act similarly, with the result that commercial animal agriculture, from vast agribusiness operations to the traditional family farm, will go the way of the slave trade—will, that is, cease to exist. But the *individual's* duty to cease to support those who violate the rights of animals does not depend on humanity in general doing so as well.

The rights view is, one might say, a "radical" position, calling, as it does, for the total abolition of a culturally accepted institution to wit, commercial animal farming. The way to "clean up" this institution is not by giving animals bigger cages, cleaner stalls, a place to roost, thus and so much hay, etc. When an institution is grounded in injustices, because it fails to respect the rights of those involved, there is no room for internal house cleaning. Morality will not be satisfied with anything less than its total abolition. And that, for the reasons given, is the rights view's verdict regarding commercial animal agriculture.

Notes

1. Immanuel Kant, "Duties to Animals and Spirits," *Lectures on Ethics,* trans. Louis Infield (New York: Harper and Row, 1963), pp. 239–41. Collected in *Animal Rights and Human Obligations,* Tom Regan and Peter Singer, eds. (Englewood Cliffs, NJ: Prentice-Hall Inc., 1976), pp. 122–23.
2. St. Thomas Aquinas, *Summa Contra Gentiles,* literally translated by the English Dominican Fathers (Benzinger Books, 1928), Third Book, Part II, Chap. C XII. Collected in *Animal Rights and Human Obligations,* op. cit., pp. 58–59.
3. Jeremy Bentham, *The Principles of Morals and Legislation* (1789; many editions), Chapter XVII, Section 1. Collected in *Animal Rights and Human Obligations,* op. cit., pp. 129–30.
4. John Stuart Mill, "Whewell on Moral Philosophy," *Collected Works,* Vol. X, pp. 185–87. Collected in *Animal Rights and Human Obligations,* op. cit., pp. 131–32.
5. Peter Singer, *Animal Liberation* (New York: Avon Books, 1975). By far the best factual account of factory farming is J. Mason and Peter Singer, *Animal Factories* (New York: Collier Books, 1982).
6. Richard Ryder, "Experiments on Animals," in *Animals, Men and Morals,* ed. S. and R. Godlovitch and J. Harris (New York: Taplinger, 1972). Collected in *Animal Rights and Human Obligations,* op. cit., pp. 33–47.
7. These criticisms of utilitarianism are developed at greater length in my *Case for Animal Rights* (Berkeley: University of California Press. London: Routledge and Kegan Paul, 1983).
8. The rights view is developed at length in *The Case for Animal Rights,* ibid.
9. I use the familiar idea of "person" here because it is helpful. I do not use it in *The Case for Animal Rights.* I do not believe anything of substance turns on its use or nonuse.

11

Famine, Affluence, and Morality

Peter Singer is professor of philosophy and director of the Centre for Human Bioethics at Monash University, Melbourne, Australia. His books include *Animal Liberation* (1975), *Practical Ethics* (1979), and *The Expanding Circle* (1981). He has also edited *A Companion to Ethics* (1991).

As I write this, in November 1971, people are dying in East Bengal from lack of food, shelter, and medical care. The suffering and death that are occurring there now are not inevitable, not unavoidable in any fatalistic sense of the term. Constant poverty, a cyclone, and a civil war have turned at least nine million people into destitute refugees; nevertheless, it is not beyond the capacity of the richer nations to give enough assistance to reduce any further suffering to very small proportions. The decisions and actions of human beings can prevent this kind of suffering. Unfortunately, human beings have not made the necessary decisions. At the individual level, people have, with very few exceptions, not responded to the situation in any significant way.

Generally speaking, people have not given large sums to relief funds; they have not written to their parliamentary representatives demanding increased government assistance; they have not demonstrated in the streets, held symbolic fasts, or done anything else directed toward providing the refugees with the means to satisfy their essential needs. At the government level, no government has given the sort of massive aid that would enable the refugees to survive for more than a few days. Britain, for instance, has given rather more than most countries. It has, to date, given £14,750,000. For comparative purposes, Britain's share of the nonrecoverable development costs of the Anglo-French Concorde project is already in excess of £275,000,000, and on present estimates will reach £440,000,000. The implication is that the British government values a supersonic transport more than thirty times as highly as it values the lives of the nine million refugees. Australia is another country which, on a per capita

From Peter Singer, "Famine, Affluence, and Morality," *Philosophy & Public Affairs*, Vol. 1, No. 3 (Spring 1972). Copyright © 1972 by Princeton University Press. Reprinted by permission of Princeton University Press.

basis, is well up in the "aid to Bengal" table. Australia's aid, however, amounts to less than one-twelfth of the cost of Sydney's new opera house. The total amount given, from all sources, now stands at about £65,000,000. The estimated cost of keeping the refugees alive for one year is £464,000,000. Most of the refugees have now been in the camps for more than six months. The World Bank has said that India needs a minimum of £300,000,000 in assistance from other countries before the end of the year. It seems obvious that assistance on this scale will not be forthcoming. India will be forced to choose between letting the refugees starve or diverting funds from her own development program, which will mean that more of her own people will starve in the future.[1]

These are the essential facts about the present situation in Bengal. So far as it concerns us here, there is nothing unique about this situation except its magnitude. The Bengal emergency is just the latest and most acute of a series of major emergencies in various parts of the world, arising both from natural and from man-made causes. There are also many parts of the world in which people die from malnutrition and lack of food independent of any special emergency. I take Bengal as my example only because it is the present concern, and because the size of the problem has ensured that it has been given adequate publicity. Neither individuals nor governments can claim to be unaware of what is happening there.

What are the moral implications of a situation like this? In what follows, I shall argue that the way people in relatively affluent countries react to a situation like that in Bengal cannot be justified; indeed, the whole way we look at moral issues—our moral conceptual scheme—needs to be altered, and with it, the way of life that has come to be taken for granted in our society.

In arguing for this conclusion I will not, of course, claim to be morally neutral. I shall, however, try to argue for the moral position that I take, so that anyone who accepts certain assumptions, to be made explicit, will, I hope, accept my conclusion.

I begin with the assumption that suffering and death from lack of food, shelter, and medical care are bad. I think most people will agree about this, although one may reach the same view by different routes. I shall not argue for this view. People can hold all sorts of eccentric positions, and perhaps from some of them it would not follow that death by starvation is in itself bad. It is difficult, perhaps impossible, to refute such positions, and so for brevity I will henceforth take this assumption as accepted. Those who disagree need read no further.

My next point is this: if it is in our power to prevent something bad from happening, without thereby sacrificing anything of comparable moral importance, we ought, morally, to do it. By "without sacrificing anything of comparable moral importance" I mean without causing anything else comparably bad to happen, or doing something that is wrong in itself, or failing to pro-

---

[1] There was also a third possibility: that India would go to war to enable the refugees to return to their lands. Since I wrote this paper, India has taken this way out. The situation is no longer that described above, but this does not affect my argument, as the next paragraph indicates.

mote some moral good, comparable in significance to the bad thing that we can prevent. This principle seems almost as uncontroversial as the last one. It requires us only to prevent what is bad, and not to promote what is good, and it requires this of us only when we can do it without sacrificing anything that is, from the moral point of view, comparably important. I could even, as far as the application of my argument to the Bengal emergency is concerned, qualify the point so as to make it: if it is in our power to prevent something very bad from happening, without thereby sacrificing anything morally significant, we ought, morally, to do it. An application of this principle would be as follows: if I am walking past a shallow pond and see a child drowning in it, I ought to wade in and pull the child out. This will mean getting my clothes muddy, but this is insignificant, while the death of the child would presumably be a very bad thing.

The uncontroversial appearance of the principle just stated is deceptive. If it were acted upon, even in its qualified form, our lives, our society, and our world would be fundamentally changed. For the principle takes, firstly, no account of proximity or distance. It makes no moral difference whether the person I can help is a neighbor's child ten yards from me or a Bengali whose name I shall never know, ten thousand miles away. Secondly, the principle makes no distinction between cases in which I am the only person who could possibly do anything and cases in which I am just one among millions in the same position.

I do not think I need to say much in defense of the refusal to take proximity and distance into account. The fact that a person is physically near to us, so that we have personal contact with him, may make it more likely that we *shall* assist him, but this does not show that we *ought* to help him rather than another who happens to be further away. If we accept any principle of impartiality, universalizability, equality, or whatever, we cannot discriminate against someone merely because he is far away from us (or we are far away from him). Admittedly, it is possible that we are in a better position to judge what needs to be done to help a person near to us than one far away, and perhaps also to provide the assistance we judge to be necessary. If this were the case, it would be a reason for helping those near to us first. This may once have been a justification for being more concerned with the poor in one's own town than with famine victims in India. Unfortunately for those who like to keep their moral responsibilities limited, instant communication and swift transportation have changed the situation. From the moral point of view, the development of the world into a "global village" has made an important, though still unrecognized, difference to our moral situation. Expert observers and supervisors, sent out by famine relief organizations or permanently stationed in famine-prone areas, can direct our aid to a refugee in Bengal almost as effectively as we could get it to someone in our own block. There would seem, therefore, to be no possible justification for discriminating on geographical grounds.

There may be a greater need to defend the second implication of my principle—that the fact that there are millions of other people in the same position, in respect to the Bengali refugees, as I am, does not make the situation significantly different from a situation in which I am the only person who can prevent something very bad from occurring. Again, of course, I admit that there is a psychological difference between the cases; one feels less guilty about doing nothing if one can point to others, similarly placed, who have also done nothing. Yet this can make no real difference to our moral obligations. Should I consider that I am less obliged to pull the drowning child out of the pond if on looking around I see other people, no further away than I am, who have also noticed the child but are doing nothing? One has only to ask this question to see the absurdity of the view that numbers lessen obligation. It is a view that is an ideal excuse for inactivity; unfortunately most of the major evils—poverty, overpopulation, pollution—are problems in which everyone is almost equally involved.

The view that numbers do make a difference can be made plausible if stated in this way: if everyone in circumstances like mine gave £5 to the Bengal Relief Fund, there would be enough to provide food, shelter, and medical care for the refugees: there is no reason why I should give more than anyone else in the same circumstances as I am: therefore I have no obligation to give more than £5. Each premise in this argument is true, and the argument looks sound. It may convince us, unless we notice that it is based on a hypothetical premise, although the conclusion is not stated hypothetically. The argument would be sound if the conclusion were: if everyone in circumstances like mine were to give £5, I would have no obligation to give more than £5. If the conclusion were so stated, however, it would be obvious that the argument has no bearing on a situation in which it is not the case that everyone else gives £5. This, of course, is the actual situation. It is more or less certain that not everyone in circumstances like mine will give £5. So there will not be enough to provide the needed food, shelter, and medical care. Therefore by giving more than £5 I will prevent more suffering than I would if I gave just £5.

It might be thought that this argument has an absurd consequence. Since the situation appears to be that very few people are likely to give substantial amounts, it follows that I and everyone else in similar circumstances ought to give as much as possible, that is, at least up to the point at which by giving more one would begin to cause serious suffering for oneself and one's dependents—perhaps even beyond this point to the point of marginal utility, at which by giving more one would cause oneself and one's dependents as much suffering as one would prevent in Bengal. If everyone does this, however, there will be more than can be used for the benefit of the refugees, and some of the sacrifice will have been unnecessary. Thus, if everyone does what he ought to do, the result will not be as good as it would be if everyone did a little less than he ought to do, or if only some do all that they ought to do.

The paradox here arises only if we assume that the actions in question—sending money to the relief funds—are performed more or less simultaneously, and are also unexpected. For if it is to be expected that everyone is going to contribute something, then clearly each is not obliged to give as much as he would have been obliged to had others not been giving too. And if everyone is not acting more or less simultaneously, then those giving later will know how much more is needed, and will have no obligation to give more than is necessary to reach this amount. To say this is not to deny the principle that people in the same circumstances have the same obligations, but to point out that the fact that others have given, or may be expected to give, is a relevant circumstance: those giving after it has become known that many others are giving and those giving before are not in the same circumstances. So the seemingly absurd consequence of the principle I have put forward can occur only if people are in error about the actual circumstances—that is, if they think they are giving when others are not, but in fact they are giving when others are. The result of everyone doing what he really ought to do cannot be worse than the result of everyone doing less than he ought to do, although the result of everyone doing what he reasonably believes he ought to do could be.

If my argument so far has been sound, neither our distance from a preventable evil nor the number of other people who, in respect to that evil, are in the same situation as we are, lessens our obligation to mitigate or prevent that evil. I shall therefore take as established the principle I asserted earlier. As I have already said, I need to assert it only in its qualified form: if it is in our power to prevent something very bad from happening, without thereby sacrificing anything else morally significant, we ought, morally, to do it.

The outcome of this argument is that our traditional moral categories are upset. The traditional distinction between duty and charity cannot be drawn, or at least, not in the place we normally draw it. Giving money to the Bengal Relief Fund is regarded as an act of charity in our society. The bodies which collect money are known as "charities." These organizations see themselves in this way—if you send them a check, you will be thanked for your "generosity." Because giving money is regarded as an act of charity, it is not thought that there is anything wrong with not giving. The charitable man may be praised, but the man who is not charitable is not condemned. People do not feel in any way ashamed or guilty about spending money on new clothes or a new car instead of giving it to famine relief. (Indeed, the alternative does not occur to them.) This way of looking at the matter cannot be justified. When we buy new clothes not to keep ourselves warm but to look "well-dressed" we are not providing for any important need. We would not be sacrificing anything significant if we were to continue to wear our old clothes, and give the money to famine relief. By doing so, we would be preventing another person from starving. It follows from what I have said earlier that we ought to give money away, rather than spend it on clothes which we do not need to keep us warm. To do so is not charitable, or generous. Nor is it the kind of act which philosophers and theologians have called "supererogatory"—an act which it would be good to do, but not wrong not to do. On the contrary, we ought to give the money away, and it is wrong not to do so.

I am not maintaining that there are no acts which are charitable, or that there are no acts which it would be good to do but not wrong not to do. It may be possible to redraw the distinction between duty and charity in some other place. All I am arguing here is that the present way of drawing the distinction, which makes it an act of charity for a man living at the level of affluence which most people in the "developed nations" enjoy to give money to save someone else from starvation, cannot be supported. It is beyond the scope of my argument to consider whether the distinction should be redrawn or abolished altogether. There would be many other possible ways of drawing the distinction—for instance, one might decide that it is good to make other people as happy as possible, but not wrong not to do so.

Despite the limited nature of the revision in our moral conceptual scheme which I am proposing, the revision would, given the extent of both affluence and famine in the world today, have radical implications. These implications may lead to further objections, distinct from those I have already considered. I shall discuss two of these.

One objection to the position I have taken might be simply that it is too drastic a revision of our moral scheme. People do not ordinarily judge in the way I have suggested they should. Most people reserve their moral condemnation for those who violate some moral norm, such as the norm against taking another person's property. They do not condemn those who indulge in luxury instead of giving to famine relief. But given that I did not set out to present a morally neutral description of the way people make moral judgments, the way people do in fact judge has nothing to do with the validity of my conclusion. My conclusion follows from the principle which I advanced earlier, and unless that principle is rejected, or the arguments shown to be unsound, I think the conclusion must stand, however strange it appears. . . .

The second objection to my attack on the present distinction between duty and charity is one which has from time to time been made against utilitarianism. It follows from some forms of utilitarian theory that we all ought, morally, to be working full time to increase the balance of happiness over misery. The position I have taken here would not lead to this conclusion in all circumstances, for if there were no bad occurrences that we could prevent without sacrificing something of comparable moral importance, my argument would have no application. Given the present conditions in many parts of the world, however, it does follow from my argument that we ought, morally, to be working full time to relieve great suffering of the sort that occurs as a result of famine or other disasters. Of course, mitigating circumstances can be adduced—for instance, that if we wear ourselves out through overwork, we shall be less effective than we would otherwise have been. Nevertheless, when all considerations of this sort have been taken into account, the conclusion remains: we ought to be preventing as much suffering as we can without sacrificing something else of comparable moral importance. This conclusion is one which we may be reluctant to face. I cannot see, though, why it should be regarded as a criticism of the position for which I have argued, rather than a criticism of our ordinary standards of behavior. Since most people are self-interested to some degree, very few of us are likely to do everything that we ought to do. It would, however, hardly be honest to take this as evidence that it is not the case that we ought to do it. . . .

The conclusion reached earlier [raises] the question of just how much we all ought to be giving away. One possibility, which has already been mentioned, is that we ought to give until we reach the level of marginal utility—

that is, the level at which, by giving more, I would cause as much suffering to myself or my dependents as I would relieve by my gift. This would mean, of course, that one would reduce oneself to very near the material circumstances of a Bengali refugee. It will be recalled that earlier I put forward both a strong and a moderate version of the principle of preventing bad occurrences. The strong version, which required us to prevent bad things from happening unless in doing so we would be sacrificing something of a comparable moral significance, does seem to require reducing ourselves to the level of marginal utility. I should also say that the strong version seems to me to be the correct one. I proposed the more moderate version—that we should prevent bad occurrences unless, to do so, we had to sacrifice something morally significant—only in order to show that even on this surely undeniable principle a great change in our way of life is required. On the more moderate principle, it may not follow that we ought to reduce ourselves to the level of marginal utility, for one might hold that to reduce oneself and one's family to this level is to cause something significantly bad to happen. Whether this is so I shall not discuss, since, as I have said, I can see no good reason for holding the moderate version of the principle rather than the strong version. Even if we accepted the principle only in its moderate form, however, it should be clear that we would have to give away enough to ensure that the consumer society, dependent as it is on people spending on trivia rather than giving to famine relief, would slow down and perhaps disappear entirely. There are several reasons why this would be desirable in itself. The value and necessity of economic growth are now being questioned not only by conservationists, but by economists as well.[2] There is no doubt, too, that the consumer society has had a distorting effect on the goals and purposes of its members. Yet looking at the matter purely from the point of view of overseas aid, there must be a limit to the extent to which we should deliberately slow down our economy; for it might be the case that if we gave away, say, forty percent of our Gross National Product, we would slow down the economy so much that in absolute terms we would be giving less than if we gave twenty-five percent of the much larger GNP that we would have if we limited our contribution to this smaller percentage.

I mention this only as an indication of the sort of factor that one would have to take into account in working out an ideal. Since Western societies generally consider one percent of the GNP an acceptable level for overseas aid, the matter is entirely academic. Nor does it affect the question of how much an individual should give in a society in which very few are giving substantial amounts.

It is sometimes said, though less often now than it used to be, that philosophers have no special role to play in public affairs, since most public issues depend primarily on an assessment of facts. On questions of fact, it is said, philosophers as such have no special expertise, and so it has been possible to engage in philosophy without committing oneself to any position on

---

[2] See, for instance, John Kenneth Galbraith, *The New Industrial State* (Boston, 1967); and E. J. Mishan, *The Costs of Economic Growth* (London, 1967).

major public issues. No doubt there are some issues of social policy and foreign policy about which it can truly be said that a really expert assessment of the facts is required before taking sides or acting, but the issue of famine is surely not one of these. The facts about the existence of suffering are beyond dispute. Nor, I think, is it disputed that we can do something about it, either through orthodox methods of famine relief or through population control or both. This is therefore an issue on which philosophers are competent to take a position. The issue is one which faces everyone who has more money than he needs to support himself and his dependents, or who is in a position to take some sort of political action. These categories must include practically every teacher and student of philosophy in the universities of the Western world. If philosophy is to deal with matters that are relevant to both teachers and students, this is an issue that philosophers should discuss.

Discussion, though, is not enough. What is the point of relating philosophy to public (and personal) affairs if we do not take our conclusions seriously? In this instance, taking our conclusion seriously means acting upon it. The philosopher will not find it any easier than anyone else to alter his attitudes and way of life to the extent that, if I am right, is involved in doing everything that we ought to be doing. At the very least, though, one can make a start. The philosopher who does so will have to sacrifice some of the benefits of the consumer society, but he can find compensation in the satisfaction of a way of life in which theory and practice, if not yet in harmony, are at least coming together.

12

Execution

Jonathan Glover is a fellow and tutor in philosophy at New College, Oxford. He is the author of *Responsibility* (1970) and *Causing Death and Saving Lives* (1977).

The debate about capital punishment for murder is, emotionally at least, dominated by two absolutist views. On the retributive view, the murderer must be given the punishment he deserves, which is death. On the other view, analogous to pacifism about war, there is in principle no possibility of justifying capital punishment: in execution there is only "the unspeakable wrongness of cutting a life short when it is in full tide." Supporters of these two approaches agree only in rejecting the serpent-windings of utilitarianism.

Let us look first at the retributive view. According to retributivism in its purest form, the aim of punishment is quite independent of any beneficial social consequences it may have. To quote Kant . . . :

> Even if a Civil Society resolved to dissolve itself with the consent of all its members—as might be supposed in the case of a people inhabiting an island resolving to separate and scatter themselves throughout the whole world—the last Murderer lying in the prison ought to be executed before the resolution was carried out. This ought to be done in order that everyone may realize the desert of his deeds, and that blood-guiltiness may not remain upon the people; for otherwise they might all be regarded as participators in the murder as a public violation of justice.

This view of punishment, according to which it has a value independent of its contribution to reducing the crime rate, is open to the objection that acting on it leads to what many consider to be pointless suffering. To impose suffering or deprivation on someone, or to take his life, is something that those of us who are not retributivists think needs very strong justification in terms of benefits, either to the person concerned or to other people. The retributivist

has to say either that the claims of justice can make it right to harm someone where no one benefits, or else to cite the curiously metaphysical "benefit"' of justice being done, such as Kant's concern that we should have
"blood-guiltiness" removed. I have no way of refuting these positions, as they
seem to involve no clear intellectual mistake. I do not expect to win the agreement of those who hold them, and I am simply presupposing the other view,
that there is already enough misery in the world, and that adding to it requires
a justification in terms of non-metaphysical benefits to people.

This is not to rule out retributive moral principles perhaps playing a limiting role in a general theory of punishment. There is a lot to be said for the retributive restrictions that *only* those who deserve punishment should receive it
and that they should never get more punishment than they deserve. (The case
for this, which at least partly rests on utilitarian considerations, has been powerfully argued by H.L.A. Hart.)[1] But the approach to be adopted here rules out
using retributive considerations to justify any punishment not already justifiable in terms of social benefits. In particular it rules out the argument that
capital punishment can be justified, whether or not it reduces the crime rate,
because the criminal deserves it.

This approach also has the effect of casting doubt on another way of defending capital punishment, which was forthrightly expressed by Lord Denning:
"The ultimate justification of any punishment is not that it is a deterrent, but
that it is the emphatic denunciation by the community of a crime: and from
this point of view, there are some murders which, in the present state of public opinion, demand the most emphatic denunciation of all, namely the death
penalty."[2] The question here is whether the point of the denunciation is to reduce the murder rate, in which case this turns out after all to be a utilitarian
justification, or whether denunciation is an end in itself. If it is an end in itself,
it starts to look like the retributive view in disguise, and should be rejected for
the same reasons.

If we reject retribution for its own sake as a justification for capital punishment, we are left with two alternative general approaches to the question.
One is an absolute rejection in principle of any possibility of capital punishment being justified, in the spirit of Orwell's remarks. The other is the rather
more messy approach, broadly utilitarian in character, of weighing up likely
social costs and benefits.

The Absolutist Rejection of Capital Punishment

To some people, it is impossible to justify the act of killing a fellow human
being. They are absolute pacifists about war and are likely to think of capital
punishment as "judicial murder." They will sympathize with Beccaria's ques-

---

[1] H.L.A. Hart: "Prolegomenon to the Principles of Punishment," *Proceedings of the Aristotelian
Society*, 1959–60.
[2] Quoted in the *Report of the Royal Commission on Capital Punishment*, 1953.

tion: "Is it not absurd that the laws which detest and punish homicide, in order to prevent murder, publicly commit murder themselves?"

The test of whether an opponent of capital punishment adopts this absolutist position is whether he would still oppose it if it could be shown to save many more lives than it cost: if, say, every execution deterred a dozen potential murderers. The absolutist, unlike the utilitarian opponent of the death penalty, would be unmoved by any such evidence. This question brings out the links between the absolutist position and the acts and omissions doctrine. For those of us who reject the acts and omissions doctrine, the deaths we fail to prevent have to be given weight, as well as the deaths we cause by execution. So those of us who do not accept the acts and omissions doctrine cannot be absolutist opponents of capital punishment.

There is a variant on the absolutist position which at first sight seems not to presuppose the acts and omissions doctrine. On this view, while saving a potential murder victim is in itself as important as not killing a murderer, there is something so cruel about the kind of death involved in capital punishment that this rules out the possibility of its being justified. Those of us who reject the acts and omissions doctrine have to allow that sometimes there can be side-effects associated with an act of killing, but not with failure to save a life, which can be sufficiently bad to make a substantial moral difference between the two. When this view is taken of the cruelty of the death penalty, it is not usually the actual method of execution which is objected to, though this can seem important, as in the case where international pressure on General Franco led him to substitute shooting for the garrotte. What seems peculiarly cruel and horrible about capital punishment is that the condemned man has the period of waiting, knowing how and when he is to be killed. Many of us would rather die suddenly than linger for weeks or months knowing we were fatally ill, and the condemned man's position is several degrees worse than that of the person given a few months to live by doctors. He has the additional horror of knowing exactly when he will die, and of knowing that his death will be in a ritualized killing by other people, symbolizing his ultimate rejection by the members of his community. The whole of his life may seem to have a different and horrible meaning when he sees it leading up to this end.

For reasons of this kind, capital punishment can plausibly be claimed to fall under the United States constitution's ban on "cruel and unusual punishments," so long as the word "unusual" is not interpreted too strictly. The same reasons make the death penalty a plausible candidate for falling under a rather similar ethical ban, which has been expressed by H.L.A. Hart: "There are many different ways in which we think it morally incumbent on us to *qualify* or *limit* the pursuit of the utilitarian goal by methods of punishment. Some punishments are ruled out as too barbarous to use *whatever their social utility*"[3] (final italics mine). Because of the extreme cruelty of capital punishment, many

---

[3] H.L.A. Hart: "Murder and the Principles of Punishment," *Northwestern Law Review*, 1958.

of us would, if forced to make a choice between two horrors, prefer to be suddenly murdered rather than be sentenced to death and executed. This is what makes it seem reasonable to say that the absolutist rejection of the death penalty need not rest on the acts and omissions doctrine.

But this appearance is illusory. The special awfulness of capital punishment may make an execution even more undesirable than a murder (though many would disagree on the grounds that this is outweighed by the desirability that the guilty rather than the innocent should die). Even if we accept that an execution is worse than an average murder, it does not follow from this that capital punishment is too barbarous to use *whatever its social utility*. For supposing a single execution deterred many murders? Or suppose that some of the murders deterred would themselves have been as cruel as an execution? When we think of the suffering imposed in a famous kidnapping case, where the mother received her son's ear through the post, we may feel uncertain even that capital punishment is more cruel than some "lesser" crimes than murder. The view that some kinds of suffering are too great to impose, whatever their social utility, rules out the possibility of justifying them, however much more suffering they would prevent. And this does presuppose the acts and omissions doctrine, and so excludes some of us even from this version of absolutism.

A Utilitarian Approach

It is often supposed that the utilitarian alternative to absolutism is simply one of adopting an unqualified maximizing policy. On such a view, the death penalty would be justified if, and only if, it was reasonable to think the number of lives saved exceeded the number of executions. (The question of what to do where the numbers exactly balance presupposes a fineness of measurement that is unattainable in these matters.) On any utilitarian view, numbers of lives saved must be a very important consideration. But there are various special features that justify the substantial qualification of a maximizing policy.

The special horror of the period of waiting for execution may not justify the absolutist rejection of the death penalty, but it is a powerful reason for thinking that an execution may normally cause more misery than a murder, and so for thinking that, if capital punishment is to be justified, it must do better than break even when lives saved through deterrence are compared with lives taken by the executioner.

This view is reinforced when we think of some of the other side-effects of the death penalty. It must be appalling to be told that your husband, wife or child has been murdered, but this is surely less bad than the experience of waiting a month or two for your husband, wife or child to be executed. And those who think that the suffering of the murderer himself matters less than that of an innocent victim will perhaps not be prepared to extend this view to the suffering of the murderer's parents, wife and children.

There is also the possibility of mistakenly executing an innocent man, something which it is very probable happened in the case of Timothy Evans.

The German Federal Ministry of Justice is quoted in the Council of Europe's report on *The Death Penalty in European Countries* as saying that in the hundred years to 1953, there were twenty-seven death sentences "now established or presumed" to be miscarriages of justice. This point is often used as an argument against capital punishment, but what is often not noticed is that its force must depend on the special horrors of execution as compared with other forms of death, including being murdered. For the victim of murder is innocent too, and he also has no form of redress. It is only the (surely correct) assumption that an innocent man faces something much worse in execution than in murder that gives this argument its claim to prominence in this debate. For, otherwise, the rare cases of innocent men being executed would be completely overshadowed by the numbers of innocent men being murdered. (Unless, of course, the acts and omissions doctrine is again at work here, for execution is something that we, as a community, *do,* while a higher murder rate is something we at most *allow*.)

The death penalty also has harmful effects on people other than the condemned man and his family. For most normal people, to be professionally involved with executions, whether as judge, prison warder or chaplain, or executioner, must be highly disturbing. Arthur Koestler quotes the case of the executioner Ellis, who attempted suicide a few weeks after he executed a sick woman "whose insides fell out before she vanished through the trap."[4] (Though the chances must be very small of the experience of Mr. Pierrepoint, who describes in his autobiography how he had to execute a friend with whom he often sang duets in a pub.[5]) And there are wider effects on society at large. When there is capital punishment, we are all involved in the horrible business of a long-premeditated killing, and most of us will to some degree share in the emotional response George Orwell had so strongly when he had to be present. It cannot be good for children at school to know that there is an execution at the prison down the road. And there is another bad effect, drily stated in the *Report of the Royal Commission on Capital Punishment*: "No doubt the ambition that prompts an average of five applications a week for the post of hangman, and the craving that draws a crowd to the prison where a notorious murderer is being executed, reveal psychological qualities that no state would wish to foster in its citizens."

Capital punishment is also likely to operate erratically. Some murderers are likely to go free because the death penalty makes juries less likely to convict. (Charles Dickens, in a newspaper article quoted in the 1868 Commons debate, gave the example of a forgery case, where a jury found a £10 note to be worth 39 shillings, in order to save the forger's life.) There are also great problems in operating a reprieve system without arbitrariness, say, in deciding whether being pregnant or having a young baby should qualify a woman for a reprieve.

---

[4] Arthur Koestler: *Reflections on Hanging*, London, 1956.
[5] Albert Pierrepoint: *Executioner: Pierrepoint*, London, 1974.

Finally, there is the drawback that the retention or re-introduction of capital punishment contributes to a tradition of cruel and horrible punishment which we might hope would wither away. Nowadays we never think of disembowelling people or chopping off their hands as a punishment. Even if these punishments would be specially effective in deterring some very serious crimes, they are not regarded as a real possibility. To many of us, it seems that the utilitarian benefits from this situation outweigh the loss of any deterrent power they might have if re-introduced for some repulsive crime like kidnapping. And the longer we leave capital punishment in abeyance, the more its use will seem as out of the question as the no more cruel punishment of mutilation. (At this point, I come near to Hart's view that some punishments are too barbarous to use whatever their social utility. The difference is that I think that arguments for and against a punishment should be based on social utility, but that a widespread view that some things are unthinkable is itself of great social utility.)

For these reasons, a properly thought-out utilitarianism does not enjoin an unqualified policy of seeking the minimum loss of life, as the no trade-off view does. Capital punishment has its own special cruelties and horrors, which change the whole position. In order to be justified, it must be shown, with good evidence, that it has a deterrent effect not obtainable by less awful means, and one which is quite substantial rather than marginal.

Deterrence and Murder

The arguments over whether capital punishment deters murder more effectively than less drastic methods are of two kinds: statistical and intuitive. The statistical arguments are based on various kinds of comparisons of murder rates. Rates are compared before and after abolition in a country, and, where possible, further comparisons are made with rates after re-introduction of capital punishment. Rates are compared in neighbouring countries, or neighbouring states of the U.S.A., with and without the death penalty. I am not a statistician and have no special competence to discuss the issue, but will merely purvey the received opinion of those who have looked into the matter. Those who have studied the figures are agreed that there is no striking correlation between the absence of capital punishment and any alteration in the curve of the murder rate. Having agreed on this point, they then fall into two schools. On one view, we can conclude that capital punishment is not a greater deterrent to murder than the prison sentences that are substituted for it. On the other, more cautious, view, we can only conclude that we do not know that capital punishment is a deterrent. I shall not attempt to choose between these interpretations. For, given that capital punishment is justified only where there is good evidence that it is a substantial deterrent, either interpretation fails to support the case for it.

If the statistical evidence were conclusive that capital punishment did not deter more than milder punishments, this would leave no room for any further discussion. But, since the statistical evidence may be inconclusive, many people feel there is room left for intuitive arguments. Some of these deserve examination. The intuitive case was forcefully stated in 1864 by Sir James Fitzjames Stephen:[6]

> No other punishment deters men so effectually from committing crimes as the punishment of death. This is one of those propositions which it is difficult to prove, simply because they are in themselves more obvious than any proof can make them. It is possible to display ingenuity in arguing against it, but that is all. The whole experience of mankind is in the other direction. The threat of instant death is the one to which resort has always been made when there was an absolute necessity for producing some result . . . No one goes to certain inevitable death except by compulsion. Put the matter the other way. Was there ever yet a criminal who, when sentenced to death and brought out to die, would refuse the offer of a commutation of his sentence for the severest secondary punishment? Surely not. Why is this? It can only be because: "All that a man has will he give for his life." In any secondary punishment, however terrible, there is hope; but death is death; its terrors cannot be described more forcibly.

These claims turn out when scrutinized to be much more speculative and doubtful than they at first sight appear.

The first doubt arises when Stephen talks of "certain inevitable death." The Royal Commission, in their *Report,* after quoting the passage from Stephen above, quote figures to show that, in the fifty years from 1900 to 1949, there was in England and Wales one execution for every twelve murders known to the police. In Scotland in the same period there was less than one execution for every twenty-five murders known to the police. Supporters of Stephen's view could supplement their case by advocating more death sentences and fewer reprieves, or by optimistic speculations about better police detection or greater willingness of juries to convict. But the reality of capital punishment as it was in these countries, unmodified by such recommendations and speculations, was not one where the potential murderer faced certain, inevitable death. This may incline us to modify Stephen's estimate of its deterrent effect, unless we buttress his view with the further speculation that a fair number of potential murderers falsely believed that what they would face was certain, inevitable death.

The second doubt concerns Stephen's talk of "the threat of instant death." The reality again does not quite fit this. By the time the police conclude their investigation, the case is brought to trial, and verdict and sentence are followed by appeal, petition for reprieve and then execution, many months have probably elapsed, and when this time factor is added to the low probability of the murderers being executed, the picture looks very different. For we often have a time bias, being less affected by threats of future catastrophes than by threats of instant ones. The certainty of immediate death is one thing; it is another thing merely to increase one's chances of death in the future. Unless this were so, no one would smoke or take on such high-risk jobs as diving in the North Sea.

---

[6] James Fitzjames Stephen: Capital Punishments, *Fraser's Magazine,* 1864.

There is another doubt when Stephen very plausibly says that virtually all criminals would prefer life imprisonment to execution. The difficulty is over whether this entitles us to conclude that it is therefore a more effective deterrent. For there is the possibility that, compared with the long term of imprisonment that is the alternative, capital punishment is what may appropriately be called an "overkill." It may be that, for those who will be deterred by threat of punishment, a long prison sentence is sufficient deterrent. I am not suggesting that this is so, but simply that it is an open question whether a worse alternative here generates any additional deterrent effect. The answer is *not* intuitively obvious.

Stephen's case rests on the speculative psychological assumptions that capital punishment is not an overkill compared with a prison sentence; and that its additional deterrent effect is not obliterated by time bias, nor by the low probability of execution, nor by a combination of these factors. Or else it must be assumed that, where the additional deterrent effect would be obliterated by the low probability of death, either on its own or in combination with time bias, the potential murderer thinks the probability is higher than it is. Some of these assumptions may be true, but, when they are brought out into the open, it is by no means obvious that the required combination of them can be relied upon.

Supporters of the death penalty also sometimes use what David A. Conway, in his valuable discussion of this issue, calls "the best-bet argument,"[7] On this view, since there is no certainty whether or not capital punishment reduces the number of murders, either decision about it involves gambling with lives. It is suggested that it is better to gamble with the lives of murderers than with the lives of their innocent potential victims. This presupposes the attitude, rejected here, that a murder is a greater evil than the execution of a murderer. But, since this attitude probably has overwhelmingly widespread support, it is worth noting that, even if it is accepted, the best-bet argument is unconvincing. This is because, as Conway has pointed out, it overlooks the fact that we are not choosing between the chance of a murderer dying and the chance of a victim dying. In leaving the death penalty, we are opting for the certainty of the murderer dying which we hope will give us a chance of a potential victim being saved. This would look like a good bet only if we thought an execution substantially preferable to a murder and either the statistical evidence or the intuitive arguments made the effectiveness of the death penalty as a deterrent look reasonably likely.

Since the statistical studies do not give any clear indication that capital punishment makes any difference to the numbers of murders committed, the only chance of its supporters discharging the heavy burden of justification would be if the intuitive arguments were extremely powerful. We might then feel justified in supposing that other factors distorted the murder rate,

---

[7] David A. Conway: "Capital Punishment and Deterrence," *Philosophy and Public Affairs,* 1974.

masking the substantial deterrent effect of capital punishment. The intuitive arguments, presented as the merest platitudes, turn out to be speculative and unobvious. I conclude that the case for capital punishment as a substantial deterrent fails.

Deterrence and Political Crimes by Opposition Groups

It is sometimes suggested that the death penalty may be an effective deterrent in the case of a special class of "political" crimes. The "ordinary" murder (killing one's wife in a moment of rage, shooting a policeman in panic after a robbery, killing someone in a brawl) may not be particularly sensitive to different degrees of punishment. But some killings for political purposes have a degree of preparation and thought which may allow the severity of the penalty to affect the calculation. Two different kinds of killing come to mind here. There are killings as part of a political campaign, ranging from assassination through terrorist activities up to full-scale guerrilla war. And then there are policies carried out by repressive governments, varying from "liquidation" of individual opponents with or without "trial" to policies of wholesale extermination, sometimes, but not always, in wartime.

Let us look first at killings by groups opposed to governments. Would the various sectarian terrorist groups in Ireland stop their killings if those involved were executed? Would independence movements in countries like Algeria or Kenya have confined themselves to non-violent means if more executions had taken place? Could the Nazis have deterred the French resistance by more executions? Could the Americans have deterred guerrilla war in Vietnam by more executions?

To ask these questions is to realize both the variety of different political situations in which the question of deterrent killing arises, and also to be reminded, if it is necessary, that moral right is not always on the side of the authorities trying to do the deterring. But let us, for the sake of argument, assume a decent government is trying to deal with terrorists or guerrillas whose cause has nothing to be said for it. People have always gone to war knowing they risk their lives, and those prepared to fight in a guerrilla war seem scarcely likely to change their mind because of the marginal extra risk of capital punishment if they are arrested. If the case is to be made, it must apply to lower levels of violence than full-scale guerrilla war.

Given the death penalty's drawbacks, is there any reason to think it would be sufficiently effective in deterring a campaign of terrorist violence to be justified? The evidence is again inconclusive. In many countries there have been terrorist campaigns where the authorities have responded with executions without stopping the campaign. It is always open to someone to say that the level of terrorist activity might have been even higher but for the executions, but it is hard to see why this should be likely. Those who do the shooting or the planting of bombs are not usually the leaders and can be easily replaced by others willing to risk their lives. Danger to life does not deter people from fighting in wars, and a terrorist gunman may be just as committed to his cause as a soldier. And executions create martyrs, which helps the terrorist cause. They may even raise the level of violence by leading to reprisals.

But it may be that a sufficiently ruthless policy of executions would be effective enough to overcome these drawbacks. It has been claimed that the policy of the Irish government in 1922–3 is an instance of this. David R. Bates describes it as follows:[8]

> In the turbulent period following the establishment of the Irish Free State, military courts with power to inflict the death penalty were set up to enable the Irregulars (opposing the Treaty) to be crushed. These powers were first used on 17 November 1922, when four young men were arrested in Dublin and, on being found to be armed, were executed. Shortly afterwards the Englishman, Erskine Childers, captured while carrying a revolver, was also executed. On 7 December two Deputies were shot (one fatally) by the Irregulars. The Minister for Defence, with the agreement of the Cabinet, selected four Irregular leaders who had been in prison since the fall of the Four Courts on 29 June. They were wakened, told to prepare themselves, and were executed by firing squad at dawn. During a six-month period, almost twice as many Irregular prisoners were executed as had been executed by the British from 1916 to 1921. At the end of April 1923, the Irregulars sought a ceasefire to discuss terms. The Free State Government refused. In May 1924, the Irregulars conceded military defeat.

This is an impressive case, and it may be that this degree of ruthlessness by the government involved fewer deaths than would have taken place during a prolonged terrorist campaign. But against this must be set some doubts. What would have happened if the terrorists had been as ruthless in reprisal as the government, perhaps announcing that for every man executed there would be two murders? Is it clear that after a period of such counter-retaliation it would have been the Irregulars rather than the government who climbed down? Does not any net saving of lives by the government's ruthless policy depend on the terrorists refraining from counter-retaliation, and can this be relied on in other cases? And is there not something dangerous in the precedent set when a government has prisoners executed without their having been convicted and sentenced for a capital offence? And, in this case, is it even clear that the defeat of the Irregulars ended once and for all the violence associated with the issues they were campaigning about? I raise these questions, not to claim that the government policy was clearly wrong, but to show how even a case like this is ambiguous in the weight it lends to the argument for using the death penalty against terrorism.

I do not think that the chance of a net saving of lives will in general outweigh the combination of the general drawbacks of capital punishment combined with the danger of its merely leading to a higher level of violence in a

---

[8] Professor David R. Bates, Letter to *The Times*, 14 October 1975.

terrorist situation. But this is a matter of judgement rather than proof, and I admit that it *may* be that the opposite view had better results than mine would have had in 1922.

Deterrence and Political Crimes by the Authorities

The other category of political crimes which sometimes seems so special as to justify the death penalty is atrocities committed by governments or their agents. The executions of leading Nazis after the Nuremberg trials and the execution of Eichmann after his trial in Jerusalem come to mind. The justification usually advanced for these executions is retributive, and it is hard to imagine any more deserving candidates for the death penalty. But, for those of us who do not consider retribution an acceptable aim of punishment, the question must be whether executing them made their kind of activity less likely to happen again in the future. For, if not, we have no answer to the question asked by Victor Gollancz at the time of the Eichmann trial: why should we think we improve the world by turning six million deaths into six million and one?

The chances of people who design or carry out governmental policies of murder being tried and sentenced must often be very small. Sometimes this happens as the result of revolution or defeat in war, but those in power stand a fairly good chance of being killed under these circumstances anyway, and the additional hazard of capital punishment may not have much deterrent effect. As with "ordinary" murderers, the hope of not being caught reduces the punishment's terrors. Some of those who murdered for Hitler were executed; their opposite numbers under Stalin paid no penalty. The torturers who worked for the Greek colonels were brought to trial, but those now at work in Chile, Brazil and South Africa have every expectation of not being punished.

When considering isolated cases of governmental murder (perhaps the assassination of a troublesome foreign leader by a country's intelligence agency, or the single killing of a political opponent) there seems no reason to think capital punishment more of a deterrent than it is of "ordinary" non-political murder. If anything, it is likely to be less of a deterrent because of the reduced chance of a murder charge ever being brought. So there seems to be no case for treating these crimes as other than ordinary murders. But when considering large-scale atrocities, on the scale of those of Hitler or Stalin, or even on the scale of Lyndon Johnson in Vietnam or General Gowon in Nigeria, a version of the best-bet argument comes into play. There are two possible advantages to the death penalty here. One is simply that of totally eliminating the chance of the same mass murderer occupying a position of leadership again. Suppose Hitler had been captured at the end of the Second World War and the question of executing him had arisen. If he had not been executed, it is overwhelmingly probable that he would have spent the rest of his life in Spandau prison, writing his memoirs and giving increasingly senile lectures on world history to visiting journalists. But there would always be the very slight risk of an escape and return to power in the style of Napoleon. This slight risk is removed by execution. The other advantage of the death penalty is the chance, which we have seen to be probably very slight, of deterring repetition of such policies by other leaders.

The best-bet argument in these cases can be used by someone who accepts that the dangers of a defeated leader returning to power are very small and that the chances of execution deterring future leaders from similar policies are also very small. The argument is simply that, where the prevention of such enormous atrocities is in question, even an extremely small probability of prevention is valuable. Consider a case where numbers and probabilities are parallel, but where act and omission are reversed. Suppose someone in hospital can have his life saved only by the making of some organism which has previously been banned. The reason for the ban is that there is a danger, but only a very faint one, of the organism getting out of control. If it does this, the death rate will run into millions. Let us suppose that our intuitive estimate of the unquantifiable risk here is the same as our intuitive estimate of the unquantifiable reduction of risk caused by executing the murdering leader. Those who would rather let the hospital patient die than breach the ban on the dangerous organism must either rely on the acts and omissions doctrine, or else rely on some difference of side-effects, if they are not prepared to support executing the murdering politician or official.

Part of the difficulty in interpreting comparisons of this sort arises from the fact that we are dealing with probabilities that cannot be measured. And, even if they could be measured, most of us are unclear what sacrifices are worth making for the reduction of some risk that is already very small. But if we make the highly artificial assumption that the alterations in probability of risk are the same in the medical case as in the execution case, the dilemma remains. Let us suppose that the risk is one that we would not take in the medical case to save a single life. Those of us who do not accept the acts and omissions doctrine must then either find some difference of side-effects or else support the execution.

Side-effects do go some way towards separating the two cases. For, to breach the ban on producing the organism, even if it does no harm itself, contributes by example to a less strict observance of that ban (and possibly others) in cases where the risk may be much greater. While, in the case of the Nazi leaders, such bad side-effects as exist follow from execution rather than from saving their lives. These side-effects include the contribution made to a climate of opinion where the death penalty seems more acceptable in other contexts, and the precedent which may encourage politicians to have their overthrown rivals, at home or abroad, executed. This last effect could be mitigated by more effort than was made at Nuremberg to remove the impression of the defeated being tried by the victors. It would be possible to set up a court of a genuinely international kind, independent of governmental pressure, to which prosecutions for a large-scale murder could be brought. But the general effect on the public consciousness of having capital punishment as a serious possibility would remain. I am uncertain how to weigh this against the small chance of helping to avert a great evil. For this reason my own views on this question are undecided.

13

Homosexuality and the "Unnaturalness" Argument

Burton M. Leiser is professor of philosophy at Pace University. He is the author of *Custom, Law, and Morality* (1969) and *Liberty, Justice, and Morals* (3d ed., 1986). He is also the editor of *Values in Conflict* (1981).

. . . The "unnaturalness" of homosexuality raises the question of the meaning of *nature, natural,* and similar terms. Theologians and other moralists have said homosexual acts violate the "natural law," and that they are therefore immoral and ought to be prohibited by the state.

The word *nature* has a built-in ambiguity that can lead to serious misunderstandings. When something is said to be "natural" or in conformity with "natural law" or the "law of nature," this may mean either (1) that it is in conformity with the descriptive laws of nature, or (2) that it is not artificial, that man has not imposed his will or his devices upon events or conditions as they exist or would have existed without such interference.

1. *The descriptive laws of nature.* The laws of nature, as these are understood by the scientist, differ from the laws of man. The former are purely descriptive, where the latter are prescriptive. When a scientist says that water boils at 212° Fahrenheit or that the volume of a gas varies directly with the heat that is applied to it and inversely with the pressure, he means merely that as a matter of recorded and observable fact, pure water under standard conditions always boils at precisely 212° Fahrenheit and that as a matter of observed fact, the volume of a gas rises as it is heated and falls as pressure is applied to it. These "laws" merely *describe* the manner in which physical substances *actually behave.* They differ from municipal and federal laws in that they *do not prescribe* behavior. Unlike man-made laws, natural laws are not passed by any legislator or group of legislators; they are not proclaimed or announced; they impose

no obligation upon anyone or anything; their violation entails no penalty, and there is no reward for following them or abiding by them. When a scientist says that the air in a tire obeys the laws of nature that govern gases, he does *not* mean that the air, having been informed that it *ought* to behave in a certain way, behaves appropriately under the right conditions. He means, rather, that as a matter of fact, the air in a tire *will* behave like all other gases. In saying that Boyle's law governs the behavior of gases, he means merely that gases do, as a matter of fact, behave in accordance with Boyle's law, and that Boyle's law enables one to predict accurately what will happen to a given quantity of gas as its pressure is raised; he does *not* mean to suggest that some heavenly voice has proclaimed that all gases should henceforth behave in accordance with the terms of Boyle's law and that a ghostly policeman patrols the world, ready to mete out punishments to any gases that violate the heavenly decree. In fact, according to the scientist, it does not make sense to speak of a natural law being violated. For if there were a true exception to a so-called law of nature, the exception would require a change in the description of those phenomena, and the law would have been shown to be no law at all. The laws of nature are revised as scientists discover new phenomena that require new refinements in their descriptions of the way things actually happen. In this respect they differ fundamentally from human laws, which are revised periodically by legislators who are not so interested in *describing* human behavior as they are in *prescribing* what human behavior *should* be.

2. *The artificial as a form of the unnatural.* On occasion when we say that something is not natural, we mean that it is a product of human artifice. A typewriter is not a natural object, in this sense, for the substances of which it is composed have been removed from their natural state—the state in which they existed before men came along—and have been transformed by a series of chemical and physical and mechanical processes into other substances. They have been rearranged into a whole that is quite different from anything found in nature. In short, a typewriter is an artificial object. In this sense, clothing is not natural, for it has been transformed considerably from the state in which it was found in nature; and wearing clothing is also not natural, in this sense, for in one's natural state, before the application of anything artificial, before any human interference with things as they are, one is quite naked. Human laws, being artificial conventions designed to exercise a degree of control over the natural inclinations and propensities of men, may in this sense be considered to be unnatural.

When theologians and moralists speak of homosexuality, contraception, abortion, and other forms of human behavior as being unnatural and say that for that reason such behavior must be considered to be wrong, in what sense are they using the word *unnatural*? Are they saying that homosexual behavior and the use of contraceptives are contrary to the scientific laws of nature, are they saying that they are artificial forms of behavior, or are they using the terms *natural* and *unnatural* in some third sense?

They cannot mean that homosexual behavior (to stick to the subject presently under discussion) violates the laws of nature in the first sense, for, as has been pointed out, in *that* sense it is impossible to violate the laws of nature.

Those laws, being merely descriptive of what actually does happen, would have to *include* homosexual behavior if such behavior does actually take place. Even if the defenders of the theological view that homosexuality is unnatural were to appeal to a statistical analysis by pointing out that such behavior is not normal from a statistical point of view, and therefore not what the laws of nature require, it would be open to their critics to reply that any descriptive law of nature must account for and incorporate all statistical deviations, and that the laws of nature, in this sense, do not *require* anything. These critics might also note that the best statistics available reveal that about half of all American males engage in homosexual activity at some time in their lives, and that a very large percentage of American males have exclusively homosexual relations for a fairly extensive period of time; from which it would follow that such behavior is natural, for them, at any rate, in this sense of the word *natural*.

If those who say that homosexual behavior is unnatural are using the term *unnatural* in the second sense as artificial, it is difficult to understand their objection. That which is artificial is often far better than what is natural. Artificial homes seem, at any rate, to be more suited to human habitation and more conducive to longer life and better health than are caves and other natural shelters. There are distinct advantages to the use of such unnatural (artificial) amenities as clothes, furniture, and books. Although we may dream of an idyllic return to nature in our more wistful moments, we would soon discover, as Thoreau did in his attempt to escape from the artificiality of civilization, that needles and thread, knives and matches, ploughs and nails, and countless other products of human artifice are essential to human life. We would discover, as Plato pointed out in the *Republic,* that no man can be truly self-sufficient. Some of the by-products of industry are less than desirable, but neither industry nor the products of industry are intrinsically evil, even though both are unnatural in this sense of the word.

Interference with nature is not evil in itself. Nature, as some writers have put it, must be tamed. In some respects man must look upon it as an enemy to be conquered. If nature were left to its own devices, without the intervention of human artifice, men would be consumed by disease, they would be plagued by insects, they would be chained to the places where they were born with no means of swift communication or transport, and they would suffer the discomforts and the torments of wind and weather and flood and fire with no practical means of combating any of them. Interfering with nature, doing battle with nature, using human will and reason and skill to thwart what might otherwise follow from the conditions that prevail in the world is a peculiarly human enterprise, one that can hardly be condemned merely because it does what is not natural.

Homosexual behavior can hardly be considered to be unnatural in this sense. There is nothing artificial about such behavior. On the contrary, it is quite natural, in this sense, to those who engage in it. And even if it were not, even if it were quite artificial, this is not in itself a ground for condemning it.

It would seem, then, that those who condemn homosexuality as an unnatural form of behavior must mean something else by the word *unnatural,* something not covered by either of the preceding definitions. A third possibility is this:

3. *Anything uncommon or abnormal is unnatural.* If this is what is meant by those who condemn homosexuality on the ground that it is unnatural, it is quite obvious that their condemnation cannot be accepted without further argument. The fact that a given form of behavior is uncommon provides no justification for condemning it. Playing viola in a string quartet may be an uncommon form of human behavior. Yet there is no reason to suppose that such uncommon behavior is, by virtue of its uncommonness, deserving of condemnation or ethically or morally wrong. On the contrary, many forms of behavior are praised precisely because they are so uncommon. Great artists, poets, musicians, and scientists are uncommon in this sense; but clearly the world is better off for having them, and it would be absurd to condemn them or their activities for their failure to be common and normal. If homosexual behavior is wrong, then, it must be for some reason other than its unnaturalness in this sense of the word.

4. *Any use of an organ or an instrument that is contrary to its principal purpose or function is unnatural.* Every organ and every instrument—perhaps even every creature—has a function to perform, one for which it is particularly designed. Any use of those instruments and organs that is consonant with their purposes is natural and proper, but any use that is inconsistent with their principal functions is unnatural and improper, and to that extent, evil or harmful. Human teeth, for example, are admirably designed for their principal functions—biting and chewing the kinds of food suitable for human consumption. But they are not particularly well suited for prying the caps from beer bottles. If they are used for that purpose, which is not natural to them, they are likely to crack or break under the strain. The abuse of one's teeth leads to their destruction and to a consequent deterioration in one's overall health. If they are used only for their proper function, however, they may continue to serve well for many years. Similarly, a given drug may have a proper function. If used in the furtherance of that end, it can preserve life and restore health. But if it is abused and employed for purposes for which it was never intended, it may cause serious harm and even death. The natural uses of things are good and proper, but their unnatural uses are bad and harmful.

What we must do, then, is to find the proper use, or the true purpose, of each organ in our bodies. Once we have discovered that, we will know what constitutes the natural use of each organ and what constitutes an unnatural, abusive, and potentially harmful employment of the various parts of our bodies. If we are rational, we will be careful to confine behavior to the proper functions and to refrain from unnatural behavior. According to those philosophers who follow this line of reasoning, the way to discover the proper use of any organ is to determine what it is peculiarly suited to do. The eye is suited for seeing, the ear for hearing, the nerves for transmitting impulses from one part of the body to another, and so on.

What are the sex organs peculiarly suited to do? Obviously, they are peculiarly suited to enable men and women to reproduce their own kind. No other organ in the body is capable of fulfilling that function. It follows, according to those who follow the natural-law line, that the proper or natural function of the sex organs is reproduction, and that strictly speaking, any use of those organs for other purposes is unnatural, abusive, potentially harmful, and therefore wrong. The sex organs have been given to us in order to enable us to maintain the continued existence of mankind on this earth. All perversions— including masturbation, homosexual behavior, and heterosexual intercourse that deliberately frustrates the design of the sexual organs—are unnatural and bad. As Pope Pius XI once said, "Private individuals have no other power over the members of their bodies than that which pertains to their natural ends."

But the problem is not so easily resolved. Is it true that every organ has one and only one proper function? A hammer may have been designed to pound nails, and it may perform that particular job best. But it is not sinful to employ a hammer to crack nuts if you have no other more suitable tool immediately available. The hammer, being a relatively versatile tool, may be employed in a number of ways. It has no one proper or natural function. A woman's eyes are well adapted to seeing, it is true. But they seem also to be well adapted to flirting. Is a woman's use of her eyes for the latter purpose sinful merely because she is not using them, at that moment, for their "primary" purpose of seeing? Our sexual organs are uniquely adapted for procreation, but that is obviously not the only function for which they are adapted. Human beings may—and do—use those organs for a great many other purposes, and it is difficult to see why any *one* use should be considered to be the only proper one. The sex organs seem to be particularly well adapted to give their owners and others intense sensations of pleasure. Unless one believes that pleasure itself is bad, there seems to be little reason to believe that the use of the sex organs for the production of pleasure in oneself or in others is evil. In view of the peculiar design of these organs, with their great concentration of nerve endings, it would seem that they were designed (if they *were* designed) with that very goal in mind, and that their use for such purposes would be no more unnatural than their use for the purpose of procreation.

Nor should we overlook the fact that human sex organs may be and are used to express, in the deepest and most intimate way open to man, the love of one person for another. Even the most ardent opponents of "unfruitful" intercourse admit that sex does serve this function. They have accordingly conceded that a man and his wife may have intercourse even though she is pregnant, or past the age of child bearing, or in the infertile period of her menstrual cycle.

Human beings are remarkably complex and adaptable creatures. Neither they nor their organs can properly be compared to hammers or to other tools. The analogy quickly breaks down. The generalization that a given organ or instrument has one and only one proper function does not hold up, even with regard to the simplest manufactured tools, for, as we have seen, a tool may be used for more than one purpose—less effectively than one especially designed for a given task, perhaps, but properly and certainly not *sinfully*. A woman may use her eyes not only to see and to flirt, but also to earn money—if she is, for example, an actress or a model. Though neither of the latter functions seems to have been a part of the original design, if one may speak sensibly of *design* in this context, of the eye, it is difficult to see why such a use of the eyes of a woman should be considered sinful, perverse, or unnatural. Her sex organs have the unique capacity of producing ova and nurturing human embryos, under the right conditions; but why should any other use of those organs, including their use to bring pleasure to their owner or to someone else, or to manifest love to another person, or even, perhaps, to earn money, be regarded as perverse, sinful, or unnatural? Similarly, a man's sexual organs possess the unique capacity of causing the generation of another human being, but if a man chooses to use them for pleasure, or for the expression of love, or for some other purpose—so long as he does not interfere with the rights of some other person—the fact that his sex organs do have their unique capabilities does not constitute a convincing justification for condemning their other uses as being perverse, sinful, unnatural or criminal. If a man "perverts" himself by wiggling his ears for the entertainment of his neighbors instead of using them exclusively for their "natural" function of hearing, no one thinks of consigning him to prison. If he abuses his teeth by using them to pull staples from memos—a function for which teeth were clearly not designed—he is not accused of being immoral, degraded, and degenerate. The fact that people *are* condemned for using their sex organs for their own pleasure or profit, or for that of others, may be more revealing about the prejudices and taboos of our society than it is about our perception of the true nature or purpose of our bodies.

In this connection, it may be worthwhile to note that with the development of artificial means of reproduction (that is, test tube babies), the sex organs may become obsolete for reproductive purposes but would still contribute greatly to human pleasure. In addition, studies of animal behavior and anthropological reports indicate that such nonreproductive sex acts as masturbation, homosexual intercourse, and mutual fondling of genital organs are widespread, both among human beings and among lower animals. Under suitable circumstances, many animals reverse their sex roles, males assuming the posture of females and presenting themselves to others for intercourse, and females mounting other females and going through all the actions of a male engaged in intercourse. Many peoples all around the world have sanctioned and even ritualized homosexual relations. It would seem that an excessive readiness to insist that human sex organs are designed only for reproductive purposes and therefore ought to be used only for such purposes must be based upon a very narrow conception that is conditioned by our own society's peculiar history and taboos.

To sum up, then, the proposition that any use of an organ that is contrary to its principal purpose or function is unnatural assumes that organs *have* a principal purpose or function, but this may be denied on the ground that the purpose or function of a given organ may vary according to the needs or desires of its owner. It may be denied on the ground that a given organ may have more than one principal purpose or function, and any attempt to call one use or another the only natural one seems to be arbitrary, if not question-begging. Also, the proposition suggests that what is unnatural is evil or depraved. This goes beyond the pure description of things, and enters into the problem of the evaluation of human behavior, which leads us to the fifth meaning of *natural*.

5. *That which is natural is good, and whatever is unnatural is bad.* When one condemns homosexuality or masturbation or the use of contraceptives on the ground that it is unnatural, one implies that whatever is unnatural is bad, wrongful, or perverse. But as we have seen, in some senses of the word, the unnatural (the artificial) is often very good, whereas that which is natural (that which has not been subjected to human artifice or improvement) may be very bad indeed. Of course, interference with nature may be bad. Ecologists have made us more aware than we have ever been of the dangers of unplanned and uninformed interference with nature. But this is not to say that *all* interference with nature is bad. Every time a man cuts down a tree to make room for a home for himself, or catches a fish to feed himself or his family, he is interfering with nature. If men did not interfere with nature, they would have no homes, they could eat no fish, and, in fact, they could not survive. What, then, can be meant by those who say that whatever is natural is good and whatever is unnatural is bad? Clearly, they cannot have intended merely to reduce the word *natural* to a synonym of *good, right,* and *proper,* and *unnatural* to a synonym of *evil, wrong, improper, corrupt,* and *depraved.* If that were all they had intended to do, there would be very little to discuss as to whether a given form of behavior might be proper even though it is not in strict conformity with someone's views of what is natural; for *good* and *natural* being synonyms, it would follow inevitably that whatever is good must be natural, and vice versa, by definition. This is certainly not what the opponents of homosexuality have been saying when they claim that homosexuality, being unnatural, is evil. For if it were, their claim would be quite empty. They would be saying merely that homosexuality, being evil, is evil—a redundancy that could as easily be reduced to the simpler assertion that homosexuality is evil. This assertion, however, is not an argument. Those who oppose homosexuality and other sexual "perversions" on the ground that they are "unnatural" are saying that there is some objectively identifiable quality in such behavior that is unnatural; and that that quality, once it has been identified by some kind of scientific observation, can be seen to be detrimental to those who engage in such behavior, or to those around them; and that *because* of the harm (physical, mental, moral, or spiritual) that results from engaging in any behavior possessing the attribute of unnaturalness, such behavior must be considered to be wrongful, and should be discouraged by society. "Unnaturalness" and "wrongfulness" are not synonyms, then, but different concepts. The problem with which we are wrestling is that we are unable to find a meaning for *unnatural* that enables us to arrive at the conclusion that homosexuality is unnatural or that if homosexuality is unnatural, it is therefore wrongful behavior. We have examined four common meanings of *natural* and *unnatural,* and have seen that none of them performs the task that it must perform if advocates of this argument are to prevail. Without some more satisfactory explanation of the connection between the wrongfulness of homosexuality and its alleged unnaturalness, the argument . . . must be rejected.

14

Distributive Justice[1]

John Rawls is professor of philosophy at Harvard University. He is the author of *A Theory of Justice* (1971), a book that has attracted widespread interest among philosophers and social scientists. Although written before his book, the following reading summarizes many of the basic points of Rawls's theory and works out some of its implications for the problem of distributive justice.

We may think of a human society as a more or less self-sufficient association regulated by a common conception of justice and aimed at advancing the good of its members. As a co-operative venture for mutual advantage, it is characterized by a conflict as well as an identity of interests. There is an identity of interests since social co-operation makes possible a better life for all than any would have if everyone were to try to live by his own efforts; yet at the same time men are not indifferent as to how the greater benefits produced by their joint labours are distributed, for in order to further their own aims each prefers a larger to a lesser share. A conception of justice is a set of principles for choosing between the social arrangements which determine this division and for underwriting a consensus as to the proper distributive shares.

Now at first sight the most rational conception of justice would seem to be utilitarian. For consider: each man in realizing his own good can certainly balance his own losses against his own gains. We can impose a sacrifice on ourselves now for the sake of a greater advantage later. A man quite properly acts, as long as others are not affected, to achieve his own greatest good, to advance his ends as far as possible. Now, why should not a society act on precisely the same principle? Why is not that which is rational in the case of one

<hr />

[1] In this essay I try to work out some of the implications of the two principles of justice discussed in "Justice as Fairness" which first appeared in the *Philosophical Review*, 1958, and which is reprinted in *Philosophy, Politics and Society*, Series II, pp. 132-57.

<hr />

man right in the case of a group of men? Surely the simplest and most direct conception of the right, and so of justice, is that of maximizing the good. This assumes a prior understanding of what is good, but we can think of the good as already given by the interests of rational individuals. Thus just as the principle of individual choice is to achieve one's greatest good, to advance so far as possible one's own system of rational desires, so the principle of social choice is to realize the greatest good (similarly defined) summed over all the members of society. We arrive at the principle of utility in a natural way: by this principle a society is rightly ordered, and hence just, when its institutions are arranged so as to realize the greatest sum of satisfactions.

The striking feature of the principle of utility is that it does not matter, except indirectly, how this sum of satisfactions is distributed among individuals, any more than it matters, except indirectly, how one man distributes his satisfactions over time. Since certain ways of distributing things affect the total sum of satisfactions, this fact must be taken into account in arranging social institutions; but according to this principle the explanation of common-sense precepts of justice and their seemingly stringent character is that they are those rules which experience shows must be strictly respected and departed from only under exceptional circumstances if the sum of advantages is to be maximized. The precepts of justice are derivative from the one end of attaining the greatest net balance of satisfactions. There is no reason in principle why the greater gains of some should not compensate for the lesser losses of others; or why the violation of the liberty of a few might not be made right by a greater good shared by many. It simply happens, at least under most conditions, that the greatest sum of advantages is not generally achieved in this way. From the standpoint of utility the strictness of common-sense notions of justice has a certain usefulness, but as a philosophical doctrine it is irrational.

If, then, we believe that as a matter of principle each member of society has an inviolability founded on justice which even the welfare of everyone else cannot over-ride, and that a loss of freedom for some is not made right by a greater sum of satisfactions enjoyed by many, we shall have to look for another account of the principles of justice. The principle of utility is incapable of explaining the fact that in a just society the liberties of equal citizenship are taken for granted, and the rights secured by justice are not subject to political bargaining nor to the calculus of social interests. Now, the most natural alternative to the principle of utility is its traditional rival, the theory of the social contract. The aim of the contract doctrine is precisely to account for the strictness of justice by supposing that its principles arise from an agreement among free and independent persons in an original position of equality and hence reflect the integrity and equal sovereignty of the rational persons who are the contractees. Instead of supposing that a conception of right, and so a conception of justice, is simply an extension of the principle of choice for one man to society as a whole, the contract doctrine assumes that the rational individuals who belong to society must choose together, in one joint act, what is to count among them as just and unjust. They are to decide among themselves once and for all what is to be their conception of justice. This decision is thought of as being made in a suitably defined initial situation one of the significant features of which is that no one knows his position in society, nor even his place in the distribution of natural talents and abilities. The principles of justice to which all are forever bound are chosen in the absence of this sort of specific information. A veil of ignorance prevents anyone from being advantaged or disadvantaged by the contingencies of social class and fortune; and hence the bargaining problems which arise in everyday life from the possession of this knowledge do not affect the choice of principles. On the contract doctrine, then, the theory of justice, and indeed ethics itself, is part of the general theory of rational choice, a fact perfectly clear in its Kantian formulation.

Once justice is thought of as arising from an original agreement of this kind, it is evident that the principle of utility is problematical. For why should rational individuals who have a system of ends they wish to advance agree to a violation of their liberty for the sake of a greater balance of satisfactions enjoyed by others? It seems more plausible to suppose that, when situated in an original position of equal right, they would insist upon institutions which returned compensating advantages for any sacrifices required. A rational man would not accept an institution merely because it maximized the sum of advantages irrespective of its effect on his own interests. It appears, then, that the principle of utility would be rejected as a principle of justice, although we shall not try to argue this important question here. Rather, our aim is to give a brief sketch of the conception of distributive shares implicit in the principles of justice which, it seems, would be chosen in the original position. The philosophical appeal of utilitarianism is that it seems to offer a single principle on the basis of which a consistent and complete conception of right can be developed. The problem is to work out a contractarian alternative in such a way that it has comparable if not all the same virtues.

In our discussion we shall make no attempt to derive the two principles of justice which we shall examine; that is, we shall not try to show that they would be chosen in the original position.[2] It must suffice that it is plausible that they would be, at least in preference to the standard forms of traditional theories. Instead we shall be mainly concerned with three questions: first, how to interpret these principles so that they define a consistent and complete conception of justice; second, whether it is possible to arrange the institutions of a constitutional democracy so that these principles are satisfied, at least approximately; and third, whether the conception of distributive shares which they define is compatible with common-sense notions of justice. The significance of these

---

[2] This question is discussed very briefly in "Justice as Fairness," see pp. 138-41. The intuitive idea is as follows. Given the circumstances of the original position, it is rational for a man to choose as if he were designing a society in which his enemy is to assign him his place. Thus, in particular, given the complete lack of knowledge (which makes the choice one under uncertainty), the fact that the decision involves one's life-prospects as a whole and is constrained by obligations to third parties (e.g. one's descendants) and duties to certain values (e.g. to religious truth), it is rational to be conservative and so to choose in accordance with an analogue of the maximin principle.

principles is that they allow for the strictness of the claims of justice; and if they can be understood so as to yield a consistent and complete conception, the contractarian alternative would seem all the more attractive.

The two principles of justice which we shall discuss may be formulated as follows: first, each person engaged in an institution or affected by it has an equal right to the most extensive liberty compatible with a like liberty for all; and second, inequalities as defined by the institutional structure or fostered by it are arbitrary unless it is reasonable to expect that they will work out to everyone's advantage and provided that the positions and offices to which they attach or from which they may be gained are open to all. These principles regulate the distributive aspects of institutions by controlling the assignment of rights and duties throughout the whole social structure, beginning with the adoption of a political constitution in accordance with which they are then to be applied to legislation. It is upon a correct choice of a basic structure of society, its fundamental system of rights and duties, that the justice of distributive shares depends.

The two principles of justice apply in the first instance to this basic structure, that is, to the main institutions of the social system and their arrangement, how they are combined together. Thus this structure includes the political constitution and the principal economic and social institutions which together define a person's liberties and rights and affect his life-prospects, what he may expect to be and how well he may expect to fare. The intuitive idea here is that those born into the social system at different positions, say in different social classes, have varying life-prospects determined, in part, by the system of political liberties and personal rights, and by the economic and social opportunities which are made available to these positions. In this way the basic structure of society favours certain men over others, and these are the basic inequalities, the ones which affect their whole life-prospects. It is inequalities of this kind, presumably inevitable in any society, with which the two principles of justice are primarily designed to deal.

Now the second principle holds that an inequality is allowed only if there is reason to believe that the institution with the inequality, or permitting it, will work out for the advantage of every person engaged in it. In the case of the basic structure this means that all inequalities which affect life-prospects, say the inequalities of income and wealth which exist between social classes, must be to the advantage of everyone. Since the principle applies to institutions, we interpret this to mean that inequalities must be to the advantage of the representative man for each relevant social position; they should improve each such man's expectation. Here we assume that it is possible to attach to each position an expectation, and that this expectation is a function of the whole institutional structure: it can be raised and lowered by reassigning rights and duties throughout the system. Thus the expectation of any position depends upon the expectations of the others, and these in turn depend upon the pattern of rights and duties established by the basic structure. But it is not clear what is meant by saying that inequalities must be to the advantage of every representative man, and hence our first question. . . .

... [One] interpretation ... is to choose some social position by reference to which the pattern of expectations as a whole is to be judged, and then to maximize with respect to the expectations of this representative man consistent with the demands of equal liberty and equality of opportunity. Now, the one obvious candidate is the representative man of those who are least favoured by the system of institutional inequalities. Thus we arrive at the following idea: the basic structure of the social system affects the life-prospects of typical individuals according to their initial places in society, say the various income classes into which they are born, or depending upon certain natural attributes, as when institutions make discriminations between men and women or allow certain advantages to be gained by those with greater natural abilities. The fundamental problem of distributive justice concerns the differences in life-prospects which come about in this way. We interpret the second principle to hold that these differences are just if and only if the greater expectations of the more advantaged, when playing a part in the working of the whole social system, improve the expectations of the least advantaged. The basic structure is just throughout when the advantages of the more fortunate promote the well-being of the least fortunate, that is, when a decrease in their advantages would make the least fortunate even worse off than they are. The basic structure is perfectly just when the prospects of the least fortunate are as great as they can be.

In interpreting the second principle (or rather the first part of it which we may, for obvious reasons, refer to as the difference principle), we assume that the first principle requires a basic equal liberty for all, and that the resulting political system, when circumstances permit, is that of a constitutional democracy in some form. There must be liberty of the person and political equality as well as liberty of conscience and freedom of thought. There is one class of equal citizens which defines a common status for all. We also assume that there is equality of opportunity and a fair competition for the available positions on the basis of reasonable qualifications. Now, given this background, the differences to be justified are the various economic and social inequalities in the basic structure which must inevitably arise in such a scheme. These are the inequalities in the distribution of income and wealth and the distinctions in social prestige and status which attach to the various positions and classes. The difference principle says that these inequalities are just if and only if they are part of a larger system in which they work out to the advantage of the most unfortunate representative man. The just distributive shares determined by the basic structure are those specified by this constrained maximum principle.

Thus, consider the chief problem of distributive justice, that concerning the distribution of wealth as it affects the life-prospects of those starting out in the various income groups. These income classes define the relevant representative men from which the social system is to be judged. Now, a son of a member of the entrepreneurial class (in a capitalist society) has a better prospect than that of the son of an unskilled labourer. This will be true, it seems, even when the social injustices which presently exist are removed and the two men are of equal talent and ability; the inequality cannot be done away with as long as something like the family is maintained. What, then, can justify this inequality in life-prospects? According to the second principle it is justified only if it is to the advantage of the representative man who is worst off, in this case the representative unskilled labourer. The inequality is permissible because lowering it would, let's suppose, make the working man even worse off than he is. Presumably, given the principle of open offices (the second part of the second principle), the greater expectations allowed to entrepreneurs has the effect in the longer run of raising the life-prospects of the labouring class. The inequality in expectation provides an incentive so that the economy is more efficient, industrial advance proceeds at a quicker pace, and so on, the end result of which is that greater material and other benefits are distributed throughout the system. Of course, all of this is familiar, and whether true or not in particular cases, it is the sort of thing which must be argued if the inequality in income and wealth is to be acceptable by the difference principle.

We should now verify that this interpretation of the second principle gives a natural sense in which everyone may be said to be made better off. Let us suppose that inequalities are chain-connected: that is, if an inequality raises the expectations of the lowest position, it raises the expectations of all positions in between. For example, if the greater expectations of the representative entrepreneur raises that of the unskilled labourer, it also raises that of the semi-skilled. Let us further assume that inequalities are close-knit: that is, it is impossible to raise (or lower) the expectation of any representative man without raising (or lowering) the expectations of every other representative man, and in particular, without affecting one way or the other that of the least fortunate. There is no loose-jointedness, so to speak, in the way in which expectations depend upon one another. Now, with these assumptions, everyone does benefit from an inequality which satisfies the difference principle, and the second principle as we have formulated it reads correctly. For the representative man who is better off in any pair-wise comparison gains by being allowed to have his advantage, and the man who is worse off benefits from the contribution which all inequalities make to each position below. Of course, chain-connection and close-knitness may not obtain; but in this case those who are better off should not have a veto over the advantages available for the least advantaged. The stricter interpretation of the difference principle should be followed, and all inequalities should be arranged for the advantage of the most unfortunate even if some inequalities are not to the advantage of those in middle positions. Should these conditions fail, then, the second principle would have to be stated in another way.

It may be observed that the difference principle represents, in effect, an original agreement to share in the benefits of the distribution of natural talents and abilities, whatever this distribution turns out to be, in order to alleviate as far as possible the arbitrary handicaps resulting from our initial starting places in society. Those who have been favoured by nature, whoever they are, may gain from their good fortune only on terms that improve the well-being of those who have lost out. The naturally advantaged are not to gain simply because they are more gifted, but only to cover the costs of training and cultivating their endowments and for putting them to use in a way which improves the position of the less fortunate. We are led to the difference principle if we wish to arrange the basic social structure so that no one gains (or loses) from his luck in the natural lottery of talent and ability, or from his initial place in society, without giving (or receiving) compensating advantages in return. (The parties in the original position are not said to be attracted by this idea and so agree to it; rather, given the symmetries of their situation, and particularly their lack of knowledge, and so on, they will find it to their interest to agree to a principle which can be understood in this way.) And we should note also that when the difference principle is perfectly satisfied, the basic structure is optimal by the efficiency principle. There is no way to make anyone better off without making someone else worse off, namely, the least fortunate representative man. Thus the two principles of justice define distributive shares in a way compatible with efficiency, at least as long as we move on this highly abstract level. If we want to say (as we do, although it cannot be argued here) that the demands of justice have an absolute weight with respect to efficiency, this claim may seem less paradoxical when it is kept in mind that perfectly just institutions are also efficient.

Our second question is whether it is possible to arrange the institutions of a constitutional democracy so that the two principles of justice are satisfied, at least approximately. We shall try to show that this can be done provided the government regulates a free economy in a certain way. More fully, if law and government act effectively to keep markets competitive, resources fully employed, property and wealth widely distributed over time, and to maintain the appropriate social minimum, then if there is equality of opportunity underwritten by education for all, the resulting distribution will be just. Of course, all of these arrangements and policies are familiar. The only novelty in the following remarks, if there is any novelty at all, is that this framework of institutions can be made to satisfy the difference principle. To argue this, we must sketch the relations of these institutions and how they work together.

First of all, we assume that the basic social structure is controlled by a just constitution which secures the various liberties of equal citizenship. Thus the legal order is administered in accordance with the principle of legality, and liberty of conscience and freedom of thought are taken for granted. The political process is conducted, so far as possible, as a just procedure for choosing between governments and for enacting just legislation. From the standpoint of distributive justice, it is also essential that there be equality of opportunity in several senses. Thus, we suppose that, in addition to maintaining the usual social overhead capital, government provides for equal educational opportunities for all either by subsidizing private schools or by operating a public school system. It also enforces and underwrites equality of opportunity in commercial ventures and in the free choice of occupation. This result is achieved by policing business behaviour and by preventing the establishment of barriers and restriction to the desirable positions and markets. Lastly, there is a guarantee of a social minimum which the government meets by family allowances and special payments in times of unemployment, or by a negative income tax.

In maintaining this system of institutions the government may be thought of as divided into four branches. Each branch is represented by various agencies (or activities thereof) charged with preserving certain social and economic conditions. These branches do not necessarily overlap with the usual organization of government, but should be understood as purely conceptual. Thus the allocation branch is to keep the economy feasibly competitive, that is, to prevent the formation of unreasonable market power. Markets are competitive in this sense when they cannot be made more so consistent with the requirements of efficiency and the acceptance of the facts of consumer preferences and geography. The allocation branch is also charged with identifying and correcting, say by suitable taxes and subsidies, wherever possible, the more obvious departures from efficiency caused by the failure of prices to measure accurately social benefits and costs. The stabilization branch strives to maintain reasonably full employment so that there is no waste through failure to use resources and the free choice of occupation and the deployment of finance is supported by strong effective demand. These two branches together are to preserve the efficiency of the market economy generally.

The social minimum is established through the operations of the transfer branch. Later on we shall consider at what level this minimum should be set, since this is a crucial matter; but for the moment, a few general remarks will suffice. The main idea is that the workings of the transfer branch take into account the precept of need and assign it an appropriate weight with respect to the other common-sense precepts of justice. A market economy ignores the claims of need altogether. Hence there is a division of labour between the parts of the social system as different institutions answer to different common-sense precepts. Competitive markets (properly supplemented by government operations) handle the problem of the efficient allocation of labour and resources and set a weight to the conventional precepts associated with wages and earnings (the precepts of each according to his work and experience, or responsibility and the hazards of the job, and so on), whereas the transfer branch guarantees a certain level of well-being and meets the claims of need. Thus it is obvious that the justice of distributive shares depends upon the whole social system and how it distributes total income, wages plus transfers. There is with reason strong objection to the competitive determination of total income, since this would leave out of account the claims of need and of a decent standard of life. From the standpoint of the original position it is clearly rational to insure oneself against these contingencies. But now, if the appropriate minimum is provided by transfers, it may be perfectly fair that the other part of total income is competitively determined. Moreover, this way of dealing with the claims of need is doubtless more efficient, at least from a theoretical point of view, than trying to regulate prices by minimum wage standards and so on. It is preferable to handle these claims by a separate branch which supports a social minimum. Henceforth, in considering whether the second principle of justice is satisfied, the answer turns on whether the total income of the least advantaged, that is, wages plus transfers, is such as to maximize their long-term expectations consistent with the demands of liberty.

Finally, the distribution branch is to preserve an approximately just distribution of income and wealth over time by affecting the background conditions of the market from period to period. Two aspects of this branch may be distinguished. First of all, it operates a system of inheritance and gift taxes. The aim of these levies is not to raise revenue, but gradually and continually to correct the distribution of wealth and to prevent the concentrations of power to the detriment of liberty and equality of opportunity. It is perfectly true, as some have said,[3] that unequal inheritance of wealth is no more inherently unjust than unequal inheritance of intelligence; as far as possible the inequalities founded on either should satisfy the difference principle. Thus, the inheritance of greater wealth is just as long as it is to the advantage of the worst off and consistent with liberty, including equality of opportunity. Now by the latter we do not mean, of course, the equality of expectations between classes, since differences in life-prospects arising from the basic structure are inevitable, and it is precisely the aim of the second principle to say when these differences are just. Instead, equality of opportunity is a certain set of institutions which assures equally good education and chances of culture for all and which keeps open the competition for positions on the basis of qualities reasonably related to performance, and so on. It is these institutions which are put in jeopardy when inequalities and concentrations of wealth reach a certain limit; and the taxes imposed by the distribution branch are to prevent this limit from being exceeded. Naturally enough where this limit lies is a matter for political judgment guided by theory, practical experience, and plain hunch; on this questions the theory of justice has nothing to say.

The second part of the distribution branch is a scheme of taxation for raising revenue to cover the costs of public goods, to make transfer payments, and the like. This scheme belongs to the distribution branch since the burden of taxation must be justly shared. Although we cannot examine the legal and economic complications involved, there are several points in favour of proportional expenditure taxes as part of an ideally just arrangement. For one thing, they are preferable to income taxes at the level of common-sense precepts of justice, since they impose a levy according to how much a man takes out of the common store of goods and not according to how much he contributes (assuming that income is fairly earned in return for productive efforts). On the other hand, proportional taxes treat everyone in a clearly defined uniform way (again assuming that income is fairly earned) and hence it is preferable to use progressive rates only when they are necessary to preserve the justice of the system as a whole, that is, to prevent large fortunes hazardous to liberty and equality of opportunity, and the like. If proportional expenditure taxes should also prove more efficient, say because they interfere less with incentives, or whatever, this would make the case for them decisive provided a feasible scheme could be worked out.[4] Yet these are questions of political judgment which are not our concern; and, in any case, a proportional expendi-

---

[3] See, for example, F. von Hayek, *The Constitution of Liberty* (1960), p. 90.

[4] See N. Kaldor, *An Expenditure Tax* (1955).

ture tax is part of an idealized scheme which we are describing. It does not follow that even steeply progressive income taxes, given the injustice of existing systems, do not improve justice and efficiency all things considered. In practice we must usually choose between unjust arrangements and then it is a matter of finding the lesser injustice.

Whatever form the distribution branch assumes, the argument for it is to be based on justice: we must hold that once it is accepted the social system as a whole—the competitive economy surrounded by a just constitutional and legal framework—can be made to satisfy the principles of justice with the smallest loss in efficiency. The long-term expectations of the least advantaged are raised to the highest level consistent with the demands of equal liberty. In discussing the choice of a distribution scheme we have made no reference to the traditional criteria of taxation according to ability to pay or benefits received; nor have we mentioned any of the variants of the sacrifice principle. These standards are subordinate to the two principles of justice; once the problem is seen as that of designing a whole social system, they assume the status of secondary precepts with no more independent force than the precepts of common sense in regard to wages. To suppose otherwise is not to take a sufficiently comprehensive point of view. In setting up a just distribution branch these precepts may or may not have a place depending upon the demands of the two principles of justice when applied to the entire system. . . .

The sketch of the system of institutions satisfying the two principles of justice is now complete. . . .

In order . . . to establish just distributive shares a just total system of institutions must be set up and impartially administered. Given a just constitution and the smooth working of the four branches of government, and so on, there exists a procedure such that the actual distribution of wealth, whatever it turns out to be, is just. It will have come about as a consequence of a just system of institutions satisfying the principles to which everyone would agree and against which no one can complain. The situation is one of pure procedural justice, since there is no independent criterion by which the outcome can be judged. Nor can we say that a particular distribution of wealth is just because it is one which could have resulted from just institutions although it has not, as this would be to allow too much. Clearly there are many distributions which may be reached by just institutions, and this is true whether we count patterns of distributions among social classes or whether we count distributions of particular goods and services among particular individuals. There are indefinitely many outcomes and what makes one of these just is that it has been achieved by actually carrying out a just scheme of co-operation as it is publicly understood. It is the result which has arisen when everyone receives that to which he is entitled given his and others' actions guided by their legitimate expectations and their obligations to one another. We can no more arrive at a just distribution of wealth except by working together within the framework of a just system of institutions than we can win or lose fairly without actually betting.

This account of distributive shares is simply an elaboration of the familiar idea that economic rewards will be just once a perfectly competitive price system is organized as a fair game. But in order to do this we have to begin with the choice of a social system as a whole, for the basic structure of the entire arrangement must be just. The economy must be surrounded with the appropriate framework of institutions, since even a perfectly efficient price system has no tendency to determine just distributive shares when left to itself. Not only must economic activity be regulated by a just constitution and controlled by the four branches of government, but a just saving-function must be adopted to estimate the provision to be made for future generations. Thus, we cannot, in general, consider only piecewise reforms, for unless all of these fundamental questions are properly handled, there is no assurance that the resulting distributive shares will be just; while if the correct initial choices of institutions are made, the matter of distributive justice may be left to take care of itself. Within the framework of a just system men may be permitted to form associations and groupings as they please so long as they respect the like liberty of others. With social ingenuity it should be possible to invent many different kinds of economic and social activities appealing to a wide variety of tastes and talents; and as long as the justice of the basic structure of the whole is not affected, men may be allowed, in accordance with the principle of free association, to enter into and to take part in whatever activities they wish. The resulting distribution will be just whatever it happens to be. The system of institutions which we have described is, let's suppose, the basic structure of a well-ordered society. This system exhibits the content of the two principles of justice by showing how they may be perfectly satisfied; and it defines a social ideal by reference to which political judgment among second-bests, and the long range direction of reform, may be guided. . . .

Questions for Discussion

1. Tom Regan seems to think that some (nonhuman) animals are persons. Do you agree with him? Might there be humans who are not persons? What is the difference between humans and persons and what might such difference mean for issues other than the one of how to treat animals?

2. Does Regan refute utilitarianism? Explain.

3. Imagine there to be a highly sophisticated and powerful space traveler who enjoys feasting on the inhabitants of certain planets but who does not need this nourishment to live a good life. Imagine further that this space traveler has announced his intention to consume human beings in order to satisfy his palate. Would the fact that we are as inferior to him as animals are to us be morally relevant in our effort to persuade him to spare our lives? If not, what implications does this have for our treatment of animals?

4. Most of us regard charity as something it is good to give but not wrong not to give. For Singer, however, giving charity is a moral duty—if we fail

to give charity we have done something wrong. Do you agree? Does this set a standard that is too high for most of us to follow?

5. If people are geographically remote from us, does that absolve us from responsibility for their welfare?

6. How would Peter Singer respond to the third-century theologian Tertullian who wrote, "The scourges of pestilence, famine, wars, and earthquakes have come to be regarded as a blessing to overcrowded nations, since they serve to prune away the luxuriant growth of the human race?"

7. Compare and contrast the retributivist view of capital punishment with the deterrence view. With which position do you sympathize? Why?

8. Jonathan Glover argues that the case for capital punishment as a substantial deterrence fails. Do you agree? Defend your answer.

9. Is capital punishment legalized murder as some of its critics sometimes suggest? Analyze the concept of murder and determine whether capital punishment is a species thereof.

10. Can the "unnaturalness" argument be developed in a way that is immune to Burton M. Leiser's criticisms? If so, how?

11. Might homosexuality be immoral on grounds other than those of natural law? If so, on what grounds?

12. Is society justified in limiting the rights and privileges of individuals on the basis of their sexual preferences? If so, how, and on what basis?

13. Why does John Rawls believe that his view is morally preferable to that of utilitarianism? Do you agree?

14. According to Rawls, a distribution of wealth is just if its pattern of distribution is just. What place, if any, does this leave for the manner in which wealth is acquired and transferred?

15. What principles of justice can you think of that might fairly govern the distribution of wealth in society?

Selected Bibliography
Animal Rights

Clark, S. *The Moral Status of Animals*. Oxford, England: Clarendon Press, 1977.

Feinberg, Joel. "The Rights of Animals and Unborn Generations." In *Philosophy and Environmental Crisis*, edited by W. Blackstone; 48-68. Athens: University of Georgia Press, 1974.

Francis, Leslie Pickering, and Richard Norman. "Some Animals Are More Equal Than Others." *Philosophy* 53 (October 1978); 507–27.

Frey, R. G. *Interests and Rights: The Case Against Animals*. Oxford, England: Clarendon Press, 1980.

McCloskey, H. J. "Moral Rights and Animals." *Inquiry* 22 (Spring–Summer, 1979); 25–54.

Midgley, Mary. *Animals and Why They Matter*. Athens: University of Georgia Press, 1983.

Regan, Tom. *The Case for Animal Rights*. Berkeley, Calif.: University of California Press, 1983.

Regan, Tom, and Peter Singer, eds. *Animal Rights and Human Obligations*. Englewood Cliffs, N.J.: Prentice-Hall, 1976.

Rollin, Bernard. *Animal Rights and Human Morality*. Buffalo, N.Y.: Prometheus, 1981.

Singer, Peter. *Animal Liberation*. New York: Avon Books, 1975.

World Hunger

Aiken, William, and Hugh Lafollette, eds. *World Hunger and Moral Obligation*. Englewood Cliffs, N.J.: Prentice-Hall, 1977.

Bayles, Michael. *Morality and Population Policy*. Birmingham: University of Alabama Press, 1980.

Elfstrom, Gerald. *Ethics for a Shrinking World*. New York: St. Martin's Press, 1990.

Hardin, Garrett. "Lifeboat Ethics: The Case Against Helping the Poor." *Psychology Today* 8 (September 1974); 38–43.

———. *Promethean Ethics*. Seattle: University of Washington Press, 1979.

Lucas, George R., Jr., and Thomas Ogletree, eds. *Lifeboat Ethics*. New York: Harper and Row, 1976.

Rachels, James. "Killing and Starving to Death." *Philosophy* 54 (April 1979); 159–71.

Shuman, Charles B. "Food Aid and the Free Market." In *Food Policy*, edited by Peter G. Brown, and Henry Shue, 145–63. New York: The Free Press, 1977.

Singer, Peter. *Practical Ethics*; 158–81. Cambridge, Mass.: Cambridge University Press, 1979.

Sterba, James. "The Welfare Rights of Distant Peoples and Future Generations." In *Morality in Practice*, edited by James Sterba; 106–18. Belmont, Calif.: Wadsworth, 1991.

Capital Punishment

Bedau, Hugo. *The Death Penalty in America*. New York: Oxford University Press, 1982.

Bedau, Hugo, and C. M. Pierce, eds. *Capital Punishment in the United States*. New York: AMS Press, 1976.

Black, Charles L., Jr. *Capital Punishment*. New York: W. W. Norton, 1974.

Davis, Michael. "Death, Deterrence, and the Method of Common Sense." *Social Theory and Practice* 7 (Summer 1981); 145–77.

Ezorsky, Gertrude, ed. *Philosophical Perspectives on Punishment*. Albany: State University of New York Press, 1972.

Goldberg, Steven. "On Capital Punishment." *Ethics* 85 (October 1974); 67–74.

Murphy, Jeffrie G. *Punishment and Rehabilitation*. Belmont, Calif.: Wadsworth, 1984.

Nathanson, Stephen. *The Morality of Punishment by Death*. Savage, Md.: Rowman and Littlefield, 1987.

Van den Haag, Ernest. *Punishing Criminals*. New York: Basic Books, 1975.

Van den Haag, Ernest and John P. Conrad. *The Death Penalty: A Debate*. New York: Plenum, 1983.

PART II

Doing or Being?

Rival Approaches to Moral Philosophy

Doing or Being?

In Part I, we examined action-based approaches to the question, "What should we do when confronted with choices involving right and wrong conduct?" The theories behind these approaches answer the question by focusing on moral principles that should govern our actions. The *ethical relativist* answers the question by defining moral conduct in sociological terms; the *ethical egoist*, by what satisfies a person's selfish desires; the *utilitarian*, by what maximizes overall happiness; and the *Kantian*, by whether the principle of one's actions can be applied universally. Many of these theories have practical applications to such vexing moral issues as abortion, capital punishment, and the welfare of animals.

In this part, we examine whether the question "What should I do?" is the right one to ask. In recent years a growing number of moral philosophers, called virtue-theorists, have become disenchanted with an action-based approach. They note that we often make judgments about good and evil people apart from the actions these people perform. For them, the central question of ethics is not "What should I do?" but "What kind of person should I be?" A theory that emphasizes the former question is sometimes referred to as an *ethics of doing* (also known as action-based, duty-based, or principle-based ethics). A theory that emphasizes the latter question is sometimes referred to as an *ethics of being* (also known as virtue-based, agent-based, or character-based ethics).

It is not difficult to understand what motivates an ethics of being. Consider, for instance, the following story that Richard Taylor tells in his *Good and Evil*:

> A boy, strolling over the countryside on his way from Sunday school, came across a large beetle lumbering over the ground. Fascinated by its size and beauty, he took a pin, stabbed the insect through the back, ran it up to the head of the pin, and impaled it on a nearby tree. Several days later, having forgotten this, while he was going about his daily play, the boy found himself again in the same place and curiosity led him again to the tree. There was the beetle, its legs still moving, although very slowly, against the empty air.[1]

What is it about this story that stirs moral sentiments? It is not the boy's failure to comply with the *principles* of morality, for it is arguable whether there are any principles at all that prohibit such conduct. Torturing animals is not explicitly prohibited by any of the action-based theories. Even if it were, what gives this tale its "stamp of moral evil" is the boy's delight in torturing the insect. It is the cruelty of the *person* that fills us with abhorrence.

---

[1] Richard Taylor, *Good and Evil* (New York: Macmillan), 1970, 207. (See also Part III, p. 329.)

The moral of the story is this: in addition to making judgments about right and wrong *conduct*, we also make judgments about the *agent* involved. We make judgments about good and evil persons, their character traits, and their willingness to perform certain actions. For this reason, moral philosophers have come to debate the question of how best to approach moral theory. Is the fundamental question of moral philosophy "What should I do?" as suggested by action-theorists? Or is it "What should I be?" as suggested by virtue-theorists?

We have already seen, in Part I, how action-theorists go about their business. In contrast, virtue-theorists proceed by putting forward an exemplary individual (i.e., a hero or saint such as Socrates, Mother Teresa, or St. Francis of Assisi), explaining what it is that makes this person good, and exhorting us to be like the person. The claim is that the person's character is at least as basic as any principle of action that explains right conduct, and that this approach to ethics has methodological advantages.

Of course, action-theorists would not agree with this claim. How, they might ask, are we to identify good persons without prior knowledge of right and wrong conduct? To call a person good presupposes that the person is disposed to do good, and doing good implies that we have the ability to distinguish right from wrong. Furthermore, the kind of person we are depends in part on the actions we perform. Mother Teresa would hardly be considered a moral saint if she never engaged in charitable acts.

We see, then, that the question of "Doing or Being?" is difficult to answer. It is impossible to separate completely who one is from what one does. On the one hand, a person can do all the right things yet not be considered morally good. On the other hand, a person may be considered morally good yet sometimes fail to do what is right. Furthermore, there are certain acts that automatically render one morally evil. Torturing children is an obvious example.

In fairness, it would be a mistake to assume that action-theorists completely ignore the importance of the agent. Kant, for instance, insisted that actions be performed from the right kind of motive, and Mill distinguished between judging an action and judging a person. In discussing motive, Mill specifically stated that "utilitarian moralists have gone beyond almost all others in affirming that the motive has nothing to do with the morality of the action, though much with the worth of the agent."[2] However, Mill's point is that we do not need to know anything about the character of the agent to know whether the actions are right or wrong. Today, many moral theorists follow Mill in distinguishing the rightness of the act from the goodness of the agent.

It is, then, somewhat misleading to pit action-theorists against virtue-theorists in the manner we have shown. Action-theorists allow for character judgments although they often assign them a secondary status. Typically, for instance, they will distinguish between first- and second-order moral judgments. First-order moral judgments are made about the acts in question

---

[2] John Stuart Mill, *Utilitarianism* (1863), Chapter 2, paragraph 19.

whereas second-order moral judgments are made about the agent who performs them. But the important point is that second-order judgments logically depend on first-order ones—a claim virtue-theorists deny.

Summary of Readings

The readings in this part address the question of whether moral theory is best served by focusing on an ethics of doing, of being, or both. Some philosophers see the concern with virtue as a summons to change the focus on doing to one on being. Others see it as a plea for balance in our moral deliberations. Both approaches emphasize the need to identify the traits and attitudes that reflect good character, rather than simply formulating the principles of conduct that distinguish right from wrong actions independent of the agent.

In the first reading, "Negative and Positive Morality," Bernard Mayo points out that the classical philosophers did not lay down action-guiding principles but concentrated instead on the character of the agent. Mayo's claim is that this approach has distinct advantages. Admitting that an ethics of doing has a simplicity to recommend it (we determine what we should do by seeing whether it maximizes happiness [utilitarianism], whether it is universalizable [Kantianism], etc.), an ethics of being has its own simplicity, which Mayo refers to as "the unity of character." Persons of character, says Mayo, do not merely give us principles to follow; they set us examples to follow. And because there is more than one way to follow an example, an ethics of being is more flexible than one of doing. For this reason, Mayo urges us not to overemphasize an ethics of doing and demonstrates how an ethics of being adds an important perspective to moral philosophy.

In the next reading, "Quandary Ethics," Edmund L. Pincoffs takes issue with what he refers to as *quandary ethics*, in which the concern is the resolution of problems by the application of a theory. According to Pincoffs, classical moral philosophers were not "quandarists" but were chiefly concerned with what was good for humanity. This being so, quandary ethics is a relative newcomer to moral philosophy, arising in response to the problems created by social changes and technological advances. Its underlying assumption is that the best way of handling moral problems is by formulating principles of conduct that are appropriate to whatever circumstances we find ourselves in.

For Pincoffs, however, this conception is more a hindrance than a help. In his view, moral judgment is not so much the application of a principle to the facts as it is an expression of the character of the agent. Put another way, we do not solve moral dilemmas by impartially applying principles to facts as a judge might do in deciding a case; rather, we solve them by determining what would be right for a particular person, taking into account such features as that person's conception of his or her own moral character. For such reasons, Pincoffs suggests that we take an alternative approach to ethics—one that makes "virtue" the fundamental concept of moral philosophy.

In "The Schizophrenia of Modern Ethical Theories," Michael Stocker argues that the primary purpose of a moral theory is to provide us with a reason for moral action. However, none of the action-theories succeeds on this score because they cannot be integrated into a person's moral life. Because this is true, none of these theories is particularly satisfying. Furthermore, to the extent that we can integrate such theories into our lives, something is lost that is vital to morality. Suppose, for instance, that we succeed in being moved by considerations of self-interest (egoism), happiness (utilitarianism), or duty (Kantianism). What follows is that we focus on the consideration and we lose the person-relatedness of our actions and attitudes—we lose the love, affection, and feeling that ordinarily move us. The effort, for example, to be a friend to someone out of the desire to maximize utility or out of a sense of duty impedes our ability to achieve true friendship. Thus, Stocker concludes that we need an ethical theory that we can actually *live by*, suggesting an emphasis on the concept of virtue.

Mayo, Pincoffs, and Stocker are all critical of an ethics of doing. In contrast, as the title of Robert B. Louden's piece suggests—"On Some Vices of Virtue Ethics"—this author is critical of an ethics of being. He argues that an ethics of being cannot meet some of the needs that an ethics of doing has typically met. If, says Louden, we concentrate exclusively on evaluating agents as opposed to acts, the theory will fail in several respects. It will, for example, fail to provide the guidance for finding our way out of practical quandaries. Because of this and other problems that virtue-theorists encounter, Louden concludes that we should study the virtues but not, as virtue-theorists do, in a way that makes the virtues themselves morally basic.

William Frankena's "To Be or to Do, That Is the Question," although generally supportive of an ethics of doing, nonetheless sympathizes with an ethics of being. He argues that an ethics of doing and an ethics of being need not be construed as rival moralities but as complementary aspects of the same morality. As he sees it, an ethics of doing could not get started without the disposition to act in accordance with principles ("principles without traits are impotent"). On the other hand, it is hard to understand traits of character except as dispositions to behave in specified ways ("traits without principles are blind"). He proposes, therefore, a "double-aspect" conception of morality that says that for every moral principle there will be a morally good trait consisting of a disposition to act according to the principle, and for every moral trait there will be a principle of action telling us how to express the trait.

In the final reading of this section, "What's So Special About the Virtues?," Thomas L. Beauchamp is concerned with warding off what he considers the overemphasis philosophers attach to their preferred moral theories. To counteract this tendency, Beauchamp—like Frankena—argues that an ethics of doing and an ethics of being need not be construed as rivals but should be viewed as correlative theories. "A morality of principles," he says, "should enthusiastically recommend settled dispositions to act in accordance with that which is morally required, and a proponent of virtue ethics should encourage the development of principles that express how one ought to act." As Beauchamp sees it, virtues and principles are both instruments to achieve the ends of life that it is the business of moral theory to identify and promulgate. Within some contexts, some features of the good life will best be served by emphasizing an ethics of doing; within other contexts, by an ethics of being. For this reason, Beauchamp advises tolerance rather than favoritism in the evaluation of moral theories.

15

Negative and Positive Morality

Bernard Mayo was an English philosopher. He is the author of *Ethics and the Moral Life* (1958).

Duty and Virtue

It has been said that the whole of Western philosophy is a set of footnotes to Plato. This is a pardonable half-truth for, say, metaphysics, but it is very far from true of moral philosophy. The philosophy of moral principles, which is characteristic of Kant and the post-Kantian era, is something of which hardly a trace exists in Plato. Plato speaks at great length of goodness and the good; we also speak of the word "good" as a moral word, but . . . it is an evaluative and not an imperative word, and is less at home in the context of moral principles than are such words as "right" and "wrong." These words, on the other hand, do not occur in Platonic ethics. Plato says nothing about rules or principles or laws, except when he is talking politics. Instead he talks about virtues and vices, and about certain types of human character. The key word in Platonic ethics is Virtue; the key word in Kantian ethics is Duty. And modern ethics is a set of footnotes, not to Plato, but to Kant, and, more remotely, to the Old Testament and Roman Law.

We shall now consider a family of objections to the philosophy of moral principles, some of which point to genuine shortcomings of that philosophy. I consider them all under the heading of "Positive and Negative Morality" because their general trend is to suggest that Duty and its related concepts (obligation, principle, and so on) refer only to the negative aspect of morality; that there is a positive aspect; and that the concept of virtue, unjustly neglected recently, may point to the missing positive factor. . . .

Doing and Being

Attention to the novelists can be a welcome correction to a tendency of philosophical ethics of the last generation or two to lose contact with the ordinary life of man which is just what the novelists, in their own way, are concerned with. Of course there are writers who can be called in to illustrate problems about Duty (Graham Greene is a good example). But there are more who perhaps never mention the words duty, obligation or principle. Yet they are all concerned—Jane Austen, for instance, entirely and absolutely—with the moral qualities or defects of their heroes and heroines and other characters. This points to a radical one-sidedness in the philosophers' account of morality in terms of principles: it takes little or no account of qualities, of what people *are*. It is just here that the old-fashioned word Virtue used to have a place; and it is just here that the work of Plato and Aristotle can be instructive. Justice, for Plato, though it is closely connected with acting according to law, does not *mean* acting according to law: it is a quality of character, and a just action is one such as a just man would do. Telling the truth, for Aristotle, is not, as it was for Kant, fulfilling an obligation; again it is a quality of character, or, rather, a whole range of qualities of character, some of which may actually be defects, such as tactlessness, boastfulness, and so on—a point which can be brought out, in terms of principles, only with the greatest complexity and artificiality, but quite simply and naturally in terms of character.

If we wish to enquire about Aristotle's moral views, it is no use looking for a set of principles. Of course we can find *some* principles to which he must have subscribed—for instance, that one ought not to commit adultery. But what we find much more prominently is a set of character-traits, a list of certain types of person—the courageous man, the niggardly man, the boaster, the lavish spender and so on. The basic moral question, for Aristotle, is not, What shall I do? but, What shall I be?

These contrasts between doing and being, negative and positive, and modern as against Greek morality were noted by John Stuart Mill; I quote from the *Essay on Liberty*:

> Christian morality (so-called) has all the characters of a reaction; it is, in great part, a protest against Paganism. Its ideal is negative rather than positive; passive rather than active; Innocence rather than Nobleness; Abstinence from Evil, rather than energetic Pursuit of the Good; in its precepts (as has been well said) "Thou shalt not" predominates unduly over "Thou shalt." . . . Whatever exists of magnanimity, highmindedness, personal dignity, even the sense of honour, is derived from the purely human, not the religious part of our education, and never could have grown out of a standard of ethics in which the only worth, professedly recognised, is that of obedience.

Of course, there are connections between being and doing. It is obvious that a man cannot just *be*; he can only be what he is by doing what he does; his moral qualities are ascribed to him because of his actions, which are said to manifest those qualities. But the point is that an ethics of Being must include this obvious fact, that Being involves Doing; whereas an ethics of Doing, such as I have been examining, may easily overlook it. As I have suggested, a morality of principles is concerned only with what people do or fail to do, since that is what rules are for. And as far as this sort of ethics goes, people might well have no moral qualities at all except the possession of principles and the will (and capacity) to act accordingly.

Principles and Ideals

When we speak of a moral quality such as courage, and say that a certain action was courageous, we are not merely saying something about the action. We are referring, not so much to what is done, as to the kind of person by whom we take it to have been done. We connect, by means of imputed motives and intentions, with the character of the agent as courageous. This explains, incidentally, why both Kantians and Utilitarians encounter, in their different ways, such difficulties in dealing with motives, which their principles, on the face of it, have no room for. A Utilitarian, for example, can only praise a courageous action in some such way as this: the action is of a sort such as a person of courage is likely to perform, and courage is a quality of character the cultivation of which is likely to increase rather than diminish the sum total of human happiness. But Aristotelians have no need of such circumlocution. For them a courageous action just is one which proceeds from and manifests a certain type of character, and is praised because such a character-trait is good, or better than others, or is a virtue. An evaluative criterion is sufficient: there is no need to look for an imperative criterion as well, or rather instead, according to which it is not the character which is good, but the cultivation of the character which is right.

Dispositions of the special sort applicable to human beings are . . . in an important sense "elastic"; that is, from the information that someone is timid we cannot rigorously deduce that he will be frightened on a given occasion, as we can rigorously deduce from the solubility of sugar that it will dissolve when immersed in water. Timid people sometimes act courageously, that is, as courageous people behave; in general, people can act "out of character." Acting out of character is interestingly different from breaking a principle. There are no degrees about rule-breaking: the rule is either kept or broken. In terms of rules, all we are entitled to consider is the relation between an action (the subject of judgment) and a rule (the criterion of judgment), and the verdict is either Right or Wrong. But in considering action by an agent, we have to take into account as well a whole range of other actions by the agent, on the basis of which we form a judgment of character. Actions are "in character" or "out of character" in varying degrees, and, further, we can never state precisely what a person's character is. Instead of the extreme simplicity of the moral judgment based on a moral principle and an instance of conduct which either does or does not conform to that principle, we have a double complexity. Corresponding to the moral principle (which represents the conduct of an ideally righteous man) we have, instead, the idea of a virtue (which represents the conduct and conduct-tendency of an ideally good man). But whereas a man's action can be compared directly with the principle and only two possible verdicts result (or three, if we include "indifferent"), it cannot be compared in this way with the standard of virtue. For we cannot say exactly either how far the action is "in character" for the man, nor how far the character of the man matches or fails to match the idea. It is not surprising that moral principles, with their superior logical manageability, have proved more attractive than moral ideals as material for ethical theory.

No doubt the fundamental moral question is just "What ought I to do?" And according to the philosophy of moral principles, the answer (which must be an imperative "Do this") must be derived from a conjunction of premises, consisting (in the simplest case) firstly of a rule, or universal imperative, enjoining (or forbidding) all actions of a certain type in situations of a certain type, and, secondly, a statement to the effect that this is a situation of that type, falling under that rule. In practice the emphasis may be on supplying only one of these premises, the other being assumed or taken for granted: one may answer the question "What ought I to do?" either by quoting a rule which I am to adopt, or by showing that my case is legislated for by a rule which I do adopt. To take a previous example of moral perplexity, if I am in doubt whether to tell the truth about his condition to a dying man, my doubt may be resolved by showing that the case comes under a rule about the avoidance of unnecessary suffering, which I am assumed to accept. But if the case is without precedent in my moral career, my problem may be soluble only by adopting a new principle about what I am to do now and in the future about cases of this kind.

This second possibility offers a connection with moral ideals. Suppose my perplexity is not merely an unprecedented situation which I could cope with by adopting a new rule. Suppose the new rule is thoroughly inconsistent with my existing moral code. This may happen, for instance, if the moral code is one to which I only pay lip-service; if . . . its authority is not yet internalised, or if it has ceased to be so; it is ready for rejection, but its final rejection awaits a moral crisis such as we are assuming to occur. What I now need is not a rule for deciding how to act in this situation and others of its kind. I need a whole set of rules, a complete morality, new principles to live by.

Now according to the philosophy of moral character, there is another way of answering the fundamental question "What ought I to do?" Instead of quoting a rule, we quote a quality of character, a virtue: we say "Be brave," or "Be patient" or "Be lenient." We may even say "Be a man": if I am in doubt, say, whether to take a risk, and someone says "Be a man," meaning a morally sound man, in this case a man of sufficient courage. (Compare the very different ideal invoked in "Be a gentleman." I shall not discuss whether this is a *moral* ideal.) Here, too, we have the extreme cases, where a man's moral perplexity extends not merely to a particular situation but to his whole way of living. And now the question "What ought I to do?" turns into the question "What ought I to be?"—as, indeed, it was treated in the first place. ("Be brave.") It is answered, not by quoting a rule or a set of rules, but by describing a quality of character or a type of person. And here the ethics of character gains a practical simplicity which offsets the greater logical simplicity of the ethics of principles. We do not have to give a list of characteristics or virtues, as we might list a set of principles. We can give a unity to our answer.

Of course we can in theory give a unity to our principles: this is implied by speaking of a *set* of principles. But if such a set is to be a system and not a mere aggregate, the unity we are looking for is a logical one, namely the possibility that some principles are deducible from others, and ultimately from one. But the attempt to construct a deductive moral system is notoriously difficult, and in any case ill-founded. Why should we expect that all rules of conduct should be ultimately reducible to a few?

Saints and Heroes

But when we are asked "What shall I be?" we can readily give a unity to our answer, though not a logical unity. It is the unity of character. A person's character is not merely a list of dispositions; it has the organic unity of something that is more than the sum of its parts. And we can say, in answer to our morally perplexed questioner, not only "Be this" and "Be that," but also "Be like So-and-So"—where So-and-So is either an ideal type of character, or else an actual person taken as representative of the ideal, an exemplar. Examples of the first are Plato's "just man" in the Republic; Aristotle's man of practical wisdom, in the Nicomachean Ethics; Augustine's citizen of the City of God; the good Communist; the American way of life (which is a collective expression for a type of character). Examples of the second kind, the exemplar, are Socrates, Christ, Buddha, St. Francis, the heroes of epic writers and of novelists. Indeed the idea of the Hero, as well as the idea of the Saint, are very much the expression of this attitude to morality. Heroes and saints are not merely people who did things. They are people whom we are expected, and expect ourselves, to imitate. And imitating them means not merely doing what they did; it means being like them. Their status is not in the least like that of legislators whose laws we admire; for the character of a legislator is irrelevant to our judgment about his legislation. The heroes and saints did not merely give us principles to live by (though some of them did that as well): they gave us examples to follow.

Kant, as we should expect, emphatically rejects this attitude as "fatal to morality" (*Groundwork*, p. 76). According to him, examples serve only to render *visible* an instance of the moral principle, and thereby to demonstrate its practical feasibility. But every exemplar, such as Christ himself, must be judged by the independent criterion of the moral law, before we are entitled to recognize him as worthy of imitation. I am not suggesting that the subordination of exemplars to principles is incorrect, but that it is one-sided and fails to do justice to a large area of moral experience.

Imitation can be more or less successful. And this suggests another defect of the ethics of principles. It has no room for ideals, except the ideal of a perfect set of principles (which, as a matter of fact, is intelligible only in terms of an ideal character or way of life), and the ideal of perfect conscientiousness (which is itself a character-trait). This results, of course, from the "biack-or-white" nature of moral verdicts based on rules. There are no degrees of rule-keeping and rule-breaking. But there certainly are degrees by which we approach or recede from the attainment of a certain quality or virtue; if there were not, the word "ideal" would have no meaning. Heroes and saints are not people whom we try to be *just* like, since we know that is impossible. It is precisely because it is impossible for ordinary human beings to achieve the same qualities as the saints, and in the same degree, that we do set them apart from the rest of humanity. It is enough if we try to be a little like them. . . .

16

Quandary Ethics

Edmund L. Pincoffs was professor of philosophy at the University of Texas at Austin. Past president of AMINTAPHIL, his writings in ethics include "Virtue, the Quality of Life, and Punishment" (1960), "Quandary Ethics" (1971), *Quandaries and Virtues* (1986), and *Philosophy of Law: A Brief Introduction* (1991).

> Ethics is everybody's concern. . . . Everyone . . . is faced with moral problems—problems about which, after more or less reflection, a decision must be reached.
> —S. E. Toulmin, *Reason in Ethics*, p. 1

> I ask the reader to start by supposing that someone (himself perhaps) is faced with a serious moral problem.
> —R. M. Hare, *Freedom and Reason*, p. 1

> What is ethical theory about? Someone might propose as an answer: "Everyone knows what an ethical problem is; ethical theory must be about the solutions to such problems." . . . But do we really know precisely what an "ethical problem" is?
> —R. M. Brandt, *Ethical Theory*, p. 1

> My ultimate aim is to determine . . . how moral judgments can rationally be supported, how moral perplexities can be resolved, and how moral disputes can rationally be settled.
> —M. G. Singer, *Generalization in Ethics*, p. 6

> Only when he has linked these parts together in well-tempered harmony and has made himself one man instead of many, will he be ready to go about whatever he may have to do, whether it be making money and satisfying bodily wants, or business transactions, or the affairs of state. In all these fields when he speaks of just and honorable conduct, he will mean the behavior that helps to produce and

preserve this habit of mind. . . . Any action which tends to break
down this habit will be unjust; and the notion governing it he will
call ignorance and folly.

—Plato, *The Republic*

There is a consensus concerning the subject matter of ethics so general that it
would be tedious to document it. It is that the business of ethics is with 'problems', that is, situations in which it is difficult to know what one should do;
that the ultimate beneficiary of ethical analysis is the person who, in one of
these situations, seeks rational ground for the decision he must make; that
ethics is therefore primarily concerned to find such grounds, often conceived
of as moral rules and the principles from which they can be derived; and that
meta-ethics consists in the analysis of the terms, claims, and arguments that
come into play in moral disputation, deliberation, and justification in problematic contexts. It is my purpose in this chapter to raise some questions about
this conception of ethics, which I shall refer to, for convenience and disparage-
ment, as 'quandary ethics'.

Before proceeding to more philosophical matters it may be well to attend
to rhetorical ones—to present considerations that might cause the reader to
hesitate before replying, "Of course ethics is concerned to resolve problems on
rational grounds! With what else would it be concerned? To abandon the
search for rationally defensible rules and principles is to abandon moral philosophy," and so forth.

The first and most obvious rhetorical point is that quandary ethics is a
newcomer, that the 'quandarist' is fighting a very long tradition with which
he is at odds. Plato, Aristotle, the Epicureans, the Stoics, Augustine, Aquinas,
Shaftesbury, Hume, and Hegel do not conceive of ethics as the quandarists do.
If they are read for their theories—that is, for the grounds that they give for
making particular difficult moral decisions—their teachings are inevitably distorted. To give such grounds, such justifications of particular difficult choices,
was not their objective. They were, by and large, not so much concerned with
problematic situations as with moral enlightenment, education, and the good
for man. Again, the shift in emphasis is too patent to require documentation, but
we may illustrate the point by means of a brief glance at the ethics of Aristotle.

He, as is well known, thought of ethics as a branch of politics, which in
turn he thought of as a very wide-ranging subject having to do generally with
the planning of human life so that it could be lived as well as possible. In the
Politics the question concerns the best political arrangements, and a large and
important preliminary is the comparative study of constitutions, so that one
will know what kinds of arrangements are possible, with their advantages and
disadvantages, so that a choice may be made. Similarly in ethics, the leading
question concerns the best kind of individual life and the qualities of character
exhibited by the man who leads it. Again, a necessary preliminary is the study
of types of men, of characters, and possible exemplars of the sort of life to be
pursued or avoided. This study occupies a large part of the *Nicomachean Ethics*.

Moral problems are given their due but are by no means at stage center. The question is not so much how we should resolve perplexities as how we should live. Both the 'we' and the 'perplexity' or 'quandary' must be carefully qualified. The 'we' in question is not a mere place holder; rather, it refers to those of us who were well brought up, who have had some experience of life, who know something of the way in which the social order operates, who have some control over the direction of our lives in that we are capable of living according to a pattern and are not washed about by emotional tides or pulled hither and yon by capricious whim. So that if Aristotle is presented with a moral quandary, he has a right to presuppose a great deal concerning the upbringing, knowledge, and self-control of the persons concerned. But the notion of presenting Aristotle with a quandary is blurred if looked at through our spectacles. The kind of problems that Aristotle's qualified agents typically have are concerned not so much with what is to be done by anyone, qualified or not, in certain sorts of circumstances as with how not to fall into the traps that seize the unwary and convert them into one or another kind of undesirable character. When Aristotle discusses moral deliberation, it is not so much in the interest of finding grounds for the solution of puzzles as of determining when we may assign responsibility or of determining what it is that sets off practical from scientific reasoning.

But if Aristotle does not present us with quandaries into which the individual may fall and which he must puzzle and pry his way out of, this may be just because Aristotle does not value the qualities that allow or require a man to become bogged down in a marsh of indecision. There is, after all, the question of when we should and should not be involved in perplexities, when to avoid, as we often should, the *occasion* of perplexity. People can be perplexed because they are sensitive and conscientious, because they do not have the sense to avoid perplexity, or because they are pathologically immobilized by moral questions. A well-founded ethics would encourage the development of moral sensitivity but would discourage the entertainment of moral quandaries that arise out of moral ineptness or pathological fixation. The quandarists do not insist upon these distinctions, yet they are as important and obvious as the distinction between preventive and curative medicine. That the moral philosopher can be thought of as prescribing a regimen for a healthy moral life, rather than a cure for particular moral illnesses, would surely not be news to Aristotle.

The second rhetorical point to be made is that even though there may be philosophers who have thought through their reasons for accepting the present posture of ethics, very little argument can be found in defense of it. In fact, it rests, as far as I can tell, on unexamined assumptions that are perpetuated more by scholarly convention than by reasoned agreement. This posture, it may be well to emphasize, is not that of the casuist but one in which the ultimate objective of ethics is conceived to be the resolution of quandaries. It may be felt, indeed, that the nature of the times dictates what ethics must be and that therefore no critical examination of the role of ethics is in order. It may be believed that the era in which we live, beset by problems if men ever were, somehow militates in itself against any form of ethics but a problem-oriented one; that in this respect our time differs from all previous less-problem-plagued ones; that these problems are being loosed upon us by technological and social change; and that since change is so rapid and unpredictable, the best we can do for ourselves is to learn how to make decisions as they come along, to discover the form of a good decision; and the best we can do for our children is to teach them how to go about making decisions in the tight places into which they are sure to be crowded. This means that the tools for decision making must be put into their hands: the very general, and quite empty, principles from which rules that are appropriate to the occasion, whatever it is, may be derived. It may be felt, also, that the kaleidoscopic character of the times rules out an ethics focused, as such systems have been in most of the long tradition, on qualities of character and their development, since the inculcation of traits presupposes precisely the social stability that we do not have, because if we cannot count on social stability, we cannot know what character traits will be appropriate to the times in which our children will live.

This argument, which I have heard but not read, fails for two reasons, either of which is conclusive. The first is that it rests on a premise that is historically false. Character ethics has flourished in times of change that are comparable in their kaleidoscopic quality to our own. The Stoic ethic was taught and practiced over five hundred years, during which there were periods of violent change in the ancient world. These changes were often of such scope as to make individual citizens uncertain what kind of world their children were likely to inhabit. Athens, the original home of the movement, fluttered about in the surgings and wanings of empires, now moving forward with a democratic form of government, now languishing under tyrants supported by armies of occupation. The form that Stoicism took in Rome during the early empire, with its emphasis on the individual's control of his own soul no matter what the external circumstances might be like, is ample testimony to the insecurity that even the privileged classes felt in a time of tyranny and corruption.

The second reason is that the argument, even if it were sound, would militate as effectively against quandary ethics as against character ethics. Quandary ethics must, according to the argument, provide some stable means of arriving at decisions, no matter how circumstances may change. This is usually interpreted as requiring that rules and principles (or anyway 'good reasons') of universal application should be provided. But it is not at all clear why rules and principles will transcend change when qualities of character will not. If there are principles that would seem to apply in any conceivable world, why should there not exist qualities of character that are equally universal in scope? If there are character traits of narrower application, then there are principles that would be applicable in some circumstances but not in others. Indeed, it would be hard to imagine a world in which we should not make it a principle not to do to others what we would not want them to do to us; but it would be equally hard to imagine a world in which the quality of justice was without relevance. If there could be a world in which there was no place for justice, might there not also be a world in which there was no place for the

Silver Rule? The argument works not so much to demonstrate the advantages of principles and rules in an uncertain world as to point up the limits of any form of moral education in times of change.

The rhetorical points, then, are that quandary ethics diverges from the main lines of discussion followed through most of the history of ethics and that there seems to be little offered in justification of this change of orientation—and that little is not convincing. Of course, it may well be that there are excellent reasons why ethics should now be focused on disputation, deliberation, and justification, to the exclusion of questions of moral character. At best, the rhetorical arguments can challenge the defender of the contemporary trend to produce those reasons.

But there are philosophical questions as well, questions that at least have the advantage that they point up some of the presuppositions of quandary ethics and at most reveal that indefensible distortions of ethics result from the contemporary fixation on problems and their resolution. Quandary ethics, remember, supposes that the ultimate relevance of ethics is to the resolution of the problematic situations into which we fall. The problems in question are practical, not philosophical. Moral philosophers, like other philosophers, must deal with philosophical quandaries, which are not escaped, although they may be emphasized or de-emphasized, by changing the focus of ethics. For example, questions about the logical status of 'moral assertions' will present as much of a problem for the nonquandarist as for the quandarist. But the assertions in question are as likely to be about ideal standards as about the duties and obligations that are incumbent upon everyone.

The questions I want to raise are: What is a problematic situation? and Who are 'we' who find ourselves in these situations? Discussion of these questions, however, will require that I rehearse briefly some time-honored distinctions.

The quandarist typically thinks of the problem question as What is the right thing to do? or What would be a good thing to do? or What ought I to do? But these questions are recognized to be ambiguous, at least in the sense that they fail to distinguish between queries concerning what is the morally *correct* (rule-required, expected, proper, appropriate, fitting) thing to do and queries concerning the morally *useful* (fruitful, helpful, practical, optimum) thing to do. The questions concerning rightness, goodness, and oughtness can be questions about correctness or usefulness, or both. The discussion of these questions is likely to be informed by general theories concerning correctness and usefulness: in particular the theory that the correct thing to do is the thing that it would be correct for any person in similar circumstances to do and the theory that the useful thing to do is the thing that will, directly or indirectly, increase the happiness and decrease the misery of everyone concerned as much as possible.

Now if we ask the quandarist what a moral problem is and who 'we' are who are enmeshed in the problem, certain difficulties arise for the quandarist conception of ethics. The quandarist might hold that a moral problem con-

cerns what it is correct or what it is useful to do, or both. Whether he holds
that correctness entails usefulness, or vice versa, need not concern us. Let us consider the correctness question, through the examination of a typical quandary.

I have made a promise, one of these promises encountered so frequently
in the literature and so infrequently in life. It is to meet a friend to attend a
concert. That is to say, I have solemnly averred, using the words, 'I promise',
that this time I will not disappoint him, as I did the last time, and that I will
indeed be on hand at eight o'clock at the theater. Meantime (back at the ranch)
a neighbor calls to remind me of my agreement to attend an eight-o'clock
meeting of the school board, to argue that a proposed desegregation plan is
inadequate. What is the correct thing to do? How shall I decide? What is and
is not relevant in my deliberations? Roughly: what is supposedly relevant
is the agreements that I have made; what is supposedly not relevant is any
personal wants or desires or characteristics that I may have. The question is
whether a promise of this-and-that sort may be violated so that I may keep an
agreement of that-and-that sort: whether anyone should violate the promise to
keep the agreement, whether there is an exception to the rule that one should
keep promises, or whether there is another, more stringent, rule that would
justify my keeping the agreement and not the promise.

The analogy with the law is never far beneath the surface. A case in which
I must decide whether or not to keep a promise is regarded as analogous to a
case in which I must decide whether or not I have the right of way at an intersection. I have the right of way if I am approaching from the right. I must keep
the promise if I have made it. There are, however, appropriate exceptions in
both cases. I do not have the right of way, even though approaching from the
right, if I have a 'yield' sign against me. I need not keep the promise, even
though made, if to do so would result in my failing to keep an even-more-
binding promise. For example, I need not keep a promise made in passing on
a trivial matter, if to do so would result in my violating a promise made in
great solemnity on a matter of real importance. In both the moral and the legal
case, what count are the rule and its exceptions (or, understood differently, the
rule and other rules with which it can conflict). What count as relevant are differences in the situation; what do not count as relevant are differences in the
personal descriptions of the persons involved. In a court of law, that I am in a
hurry to get home is irrelevant to the question of whether I have the right of
way. That I am very fond of music is irrelevant to the question of whether I
should keep the promise to attend the concert. What is relevant must have
nothing to do with *me*, but only with the situation: a situation in which anyone
could find himself. What is right for me must be right for anyone.

On the courtroom board, the model cars are moved through the dia-
gramed intersection so as to represent the movement of the cars that collided.
What are relevant are direction, signals given, signs, lighting conditions.
Similarly we rehearse promise breaking. What are relevant are the nature of
the emergency, the conflict of agreements, the likelihood of injury or damage
if the promise is kept. These are relevant matters in that a general rule can be
formulated governing any one of them. For example, it is a general rule that if

a promise is a trivial one and if serious injury is likely to result from its being kept, then it need not be kept.

The analogy with law, with respect to the impersonality of the decision as to whether an action is or is not correct, is, I believe, widely accepted. It informs the quandarist conception of what a problematic situation is. According to this conception, it is irrelevant who the person is who is in the situation. Relevant, at most, are what tacit or explicit agreements he has made and what role—for example, father, employer, judge—he finds himself playing. The conflicts of rules or conflicts of duties are conflicts into which anyone can fall; and the resolution of the conflicts must be right for anyone who falls into them. This consensus seems to me to hide a confusion.

There is, in fact, an important disanalogy between moral and legal correctness decisions. There are considerations that are in a sense personal, that would be irrelevant in legal cases, but that are relevant in moral ones. They have to do with what the agent will allow himself to do and to suffer in accordance with the conception that he has of his own moral character. The quandarist cannot, I think, ignore these considerations; but to give them their due is to shift the focus of ethics away from problematics toward character—away from Hobbes and toward Aristotle.

The moral question, inevitably, is What would it be correct for me to do? It may be, indeed, that I cannot both keep my promise to my friend and my agreement with my neighbor. So, I will have to decide. Say I decide to keep the agreement. How can I justify this decision to my friend? If I can do so at all, I must make use of principles that I set for myself, but not necessarily for other people, and of moral ideals that I have but that I do not necessarily attribute to other people. I must justify myself to him for what I have done. I cannot do this by talking only about what anyone should have done in the same circumstances. Indeed, if what I did would have been wrong for anyone in the same circumstances to do, then it would have been wrong for me. If there had been no conflicting agreement and if I simply broke the promise to avoid the perturbation of my soul that would likely have been caused by rushing to be on time, then I decided incorrectly. But *it does not follow that because my decision would have been right for anyone in the same circumstances, it would have been right for me.* It follows only that almost no one could rightly blame me for what I did, that what I did was permissible. But I can blame myself. Those persons who are close enough to me to understand and to share my special moral ideals can blame me too.

Suppose that I have devoted my life to the cause of desegregation, that all of my spare time and energy and means are devoted to it. Suppose that I have taken a particular interest in the development of school policy in my town. Suppose that it is a part both of my self-conception and of the conception that others have of me that I could not miss an opportunity to press the cause of desegregation, that if I did so I would have to question my own integrity as a person. Suppose that I know that this particular meeting of the school board is a crucial one, one at which the final decision on a plan will be made. Suppose that I am recognized as the chief spokesman for the cause of meaningful desegregation. Suppose that I have built a deserved reputation with others and with myself for persistence and courage in the face of obstacles, for being a man of principle, for sensitivity to the needs of others. Then what would be right for someone else in a situation in which a solemnly given promise conflicts with an agreement to attend a meeting might well not be right for me. If my personal ideals and my conception of myself as a moral person are to be excluded from consideration as merely personal and if nothing is to remain but considerations that have to do with the situation as it would appear to anyone regardless of his former character, then the decision process has been distorted in the interest of a mistaken conception of ethics. The legal analogy has been taken too seriously.

It is easy to be misunderstood here. I am not glorifying the prig, nor do I intend to offer him comfort. I am not suggesting that the person who takes into account his ideals of character should agonize in public over them or that he should be pointedly or even obnoxiously rigid in his adherence to his standards. In fact, his ideals of character may rule out priggishness too. Nevertheless, even though he should not take his ideals inappropriately into account, he should take them into account.

But suppose the quandarist is quite willing to allow all of the sorts of considerations that I have mentioned in the previous paragraph. Suppose he insists that there is nothing inherent in his conception of ethics as being focused upon the resolution of moral difficulties that prevents him from taking these matters into account. Well, fine! That is all that I am arguing for. Then ethics must take seriously the formation of character and the role of personal ideals. And these matters must be discussed at length before decision making is discussed. Moral decision making will no longer appear in the literature as an exercise in a special form of reasoning by agents of undefined character.

But the quandarist might take a different tack, arguing that the distinction between considerations having to do with the situation and considerations having to do with the character of the agent breaks down. "Why should not my formed character be a part of the situation?" he might ask. My response must be a qualified one. In courts of law, such a distinction is maintained, even though it may not always be clear what is and is not relevant to the issue of guilt (that is one reason we must have judges). In the 'court of morals' we maintain it fairly well, although there is a wide twilight zone between the two. But again, this is an objection that works more in my direction than in his. To whatever extent it is impossible to maintain the distinction, to that extent we must pay more attention in ethics to character and its formation.

The general point I have made is that what would be right for anyone in the same circumstances (understanding 'circumstances' to refer to what in law would be the 'collision situation' only, but not to refer to what is 'merely personal') is not necessarily right for me. Because I have to take into account, as well as the situation, the question of what is worthy of me. What may I permit myself to do or suffer in the light of the conception I have of my own so-far-formed and still forming moral character?

It may be useful in expanding this point to return for a time to the concept of rules. It is here that the legal analogy has the strongest grip on the imagination. We say to ourselves: If I want to know what is the correct thing to do, then I must know whether there is a rule that covers this situation—or two rules or a rule and an exception. But even if—which I would deny—we are tied by some kind of logical necessity to the concept of rule abiding in thinking what is and is not correct, we would still have to let in considerations of character by the back door. Let me explain.

To do so, it is necessary to distinguish between different ways in which a rule may come to bear upon an agent. An analogous distinction could be made for prescriptions. In the armed services, as I remember dimly from an ancient war, it is customary to distinguish between orders and commands. A command tells us what to do or to refrain from doing in such explicit terms that there is either no or very little room for variation in the way in which it is obeyed or disobeyed. An order, on the other hand, does not so much specifically tell us what to do as what to accomplish or at what we should aim. "Report at 10.00" is a command; "Provide protective screen for the convoy" is an order. There can, of course, be general and standing orders and commands. A general command would be "All hands report at 10.00 tomorrow morning," and a general standing command would require all hands to report every morning at 10.00. "Exercise extreme caution when in enemy waters" can serve as a general standing order. General commands and orders apply to everyone; standing orders and commands apply to recurrent situations. Rules may be like general standing commands or like general standing orders; analogously, they may be like general standing specific and nonspecific prescriptions. They may allow no leeway in compliance, or they may allow a great deal of leeway.

Some moral rules are more like general standing orders than like general standing commands: for example, "Love thy neighbor" or "Do not cause suffering." They say what is wanted but do not say what to do. If, however, we concentrate upon rules that are like commands, such as "Do not kill" or "Never break promises," we are likely to think of moral rules much like criminal laws, in that they will consist, for us, largely of specific injunctions and directions. But if we recognize that they can also be like orders, we will be more aware of the discretion they sometimes allow. They do not tell us exactly what to do so much as they indicate what we should struggle toward in our own way. But since we are already moral beings with characters formed, the way in which I will abide by an order/rule is not the same as the way in which you will. In fact, I have to decide not only what the rule is that governs the case but also how to go about honoring it. In deciding this, it is inevitable that I will not approach the problem in a vacuum, as any anonymous agent would, but in the light of my conception of what is and is not worthy of me. So, considerations of character, of my own character, do enter in by the back door, even if, as I have assumed for the sake of argument, the notion is that being moral is nothing but following a set of moral rules.

Personal considerations, then, in moral decisions, as opposed to legal decisions, need not be merely personal. It is often not irrelevant to the correctness of my moral decision that I take into account what I am—the conception that I have of myself as a moral being. In fact, the recognition of these considerations of worthiness leads us away from the typical examples of quandary ethics. We may now also consider not so much examples in which the individual is faced with a quandary concerning what he should do as ones in which he is reacting as an admirable moral character would to a situation that might call forth less admirable responses on the part of another. He turns the other cheek, walks the second mile, storms the impossible bastion, exhibits his finely tuned sense of justice by his decision, refrains from pleasurable recreation until the last job of his work is done. He exhibits his character in doing these things: he shows forth the kind of man that he is.

Now it might be said, in weary professional tones, that I have simply insisted upon a distinction that is quite familiar to the contemporary moral philosopher—the distinction, which has been with us at least since Aristotle, between the rightness of the act and the praiseworthiness of the agent. The act, it will be said, may be right, even though the agent is not necessarily praise-worthy for having done it. Or it will be said that I have failed to distinguish between obligation and supererogation: that what a person is obliged to do is one thing, but that if he is a saint or a hero, he may of course exceed the demands of duty and be accorded a halo or a garland, as the case may be.

In response, I want to say that both of these distinctions, while in other ways useful, may lead us to miss the point that I want to make. Consider first the distinction between the rightness of the act and the praiseworthiness of the agent. I want to insist that the question of whether the act is right may only with care be severed from the question of whether the agent is praiseworthy. The agent earns praise by doing what, in his lights, is only right, by doing what he could not conceive of himself as not doing. In considering whether the action is right, he brings in considerations beyond those of the generaliz-ability of a rule. He wants to know not merely whether anyone may do it but also whether he may. Indeed, we would not blame him for failing to go the second mile, but from his standpoint he is convinced that this is what was right for him to do. He, in fact, exhibits himself as the moral character that he is by the demands that he makes upon himself and by his taking it for granted that these demands must be met.

Now take the distinction between obligation and supererogation. Again, it does not follow that because a person has more guide rails than the rules that in his opinion should apply to everyone, he is either a saint or a hero, that he is morally extraordinary. In fact, a person's character is likely to exhibit itself in his making obligatory for himself what he would not hold others obligated to do. A person does not attain moral stature by what he demands of others but by what he demands of himself; that he demands more of himself than others is not something in itself admirable, but is what is to be expected if he is to have a distinct moral character. The question of whether an act would be right for anyone in the same circumstances can show only that it would be permissible for everyone or that it would be mandatory for everyone. What is permissible or mandatory for everyone is so for the moral man, but even leav-ing aside the question of leeway discussed above, he may not consider it right for him to do what would be permissible for anyone, or he may regard it as mandatory for him to go the second mile, rather than merely the first, which is mandatory for everyone. The question of what is right for anyone in the same circumstances therefore provides the agent with but the beginnings of an answer to the question of what he should do.

The special requirements that I place upon myself in virtue of the conception that I have of what is and is not worthy of me must not be confused, either, with the special requirements incumbent upon me in virtue of "my station and its duties." There, requirements deal with duties that I have as a father, a judge, a village lamplighter, a sergeant at arms, or what have you. Again, these are in the realm of the minimal requirements that should be met by anyone: anyone, this time, who falls into the same role as I do.

Quandary ethics, then, conceives of a quandary that arises because I fall into a certain situation. The situation is such that it can be described in perfectly general terms, without any reference to me as an individual, including my personal conceptions of what are and are not worthy deeds and attitudes and feelings—that is, worthy of me. I may, according to this conception, fall into the situation in virtue of my falling under a rule that would apply to any person or in virtue of my falling under a rule that would apply to any person playing a particular role. The general situation is what gives rise to the quandary; and it is only by reference to the features of the situation that I may deliberate concerning what I should do or that I may justify my action. Just as I may refer only to the position of my car at the intersection and not to my personal standards or ideals, so I may refer only to the promising and to the nature of the emergency that caused its violation, with no reference to my standards or ideals. But I contend that reference to my standards and ideals is an essential, not an accidental, feature of my moral deliberation. An act is or is not right from my standpoint, which is where I stand when I deliberate, not merely as it meets or fails to meet the requirements of an ideal universal legislation, but also as it meets or fails to meet the standards that I have set for myself. I am not judged morally by the extent to which I abide by the rules (those which are like general standing commands) which set the minimal limits that anyone should observe in his conduct, even though it may be a necessary condition of my having any degree of moral worth that I should abide by such rules.

The person who is concerned in nonstupid and nonpathological ways over what he should and should not do is, to that extent, a conscientious person. Quandary ethics is addressed to the conscientious person. He is its ultimate customer. But two things should be said here: that the truly conscientious man is concerned not just with what anyone should do but also with what he should do (this I have discussed) and that conscientiousness is but one feature of moral character. Loyalty, generosity, courage, and a great many other qualities may figure as well. We cannot identify morality with conscientiousness. This, I charge, is what quandary ethics does. By starting from problems and their resolution and by confining the description of problematic situations to those features of which a general description can be given, the whole of the question of morality of character is restricted to judgments concerning the conscientiousness of the agent. Since it may be somehow possible to reduce being moral to being conscientious, we should examine the plausibility of such a reductivist claim. But it is worth mentioning that the quandarists do not so much as recognize as such the question of what gives conscientiousness the sole claim to moral worth. It is worth repeating that in speaking of conscientiousness, we are not speaking of those degenerate forms, seldom recognized by the quandarist, in which there is a mere moral dithering (the Buridan's Ass Complex) or in which there is a seeking out of occasions for moral puzzlement when there is no real ground for such puzzlement (pathological conscientiousness).

Why is it, then, that conscientiousness gets the nod from contemporary moral philosophers over such qualities as loyalty, integrity, and kindness? Why would not honesty have equal claim to consideration? Or sensitivity to suffering? The answer may be obvious to others, but it is not so to me. I suspect that the best answer would take the form of an historical-sociological disquisition upon the increasing complexity of the social order, the increase in the possibilities of breakdown and disorder, the resultant need for more and more complex rules, and finally, the consequent demand for the kind of individual who will not only be rule abiding but also 'rule responsible', in that he does not flap, panic, or throw up his hands when—as is inevitable—the rules conflict in a given situation in which he may find himself. He should be rule responsible also in that where there is no rule to govern a given choice, he will create a rule that is consistent with the other rules that he accepts, and in that he has at heart the attainment of a community governed by an ideal set of rules, and that he evinces this interest in the legislation for himself of rules that would be consistent with the rules governing such a community. Such a person would have an intense regard for rules—for the enactment, interpretation, and application of them. This regard would extend not only to 'public' rules—rules that govern everyone's action in recurrent situations—but to 'private' rules as well—rules that result from particular relationships with other persons into which he voluntarily enters. These rules, which might be distinguished from others by being called 'obligations', rest on tacit or explicit commitment to do or refrain and require constant interpretation, since the implications of our commitments in future contingencies are often far from clear at the time when we make them (e.g., "Love, honor, and obey," ". . . help you get started").

Surely the disquisition need not extend farther. It could easily be expanded into a convincing case for the importance of rule responsibility in our culture. But it would show at best that one desirable, even socially necessary, quality is rule responsibility, or conscientiousness. It does not have the consequence that we must confine our assessments of moral character to judgments of the extent to which the individual is rule responsible.

Suppose that a person wants to know what he should do about the moral education of his children. What will he learn from the quandarists? He will learn, as might be expected, that he should teach them how to make decisions: that is, according to one popular version, he will impart to his children as stable a set of principles as is possible in the changing circumstances in which he lives; but he will also give them the idea that they must learn to make their own decisions of principle when the occasion arises, even though he cannot teach them how to do so. We later learn that the principles in question must be universalizable prescriptions, applicable to any persons similarly situated. But is moral education best understood as teaching children how to make moral decisions? One might also reply that the problem of moral education is not so much teaching children how to make moral decisions as giving them the background out of which arise the demands that decisions be made. The focus of moral education might well be, not so much decisions, as the inculcation of excellences of character. The adult of good moral character must indeed be able to handle difficult situations as they arise and to reason about problems unforeseeable by his parents; but to reason well, he must already be an adult of good moral character: loyal, just, honest, sensitive to suffering, and the rest. Everything is not up for grabs! Unless he has these qualities, moral dilemmas will not arise for him. Unless he has a well-formed character, his prescriptions for himself and others are not likely to be morally acceptable. It is, as Aristotle notes, the prescriptions of qualified moral agents to which we should bend our ears.

One aim of moral education that the quandarists are apt to overlook is the development of the sense of the moral self as the product of continuous cultivation. It is as a formed and still-forming self that one either confronts or properly avoids moral problems. There are no moral problems for the child whose character is yet to be formed. For the quandarist, problems may arise for anyone at whatever stage of development he may be, when there is a conflict of rules or principles. What is socially essential is that there should be a workable and working set of rules and that there should be principles that can serve as arbitrators between them. The argument that there is a need for such rules and principles is inevitably a Hobbesian one. But precisely the source of the discomfort with Hobbes was that he approached ethics from this administrative point of view. He abandoned the cultivated moral self and insisted on reducing ethics to a code of minimal standards of behavior, standards that cannot be ignored without social disaster.

Very close to the surface in quandary ethics is the presupposition that there is an essence of morality—that being moral can be reduced to being rule responsible. But no more reason exists to believe that there is an essence of morality than that there is an essence of beauty. The suspect notion that there is an essence of morality is confused with the defensible idea that some moral rules are socially essential. However men may conceive their moral characters, whatever moral education they may have had, whatever moral models they may hold dear, whatever may be their religious beliefs, whatever virtues they may consider paramount, it is socially essential that they should be rule responsible. But to grant that rule responsibility is socially essential is not to grant that it is the essence of morality, in that all other moral character traits can be reduced to or derived from some form of this one. We may, even if we hold to the administrative point of view, expand our list of socially necessary character traits beyond rule responsibility. Chaos also threatens in the absence of tolerance, temperance, and justice, for example. These, too, are socially essential virtues.

To say that they are socially essential is to speak elliptically. What is essential is that everyone should exhibit some virtues to a certain degree and that some persons should exhibit others to a certain degree. It is not essential that everyone be as honest as Lincoln, nor is it essential that anyone but judges or others who have something to distribute should be just in any degree, since the opportunity for justice or injustice does not otherwise arise. It is clearly socially essential that everyone should be rule responsible to a degree commensurate with the complexity of the society; and it is socially desirable that everyone should be rule responsible to as high a degree as possible and that moral models or prophets should show the way. But it does not follow from any of this that morality can be reduced to rule responsibility. The attempt to reduce moral character to any given trait by philosophical fiat is open to suspicion. Individuals may, and perhaps should, give focus to their moral lives by centering them around some particular virtues—for example, honesty or sensitivity to suffering. But to contend that morality is nothing but honesty or sensitivity to suffering is to attempt to legislate for everyone what cannot be legislated. We may encourage children and ourselves in the development of certain virtues, but the form that each person's character assumes will inevitably be the result of his own selective cultivation and his own conception of what is and is not worthy of himself. It is, once we move beyond the minimal needs of society, his problem, peculiar to him, his training, and his ideals. To insist otherwise is to espouse the cause of the moral leveler.

The remark that certain virtues are socially essential is also elliptical in that it fails to distinguish between virtues that are essential, to a certain degree, in all or some men and to the very existence of any social order and those that are essential to the continued existence of a particular social order. The distinction is, as Hobbes recognized, a crucial one. 'Gentility,' as that term was understood in the pre-Civil War South, was necessary to the existence of the social order created by white landholders. When the nongentile Snopses appeared, that social order collapsed. It may be that people are either so attached to a particular social order or so averse to another that they are willing to entertain the possibility of the absence of any social order, rather than see the one collapse or the other prevail. This is social nihilism, but it does not entail moral nihilism. The individual may prize non-socially-essential virtues over socially essential ones. In the interest of the continued existence of society, we cannot allow such moralities to prevail.

Earlier I distinguished between questions of correctness and questions of usefulness. I have confined my discussion to the former sort of question, but it could be extended with little difficulty to the latter. Suppose that the conception of decision making is that it has to do with the best way to use the circumstances, to take advantage of the situation, to maximize the happiness of everyone concerned. Again, the question will be, not What should I—in the light of my moral character and ideals—do? but What might anyone who finds himself in this situation most usefully do? It is a question about means to ends: a question not about how I might be most useful in the circumstances but about how anyone might increase happiness. Conceived this way and supposing the goal of happiness to be one that we all understand in the same way, then the question of what I should do is not a moral question at all; it is one that could best be answered by a social engineer familiar with the circumstances. Even if the question of what would be the most useful does not trail behind it a general theory to the effect that there is only one kind of thing that is ultimately useful, and if the possibility that there are a great many useful kinds of things that one may do is left open, as it should be, there is still a tendency to regard the question of what 'one' may do which is most useful in a given 'situation', as if it could be answered without regard to the moral character of the agent. Again: granting that the promotion of a given state of affairs would be useful and that a given line of action would promote that state of affairs, it might seem to follow that I should undertake that line of action. It does not. All that follows is that it would be generally desirable if I, or anyone, should. But in the light of the commitments, interests, and tendencies that I have already developed, it might seem a great deal more desirable that I should follow some alternative course of action. It might be generally desirable that I—and others—should join in a general demonstration against a war; but it might be more desirable that I should follow my already developed moral commitment to the abolition of capital punishment. I cannot decide what would be most useful without taking into account my conception of myself as a committed moral agent who has already for some time been active in the world. . . .

17

The Schizophrenia of Modern Ethical Theories

Michael Stocker is professor of philosophy at Syracuse University. He has written several articles on ethics and is the author of *Plural and Conflicting Values* (1990).

Modern ethical theories, with perhaps a few honorable exceptions, deal only with reasons, with values, with what justifies. They fail to examine motives and the motivational structures and constraints of ethical life. They not only fail to do this, they fail as ethical theories by not doing this—as I shall argue in this paper. I shall also attempt two correlative tasks: to exhibit some constraints that motivation imposes on ethical theory and life; and to advance our understanding of the relations between reason and motive.

One mark of a good life is a harmony between one's motives and one's reasons, values, justifications. Not to be moved by what one values—what one believes good, nice, right, beautiful, and so on—bespeaks a malady of the spirit. Not to value what moves one also bespeaks a malady of the spirit. Such a malady, or such maladies, can properly be called *moral schizophrenia*—for they are a split between one's motives and one's reasons. (Here and elsewhere, 'reasons' will stand also for 'values' and 'justifications'.)

An extreme form of such schizophrenia is characterized, on the one hand, by being moved to do what one believes bad, harmful, ugly, abasing; on the other, by being disgusted, horrified, dismayed by what one wants to do. Perhaps such cases are rare. But a more modest schizophrenia between reason and motive is not, as can be seen in many examples of weakness of the will, indecisiveness, guilt, shame, self-deception, rationalization, and annoyance with oneself.

At the very least we should be moved by our major values and we should value what our major motives seek. Should, that is, if we are to lead a good life.

From Michael Stocker, "The Schizophrenia of Modern Ethical Theories," *Journal of Philosophy,* LXXIII, 14 (August 12, 1976):453-466. Copyright 1976. Reprinted by permission of the author and the publisher.

To repeat, such harmony is a mark of a good life. Indeed, one might wonder whether human life—good or bad—is possible without some such integration.

This is not, however, to say that in all cases it is better to have such harmony. It is better for us if self-seeking authoritarians feel fettered by their moral upbringing; better, that is, than if they adopt the reason of their motives. It would have been far better for the world and his victims had Eichmann not wanted to do what he thought he should do.[1]

Nor is this to say that in all areas of endeavor such harmony is necessary or even especially conducive to achieving what is valued. In many cases, it is not. For example, one's motives in fixing a flat tire are largely irrelevant to getting under way again. (In many such cases, one need not even value the intended outcome.)

Nor is this even to say that in all "morally significant" areas such harmony is necessary or especially conducive to achieving what is valued. Many morally significant jobs, such as feeding the sick, can be done equally well pretty much irrespective of motive. And, as Ross, at times joined by Mill, argues, for a large part of ethics, there simply is no philosophical question of harmony or disharmony between value and motive: you can do what is right, obligatory, your duty no matter what your motive for so acting. If it is your duty to keep a promise, you fulfill that duty no matter whether you keep the promise out of respect for duty, fear of losing your reputation, or whatever. What motivates is irrelevant so far as rightness, obligatoriness, duty are concerned.

Notwithstanding the very questionable correctness of this view so far as rightness, obligatoriness, duty are concerned,[2] there remain at least two problems. The first is that even here there is still a question of harmony. What sort of life would people have who did their duties but never or rarely wanted to? Second, duty, obligation, and rightness are only one part—indeed, only a small part, a dry and minimal part—of ethics. There is the whole other area of the values of personal and interpersonal relations and activities; and also the area of moral goodness, merit, virtue. In both, motive is an essential part of what is valuable; in both, motive and reason must be in harmony for the values to be realized.

For this reason and for the reason that such harmony is a mark of a good life, any theory that ignores such harmony does so at great peril. Any theory that makes difficult, or precludes, such harmony stands, if not convicted, then in need of much and powerful defense. What I shall now argue is that modern ethical theories—those theories prominent in the English-speaking philosophical world—make such harmony impossible.

---

[1] It might be asked what is better for such people, to have or lack this harmony, given their evil motives or values; in which way they would be morally better. Such questions may not be answerable.

[2] See my "Act and Agent Evaluations," *Review of Metaphysics*, XXVII, 1, 105 (September 1973): 42–61.

Criticism of Modern Ethics

Reflection on the complexity and vastness of our moral life, on what has value, shows that recent ethical theories have by far overconcentrated on duty, rightness, and obligation.[3] This failure—of overconcentrating—could not have been tolerated but for the failure of not dealing with motives or with the relations of motives to values. (So too, the first failure supports and explains the second.) In this second failure, we find a far more serious defect of modern ethical theories than such overconcentration: they necessitate a schizophrenia between reason and motive in vitally important and pervasive areas of value, or alternatively they allow us the harmony of a morally impoverished life, a life deeply deficient in what is valuable. It is not possible for moral people, that is, people who would achieve what is valuable, to act on these ethical theories, to let them comprise their motives. People who do let them comprise their motives will, for that reason, have a life seriously lacking in what is valuable.

These theories are, thus, doubly defective. As ethical theories, they fail by making it impossible for a person to achieve the good in an integrated way. As theories of the mind, of reasons and motives, of human life and activity, they fail, not only by putting us in a position that is psychologically uncomfortable, difficult, or even untenable, but also by making us and our lives essentially fragmented and incoherent.

The sort of disharmony I have in mind can be brought out by considering a problem for egoists, typified by hedonistic egoists. Love, friendship, affection, fellow feeling, and community are important sources of personal pleasure. But can such egoists get these pleasures? I think not—not so long as they adhere to the motive of pleasure-for-self.

The reason for this is not that egoists cannot get together and decide, as it were, to enter into a love relationship. Surely they can (leaving aside the irrelevant problems about deciding to do such a thing). And they can do the various things calculated to bring about such pleasure: have absorbing talks, make love, eat delicious meals, see interesting films, and so on, and so on.

Nonetheless, there is something necessarily lacking in such a life: love. For it is essential to the very concept of love that one care for the beloved, that one be prepared to act for the sake of the beloved. More strongly, one must care for the beloved and act for that person's sake as a final goal; the beloved, or the beloved's welfare or interest, must be a final goal of one's concern and action.

To the extent that my consideration for you—or even my trying to make you happy—comes from my desire to lead an untroubled life, a life that is personally pleasing for me, I do not act for your sake. In short, to the extent that I

---

[3]See *ibid.* and my "Rightness and Goodness: Is There a Difference?," *American Philosophical Quarterly*, x, 2 (April 1973): 87–98.

act in various ways toward you with the final goal of getting pleasure—or, more generally, good—for myself, I do not act for your sake.

When we think about it this way, we may get some idea of why egoism is often claimed to be essentially lonely. For it is essentially concerned with external relations with others, where, except for their effects on us, one person is no different from, nor more important, valuable, or special than any other person or even any other thing. The individuals as such are not important, only their effects on us are; they are essentially replaceable, anything else with the same effects would do as well. And this, I suggest, is intolerable personally. To think of yourself this way, or to believe that a person you love thinks of you this way, is intolerable. And for conceptual, as well as psychological, reasons it is incompatible with love.

It might be suggested that it is rather unimportant to have love of this sort. But this would be a serious error. The love here is not merely modern-romantic or sexual. It is also the love among members of a family, the love we have for our closest friends, and so on. Just what sort of life would people have who never "cared" for anyone else, except as a means to their own interests? And what sort of life would people have who took it that no one loved them for their own sake, but only for the way they served the other's interest?

Just as the notion of doing something for the sake of another, or of caring for the person for that person's sake, is essential for love, so too is it essential for friendship and all affectionate relations. Without this, at best we could have good relations, friendly relations. And similarly, such caring and respect is essential for fellow feeling and community.

Before proceeding, let us contrast this criticism of egoism with a more standard one. My criticism runs as follows: Hedonistic egoists take their own pleasure to be the sole justification of acts, activities, ways of life; they should recognize that love, friendship, affection, fellow feeling, and community are among the greatest (sources of) personal pleasures. Thus, they have good reason, on their own grounds, to enter such relations. But they cannot act in the ways required to get those pleasures, those great goods, if they act on their motive of pleasure-for-self. They cannot act for the sake of the intended beloved, friend, and so on; thus, they cannot love, be or have a friend, and so on. To achieve these great personal goods, they have to abandon that egoistical motive. They cannot embody their reason in their motive. Their reasons and motives make their moral lives schizophrenic.

The standard criticism of egoists is that they simply cannot achieve such nonegoistical goods, that their course of action will, as a matter of principle, keep them from involving themselves with others in the relevant ways, and so on. This criticism is not clearly correct. For there may be nothing inconsistent in egoists' adopting a policy that will allow them to forget, as it were, that they are egoists, a policy that will allow and even encourage them to develop such final goals and motives as caring for another for that person's own sake. Indeed, as has often been argued, the wise egoist would do just this.

Several questions should be asked of this response: would the transformed person still be an egoist? Is it important, for the defense of egoism, that the person remain an egoist? Or is it important only that the person live in a way that would be approved of by an egoist? It is, of course, essential to the transformation of the person from egoistical motivation to caring for others that the person-as-egoist lose conscious control of him/ herself. This raises the question of whether such people would be able to check up and see how their transformed selves are getting on in achieving egoistically approved goals. Will they have a mental alarm clock which wakes them up from their nonegoistical transforms every once in a while, to allow them to reshape these transforms if they are not getting enough personal pleasure—or, more generally, enough good? I suppose that this would not be impossible. But it hardly seems an ideal, or even a very satisfactory, life. It is bad enough to have a private personality, which you must hide from others; but imagine having a personality that you must hide from (the other parts of) yourself. Still, perhaps this is possible. If it is, then it seems that egoists may be able to meet this second criticism. But this does not touch my criticism: that they will not be able to embody their reason in their motives; that they will have to lead a bifurcated, schizophrenic life to achieve what is good.

This might be thought a defect of only such ethical theories as egoism. But consider those utilitarianisms which hold that an act is right, obligatory, or whatever if and only if it is optimific in regard to pleasure and pain (or weighted expectations of them). Such a view has it that the only good reason for acting is pleasure vs. pain, and thus should highly value love, friendship, affection, fellow feeling, and community. Suppose, now, you embody this utilitarian reason as your motive in your actions and thoughts toward someone. Whatever your relation to that person, it is necessarily not love (nor is it friendship, affection, fellow feeling, or community). The person you supposedly love engages your thought and action not for him/herself, but rather as a source of pleasure. . . .

Just as egoism and the above sorts of utilitarianisms necessitate a schizophrenia between reason and motive—and just as they cannot allow for love, friendship, affection, fellow feeling, and community—so do current rule utilitarianisms. And so do current deontologies.

What is lacking in these theories is simply—or not so simply—the person. For, love, friendship, affection, fellow feeling, and community all require that the other person be an essential part of what is valued. The person—not merely the person's general values nor even the person-qua-producer-or-possessor-of-general-values—must be valued. The defect of these theories in regard to love, to take one case, is not that they do not value love (which, often, they do not) but that they do not value the beloved. Indeed, a person who values and aims at simply love, that is, love-in-general or even love-in-general-exemplified-by-this-person "misses" the intended beloved as surely as does an adherent of the theories I have criticized.

The problem with these theories is not, however, with *other*-people-as-valuable. It is simply—or not so simply—with *people*-as-valuable. Just as they would do *vis-à-vis* other people, modern ethical theories would prevent each of us from loving, caring for, and valuing ourself—as opposed to loving, caring for, and valuing our general values or ourself-qua-producer-or-possessor-of-general-values. In these externality-ridden theories, there is as much a disappearance or nonappearance of the self as of other people. Their externality-ridden universes of what is intrinsically valuable are not solipsistic; rather, they are devoid of all people.[4]

It is a truism that it is difficult to deal with people as such. It is difficult really to care for them for their own sake. It is psychically wearing and exhausting. It puts us in too open, too vulnerable a position. But what must also be looked at is what it does to us—taken individually and in groups as small as a couple and as large as society—to view and treat others externally, as essentially replaceable, as mere instruments or repositories of general and nonspecific value; and what it does to us to be treated, or believe we are treated, in these ways.

At the very least, these ways are dehumanizing. To say much more than this would require a full-scale philosophical anthropology showing how such personal relations as love and friendship are possible, how they relate to larger ways and structures of human life, and how they—and perhaps only they—allow for the development of those relations which are constitutive of a human life worth living: how, in short, they work together to produce the fullness of a good life, a life of eudaimonia.

Having said this, it must be acknowledged that there are many unclarities and difficulties in the notion of valuing a person, in the notion of a person-as-valuable. When we think about this—e.g., what and why we value—we seem driven either to omitting the person and ending up with a person-qua-producer-or-possessor-of-general-values or with a person's general values, or to omitting them and ending up with a bare particular ego.

In all of this, perhaps we could learn from the egoists. Their instincts, at least, must be to admit themselves, each for self, into their values. At the risk of absurdity—indeed, at the risk of complete loss of appeal of their view—what they find attractive and good about good-for-self must be, not only the good, but also and preeminently the for-self.

At this point, it might help to restate some of the things I have tried to do and some I have not. Throughout I have been concerned with what sort of motives people can have if they are to be able to realize the great goods of love, friendship, fellow feeling, and community. And I have argued that, if we take as motives, embody in our motives, those various things which recent

---

[4] G.E. Moore's taking friendship to be an intrinsic good is an exception to this. But his so taking friendship also introduces serious strains, verging on inconsistencies, into his theory.

ethical theories hold to be ultimately good or right, we will, of necessity, be unable to have those motives. Love, friendship, affection, fellow feeling, and community, like many other states and activities, essentially contain certain motives and essentially preclude certain others; among those precluded we find motives comprising the justifications, the goals, the goods of those ethical theories most prominent today. To embody in one's motives the values of current ethical theories is to treat people externally and to preclude love, friendship, affection, fellow feeling, and community—both with others and with oneself. To get these great goods while holding those current ethical theories requires a schizophrenia between reason and motive.

I have not argued that if you have a successful love relationship, friendship, . . . then you will be unable to achieve the justifications, goals, goods posited by those theories. You can achieve them, but not by trying to live the theory directly. Or, more exactly, to the extent that you live the theory directly, to that extent you will fail to achieve its goods. . . .

It might be expected that, in those areas explicitly concerned with motives and their evaluation, ethical theories would not lead us into this disharmony or the corresponding morally defective life. And to some extent this expectation is met. But even in regard to moral merit and demerit, moral praise and blameworthiness, the moral virtues and vices, the situation is not wholly dissimilar. Again, the problem of externality and impersonality, and the connected disharmony, arises.

The standard view has it that a morally good intention is an essential constituent of a morally good act. This seems correct enough. On that view, further, a morally good intention is an intention to do an act for the sake of its goodness or rightness. But now, suppose you are in a hospital, recovering from a long illness. You are very bored and restless and at loose ends when Smith comes in once again. You are now convinced more than ever that he is a fine fellow and a real friend—taking so much time to cheer you up, traveling all the way across town, and so on. You are so effusive with your praise and thanks that he protests that he always tries to do what he thinks is his duty, what he thinks will be best. You at first think he is engaging in a polite form of self-deprecation, relieving the moral burden. But the more you two speak, the more clear it becomes that he was telling the literal truth: that it is not essentially because of you that he came to see you, not because you are friends, but because he thought it his duty, perhaps as a fellow Christian or Communist or whatever, or simply because he knows of no one more in need of cheering up and no one easier to cheer up.

Surely there is something lacking here—and lacking in moral merit or value. The lack can be sheeted home to two related points: again, the wrong sort of thing is said to be the proper motive; and, in this case at least, the wrong sort of thing is, again, essentially external.[5]

---

[5] For a way to evade this problem, see my "Morally Good Intentions," *The Monist*, LIV, 1 (January 1970): 124–141, where it is argued that goodness and rightness need not be the object of a morally good intention, but rather that various goods or right acts can be.

Some Questions and Concluding Remarks

I have assumed that the reasons, values, justifications of ethical theories should be such as to allow us to embody them in our motives and still act morally and achieve the good. But why assume this? Perhaps we should take ethical theories as encouraging indirection—getting what we want by seeking something else: e.g., some say the economic well-being of all is realized, not by everyone's seeking it but by everyone's seeking his/her own well-being. Or perhaps we should take ethical theories as giving only indices, not determinants, of what is right and good.

Theories of indirection have their own special problems. There is always a great risk that we will get the something else, not what we really want. There are, also, these two related problems. A theory advocating indirection needs to be augmented by another theory of motivation, telling us which motives are suitable for which acts. Such a theory would also have to explain the connections, the indirect connections, between motive and real goal.

Second, it may not be very troubling to talk about indirection in such large-scale and multi-person matters as the economics of society. But in regard to something of such personal concern, so close to and so internal to a person as ethics, talk of indirection is both implausible and baffling. Implausible in that we do not seem to act by indirection, at least not in such areas as love, friendship, affection, fellow feeling, and community. In these cases, our motive has to do directly with the loved one, the friend, . . . as does our reason. In doing something for a loved child or parent, there is no need to appeal to, or even think of, the reasons found in contemporary ethical theories. Talk of indirection is baffling, in an action- and understanding-defeating sense, since, once we begin to believe that there is something beyond such activities as love which is necessary to justify them, it is only by something akin to self-deception that we are able to continue them.

One partial defense of these ethical theories would be that they are not intended to supply what can serve as both reasons and motives; that they are intended only to supply indices of goodness and rightness, not determinants. Formally, there may be no problems in taking ethical theories this way. But several questions do arise. Why should we be concerned with such theories, theories that cannot be acted on? Why not simply have a theory that allows for harmony between reason and motive? A theory that gives determinants? And indeed, will we not need to have such a theory? True, our pre-analytic views might be sufficient to judge among index theories; we may not need a determinant theory to pick out a correct index theory. But will we not need a determinant theory to know why the index is correct, why it works, to know what is good about what is so indexed?[6]

---

[6] Taking contemporary theories to be index theories would help settle one of the longest-standing disputes in ethical philosophy—a dispute which finds Aristotle and Marx on the winning side and many if not most contemporary ethicists on the other. The dispute concerns the relative explanatory roles of pleasure and good activity and good life. Put crudely, many utilitarians and others

Another partial defense of recent theories would be that, first, they are concerned almost entirely with rightness, obligation, and duty, and not with the whole of ethics; and, second, that within this restricted area, they do not suffer from disharmony or schizophrenia. To some extent this defense, especially its second point, has been dealt with earlier. But more should be said. It is perhaps clear enough by now that recent ethicists have ignored large and extremely important areas of morality—e.g., that of personal relations and that of merit. To this extent, the first point of the defense is correct. What is far from clear, however, is whether these theories were advanced only as partial theories, or whether it was believed by their proponents that duty and so on were really the whole, or at least the only important part, of ethics.

We might be advised to forget past motivation and belief, and simply look at these theories and see what use can be made of them. Perhaps they were mistaken about the scope and importance of duty and so on. Nonetheless they could be correct about the concepts involved. In reply, several points should be made. First, they were mistaken about these concepts, as even a brief study of supererogation and self-regarding notions would indicate. Second, these theories are dangerously misleading; for they can all too readily be taken as suggesting that all of ethics can be treated in an external, legislation-model, index way. (On 'legislation-model' see below.) Third, the acceptance of such theories as partial theories would pose severe difficulties of integration within ethical theory. Since these theories are so different from those concerning, e.g., personal relations, how are they all to be integrated? Of course, this third point may not be a criticism of these theories of duty, but only a recognition of the great diversity and complexity of our moral life.[7]

In conclusion, it might be asked how contemporary ethical theories come to require either a stunted moral life or disharmony, schizophrenia. One cluster of (somewhat speculative) answers surrounds the preeminence of duty, rightness, and obligation in these theories. This preeminence fits naturally

---

have held that an activity is good only because and insofar as it is productive of pleasure; Aristotle and Marx hold of at least many pleasures that if they are good this is because they are produced by good activity. The problem of immoral pleasures has seemed to many the most important test case for this dispute. To the extent that my paper is correct, we have another way to settle the dispute. For, if I am correct, pleasure cannot be what makes all good activity good, even prescinding from immoral pleasures. It must be activity, such as love and friendship, which makes some pleasures good.

[7] Part of this complexity can be seen as follows: Duty seems relevant in our relations with our loved ones and friends, only when our love, friendship, and affection lapse. If a family is "going well," its members "naturally" help each other; that is, their love, affection, and deep friendship are sufficient for them to care for and help one another (to put it a bit coolly). Such "feelings" are at times worn thin. At these times, duty may have to be looked to or called upon (by the agent or by others) to get done at least a modicum of those things which love would normally provide. To some rough extent, the frequency with which a family member acts out of duty, instead of love, toward another in the family is a measure of the lack of love the first has for the other. But this is not to deny that there are duties of love, friendship, and the like.

with theories developed in a time of diminishing personal relations; of a time when the ties holding people together and easing the frictions of their various enterprises were less and less affection; of a time when commercial relations superseded family (or family-like) relations; of a time of growing individualism. It also fits naturally with a major concern of those philosophers: legislation. When concerned with legislation, they were concerned with duty, rightness, obligation. (Of course, the question then is, Why were they interested in legislation, especially of this sort? To some small extent this has been answered, but no more will be said on this score.) When viewing morality from such a legislator's point of view, taking such legislation to be the model, motivation too easily becomes irrelevant. The legislator wants various things done or not done; it is not important why they are done or not done; one can count on and know the actions, but not the motives. (This is also tied up with a general devaluing of our emotions and emotional possibilities—taking emotions to be mere feelings or urges, without rational or cognitive content or constraint; and taking us to be pleasure-seekers and pain-avoiders—forgetting or denying that love, friendship, affection, fellow feeling, and desire for virtue are extremely strong movers of people.) Connected with this is the legislative or simply the third-person's-eye view, which assures us that others are getting on well if they are happy, if they are doing what gives them pleasure, and the like. The effect guarantees the cause—in the epistemic sense. (One might wonder whether the general empiricist confusion of *ratio cognescendi* and *ratio essendi* is at work here.)

These various factors, then, may help explain this rather remarkable inversion (to use Marx's notion): of taking the "effect," pleasure and the like, for the "cause," good activity.

Moore's formalistic utilitarianism and the traditional views of morally good action also suffer from something like an inversion. Here, however, it is not causal, but philosophical. It is as if these philosophers have taken it at that, because these various good things can all be classified as good, their goodness consists in this, rather than conversely. The most general classification seems to have been reified and itself taken as the morally relevant goal.

These inversions may help answer a question which afflicts this paper: Why have I said that contemporary ethics suffers from schizophrenia, bifurcation, disharmony? Why have I not claimed simply that these theories are mistaken in their denomination of what is good and bad, right- and wrong-making? For it is clear enough that, if we aim for the wrong goal, then (in all likelihood) we will not achieve what we really want, what is good, and the like. My reason for claiming more than a mere mistake is that the mistake is well reasoned; it is closely related to the truth, it bears many of the features of the truth. To take only two examples (barring bad fortune and bad circumstances), good activity does bring about pleasure; love clearly benefits the lover. There is, thus, great plausibility in taking as good what these theories advance as good. But when we try to act on the theories, try to embody their reasons in our motives—as opposed to simply seeing whether our or others' lives would be approved of by the theories—then in a quite mad way, things start going wrong. The personalities of loved ones get passed over for their effects, moral action becomes self-stultifying and self-defeating. And perhaps the greatest madnesses of all are—and they stand in a vicious interrelation— first, the world is increasingly made such as to make these theories correct; and, second, we take these theories to be correct and thus come to see love, friendship, and the like only as possible, and not very certain, sources of plea- sure or whatever. We mistake the effect for the cause and when the cause- seen-as-effect fails to result from the effect-seen-as-cause, we devalue the former, relegating it, at best, to good as a means and embrace the latter, won- dering why our chosen goods are so hollow, bitter, and inhumane.

18

On Some Vices of Virtue Ethics

Robert B. Louden teaches philosophy at the University of Southern Maine. He has published a number of articles in ethical theory and the history of ethics and is the author of *Morality and Moral Theory: A Reappraisal and Reaffirmation* (1992).

It is common knowledge by now that recent philosophical and theological writing about ethics reveals a marked revival of interest in the virtues. But what exactly are the distinctive features of a so-called virtue ethics? Does it have a special contribution to make to our understanding of moral experience? Is there a price to be paid for its different perspective, and if so, is the price worth paying?

Contemporary textbook typologies of ethics still tend to divide the terrain of normative ethical theory into the teleological and deontological. Both types of theory, despite their well-defined differences, have a common focus on acts as opposed to qualities of agents. The fundamental question that both types of theory are designed to answer is: What ought I to do? What is the correct analysis and resolution of morally problematic situations? A second feature shared by teleological and deontological theories is conceptual reductionism. Both types of theory start with a primary irreducible element and then proceed to introduce secondary derivative concepts which are defined in terms of their relations to the beginning element. Modern teleologists (the majority of whom are utilitarians) begin with a concept of the good—here defined with reference to states of affairs rather than persons. After this criterion of the good is established, the remaining ethical categories are defined in terms of this starting point. Thus, according to the classic maxim, one ought always to promote the greatest good for the greatest number. Duty, in other words, is defined in terms of the element of ends—one ought always to maximize utility. The concepts of virtue and rights are also treated as derivative categories of secondary importance, definable in terms of utility. For the classic utilitarian, a right is upheld "so long as it is upon the whole advantageous to the society that it should be maintained," while virtue is construed as a "tendency to give a net increase to the aggregate quantity of happiness in all its shapes taken together."[1]

For the deontologist, on the other hand, the concept of duty is the irreducible starting point, and any attempt to define this root notion of being morally bound to do something in terms of the good to be achieved is rejected from the start. The deontologist is committed to the notion that certain acts are simply inherently right. Here the notion of the good is only a derivative category, definable in terms of the right. The good that we are to promote is right action for its own sake—duty for duty's sake. Similarly, the virtues tend to be defined in terms of pro-attitudes towards one's duties. Virtue is important, but only because it helps us do our duty.

But what about virtue ethics? What are the hallmarks of this approach to normative ethics? One problem confronting anyone who sets out to analyze the new virtue ethics in any detail is that we presently lack fully developed examples of it in the contemporary literature. Most of the work done in this genre has a negative rather than positive thrust—its primary aim is more to criticize the traditions and research programs to which it is opposed rather than to state positively and precisely what its own alternative is. A second hindrance is that the literature often has a somewhat misty antiquarian air. It is frequently said, for instance, that the Greeks advocated a virtue ethics, though what precisely it is that they were advocating is not always spelled out. In describing contemporary virtue ethics, it is therefore necessary, in my opinion, to do some detective work concerning its conceptual shape, making inferences based on the unfortunately small number of remarks that are available.

For purposes of illustration, I propose to briefly examine and expand on some key remarks made by two contemporary philosophers—Elizabeth Anscombe and Philippa Foot—whose names have often been associated with the revival of virtue movement. Anscombe, in her frequently cited article, "Modern Moral Philosophy," writes: "you can do ethics without it [viz., the notion of 'obligation' or 'morally ought'], as is shown by the example of Aristotle. It would be a great improvement if, instead of 'morally wrong,' one always named a genus such as 'untruthful,' 'unchaste,' 'unjust.'"[2] Here we find an early rallying cry for an ethics of virtue program, to be based on contemporary efforts in philosophical psychology and action theory. On the Anscombe model, strong, irreducible duty and obligation notions drop out of the picture, and are to be replaced by vices such as unchasteness and untruthfulness. But are we to take the assertion literally, and actually attempt to do moral theory without any concept of duty whatsoever? On my reading, Anscombe is not really proposing that we entirely dispose of moral oughts. Suppose one follows her advice, and replaces "morally wrong" with "untruthful," "unchaste," etc. Isn't this merely shorthand for saying that agents *ought* to be truthful and chaste, and that untruthful and unchaste acts are *morally wrong* because good agents don't perform such acts? The concept of the moral ought, in other words, seems now to be explicated in terms of what the good person would do.[3]

A similar strategy is at work in some of Foot's articles. In the Introduction to her recent collection of essays, *Virtues and Vices and Other Essays in Moral Philosophy*, she announces that one of the two major themes running throughout her work is "the thought that a sound moral philosophy should start from a theory of virtues and vices."[4] When this thought is considered in conjunction with the central argument in her article, "Morality as a System of Hypothetical Imperatives," the indication is that another virtue-based moral theory is in the making. For in this essay Foot envisions a moral community composed of an "army of volunteers," composed, that is, of agents who voluntarily commit themselves to such moral ideals as truth, justice, generosity, and kindness.[5] In a moral community of this sort, all moral imperatives become hypothetical rather than categorical: there are things an agent morally ought to do if he or she wants truth, justice, generosity, or kindness, but no things an agent morally ought to do if he or she isn't first committed to these (or other) moral ideals. On the Foot model (as presented in "Morality as a System"), what distinguishes an ethics of virtue from its competitors is that it construes the ideal moral agent as acting from a direct desire, without first believing that he or she morally ought to perform that action or have that desire. However, in a more recent paper, Foot has expressed doubts about her earlier attempts to articulate the relationship between oughts and desires. In "William Frankena's Carus Lectures" (1981), she states that *"thoughts* [my emphasis] about what is despicable or contemptible, or low, or again admirable, glorious or honourable may give us the key to the problem of rational moral action."[6] But regardless of whether she begins with desires or with thoughts, it seems clear her strategy too is not to dispense with oughts entirely, but rather to employ softer, derivative oughts.

In other words, conceptual reductionism is at work in virtue ethics too. Just as its utilitarian and deontological competitors begin with primitive concepts of the good state of affairs and the intrinsically right action respectively and then derive secondary concepts out of their starting points, so virtue ethics, beginning with a root conception of the morally good person, proceeds to introduce a different set of secondary concepts which are defined in terms of their relationship to the primitive element. Though the ordering of primitive and derivatives differs in each case, the overall strategy remains the same. Viewed from this perspective, virtue ethics is not unique at all. It has adopted the traditional mononomic strategy of normative ethics. What sets it apart from other approaches, again, is its strong agent orientation.

So for virtue ethics, the primary object of moral evaluation is not the act or its consequences, but rather the agent. And the respective conceptual starting points of agent and act-centered ethics result in other basic differences as well, which may be briefly summarized as follows. First of all, the two camps are likely to employ different models of practical reasoning. Act theorists, because they focus on discrete acts and moral quandaries, are naturally very interested in formulating decision procedures for making practical choices. The agent, in their conceptual scheme, needs a guide—hopefully a determinate decision procedure—for finding a way out of the quandary. Agent-centered ethics, on the other hand, focuses on long-term characteristic patterns of action, intentionally downplaying atomic acts and particular choice situations in the process. They are not as concerned with portraying practical reason as a rule-governed enterprise which can be applied on a case-by-case basis.

Secondly, their views on moral motivation differ. For the deontological act theorist, the preferred motive for moral action is the concept of duty itself; for the utilitarian act theorist, it is the disposition to seek the happiness of all sentient creatures. But for the virtue theorist, the preferred motivation factor is the virtues themselves (here understood non-reductionistically). The agent who correctly acts from the disposition of charity does so (according to the virtue theorist) not because it maximizes utility or because it is one's duty to do so, but rather out of a commitment to the value of charity for its own sake.

While I am sympathetic to recent efforts to recover virtue from its long-standing neglect, my purpose in this essay is not to contribute further to the campaign for virtue. Instead, I wish to take a more critical look at the phenomenon, and to ask whether there are certain important features of morality which a virtue-based ethics either handles poorly or ignores entirely. In the remainder of this essay, I shall sketch some objections which (I believe) point to genuine shortcomings of the virtue approach to ethics. My object here is not to offer an exhaustive or even thoroughly systematic critique of virtue ethics, but rather to look at certain mundane regions of the moral field and to ask first what an ethics of virtue might say about them, and second whether what it says about them seems satisfactory.

Agents vs. Acts

As noted earlier, it is a commonplace that virtue theorists focus on good and bad agents rather than on right and wrong acts. In focusing on good and bad agents, virtue theorists are thus forced to de-emphasize discrete acts in favor of long-term, characteristic patterns of behavior. Several related problems arise for virtue ethics as a result of this particular conceptual commitment.

a. *Casuistry and Applied Ethics.* It has often been said that for virtue ethics the central question is not "What ought I to *do*?" but rather "What sort of person ought I to *be*?"[7] However, people have always expected ethical theory to tell them something about what they ought to do, and it seems to me that virtue ethics is structurally unable to say much of anything about this issue. If I'm right, one consequence of this is that a virtue-based ethics will be particularly weak in the areas of casuistry and applied ethics. A recent reviewer of Foot's *Virtues and Vices*, for instance, notes that "one must do some shifting to gather her view on the virtues." "Surprisingly," he adds, "the studies of abortion and euthanasia are not of much use."[8] And this is odd, when one considers Foot's demonstrated interest in applied ethics in conjunction with her earlier cited prefatory remark that a "sound moral theory should start from a theory of virtues and vices." But what can a virtues and vices approach say about specific moral dilemmas? As virtue theorists from Aristotle onward have rightly emphasized, virtues are not simply dispositions to behave in specified ways, for which rules and principles can always be cited. In addition, they involve skills of perception and articulation, situation-specific "know-how," all of which are developed only through recognizing and acting on what is relevant in concrete moral contexts as they arise. These skills of moral perception and practical reason are not completely routinizable, and so cannot be transferred from agent to agent as any sort of decision procedure "package deal." Due to the very nature of the moral virtues, there is thus a very limited amount of advice on moral quandaries that one can reasonably expect from the virtue-oriented approach. We ought, of course, to do what the virtuous person would do, but it is not always easy to fathom what the hypothetical moral exemplar would do were he in our shoes, and sometimes even he will act out of character. Furthermore, if one asks him why he did what he did, or how he knew what to do, the answer—if one is offered—might not be very enlightening. One would not necessarily expect him to appeal to any rules or principles which might be of use to others.

We can say, à la Aristotle, that the virtuous agent acts for the sake of the noble (*tou kalou heneka*), that he will not do what is base or depraved, etc. But it seems to me that we cannot intelligently say things like: "The virtuous person (who acts for the sake of the noble) is also one who recognizes that all mentally deficient eight-month-old fetuses should (or should not) be aborted, that the doctor/patient principle of confidentiality must always (or not always) be respected, etc." The latter simply sound too strange, and their strangeness stems from the fact that motives of virtue and honor cannot be fully routinized.

Virtue theory is not a problem-oriented or quandary approach to ethics: it speaks of rules and principles of action only in a derivative manner. And its derivative oughts are frequently too vague and unhelpful for persons who have not yet acquired the requisite moral insight and sensitivity. Consequently, we cannot expect it to be of great use in applied ethics and casuistry. The increasing importance of these two subfields of ethics in contemporary society is thus a strike against the move to revive virtue ethics.

b. *Tragic Humans.* Another reason for making sure that our ethical theory allows us to talk about features of acts and their results in abstraction from the agent and his conception of what he is doing is that sometimes even the best person can make the wrong choices. There are cases in which a man's choice is grounded in the best possible information, his motives honorable and his action not at all out of character. And yet his best laid plans may go sour. Aristotle, in his *Poetics*, suggests that here lies the source of tragedy: we are confronted with an eminent and respected man, "whose misfortune, however, is brought upon him not by vice (*kakia*) and depravity (*moktheira*) but by some error of judgment (*amartia*)" (1453a8–9). But every human being is morally fallible, for there is a little Oedipus in each of us. So Aristotle's point is that *regardless of character*, anyone can fall into the sort of mistake of which tragedies are made. Virtue ethics, however, since its conceptual scheme is rooted in the notion of the good person, is unable to assess correctly the occasional (inevitable) tragic outcomes of human action.

Lawrence Becker, in his article, "The Neglect of Virtue," seems at first to draw an opposite conclusion from similar reflections about virtue theory and tragedy, for it is his view that virtue ethics makes an indispensable contribution to our understanding of tragedy. According to him, "there are times when the issue is not how much harm has been done, or the value to excusing the wrongdoer, or the voluntary nature of the offending behavior, but rather whether the sort of character indicated by the behavior is 'acceptable' or not—perhaps even ideal—so that the 'wrongful' conduct must be seen simply as an unavoidable defect of it."[9] As Becker sees it, Oedipus merely comes off as a fool who asked too many questions when viewed from the perspective of act theories. Only a virtue ethics, with its agent perspective, allows us to differentiate tragic heroes from fools, and to view the acts that flow from each character type in their proper light. And the proper light in the case of tragic heroes is that there are unavoidable defects in this character type, even though it represents a human ideal. Becker's point is well taken, but its truth does not cancel out my criticism. My point is that virtue ethics is in danger of blinding itself to the wrongful conduct in Oedipal acts, simply because it views the Oedipuses of the world as honorable persons *and* because its focus is on long-term character manifestations rather than discrete acts. To recognize the wrong in Oedipal behavior, a theory with the conceptual tools enabling one to focus on discrete acts is needed. (Notice, incidentally, that Becker's own description does just this.)

c. *Intolerable Actions.* A third reason for insisting that our moral theory enable us to assess acts in abstraction from agents is that we need to be able to identify certain types of action which produce harms of such magnitude that they destroy the bonds of community and render (at least temporarily) the achievement of moral goods impossible. In every traditional moral community one encounters prohibitions or "barriers to action" which mark off clear boundaries in such areas as the taking of innocent life, sexual relations, and the administration of justice according to local laws and customs.[10] Such rules are needed to teach citizens what kinds of actions are to be regarded not simply as bad (a table of vices can handle this) but as intolerable.[11] Theorists must resort to specific lists of offenses to emphasize the fact that there are some acts which are absolutely prohibited. We cannot articulate this sense of absolute prohibition by referring merely to characteristic patterns of behavior.

In rebuttal here, the virtue theorist may reply by saying: "Virtue ethics does not need to articulate these prohibitions—let the law do it, with its list of do's and don't's." But the sense of requirement and prohibition referred to above seems to me to be at bottom inescapably moral rather than legal. Morality can (and frequently does) invoke the aid of law in such cases, but when we ask *why* there is a law against, e.g., rape or murder, the proper answer is that it is morally intolerable. To point merely to a legal convention when asked why an act is prohibited or intolerable raises more questions than it answers.

d. *Character Change.* A fourth reason for insisting that a moral theory be able to assess acts in abstraction from agents and their conception of what they're doing is that peoples' moral characters may sometimes change. Xenophon, toward the beginning of his *Memorabilia* (I.II.21), cites an unknown poet who says, "Ah, but a good man is at one time noble (*esthios*), at another wicked (*kakos*)." Xenophon himself agrees with the poet: ". . . many alleged (*phaskonton*) philosophers may say: A just (*dikaios*) man can never become unjust; a self-controlled (*sophron*) man can never become wanton (*hubristes*); in fact no one having learned any kind of knowledge (*mathesis*) can become ignorant of it. I do not hold this view. . . . For I see that, just as poetry is forgotten unless it is often repeated, so instruction, when no longer needed, fades from the mind."[12]

Xenophon was a practical man who was not often given to speculation, but he arrived at his position on character change in the course of his defense of Socrates. One of the reasons Socrates got into trouble, Xenophon believed, was due to his contact with Critias and Alcibiades during their youth. For of all Athenians, "none wrought so many evils to the *polis*." However, Xenophon reached the conclusion that Socrates should not be blamed for the disappearance of his good influence once these two had ceased their close contact with him.

If skills can become rusty, it seems to me that virtues can too. Unless we stay in practice we run the risk of losing relative proficiency. We probably can't forget them completely (in part because the opportunities for exercising virtues are so pervasive in everyday life), but we can lose a certain sensitivity. People do become morally insensitive, relatively speaking—missing opportunities they once would have noticed, although perhaps when confronted with a failure they might recognize that they had failed, showing at least that they hadn't literally "forgotten the difference between right and wrong." If the moral virtues are acquired habits rather than innate gifts, it is always possible that one can lose relative proficiency in these habits. Also, just as one's interests and skills sometimes change over the course of a life as new perceptions and influences take hold, it seems too that aspects of our moral characters can likewise alter. (Consider religious conversion experiences.) Once we grant the possibility of such changes in moral character, the need for a more "character free" way of assessing action becomes evident. Character is not a permanent fixture, but rather plastic. A more reliable yardstick is sometimes needed.[13]

e. *Moral Backsliding.* Finally, the focus on good and bad agents rather than on right and wrong actions may lead to a peculiar sort of moral backsliding. Because the emphasis in agent ethics is on long-term, characteristic patterns of behavior, its advocates run the risk of overlooking occasional lies or acts of selfishness on the ground that such performances are mere temporary aberrations—acts out of character. Even the just man may on occasion act unjustly, so why haggle over specifics? It is unbecoming to a virtue theorist to engage in such pharisaic calculations. But once he commits himself to the view that assessments of moral worth are not simply a matter of whether we have done the right thing, backsliding may result: "No matter how many successes some people have, they still feel they 'are' fundamentally honest."[14] At some point, such backsliding is bound to lead to self-deception.

I have argued that there is a common source behind each of these vices. The virtue theorist is committed to the claim that the primary object of moral evaluation is not the act or its consequences but rather the agent—specifically, those character traits of the agent which are judged morally relevant. This is not to say that virtue ethics does not ever address the issue of right and wrong actions, but rather that it can only do so in a derivative manner. Sometimes, however, it is clearly acts rather than agents which ought to be the primary focus of moral evaluation.

Who Is Virtuous?

There is also an epistemological issue which becomes troublesome when one focuses on qualities of persons rather than on qualities of acts. Baldly put, the difficulty is that we do not seem to be able to know with any degree of certainty who really is virtuous and who vicious. For how is one to go about establishing an agent's true moral character? The standard strategy is what might be called the "externalist" one: we try to infer character by observing conduct. While not denying the existence of some connection between character and conduct, I believe that the connection between the two is not nearly as tight as externalists have assumed. The relationship is not a necessary one, but merely contingent. Virtue theorists themselves are committed to this claim, though they have not always realized it. For one central issue behind the "Being vs. Doing" debate is the virtue theorist's contention that the moral value of Being is not reducible to or dependent on Doing: that the measure of an agent's character is not exhausted by or even dependent on the values of the actions which he may perform. On this view, the most important moral traits are what may be called "spiritual" rather than "actional."[15]

Perhaps the most famous example of a spiritual virtue would be Plato's definition of justice (*dikaiosunē*). Plato, it will be remembered, argued that attempts to characterize *dikaiosunē* in terms of an agent's conduct are misguided and place the emphasis in the wrong place. *Dikaiosunē* for Plato is rather a matter of the correct harmonious relationship between the three parts of the soul: "It does not lie in a man's external actions, but in the way he acts within himself (*tēn entos*), really concerned with himself and his inner parts (*peri eauton kai ta eautou*)" (*Rep.* 443d). Other spiritual virtues would include such attitudes as self-respect and integrity. These are traits which do have a significant impact on what we do, but whose moral value is not wholly derivable from the actions to which they may give rise.

If there are such spiritual virtues, and if they rank among the most important of moral virtues, then the externalist strategy is in trouble. For those who accept spiritual virtues, the Inner is not reducible to or dependent on the Outer. We cannot always know the moral value of a person's character by assessing his or her actions.

But suppose we reject the externalist approach and take instead the allegedly direct internalist route. Suppose, that is, that we could literally "see inside" agents and somehow observe their character traits first-hand. (The easiest way to envision this is to assume that some sort of identity thesis with respect to moral psychology and neurophysiology is in principle correct. Lest the reader object that this is only a modern materialist's silly pipe dream, I might add that at least one commentator has argued that Aristotle's considered view was that the presence of the virtues and vices depends on modifications of the brain and nervous system; and that the relevant mental processes in ethics have accompanying bodily states.)[16] Here the goal will be to match specific virtues with specific chemicals, much in the manner that identity theorists have sought to match other types of mental events with other specific neurophysiological events. However, even on this materialistic reading of the internalist strategy, nothing could be settled about virtues by analyzing chemicals without first deciding who has what virtue. For we would first need to know who possessed and exhibited which virtue, and then look for specific physical traces in him that were missing in other agents. But as indicated earlier in my discussion of the externalist strategy, this is precisely what we don't know. An analogy might be the attempt to determine which objects have which colors. Regardless of how much we know about the physical make-up of the objects in question, we must first make color judgments. However, at this point the analogy breaks down, for the epistemological problems involved in making color judgments are not nearly as troublesome as are those involved in making virtue judgments.[17]

To raise doubts about our ability to know who is virtuous is to bring skepticism into the center of virtue ethics, for it is to call into question our ability to identify the very object of our inquiry. This is not the same skepticism which has concerned recent writers such as Bernard Williams and Thomas Nagel, when they reflect on the fact that "the natural objects of moral assessment are disturbingly subject to luck."[18] Theirs is more a skepticism *about* morality, while mine is a skepticism *within* morality. The sort of skepticism to which I am drawing attention occurs after one has convinced oneself that there are genuine moral agents who really do things rather than have things happen to them. As such, my skepticism is narrower but also more morality-specific: it concerns not so much queries about causality and free will as doubts about our ability to know the motives of our own behavior. As Kant wrote, "the real morality of actions, their merit or guilt, even that of our own conduct, . . . remains entirely hidden from us."[19] Aquinas too subscribed to a similar skepticism: "Man is not competent to judge of interior movements, that are hidden, but only of exterior acts which are observable; and yet for the perfection of virtue it is necessary for man to conduct himself rightly in both kinds of acts."[20]

Now it may be objected here that I am making too much of this epistemological error, that no one actually "lives it" or contests the fact that it is an error. But I think not. To advocate an ethics of virtue is, among other things, to presuppose that we can clearly differentiate the virtuous from the vicious. Otherwise, the project lacks applicability.

Consider for a moment the Aristotelian notion of the *spoudaios* (good man) or *phronimos* (man of practical wisdom)—two essentially synonymous terms which together have often been called the touchstone of Aristotle's ethics. Again and again in the *Nicomachean Ethics* the *spoudaios/phronimos* is pointed to as the solution to a number of unanswered problems in Aristotle's ethical theory. For instance, we are told to turn to the *spoudaios* in order to learn what really is pleasurable (1113a26–28). And we must turn to an actual *phronimos* in order to find out what the abstract and mysterious *orthos logos* really is (right reason or rational principle—a notion which plays a key role in the definition of virtue) (1107a2, 1144b24). Even in discussing the intellectual virtue of *phronēsis* or practical wisdom, Aristotle begins by announcing that "we shall get at the truth by considering who are the persons we credit with it" (1140a24). But who are the *phronimoi*, and how do we know one when we see one? Aristotle does say that Pericles "and men like him" are *phronimoi*, "because they can see what is good for themselves and what is good for men in general" (1140b8–10). However, beyond this rather casual remark he does not give the reader any hints on how to track down a *phronimos*. Indeed, he does not even see it as a problem worth discussing.

The reasons for this strange lacuna, I suggest, are two. First, Aristotle is dealing with a small face to face community, where the pool of potential *phronimoi* generally come from certain well established families who are well known throughout the *polis*. Within a small face to face community of this sort, one would naturally expect to find wide agreement about judgments of character. Second, Aristotle's own methodology is itself designed to fit this sort of moral community. He is not advocating a Platonic ethics of universal categories.

Within the context of a *polis* and an ethical theory intended to accompany it, the strategy of pointing to a *phronimos* makes a certain sense. However, to divorce this strategy from its social and economic roots and to then apply it to a very different sort of community—one where people really do not know each other all that well, and where there is wide disagreement on values—does not. And this, I fear, is what contemporary virtue ethicists have tried to do.[21]

Style Over Substance

In emphasizing Being over Doing, the Inner over the Outer, virtue theorists also lay themselves open to the charge that they are more concerned with style than with substance. For as I argued earlier, virtue theorists are committed to the view that the moral value of certain key character traits is not exhausted by or even dependent on the value of the actions to which they may give rise. When this gulf between character and conduct is asserted, and joined with the claim that it is agents rather than actions which count morally, the conclusion is that it is not the substance of an agent's actions which is the focus of moral appraisal. The implication here seems to be that if you have style, i.e., the style of the virtuous person, as defined in the context of a concrete moral tradition, it doesn't so much matter what the results are. ("It's not whether you win or lose, but how you play the game that counts.") As Frankena remarks, in a passage which underscores an alleged basic difference between ancient and contemporary virtue ethics:

> The Greeks held . . . that being virtuous entails not just having good motives or intentions but also doing the right thing. Modern views typically differ from Greek views here; perhaps because of the changed ways of thinking introduced by the Judeo-Christian tradition, we tend to believe that being morally good does not entail doing what is actually right . . . even if we believe (as I do) that doing what is actually right involves more than only having a good motive or intention. Today many people go so far as to think that in morality it does not matter much *what* you do; all that matters, they say, is *how* you do it. To parody a late cigarette advertisement: for them it's not how wrong you make it, it's how you make it wrong."[22]

But it is sophistry to claim that the consequences of the lies of gentlemen or Aristotelian *kaloikagathoi* aren't very important, or that the implications of their rudeness are somehow tempered by the fact that they are who they are. This line of thought flies in the face of our basic conviction that moral assessment must strive toward impartiality and the bracketing of morally irrelevant social and economic data.

It seems to me that this particular vice of virtue ethics is analogous to the Hegelian "duty for duty's sake" critique of formalist deontologies. Virtue-based and duty-based theories are both subject to the "style over substance" charge because their notion of ends is too weak. Both types of theory speak of ends only in a derivative sense. For the duty-based theorist, the good is an inherent feature of dutiful action, so that the only proclaimed end is right action itself. For the virtue-based theorist, the good is defined in terms of the virtuous agent. ("Virtue is its own reward.") Aristotle, as noted earlier, in distinguishing the true from the apparent good, remarks that "that which is in truth an object of wish is an object of wish to the good man (*spoudaios*), while any chance thing may be so to the bad man" (*EN* 1113a26–28).

While no one (except the most obstinate utilitarian) would deny these two respective ends their place in a list of moral goods, it appears that there is another important type of end which is left completely unaccounted for. This second type of end is what may be called a *product-end*, a result or outcome of action which is distinct from the activity that produces it. (An example would be a catastrophe or its opposite.) Virtue-based and duty-based theories, on the other hand, can account only for *activity-ends*, ends which are inherent features of (virtuous or dutiful) action. Virtue-based theories then, like their duty-based competitors, reveal a structural defect in their lack of attention to product-ends.[23]

Now it might be said that the "style over substance" charge is more appropriately directed at those who emphasize Doing over Being, since one can do the right things just to conform or for praise. One can cultivate the externalities, but be inwardly wretched or shallow. I grant that this is a problem for act theorists, but it is a slightly different criticism than mine, using different senses of the words "style" and "substance." "Style," as used in my criticism, means roughly: "morally irrelevant mannerisms and behavior, while "substance," as I used it, means something like: "morally relevant results of action." The "substance" in this new criticism refers to good moral character and the acts which flow from it, while "style" here means more "doing the right thing, but without the proper fixed trait behind it." However, granted that both "style over substance" criticisms have some validity, I would also argue that mine points to a greater vice. It is one thing to do what is right without the best disposition, it is another not to do what is right at all.

Utopianism

The last vice I shall mention has a more socio-historical character. It seems to me that there is a bit of utopianism behind the virtue theorist's complaints about the ethics of rules. Surely, one reason there is more emphasis on rules and regulations in modern society is that things have gotten more complex. Our moral community (insofar as it makes sense to speak of "community" in these narcissistic times) contains more ethnic, religious, and class groups than did the moral community which Aristotle theorized about. Unfortunately, each segment of society has not only its own interests but its own set of virtues as well. There is no general agreed upon and significant expression of desirable moral character in such a world. Indeed, our pluralist culture prides itself on and defines itself in terms of its alleged value neutrality and its lack of allegiance to any one moral tradition. This absence of agreement regarding human purposes and moral ideals seems to drive us (partly out of lack of alternatives) to a more legalistic form of morality. To suppose that academic theorists can alter the situation simply by reemphasizing certain concepts is illusory. Our world lacks the sort of moral cohesiveness and value unity which traditional virtue theorists saw as prerequisites of a viable moral community.[24]

The table of vices sketched above is not intended to be exhaustive, but even in its incomplete state I believe it spells trouble for virtue-based moral theories. For the shortcomings described are not esoteric—they concern mundane features of moral experience which any minimally adequate moral theory should be expected to account for. While I do think that contemporary virtue theorists are correct in asserting that any adequate moral theory must account for the fact of character, and that no ethics of rules, pure and unsupplemented, is up to this job, the above analysis also suggests that no ethics of virtue, pure and unsupplemented, can be satisfactory.

My own view (which can only be stated summarily here) is that we need to begin efforts to coordinate irreducible or strong notions of virtue along with irreducible or strong conceptions of the various act notions into our conceptual scheme of morality. This appeal for coordination will not satisfy those theorists who continue to think in the single-element or mononomic tradition (a tradition which contemporary virtue-based theorists have inherited from their duty-based and goal-based ancestors), but I do believe that it will result in a more realistic account of our moral experience. The moral field is not unitary, and the values we employ in making moral judgments sometimes have fundamentally different sources. No single reductive method can offer a realistic means of prioritizing these different values. There exists no single scale by means of which disparate moral considerations can always be measured, added, and balanced.[25] The theoretician's quest for conceptual economy and elegance has been won at too great a price, for the resulting reductionist definitions of the moral concepts are not true to the facts of moral experience. It is important now to see the ethics of virtue and the ethics of rules as adding up, rather than as cancelling each other out.[26]

Notes

1. The rights definition is from Bentham's "Anarchical Fallacies," reprinted in A. I. Melden, (ed.), *Human Rights* (Belmont: Wadsworth, 1970), p. 32. The virtue definition is from Bentham's "The Nature of Virtue," reprinted in Bhiku Parekh, (ed.), *Bentham's Political Thought* (New York: Barnes and Noble, 1973), p. 89.
2. G. E. M. Anscombe, "Modern Moral Philosophy," *Philosophy*, Vol. 33 (1958), pp. 1–19; reprinted in J. J. Thomson and G. Dworkin, (eds.), *Ethics* (New York: Harper & Row, 1968), p. 196.
3. Anscombe appears to believe also that moral oughts and obligations only make sense in a divine law context, which would mean that only divine command theories of ethics employ valid concepts of obligation. I see no reason to accept such a narrow definition of duty. See pp. 192, 202 of "Modern Moral Philosophy." For one argument against her restrictive divine law approach to moral obligation, see Alan Donagan, *The Theory of Morality* (Chicago: University of Chicago Press, 1977), p. 3.
4. Philippa Foot, *Virtues and Vices and Other Essays in Moral Philosophy* (Berkeley and Los Angeles: University of California Press, 1978), p. xi.
5. Foot, "Morality as a System of Hypothetical Imperatives," *The Philosophical Review*, Vol. 81 (1972), pp. 305–16; reprinted in *Virtues and Vices*, pp. 157–73. See especially the long concluding footnote, added in 1977.
6. Foot, "William Frankena's Carus Lectures," *The Monist*, Vol. 64 (1981), p. 311.
7. For background on this "Being vs. Doing" debate, see Bernard Mayo, *Ethics and the Moral Life* (London: Macmillan & Co., Ltd., 1958), pp. 211–14, and William K. Frankena, *Ethics* second ed. (Englewood Cliffs, N.J.: Prentice-Hall, 1973), pp. 65–66.
8. Arthur Flemming, "Reviving the Virtues," Review of Foot's *Virtues and Vices* and James Wallace's *Virtues and Vices. Ethics*, Vol. 90 (1980), p. 588.
9. Lawrence Becker, "The Neglect of Virtue," *Ethics*, Vol. 85 (1975), p. 111.
10. Stuart Hampshire (ed.), *Private and Public Morality* (New York: Cambridge University Press, 1978), p. 7.
11. Alasdair MacIntyre, *After Virtue* (Notre Dame: University of Notre Dame Press, 1981), p. 142.
12. It is curious to note that contemporary philosophers as different as Gilbert Ryle and H. G. Gadamer have argued, against Xenophon and myself, that character cannot change. See H. G. Gadamer, "The Problem of Historical Consciousness," p. 140 in P. Rabinow and W. M. Sullivan (eds.) *Interpretive Social Science* (Berkeley and Los Angeles: University of California Press, 1979), and Gilbert Ryle, "On Forgetting the Difference Between Right and Wrong" in A. I. Melden, (ed.) *Essays in Moral Philosophy* (Seattle: University of Washington Press, 1958).
13. One possibility here might be to isolate specific traits and then add that the virtuous agent ought to *retain* such traits throughout any character changes. (E.g.: "The good man will not do what is base, regardless of whether he be Christian, Jew, or atheist.") However, it is my view that very few if any moral traits have such a "transcharacter" status. The very notion of what counts as a virtue or vice itself changes radically when one looks at different traditions. (Compare Aristotle's praise for *megalopsuchia* or pride as the "crown of the virtues" with the New Testament on humility.) Also, one would expect basic notions about what is base or noble to themselves undergo shifts of meaning as they move across traditions.

204 Doing or Being?

14. Becker, "The Neglect of Virtue," p. 112.
15. I have borrowed this terminology from G. W. Trianosky-Stillwell, *Should We Be Good? The Place of Virtue in Our Morality* (Doctoral Dissertation, University of Michigan, 1980).
16. W. F. R. Hardie, *Aristotle's Ethical Theory*, 2nd edition (Oxford: Clarendon Press, 1980), Ch. VI, esp. pp. 111–13.
17. I am indebted to Bill Robinson for help on this criticism of the internalist strategy.
18. Thomas Nagel, "Moral Luck" in *Mortal Questions* (New York: Cambridge University Press, 1979), p. 28. See also Bernard Williams, "Moral Luck," in *Moral Luck: Philosophical Papers 1973–1980* (New York: Cambridge University Press, 1981).
19. Kant, *Critique of Pure Reason*, A552 = B580, n. 1.
20. Thomas Aquinas, Saint. *Summa Theologica*, I–II Q. 91. a. 4.
21. I would like to thank Arthur Adkins for discussion on these points.
22. William K. Frankena, *Thinking About Morality* (Ann Arbor: University of Michigan Press, 1980), pp. 52–53.
23. My own position on this topic is contra that of utilitarianism. I believe that activity-ends are clearly the more important of the two, and that most product-ends ultimately derive their moral value from more fundamental activity-ends. (The importance of saving lives, for instance, borrows its value from the quality of life it makes possible. "Life at any price" is nonsense.) But I also believe, contra deontology and virtue ethics, that any adequate moral theory must find room for both types of ends.
24. For similar criticism, see Mayo, *Ethics and the Moral Life*, p. 217; and MacIntyre, *After Virtue*.
25. See Thomas Nagel, "The Fragmentation of Value," pp. 131–32, 135 in *Mortal Questions* (New York: Cambridge University Press, 1979). A similar position is defended by Charles Taylor in his recent essay, "The Diversity of Goods," in A. Sen and B. Williams, (eds.), *Utilitarianism and Beyond* (New York: Cambridge University Press, 1982).
26. Earlier versions of this essay were read at the 1982 American Philosophical Association Pacific Division Meetings, and at the 1981 Iowa Philosophical Society Meeting at Grinnell College. I am very grateful for useful criticisms and suggestions offered on these occasions. I would also like to thank Marcia Baron, Lawrence Becker, James Gustafson, W. D. Hamlyn, Bob Hollinger, Joe Kupfer, and Warner Wick for criticisms of earlier drafts. Portions of the present version are taken from my doctoral dissertation, *The Elements of Ethics: Towards a Topography of the Moral Field* (University of Chicago, 1981).

19

To Be or to Do, That Is the Question

William Frankena is professor emeritus of philosophy at the University of
Michigan where he has taught since 1937. Among his many publications are
Ethics (1973), *Perspectives on Morality* (1976), and *Thinking About Morality*
(1980).

. . . Throughout its history morality has been concerned about the cultivation
of certain dispositions, or traits, among which are "character" and such "virtues" (an old-fashioned but still useful term) as honesty, kindness, and conscientiousness. Virtues are dispositions or traits that are not wholly innate;
they must all be acquired, at least in part, by teaching and practice, or,
perhaps, by grace. They are also traits of "character," rather than traits of "personality" like charm or shyness, and they all involve a tendency to do certain
kinds of action in certain kinds of situations, not just to think or feel in certain ways. They are not just abilities or skills, like intelligence or carpentry,
which one may have without using.

In fact, it has been suggested that morality is or should be conceived as
primarily concerned, not with rules or principles as we have been supposing
so far, but with the cultivation of such dispositions or traits of character. Plato
and Aristotle seem to conceive of morality in this way, for they talk mainly in
terms of virtues and the virtuous, rather than in terms of what is right or obligatory. Hume uses similar terms, although he mixes in some nonmoral traits
like cheerfulness and wit along with moral ones like benevolence and justice.
More recently, Leslie Stephen stated the view in these words:

> . . . morality is internal. The moral law. . . has to be expressed in the form, "be this,"
> not in the form, "do this.". . . the true moral law says "hate not," instead of "kill
> not.". . . the only mode of stating the moral law must be as a rule of character.[1]

---

[1] *The Science of Ethics* (New York: G. P. Putnam's Sons, 1882), pp. 155, 158.

From William Frankena, *Ethics*, 2d ed., (C) 1973, pp. 62–70. Reprinted by permission of Prentice-
Hall, Englewood Cliffs, New Jersey.

Those who hold this view are advocating an *ethics of virtue* or being, in opposition to an ethics of duty, principle, or doing. . . . The notion of an ethics of virtue is worth looking at here, not only because it has a long history but also because some spokesmen of "the new morality" seem to espouse it. What would an ethics of virtue be like? It would, of course, not take deontic judgments or principles as basic in morality; instead, it would take as basic aretaic judgments like "That was a courageous deed," "His action was virtuous," or "Courage is a virtue," and it would insist that deontic judgments are either derivative from such aretaic ones or can be dispensed with entirely. Moreover, it would regard aretaic judgments about actions as secondary and as based on aretaic judgments about agents and their motives or traits, as Hume does when he writes:

> . . . when we praise any actions, we regard only the motives that produced them. . . . The external performance has no merit. . . . all virtuous actions derive their merit only from virtuous motives.[2]

For an ethics of virtue, then, what is basic in morality is judgments like "Benevolence is a good motive," "Courage is a virtue," "The morally good man is kind to everyone" or, more simply and less accurately, "Be loving!"— not judgments or principles about what our duty is or what we ought to do. But, of course, it thinks that its basic instructions will guide us, not only about what to be, but also about what to do.

It looks as if there would be three kinds of ethics of virtue, corresponding to the three kinds of ethics of duty. The question to be answered is: What dispositions or traits are moral virtues? *Trait-egoism* replies that the virtues are the dispositions that are most conducive to one's own good or welfare, or, alternatively, that prudence or a careful concern for one's own good is the cardinal or basic moral virtue, other virtues being derivative from it. *Trait-utilitarianism* asserts that the virtues are those traits that most promote the general good, or, alternatively, that benevolence is the basic or cardinal moral virtue. These views may be called *trait-teleological*, but, of course, there are also *trait-deontological theories*, which will hold that certain traits are morally good or virtuous simply as such, and not just because of the nonmoral value they may have or promote, or, alternatively, that there are other cardinal or basic virtues besides prudence or benevolence, for example, obedience to God, honesty, or justice. If they add that there is only one such cardinal virtue, they are monistic, otherwise pluralistic.

To avoid confusion, it is necessary to notice here that we must distinguish between *virtues* and *principles of duty* like "We ought to promote the good" and "We ought to treat people equally." A virtue is not a principle of this kind; it is a disposition, habit, quality, or trait of the person or soul, which an individual either has or seeks to have. Hence, I speak of the principle of *beneficence* and

---

[2] *Treatise of Human Nature*, Book III, Part II, opening of Sec. I.

the virtue of *benevolence*, since we have two words with which to mark the difference. In the case of justice, we do not have different words, but still we must not confuse the principle of equal treatment with the disposition to treat people equally.

We may assume at this point that views of the first two kinds are unsatisfactory, and that the most adequate ethics of virtue would be one of the third sort, one that would posit two cardinal virtues, namely, benevolence and justice, considered now as dispositions or traits of character rather than as principles of duty. By a set of cardinal virtues is meant a set of virtues such that (1) they cannot be derived from one another and (2) all other moral virtues can be derived from or shown to be forms of them. Plato and other Greeks thought there were four cardinal virtues in this sense: wisdom, courage, temperance, and justice. Christianity is traditionally regarded as having seven cardinal virtues: three "theological" virtues—faith, hope, and love; and four "human" virtues—prudence, fortitude, temperance, and justice. This was essentially St. Thomas Aquinas's view; since St. Augustine regarded the last four as forms of love, only the first three were really cardinal for him. However, many moralists, among them Schopenhauer, have taken benevolence and justice to be the cardinal moral virtues, as I would. It seems to me that all of the usual virtues (such as love, courage, temperance, honesty, gratitude, and considerateness), at least insofar as they are *moral* virtues, can be derived from these two. Insofar as a disposition cannot be derived from benevolence and justice, I should try to argue either that it is not a *moral* virtue (e.g., I take faith, hope, and wisdom to be religious or intellectual, not moral, virtues) or that it is not a virtue at all.

We may now return to the issue posed by the quotation from Stephen, though we cannot debate it as fully as we should.[3] To be or to do, that is the question. Should we construe morality as primarily a following of certain principles or as primarily a cultivation of certain dispositions and traits? Must we choose? It is hard to see how a morality of principles can get off the ground except through the development of dispositions to act in accordance with its principles, else all motivation to act on them must be of an *ad hoc* kind, either prudential or impulsively altruistic. Moreover, morality can hardly be content with a mere conformity to rules, however willing and self-conscious it may be, unless it has no interest in the spirit of its law but only in the letter. On the other hand, one cannot conceive of traits of character except as including dispositions and tendencies to act in certain ways in certain circumstances. Hating involves being disposed to kill or harm, being just involves tending to do just acts (acts that conform to the principle of justice) when the occasion calls. Again, it is hard to see how we could know what traits to encourage or inculcate if we did not subscribe to principles, for example, to the principle of utility, or to those of benevolence and justice.

---

[3] For a fuller discussion see my "Prichard and the Ethics of Virtue," *Monist* (1971), 54, 1–17.

I propose therefore that we regard the morality of duty and principles and the morality of virtues or traits of character not as rival kinds of morality between which we must choose, but as two complementary aspects of the same morality. Then, for every principle there will be a morally good trait, often going by the same name, consisting of a disposition or tendency to act according to it; and for every morally good trait there will be a principle defining the kind of action in which it is to express itself. To parody a famous dictum of Kant's, I am inclined to think that principles without traits are impotent and traits without principles are blind.

Even if we adopt this double-aspect conception of morality, in which principles are basic, we may still agree that morality does and must put a premium on *being* honest, conscientious, and so forth. If its sanctions or sources of motivation are not to be entirely external (for example, the prospect of being praised, blamed, rewarded, or punished by others) or adventitious (for example, a purely instinctive love of others), if it is to have adequate "internal sanctions," as Mill called them, then morality must foster the development of such dispositions and habits as have been mentioned. It could hardly be satisfied with a mere conformity to its principles even if it could provide us with fixed principles of actual duty. For such a conformity might be motivated entirely by extrinsic or nonmoral considerations, and would then be at the mercy of these other considerations. It could not be counted on in a moment of trial. Besides, since morality cannot provide us with fixed principles of actual duty but only with principles of prima facie duty, it cannot be content with the letter of its law, but must foster in us the dispositions that will sustain us in the hour of decision when we are choosing between conflicting principles of prima facie duty or trying to revise our working rules of right and wrong.

There is another reason why we must cultivate certain traits of character in ourselves and others, or why we must be certain sorts of persons. Although morality is concerned that we act in certain ways, it cannot take the hard line of insisting that we act precisely in those ways, even if those ways could be more clearly defined. We cannot praise and blame or apply other sanctions to an agent simply on the ground that he has or has not acted in conformity with certain principles. It would not be right. Through no fault of his own, the agent may not have known all the relevant facts. What action the principles of morality called for in the situation may not have been clear to him, again through no fault of his own, and he may have been honestly mistaken about his duty. Or his doing what he ought to have done might have carried with it an intolerable sacrifice on his part. He may even have been simply incapable of doing it. Morality must therefore recognize various sorts of excuses and extenuating circumstances. All it can really insist on, then, except in certain critical cases, is that we develop and manifest fixed dispositions to find out what the right thing is and to do it if possible. In this sense a person must "be this" rather than "do this." But it must be remembered that "being" involves at least *trying* to "do." Being without doing, like faith without works, is dead.

At least it will be clear from this discussion that an ethics of duty or principles also has an important place for the virtues and must put a premium on their cultivation as a part of moral education and development. The place it has for virtue and/or the virtues is, however, different from that accorded them by an ethics of virtue. Talking in terms of . . . an ethics of duty, we may say that, if we ask for *guidance* about what to do or not do, then the answer is contained, at least primarily, in two deontic principles and their corollaries, namely, the principles of beneficence and equal treatment. Given these two deontic principles, plus the necessary clarity of thought and factual knowledge, we can know what we morally ought to do or not do, except perhaps in cases of conflict between them. We also know that we should cultivate two virtues, a disposition to be beneficial (i.e., benevolence) and a disposition to treat people equally (justice as a trait). But the point of acquiring these virtues is not further guidance or instruction; the function of the virtues in an ethics of duty is not to tell us what to do but to ensure that we will do it willingly in whatever situations we may face. In an ethics of virtue, on the other hand, the virtues play a dual role—they must not only move us to do what we do, they must also tell us what to do. To parody Alfred Lord Tennyson:

Theirs not (only) to do or die,
Theirs (also) to reason why.

This is the place to mention ideals again, which are among what we called the ingredients of morality. One may, perhaps, identify moral ideals with moral principles, but, more properly speaking, moral ideals are ways of being rather than of doing. Having a moral ideal is wanting to be a person of a certain sort, wanting to have a certain trait of character rather than others, for example, moral courage or perfect integrity. That is why the use of exemplary persons like Socrates, Jesus, or Martin Luther King has been such an important part of moral education and self-development, and it is one of the reasons for the writing and reading of biographies or of novels and epics in which types of moral personality are portrayed, even if they are not all heroes or saints. Often such moral ideals of personality go beyond what can be demanded or regarded as obligatory, belonging among the things to be praised rather than required, except as one may require them of oneself. It should be remembered, however, that not all personal ideals are moral ones. Achilles, Hercules, Napoleon, and Prince Charming may all be taken as ideals, but the ideals they represent are not moral ones, even though they may not be immoral ones either. Some ideals, e.g., those of chivalry, may be partly moral and partly nonmoral. There is every reason why one should pursue nonmoral as well as moral ideals, but there is no good reason for confusing them.

When one has a moral ideal, wanting to be a certain sort of moral person, one has at least some motivation to live in a certain way, but one also has something to guide him in living. Here the idea of an ethics of virtue may have a point. One may, of course, take as one's ideal that of being a good man who always does his duty from a sense of duty, perhaps gladly, and perhaps even going a second mile on occasion. Then one's guidance clearly comes entirely from one's rules and principles of duty. However, one may also have an ideal that goes beyond anything that can be regarded by others or even oneself as strict duty or obligation, a form or style of personal being that may be morally good or virtuous, but is not morally required of one. An ethics of virtue seems to provide for such an aspiration more naturally than an ethics of duty or principle, and perhaps an adequate morality should at least contain a region in which we can follow such an ideal, over and beyond the region in which we are to listen to the call of duty. There certainly should be moral heroes and saints who go beyond the merely good man, if only to serve as an inspiration to others to be better and do more than they would otherwise be or do. Granted all this, however, it still seems to me that, if one's ideal is truly a moral one, there will be nothing in it that is not covered by the principles of beneficence and justice conceived as principles of what we ought to do in the wider sense referred to earlier.

Are there any other moral virtues to be cultivated besides benevolence and justice? No cardinal ones, of course. In this sense our answer to Socrates' question whether virtue is one or many is that it is two. We saw, however, that the principles of beneficence and equality have corollaries like telling the truth, keeping promises, etc. It follows that character traits like honesty and fidelity are virtues, though subordinate ones, and should be acquired and fostered. There will then be other such virtues corresponding to other corollaries of our main principles. Let us call all of these virtues, cardinal and non-cardinal, first-order moral virtues. Besides first-order virtues like these, there are certain other moral virtues that ought also to be cultivated, which are in a way more abstract and general and may be called second-order virtues. Conscientiousness is one such virtue; it is not limited to a certain sector of the moral life, as gratitude and honesty are, but is a virtue covering the whole of the moral life. Moral courage, or courage when moral issues are at stake, is another such second-order virtue; it belongs to all sectors of the moral life. Others that overlap with these are integrity and good-will, understanding good-will in Kant's sense of respect for the moral law.

We must list two other second-order traits: a disposition to find out and respect the relevant facts and a disposition to think clearly. These are not just abilities but character traits; one might have the ability to think intelligently without having a disposition to use it. They are therefore virtues, though they are intellectual virtues, not moral ones. Still, though their role is not limited to the moral life, they are necessary to it. More generally speaking, we should cultivate the virtue Plato called wisdom and Aristotle practical wisdom, which they thought of as including all of the intellectual abilities and virtues essential to the moral life.

Still other second-order qualities, which may be abilities rather than virtues, but which must be cultivated for moral living, and so may, perhaps, best be mentioned here, are moral autonomy, the ability to make moral decisions and to revise one's principles if necessary, and the ability to realize vividly, in imagination and feeling, the "inner lives" of others. Of these second-order qualities, the first two have been amply discussed by moral philosophers, but something should be said about the last.

If our morality is to be more than a conformity to internalized rules and principles, if it is to include and rest on an understanding of the point of these rules and principles, and certainly if it is to involve *being* a certain kind of person and not merely *doing* certain kinds of things, then we must somehow attain and develop an ability to be aware of others as persons, as important to themselves as we are to ourselves, and to have a lively and sympathetic representation in imagination of their interests and of the effects of our actions on their lives. The need for this is particularly stressed by Josiah Royce and William James. Both men point out how we usually go our own busy and self-concerned ways, with only an external awareness of the presence of others, much as if they were things, and without any realization of their inner and peculiar worlds of personal experience; and both emphasize the need and the possibility of a "higher vision of an inner significance" which pierces this "certain blindness in human beings" and enables us to realize the existence of others in a wholly different way, as we do our own.

> What then is thy neighbor? He too is a mass of states, of experiences, thoughts and desires, just as concrete, as thou art. . . . Dost thou believe this? Art thou sure what it means? This is for thee the turning-point of thy whole conduct towards him.[4]

These are Royce's quaint old-fashioned words. Here are James's more modern ones.

> This higher vision of an inner significance in what, until then, we had realized only in the dead external way, often comes over a person suddenly; and, when it does so, it makes an epoch in his history.[5]

Royce calls this more perfect recognition of our neighbors "the moral insight" and James says that its practical consequence is "the well-known democratic respect for the sacredness of individuality." It is hard to see how either a benevolent (loving) or a just (equalitarian) disposition could come to fruition without it. To quote James again,

> We ought, all of us, to realize each other in this intense, pathetic, and important way.[6]

Doing this is part of what is involved in fully taking the moral point of view.

---

[4] *The Religious Aspect of Philosophy,* (New York: Harper & Row, Publishers, 1958), Harper Torchbook edition, pp. 156–57. See selections in Frankena and Granrose, Chap. IV.
[5] *On Some of Life's Ideals* (New York: Holt, Rinehart and Winston, Inc., 1899), p. 20.
[6] *Life's Ideals,* p. 51.

20

What's So Special About the Virtues?

Tom L. Beauchamp is professor of philosophy and senior research scholar at the Kennedy Institute of Ethics, Georgetown University. He has written extensively in the area of bioethics. Among the many texts he has authored and edited are *Philosophical Ethics* (1991), *Principles of Biomedical Ethics* (with James Childress) (1989), and *Contemporary Issues in Bioethics* (with LeRoy Walters) (1989).

What Value Shall We Place on the Virtues?

[The] problem about whether duty depends on virtue, or virtue on duty, raises profoundly important questions that deserve sustained reflection in contemporary philosophy. There is much to command both viewpoints. . . . Yet I believe there is more to be said *against* both viewpoints, because each overvalues its preferred basic category. One of my purposes is to show how misleading it can be to make any such category "fundamental to" or "prior in" a moral theory. The virtues serve an important function in the moral life, but they do not serve either as primary action guides or as primary sources of moral appraisal. I shall also argue for a consequentialist view that integrates these moral notions in a single system, without the fragmentation that MacIntyre and others have proclaimed. . . .

I shall defend this claim by showing that the virtues are of a less unique importance than many believe, precisely because they *correspond to* or are *correlative to* other forms of moral action guides, including moral principles and moral rights. If I am right, then the virtues should be accorded no higher priority status than "competing" categories—which, on my analysis, turn out not to be in serious competition at all.

Virtue Over Duty?

The moral virtues seem profoundly important because they are integral to a person's moral character. . . . [A]ll persons have characters that exhibit various levels of the virtues and vices, where virtues are understood as established dispositions or habits to do that which is morally commendable. . . . One important objective of the cultivation of virtue is to render fulfillment of duty a routine matter, rather than a continuous struggle to do one's duty, and this is one reason why Aristotle's ethics rightly has a greater appeal to some—myself included—than Kant's. Aristotle's is a more realistic and appealing picture of the human condition, because morality flows from cultivated or natural habit rather than a powerful struggle against inclinations in the attempt to emulate the habits of a holy will—a goal one can approximate but never achieve.

The person who acts charitably because duty demands it seems less admirable than the person who contributes spontaneously from well-formed habits of virtue, and without need of a strict moral law. As Philippa Foot rightly says, "The man who acts charitably out of a sense of duty is not to be undervalued, but it is the [spontaneous contributor] who most shows virtue and therefore to the other that most moral worth is attributed" ([5], pp. 12–14). Not surprisingly, Foot finds Aristotle's theory more prescient and congruent with our intuitions about the moral life than Kant's, particularly because the Kantian quasi-legal metaphors of law, duty, and command seem disembodied and inadequate to the moral life. Is it not better to be generous-spirited than to act from the prod of duty?

The merits of Foot's view are considerable, but there is an important respect in which a sweeping dismissal of Kant and other theories that appeal to principles of duty (including virtually all prominent deontological and utilitarian theories) is too harsh and one-sided. No principle-of-duty-based— hereinafter simply duty-based—theory need deny the importance of virtues, and any viable theory of principles of duty, in my judgment, will include an account of virtue. If I am right, then we should not set up stereotypes of theories . . . such that one must be either a defender of duty-based *or* virtue-based—*or* rights-based—theories. A morality of principles of duty should enthusiastically recommend settled dispositions to act in accordance with that which is morally required, and a proponent of virtue ethics should encourage the development of principles that express how one ought to act. It is a defect in any theory to overlook all of these ways of expressing what is important in the moral life.

As noted above, some writers in ethical theory suggest that we need only some one or the other of these categories; but the more prudent course is to view these approaches as the reverse sides of a nickel, and neither as worth less than 5¢. Let me now proceed to an argument for this view.

The Correspondence Between Virtue Standards and Principles of Duty

I am suggesting that principles of duty correspond to virtue standards. Yet virtue standards such as kindness, generosity, and affection often function to express ideals of conduct rather than duties—and so do not cleanly correspond to duties. I shall argue momentarily that the problem is that these virtues function, in part, as the complement of supererogatory actions in duty-based theories. A principle like beneficence is a better starting point because it directly corresponds to the virtue standard of benevolence: They function both as supererogatory moral ideals *and* as basic standards in a shared morality. In the shared—or what I shall call the "ordinary"—morality, for every moral principle, such as nonmaleficence and respect for persons, there corresponds or can be made to correspond one or more virtue standards. Virtues such as nonmalevolence and respectfulness, then, are dispositions to act in accordance with duties.

I am not contending that actions are virtues or that virtue standards are logically equivalent to moral principles. But I am maintaining the following: Principles and virtues standards are *both* alike general action guides; virtues in the context of ordinary morality are dispositions to do what persons ought to do as a matter of duty; and principles of duty express our convictions about the proper character that persons should cultivate. It will not do to object to this account that it is *duty*-based because *action*-based, while virtue has to do with character ("being") rather than action ("doing"). As Aristotle repeatedly says, virtue is integrally tied to *actions* that *ought* to be performed. . . .

The two categories of virtue standards and principles of duty can in principle be conceived as in a relation of *perfect* correspondence: For *every* principle of duty there is a corresponding trait of character or virtue, which is simply a disposition to act as specified in the principle; and for *every* virtue of character, there is a corresponding action that conforms to a principle of duty. This may be diagrammed as follows (cf.[2], pp. 165–66):

Duty-Based Theories [Correspond to] Virtue-Based Theories

Ordinary Moral Guides	Principles of Duty as Guides of Conduct	Virtue Standards as Guides of Conduct
Extraordinary Moral Guides	Supererogatory Principles as Guides of Conduct	Supererogatory Virtue Standards as Guides of Conduct

"Ordinary moral guides" refers to (1) those (prima facie) moral principles shared in common by all persons and (2) those principles that are shared in common by persons in special roles or professions—such as physicians, nurses, public health officials, and the like. Both (1) and (2) are principles of duty. I shall take *"duties"* to be synonymous with *"obligations,"* because both function to assert what *must* be done by all moral agents. This form of assertion covers only part of the moral ground of what *should* or *ought* to be done. The "extraordinary moral guides" designated above function as ideal standards of what should or ought to be done, not as a matter of the common shared morality but as a matter of what uncommonly exceeds that morality by doing more than it demands. Supererogatory conduct, then, is neither morally required nor morally wrong, is morally praiseworthy, is not morally blameworthy, and voluntarily exceeds what is morally required (cf. [7], p. 115). In the case of superogatory acts that exceed dutiful acts, "principles of duty" are *extended as* moral *ideals* and the *duty* part fades from significance. Those who fail at the level of self-imposed, exceptional moral "oughts," obviously need not also fail at the level of execution of moral duties.

This general category of supererogation need not entail the heroic, saintly, or extraordinary in the sense of exceptionally excellent. If you give aid to a tourist who stops you on the street and asks for directions, or if you invite a blind man to move ahead of you in line, nothing in morality requires this behavior, but you do not so far exceed the demands of morality that you require exceptional praise either. Here we find something of a no man's land in the moral terrain: Morality does not require the action, but a failure to be of aid is nonetheless a moral defect. For those in the role of parents, morality tends to be more demanding. A parent is not required to donate a needed organ to a child, but is required in a wide variety of circumstances to volunteer aid to a child in danger or need. This indicates that we should not divide the moral life too *bluntly* into ordinary moral guides and extra-ordinary moral guides, as the above chart suggests. The imperatives of the moral life rest on an ill-formed continuum of stringency, and there are many points on the continuum.

The program of correspondence suggested in the above chart can be outlined by listing a few select principles and virtues:

The Principle or Duty of	corresponds to	*The Virtue Standard of*
Beneficence		Benevolence
Truth-telling		Truthfulness
Gratitude		Gratefulness
Fidelity		Faithfulness
Confidentiality		Confidentialness

. . . Critics of this conception will argue that virtues such as sincerity, integrity, fortitude, rectitude, conscientiousness, hopefulness, and perseverance have no clear corresponding duty . . . This criticism is partially right, but misleading and not damaging to the case I have made. I believe that many duties *do* correspond to such virtues. For example, I think there are ordinary moral requirements of thoroughness, scrupulousness, objectivity, and fairness. More important is that there is no reason to think that each virtue singled out in the English language has a corresponding principle that is likewise singled out in the language. Many virtues are not moral virtues, and some virtues—as

Michael Slote has recently shown—are contra-moral in nature ([11], pp. 77–107). But even in the case of exclusively moral virtues, our moral language is untidy: One virtue may encompass many duties, and one duty may correspond to many virtues. . . .

The Correlativity of Rights, Duties, and Virtues

A similar correspondence theory can be developed for rights-based approaches to ethics, which are also often said to rest on a different "foundation" than either virtue-based or duty-based theories. According to the correlativity theory of rights and duties . . . one person's right entails the duty of another to refrain from interfering or to provide some benefit, and any duty similarly entails a right. (A weaker version is that rights entail duties, although not all duties entail rights, but I shall not discuss this version.) The language of rights is thus always translatable into the language of duties.

By adopting this correlativity thesis, we can construct the following abstract schema of the relationship between virtue standards, principles of duty, and rights:

	Duty-Based Theories [correspond to]	Virtue-Based Theories	Rights-Based Theories [and are both correlative to]
Ordinary Moral Guides	Principles of Duty as Guides of Conduct	Virtue Standards as Guides of Conduct	Rights Claims as Guides of Conduct
Extraordinary Moral Guides	Supererogatory Principles as Guides of Conduct	Supererogatory Virtue Standards as Guides of Conduct	

Under this conception, there can be fundamental moral virtues that correspond to fundamental principles and to fundamental rights, and there can be derivative rules in each category that are derived from the fundamental standard(s). . . .

The correlativity thesis has been challenged on grounds that several classes of duties to do not entail rights, and that certain rights do not entail duties. Duties of charity, kindness to animals, and duties of conscience are the staple of such objections. However, this problem can be handled by distinguishing between duty required by a shared principle of ordinary morality and "duty" required by a self-imposed principle of extraordinary morality. For example, duties of charity and conscience are often supererogatory, and duties of kindness to animals occupy an uncertain status. Thus, the same distinction between supererogatory or extraordinary morality and ordinary (nonsupererogatory) morality discussed earlier again rescues us from theoretical problems: The correlativity thesis holds for all and only duties of ordinary, non-supererogatory morality. It will of course not always be easy to determine the class in which a particular obligation (or virtue) properly belongs, and there may be several obligations and several persons having obligations that correspond to a single right. But this untidiness does not impair the correlativity thesis; it only shows that correlativity is complex.

I conclude that the correspondence and correlativity theses developed above provide the outlines of an integrated theory of morality according to which virtue standards, principles of duty, and valid claims of right express different emphases in the moral life and are complementary categories.

Rights, for example, are particularly appropriate for contexts in which a good, service, or liberty can rightfully, and if necessary forcefully, be demanded as one's due; the bearer of a right can validly make demands, and others are validly constrained from interferences with the exercise of that right and from failures to provide that which the person is owed. Protection-by-rights is a highly suitable model for certain contexts, while generally unsuitable for those in which virtue is most suitable. It does not follow that one does not have rights that correspond to virtue standards, but only that the distinct emphases attached to our various moral standards are fashioned for and peculiarly suited for certain purposes. For example, we have a right to be treated kindly by others, but contexts in which kindness is appropriate are not usually contexts suited for forcefully demanding something as one's due. . . .

John Stuart Mill held that the "object of virtue" is the "multiplication of happiness"[10]. He viewed the principle of utility and the virtues and rules derived from it as instruments of the happy life. This great exponent of the principle of utility, and the duties derived from it, had no trouble accommodating virtues in his system. Mill knew that the purpose of general moral standards—whether in the form of virtues, duties, or rights—is to achieve certain desirable outcomes and to avoid certain undesirable outcomes. This is the reason, and ultimately the justification of our scheme of moral duties, virtues, and rights. Contemporary consequentialists have not abandoned this perspective as a relic of 19th century philosophy. For example, in his recent book, *Moral Thinking*, R. M. Hare relies on a strikingly similar approach. He holds that "intrinsic moral virtues" have "corresponding principles" and that in the training of children we want them most to learn not merely to adopt a policy or practice of obeying principles but rather to possess "firm dispositions of character"—i.e., virtues—that accord with the principles. As with Mill, the justification of both training in duty and virtue is human happiness ([6], pp. 194–197, 103–105).

The Greek tradition too has emphasized the connection between the virtues and a life of happiness or human flourishing. . . . Ethics has a use and objective for Aristotle: to order individual and (as a branch of politics) communal life so that we can live as well as possible through conventions and practices specifically arranged to promote well-being (*eudaimonia*). Human excellences, including moral virtues, are capacities for living according to the goals and purposes of human activities. The virtues are general *dispositions* leading to *states* of well-being or of preventing the reverse. Aristotle's whole moral theory in this interpretation is teleological ([1], Book 2).

Properly qualified, I accept such a consequentialist approach to justification. Following both Mill and Aristotle, I take the object of morality to be closely tied to the creation and maintenance of conditions that allow the pursuit of a well-structured life of well-being, including conditions that minimize the threat of injury and pain. And, with a debt to both Hume [8] and G. J. Warnock [12], I believe that the specific purpose of moral principles and of standards such as virtue is to minimize the tendency for things to go wrong or badly in interpersonal human relationships. Because humans are not characterized by what Hume calls "extensive benevolence," conditions can seriously deteriorate in human affairs as a result of limited resources, limited time, limited information, and, most importantly, sharply limited sympathies with the plight or needs of others. Moral action guides are needed in a culture to counter the limited sympathies of the human condition, because human motivations can lead to unfortunate and even tragic circumstances, especially if self-interest is allowed to be the overriding factor.

. . . Duties, virtues, and rights prevent things from going wrong, in ways they otherwise might, by directing people toward the protection of the interests of others rather than becoming mired in their self-centered interests. . . .

Warnock has shown that the point of moral standards for action and character is to make things better than they otherwise might be. Ethical principles, moral rights, and dispositions of virtue function to countervail limited sympathies. Good principles, good dispositions, good protections, and the like are our tools to the countervailing of many limited human tendencies, such as the infliction of damage, discrimination, deception, and indifference. This conception, which I believe in all essentials to be correct, leads Warnock to the following claims about the relationship between virtues and principles:

> We seem to be led to four (at least) general types of *good disposition*. . . . Somewhat crudely named, those of (1) non-maleficence, (2) fairness, (3) beneficence, and (4) non-deception. We venture the hypothesis that these (at least) are fundamental *moral virtues*.

> But we can now manipulate this conclusion about "good [moral] dispositions". . . to derive from this the proposition that we have here, by the same token, four fundamental moral *standards*, or moral principles. To have and to display, say, the moral virtue of non-deception could be said to regulate one's conduct in conformity to a *principle* of non-deception [12].

My claim is that virtues, principles, and rights are all instruments, or means, to these ends of the moral life. These objectives determine our choices of means, and in some contexts the subtle differences of emphasis appropriate to virtues, principles, and rights motivate us to select one category as more suitable than another for the context at hand. Consider as an example of an argument that emphasizes virtue Henry Beecher's pioneering monograph,

Experimentation in Man. Beecher was worried about the consequences of rule-based or regulatory approaches to the control of experimentation involving human subjects. He held that rules and regulations are "more likely to do harm than good," and will utterly fail to "curb the unscrupulous." Beecher argued that the Nuremberg Code's unqualified insistence on the consent of all subjects "would effectively cripple if not eliminate most research in the field of mental disease," as well as throw out the use of placebos. "Even the 'obvious' matter of consent," he held, "is not so easy to live up to as it sounds" ([3], pp. 52–58). The thrust of his essay was to heighten awareness of the complex character of the problem, to insist on the overwhelming importance of sound training in scientific methodology, to make the scientific practices consonant with moral sensitivity, and to suggest that we cultivate virtue in physicians ([9], pp. 15–17, 43–44, 50). He went on in his subsequent writings to propose that we stem the tide of "thoughtlessness" and "carelessness" through the most "reliable safeguard" against abuses in research involving human subjects, viz. "the presence of an intelligent, informed, conscientious, compassionate, responsible researcher" ([4], pp. 1354–1355). Beecher's approach relies on an argument that the best outcome will be achieved by educating physicians through a virtue-based ethic rather than a rule- or duty-based one. There is a notable absence in his work of any approach based on the *rights* of subjects—an absence that led to subsequent criticism of Beecher's suggestions.

Beecher's approach resembles the views of Allen Dyer in this volume, who argues that "The doctor-patient relationship is in fact based on trust in the ethics of 'virtuous men (and women) of spontaneous good conscience,' a much higher standard than could possibly be achieved by explicit group sanctions. Trust or trustworthiness is the keystone of medical virtue in the traditional canons . . ." (p. 230). Like Beecher—and MacIntyre and Hauerwas—Dyer is worried that duties, sanctions, rights, and the like are not as well *suited* to the medical context as the virtues. Placed in the perspective of appropriate emphases, as discussed previously, this claim seems unproblematic. An emphasis on character can serve clinical medical ethics well, especially if we have the objective of minimizing the line between the required and the supererogatory. It would not serve well to protect the interests of citizens who have a right to food under a government-sponsored food-stamp program.

In many contexts, principles that permit "ought" statements and rigidly formulated duties serve our ends better than the language of virtue. For example, in the years following the publication of Beecher's monograph, the very people that it influenced the most—officials at N.I.H.—adapted his ideas to schemes of government research with human subjects. Shortly therefore, we saw the appearance of a long chain of moral rules and regulations—e.g., The Yellow Book (1971) as well as the moral guidelines proposed by the National Commission for the Protection of Human Subjects. N.I.H. officials were convinced—after years of experience, and rightly in my judgment—that an approach based on the virtues-of-the-investigator had insufficient teeth and bite. Moral imperatives—like statements of rights—are blunter and more effective instruments for guiding conduct where exhortations to virtue are hard to transmit or need a disinterested audience. One chooses an instrument or tool for the job at hand—which is why rights are so often listed in political and adversarial contexts: They are our most direct and forceful instruments, because fashioned to allow us to demand what is our due.

To summarize: In those contexts in which reliance on a person of good character is most likely to achieve the moral ends we desire, then a theory of the virtues may be the superior account. This belief underlies Beecher's proposal. On the other hand, the person of virtue may often be perplexed about what should be done, or which course of action is the right one. Indeed, the person of good character may be the first to know that his or her character is insufficient to yield the answer. Hence, a discussion of duty, right, or the morality of actions may seem in some contexts to be more important than a doctrine of the virtues for achieving our ends. In still other contexts where the prod of duty or the protection of rights best achieves our objectives, these moral standards will surpass appeals to virtue. . . .

Bibliography

1. Aristotle: 1963, *Nichomachean Ethics*, in *The Philosophy of Aristotle*, trans. A. E. Wardman, Mentor Books, New York.
2. Beauchamp, T. L.: 1982, *Philosophical Ethics*, McGraw-Hill, New York.
3. Beecher, H.: 1959, *Experimentation in Man*, Charles C Thomas, Springfield, Ill.
4. Beecher, H.: 1966, "Ethics and Clinical Research," *New England Journal of Medicine* 274, 1354–1360.
5. Foot, P.: 1978, *Virtues and Vices*, Basil Blackwell, Oxford.
6. Hare, R. M.: 1981, *Moral Thinking: Its Levels, Method and Point*, Oxford University Press, Oxford.
7. Heyd, D.: 1982, *Supererogation: Its Status in Ethical Theory*, Cambridge University Press, Cambridge.
8. Hume, D.: 1894/1975, *An Enquiry Concerning the Principles of Morals*, ed. L. A. Selby-Bigge, 3rd edition, Ph. D. Nidditch, Oxford University Press, Oxford.
9. Jonsen, A. and Hellegers, A. E.: 1974, "Conceptual Foundations for an Ethics of Medical Care," in L. Tancredi (ed.), *Ethics of Health Care: Papers of the Conference on Health Care and Changing Values*, National Academy of Sciences, Washington, pp. 3–20.
10. Mill, J. S.: 1974, *Utilitarianism*, in *Utilitarianism, On Liberty, and Essay on Bentham*, ed. with an Introduction by Mary Warnock, New American Library, New York.
11. Slote, M.: 1983, *Goods and Virtues*, Clarendon Press, Oxford.
12. Warnock, G. J.: 1971, *The Object of Morality*, Methuen & Co., London.

Questions for Discussion

1. What is the difference between an ethics of doing and an ethics of being? Which approach do you find more appealing? Why?

2. Should we be judged for our feelings and attitudes in addition to our actions? Suppose you desire to steal a book from the library but never act on that desire. Should you be held accountable?

3. Imagine a society whose members evaluate each other's moral character but lack the conceptual resources to evaluate the rightness or wrongness of each other's actions. How would day-to-day life in this imaginary society differ from our own?

4. According to Bernard Mayo, an ethics of being has distinct advantages over an ethics of doing—we need merely follow the examples set for us by moral heroes and saints. How would this advice help us solve such vexing questions as whether it is permissible to abort a mentally retarded fetus or to discontinue the life-support system of a comatose relative?

5. Mayo suggests that novelists can help us in our understanding of ethics because they are often concerned with the moral qualities of their characters. He specifically mentions Jane Austen. What other novelists can you think of who are concerned with the moral qualities of their heroes and heroines?

6. What does Edmund L. Pincoffs mean by "quandary ethics" and how does it differ from the conception of ethics that Pincoffs is defending?

7. According to Pincoffs, quandary ethics is in some way analogous with the law. What is this analogy and what does Pincoffs have to say about it?

8. According to Michael Stocker, a moral theory is deficient if it fails to move us. It could be argued, however, that it is no more a strike against a moral theory if it fails to move us than it is strike against a theory of physics if it fails to move us—a moral theory is simply one that explains morality in much the way a theory of physics explains matter and energy. With whom do you agree and why?

9. Do you agree with Stocker that modern ethical theories are incompatible with such values as love and friendship? How might these theories answer this charge?

10. One of the alleged vices of virtue-ethics on which Robert B. Louden comments is that of character change. According to Louden, our moral characters can change, and thus we need a more "character-free" way of assessing action. However, Aristotle holds that acts that are in accordance with virtue "must proceed from a firm and unchangeable character" (*Nicomachean Ethics* 1105a33). What do you think? Is it possible for an adult's moral character to change? Why or why not?

11. Do you agree with Louden that we cannot identify virtuous individuals except by their actions? If so, can we say of certain people that they "acted out of character"?

12. What does William Frankena mean when he says that "principles without traits are impotent" and "traits without principles are blind"?

13. Frankena believes that for every principle of action there is a corresponding virtue that includes a disposition to act according to it. Do you agree? Can you think of a virtue that does not correspond to some principle of action?

14. What does Tom L. Beauchamp mean by a rights-based approach to ethics and how does it differ from a duty-based or virtue-based approach?

15. Beauchamp suggests that moral virtues correspond to principles of duty; the virtue of truthfulness, for example, corresponds to the duty to tell the truth; the virtue of benevolence to the duty of beneficence. To what principle does the virtue of forgiveness correspond? Of integrity? modesty?

Selected Bibliography

Baron, Marcia. "The Alleged Moral Repugnance of Acting from Duty." *Journal of Philosophy* 81 (April 1984): 197–220.

Becker, Lawrence C. "Axiology, Deontology, and Agent Morality: The Need for Coordination." *Journal of Value Inquiry* 4 (Fall 1972): 213–20.

Brandt, Richard B. "W. K. Frankena and Ethics of Virtue." *The Monist* 64 (July 1981): 271–92.

Brown, James. "Right and Virtue." *Proceedings of the Aristotelian Society* 82 (1981–1982): 143–58.

Conly, Sarah. "The Objectivity of Morals and the Subjectivity of Agents." *American Philosophical Quarterly* 22 (October 1985): 275–86.

Davie, William E. "Does Morality Focus on Action?" *Southwestern Journal of Philosophy* 8 (Winter 1977): 33–47.

Gewirth, Alan. "Rights and Virtues." *Review of Metaphysics* 38 (June 1985): 739–62.

Hauerwas, Stanley. "Obligation and Virtue Once More." *Journal of Religious Ethics* 3 (Spring 1975): 27–44.

Herman, Barbara. "Rules, Motives and Helping Actions." *Philosophical Studies* 45 (May 1984): 367–77.

Hudson, Stephen D. "Taking Virtues Seriously." *Australian Journal of Philosophy* 59 (June 1981): 189–202.

Kalin, Jesse. "Lies, Secrets, and Love: The Inadequacy of Contemporary Moral Philosophy." *Journal of Value Inquiry* 4 (Winter 1976): 235–65.

Kekes, John. " 'Ought Implies Can' and Two Kinds of Morality." *The Personalist* 34 (October 1984): 460–67.

Kilcullen, John. "Utilitarianism and Virtue." *Ethics* 93 (April 1983): 451–66.

Koehn, Donald R. "Normative Ethics That Are Neither Teleological Nor Deontological." *Metaphilosophy* 5 (July 1974): 173–80.

Laird, J. "Act-Ethics and Agent-Ethics." *Mind* 55 (April 1946): 113–32.

O'Neill, Onora. "Kant After Virtue." *Inquiry* 26 (December 1983): 387–406.

Pincoffs, Edmund L. "Quandary Ethics." *Mind* 80 (October 1971): 552–71. Reprinted in *Revisions*, edited by Stanley Hauerwas, and Alasdair MacIntyre, 92–112. Notre Dame, Ind.: University of Notre Dame Press, 1983.

Robbines, Wesley. "Frankena on the Difference Between an Ethic of Virtue and an Ethic of Duty." *Journal of Religious Ethics* 4 (Spring 1976): 57–62.

Schenk, David, Jr. "Recasting the Ethics of Virtue/Ethics of Duty Debate." *Journal of Religious Ethics* 4 (Fall 1976): 269–86.

Slote, Michael A. "Morality Not a System of Imperatives." *American Philosophical Quarterly* 19 (October 1982): 331–40.

Stocker, Michael. "Rightness and Goodness: Is There a Difference?" *American Philosophical Quarterly* 10 (April 1973): 87–98.

———. "Act and Agent Evaluations." *Review of Metaphysics* 27 (September 1983): 42–61.

Wolf, Susan. "Above and Below the Line of Duty." *Philosophical Topics* 14 (Fall 1986): 131–48.

PART III

Being

Virtue-Based Approaches to Moral Philosophy:
Theories and Applications

A. THEORIES

Virtue-based approaches to moral philosophy take the central question of ethics as asking, "What kind of persons ought we to be?" They answer this question by listing the traits that contribute to human fulfillment along with the reasons that support this list. Section A of this part examines some of the more prominent of these approaches. Section B considers how virtue-theory impacts on particular virtues and vices.

Virtue-Based Theories of Moral Philosophy

For most of the twentieth century, moral philosophy has been dominated by a concern with *metaethics*; that is, with the meaning and logic of ethical statements. Many philosophers assumed that an analysis of moral language could be pursued in a morally neutral way, and many of them assumed that their conclusions held no implications for substantive moral theory. Other philosophers concerned themselves with *normative ethics*; that is, with the attempt to provide systematic and justifiable answers to moral questions. Recently, dissatisfied with both of these approaches, a number of philosophers have turned to a study of the virtues with an emphasis not on the meaning and logic of moral terms or on how we might answer moral questions but on what kind of persons we ought to be and what kind of lives we ought to live.

What, then, is virtue-ethics and why is it important? One way to answer this question is to say that virtue-ethics is what concerned Plato and Aristotle as well as those who followed them. For them, cultivation of the virtues was among the primary functions of moral behavior. In his great work *The Republic*, Plato argued that the four cardinal virtues (wisdom, justice, courage, and temperance) are the traits that are essential to moral goodness. He claimed that only a person of virtue is capable of rational living and of achieving inner harmony. In *The Nicomachean Ethics*, Aristotle argued that virtues are the traits that enable a person to flourish, to achieve what he called *eudaimonia* (happiness). Not unlike acorns, which have a distinct function enabling them to flourish in the right environment, Aristotle believed that humans, too, have a function enabling them to flourish in an appropriate environment.

Further on in history, Christianity introduced a new understanding of virtue. To the four cardinal virtues, St. Thomas Aquinas added three theological ones: faith, hope, and charity (love). According to Aquinas, these virtues have value in and of themselves but also are needed to achieve salvation. Thus, he added a theological reality to the naturalistic one put forward by Aristotle.

A virtue-based ethics was, then, the primary way in which ancient philosophers answered the questions that pertained to morality. However, with the rise of modern science an increased scepticism was brought to bear on the world view of the ancient philosophers. Such factors as the growth of capitalism, the Industrial Revolution, and the emergence of Protestantism brought in their train a new way of viewing morality. No longer was it fashionable to construe human beings as having a distinct function that would enable them to flourish as human beings. Nor was it fashionable to construe them as actors on a stage enacting a drama with God as director. Rather, the emphasis shifted to a liberal individualism highly mindful of cultural diversity.

But if the new world order was an advance on the old, it also ushered in a new set of problems. Not having God or human nature on which to ground the moral law, it became necessary to find an acceptable alternative. This led to the great moral systems of the seventeenth, eighteenth, and nineteenth centuries. Hobbes grounded morality in the social contract; Hume in the sympathetic judgments of an impartial observer; Kant in the dictates of pure reason; Mill in the satisfaction of desires; and so forth.

Notwithstanding the achievements of these systems, none of them has been entirely successful. Many philosophers believe that we still lack a defensible account of morality. As MacIntyre observes (*After Virtue*, p. 227f.), we still have no idea how to rationally settle the kinds of moral disagreements that pervade our culture. Because of this, many philosophers are now turning back to the Aristotelian approach, with an emphasis on the kinds of persons we ought to be and the kinds of lives we ought to live.

For some philosophers, virtue-theory is thought of as an alternative to the theories of which it is critical. For these philosophers, the question "What kind of persons ought we to be?" is the fundamental question of moral philosophy. Virtue-theorist Harold Alderman, for instance, has argued that since all moral theories ultimately appeal to the obvious, why not appeal to the obviously good character? As he sees it, using the character of a Socrates, Buddha, or Confucious is the best way to approach moral philosophy.[1] Others see virtue-theory as supplementing the moral theories they find deficient.

But however we construe a virtue-based ethics, it goes without saying that the work to be done will necessarily differ from that of its historical ancestry. It will not do, for instance, to return to an Aristotelian conception of human nature in which humans have a purpose it is their destiny to fulfill. For moderns, humans have purpose only if they give themselves one. A virtue-based ethics will, however, share methodological features that characterized those earlier theories. It will focus on characters, their psychological makeup, and the conditions needed for their flourishing. But it will recognize and employ a scheme of moral categories different from the current one.

Summary of Readings

The first selection, "Virtue and Happiness," is from Aristotle's *Nicomachean Ethics*. Aristotle begins by investigating what it is that people desire above all else and concludes that it must be happiness. His reasoning is that all our activities

---

[1] See Harold Alderman, "By Virtue of a Virtue," *Review of Metaphysics* 36 (September 1982): 127–53.

are pursued so that we may be happy, yet we do not pursue happiness for some other reason. Having shown this, he then discusses the nature of happiness.

As Aristotle sees it, happiness is to be explained in terms of actualizing a defining potential or function. For example, an acorn's defining function is its ability to become an oak tree so that if we were to predicate happiness of acorns, we would say they would be happy if they actualized this potential. So, too, Aristotle believes that human beings are happy when they actualize their defining potential. For him, this means living a life in which desires are governed by reason because humans, characteristically, are rational animals.

Considerations of the conditions required for the attainment of happiness lead Aristotle next to a discussion of virtue. For Aristotle, "virtue" refers to the excellence of a thing, or its capacity to effectively perform its defining function. Thus, acorns are "virtuous" (read: good) if they perform their function well; that is, grow into flourishing oak trees. Analogously, humans are virtuous (good) if they perform their function well and flourish as rational animals.

For Aristotle, flourishing as a human being means acting in accordance with reason and this, in turn, means living a life of moderation. Thus, humans flourish when, for instance, they are courageous rather than cowardly or rash; proud, rather than vain or humble. Means between extremes thus become the defining characteristic of the virtues, with vices being extremes of excess and deficiency. (See the chart that follows the reading.)

The next selection, "Virtue and Theology," is by St. Thomas Aquinas, a medieval philosopher in the Christian tradition. In this selection, Aquinas adds to the Aristotelian virtues the theological virtues of faith, hope, and love. According to Aquinas, these virtues are theological because they are a means of achieving eternal salvation. He is compelled to add to Aristotle's list because the Christian cosmology requires an expanded conception of virtue to properly situate humankind within it.

The next selection is G. E. M. Anscombe's influential "Modern Moral Philosophy." It is this essay that has signaled the renewed interest in virtue-theory by contemporary Anglo-American philosophers. Anscombe begins by observing that the terms *right*, *wrong*, and *obligation* are problematic for several reasons, chief among them that they function best as legal terms, implying the existence of some legal authority. But, says Anscombe, modern moral philosophers do not want to tie these terms to the notion of a legislator. Yet if one has an obligation, she says, then surely it must be with respect to an obliging *authority*—one who posits the law and has authority to do so.

Traditionally, moral law has been grounded in God. He is the one who creates obligations by His acts of legislation. But many modern philosophers deny the existence of God, and even when they don't, they believe that God Himself is bound by his laws.[2] They are thus left with the concept of legislation without a legislator and with moral terms devoid of content.

---

[2] See Plato's *Euthyphro* in Plato's *Euthyphro, Apology, Crito*, trans. F. J. Church (New York: Macmillan, 1989).

Having abandoned God as the source of legislation, modern philosophers have tried to find the source of moral legislation in society, nature, or the social contract. But each of these theories is problematic at best. This being so, Anscombe argues that there is only one way to have ethical "norms" and that is by way of the virtues. As Anscombe puts it, "It might remain to look for 'norms' in human virtues: just as *man* has so many teeth, which is certainly not the average number of teeth men have, but is the number of teeth for the species, so perhaps the species *man*, regarded not just biologically, but from the point of view of the activity of thought and choice in regard to the various departments of life—powers and faculties and use of things needed—'has' such-and-such virtues: and this 'man' with the complete set of virtues is the 'norm,' as 'man' with, e.g., a complete set of teeth is a norm" (p. 271). This way of securing norms for ethics is unlike that of most modern philosophers. To say, for instance, that "one ought to be courageous" is not to say that one has a duty or an obligation to be courageous. Rather, it is to say that courage is a feature of human flourishing.

Twenty-three years after Anscombe's essay appeared, Alasdair MacIntyre published *After Virtue*, from which the next selection is taken. This book, like Anscombe's essay, stands at the forefront of the renewed interest in virtue-theory.[3] Like Anscombe, MacIntyre's point of departure is the bankruptcy of modern moral philosophy. As MacIntyre sees it, moral debate about social issues tends to go on endlessly, with neither side winning by rational argument. It is as if there was once a time, he suggests, in which we all shared a moral tradition, a time that was followed by a great catastrophe that left us with only the *language* of morality with which to try to rebuild the tradition, but with no *understanding* of it. Following this catastrophe, we now mistakenly believe there is some single body of concepts called "morality" on which we should draw to make moral decisions, whereas, in fact, there is nothing of the sort.

Despite this predicament, MacIntyre believes that we can be rescued. What we need, he believes, is a vision of the human good supporting a new conception of human virtues. This he finds in his account of practices, narrative order, and moral tradition.

Practices, says MacIntyre, are complex and demanding activities with standards of excellence and goods "internal" to them. By goods internal to practices, he means such goods as are "appropriate to and partially definitive of" the practice in question. For example, some goods internal to the practice of medicine are the abilities to make an accurate diagnosis and to apply certain kinds of knowledge. (Some goods "external" to the practice of medicine are financial security and status among friends.)

---

[3] MacIntyre, however, takes issue with those who claim he is offering a morality of the virtues *as an alternative* to a morality of principles. See his *After Virtue*, 2d ed. (Notre Dame, Ind.: University of Notre Dame Press, 1984), 150–52, and *Whose Justice? Which Rationality?* (Notre Dame, Ind.: University of Notre Dame Press, 1988), ix, 108–18.

Having discussed what he means by a practice, MacIntyre next explains that the concept needs to be supplemented because there are rival practices from which we must choose, and some are more important than others. Thus, even after we have identified the goods internal to them, we must still order such goods and choose among the practices. We deal with this problem by using the concepts of narrative order and moral tradition.

According to MacIntyre, there is no such thing as an abstract universal morality. We each find ourselves in a particular moral tradition and a particular place within that tradition. By virtue of being placed within a tradition, we come to a sense of personal identity. Our lives, in turn, must then be thought of as structured wholes with a past we are tied to and a future that reflects our goals and aspirations.

But what is a good life? What is the purpose of such a life? MacIntyre's answer is that a life spent in pursuit of the good life *is* the good life. "The virtues therefore are to be understood as those dispositions which will not only sustain practices and enable us to achieve goods internal to practices, but which will also sustain us in the relevant kind of quest for the good."

Thus far, we have seen a classical account of virtue-theory (Aristotle), a medieval account (Aquinas), and two contemporary accounts (Anscombe and MacIntyre). The next selection, "Virtues and Vices" by Philippa Foot, is an attempt to clarify the concept of virtue. To begin with, Foot construes virtues to be beneficial character traits—traits that humans need for their own sake and for the sake of others. But not all beneficial character traits are virtues. Health and good memory, for instance, are beneficial traits but neither is considered a virtue. Thus, Foot says that in addition to being beneficial, virtues "belong to the will." By this, she means that virtues include such things as volition, intentions, desires, and attitudes. It is in the light of these that a person is judged. Thus, unlike health and good memory, whose possession reflects neither well nor badly on their owners, generosity, charity, gratitude, and the like are occasion for moral praise. Finally, Foot mentions that virtues are *corrective*: they check temptations to be resisted and correct deficiencies in motivation.

Peter Geach's "Why We Need the Virtues" is concerned with shedding light on the role the virtues play in the moral life. In doing this, Geach uses a teleological or functional analysis that provides that something is good if it performs its function well. However, the question "What is the function of human beings?" ("What are human beings for?") is not like the question "What are knives for?" or even "What are hearts for?" because people may not have functions in the sense needed to answer this question. However, the fact that people *have* purposes convinces Geach that they need the virtues.

According to Geach, all that is required to understand the need for the virtues is that many human goals involve social cooperation. Thus, even people who have different values can agree on the goal of running a hospital, even if they cannot agree on a host of other things. But if this is true, then cooperation will be possible only against a background of some fundamental agreement that includes a commitment to such virtues as wisdom, temperance, justice, and courage. The function of the virtues, then, is to make life possible in a social community.

The final reading in this section is Christine McKinnon's "Ways of Wrongdoing: A Theory of the Vices." In this essay, McKinnon attempts to develop a theory of the vices. She observes that although virtue-theorists have had much to say on the subject of virtue, they have had little to say on the subject of vices.

"It would appear," says McKinnon, "that the presupposition [of virtue-theorists] is either that a study of vice is deemed to be unimportant for moral philosophy or that once one has a theory of the virtues one thereby has, by default, a theory of the vices. . . . " However, McKinnon believes this presupposition is false. There are, she argues, important differences between virtues and vices, good and bad characters. But if this is so, then we need a theory of the vices to supplement a theory of the virtues.

21

Virtue and Happiness

Aristotle (384–322 B.C.) was born in Stagira in Macedon although he spent most of his life in Athens. The son of a physician to the royal court, Aristotle was a member of Plato's Academy and the personal tutor of Alexander the Great. Founder of a school called the Lyceum, he pioneered work on a wide range of subjects including logic, physics, metaphysics, biology, ethics, politics, and rhetoric. The following selection is from his *Nicomachean Ethics*, which is thought to be named after or dedicated to the editor of the work, Nicomachus.

Book I

1. The Good As the Aim of Action. Every art or applied science and every systematic investigation, and similarly every action and choice, seem to aim at some good; the good, therefore, has been well defined as that at which all things aim. But it is clear that there is a difference in the ends at which they aim: in some cases the activity is the end, in others the end is some product beyond the activity. In cases where the end lies beyond the action the product is naturally superior to the activity.

Since there are many activities, arts, and sciences, the number of ends is correspondingly large: of medicine the end is health, of shipbuilding a vessel, of strategy, victory, and of household management, wealth. In many instances several such pursuits are grouped together under a single capacity: the art of bridle-making, for example, and everything else pertaining to the equipment of a horse are grouped together under horsemanship; horsemanship in turn, along with every other military action, is grouped together under strategy; and other pursuits are grouped together under other capacities. In all these cases the ends of the master sciences are preferable to the ends of the subordinate sciences, since the latter are pursued for the sake of the former. This is true whether the ends of the actions lie in the activities themselves or, as is the case in the disciplines just mentioned, in something beyond the activities.

Reprinted with the permission of Macmillan Publishing Company from *Nicomachean Ethics* by Aristotle, translated by Martin Ostwald. Copyright © 1986 by Macmillan Publishing Company. Copyright © 1962 by The Liberal Arts Press, Inc.

2. Politics As the Master Science of the Good. Now, if there exists an end in the realm of action which we desire for its own sake, an end which determines all our other desires; if, in other words, we do not make all our choices for the sake of something else—for in this way the process will go on infinitely so that our desire would be futile and pointless—then obviously this end will be the good, that is, the highest good. Will not the knowledge of this good, consequently, be very important to our lives? Would it not better equip us, like archers who have a target to aim at, to hit the proper mark? If so, we must try to comprehend in outline at least what this good is and to which branch of knowledge or to which capacity it belongs.

This good, one should think, belongs to the most sovereign and most comprehensive master science, and politics clearly fits this description. For it determines which sciences ought to exist in states, what kind of sciences each group of citizens must learn, and what degree of proficiency each must attain. We observe further that the most honored capacities, such as strategy, household management, and oratory, are contained in politics. Since this science uses the rest of the sciences, and since, moreover, it legislates what people are to do and what they are not to do, its end seems to embrace the ends of the other sciences. Thus it follows that the end of politics is the good for man. For even if the good is the same for the individual and the state, the good of the state clearly is the greater and more perfect thing to attain and to safeguard. The attainment of the good for one man alone is, to be sure, a source of satisfaction; yet to secure it for a nation and for states is nobler and more divine. In short, these are the aims of our investigation, which is in a sense an investigation of social and political matters.

3. The Limitations of Ethics and Politics. Our discussion will be adequate if it achieves clarity within the limits of the subject matter. For precision cannot be expected in the treatment of all subjects alike, any more than it can be expected in all manufactured articles. Problems of what is noble and just, which politics examines, present so much variety and irregularity that some people believe that they exist only by convention and not by nature. The problem of the good, too, presents a similar kind of irregularity, because in many cases good things bring harmful results. There are instances of men ruined by wealth, and others by courage. Therefore, in a discussion of such subjects, which has to start from a basis of this kind, we must be satisfied to indicate the truth with a rough and general sketch: when the subject and the basis of a discussion consist of matters that hold good only as a general rule, but not always, the conclusions reached must be of the same order. The various points that are made must be received in the same spirit. For a well-schooled man is one who searches for that degree of precision in each kind of study which the nature of the subject at hand admits: it is obviously just as foolish to accept arguments of probability from a mathematician as to demand strict demonstrations from an orator.

Each man can judge competently the things he knows, and of these he is a good judge. Accordingly, a good judge in each particular field is one who has been trained in it, and a good judge in general, a man who has received an all-round schooling. For that reason, a young man is not equipped to be a student of politics; for he has no experience in the actions which life demands of him, and these actions form the basis and subject matter of the discussion. Moreover, since he follows his emotions, his study will be pointless and unprofitable, for the end of this kind of study is not knowledge but action. Whether he is young in years or immature in character makes no difference; for his deficiency is not a matter of time but of living and of pursuing all his interests under the influence of his emotions. Knowledge brings no benefit to this kind of person, just as it brings none to the morally weak. But those who regulate their desires and actions by a rational principle will greatly benefit from a knowledge of this subject. So much by way of a preface about the student, the limitations which have to be accepted, and the objective before us.

4. Happiness Is the Good, but Many Views Are Held about It. To resume the discussion: since all knowledge and every choice is directed toward some good, let us discuss what is in our view the aim of politics, i.e., the highest good attainable by action. As far as its name is concerned, most people would probably agree: for both the common run of people and cultivated men call it happiness, and understand by "being happy" the same as "living well" and "doing well." But when it comes to defining what happiness is, they disagree, and the account given by the common run differs from that of the philosophers. The former say it is some clear and obvious good, such as pleasure, wealth, or honor; some say it is one thing and others another, and often the very same person identifies it with different things at different times: when he is sick he thinks it is health, and when he is poor he says it is wealth; and when people are conscious of their ignorance, they admire those who talk above their heads in accents of greatness. Some thinkers used to believe that there exists over and above these many goods another good, good in itself and by itself, which also is the cause of good in all these things. An examination of all the different opinions would perhaps be a little pointless, and it is sufficient to concentrate on those which are most in evidence or which seem to make some sort of sense.

Nor must we overlook the fact that arguments which proceed from fundamental principles are different from arguments that lead up to them. Plato, too, rightly recognized this as a problem and used to ask whether the discussion was proceeding from or leading up to fundamental principles, just as in a race course there is a difference between running from the judges to the far end of the track and running back again. Now, we must start with the known. But this term has two connotations: "what is known to us" and "what is known" pure and simple. Therefore, we should start perhaps from what is known to us. For that reason, to be a competent student of what is right and just, and of politics generally, one must first have received a proper upbringing in moral conduct. The acceptance of a fact as a fact is the starting point, and if this is sufficiently clear, there will be no further need to ask why it is so. A man with this kind of background has or can easily acquire the foundations from which he must start. But if he neither has nor can acquire them, let him lend an ear to Hesiod's words:

That man is all-best who himself works out every problem. . . .
That man, too, is admirable who follows one who speaks well.
He who cannot see the truth for himself, nor, hearing it from others,
store it away in his mind, that man is utterly useless.

5. *Various Views on the Highest Good.* But to return to the point from which
we digressed. It is not unreasonable that men should derive their concept of
the good and of happiness from the lives which they lead. The common run
of people and the most vulgar identify it with pleasure, and for that reason are
satisfied with a life of enjoyment. For the most notable kinds of life are three:
the life just mentioned, the political life, and the contemplative life.

The common run of people, as we saw, betray their utter slavishness in
their preference for a life suitable to cattle; but their views seem plausible
because many people in high places share the feelings of Sardanapallus.
Cultivated and active men, on the other hand, believe the good to be honor,
for honor, one might say, is the end of the political life. But this is clearly
too superficial an answer: for honor seems to depend on those who confer it
rather than on him who receives it, whereas our guess is that the good is a
man's own possession which cannot easily be taken away from him. Furthermore, men seem to pursue honor to assure themselves of their own worth; at
any rate, they seek to be honored by sensible men and by those who know
them, and they want to be honored on the basis of their virtue or excellence.
Obviously, then, excellence, as far as they are concerned, is better than honor.
One might perhaps even go so far as to consider excellence rather than honor
as the end of political life. However, even excellence proves to be imperfect as
an end: for a man might possibly possess it while asleep or while being inac-
tive all his life, and while, in addition, undergoing the greatest suffering and
misfortune. Nobody would call the life of such a man happy, except for the
sake of maintaining an argument. But enough of this: the subject has been
sufficiently treated in our publications addressed to a wider audience. In the
third place there is the contemplative life, which we shall examine later on. As
for the money-maker, his life is led under some kind of constraint: clearly,
wealth is not the good which we are trying to find, for it is only useful, i.e., it
is a means to something else. Hence one might rather regard the aforementioned objects as ends, since they are valued for their own sake. But even they
prove not to be the good, though many words have been wasted to show that
they are. Accordingly, we may dismiss them. . . .

6. *The Good Is Final and Self-sufficient; Happiness Is Defined.* Let us return
again to our investigation into the nature of the good which we are seeking. It
is evidently something different in different actions and in each art: it is one
thing in medicine, another in strategy, and another again in each of the other
arts. What, then, is the good of each? Is it not that for the sake of which everything else is done? That means it is health in the case of medicine, victory
in the case of strategy, a house in the case of building, a different thing in the
case of different arts, and in all actions and choices it is the end. For it is for
the sake of the end that all else is done. Thus, if there is some one end for all

that we do, this would be the good attainable by action: if there are several ends, they will be the goods attainable by action.

Our argument has gradually progressed to the same point at which we were before, and we must try to clarify it still further. Since there are evidently several ends, and since we choose some of these—e.g., wealth, flutes, and instruments generally—as a means to something else, it is obvious that not all ends are final. The highest good, on the other hand, must be something final. Thus, if there is only one final end, this will be the good we are seeking; if there are several, it will be the most final and perfect of them. We call that which is pursued as an end in itself more final than an end which is pursued for the sake of something else; and what is never chosen as a means to something else we call more final than that which is chosen both as an end in itself and as a means to something else. What is always chosen as an end in itself and never as a means to something else is called final in an unqualified sense. This description seems to apply to happiness above all else: for we always choose happiness as an end in itself and never for the sake of something else. Honor, pleasure, intelligence, and all virtue we choose partly for themselves—for we would choose each of them even if no further advantage would accrue from them—but we also choose them partly for the sake of happiness, because we assume that it is through them that we will be happy. On the other hand, no one chooses happiness for the sake of honor, pleasure, and the like, nor as a means to anything at all.

We arrive at the same conclusion if we approach the question from the standpoint of self-sufficiency. For the final and perfect good seems to be self-sufficient. However, we define something as self-sufficient not by reference to the "self" alone. We do not mean a man who lives his life in isolation, but a man who also lives with parents, children, a wife, and friends and fellow citizens generally, since man is by nature a social and political being. But some limit must be set to these relationships; for if they are extended to include ancestors, descendants, and friends of friends, they will go on to infinity. However, this point must be reserved for investigation later. For the present we define as "self-sufficient" that which taken by itself makes life something desirable and deficient in nothing. It is happiness, in our opinion, which fits this description. Moreover, happiness is of all things the one most desirable, and it is not counted as one good thing among many others. But if it were counted as one among many others, it is obvious that the addition of even the least of the goods would make it more desirable; for the addition would produce an extra amount of good, and the greater amount of good is always more desirable than the lesser. We see then that happiness is something final and self-sufficient and the end of our actions.

To call happiness the highest good is perhaps a little trite, and a clearer account of what it is, is still required. Perhaps that is best done by first ascertaining the proper function of man. For just as the goodness and performance of a flute player, a sculptor, or any kind of expert, and generally of anyone who fulfills some function or performs some action, are thought to reside in his proper function, so the goodness and performance of man would seem to reside in whatever is his proper function. Is it then possible that while a carpenter and a shoemaker have their own proper functions and spheres of action, man as man has none, but was left by nature a good-for-nothing without a function? Should we not assume that just as the eye, the hand, the foot, and in general each part of the body clearly has its own proper function, so man too has some function over and above the functions of his parts? What can this function possibly be? Simply living? He shares that even with plants, but we are now looking for something peculiar to man. Accordingly, the life of nutrition and growth must be excluded. Next in line there is a life of sense perception. But this, too, man has in common with the horse, the ox, and every animal. There remains then an active life of the rational element. The rational element has two parts: one is rational in that it obeys the rule of reason, the other in that it possesses and conceives rational rules. Since the expression "life of the rational element" also can be used in two senses, we must make it clear that we mean a life determined by the activity, as opposed to the mere possession, of the rational element. For the activity, it seems, has a greater claim to be the function of man.

The proper function of man, then, consists in an activity of the soul in conformity with a rational principle or, at least, not without it. In speaking of the proper function of a given individual we mean that it is the same in kind as the function of an individual who sets high standards for himself: the proper function of a harpist, for example, is the same as the function of a harpist who has set high standards for himself. The same applies to any and every group of individuals: the full attainment of excellence must be added to the mere function. In other words, the function of the harpist is to play the harp; the function of the harpist who has high standards is to play it well. On these assumptions, if we take the proper function of man to be a certain kind of life, and if this kind of life is an activity of the soul and consists in actions performed in conjunction with the rational element, and if a man of high standards is he who performs these actions well and properly, and if a function is well performed when it is performed in accordance with the excellence appropriate to it; we reach the conclusion that the good of man is an activity of the soul in conformity with excellence or virtue, and if there are several virtues, in conformity with the best and most complete.

But we must add "in a complete life." For one swallow does not make a spring, nor does one sunny day; similarly, one day or a short time does not make a man blessed and happy. . . .

7. Popular Views about Happiness Confirm Our Position.
We must examine the fundamental principle with which we are concerned (happiness) not only on the basis of the logical conclusion we have reached and on the basis of the elements which make up its definition, but also on the basis of the views commonly expressed about it. For in a true statement, all the facts are in harmony; in a false statement, truth soon introduces a discordant note.

Good things are commonly divided into three classes: (1) external goods, (2) goods of the soul, and (3) goods of the body. Of these, we call the goods pertaining to the soul goods in the highest and fullest sense. But in speaking of "soul," we refer to our soul's actions and activities. Thus, our definition tallies with this opinion which has been current for a long time and to which philosophers subscribe. We are also right in defining the end as consisting of actions and activities; for in this way the end is included among the goods of the soul and not among external goods.

Also the view that a happy man lives well and fares well fits in with our definition; for we have all but defined happiness as a kind of good life and well-being.

Moreover, the characteristics which one looks for in happiness are all included in our definition. For some people think that happiness is virtue, others that it is practical wisdom, others that it is some kind of theoretical wisdom; others again believe it to be all or some of these accompanied by, or not devoid of, pleasure; and some people also include external prosperity in its definition. Some of these views are expressed by many people and have come down from antiquity, some by a few men of high prestige, and it is not reasonable to assume that both groups are altogether wrong; the presumption is rather that they are right in at least one or even in most respects.

Now, in our definition we are in agreement with those who describe happiness as virtue or as some particular virtue, for our term "activity in conformity with virtue" implies virtue. But it does doubtless make a considerable difference whether we think of the highest good as consisting in the possession or in the practice of virtue, viz., as being a characteristic or an activity. For a characteristic may exist without producing any good result, as for example, in a man who is asleep or incapacitated in some other respect. An activity, on the other hand, must produce a result: (an active person) will necessarily act and act well. Just as the crown at the Olympic Games is not awarded to the most beautiful and the strongest but to the participants in the contests—for it is among them that the victors are found—so the good and noble things in life are won by those who act rightly.

The life of men active in this sense is also pleasant in itself. For the sensation of pleasure belongs to the soul, and each man derives pleasure from what he is said to love: a lover of horses from horses, a lover of the theater from plays, and in the same way a lover of justice from just acts, and a lover of virtue in general from virtuous acts. In most men, pleasant acts conflict with one another because they are not pleasant by nature, but men who love what is noble derive pleasure from what is naturally pleasant. Actions which conform to virtue are naturally pleasant, and, as a result, such actions are not only pleasant for those who love the noble but also pleasant in themselves. The life of such men has no further need of pleasure as an added attraction, but it contains pleasure within itself. We may even go so far as to state that the man who does not enjoy performing noble actions is not a good man at all. Nobody would call a man just who does not enjoy acting justly, nor generous who does not enjoy generous actions, and so on. If this is true, actions performed in conformity with virtue are in themselves pleasant.

Of course it goes without saying that such actions are good as well as noble, and they are both in the highest degree, if the man of high moral standards displays any right judgment about them at all; and his judgment corresponds to our description. So we see that happiness is at once the best, noblest, and most pleasant thing, and these qualities are not separate, as the inscription at Delos makes out:

The most just is most noble, but health is the best,
and to win what one loves is pleasantest.

For the best activities encompass all these attributes, and it is in these, or in the best one of them, that we maintain happiness consists.

Still, happiness, as we have said, needs external goods as well. For it is impossible or at least not easy to perform noble actions if one lacks the wherewithal. Many actions can only be performed with the help of instruments, as it were: friends, wealth, and political power. And there are some external goods the absence of which spoils supreme happiness, e.g., good birth, good children, and beauty: for a man who is very ugly in appearance or ill-born or who lives all by himself and has no children cannot be classified as altogether happy; even less happy perhaps is a man whose children and friends are worthless, or one who has lost good children and friends through death. Thus, as we have said, happiness also requires well-being of this kind, and that is the reason why some classify good fortune with happiness, while others link it to virtue.

8. How Happiness Is Acquired. This also explains why there is a problem whether happiness is acquired by learning, by discipline, or by some other kind of training, or whether we attain it by reason of some divine dispensation or even by chance. Now, if there is anything at all which comes to men as a gift from the gods, it is reasonable to suppose that happiness above all else is god-given; and of all things human it is the most likely to be god-given, inasmuch as it is the best. But although this subject is perhaps more appropriate to a different field of study, it is clear that happiness is one of the most divine things, even if it is not god-sent but attained through virtue and some kind of learning or training. For the prize and end of excellence and virtue is the best thing of all, and it is something divine and blessed. Moreover, if happiness depends on excellence, it will be shared by many people; for study and effort will make it accessible to anyone whose capacity for virtue is unimpaired. And if it is better that happiness is acquired in this way rather than by chance, it is reasonable to assume that this is the way in which it is acquired. For, in the realm of nature, things are naturally arranged in the best way possible—and the same is also true of the products of art and of any kind of causation, especially the highest. To leave the greatest and noblest of things to chance would hardly be right.

A solution of this question is also suggested by our earlier definition, according to which the good of man, happiness, is some kind of activity of the soul in conformity with virtue. All the other goods are either necessary prerequisites for happiness, or are by nature co-workers with it and useful instruments for attaining it. Our results also tally with what we said at the outset: for we stated that the end of politics is the best of ends; and the main concern of politics is to engender a certain character in the citizens and to make them good and disposed to perform noble actions.

We are right, then, when we call neither a horse nor an ox nor any other animal happy, for none of them is capable of participating in an activity of this kind. For the same reason, a child is not happy, either; for, because of his age, he cannot yet perform such actions. When we do call a child happy, we do so by reason of the hopes we have for his future. Happiness, as we have said, requires completeness in virtue as well as a complete lifetime. . . .

9. The Psychological Foundations of the Virtues. Since happiness is a certain activity of the soul in conformity with perfect virtue, we must now examine what virtue or excellence is. For such an inquiry will perhaps better enable us to discover the nature of happiness. Moreover, the man who is truly concerned about politics seems to devote special attention to excellence, since it is his aim to make the citizens good and law-abiding. We have an example of this in the lawgivers of Crete and Sparta and in other great legislators. If an examination of virtue is part of politics, this question clearly fits into the pattern of our original plan.

There can be no doubt that the virtue which we have to study is human virtue. For the good which we have been seeking is a human good and the happiness a human happiness. By human virtue we do not mean the excellence of the body, but that of the soul, and we define happiness as an activity of the soul. If this is true, the student of politics must obviously have some knowledge of the workings of the soul, just as the man who is to heal eyes must know something about the whole body. In fact, knowledge is all the more important for the former, inasmuch as politics is better and more valuable than medicine, and cultivated physicians devote much time and trouble to gain knowledge about the body. Thus, the student of politics must study the soul, but he must do so with his own aim in view, and only to the extent that the objects of his inquiry demand: to go into it in greater detail would perhaps be more laborious than his purposes require.

Some things that are said about the soul in our less technical discussions are adequate enough to be used here, for instance, that the soul consists of two elements, one irrational and one rational. Whether these two elements are separate, like the parts of the body or any other divisible thing, or whether they are only logically separable though in reality indivisible, as convex and concave are in the circumference of a circle, is irrelevant for our present purposes.

Of the irrational element, again, one part seems to be common to all living things and vegetative in nature: I mean that part which is responsible for nurture and growth. We must assume that some such capacity of the soul exists in everything that takes nourishment, in the embryonic stage as well as when the organism is fully developed; for this makes more sense than to assume the existence of some different capacity at the latter stage. The excellence of this part of the soul is, therefore, shown to be common to all living things and is not exclusively human. This very part and this capacity seem to be most active in sleep. For in sleep the difference between a good man and a bad is least apparent—whence the saying that for half their lives the happy are no better off than the wretched. This is just what we would expect, for sleep is an inactivity of the soul in that it ceases to do things which cause it to be called good or bad. However, to a small extent some bodily movements do penetrate to the soul in sleep, and in this sense the dreams of honest men are better than those of average people. But enough of this subject: we may pass by the nutritive part, since it has no natural share in human excellence or virtue.

In addition to this, there seems to be another integral element of the soul which, though irrational, still does partake of reason in some way. In morally strong and morally weak men we praise the reason that guides them and the rational element of the soul, because it exhorts them to follow the right path and to do what is best. Yet we see in them also another natural strain different from the rational, which fights and resists the guidance of reason. The soul behaves in precisely the same manner as do the paralyzed limbs of the body. When we intend to move the limbs to the right, they turn to the left, and similarly, the impulses of morally weak persons turn in the direction opposite to that in which reason leads them. However, while the aberration of the body is visible, that of the soul is not. But perhaps we must accept it as a fact, nevertheless, that there is something in the soul besides the rational element, which opposes and reacts against it. In what way the two are distinct need not concern us here. But, as we have stated, it too seems to partake of reason; at any rate, in a morally strong man it accepts the leadership of reason, and is perhaps more obedient still in a self-controlled and courageous man, since in him everything is in harmony with the voice of reason.

Thus we see that the irrational element of the soul has two parts: the one is vegetative and has no share in reason at all, the other is the seat of the appetites and of desire in general and partakes of reason insofar as it complies with reason and accepts its leadership; it possesses reason in the sense that we say it is "reasonable" to accept the advice of a father and of friends, not in the sense that we have a "rational" understanding of mathematical propositions. That the irrational element can be persuaded by the rational is shown by the fact that admonition and all manner of rebuke and exhortation are possible. If it is correct to say that the appetitive part, too, has reason, it follows that the rational element of the soul has two subdivisions: the one possesses reason in the strict sense, contained within itself, and the other possesses reason in the sense that it listens to reason as one would listen to a father.

Virtue, too, is differentiated in line with this division of the soul. We call some virtues "intellectual" and others "moral": theoretical wisdom, understanding, and practical wisdom are intellectual virtues, generosity and self-control moral virtues. In speaking of a man's character, we do not describe him as wise or understanding, but as gentle or self-controlled; but we praise the wise man, too, for his characteristic, and praiseworthy characteristics are what we call virtues.

Book II

1. Moral Virtue As the Result of Habits. Virtue, as we have seen, consists of two kinds, intellectual virtue and moral virtue. Intellectual virtue or excellence owes its origin and development chiefly to teaching, and for that reason requires experience and time. Moral virtue, on the other hand, is formed by habit, *ethos*, and its name, *ēthikē*, is therefore derived, by a slight variation, from *ethos*. This shows, too, that none of the moral virtues is implanted in us by nature, for nothing which exists by nature can be changed by habit. For example, it is impossible for a stone, which has a natural downward movement, to become habituated to moving upward, even if one should try ten thousand times to inculcate the habit by throwing it in the air; nor can fire be made to move downward, nor can the direction of any nature-given tendency be changed by habituation. Thus, the virtues are implanted in us neither by nature nor contrary to nature: we are by nature equipped with the ability to receive them, and habit brings this ability to completion and fulfillment.

Furthermore, of all the qualities with which we are endowed by nature, we are provided with the capacity first, and display the activity afterward. That this is true is shown by the senses: it is not by frequent seeing or frequent hearing that we acquired our senses, but on the contrary we first possess and then use them; we do not acquire them by use. The virtues, on the other hand, we acquire by first having put them into action, and the same is also true of the arts. For the things which we have to learn before we can do them we learn by doing: men become builders by building houses, and harpists by playing the harp. Similarly, we become just by the practice of just actions, self-controlled by exercising self-control, and courageous by performing acts of courage.

This is corroborated by what happens in states. Lawgivers make the citizens good by inculcating (good) habits in them, and this is the aim of every lawgiver; if he does not succeed in doing that, his legislation is a failure. It is in this that a good constitution differs from a bad one.

Moreover, the same causes and the same means that produce any excellence or virtue can also destroy it, and this is also true of every art. It is by playing the harp that men become both good and bad harpists, and correspondingly with builders and all the other craftsmen: a man who builds well will be a good builder, one who builds badly a bad one. For if this were not so, there would be no need for an instructor, but everybody would be born as a good or a bad craftsman. The same holds true of the virtues: in our transactions with other men it is by action that some become just and others unjust, and it is by acting in the face of danger and by developing the habit of feeling fear or confidence that some become brave men and others cowards. The same applies to the appetites and feelings of anger: by reacting in one way or in another to given circumstances some people become self-controlled and gentle, and others self-indulgent and short-tempered. In a word, characteristics develop from corresponding activities. For that reason, we must see to it that our activities are of a certain kind, since any variations in them will be reflected in our characteristics. Hence it is no small matter whether one habit or another is inculcated in us from early childhood; on the contrary, it makes a considerable difference, or, rather, all the difference.

2. Method in the Practical Sciences.

The purpose of the present study is not, as it is in other inquiries, the attainment of theoretical knowledge: we are not conducting this inquiry in order to know what virtue is, but in order to become good, else there would be no advantage in studying it. For that reason, it becomes necessary to examine the problem of actions, and to ask how they are to be performed. For, as we have said, the actions determine what kind of characteristics are developed.

That we must act according to right reason is generally conceded and may be assumed as the basis of our discussion. We shall speak about it later and discuss what right reason is and examine its relation to the other virtues. But let us first agree that any discussion on matters of action cannot be more than an outline and is bound to lack precision; for as we stated at the outset, one can demand of a discussion only what the subject matter permits, and there are no fixed data in matters concerning action and questions of what is beneficial, any more than there are in matters of health. And if this is true of our general discussion, our treatment of particular problems will be even less precise, since these do not come under the head of any art which can be transmitted by precept, but the agent must consider on each different occasion what the situation demands, just as in medicine and in navigation. But although such is the kind of discussion in which we are engaged, we must do our best.

First of all, it must be observed that the nature of moral qualities is such that they are destroyed by defect and by excess. We see the same thing happen in the case of strength and of health, to illustrate, as we must, the invisible by means of visible examples: excess as well as deficiency of physical exercise destroys our strength, and similarly, too much and too little food and drink destroys our health; the proportionate amount, however, produces, increases, and preserves it. The same applies to self-control, courage, and the other virtues: the man who shuns and fears everything and never stands his ground becomes a coward, whereas a man who knows no fear at all and goes to meet every danger becomes reckless. Similarly, a man who revels in every pleasure and abstains from none becomes self-indulgent, while he who avoids every pleasure like a boor becomes what might be called insensitive. Thus we see that self-control and courage are destroyed by excess and by deficiency and are preserved by the mean.

Not only are the same actions which are responsible for and instrumental in the origin and development of the virtues also the causes and means of their destruction, but they will also be manifested in the active exercise of the virtues. We can see the truth of this in the case of other more visible qualities, e.g., strength. Strength is produced by consuming plenty of food and by enduring much hard work, and it is the strong man who is best able to do these things. The same is also true of the virtues: by abstaining from pleasures we become self-controlled, and once we are self-controlled we are best able to abstain from pleasures. So also with courage: by becoming habituated to despise and to endure terrors we become courageous, and once we have become courageous we will best be able to endure terror.

3. Pleasure and Pain As the Test of Virtue.

An index to our characteristics is provided by the pleasure or pain which follows upon the tasks we have achieved. A man who abstains from bodily pleasures and enjoys doing so is self-controlled: if he finds abstinence troublesome, he is self-indulgent; a man who endures danger with joy, or at least without pain, is courageous; if he endures it with pain, he is a coward. For moral excellence is concerned with pleasure and pain; it is pleasure that makes us do base actions and pain that prevents us from doing noble actions. For that reason, as Plato says, men must be brought up from childhood to feel pleasure and pain at the proper things; for this is correct education.

Furthermore, since the virtues have to do with actions and emotions, and since pleasure and pain are a consequence of every emotion and of every action, it follows from this point of view, too, that virtue has to do with pleasure and pain. This is further indicated by the fact that punishment is inflicted by means of pain. For punishment is a kind of medical treatment and it is the nature of medical treatments to take effect through the introduction of the opposite of the disease. Again, as we said just now, every characteristic of the soul shows its true nature in its relation to and its concern with those factors which naturally make it better or worse. But it is through pleasures and pains that men are corrupted, i.e., through pursuing and avoiding pleasures and pains either of the wrong kind or at the wrong time or in the wrong manner, or by going wrong in some other definable respect. For that reason some people define the virtues as states of freedom from emotion and of quietude. However, they make the mistake of using these terms absolutely and without adding such qualifications as "in the right manner," "at the right or wrong time," and so forth. We may, therefore, assume as the basis of our discussion that virtue, being concerned with pleasure and pain in the way we have described, makes us act in the best way in matters involving pleasure and pain, and that vice does the opposite.

The following considerations may further illustrate that virtue is concerned with pleasure and pain. There are three factors that determine choice and three that determine avoidance: the noble, the beneficial, and the pleasurable, on the one hand, and on the other their opposites: the base, the harmful, and the painful. Now a good man will go right and a bad man will go wrong when any of these, and especially when pleasure is involved. For pleasure is not only common to man and the animals, but also accompanies all objects of choice: in fact, the noble and the beneficial seem pleasant to us. Moreover, a love of pleasure has grown up with all of us from infancy. Therefore, this emotion has come to be ingrained in our lives and is difficult to erase. Even in our actions we use, to a greater or smaller extent, pleasure and pain as a criterion. For this reason, this entire study is necessarily concerned with pleasure and pain; for it is not unimportant for our actions whether we feel joy and pain in the right or the wrong way. Again, it is harder to fight against pleasure than against anger, as Heraclitus says; and both virtue and art are always concerned with what is harder, for success is better when it is hard to achieve. Thus, for this reason also, every study both of virtue and of politics must deal with pleasures and pains, for if a man has the right attitude to them, he will be good; if the wrong attitude, he will be bad.

We have now established that virtue or excellence is concerned with pleasures and pains; that the actions which produce it also develop it and, if differently performed, destroy it; and that it actualizes itself fully in those activities to which it owes its origin.

4. *Virtuous Action and Virtue.* However, the question may be raised what we mean by saying that men become just by performing just actions and self-controlled by practicing self-control. For if they perform just actions and exercise self-control, they are already just and self-controlled, in the same way as they are literate and musical if they write correctly and practice music.

But is this objection really valid, even as regards the arts? No, for it is possible for a man to write a piece correctly by chance or at the prompting of another: but he will be literate only if he produces a piece of writing in a literate way, and that means doing it in accordance with the skill of literate composition which he has in himself.

Moreover, the factors involved in the arts and in the virtues are not the same. In the arts, excellence lies in the result itself, so that it is sufficient if it is of a certain kind. But in the case of the virtues an act is not performed justly or with self-control if the act itself is of a certain kind, but only if in addition the agent has certain characteristics as he performs it: first of all, he must know what he is doing; secondly, he must choose to act the way he does, and he must choose it for its own sake; and in the third place, the act must spring from a firm and unchangeable character. With the exception of knowing what one is about, these considerations do not enter into the mastery of the arts; for the mastery of the virtues, however, knowledge is of little or no importance, whereas the other two conditions count not for a little but are all-decisive, since repeated acts of justice and self-control result in the possession of these virtues. In other words, acts are called just and self-controlled when they are the kind of acts which a just or self-controlled man would perform; but the just and self-controlled man is not he who performs these acts, but he who also performs them in the way just and self-controlled men do.

Thus our assertion that a man becomes just by performing just acts and self-controlled by performing acts of self-control is correct; without performing them, nobody could even be on the way to becoming good. Yet most men do not perform such acts, but by taking refuge in argument they think that they are engaged in philosophy and that they will become good in this way. In so doing, they act like sick men who listen attentively to what the doctor says, but fail to do any of the things he prescribes. That kind of philosophical activity will not bring health to the soul any more than this sort of treatment will produce a healthy body.

5. *Virtue Defined: The Genus.* The next point to consider is the definition of virtue or excellence. As there are three kinds of things found in the soul: (1) emotions, (2) capacities, and (3) characteristics, virtue must be one of these. By "emotions" I mean appetite, anger, fear, confidence, envy, joy, affection, hatred, longing, emulation, pity, and in general anything that is followed by pleasure or pain; by "capacities" I mean that by virtue of which we are said to be affected by these emotions, for example, the capacity which enables us to feel anger, pain, or pity; and by "characteristics" I mean the condition, either good or bad, in which we are, in relation to the emotions: for example, our condition in relation to anger is bad, if our anger is too violent or not violent enough, but if it is moderate, our condition is good; and similarly with our condition in relation to the other emotions.

Now the virtues and vices cannot be emotions, because we are not called good or bad on the basis of our emotions, but on the basis of our virtues and vices. Also, we are neither praised nor blamed for our emotions: a man does not receive praise for being frightened or angry, nor blame for being angry pure and simple, but for being angry in a certain way. Yet we are praised or blamed for our virtues and vices. Furthermore, no choice is involved when we experience anger or fear, while the virtues are some kind of choice or at least involve choice. Moreover, with regard to our emotions we are said to be "moved," but with regard to our virtues and vices we are not said to be "moved" but to be "disposed" in a certain way.

For the same reason, the virtues cannot be capacities, either, for we are neither called good or bad nor praised or blamed simply because we are capable of being affected. Further, our capacities have been given to us by nature, but we do not by nature develop into good or bad men. We have discussed this subject before. Thus, if the virtues are neither emotions nor capacities, the only remaining alternative is that they are characteristics. So much for the genus of virtue.

6. *Virtue Defined: The Differentia.* It is not sufficient, however, merely to define virtue in general terms as a characteristic: we must also specify what kind of characteristic it is. It must, then, be remarked that every virtue or excellence (1) renders good the thing itself of which it is the excellence, and (2) causes it to perform its function well. For example, the excellence of the eye makes both the eye and its function good, for good sight is due to the excellence of the eye. Likewise, the excellence of a horse makes it both good as a horse and good at running, at carrying its rider, and at facing the enemy. Now, if this is true of all things, the virtue or excellence of man, too, will be a characteristic which makes him a good man, and which causes him to perform his own function well. To some extent we have already stated how this will be true; the rest will become clear if we study what the nature of virtue is.

Of every continuous entity that is divisible into parts it is possible to take the larger, the smaller, or an equal part, and these parts may be larger, smaller, or equal either in relation to the entity itself, or in relation to us. The "equal" part is something median between excess and deficiency. By the median of an entity I understand a point equidistant from both extremes, and this point is one and the same for everybody. By the median relative to us I understand an amount neither too large nor too small, and this is neither one nor the same for everybody. To take an example: if ten is many and two is few, six is taken as the median in relation to the entity, for it exceeds and is exceeded by the same amount, and is thus the median in terms of arithmetical proportion. But the median relative to us cannot be determined in this manner: if ten pounds of food is much for a man to eat and two pounds little, it does not follow that the trainer will prescribe six pounds, for this may in turn be much or little for him to eat; it may be little for Milo and much for someone who has just begun to take up athletics. The same applies to running and wrestling. Thus we see that an expert in any field avoids excess and deficiency, but seeks the median and chooses it—not the median of the object but the median relative to us.

If this, then, is the way in which every science perfects its work, by looking to the median and by bringing its work up to that point—and this is the reason why it is usually said of a successful piece of work that it is impossible to detract from it or to add to it, the implication being that excess and deficiency destroy success while the mean safeguards it (good craftsmen, we say, look toward this standard in the performance of their work)—and if virtue, like nature, is more precise and better than any art, we must conclude that virtue aims at the median. I am referring to moral virtue: for it is moral virtue that is concerned with emotions and actions, and it is in emotions and actions that excess, deficiency, and the median are found. Thus we can experience fear, confidence, desire, anger, pity, and generally any kind of pleasure and pain either too much or too little, and in either case not properly. But to experience all this at the right time, toward the right objects, toward the right people, for the right reason, and in the right manner—that is the median and the best course, the course that is a mark of virtue.

Similarly, excess, deficiency, and the median can also be found in actions. Now virtue is concerned with emotions and actions; and in emotions and actions excess and deficiency miss the mark, whereas the median is praised and constitutes success. But both praise and success are signs of virtue or excellence. Consequently, virtue is a mean in the sense that it aims at the median. This is corroborated by the fact that there are many ways of going wrong, but only one way which is right—for evil belongs to the indeterminate, as the Pythagoreans imagined, but good to the determinate. This, by the way, is also the reason why the one is easy and the other hard: it is easy to miss the target but hard to hit it. Here, then, is an additional proof that excess and deficiency characterize vice, while the mean characterizes virtue: for "bad men have many ways, good men but one."

We may thus conclude that virtue or excellence is a characteristic involving choice, and that it consists in observing the mean relative to us, a mean which is defined by a rational principle, such as a man of practical wisdom would use to determine it. It is the mean by reference to two vices: the one of excess and the other of deficiency. It is, moreover, a mean because some vices exceed and others fall short of what is required in emotion and in action, whereas virtue finds and chooses the median. Hence, in respect of its essence and the definition of its essential nature virtue is a mean, but in regard to goodness and excellence it is an extreme.

Not every action nor every emotion admits of a mean. There are some actions and emotions whose very names connote baseness, e.g., spite, shamelessness, envy; and among actions, adultery, theft, and murder. These and similar emotions and actions imply by their very names that they are bad; it is not their excess nor their deficiency which is called bad. It is, therefore, impossible ever to do right in performing them: to perform them is always to do wrong. In cases of this sort, let us say adultery, rightness and wrongness do not depend on committing it with the right woman at the right time and in the right manner, but the mere fact of committing such action at all is to do wrong. It would be just as absurd to suppose that there is a mean, an excess, and a deficiency in an unjust or a cowardly or a self-indulgent act. For if there were, we would have a mean of excess and a mean of deficiency, and an excess of excess and a deficiency of deficiency. Just as there cannot be an excess and a deficiency of self-control and courage—because the intermediate is, in a sense, an extreme—so there cannot be a mean, excess, and deficiency in their respective opposites: their opposites are wrong regardless of how they are performed; for, in general, there is no such thing as the mean of an excess or a deficiency, or the excess and deficiency of a mean.

7. Examples of the Mean in Particular Virtues. However, this general statement is not enough; we must also show that it fits particular instances. For in a discussion of moral actions, although general statements have a wider range of application, statements on particular points have more truth in them: actions are concerned with particulars and our statements must harmonize with them. Let us now take particular virtues and vices from the following table.

In feelings of fear and confidence courage is the mean. As for the excesses, there is no name that describes a man who exceeds in fearlessness—many virtues and vices have no name; but a man who exceeds in confidence is reckless, and a man who exceeds in fear and is deficient in confidence is cowardly.

In regard to pleasures and pains—not all of them and to a lesser degree in the case of pains—the mean is self-control and the excess self-indulgence. Men deficient in regard to pleasure are not often found, and there is therefore no name for them, but let us call them "insensitive."

In giving and taking money, the mean is generosity, the excess and deficiency are extravagance and stinginess. In these vices excess and deficiency work in opposite ways: an extravagant man exceeds in spending and is deficient in taking, while a stingy man exceeds in taking and is deficient in spending. For our present purposes, we may rest content with an outline and a summary, but we shall later define these qualities more precisely.

There are also some other dispositions in regard to money: magnificence is a mean (for there is a difference between a magnificent and a generous man in that the former operates on a large scale, the latter on a small); gaudiness and vulgarity are excesses, and niggardliness a deficiency. These vices differ from the vices opposed to generosity. But we shall postpone until later a discussion of the way in which they differ.

As regards honor and dishonor, the mean is high-mindedness, the excess is what we might call vanity, and the deficiency small-mindedness. The same relation which, as we said, exists between magnificence and generosity, the one being distinguished from the other in that it operates on a small scale, exists also between high-mindedness and another virtue: as the former deals with great, so the latter deals with small honors. For it is possible to desire honor as one should or more than one should or less than one should: a man who exceeds in his desires is called ambitious, a man who is deficient unambitious, but there is no name to describe the man in the middle. There are likewise no names for the corresponding dispositions except for the disposition of an ambitious man which is called ambition. As a result, the men who occupy the extremes lay claim to the middle position. We ourselves, in fact, sometimes call the middle person ambitious and sometimes unambitious; sometimes we praise an ambitious and at other times an unambitious man. The reason why we do that will be discussed in the sequel; for the present, let us discuss the rest of the virtues and vices along the lines we have indicated.

In regard to anger also there exists an excess, a deficiency, and a mean. Although there really are no names for them, we might call the mean gentleness, since we call a man who occupies the middle position gentle. Of the extremes, let the man who exceeds be called short-tempered and his vice a short temper, and the deficient man apathetic and his vice apathy.

There are, further, three other means which have a certain similarity with one another, but differ nonetheless one from the other. They are all concerned with human relations in speech and action, but they differ in that one of them is concerned with truth in speech and action and the other two with pleasantness: (*a*) pleasantness in amusement and (*b*) pleasantness in all our daily life. We must include these, too, in our discussion, in order to see more clearly that the mean is to be praised in all things and that the extremes are neither praiseworthy nor right, but worthy of blame. Here, too, most of the virtues and vices have no name, but for the sake of clarity and easier comprehension we must try to coin names for them, as we did in earlier instances.

To come to the point; in regard to youth, let us call the man in the middle position truthful and the mean truthfulness. Pretense in the form of exaggeration is boastfulness and its possessor boastful, while pretense in the form of understatement is self-depreciation and its possessor a self-depreciator.

Concerning pleasantness in amusement, the man in the middle position is witty and his disposition wittiness; the excess is called buffoonery and its possessor a buffoon; and the deficient man a kind of boor and the corresponding characteristic boorishness.

As far as the other kind of pleasantness is concerned, pleasantness in our daily life, a man who is as pleasant as he should be is friendly and the mean is friendliness. A man who exceeds is called obsequious if he has no particular purpose in being pleasant, but if he is acting for his own material advantage, he is a flatterer. And a man who is deficient and unpleasant in every respect is a quarrelsome and grouchy kind of person.

A mean can also be found in our emotional experiences and in our emotions. Thus, while a sense of shame is not a virtue, a bashful or modest man is praised. For even in these matters we speak of one kind of person as intermediate and of another as exceeding if he is terror-stricken and abashed at everything. On the other hand, a man who is deficient in shame or has none at all is called shameless, whereas the intermediate man is bashful or modest.

Righteous indignation is the mean between envy and spite, all of these being concerned with the pain and pleasure which we feel in regard to the fortunes of our neighbors. The righteously indignant man feels pain when someone prospers undeservedly: an envious man exceeds him in that he is pained when he sees anyone prosper; and a spiteful man is so deficient in feeling pain that he even rejoices (when someone suffers undeservedly).

But we shall have an opportunity to deal with these matters again elsewhere. After that, we shall discuss justice; since it has more than one meaning, we shall distinguish the two kinds of justice and show in what way each is a mean.

8. The Relation Between the Mean and Its Extremes.

There are, then, three kinds of disposition: two are vices (one marked by excess and one by deficiency), and one, virtue, the mean. Now, each of these dispositions is, in a sense, opposed to both the others: the extremes are opposites to the middle as well as to one another, and the middle is opposed to the extremes. Just as an equal amount is larger in relation to a smaller and smaller in relation to a larger amount, so, in the case both of emotions and of actions, the middle characteristics exceed in relation to the deficiencies and are deficient in relation to the excesses. For example, a brave man seems reckless in relation to a coward, but in relation to a reckless man he seems cowardly. Similarly, a self-controlled man seems self-indulgent in relation to an insensitive man and insensitive in relation to a self-indulgent man, and a generous man extravagant in relation to a stingy man and stingy in relation to an extravagant man. This is the reason why people at the extremes each push the man in the middle over to the other extreme: a coward calls a brave man reckless and a reckless man calls a brave man a coward, and similarly with the other qualities.

However, while these three dispositions are thus opposed to one another, the extremes are more opposed to one another than each is to the median; for they are further apart from one another than each is from the median, just as the large is further removed from the small and the small from the large than either one is from the equal. Moreover, there appears to be a certain similarity between some extremes and their median, e.g., recklessness resembles courage and extravagance generosity; but there is a very great dissimilarity between the extremes. But things that are furthest removed from one another are defined as opposites, and that means that the further things are removed from one another the more opposite they are.

In some cases it is the deficiency and in others the excess that is more opposed to the median. For example, it is not the excess, recklessness, which is more opposed to courage, but the deficiency, cowardice; while in the case of self-control it is not the defect, insensitivity, but the excess, self-indulgence which is more opposite. There are two causes for this. One arises from the nature of the thing itself: when one of the extremes is closer and more similar to the median, we do not treat it but rather the more extreme as the opposite of the median. For instance, since recklessness is believed to be more similar and closer to courage, and cowardice less similar, it is cowardice rather than recklessness which we treat as the opposite of courage. For what is further removed from the middle is regarded as being opposite. So much for the first cause which arises from the thing itself. The second reason is found in ourselves: the more we are naturally attracted to anything, the more opposed to the median does this thing appear to be. For example, since we are naturally more attracted to pleasure we incline more easily to self-indulgence than to a disciplined kind of life. We describe as more opposed to the mean those things toward which our tendency is stronger; and for that reason the excess, self-indulgence, is more opposed to self-control than is its corresponding deficiency.

9. How to Attain the Mean. Our discussion has sufficiently established (1) that moral virtue is a mean and in what sense it is a mean; (2) that it is a mean between two vices, one of which is marked by excess and the other by deficiency; and (3) that it is a mean in the sense that it aims at the median in the emotions and in actions. That is why it is a hard task to be good; in every case it is a task to find the median: for instance, not everyone can find the middle of a circle, but only a man who has the proper knowledge. Similarly, anyone can get angry—that is easy—or can give away money or spend it; but to do all this to the right person, to the right extent, at the right time, for the right reason, and in the right way is no longer something easy that anyone can do. It is for this reason that good conduct is rare, praiseworthy, and noble.

The first concern of a man who aims at the median should, therefore, be to avoid the extreme which is more opposed to it, as Calypso advises: "Keep clear your ship of yonder spray and surf." For one of the two extremes is more in error than the other, and since it is extremely difficult to hit the mean, we must, as the saying has it, sail in the second best way and take the lesser evil; and we can best do that in the manner we have described.

Moreover, we must watch the errors which have the greatest attraction for us personally. For the natural inclination of one man differs from that of another, and we each come to recognize our own by observing the pleasure and pain produced in us (by the different extremes). We must then draw ourselves away in the opposite direction, for by pulling way from error we shall reach the middle, as men do when they straighten warped timber. In every case we must be especially on our guard against pleasure and what is pleasant, for when it comes to pleasure we cannot act as unbiased judges. Our attitude toward pleasure should be the same as that of the Trojan elders was toward Helen, and we should repeat on every occasion the words they addressed to her. For if we dismiss pleasure as they dismissed her, we shall make fewer mistakes.

In summary, then, it is by acting in this way that we shall best be able to hit the median. But this is no doubt difficult, especially when particular cases are concerned. For it is not easy to determine in what manner, with what person, on what occasion, and for how long a time one ought to be angry. There are times when we praise those who are deficient in anger and call them gentle, and other times when we praise violently angry persons and call them manly. However, we do not blame a man for slightly deviating from the course of goodness, whether he strays toward excess or toward deficiency, but we do blame him if his deviation is great and cannot pass unnoticed. It is not easy to determine by a formula at what point and for how great a divergence a man deserves blame; but this difficulty is, after all, true of all objects of sense perception: determinations of this kind depend upon particular circumstances, and the decision rests with our (moral) sense.

This much, at any rate, is clear: that the median characteristic is in all fields the one that deserves praise, and that it is sometimes necessary to incline toward the excess and sometimes toward the deficiency. For it is in this way that we will most easily hit upon the median, which is the point of excellence.

Activity	Vice (Excess)	Virtue (Mean)	Vice (Deficit)
Facing death	Too much fear (i.e., cowardice)	Right amount of fear (i.e., courage)	Too little fear (i.e., foolhardiness)
Bodily actions (eating, drinking, sex, etc.)	Profligacy	Temperance	No name for this state, but it may be called "insensitivity"
Giving money	Prodigality	Liberality	Illiberality
Large-scale giving	Vulgarity	Magnificence	Meanness
Claiming honors	Vanity	Pride	Humility
Social intercourse	Obsequiousness	Friendliness	Sulkiness
According honors	Injustice	Justice	Injustice
Retribution for wrongdoing	Injustice	Justice	Injustice

Source: W. T. Jones, *The Classical Mind*, Harcourt, Brace, & World, New York, 1952, 1969, p. 268.

22

Virtue and Theology

St. Thomas Aquinas (c. 1225–1274) was the central intellectual figure of high medieval civilization and, along with St. Augustine, was one of the most important theologian-philosophers of medieval Christianity. Born in Italy to a noble family, he received his first education at the famous Abbey of Monte Cassino and from there went to the University of Naples. In 1243, he joined the Dominican order where he was later to study with Albertus Magnus. His two most important works are the *Summa Contra Gentiles* and the *Summa Theologica*. In these works, Aquinas synthesized the philosophy of Aristotle with the theology of the Christian Church.

We must now consider the Theological Virtues. Under this head there are four points of inquiry: (1) Whether there are theological virtues? (2) Whether the theological virtues are distinguished from the intellectual and moral virtues? (3) How many, and which are they? (4) Of their order.

First Article
Whether There Are Theological Virtues?

We proceed thus to the First Article:—

Objection 1. It would seem that there are not any theological virtues. For according to *Physics* vii., *virtue is the disposition of a perfect thing to that which is best; and by perfect I mean that which is disposed according to nature.*[1] But that which is divine is above man's nature. Therefore the theological virtues are not the virtues of a man.

Obj. 2. Further, theological virtues are quasi-divine virtues. But the divine virtues are exemplars, as was stated above,[2] which are not in us but in God. Therefore the theological virtues are not the virtues of man.

---

[1] Aristotle, *Phys.*, VII, 3 (246b 23).—Cf. *ibid.* (246a 13).
[2] Q. 61, a. 5.

Obj. 3. Further, the theological virtues are so called because they direct us to God, Who is the first cause and last end of all things. But by the very nature of his reason and will, man is directed to his first cause and last end. Therefore there is no need for any habits of theological virtue to direct the reason and the will to God.

On the contrary, The precepts of law are about acts of virtue. But the divine law contains precepts about the acts of faith, hope and charity: for it is written (*Ecclus.* ii. 8, *seqq.*): *Ye that fear the Lord believe Him,* and again, *hope in Him,* and again, *love Him.* Therefore faith, hope and charity are virtues directing us to God. Therefore they are theological virtues.

I answer that, Man is perfected by virtue for those actions by which he is directed to happiness, as was explained above.[3] Now man's happiness or felicity is twofold, as was also stated above.[4] One is proportioned to human nature, a happiness, namely, which man can obtain by means of the principles of his nature. The other is a happiness surpassing man's nature, and which man can obtain by the power of God alone, by a kind of participation of the Godhead; and thus it is written (2 *Pet.* i. 4) that by Christ we are made *partakers of the divine nature.* And because such happiness surpasses the power of human nature, man's natural principles, which enable him to act well according to his power, do not suffice to direct man to this same happiness. Hence it is necessary for man to receive from God some additional principles, by which he may be directed to supernatural happiness, even as he is directed to his connatural end by means of his natural principles, albeit not without the divine assistance. Such principles are called *theological virtues.*[5] They are so called, first, because their object is God, inasmuch as they direct us rightly to God; secondly, because they are infused in us by God alone; thirdly, because these virtues are not made known to us, save by divine revelation, contained in Holy Scripture.

Reply Obj. 1. A certain nature may be ascribed to a certain thing in two ways. First, essentially, and thus these theological virtues surpass the nature of man. Secondly, by participation, as kindled wood partakes of the nature of fire, and thus, after a fashion, man becomes a partaker of the divine nature, as was stated above. Hence these virtues befit man according to the nature of which he is made a partaker.

Reply Obj. 2. These virtues are called divine, not as though God were virtuous by reason of them, but because by them God makes us virtuous, and directs us to Himself. Hence they are not exemplar virtues but copies.

Reply Obj. 3. The reason and the will are naturally directed to God, inasmuch as He is the cause and the end of nature, but according to the ability of nature. But the reason and the will, according to their nature, are not sufficiently directed to Him in so far as He is the object of supernatural happiness.

---

[3] Q. 5, a. 7.
[4] Q. 5, a. 5.
[5] Cf. William of Auxerre, *Summa Aurea,* III, tr. 2, ch. 2 (fol. 130ra).

Second Article
Whether the Theological Virtues Are Distinguished from the Intellectual and Moral Virtues?

We proceed thus to the Second Article:—

Objection 1. It would seem that the theological virtues are not distinguished from moral and intellectual virtues. For the theological virtues, if they be in a human soul, must needs perfect it either as to the intellectual part or as to the appetitive part. Now the virtues which perfect the intellectual part are called intellectual, and the virtues which perfect the appetitive part are called moral. Therefore the theological virtues are not distinguished from the moral and intellectual virtues.

Obj. 2. Further, the theological virtues are those which direct us to God. Now among the intellectual virtues there is one which directs us to God, namely, wisdom, which is about divine things, since it considers the highest cause. Therefore the theological virtues are not distinguished from the intellectual virtues.

Obj. 3. Further, Augustine shows how the four cardinal virtues are the *order of love.*[6] Now love is charity, which is a theological virtue. Therefore the moral virtues are not distinct from the theological.

On the contrary, That which is above man's nature is distinguished from that which is according to his nature. But the theological virtues are above man's nature, while the intellectual and moral virtues are proportioned to his nature, as was shown above.[7] Therefore they are distinguished from one another.

I answer that, As was stated above, habits are distinguished specifically from one another according to the formal difference of their objects.[8] Now the object of the theological virtues is God Himself, Who is the last end of all, as surpassing the knowledge of our reason. On the other hand, the object of the intellectual and moral virtues is something comprehensible to human reason. Therefore the theological virtues are distinguished specifically from the moral and intellectual virtues.

Reply Obj. 1. The intellectual and moral virtues perfect man's intellect and appetite according to the power of human nature; the theological virtues, supernaturally.

Reply Obj. 2. The wisdom which the Philosopher reckons as an intellectual virtue considers divine things so far as they are open to the investigation of human reason.[9] Theological virtue, on the other hand, is about these same things so far as they surpass human reason.

Reply Obj. 3. Though charity is love, yet love is not always charity. When, then, it is stated that every virtue is the *order of love,* this can be understood

---

[6] *De Mor. Eccl.,* I, 15 (PL 32, 1322).
[7] Q. 58, a. 3.
[8] Q. 54, a. 2, ad 1.
[9] *Eth.,* VI, 3 (1139b 17).

either of love in the general sense, or of the love of charity. If it be understood of love commonly so called, then each virtue is stated to be the order of love in so far as each cardinal virtue requires an ordered affection. Now love is the root and cause of every affection, as was stated above.[10] If, however, it be understood of the love of charity, it does not mean that every other virtue is charity essentially, but that all other virtues depend on charity in some way, as we shall show further on.[11]

Third Article
Whether Faith, Hope and Charity Are Fittingly Reckoned as Theological Virtues?

We proceed thus to the Third Article:—

Objection 1. It would seem that faith, hope and charity are not fittingly reckoned as three theological virtues. For the theological virtues are in relation to divine happiness just as the inclination of nature is in relation to the connatural end. Now among the virtues directed to the connatural end there is but one natural virtue, viz., the understanding of principles. Therefore there should be but one theological virtue.

Obj. 2. Further, the theological virtues are more perfect than the intellectual and moral virtues. Now faith is not reckoned among the intellectual virtues, but is something less than a virtue, since it is imperfect knowledge. Likewise, hope is not reckoned among the moral virtues, but is something less than a virtue, since it is a passion. Much less therefore should they be reckoned as theological virtues.

Obj. 3. Further, the theological virtues direct man's soul to God. Now man's soul cannot be directed to God save through the intellectual part, in which are intellect and will. Therefore there should be only two theological virtues, one perfecting the intellect, the other, the will.

On the contrary, The Apostle says (*I Cor.* xiii. 13): *Now there remain faith, hope, charity, these three.*

I answer that, As was stated above, the theological virtues direct man to supernatural happiness in the same way as by the natural inclination man is directed to his connatural end. Now the latter direction happens in two respects. First, according to the reason or intellect, in so far as it contains the first universal principles which are known to us through the natural light of the intellect, and which are reason's starting-point, both in speculative and in practical matters. Secondly, through the rectitude of the will tending naturally to the good as defined by reason.

But these two fall short of the order of supernatural happiness, according to *I Cor.* ii. 9: *The eye hath not seen, nor ear heard, neither hath it entered into the heart of man, what things God hath prepared for them that love Him.* Consequently, in relation to both intellect and will, man needed to receive in

---

[10] Q. 27, a. 4; q. 28, a. 6, ad 2; q. 41, a. 2, ad 1.
[11] Q. 65, a. 2 and 4; II-II, q. 23, a. 7.

addition something supernatural to direct him to a supernatural end. First, as regards the intellect, man receives certain supernatural principles, which are held by means of a divine light; and these are the things which are to be believed, about which is *faith*.—Secondly, the will is directed to this end, both as to the movement of intention, which tends to that end as something attainable—this pertains to *hope*—and as to a certain spiritual union, whereby the will is, in a way, transformed into that end—and this belongs to *charity*. For the appetite of a thing is naturally moved and tends towards its connatural end and this movement is due to a certain conformity of the thing with its end.

Reply Obj. 1. The intellect requires intelligible species whereby to understand, and consequently there is need of a natural habit in addition to the power. But the very nature of the will suffices for it to be directed naturally to the end, both as to the intention of the end and as to its conformity with the end. But in relation to the things which are above nature, the nature itself of the power is insufficient. Consequently there was need for an additional supernatural habit in both respects.

Reply Obj. 2. Faith and hope imply a certain imperfection, since faith is of things unseen, and hope of things not possessed. Hence to have faith and hope in things that are subject to human power falls short of the nature of virtue. But to have faith and hope in things which are above the ability of human nature surpasses every virtue that is proportioned to man, according to *I Cor.* i. 25: *The weakness of God is stronger than men.*

Reply Obj. 3. Two things pertain to the appetite, viz., movement to the end, and conformity with the end by means of love. Hence there must needs be two theological virtues in the human appetite, namely, hope and charity.

Fourth Article
Whether Faith Precedes Hope, and Hope Charity?

We proceed thus to the Fourth Article:—

Objection 1. It would seem that the order of the theological virtues is not that faith precedes hope, and hope charity. For the root precedes that which grows from it. Now charity is the root of all virtues, according to *Ephes.* iii. 17: *Being rooted and founded in charity.* Therefore charity precedes the others.

Obj. 2. Further, Augustine says: *A man cannot love what he does not believe to exist. But if he believes and loves, by doing good works he ends in hoping.*[12] Therefore it seems that faith precedes charity, and charity hope.

Obj. 3. Further, love is the principle of all our affections, as was stated above. Now hope is a kind of affection, since it is a passion, as was stated above.[13] Therefore charity, which is love, precedes hope.

On the contrary, The Apostle enumerates them thus (*I Cor.* xiii. 13): *Now there remain faith, hope, charity.*

---

[12] *De Doct. Christ.*, I, 37 (PL 34, 35).
[13] Q. 23, a. 4.

I answer that, There is a twofold order, namely, that of generation, and that of perfection. According to the order of generation, in which matter precedes form, and the imperfect precedes the perfect, in one and the same subject faith precedes hope, and hope charity, as to their acts; for the habits are infused together. For the movement of the appetite cannot tend to anything, either by hoping or loving, unless that thing be apprehended by the sense or by the intellect. Now it is by faith that the intellect apprehends what it hopes for and loves. Hence, in the order of generation, faith must precede hope and charity. In like manner, a man loves a thing because he apprehends it as his good. Now from the very fact that a man hopes to be able to obtain some good from someone, he looks on the man in whom he hopes as a good of his own. Hence, for the very reason that a man bases his hopes in someone, he proceeds to love him; so that in order of generation, hope precedes charity as regards their respective acts.

But in the order of perfection, charity precedes faith and hope, because both faith and hope are quickened by charity, and receive from charity their full complement as virtues. For thus charity is the mother and the root of all the virtues, inasmuch as it is the form of them all, as we shall state further on.[14]

This suffices for the Reply to the First Objection.

Reply Obj. 2. Augustine is speaking of that hope by which a man hopes to obtain beatitude through the merits which he has already; and this belongs to hope quickened by, and following, charity. But it is possible for a man, before having charity, to hope through merits not already possessed, but which he hopes to possess.

Reply Obj. 3. As was stated above in treating of the passions, hope has reference to two things.[15] One is its principal object, viz., the good hoped for. With regard to this, love always precedes hope, for a good is never hoped for unless it be desired and loved.—Hope also regards the person from whom a man hopes to be able to obtain some good. With regard to this, hope precedes love at first, though afterwards hope is increased by love. Because, from the fact that a man thinks that he can obtain a good through someone, he begins to love him; and from the fact that he loves him, he then hopes all the more in him.

---

[14] *S. T.*, II–II, q. 23, a. 8.
[15] Q. 40, a. 7.

23

Modern Moral Philosophy

G. E. M. Anscombe is professor of philosophy at Cambridge University and has translated and edited many of the works of Ludwig Wittgenstein. She is the author of *Intention* (1957) and *An Introduction to Wittgenstein's "Tractatus"* (1971).

I will begin by stating three theses which I present in this paper. The first is that it is not profitable for us at present to do moral philosophy; that should be laid aside at any rate until we have an adequate philosophy of psychology, in which we are conspicuously lacking. The second is that the concepts of obligation, and duty—*moral* obligation and *moral* duty, that is to say—and of what is *morally* right and wrong, and of the *moral* sense of "ought," ought to be jettisoned if this is psychologically possible; because they are survivals, or derivatives from survivals, from an earlier conception of ethics which no longer generally survives, and are only harmful without it. My third thesis is that the differences between the well-known English writers on moral philosophy from Sidgwick to the present day are of little importance.

Anyone who has read Aristotle's *Ethics* and has also read modern moral philosophy must have been struck by the great contrasts between them. The concepts which are prominent among the moderns seem to be lacking, or at any rate buried or far in the background, in Aristotle. Most noticeably, the term "moral" itself, which we have by direct inheritance from Aristotle, just doesn't seem to fit, in its modern sense, into an account of Aristotelian ethics. Aristotle distinguishes virtues as moral and intellectual. Have some of what he calls "intellectual" virtues what *we* should call a "moral" aspect? It would seem so; the criterion is presumably that a failure in an "intellectual" virtue—like that of having good judgment in calculating how to bring about something useful, say in municipal government—may be *blameworthy*. But—it may reasonably be asked—cannot *any* failure be made a matter of blame or re-

From G. E. M. Anscombe, "Modern Moral Philosophy," *Philosophy: The Journal of the Royal Institute of Philosophy* 33 (January 1958): 1–19. Copyright 1958, Basil Blackwell. Reprinted by permission of the author and the publisher.

proach? Any derogatory criticism, say of the workmanship of a product or the design of a machine, can be called blame or reproach. So we want to put in the word "morally" again: sometimes such a failure may be *morally* blameworthy, sometimes not. Now has Aristotle got this idea of *moral* blame, as opposed to any other? If he has, why isn't it more central? There are some mistakes, he says, which are causes, not of involuntariness in actions, but of scoundrelism, and for which a man is blamed. Does this mean that there is a *moral* obligation not to make certain intellectual mistakes? Why doesn't he discuss obligation in general, and this obligation in particular? If someone professes to be expounding Aristotle and talks in a modern fashion about "moral" such-and-such, he must be very imperceptive if he does not constantly feel like someone whose jaws have somehow got out of alignment: the teeth don't come together in a proper bite.

We cannot, then, look to Aristotle for any elucidation of the modern way of talking about "moral" goodness, obligation, etc. And all the best-known writers on ethics in modern times, from Butler to Mill, appear to me to have faults as thinkers on the subject which make it impossible to hope for any direct light on it from them. I will state these objections with the brevity which their character makes possible.

Butler exalts conscience, but appears ignorant that a man's conscience may tell him to do the vilest things.

Hume defines "truth" in such a way as to exclude ethical judgments from it, and professes that he has proved that they are so excluded. He also implicitly defines "passion" in such a way that aiming at anything is having a passion. His objection to passing from "is" to "ought" would apply equally to passing from "is" to "owes" or from "is" to "needs." (However, because of the historical situation, he has a point here, which I shall return to.)

Kant introduces the idea of "legislating for oneself," which is as absurd as if in these days, when majority votes command great respect, one were to call each reflective decision a man made a *vote* resulting in a majority, which as a matter of proportion is overwhelming, for it is always 1-0. The concept of legislation requires superior power in the legislator. His own rigoristic convictions on the subject of lying were so intense that it never occurred to him that a lie could be relevantly described as anything but just a lie (e.g. as "a lie in such-and-such circumstances"). His rule about universalizable maxims is useless without stipulations as to what shall count as a relevant description of an action with a view to constructing a maxim about it.

Bentham and Mill do not notice the difficulty of the concept "pleasure." They are often said to have gone wrong through committing the "naturalistic fallacy"; but this charge does not impress me, because I do not find accounts of it coherent. But the other point—about pleasure—seems to me a fatal objection from the very outset. The ancients found this concept pretty baffling. It reduced Aristotle to sheer babble about "the bloom on the cheek of youth" because, for good reasons, he wanted to make it out both identical with and different from the pleasurable activity. Generations of modern philosophers found this concept quite unperplexing, and it reappeared in the literature as a problematic one only a year or two ago when Ryle wrote about it. The reason is simple: since Locke, pleasure was taken to be some sort of internal impression. But it was superficial, if that was the right account of it, to make it the point of actions. One might adapt something Wittgenstein said about "meaning" and say "Pleasure cannot be an internal impression, for no internal impression could have the consequences of pleasure."

Mill also, like Kant, fails to realize the necessity for stipulation as to relevant descriptions, if his theory is to have content. It did not occur to him that acts of murder and theft could be otherwise described. He holds that where a proposed action is of such a kind as to fall under some one principle established on grounds of utility, one must go by that; where it falls under none or several, the several suggesting contrary views of the action, the thing to do is to calculate particular consequences. But pretty well any action can be so described as to make it fall under a variety of principles of utility (as I shall say for short) if it falls under any.

I will now return to Hume. The features of Hume's philosophy which I have mentioned, like many other features of it, would incline me to think that Hume was a mere—brilliant—sophist; and his procedures are certainly sophistical. But I am forced, not to reverse, but to add to, this judgment by a peculiarity of Hume's philosophizing: namely that although he reaches his conclusions—with which he is in love—by sophistical methods, his considerations constantly open up very deep and important problems. It is often the case that in the act of exhibiting the sophistry one finds oneself noticing matters which deserve a lot of exploring: the obvious stands in need of investigation as a result of the points that Hume pretends to have made. In this, he is unlike, say, Butler. It was already well known that conscience could dictate vile actions; for Butler to have written disregarding this does not open up any new topics for us. But with Hume it is otherwise: hence he is a very profound and great philosopher, in spite of his sophistry. For example:

Suppose that I say to my grocer "Truth consists in *either* relations of ideas, as that 20s. = £1, *or* matters of fact, as that I ordered potatoes, you supplied them, and you sent me a bill. So it doesn't apply to such a proposition as that I *owe* you such-and-such a sum."

Now if one makes this comparison, it comes to light that the relationship of the facts mentioned to the description "X owes Y so much money" is an interesting one, which I will call that of being "brute relative to" that description. Further, the "brute" facts mentioned here themselves have descriptions relatively to which *other* facts are "brute"—as, e.g., *he had potatoes carted to my house* and *they were left there* are brute facts relative to "he supplied me with potatoes." And the fact *X owes Y money* is in turn "brute" relative to other descriptions—e.g. "X is solvent." Now the relation of "relative bruteness" is a complicated one. To mention a few points: if xyz is a set of facts brute relative to a description A, then xyz is a set out of a range some set among which holds if A holds; but the holding of some set among these does not necessarily entail

A, because exceptional circumstances can always make a difference; and what are exceptional circumstances relatively to A can generally only be explained by giving a few diverse examples, and *no* theoretically adequate provision can be made for exceptional circumstances, since a further special context can theoretically always be imagined that would reinterpret any special context. Further, though in normal circumstances, xyz would be a justification for A, that is not to say that A just comes to the same as "xyz"; and also there is apt to be an institutional context which gives its point to the description A, of which institution A is of course not itself a description. (E.g. the statement that I give someone a shilling is not a description of the institution of money or of the currency of this country.) Thus, though it would be ludicrous to pretend that there can be no such thing as a transition from, e.g., "is" to "owes," the character of the transition is in fact interesting and comes to light as a result of reflecting on Hume's arguments.[1]

That I owe the grocer such-and-such a sum would be one of a set of facts which would be "brute" in relation to the description "I am a bilker." "Bilking" is of course a species of "dishonesty" or "injustice." (Naturally the consideration will not have any effect on my actions unless I want to commit or avoid acts of injustice.)

So far, in spite of their strong associations, I conceive "bilking," "injustice" and "dishonesty" in a merely "factual" way. That I can do this for "bilking" is obvious enough; "justice" I have no idea how to define, except that its sphere is that of actions which relate to someone else, but "injustice," its defect, can for the moment be offered as a generic name covering various species. E.g.: "bilking," "theft" (which is relative to whatever property institutions exist), "slander," "adultery," "punishment of the innocent."

In present-day philosophy an explanation is required how an unjust man is a bad man, or an unjust action a bad one; to give such an explanation belongs to ethics; but it cannot even be begun until we are equipped with a sound philosophy of psychology. For the proof that an unjust man is a bad man would require a positive account of justice as a "virtue." This part of the subject-matter of ethics is, however, completely closed to us until we have an account of what *type of characteristic* a virtue is—a problem, not of ethics, but of conceptual analysis—and how it relates to the actions in which it is instanced: a matter which I think Aristotle did not succeed in really making clear. For this we certainly need an account at least of what a human action is at all, and how its description as "doing such-and-such" is affected by its motive and by the intention or intentions in it; and for this an account of such concepts is required.

The terms "should" or "ought" or "needs" relate to good and bad: e.g. machinery needs oil, or should or ought to be oiled, in that running without oil is bad for it, or it runs badly without oil. According to this conception, of course, "should" and "ought" are not used in a special "moral" sense when one says that a man should not bilk. (In Aristotle's sense of the term "moral" (ἠθικός), they are being used in connection with a *moral* subject-matter: name-

---

[1] The above two paragraphs are an abstract of a paper "On Brute Facts" *Analysis*, 18, 3 (1958).

ly that of human passions and (non-technical) actions.) But they have now acquired a special so-called "moral" sense—i.e. a sense in which they imply some absolute verdict (like one of guilty/not guilty on a man) on what is described in the "ought" sentences used in certain types of context: not merely the contexts that *Aristotle* would call "moral"—passions and actions—but also some of the contexts that he would call "intellectual."

The ordinary (and quite indispensable) terms "should," "needs," "ought," "must"—acquired this special sense by being equated in the relevant contexts with "is obliged," or "is bound," or "is required to," in the sense in which one can be obliged or bound by law, or something can be required by law.

How did this come about? The answer is in history: between Aristotle and us came Christianity, with its *law* conception of ethics. For Christianity derived its ethical notion from the Torah. (One might be inclined to think that a law conception of ethics could arise only among people who accepted an allegedly divine positive law; that this is not so is shown by the example of the Stoics, who also thought that whatever was involved in conformity to human virtues was required by divine law.)

In consequence of the dominance of Christianity for many centuries, the concepts of being bound, permitted, or excused became deeply embedded in our language and thought. The Greek word "ἁμαρτάνειν," the aptest to be turned to that use, acquired the sense "sin," from having meant "mistake," "missing the mark," "going wrong." The Latin *peccatum* which roughly corresponded to ἁμάρτημα was even apter for the sense "sin," because it was already associated with "culpa"—"guilt"—a juridical notion. The blanket term "illicit," "unlawful," meaning much the same as our blanket term "wrong," explains itself. It is interesting that Aristotle did not have such a blanket term. He has blanket terms for wickedness—"villain," "scoundrel"; but of course a man is not a villain or a scoundrel by the performance of one bad action, or a few bad actions. And he has terms like "disgraceful," "impious"; and specific terms signifying defect of the relevant virtue, like "unjust"; but no term corresponding to "illicit." The extension of this term (i.e. the range of its application) could be indicated in his terminology only by a quite lengthy sentence: that is "illicit" which, whether it is a thought or a consented-to passion or an action or an omission in thought or action, is something contrary to one of the virtues the lack of which shows a man to be bad *qua* man. That formulation would yield a concept co-extensive with the concept "illicit."

To have a *law* conception of ethics is to hold that what is needed for conformity with the virtues failure in which is the mark of being bad *qua* man (and not merely, say, *qua* craftsman or logician)—that what is needed for *this*, is required by divine law. Naturally it is not possible to have such a conception unless you believe in God as a law-giver; like Jews, Stoics, and Christians. But if such a conception is dominant for many centuries, and then is given up, it is a natural result that the concepts of "obligation," of being bound or required as by a law, should remain though they had lost their root; and if the word "ought" has become invested in certain contexts with the sense of "obligation," it too will remain to be spoken with a special emphasis and a special feeling in these contexts.

It is as if the notion "criminal" were to remain when criminal law and criminal courts had been abolished and forgotten. A Hume discovering this situation might conclude that there was a special sentiment, expressed by "criminal," which alone gave the word its sense. So Hume discovered the situation in which the notion "obligation" survived, and the notion "ought" was invested with that peculiar force having which it is said to be used in a "moral" sense, but in which the belief in divine law had long since been abandoned: for it was substantially given up among Protestants at the time of the Reformation.[2] The situation, if I am right, was the interesting one of the survival of a concept outside the framework of thought that made it a really intelligible one.

When Hume produced his famous remarks about the transition from "is" to "ought," he was, then, bringing together several quite different points. One I have tried to bring out by my remarks on the transition from "is" to "owes" and on the relative "bruteness" of facts. It would be possible to bring out a different point by enquiring about the transition from "is" to "needs"; from the characteristics of an organism to the environment that it needs, for example. To say that it needs that environment is not to say, e.g., that you want it to have that environment, but that it won't flourish unless it has it. Certainly, it all depends whether you *want* it to flourish! as Hume would say. But what "all depends" on whether you want it to flourish is whether the fact that it needs that environment, or won't flourish without it, has the slightest influence on your actions. Now *that* such-and-such "ought" to be or "is needed" is supposed to have an influence on your actions: from which it seemed natural to infer that to judge that it "ought to be" was in fact to grant what you judged "ought to be" influence on your actions. And no amount of truth as to what *is* the case could possibly have a logical claim to have influence on your actions. (It is not judgment as such that sets us in motion; but our judgment on how to get or do something we *want*.) Hence it *must* be impossible to infer "needs" or "ought to be" from "is." But in the case of a plant, let us say, the inference from "is" to "needs" is certainly not in the least dubious. It is interesting and worth examining; but not at all fishy. Its interest is similar to the interest of the relation between brute and less brute facts: these relations have been very little considered. And while you can contrast "what it needs" with "what it's got"—like contrasting *de facto* and *de iure*—that does not make its needing this environment less of a "truth."

Certainly in the case of what the plant needs, the thought of a need will only affect action if you want the plant to flourish. Here, then, there is no necessary connection between what you can judge the plant "needs" and what you want. But there is some sort of necessary connection between what you think *you* need, and what you want. The connection is a complicated one; it is

---

[2] They did not deny the existence of divine law; but their most characteristic doctrine was that it was given, not to be obeyed, but to show man's incapacity to obey it, even by grace; and this applied not merely to the ramified prescriptions of the Torah, but to the requirements of "natural divine law." Cf. in this connection the decree of Trent against the teaching that Christ was only to be trusted in as mediator, not obeyed as legislator.

possible *not* to want something that you judge you need. But, e.g., it is not possible never to want *anything* that you judge you need. This, however, is not a fact about the meaning of the word "to need," but about the phenomenon of *wanting*. Hume's reasoning, we might say, in effect, leads one to think it must be about the word "to need," or "to be good for."

Thus we find two problems already wrapped up in the remark about a transition from "is" to "ought"; now supposing that we had clarified the "relative bruteness" of facts on the one hand, and the notions involved in "needing," and "flourishing" on the other—there would *still* remain a third point. For, following Hume, someone might say: Perhaps you have made out your point about a transition from "is" to "owes" and from "is" to "needs": but only at the cost of showing "owes" and "needs" sentences to express a *kind* of truths, a *kind* of facts. And it remains impossible to infer *"morally ought"* from "is" sentences.

This comment, it seems to me, would be correct. This word "ought," having become a word of mere mesmeric force, could not, in the character of having that force, be inferred from anything whatever. It may be objected that it could be inferred from other "morally ought" sentences: but that cannot be true. The appearance that this is so is produced by the fact that the way we say "All men are ϕ" and "Socrates is a man" implies "Socrates is ϕ." But here "ϕ" is a dummy predicate. We mean that if you substitute a real predicate for "ϕ" the implication is valid. A real predicate is required; not just a word containing no intelligible thought: a word retaining the suggestion of force, and apt to have a strong psychological effect, but which no longer signifies a real concept at all.

For its suggestion is one of a *verdict* on my action, according as it agrees or disagrees with the description in the "ought" sentence. And where one does not think there is a judge or a law, the notion of a verdict may retain its psychological effect, but not its meaning. Now imagine that just this word "verdict" *were* so used—with a characteristically solemn emphasis—as to retain its atmosphere but not its meaning, and someone were to say: "For a *verdict*, after all, you need a law and a judge." The reply might be made: "Not at all, for if there were a law and a judge who gave a verdict, the question for us would be whether accepting that verdict is something that there is a *verdict* on." This is an analogue of an argument which is so frequently referred to as decisive: If someone does have a divine law conception of ethics, all the same, he has to agree that he has to have a judgment that he *ought* (morally ought) to obey the divine law; so his ethic is exactly the same position as any other: he merely has a "practical major premise"[3]: "Divine law ought to be obeyed" where someone else has, e.g., "The greatest happiness principle ought to be employed in all decisions."

I should judge that Hume and our present-day ethicists had done a considerable service by showing that no content could be found in the notion

---

[3] As it is absurdly called. Since major premise=premise containing the term which is predicate in the conclusion, it is a solecism to speak of it in the connection with practical reasoning.

"morally ought"; if it were not that the latter philosophers try to find an alternative (very fishy) content and to retain the psychological force of the term. It would be most reasonable to drop it. It has no reasonable sense outside a law conception of ethics; they are not going to maintain such a conception; and you can do ethics without it, as is shown by the example of Aristotle. It would be a great improvement if, instead of "morally wrong," one always named a genus such as "untruthful," "unchaste," "unjust." We should no longer ask whether doing something was "wrong," passing directly from some description of an action to this notion; we should ask whether, e.g., it was unjust; and the answer would sometimes be clear at once.

I now come to the epoch in modern English moral philosophy marked by Sidgwick. There is a startling change that seems to have taken place between Mill and Moore. Mill assumes, as we saw, that there is no question of calculating the particular consequences of an action such as murder or theft; and we saw too that his position was stupid, because it is not at all clear how an action *can* fall under just one principle of utility. In Moore and in subsequent academic moralists of England we find it taken to be pretty obvious that "the right action" is the action which produces the best possible consequences (reckoning among consequences the intrinsic values ascribed to certain kinds of acts by some "Objectivists"[4]). Now it follows from this that a man does well, subjectively speaking, if he acts for the best in the particular circumstances according to his judgment of the total consequences of this particular action. I say that this follows, not that any philosopher has said precisely that. For discussion of these questions can of course get extremely complicated: e.g. it can be doubted whether "such-and-such is the right action" is a satisfactory formulation, on the grounds that things have to exist to have predicates—so perhaps the best formulation is "I am obliged"; or again, a philosopher may deny that "right" is a "descriptive" term, and then take a roundabout route through linguistic analysis to reach a view which comes to the same thing as "the right action is the one productive of the best consequences" (e.g. the view that you frame your "principles" to effect the end you choose to pursue, the connexion between "choice" and "best" being supposedly such that choosing reflectively means that you choose how to act so as to produce the best consequences); further, the roles of what are called "moral principles" and of the "motive of duty" have to be described; the differences between "good" and "morally good" and "right" need to be explored, the special characteristics of "ought" sentences investigated. Such discussions generate an appearance of significant diversity of views where what is really significant is an overall similarity. The overall similarity is made clear if you consider that every one of the best known English academic philosophers has put out a philosophy according to which, e.g., it is not possible to hold that it cannot be right to kill

---

[4] Oxford Objectivists of course distinguish between "consequences" and "intrinsic values" and so produce a misleading appearance of not being "consequentialists." But they do not hold—and Ross explicitly denies—that the gravity of, e.g., procuring the condemnation of the innocent is such that it cannot be outweighed by, e.g., national interest. Hence their distinction is of no importance.

the innocent as a means to any end whatsoever and that someone who thinks otherwise is in error. (I have to mention both points; because Mr. Hare, for example, while teaching a philosophy which would encourage a person to judge that killing the innocent would be what he "ought" to choose for overriding purposes would also teach, I think, that if a man chooses to make avoiding killing the innocent for any purpose his "supreme practical principle," he cannot be impugned for error: that just is his "principle." But with that qualification, I think it can be seen that the point I have mentioned holds good of every single English academic moral philosopher since Sidgwick.) Now this is a significant thing: for it means that all these philosophies are quite incompatible with the Hebrew-Christian ethic. For it has been characteristic of that ethic to teach that there are certain things forbidden whatever *consequences* threaten, such as choosing to kill the innocent for any purpose, however good; vicarious punishment; treachery (by which I mean obtaining a man's confidence in a grave matter by promises of trustworthy friendship and then betraying him to his enemies); idolatry; sodomy; adultery; making a false profession of faith. The prohibition of certain things simply in virtue of their description as such-and-such identifiable kinds of action, regardless of any further consequences, is certainly not the whole of the Hebrew-Christian ethic; but it is a noteworthy feature of it; and if every academic philosopher since Sidgwick has written in such a way as to exclude this ethic, it would argue a certain provinciality of mind not to see this incompatibility as the most important fact about these philosophers, and the differences between them as somewhat trifling by comparison.

It is noticeable that none of these philosophers displays any consciousness that there is such an ethic, which he is contradicting: it is pretty well taken for obvious among them all that a prohibition such as that on murder does not operate in face of some consequences. But of course the strictness of the prohibition has as its point *that you are not to be tempted by fear or hope of consequences.*

If you notice the transition from Mill to Moore, you will suspect that it was made somewhere by someone; Sidgwick will come to mind as a likely name; and you will in fact find it going on, almost casually, in him. He is rather a dull author; and the important things in him occur in asides and footnotes and small bits of argument which are not concerned with his grand classification of the "method of ethics." A divine law theory of ethics is reduced to an insignificant variety by a footnote telling us that "the best theologians" (God knows whom he meant) tell us that God is to be obeyed in his capacity of a *moral* being, ἡ φορτικὸς ὁ ἔπαινος ; one seems to hear Aristotle saying: "Isn't the praise vulgar?"[5] But Sidgwick *is* vulgar in that kind of way: he thinks, for example, that humility consists in underestimating your own merits—i.e. in a species of untruthfulness; and that the ground for having laws against blasphemy was that it was offensive to believers; and that to go accurately into the virtue of purity is to offend against its canons, a thing he re-

---

[5] E.N. 1178b16.

proves "medieval theologians" for not realizing.

From the point of view of the present enquiry, the most important thing about Sidgwick was his definition of intention. He defines intention in such a way that one must be said to intend any foreseen consequences of one's voluntary action. This definition is obviously incorrect, and I dare say that no one would be found to defend it now. He uses it to put forward an ethical thesis which would now be accepted by many people: the thesis that it does not make any difference to a man's responsibility for something that he foresaw, that he felt no desire for it, either as an end or as a means to an end. Using the language of intention more correctly, and avoiding Sidgwick's faulty conception, we may state the thesis thus: it does not make any difference to a man's responsibility for an effect of his action which he can foresee, that he does not intend it. Now this sounds rather edifying; it is I think quite characteristic of very bad degenerations of thought on such questions that they sound edifying. We can see what it amounts to by considering an example. Let us suppose that a man has a responsibility for the maintenance of some child. Therefore deliberately to withdraw support from it is a bad sort of thing for him to do. It would be bad for him to withdraw its maintenance because he didn't want to maintain it any longer; *and* also bad for him to withdraw it because by doing so he would, let us say, compel someone else to do something. (We may suppose for the sake of argument that compelling that person to do that thing is in itself quite admirable.) But now he has to choose between doing something disgraceful and going to prison; if he goes to prison, it will follow that he withdraws support from the child. By Sidgwick's doctrine, there is no difference in his responsibility for ceasing to maintain the child, between the case where he does it for its own sake or as a means to some other purpose, and when it happens as a foreseen and unavoidable consequence of his going to prison rather than do something disgraceful. It follows that he must weigh up the relative badness of withdrawing support from the child and of doing the disgraceful thing; and it may easily be that the disgraceful thing is in fact a less vicious action than intentionally withdrawing support from the child would be; if then the fact that withdrawing support from the child is a side effect of his going to prison does not make any difference to his responsibility, this consideration will incline him to do the disgraceful thing; which can still be pretty bad. And of course, once he has started to look at the matter in this light, the only reasonable thing for him to consider will be the consequences and not the intrinsic badness of this or that action. So that, given that he judges reasonably that no *great* harm will come of it, he can do a much more disgraceful thing than deliberately withdrawing support from the child. And if his calculations turn out in fact wrong, it will appear that he was not responsible for the consequences, because he did not foresee them. For in fact Sidgwick's thesis leads to its being quite impossible to estimate the badness of an action except in the light of *expected* consequences. But if so, then *you* must estimate the badness in the light of the consequences *you* expect; and so it will follow that you can exculpate yourself from the *actual* consequences of the most disgraceful actions, so long as you can make out a case for not having foreseen them. Whereas I should contend that a man is responsible for the bad consequences of his bad actions, but gets no credit for the good ones; and contrariwise is not responsible for the bad consequences of good actions.

The denial of *any* distinction between foreseen and intended consequences, as far as responsibility is concerned, was not made by Sidgwick in developing any one "method of ethics"; he made this important move on behalf of everybody and just on its own account; and I think it plausible to suggest that *this* move on the part of Sidgwick explains the difference between old-fashioned Utilitarianism and that *consequentialism*, as I name it, which marks him and every English academic moral philosopher since him. By it, the kind of consideration which would formerly have been regarded as a temptation, the kind of consideration urged upon men by wives and flattering friends, was given a status by moral philosophers in their theories.

It is a necessary feature of consequentialism that it is a shallow philosophy. For there are always borderline cases in ethics. Now if you are either an Aristotelian, or a believer in divine law, you will deal with a borderline case by considering whether doing such-and-such in such-and-such circumstances is, say, murder, or is an act of injustice; and according as you decide it is or it isn't, you judge it to be a thing to do or not. This would be the method of casuistry; and while it may lead you to stretch a point on the circumference, it will not permit you to destroy the centre. But if you are a consequentialist, the question "What is right to do in such-and-such circumstances?" is a stupid one to raise. The casuist raises such a question only to ask "Would it be *permissible* to do so-and-so?" or "Would it be permissible *not* to do so-and-so?" Only if it would *not* be permissible *not* to do so-and-so could he say *"This* would be *the* thing to do."[6] Otherwise, though he may speak *against* some action, he cannot prescribe any—for in an *actual* case, the circumstances (beyond the ones imagined) might suggest all sorts of possibilities, and you can't know in advance what the possibilities are going to be. Now the consequentialist has no footing on which to say "This would be permissible, this not"; because by his own hypothesis, it is the consequences that are to decide, and he has no business to pretend that he can lay it down what possible twists a man could give doing this or that; the most he can say is: a man must not *bring about* this or that; he has no right to say he will, in an actual case, bring about such-and-such unless he does so-and-so. Further, the consequentialist, in order to be imagining borderline cases at all, has of course to assume some sort of law or standard according to which this is a borderline case. Where then does he get the standard from? In practice the answer invariably is: from the standards current in his society or his circle. And it has in fact been the mark of all these philosophers that they have been extremely conventional; they have nothing in them by which to revolt against the conventional stan-

---

[6] Necessarily a rare case: for the positive precepts, e.g. "Honour your parents," hardly ever prescribe, and seldom even necessitate, any particular action.

dards of their sort of people; it is impossible that they should be profound. But the chance that a whole range of conventional standards will be decent is small.—Finally, the point of considering hypothetical situations, perhaps very improbable ones, *seems* to be to elicit from yourself or someone else a hypothetical decision to do something of a bad kind. I don't doubt this has the effect of predisposing people—who will never get into the situations for which they have made hypothetical choices—to consent to similar bad actions, or to praise and flatter those who do them, so long as their crowd does so too, when the desperate circumstances imagined don't hold at all.

Those who recognize the origins of the notions of "obligation" and of the emphatic, "moral," *ought*, in the divine law conception of ethics, but who reject the notion of a divine legislator, sometimes look about for the possibility of retaining a law conception without a divine legislator. This search, I think, has some interest in it. Perhaps the first thing that suggests itself is the "norms" of a society. But just as one cannot be impressed by Butler when one reflects what conscience can tell people to do, so, I think, one cannot be impressed by this idea if one reflects what the "norms" of a society can be like. That legislation can be "for oneself" I reject as absurd; whatever you do "for yourself" may be admirable; but is not legislating. Once one sees this, one may say: I have to frame my own rules, and these are the best I can frame, and I shall go by them until I know something better: as a man might say "I shall go by the customs of my ancestors." Whether this leads to good or evil will depend on the *content* of the rules or of the customs of one's ancestors. If one is lucky it will lead to good. Such an attitude would be hopeful in this at any rate: it seems to have in it some Socratic doubt where, from having to fall back on such expedients, it should be clear that Socratic doubt is good; in fact rather generally it must be good for anyone to think "Perhaps in some way I can't see, I may be on a bad path, perhaps I am hopelessly wrong in some essential way."—The search for "norms" might lead someone to look for laws of nature, as if the universe were a legislator; but in the present day this is not likely to lead to good results: it might lead one to eat the weaker according to the laws of nature, but would hardly lead anyone nowadays to notions of justice; the pre-Socratic feeling about justice as comparable to the balance or harmony which keeps things going is very remote to us.

There is another possibility here: "obligation" may be contractual. Just as we look at the law to find out what a man subject to it is required by it to do, so we look at a contract to find out what the man who has made it is required by it to do. Thinkers, admittedly remote from us, might have the idea of a *foedus rerum*, of the universe not as a legislator but as the embodiment of a contract. Then if you could find out what the contract was, you would learn your obligations under it. Now, you cannot be under a law unless it has been promulgated to you; and the thinkers who believed in "natural divine law" held that it was promulgated to every grown man in his knowledge of good and evil. Similarly you cannot be in a contract without having contracted, i.e. given signs of entering upon the contract. Just possibly, it might be argued that the use of language which one makes in the ordinary conduct of life amounts in some sense to giving the signs of entering into various contracts. If anyone had this theory, we should want to see it worked out. I suspect that it would be largely formal; it might be possible to construct a system embodying the law (whose status might be compared to that of "laws" of logic): "what's sauce for the goose is sauce for the gander," but hardly one descending to such particularities as the prohibition on murder or sodomy. Also, while it is clear that you can be subject to a law that you do not acknowledge and have not thought of as law, it does not seem reasonable to say that you can enter upon a contract without knowing that you are doing so; such ignorance is usually held to be destructive of the nature of a contract.

It might remain to look for "norms" in human virtues: just as *man* has so many teeth, which is certainly not the average number of teeth men have, but is the number of teeth for the species, so perhaps the species *man*, regarded not just biologically, but from the point of view of the activity of thought and choice in regard to the various departments of life—powers and faculties and use of things needed—"has" such-and-such virtues: and this "man" with the complete set of virtues is the "norm," as "man" with, e.g., a complete set of teeth is a norm. But in *this* sense "norm" has ceased to be roughly equivalent to "law." In *this* sense the notion of a "norm" brings us nearer to an Aristotelian than a law conception of ethics. There is, I think, no harm in that; but if someone looked in this direction to give "norm" a sense, then he ought to recognize what has happened to the notion "norm," which he wanted to mean "law—without bringing God in"—it has ceased to mean "law" at all; and *so* the notions of "moral obligation," "the moral ought," and "duty" are best put on the Index, if he can manage it.

But meanwhile—is it not clear that there are several concepts that need investigating simply as part of the philosophy of psychology and,—as I should recommend—*banishing ethics totally* from our minds? Namely—to begin with: "action," "intention," "pleasure," "wanting." More will probably turn up if we start with these. Eventually it might be possible to advance to considering the concept "virtue"; with which, I suppose, we should be beginning some sort of a study of ethics.

I will end by describing the advantages of using the word "ought" in a non-emphatic fashion, and not in a special "moral" sense; of discarding the term "wrong" in a "moral" sense, and using such notions as "unjust."

It is possible, if one is allowed to proceed just by giving examples, to distinguish between the intrinsically unjust, and what is unjust given the circumstances. To arrange to get a man judicially punished for something which it can be clearly seen he has not done is intrinsically unjust. This might be done, of course, and often has been done, in all sorts of ways; by suborning false witnesses, by a rule of law by which something is "deemed" to be the case which is admittedly not the case as a matter of fact, and by open insolence on the part of the judges and powerful people when they more or less openly say: "A fig for the fact that you did not do it; we mean to sentence you for it all the same." What is unjust given, e.g., normal circumstances is to deprive people of their ostensible property without legal procedure, not to pay debts, not to keep contracts, and a host of other things of the kind. Now, the circumstances can clearly make a great deal of difference in estimating the justice or injustice of such procedures as these; and these circumstance may *sometimes* include expected consequences; for example, a man's claim to a bit of property can become a nullity when its seizure and use can avert some obvious disaster: as, e.g., if you could use a machine of his to produce an explosion in which it would be destroyed, but by means of which you could divert a flood or make a gap which fire could not jump. Now this certainly does not mean that what would ordinarily be an act of injustice, but is not intrinsically unjust, can always be rendered just by a reasonable calculation of better consequences; far from it; but the problems that would be raised in an attempt to draw a boundary line (or boundary area) here are obviously complicated. And while there are certainly some general remarks which ought to be made here, and some boundaries that can be drawn, the decision on particular cases would for the most part be determined κατὸν ὀρθον λόγον "according to what's reasonable."—E.g. that *such-and-such* a delay of payment of a *such-and-such* debt to a person *so* circumstanced, on the part of a person *so* circumstanced, would or would not be unjust, is really only to be decided "according to what's reasonable"; and for this there can *in principle* be no canon other than giving a few examples. That is to say, while it is because of a big gap in philosophy that we can give no general account of the concept of virtue and of the concept of justice, but have to proceed using the concepts, only by giving examples; still there is an area where it is not because of any gap, but is in principle the case, that there is no account except by way of examples: and that is where the canon is "what's reasonable": which of course is *not* a canon.

That is all I wish to say about what is just in some circumstances, unjust in others; and about the way in which expected consequences can play a part in determining what is just. Returning to my example of the intrinsically unjust: if a procedure *is* one of judicially punishing a man for what he is clearly understood not to have done, there can be absolutely no argument about the description of this as unjust. No circumstances, and no expected consequences, which do *not* modify the description of the procedure as one of judicially punishing a man for what he is known not to have done can modify the description of it as unjust. Someone who attempted to dispute this would only be pretending not to know what "unjust" means: for this is a paradigm case of injustice.

And here we see the superiority of the term "unjust" over the terms "morally right" and "morally wrong." For in the context of English moral philosophy since Sidgwick it appears legitimate to discuss whether it *might* be "morally right" in some circumstances to adopt that procedure; but it cannot be argued that the procedure would in any circumstance be just.

Now I am not able to do the philosophy involved—and I think that no one in the present situation of English philosophy *can* do the philosophy involved—but it is clear that a good man is a just man; and a just man is a man who habitually refuses to commit or participate in any unjust actions for fear of any consequences, or to obtain any advantage, for himself or anyone else.

Perhaps no one will disagree. But, it will be said, what *is* unjust is sometimes determined by expected consequences; and certainly that is true. But there are cases where it is not: now if someone says, "I agree, but all this wants a lot of explaining," then he is right, and, what is more, the situation at present is that we can't do the explaining; we lack the philosophic equipment. But if someone really thinks, *in advance*,[7] that it is open to question whether such an action as procuring the judicial execution of the innocent should be quite excluded from consideration—I do not want to argue with him; he shows a corrupt mind.

In such cases our moral philosophers seek to impose a dilemma upon us. "If we have a case where the term 'unjust' applies purely in virtue of a factual description, can't one raise the question whether one sometimes conceivably ought to do injustice? If 'what is unjust' is determined by consideration of whether it is *right* to do so-and-so in such-and-such circumstances, then the question whether it is 'right' to commit injustice can't arise, just because 'wrong' has been built into the definition of injustice. But if we have a case where the description 'unjust' applies purely in virtue of the facts, without bringing 'wrong' in, then the question can arise whether one 'ought' perhaps to commit an injustice, whether it might not be 'right' to? And of course 'ought' and 'right' are being used in their *moral* senses here. Now either you must decide what is 'morally right' in the light of certain *other* 'principles,' or you make a 'principle' about *this* and decide that an injustice is never 'right'; but even if you do the latter you are going beyond the facts; you are making a decision that you will not, or that it is wrong to, commit injustice. But in either case, *if* the term 'unjust' is determined simply by the facts, it is not the term 'unjust' that determines that the term 'wrong' applies, but a decision that injustice is *wrong*, together with the diagnosis of the 'factual' description as entailing injustice. But the man who makes an absolute decision that injustice is 'wrong' has no footing on which to criticize someone who does *not* make that decision as judging falsely."

In this argument "wrong" of course is explained as meaning "morally wrong," and all the atmosphere of the term is retained while its substance is guaranteed quite null. Now let us remember that "morally wrong" is the term which is the heir of the notion "illicit," or "what there is an obligation *not* to do"; which belongs in a divine law theory of ethics. Here it really does add something to the description "unjust" to say there is an obligation not to do it; for what obliges is the divine law—as rules oblige in a game. So if the divine law obliges not to commit injustice by forbidding injustice, it really does add

---

[7] If he thinks it in the concrete situation, he is of course merely a normally tempted human being. In discussion when this paper was read, as was perhaps to be expected, this case was produced: a government is required to have an innocent man tried, sentenced and executed under threat of a "hydrogen bomb war." It would seem strange to me to have much hope of so averting a war threatened by such men as made this demand. But the most important thing about the way in which cases like this are invented in discussions, is the assumption that only two courses are open: here, compliance and open defiance. No one can say in advance of such a situation what the possibilities are going to be—e.g. that there is none of stalling by a feigned willingness to comply, accompanied by a skilfully arranged "escape" of the victim.

something to the description "unjust" to say there is an obligation not to do it. And it is because "morally wrong" is the heir of this concept, but an heir that is cut off from the family of concepts from which it sprang, that "morally wrong" both goes beyond the mere factual description "unjust" and seems to have no discernible content except a certain compelling force, which I should call purely psychological. And such is the force of the term that philosophers actually suppose that the divine law notion can be dismissed as making no essential difference even if it is held—because they think that a "practical principle" running "I ought (i.e. am morally obliged) to obey divine laws" is required for the man who believes in divine laws. But actually this notion of obligation is a notion which only operates in the context of law. And I should be inclined to congratulate the present-day moral philosophers on depriving "morally ought" of its now delusive appearance of content, if only they did not manifest a detestable desire to retain the atmosphere of the term.

It may be possible, if we are resolute, to discard the notion "morally ought," and simply return to the ordinary "ought," which, we ought to notice, is such an extremely frequent term of human language that it is difficult to imagine getting on without it. Now if we do return to it, can't it reasonably be asked whether one might ever need to commit injustice, or whether it won't be the best thing to do? Of course it can. And the answers will be various. One man—a philosopher—may say that since justice is a virtue, and injustice a vice, and virtues and vices are built up by the performances of the action in which they are instanced, an act of injustice will tend to make a man bad; essentially the flourishing of a man qua man consists in his being good (e.g. in virtues); but for any X to which such terms apply, X needs what makes it flourish, so a man needs, or ought to perform, only virtuous actions; and even if, as it must be admitted may happen, he flourishes less, or not at all, in inessentials, by avoiding injustice, his life is spoiled in essentials by not avoiding injustice—so he still needs to perform only just actions. That is roughly how Plato and Aristotle talk; but it can be seen that philosophically there is a huge gap, at present unfillable as far as we are concerned, which needs to be filled by an account of human nature, human action, the type of characteristic a virtue is, and above all of human "flourishing." And it is the last concept that appears the most doubtful. For it is a bit much to swallow that a man in pain and hunger and poor and friendless is "flourishing," as Aristotle himself admitted. Further, someone might say that one at least needed to stay alive to "flourish." Another man unimpressed by all that will say in a hard case "What we need is such-and-such, which we won't get without doing this (which is unjust)—so this is what we ought to do." Another man, who does not follow the rather elaborate reasoning of the philosophers, simply says "I know it is in any case a disgraceful thing to say that one had better commit this unjust action." The man who believes in divine laws will say perhaps "It is forbidden, and however it looks, it cannot be to anyone's profit to commit injustice"; he like the Greek philosophers can think in terms of "flourishing." If he is a Stoic, he is apt to have a decidedly strained notion of what "flourishing" consists in; if he is a Jew or Christian, he need not have any very distinct notion:

the way it will profit him to abstain from injustice is something that he leaves it to God to determine, himself only saying "It can't do me any good to go against his law." (But he also hopes for a great reward in a new life later on, e.g. at the coming of Messiah; but in this he is relying on special promises.)

It is left to modern moral philosophy—the moral philosophy of all the well-known English ethicists since Sidgwick—to construct systems according to which the man who says "We need such-and-such, and will only get it this way" *may* be a virtuous character: that is to say, it is left open to debate whether such a procedure as the judicial punishment of the innocent may not in some circumstances be the "right" one to adopt; and though the present Oxford moral philosophers would accord a man *permission* to "make it his principle" not to do such a thing, they teach a philosophy according to which the particular consequences of such an action *could* "morally" be taken into account by a man who was debating what to do; and if they were such as to conflict with his "ends," it might be a step in his moral education to frame a moral principle under which he "managed" (to use Mr. Nowell-Smith's phrase[8]) to bring the action; or it might be a new "decision of principle," making which was an advance in the formulation of his moral thinking (to adopt Mr. Hare's conception), to decide: in such-and-such circumstances one ought to procure the judicial condemnation of the innocent. And that is my complaint.

---

[8] *Ethics*, p. 308.

24

After Virtue

Alasdair MacIntyre is professor of philosophy at the University of Notre Dame. He is the author of *After Virtue (1984), A Short History of Ethics* (1966), and *Whose Justice? Which Rationality? (1988).*

Imagine that the natural sciences were to suffer the effects of a catastrophe. A series of environmental disasters are blamed by the general public on the scientists. Widespread riots occur, laboratories are burnt down, physicists are lynched, books and instruments are destroyed. Finally a Know-Nothing political movement takes power and successfully abolishes science teaching in schools and universities, imprisoning and executing the remaining scientists. Later still there is a reaction against this destructive movement and enlightened people seek to revive science, although they have largely forgotten what it was. But all that they possess are fragments: a knowledge of experiments detached from any knowledge of the theoretical context which gave them significance; parts of theories unrelated either to the other bits and pieces of theory which they possess or to experiment; instruments whose use has been forgotten; half-chapters from books, single pages from articles, not always fully legible because torn and charred. Nonetheless all these fragments are reembodied in a set of practices which go under the revived names of physics, chemistry and biology. Adults argue with each other about the respective merits of relativity theory, evolutionary theory and phlogiston theory; although they possess only a very partial knowledge of each. Children learn by heart the surviving portions of the periodic table and recite as incantations some of the theorems of Euclid. Nobody, or almost nobody, realizes that what they are doing is not natural science in any proper sense at all. For everything that they do and say conforms to certain canons of consistency and coherence and those contexts which would be needed to make sense of what they are doing have been lost, perhaps irretrievably.

In such a culture men would use expressions such as "neutrino," "mass," "specific gravity," "atomic weight" in systematic and often interrelated ways which would resemble in lesser or greater degrees the ways in which such expressions had been used in earlier times before scientific knowledge had been so largely lost. But many of the beliefs presupposed by the use of these expressions would have been lost and there would appear to be an element of arbitrariness and even of choice in their application which would appear very surprising to us. What would appear to be rival and competing premises for which no further argument could be given would abound. Subjectivist theories of science would appear and would be criticized by those who held that the notion of truth embodied in what they took to be science was incompatible with subjectivism.

This imaginary possible world is very like one that some science fiction writers have constructed. We may describe it as a world in which the language of natural science, or parts of it at least, continues to be used but is in a grave state of disorder. We may notice that if in this imaginary world analytical philosophy were to flourish, it would never reveal the fact of this disorder. For the techniques of analytical philosophy are essentially descriptive and descriptive of the language of the present at that. The analytical philosopher would be able to elucidate the conceptual structures of what was taken to be scientific thinking and discourse in the imaginary world in precisely the way that he elucidates the conceptual structures of natural science as it is.

Nor again would phenomenology or existentialism be able to discern anything wrong. All the structures of intentionality would be what they are now. The task of supplying an epistemological basis for these false simulacra of natural science would not differ in phenomenological terms from the task as it is presently envisaged. A Husserl or a Merleau-Ponty would be as deceived as a Strawson or a Quine.

What is the point of constructing this imaginary world inhabited by fictitious pseudo-scientists and real, genuine philosophy? The hypothesis which I wish to advance is that in the actual world which we inhabit the language of morality is in the same state of grave disorder as the language of natural science in the imaginary world which I described. What we possess, if this view is true, are the fragments of a conceptual scheme, parts which now lack those contexts from which their significance derived. We possess indeed simulacra of morality, we continue to use many of the key expressions. But we have—very largely, if not entirely—lost our comprehension, both theoretical and practical, of morality. . . .

The most striking feature of contemporary moral utterance is that so much of it is used to express disagreements; and the most striking feature of the debates in which these disagreements are expressed is their interminable character. I do not mean by this just that such debates go on and on and on—although they do—but also that they apparently can find no terminus. There seems to be no rational way of securing moral agreement in our culture. Consider three examples of just such contemporary moral debate framed in terms of characteristic and well-known rival moral arguments:

1 (a) A just war is one in which the good to be achieved outweighs the evils involved in waging the war and in which a clear distinction can be made between combatants—whose lives are at stake—and innocent noncombatants. But in a modern war calculation of future escalation is never reliable and no practically applicable distinction between combatants and noncombatants can be made. Therefore no modern war can be a just war and we all now ought to be pacifists.

(b) If you wish for peace, prepare for war. The only way to achieve peace is to deter potential aggressors. Therefore you must build up your armaments and make it clear that going to war on any particular scale is not necessarily ruled out by your policies. An inescapable part of making *this* clear is being prepared both to fight limited wars and to go not only to, but beyond, the nuclear brink on certain types of occasion. Otherwise you will not avoid war *and* you will be defeated.

(c) Wars between the Great Powers are purely destructive; but wars waged to liberate oppressed groups, especially in the Third World, are a necessary and therefore justified means for destroying the exploitative domination which stands between mankind and happiness.

2 (a) Everybody has certain rights over his or her own person, including his or her own body. It follows from the nature of these rights that at the stage when the embryo is essentially part of the mother's body, the mother has a right to make her own decision on whether she will have an abortion or not. Therefore abortion is morally permissible and ought to be allowed by law.

(b) I cannot will that my mother should have had an abortion when she was pregnant with me, except perhaps if it had been certain that the embryo was dead or gravely damaged. But if I cannot will this in my own case, how can I consistently deny to others the right to life that I claim for myself? I would break the so-called Golden Rule unless I denied that a mother has in general a right to an abortion. I am not of course thereby committed to the view that abortion ought to be legally prohibited.

(c) Murder is wrong. Murder is the taking of innocent life. An embryo is an identifiable individual, differing from a newborn infant only in being at an earlier stage on the long road to adult capacities and, if any life is innocent, that of an embryo is. If infanticide is murder, as it is, abortion is murder. So abortion is not only morally wrong, but ought to be legally prohibited.

3 (a) Justice demands that every citizen should enjoy, so far as is possible, an equal opportunity to develop his or her talents and his or her other potentialities. But prerequisites for the provision of such equal opportunity include the provision of equal access to health care and to education. Therefore justice requires the governmental provision of health and educational services, financed out of taxation, and it also requires that no citizen should be able to buy an unfair share of such services. This in turn requires the abolition of private schools and private medical practice.

(b) Everybody has a right to incur such and only such obligations as he or she wishes, to be free to make such and only such contracts as he or she desires and to determine his or her own free choice. Physicians must therefore be free to practice on such terms as they desire and patients must be free to choose among physicians; teachers must be free to teach on such terms as they choose and pupils and parents to go where they wish for education. Freedom thus requires not only the existence of private practice in medicine and private schools in education, but also the abolition of those restraints on private practice which are imposed by licensing and regulation by such bodies as universities, medical schools, the A.M.A. and the state.

These arguments have only to be stated to be recognized as being widely influential in our society. They have of course their articulate expert spokesmen: Herman Kahn and the Pope, Che Guevara and Milton Friedman are among the authors who have produced variant versions of them. But it is their appearance in newspaper editorials and high-school debates, on radio talk shows and letters to congressmen, in bars, barracks and boardrooms, it is their typicality that makes them important examples here. What salient characteristics do these debates and disagreements share?

They are of three kinds. The first is what I shall call, adapting an expression from the philosophy of science, the conceptual incommensurability of the rival arguments in each of the three debates. Every one of the arguments is logically valid or can be easily expanded so as to be made so; the conclusions do indeed follow from the premises. But the rival premises are such that we possess no rational way of weighing the claims of one as against another. For each premise employs some quite different normative or evaluative concept from the others, so that the claims made upon us are of quite different kinds. In the first argument, for example, premises which invoke justice and innocence are at odds with premises which invoke success and survival; in the second, premises which invoke rights are at odds with those which invoke universalizability; in the third it is the claim of equality that is matched against that of liberty. It is precisely because there is in our society no established way of deciding between these claims that moral argument appears to be necessarily interminable. From our rival conclusions we can argue back to our rival premises; but when we do arrive at our premises argument ceases and the invocation of one premise against another becomes a matter of pure assertion and counter-assertion. Hence perhaps the slightly shrill tone of so much moral debate.

But that shrillness may have an additional source. For it is not only in arguments with others that we are reduced so quickly to assertion and counter-assertion; it is also in the arguments that we have within ourselves. For whenever an agent enters the forum of public debate he has already presumably, explicitly or implicitly, settled the matter in question in his own mind. Yet if we possess no unassailable criteria, no set of compelling reasons by means of which we may convince our opponents, it follows that in the process of making up our own minds we can have made no appeal to such criteria or such reasons. If I lack any good reasons to invoke against you, it must seem that I lack any good reasons. Hence it seems that underlying my own position there must be some non-rational decision to adopt that position.

Corresponding to the interminability of public argument there is at least the appearance of a disquieting private arbitrariness. It is small wonder if we become defensive and therefore shrill.

A second equally important but contrasting characteristic of these arguments is that they do none the less purport to be *impersonal*, rational arguments and as such are usually presented in a mode appropriate to that impersonality. What is that mode? Consider two different ways in which I may provide backing for an injunction to someone else to perform some specific action. In the first type of case I say, "Do so-and-so." The person addressed replies, "Why should I do so-and-so?" I reply, "Because I wish it." Here I have given the person addressed no reason to do what I command or request unless he or she independently possesses some particular reason for paying regard to my wishes. If I am your superior officer—in the police, say, or the army—or otherwise have power or authority over you, or if you love me or fear me or want something from me, then by saying "Because I wish it" I have indeed given *you* a reason, although not perhaps a sufficient reason, for doing what it is that I enjoin. Notice that in this type of case whether my utterance gives you a reason or not depends on certain characteristics possessed at the time of hearing or otherwise learning of the utterance by you. What reason-giving force the injunction has depends in this way on the personal context of the utterance.

Contrast with this the type of case in which the answer to the question "Why should I do so-and-so?" (after someone has said "Do so-and-so") is not "Because I wish it," but some such utterance as "Because it would give pleasure to a number of people" or "Because it is your duty." In this type of case the reason given for action either is or is not a good reason for performing the action in question independently of who utters it or even of whether it is uttered at all. Moreover the appeal is to a type of consideration which is independent of the relationship between speaker and hearer. Its use presupposes the existence of *impersonal* criteria—the existence, independently of the preferences or attitudes of speaker and hearer, of standards of justice or generosity or duty. The particular link between the context of utterance and the force of the reason-giving which always holds in the case of expressions of personal preferences or desire is severed in the case of moral and other evaluative utterances.

This second characteristic of contemporary moral utterance and argument, when combined with the first, imparts a paradoxical air to contemporary moral disagreement. For if we attended solely to the first characteristic, to the way in which what at first appears to be argument relapses so quickly into unargued disagreement, we might conclude that there is nothing to such contemporary disagreements but a clash of antagonistic wills, each will determined by some set of arbitrary choices of its own. But this second characteristic, the use of expressions whose distinctive function in our language is to embody what purports to be an appeal to objective standards, suggests otherwise. For even if the surface appearance of argument is only a masquerade, the question remains "Why *this* masquerade?" What is it about rational argument which is so important that it is the nearly universal appearance assumed by those who engage in moral conflict? Does not this suggest that the practice of moral argument in our culture expresses at least an aspiration to be or to become rational in this area of our lives?

A third salient characteristic of contemporary moral debate is intimately related to the first two. It is easy to see that the different conceptually incommensurable premises of the rival arguments deployed in these debates have a wide variety of historical origins. The concept of justice in the first argument has its roots in Aristotle's account of the virtues; the second argument's genealogy runs through Bismarck and Clausewitz to Machiavelli; the concept of liberation in the third argument has shallow roots in Marx, deeper roots in Fichte. In the second debate a concept of rights which has Lockean antecedents is matched against a view of universalizability which is recognizably Kantian and an appeal to the moral law which is Thomist. In the third debate an argument which owes debts to T. H. Green and to Rousseau competes with one which has Adam Smith as a grandfather. This catalogue of great names is suggestive; but it may be misleading in two ways. The citing of individual names may lead us to underestimate the complexity of the history and the ancestry of such arguments; and it may lead us to look for that history and that ancestry only in the writings of philosophers and theorists instead of in those intricate bodies of theory and practice which constitute human cultures, the beliefs of which are articulated by philosophers and theorists only in a partial and selective manner. But the catalogue of names does suggest how wide and heterogeneous the variety of moral sources is from which we have inherited. The surface rhetoric of our culture is apt to speak complacently of moral pluralism in this connection, but the notion of pluralism is too imprecise. For it may equally well apply to an ordered dialogue of intersecting viewpoints and to an unharmonious melange of ill-assorted fragments. The suspicion—and for the moment it can only be a suspicion—that it is the latter with which we have to deal is heightened when we recognize that all those various concepts which inform our moral discourse were originally at home in larger totalities of theory and practice in which they enjoyed a role and function supplied by contexts of which they have now been deprived. Moreover the concepts we employ have in at least some cases changed their character in the past three hundred years; the evaluative expressions we use have changed their meaning. In the transition from the variety of contexts in which they were originally at home to our own contemporary culture "virtue" and "justice" and "piety" and "duty" and even "ought" have become other than they once were . . .

In the Homeric account of the virtues—and in heroic societies more generally—the exercise of a virtue exhibits qualities which are required for sustaining a social role and for exhibiting excellence in some well-marked area of social practice: to excel is to excel at war or in the games, as Achilles does, in sustaining a household, as Penelope does, in giving counsel in the assembly, as Nestor does, in the telling of a tale, as Homer himself does. When Aristotle speaks of excellence in human activity, he sometimes though not always, refers to some well-defined type of human practice: flute-playing, or war, or geometry. I am going to suggest that this notion of a particular type of practice as providing the arena in which the virtues are exhibited and in terms of which they are to receive their primary, if incomplete, definition is crucial to the whole enterprise of identifying a core concept of the virtues. I hasten to add two *caveats* however.

The first is to point out that my argument will not in any way imply that virtues are *only* exercised in the course of what I am calling practices. The second is to warn that I shall be using the word "practice" in a specially defined way which does not completely agree with current ordinary usage, including my own previous use of that word. What am I going to mean by it?

By "practice" I am going to mean any coherent and complex form of socially established cooperative human activity through which goods internal to that form of activity are realized in the course of trying to achieve those standards of excellence which are appropriate to, and partially definitive of, that form of activity, with the result that human powers to achieve excellence, and human conceptions of the ends and goods involved, are systematically extended. Tic-tac-toe is not an example of a practice in this sense, nor is throwing a football with skill; but the game of football is, and so is chess. Bricklaying is not a practice; architecture is. Planting turnips is not a practice; farming is. So are the enquiries of physics, chemistry and biology, and so is the work of the historian, and so are painting and music. In the ancient and medieval worlds the creation and sustaining of human communities—of households, cities, nations—is generally taken to be a practice in the sense in which I have defined it. Thus the range of practices is wide: arts, sciences, games, politics in the Aristotelian sense, the making and sustaining of family life, all fall under the concept. But the question of the precise range of practices is not at this stage of the first importance. Instead let me explain some of the key terms involved in my definition, beginning with the notion of goods internal to a practice.

Consider the example of a highly intelligent seven-year-old child whom I wish to teach to play chess, although the child has no particular desire to learn the game. The child does however have a very strong desire for candy and little chance of obtaining it. I therefore tell the child that if the child will play chess with me once a week I will give the child 50 cents worth of candy; moreover I tell the child that I will always play in such a way that it will be difficult, but not impossible, for the child to win and that, if the child wins, the child will receive an extra 50 cents worth of candy. Thus motivated the child plays and plays to win. Notice however that, so long as it is the candy alone which provides the child with a good reason for playing chess, the child has no reason not to cheat and every reason to cheat, provided he or she can do so successfully. But, so we may hope, there will come a time when the child will find in those goods specific to chess, in the achievement of a certain highly particular kind of analytical skill, strategic imagination and competitive intensity, a new set of reasons, reasons now not just for winning on a particular occasion, but for trying to excel in whatever way the game of chess demands. Now if the child cheats, he or she will be defeating not me, but himself or herself.

There are thus two kinds of good possibly to be gained by playing chess. On the one hand there are those goods externally and contingently attached to chess-playing and to other practices by the accidents of social circumstance—in the case of the imaginary child candy, in the case of real adults such goods as prestige, status and money. There are always alternative ways for achieving such goods, and their achievement is never to be had *only* by engaging in some particular kind of practice. On the other hand there are the goods internal to the practice of chess which cannot be had in any way but by playing chess or some other game of that specific kind. We call them internal for two reasons: first, as I have already suggested, because we can only specify them in terms of chess or some other game of that specific kind and by means of examples from such games (otherwise the meagerness of our vocabulary for speaking of such goods forces us into such devices as my own resort to writing of "a certain highly particular kind of"); and secondly because they can only be identified and recognized by the experience of participating in the practice in question. Those who lack the relevant experience are incompetent thereby as judges of internal goods. . . .

A practice involves standards of excellence and obedience to rules as well as the achievement of goods. To enter into a practice is to accept the authority of those standards and the inadequacy of my own performance as judged by them. It is to subject my own attitudes, choices, preferences and tastes to the standards which currently and partially define the practice. Practices of course . . . have a history: games, sciences and arts all have histories. Thus the standards are not themselves immune from criticism, but nonetheless we cannot be initiated into a practice without accepting the authority of the best standards realized so far. If, on starting to listen to music, I do not accept my own incapacity to judge correctly, I will never learn to hear, let alone to appreciate, Bartok's last quartets. If, on starting to play baseball, I do not accept that others know better than I when to throw a fast ball and when not, I will never learn to appreciate good pitching let alone to pitch. In the realm of practices the authority of both goods and standards operates in such a way as to rule out all subjectivist and emotivist analyses of judgment. De gustibus *est* disputandum.

We are now in a position to notice an important difference between what I have called internal and what I have called external goods. It is characteristic of what I have called external goods that when achieved they are always some individual's property and possession. Moreover characteristically they are such that the more someone has of them, the less there is for other people. This is sometimes necessarily the case, as with power and fame, and sometimes the case by reason of contingent circumstance as with money. External goods are therefore characteristically objects of competition in which there must be losers as well as winners. Internal goods are indeed the outcome of competition to excel, but it is characteristic of them that their achievement is good for the whole community who participate in the practice. So when Turner transformed the seascape in painting or W. G. Grace advanced the art of batting in cricket in a quite new way their achievement enriched the whole relevant community.

But what does all or any of this have to do with the concept of the virtues? It turns out that we are now in a position to formulate a first, even if partial and tentative definition of a virtue: *A virtue is an acquired human quality the possession and exercise of which tends to enable us to achieve those goods which are internal to practices and the lack of which effectively prevents us from achieving any such goods.* Later this definition will need amplification and amendment. But as a first approximation to an adequate definition it already illuminates the place of virtues in human life. For it is not difficult to show for a whole range of key virtues that without them the goods internal to practices are barred to us, but not just barred to us generally, barred in every particular way.

It belongs to the concept of a practice as I have outlined it—and as we are all familiar with it already in our actual lives, whether we are painters or physicists or quarterbacks or indeed just lovers of good painting or first-rate experiments or a well-thrown pass—that its goods can only be achieved by subordinating ourselves within the practice in our relationship to other practitioners. We have to learn to recognize what is due to whom; we have to be prepared to take whatever self-endangering risks are demanded along the way; and we have to listen carefully to what we are told about our own inadequacies and to reply with the same carefulness for the facts. In other words we have to accept as necessary components of any practice with internal goods and standards of excellence the virtues of justice, courage and honesty. For not to accept these, to be willing to cheat as our imagined child was willing to cheat in his or her early days at chess, so far bars us from achieving the standards of excellence or the goods internal to the practice that it renders the practice pointless except as a device for achieving external goods.

We can put the same point in another way. Every practice requires a certain kind of relationship between those who participate in it. Now the virtues are those goods by reference to which, whether we like it or not, we define our relationships to those other people with whom we share the kind of purposes and standards which inform practices. Consider an example of how reference to the virtues has to be made in certain kinds of human relationship. . . . If A, a professor, gives B and C the grades that their papers deserve, but grades D because he is attracted by D's blue eyes or is repelled by D's dandruff, he has defined his relationship to D differently from his relationship to the other members of the class, whether he wishes it or not. Justice requires that we treat others in respect of merit or desert according to uniform and impersonal standards; to depart from the standards of justice in some particular instance defines our relationship with the relevant person as in some way special or distinctive.

The case with courage is a little different. We hold courage to be a virtue because the care and concern for individuals, communities and causes which is so crucial to so much in practices requires the existence of such a virtue. If someone says that he cares for some individual, community or cause, but is unwilling to risk harm or danger on his, her or its own behalf, he puts in question the genuineness of his care and concern. Courage, the capacity to risk harm or danger to oneself, has its role in human life because of this connection with care and concern. This is not to say that a man cannot genuinely care and also be a coward. It is in part to say that a man who genuinely cares and has not the capacity for risking harm or danger has to define himself, both to himself and to others, as a coward.

I take it then that from the standpoint of those types of relationship without which practices cannot be sustained truthfulness, justice and courage—and perhaps some others—are genuine excellences, are virtues in light of which we have to characterize ourselves and others, whatever our private moral standpoint or our society's particular codes may be. For this recognition that we cannot escape the definition of our relationships in terms of such goods is perfectly compatible with the acknowledgment that different societies have and have had different codes of truthfulness, justice and courage. Lutheran pietists brought up their children to believe that one ought to tell the truth to everybody at all times, whatever the circumstances or consequences, and Kant was one of their children. Traditional Bantu parents brought up their children not to tell the truth to unknown strangers, since they believed that this could render the family vulnerable to witchcraft. In our culture many of us have been brought up not to tell the truth to elderly great-aunts who invite us to admire their new hats. But each of these codes embodies an acknowledgment of the virtue of truthfulness. So it is also with varying codes of justice and of courage.

Practices then might flourish in societies with very different codes; what they could not do is flourish in societies in which the virtues were not valued, although institutions and technical skills serving unified purposes might well continue to flourish. . . . For the kind of cooperation, the kind of recognition of authority and of achievement, the kind of respect for standards and the kind of risk-taking which are characteristically involved in practices demand for example fairness in judging oneself and others . . . and willingness to trust the judgments of those whose achievement in the practice give them an authority to judge which presupposes fairness and truthfulness in those judgments, and from time to time the taking of self-endangering and even achievement-endangering risks. It is no part of my thesis that great violinists cannot be vicious or great chess-players mean-spirited. Where the virtues are required, the vices also may flourish. It is just that the vicious and mean-spirited necessarily rely on the virtues of others for the practices in which they engage to flourish and also deny themselves the experience of achieving those internal goods which may reward even not very good chess-players and violinists.

To situate the virtues any further within practices it is necessary now to clarify a little further the nature of a practice by drawing two important contrasts. The discussion so far I hope makes it clear that a practice, in the sense intended, is never just a set of technical skills, even when directed towards some unified purpose and even if the exercise of those skills can on occasion be valued or enjoyed for their own sake. What is distinctive in a practice is in part the way in which conceptions of the relevant goods and ends which the technical skills serve—and every practice does require the exercise of technical skills—are transformed and enriched by these extensions of human powers and by that regard for its own internal goods which are partially definitive of each particular practice or type of practice. Practices never have a goal or goals fixed for all time—painting has no such goal nor has physics—but the goals themselves are transmuted by the history of the activity. It therefore turns out not to be accidental that every practice has its own history and a history which is more and other than that of the improvement of the relevant technical skills. This historical dimension is crucial in relation to the virtues.

To enter into a practice is to enter into a relationship not only with its contemporary practitioners, but also with those who have preceded us in the practice, particularly those whose achievements extended the reach of the practice to its present point. It is thus the achievement, and *a fortiori* the authority, of a tradition which I then confront and from which I have to learn. And for this learning and the relationship to the past which it embodies the virtues of justice, courage and truthfulness are prerequisite in precisely the same way and for precisely the same reasons as they are in sustaining present relationships within practices.

It is not only of course with sets of technical skills that practices ought to be contrasted. Practices must not be confused with institutions. Chess, physics and medicine are practices; chess clubs, laboratories, universities and hospitals are institutions. Institutions are characteristically and necessarily concerned with what I have called external goods. They are involved in acquiring money and other material goods; they are structures in terms of power and status, and they distribute money, power and status as rewards. Nor could they do otherwise if they are to sustain not only themselves, but also the practice of which they are the bearers. For no practices can survive for any length of time unsustained by institutions. Indeed so intimate is the relationship of practices to institutions—and consequently of the goods external to the goods internal to the practices in question—that institutions and practices characteristically form a single causal order in which the ideals and the creativity of the practice are always vulnerable to the acquisitiveness of the institution, in which the cooperative care for common goods of the practice is always vulnerable to the competitiveness of the institution. In this context the essential function of the virtues is clear. Without them, without justice, courage and truthfulness, practices could not resist the corrupting power of institutions.

Yet if institutions do have corrupting power, the making and sustaining of forms of human community—and therefore of institutions—itself has all the characteristics of a practice, and moreover of a practice which stands in a peculiarly close relationship to the exercise of the virtues in two important ways. The exercise of the virtues is itself apt to require a highly determinate attitude to social and political issues; and it is always with some particular community with its own specific institutional forms that we learn or fail to learn to exercise the virtues. There is of course a crucial difference between the way in which the relationship between moral character and political community is envisaged from the standpoint of the type of ancient and medieval tradition of the virtues. . . . For liberal individualism a community is simply an arena in which individuals each pursue their own self-chosen conception of the good life, and political institutions exist to provide that degree of order which makes such self-determined activity possible. Government and law are, or ought to be, neutral between rival conceptions of the good life for man, and hence, although it is the task of government to promote law-abidingness, it is on liberal view no part of the legitimate function of government to inculcate any one moral outlook.

By contrast, on the particular ancient and medieval view . . . political community not only requires the exercise of the virtues for its own sustenance, but it is one of the tasks of parental authority to make children grow up so as to be virtuous adults. The classical statement of this analogy is by Socrates in the *Crito*. It does not of course follow from an acceptance of the Socratic view of political community and political authority that we ought to assign to the modern state the moral function which Socrates assigned to the city and its laws. Indeed the power of the liberal individualist standpoint partly derives from the evident fact that the modern state is indeed totally unfitted to act as moral educator of any community. But the history of how the modern state emerged is of course itself a moral history. If my account of the complex relationship of virtues to practices and the institutions is correct, it follows that we shall be unable to write a true history of practices and institutions unless that history is also one of the virtues and vices. For the ability of a practice to retain its integrity will depend on the way in which the virtues can be and are exercised in sustaining the institutional forms which are the social bearers of the practice. The integrity of a practice causally requires the exercise of the virtues by at least some of the individuals who embody it in their activities and conversely the corruption of institutions is always in part at least an effect of the vices. . . .

I have defined the virtues partly in terms of their place in practices. But surely, it may be suggested, some practices—that is, some coherent human activities which answer to the description of what I have called practice—are evil. So in discussions by some moral philosophers of this type of account of the virtues it has been suggested that torture and sado-masochistic sexual activities might be examples of practices. But how can a disposition be a virtue if it is the kind of disposition which sustains practices and some practices issue in evil? My answer to his objection falls into two parts.

First I want to allow that there *may* be practices—in the sense in which I understand the concept—which simply *are* evil. I am far from convinced that there are, and I do not in fact believe that either torture or sado-masochistic sexuality answer to the description of a practice which my account of the virtues employs. But I do not want to rest my case on this lack of conviction, especially since it is plain that as a matter of contingent fact many types of practice may on particular occasions be productive of evil. For the range of practices includes the arts, the sciences and certain types of intellectual and athletic game. And it is at once obvious that any of these may under certain conditions be a source of evil: the desire to excel and to win can corrupt, a man may be so engrossed by his painting that he neglects his family, what was initially an honorable resort to war can issue in savage cruelty. But what follows from this?

It certainly is not the case that my account entails *either* that we ought to excuse or condone such evils *or* that whatever flows from a virtue is right. I do have to allow that courage sometimes sustains injustice, that loyalty has been known to strengthen a murderous aggressor and that generosity has sometimes weakened the capacity to do good. . . . That the virtues need initially to be defined and explained with reference to the notion of a practice thus in no way entails approval of all practices in all circumstances. That the virtues—as the objection itself presupposed—*are* defined not in terms of good and right practices, but of practices, does not entail or imply that practices as actually carried through at particular times and places do not stand in need of moral criticism. And the resources for such criticism are not lacking. There is in the first place no inconsistency in appealing to the requirements of a virtue to criticize a practice. Justice may be initially defined as a disposition which in its particular way is necessary to sustain practices; it does not follow that in pursuing the requirement of a practice violations of justice are not to be condemned. Moreover . . . a morality of virtues requires as its counterpart a conception of moral law. Its requirements too have to be met by practices. But, it may be asked, does not all this imply that more needs to be said about the place of practices in some larger moral context? Does not this at least suggest that there is more to the core concept of a virtue than can be spelled out in terms of practices? I have after all emphasized that the scope of any virtue in human life extends beyond the practices in terms of which it is initially defined. What then is the place of the virtues in the larger arenas of human life?

Any contemporary attempt to envisage each human life as a whole, as a unity, whose character provides the virtues with an adequate *telos* encounters two different kinds of obstacle, one social and one philosophical. The social obstacles derive from the way in which modernity partitions each human life into a variety of segments, each with its own norms and modes of behavior. So work is divided from leisure, private life from public, the corporate from the personal. So both childhood and old age have been wrenched away from the rest of human life and made over into distinct realms. And all these separations have been achieved so that it is the distinctiveness of each and not the unity of the life of the individual who passes through those parts in terms of which we are taught to think and to feel.

The philosophical obstacles derive from two distinct tendencies, one chiefly, though not only, domesticated in analytical philosophy and one at home in both sociological theory and in existentialism. The former is the tendency to think atomistically about human action and to analyze complex actions and transactions in terms of simple components. Hence the recurrence in more than one context of the notion of "a basic action." That particular actions derive their character as parts of larger wholes is a point of view alien to our dominant ways of thinking and yet one which it is necessary at least to consider if we are to begin to understand how a life may be more than a sequence of individual actions and episodes.

Equally the unity of a human life becomes invisible to us when a sharp separation is made either between the individual and the roles that he or she plays—a separation characteristic not only of Sartre's existentialism, but also of the sociological theory of Ralf Dahrendorf—or between the different role— and quasi-role—enactments of an individual life so that life comes to appear as nothing but a series of unconnected episodes. . . .

For a self separated from its roles in the Sartrian mode loses that arena of social relationships in which the Aristotelian virtues function if they function at all. The patterns of a virtuous life would fall under those condemnations of conventionality which Sartre put into the mouth of Antoine Roquentin in *La Nausée* and which he uttered in his own person in *L'Etre et le néant*. Indeed the self's refusal of the inauthenticity of conventionalized social relationships becomes what integrity is diminished into in Sartre's account.

At the same time the liquidation of the self into a set of demarcated areas of role-playing allows no scope for the exercise of dispositions which could genuinely be accounted virtues in any sense remotely Aristotelian. For a virtue is not a disposition that makes for success only in some one particular type of situation. What are spoken of as the virtues of a good committee man or of a good administrator or of a gambler or a pool hustler are professional skills professionally deployed in those situations where they can be effective, not virtues. Someone who genuinely possesses a virtue can be expected to manifest it in very different types of situations, many of them situations where the practice of a virtue cannot be expected to be effective in the way that we expect a professional skill to be. Hector exhibited one and the same courage in his parting from Andromache and on the battlefield with Achilles; Eleanor Marx exhibited one and the same compassion in her relationship with her father, in her work with trade unionists and in her entanglement with Aveling. And the unity of a virtue in someone's life is intelligible only as a characteristic of a unitary life, a life that can be conceived and evaluated as a whole. Hence just as in the discussion of the changes in and fragmentation of morality accompanied the rise of modernity in the earlier parts of this book, each stage in the emergence of the characteristically modern views of the moral judgment was accompanied by a corresponding stage in the emergence of the characteristically modern conceptions of selfhood; so now, in defining the particular pre-modern concept of the virtues with which I have been pre-occupied, it has become necessary to say something of the concomitant concept of selfhood, a concept of a self whose unity resides in the unity of a narrative which links birth to life to death as narrative beginning to middle to end. . . .

It is a conceptual commonplace, both for philosophers and for ordinary agents, that one and the same segment of human behavior may be correctly characterized in a number of different ways. To the question "What is he doing?" the answers may with equal truth and appropriateness be "Digging," "Gardening," "Taking exercise," "Preparing for winter" or "Pleasing his wife." Some of these answers will characterize the agent's intentions, other unintended consequences of his actions, and of these unintended consequences some may be such that the agent is aware of them and others not. What is important to notice immediately is that any answer to the questions of how we are to understand or to explain a given segment of behavior will presuppose some prior answer to the question of how these different correct answers to the question "What is he doing?" are related to each other. For if someone's primary intention is to put the garden in order before the winter and it is only incidentally the case that in so doing he is taking exercise and pleasing his wife, we have one type of behavior to be explained; but if the agent's primary intention is to please his wife by taking exercise, we have quite another type of behavior to be explained and we will have to look in a different direction for understanding and explanation. . . .

Where intentions are concerned, we need to know which intention or intentions were primary, that is to say, of which it is the case that, had the agent intended otherwise, he would not have performed that action. Thus if we know that a man is gardening with the self-avowed purposes of healthful exercise and of pleasing his wife, we do not yet know how to understand what he is doing until we know the answer to such questions as whether he would continue gardening if he continued to believe that gardening was healthful exercise, but discovered that his gardening no longer pleased his wife, *and* whether he would continue gardening, if he ceased to believe that gardening was healthful exercise, but continued to believe that it pleased his wife, *and* whether he would continue gardening if he changed his beliefs on both points. That is to say, we need to know both what certain of his beliefs are and which of them are causally effective; and, that is to say, we need to know whether certain contrary-to-fact hypothetical statements are true or false. And until we know this, we shall not know how to characterize correctly what the agent is doing. . . .

Consider what the argument so far implies about the interrelationships of the intentional, the social and the historical. We identify a particular action only by invoking two kinds of context, implicitly if not explicitly. We place the agent's intentions, I have suggested, in causal and temporal order with reference to their role in his or her history, and we also place them with reference to their role in the history of the setting or settings to which they belong. In doing this, in determining what causal efficacy the agent's intentions had in one or more directions, and how his short-term intentions succeeded or failed to be constitutive of long-term intentions, we ourselves write a further part of these histories. Narrative history of a certain kind turns out to be the basic and essential genre for the characterization of human actions.

At the beginning . . . I argued that in successfully identifying and understanding what someone else is doing we always move towards placing a particular episode in the context of a set of narrative histories, histories both of the individuals concerned and of the settings in which they act and suffer. It is now becoming clear that we render the actions of others intelligible in this way because action itself has a basically historical character. It is because we all live out narratives in our lives and because we understand our own lives in terms of the narratives that we live out that the form of narrative is appropriate for understanding the actions of others. Stories are lived before they are told—except in the case of fiction. . . .

A central thesis then begins to emerge: man is in his action and practice, as well as in his fiction, essentially a story-telling animal. He is not essentially, but becomes through his history, a teller of stories that aspire to truth. But the key question for men is not about their own authorship; I can only answer the question "What am I to do?" if I can answer the prior question "Of what story or stories do I find myself a part?" We enter human society, that is, with one or more imputed characters—roles into which we have been drafted—and we have to learn what they are in order to be able to understand how others respond to us and how our responses to them are apt to be construed. It is through hearing stories about wicked stepmothers, lost children, good but misguided kings, wolves that suckle twin boys, youngest sons who receive no inheritance but must make their way in the world and eldest sons who waste their inheritance on riotous living and go into exile to live with the swine, that children learn or mislearn both what a child and what a parent is, what the cast of characters may be in the drama into which they have been born and what the ways of the world are. Deprive children of stories and you leave them unscripted, anxious stutterers in their actions as in their words. Hence there is no way to give us an understanding of any society, including our own, except through the stock of stories which constitute its initial dramatic resources. Mythology, in its original sense, is at the heart of things. Vico was right and so was Joyce. And so too of course is that moral tradition from heroic society to its medieval heirs according to which the telling of stories has a key part in educating us into the virtues. . . .

What the narrative concept of selfhood requires is . . . twofold. On the one hand, I am what I may justifiably be taken by others to be in the course of living out a story that runs from my birth to my death; I am the *subject* of a history that is my own and no one else's, that has its own peculiar meaning. When someone complains—as do some of those who attempt or commit suicide—that his or her life is meaningless, he or she is often and perhaps characteristically complaining that the narrative of their life has become unintelligible to them, that it lacks any point, any movement towards a climax or a *telos*. Hence the point of doing any one thing rather than another at crucial junctures in their lives seems to such person to have been lost.

To be the subject of a narrative that runs from one's birth to one's death is . . . to be accountable for the actions and experiences which compose a narratable life. It is, that is, to be open to being asked to give a certain kind of account of what one did or what happened to one or what one witnessed at any earlier point in one's life than the time at which the question is posed. Of course someone may have forgotten or suffered brain damage or simply not attended sufficiently at the relevant time to be able to give the relevant account. But to say of someone under some one description ("The prisoner of the Chateau d'If") that he is the same person as someone characterized quite differently ("The Count of Monte Cristo") is precisely to say that it makes sense to ask him to give an intelligible narrative account enabling us to understand how he could at different times and different places be one and the same person and yet be so differently characterized. Thus personal identity is just that identity presupposed by the unity of the character which the unity of a narrative requires. Without such unity there would not be subjects of whom stories could be told.

The other aspect of narrative selfhood is correlative: I am not only accountable, I am one who can always ask others for an account, who can put others to the question. I am part of their story, as they are part of mine. The narrative of any one life is part of an interlocking set of narratives. Moreover this asking for and giving of accounts itself plays an important part in constituting narratives. Asking you what you did and why, saying what I did and why, pondering the differences between your account of what I did and my account of what I did, and *vice versa*, these are essential constituents of all but the very simplest and barest of narratives. Thus without the accountability of the self those trains of events that constitute all but the simplest and barest of narratives could not occur; and without that same accountability narratives would lack that continuity required to make both them and the actions that constitute them intelligible. . . .

It is now possible to return to the question from which this enquiry into the nature of human action and identity started: In what does the unity of an individual life consist? The answer is that its unity is the unity of a narrative embodied in a single life. To ask "What is the good for me?" is to ask how best I might live out that unity and bring it to completion. To ask "What is the good for man?" is to ask what all answers to the former question must have in common. But now it is important to emphasize that it is the systematic asking of these two questions and the attempt to answer them in deed as well as in word which provide the moral life with its unity. The unity of a human life is the unity of a narrative quest. Quests sometimes fail, are frustrated, abandoned or dissipated into distractions; and human lives may in all these ways also fail. But the only criteria for success or failure in a human life as a whole are the criteria of success or failure in a narrated or to-be-narrated quest. A quest for what?

Two key features of the medieval conception of a quest need to be recalled. The first is that without some at least partly determinate conception of the final *telos* there could not be any beginning to a quest. Some conception of the good for man is required. Whence is such a conception to be drawn? Precisely from those questions which led us to attempt to transcend that limited conception of the virtues which is available in and through practices. It is in looking for a conception of *the* good which will enable us to order other goods, for a conception of *the* good which will enable us to extend our understanding of the purpose and content of the virtues, for a conception of *the* good which will enable us to understand the place of integrity and constancy in life, that we initially define the kind of life which is a quest for the good. But secondly it is clear the medieval conception of a quest is not at all that of a search for something already adequately characterized, as miners search for gold or geologists for oil. It is in the course of the quest and only through encountering and coping with the various particular harms, dangers, temptations and distractions which provide any quest with its episodes and incidents that the goal of the quest is finally to be understood. A quest is always an education both as to the character of that which is sought and in self-knowledge.

The virtues therefore are to be understood as those dispositions which will not only sustain practices and enable us to achieve the goods internal to practices, but which will also sustain us in the relevant kind of quest for the good, by enabling us to overcome the harms, dangers, temptations and distractions which we encounter, and which will furnish us with increasing self-knowledge and increasing knowledge of the good. The catalogue of the virtues will therefore include the virtues required to sustain the kind of households and the kind of political communities in which men and women can seek for the good together and the virtues necessary for philosophical enquiry about the character of the good. We have then arrived at a provisional conclusion about the good life for man: the good life for man is the life spent in seeking for the good life for man, and the virtues necessary for the seeking are those which will enable us to understand what more and what else the good life for man is. We have also completed the second stage in our account of the virtues, by situating them in relation to the good life for man and not only in relation to practices. But our enquiry requires a third stage.

For I am never able to seek for the good or exercise the virtues only *qua* individual. This is partly because what it is to live the good life concretely varies from circumstance to circumstance even when it is one and the same conception of the good life and one and the same set of virtues which are being embodied in a human life. What the good life is for a fifth-century Athenian general will not be the same as what it was for a medieval nun or a seventeenth-century farmer. But it is not just that different individuals live in different social circumstances; it is also that we all approach our own circumstances as bearers of a particular social identity. I am someone's son or daughter, someone else's cousin or uncle; I am a citizen of this or that city, a member of this or that guild or profession; I belong to this clan, that tribe, this nation. Hence what is good for me has to be the good for one who inhabits these roles. As such, I inherit from the past of my family, my city, my tribe, my nation, a variety of debts, inheritances, rightful expectations and obligations. These constitute the given of my life, my moral starting point. This is in part what gives my life its own moral particularity.

This thought is likely to appear alien and even surprising from the standpoint of modern individualism. From the standpoint of individualism I am what I myself choose to be. I can always, if I wish to, put in question what are taken to be the merely contingent social features of my existence. I may biologically be my father's son; but I cannot be held responsible for what he did unless I choose implicitly or explicitly to assume such responsibility. I may legally be a citizen of a certain country; but I cannot be held responsible for what my country does or has done unless I choose implicitly or explicitly to assume such responsibility. Such individualism is expressed by those modern Americans who deny any responsibility for the effects of slavery upon black Americans, saying "I never owned any slaves." It is more subtly the standpoint of those other modern Americans who accept a nicely calculated responsibility for such effects measured precisely by the benefits they themselves as individuals have indirectly received from slavery. In both cases "being an American" is not in itself taken to be part of the moral identity of the individual. And of course there is nothing peculiar to modern Americans in this attitude: the Englishman who says, "*I* never did any wrong to Ireland; why bring up that old history as though it had something to do with *me?*" or the young German who believes that being born after 1945 means that what Nazis did to Jews has no moral relevance to his relationship to his Jewish contemporaries, exhibit the same attitude, that according to which the self is detachable from its social and historical roles and statuses. And the self so detached is of course a self very much at home in either Sartre's or Goffman's perspective, a self that can have no history. The contrast with the narrative view of the self is clear. For the story of my life is always embedded in the story of those communities from which I derive my identity. I am born with a past; and to try to cut myself off from that past, in the individualist mode, is to deform my present relationships. The possession of an historical identity and the possession of a social identity coincide. Notice that rebellion against my identity is always one possible mode of expressing it.

Notice also that the fact that the self has to find its moral identity in and through its membership in communities such as those of the family, the neighborhood, the city and the tribe does not entail that the self has to accept the moral *limitations* of the particularity of those forms of community. Without those moral particularities to begin from there would never be anywhere to begin; but it is in moving forward from such particularity that the search for the good, for the universal, consists. Yet particularity can never be simply left behind or obliterated. The notion of escaping from it into a realm of entirely universal maxims which belong to man as such, whether in its eighteenth-century Kantian form or in the presentation of some modern analytical moral philosophies, is an illusion and an illusion with painful consequences. When men and women identify what are in fact their partial and particular causes too easily and too completely with the cause of some universal principle, they usually behave worse than they would otherwise do.

What I am, therefore, is in key part what I inherit, a specific past that is present to some degree in my present. I find myself part of a history and that is generally to say, whether I like it or not, whether I recognize it or not, one of the bearers of a tradition. It was important when I characterized the concept of a practice to notice that practices always have histories and that at any given moment what a practice is depends on a mode of understanding it which has been transmitted often through many generations. And thus, insofar as the virtues sustain the relationships required for practices, they have to sustain relationships to the past—and to the future—as well as in the present. But the traditions through which particular practices are transmitted and reshaped never exist in isolation for larger social traditions. What constitutes such traditions?

We are apt to be misled here by the ideological uses to which the concept of a tradition has been put by conservative political theorists. Characteristically such theorists have followed Burke in contrasting tradition with reason and the stability of tradition with conflict. Both contrasts obfuscate. For all reasoning takes place within the context of some traditional mode of thought, transcending through criticism and invention the limitations of what had hitherto been reasoned in that tradition; this is as true of modern physics as of medieval logic. Moreover, when a tradition is in good order it is always partially constituted by an argument about the goods the pursuit of which gives to that tradition its particular point and purpose.

So when an institution—a university, say, or a farm, or a hospital— is the bearer of a tradition of practice or practices, its common life will be partly, but in a centrally important way, constituted by a continuous argument as to what a university is and ought to be or what good farming is or what good medicine is. Traditions, when vital, embody continuities of conflict. Indeed when a tradition becomes Burkean, it is always dying or dead. . . .

A living tradition then is an historically extended, socially embodied argument, and an argument precisely in part about the goods which constitute that tradition. Within a tradition the pursuit of goods extends through generations, sometimes through many generations. Hence the individual's search for his or her good is generally and characteristically conducted within a context defined by those traditions of which the individual's life is a part, and this is true both of those goods which are internal to practices and of the goods of a single life. Once again the narrative phenomenon of embedding is crucial: the history of a practice in our time is generally and characteristically embedded in and made intelligible in terms of the larger and longer history of the tradition through which the practice in its present form was conveyed to us; the history of each of our own lives is generally and characteristically embedded in and made intelligible in terms of the larger and longer histories of a number of traditions. I have to say "generally and characteristically" rather than "always," for traditions decay, disintegrate and disappear. What then sustains and strengthens traditions? What weakens and destroys them?

The answer in key part is: the exercise or the lack of exercise of the relevant virtues. The virtues find their point and purpose not only in sustaining those relationships necessary if the variety of goods internal to practices are to be achieved and not only in sustaining the form of the individual life in which that individual may seek out his or her good as the good of his or her whole life, but also in sustaining those traditions which provide both practices and individual lives with their necessary historical context. Lack of justice, lack of truthfulness, lack of courage, lack of the relevant intellectual virtues—these corrupt traditions, just as they do those institutions and practices which derive their life from the traditions of which they are contemporary embodiments. To recognize this is of course also to recognize the existence of an additional virtue, one whose importance is perhaps most obvious when it is least present, the virtue of having an adequate sense of the traditions to which one belongs or which confront one. This virtue is not to be confused with any form of conservative antiquarianism; I am not praising those who choose the conventional conservative role of *laudator temporis acti*. It is rather the case that an adequate sense of tradition manifests itself in a grasp of those future possibilities which the past has made available to the present. Living traditions, just because they continue a not-yet-completed narrative, confront a future whose determinate and determinable character, so far as it possesses any, derives from the past. . . .

25

Virtues and Vices

Philippa Foot is Griffin Professor of Philosophy at the University of California, Los Angeles. Formerly a fellow and tutor of Somerville College, Oxford, and presently an honorary fellow there, she has written a number of articles on moral philosophy, some of which are included in her book *Virtues and Vices and Other Essays in Moral Philosophy* (1978). She is also editor of *Theories of Ethics* (1967).

I

. . . [I]t seems clear that virtues are, in some general way, beneficial. Human beings do not get on well without them. Nobody can get on well if he lacks courage, and does not have some measure of temperance and wisdom, while communities where justice and charity are lacking are apt to be wretched places to live, as Russia was under the Stalinist terror, or Sicily under the Mafia. But now we must ask to whom the benefit goes, whether to the man who has the virtue or rather to those who have to do with him? In the case of some of the virtues the answer seems clear. Courage, temperance and wisdom benefit both the man who has these dispositions and other people as well; and moral failings such as pride, vanity, worldliness, and avarice harm both their possessor and others, though chiefly perhaps the former. But what about the virtues of charity and justice? These are directly concerned with the welfare of others, and with what is owed to them; and since each may require sacrifice of interest on the part of the virtuous man both may seem to be deleterious to their possessor and beneficial to others. Whether in fact it is so has, of course, been a matter of controversy since Plato's time or earlier. It is a reasonable opinion that on the whole a man is better off for being charitable and just, but this is not to say that circumstances may not arise in which he will have to sacrifice everything for charity or justice.

Nor is this the only problem about the relation between virtue and human good. For one very difficult question concerns the relation between justice and

From Philippa Foot, "Virtues and Vices," in *Virtues and Vices and Other Essays in Moral Philosophy*, 2–18. Copyright 1978, Philippa Foot. Reprinted by permission of the author.

the common good. Justice, in the wide sense in which it is understood in discussions of the cardinal virtues, and in this paper, has to do with that to which someone has a right—that which he is owed in respect of non-interference and positive service—and rights may stand in the way of the pursuit of the common good. Or so at least it seems to those who reject utilitarian doctrines. This dispute cannot be settled here, but I shall treat justice as a virtue independent of charity, and standing as a possible limit on the scope of that virtue.

Let us say then, leaving unsolved problems behind us, that virtues are in general beneficial characteristics, and indeed ones that a human being needs to have, for his own sake and that of his fellows. This will not, however, take us far towards a definition of a virtue, since there are many other qualities of a man that may be similarly beneficial, as for instance bodily characteristics such as health and physical strength, and mental powers such as those of memory and concentration. What is it, we must ask, that differentiates virtues from such things?

As a first approximation to an answer we might say that while health and strength are excellences of the body, and memory and concentration of the mind, it is the will that is good in a man of virtue. But this suggestion is worth only as much as the explanation that follows it. What might we mean by saying that virtue belongs to the will?

In the first place we observe that it is primarily by his intentions that a man's moral dispositions are judged. If he does something unintentionally, this is usually irrelevant to our estimate of his virtue. But of course this thesis must be qualified, because failures in performance rather than intention may show a lack of virtue. This will be so when, for instance, one man brings harm to another without realizing he is doing it, but where his ignorance is itself culpable. Sometimes in such cases there will be a previous act or omission to which we can point as the source of the ignorance. Charity requires that we take care to find out how to render assistance where we are likely to be called on to do so, and thus, for example, it is contrary to charity to fail to find out about elementary first aid. But in an interesting class of cases in which it seems again to be performance rather than intention that counts in judging a man's virtue there is no possibility of shifting the judgement to previous intention. For sometimes one man succeeds where another fails not because there is some specific difference in their previous conduct but rather because his heart lies in a different place; and the disposition of the heart is part of virtue.

Thus it seems right to attribute a kind of moral failing to some deeply discouraging and debilitating people who say, without lying, that they mean to be helpful; and on the other side to see virtue *par excellence* in one who is prompt and resourceful in doing good. In his novel *A Single Pebble* John Hersey describes such a man, speaking of a rescue in a swift flowing river:

> It was the head tracker's marvellous swift response that captured my admiration at first, his split second solicitousness when he heard a cry of pain, his finding in mid-air, as it were, the only way to save the injured boy. But there was more to it

than that. His action, which could not have been mulled over in his mind, showed a deep, instinctive love of life, a compassion, an optimism, which made me feel very good . . .

What this suggests is that a man's virtue may be judged by his innermost desires as well as by his intentions; and this fits with our idea that a virtue such as generosity lies as much in someone's attitudes as in his actions. Pleasure in the good fortune of others is, one thinks, the sign of a generous spirit; and small reactions of pleasure and displeasure often the surest signs of a man's moral disposition.

None of this shows that it is wrong to think of virtues as belonging to the will; what it does show is that 'will' must here be understood in its widest sense, to cover what is wished for as well as what is sought.

A different set of considerations will, however, force us to give up any simple statement about the relation between virtue and will, and these considerations have to do with the virtue of wisdom. Practical wisdom, we said, was counted by Aristotle among the intellectual virtues, and while our *wisdom* is not quite the same as *phronēsis* or *prudentia* it too might seem to belong to the intellect rather than the will. Is not wisdom a matter of knowledge, and how can knowledge be a matter of intention or desire? The answer is that it isn't, so that there is good reason for thinking of wisdom as an intellectual virtue. But on the other hand wisdom has special connexions with the will, meeting it at more than one point.

In order to get this rather complex picture in focus we must pause for a little and ask what it is that we ourselves understand by wisdom: what the wise man knows and what he does. Wisdom, as I see it, has two parts. In the first place the wise man knows the means to certain good ends; and secondly he knows how much particular ends are worth. Wisdom in its first part is relatively easy to understand. It seems that there are some ends belonging to human life in general rather than to particular skills such as medicine or boatbuilding, ends having to do with such matters as friendship, marriage, the bringing up of children, or the choice of ways of life; and it seems that knowledge of how to act well in these matters belongs to some people but not to others. We call those who have this knowledge wise, while those who do not have it are seen as lacking wisdom. So, as both Aristotle and Aquinas insisted, wisdom is to be contrasted with cleverness because cleverness is the ability to take the right steps to any end, whereas wisdom is related only to good ends and to human life in general rather than to the ends of particular arts.

Moreover, we should add, there belongs to wisdom only that part of knowledge which is within the reach of any ordinary adult human being; knowledge that can be acquired only by someone who is clever or who has access to special training is not counted as part of wisdom, and would not be so counted even if it could serve the ends that wisdom serves. It is therefore quite wrong to suggest that wisdom cannot be a moral virtue because virtue must be within the reach of anyone who really wants it and some people are too stupid to be anything but ignorant even about the most fundamental matters of human life. Some people are wise without being at all clever or well informed: they make good decisions and they know, as we say, "what's what."

In short wisdom, in what we called its first part, is connected with the will in the following ways. To begin with it presupposes good ends: the man who is wise does not merely know *how* to do good things such as looking after his children well, or strengthening someone in trouble, but must also want to do them. And then wisdom, in so far as it consists of knowledge which anyone can gain in the course of an ordinary life, is available to anyone who really wants it. As Aquinas put it, it belongs "to a power under the direction of the will."[1]

The second part of wisdom, which has to do with values, is much harder to describe, because here we meet ideas which are curiously elusive, such as the thought that some pursuits are more worthwhile than others, and some matters trivial and some important in human life. Since it makes good sense to say that most men waste a lot of their lives in ardent pursuit of what is trivial and unimportant it is not possible to explain the important and the trivial in terms of the amount of attention given to different subjects by the average man. But I have never seen, or been able to think out, a true account of this matter, and I believe that a complete account of wisdom, and of certain other virtues and vices must wait until this gap can be filled. What we can see is that one of the things a wise man knows and a foolish man does not is that such things as social position, and wealth, and the good opinion of the world, are too dearly bought at the cost of health or friendship or family ties. So we may say that a man who lacks wisdom "has false values," and that vices such as vanity and worldliness and avarice are contrary to wisdom in a special way. There is always an element of false judgement about these vices, since the man who is vain for instance sees admiration as more important than it is, while the worldly man is apt to see the good life as one of wealth and power. Adapting Aristotle's distinction between the weak-willed man (the akratēs) who follows pleasure though he knows, in some sense, that he should not, and the licentious man (the akolastos) who sees the life of pleasure as the good life,[2] we may say that moral failings such as these are never purely "akratic." It is true that a man may criticize himself for his worldliness or vanity or love of money, but then it is his values that are the subject of his criticism.

Wisdom in this second part is, therefore, partly to be described in terms of apprehension, and even judgement, but since it has to do with a man's attachments it also characterizes his will.

The idea that virtues belong to the will, and that this helps to distinguish them from such things as bodily strength or intellectual ability has, then, survived the consideration of the virtue of wisdom, albeit in a fairly complex and slightly attenuated form. And we shall find this idea useful again if we turn to another important distinction that must be made, namely that between virtues and other practical excellences such as arts and skills.

Aristotle has sometimes been accused, for instance by von Wright, of failing to see how different virtues are from arts or skills,[3] but in fact one finds, among the many things that Aristotle and Aquinas say about this difference, the observation that seems to go to the heart of the matter. In the matter of arts and skills, they say, voluntary error is preferable to involuntary error, while in the matter of virtues (what we call virtues) it is the reverse.[4] The last part of the thesis is actually rather hard to interpret, because it is not clear what is meant by the idea of involuntary viciousness. But we can leave this aside and still have all we need in order to distinguish arts or skills from virtues. If we think, for instance, of someone who deliberately makes a spelling mistake (perhaps when writing on the blackboard in order to explain this particular point) we see that this does not in any way count against his skill as a speller: "I did it deliberately" rebuts an accusation of this kind. And what we can say without running into any difficulties is that there is no comparable rebuttal in the case of an accusation relating to lack of virtue. If a man acts unjustly or uncharitably, or in a cowardly or intemperate manner, "I did it deliberately" cannot on any interpretation lead to exculpation. So, we may say, a virtue is not, like a skill or an art, a mere capacity: it must actually engage the will.

II

I shall now turn to another thesis about the virtues, which I might express by saying that they are *corrective*, each one standing at a point at which there is some temptation to be resisted or deficiency of motivation to be made good. As Aristotle put it, virtues are about what is difficult for men, and I want to see in what sense this is true, and then to consider a problem in Kant's moral philosophy in the light of what has been said.

Let us first think about courage and temperance. Aquinas contrasted these virtues with justice in the following respect. Justice was concerned with operation, and courage and temperance with passions.[5] What he meant by this seems to have been, primarily, that the man of courage does not fear immoderately nor the man of temperance have immoderate desires for pleasure, and that there was no corresponding moderation of a passion implied in the idea of justice. This particular account of courage and temperance might be disputed on the ground that a man's courage is measured by his action and not by anything as uncontrollable as fear; and similarly that the temperate man who must on occasion refuse pleasures need not *desire* them any less than the intemperate man. Be that as it may (and something will be said about it later) it is obviously true that courage and temperance have to do with particular springs of action as justice does not. Almost any desire can lead a man to act unjustly, not even excluding the desire to help a friend or to save a life, whereas a cowardly act must be motivated by fear or a desire for safety, an act of intemperance by a desire for pleasure, perhaps even for a particular range of pleasures such as those of eating or drinking or sex. And now, going back to the idea of virtues as correctives, one may say that it is only because fear and the desire for pleasure often operate as temptations that courage and temperance exist as virtues at all. As things are we often want to run away not only where that is the right thing to do, but also where we should stand firm; and we want pleasure not only where we should seek pleasure but also where we should not. If human nature had been different there would have been no need of a corrective disposition in either place, as fear and pleasure would have been good guides to conduct throughout life. So Aquinas says, about the passions:

> They may incite us to something against reason, and so we need a curb, which we name *temperance*. Or they may make us shirk a course of action dictated by reason, through fear of dangers or hardships. Then a person needs to be steadfast and not run away from what is right; and for this *courage* is named.[6]

As with courage and temperance so with many other virtues: there is, for instance, a virtue of industriousness only because idleness is a temptation; and of humility only because men tend to think too well of themselves. Hope is a virtue because despair too is a temptation; it might have been that no one cried that all was lost except where he could really see it to be so, and in this case there would have been no virtue of hope.

With virtues such as justice and charity it is a little different, because they correspond not to any particular desire or tendency that has to be kept in check but rather to a deficiency of motivation; and it is this that they must make good. If people were as much attached to the good of others as they are to their own good there would no more be a general virtue of benevolence than there is a general virtue of self-love. And if people cared about the rights of others as they care about their own rights no virtue of justice would be needed to look after the matter, and rules about such things as contracts and promises would only need to be made public, like the rules of a game that everyone was eager to play.

On this view of the virtues and vices everything is seen to depend on what human nature is like, and the traditional catalogue of the two kinds of dispositions is not hard to understand. Nevertheless it may be defective, and anyone who accepts the thesis that I am putting forward will feel free to ask himself where the temptations and deficiencies that need correcting are really to be found. It is possible, for example, that the theory of human nature lying behind the traditional list of the virtues and vices puts too much emphasis on hedonistic and sensual impulses, and does not sufficiently take account of less straightforward inclinations such as the desire to be put upon and dissatisfied, or the unwillingness to accept good things as they come along.

It should now be clear why I said that virtues should be seen as correctives; and part of what is meant by saying that virtue is about things that are difficult for men should also have appeared. The further application of this idea is, however, controversial, and the following difficulty presents itself: that we both are and are not inclined to think that the harder a man finds it to act virtuously the more virtue he shows if he does act well. For on the one hand great virtue is needed where it is particularly hard to act virtuously; yet on the other it could be argued that difficulty in acting virtuously shows that the agent is imperfect in virtue: according to Aristotle, to take pleasure in virtuous action is the mark of true virtue, with the self-mastery of the one who finds virtue difficult only a second best. How then is this conflict to be decided? Who shows most courage, the one who wants to run away but does not, or the one who does not even want to run away? Who shows most charity, the one who finds it easy to make the good of others his object, or the one who finds it hard?

What is certain is that the thought that virtues are corrective does not constrain us to relate virtue to difficulty in each individual man. Since men in general find it hard to face great dangers or evils, and even small ones, we may count as courageous those few who without blindness or indifference are nevertheless fearless even in terrible circumstances. And when someone has a natural charity or generosity it is at least part of the virtue that he has; if natural virtue cannot be the whole of virtue this is because a kindly or fearless disposition could be disastrous without justice and wisdom, and because these virtues have to be learned, not because natural virtue is too easily acquired. I have argued that the virtues can be seen as correctives in relation to human nature in general but not that each virtue must present a difficulty to each and every man.

Nevertheless many people feel strongly inclined to say that it is for moral effort that moral praise is to be bestowed, and that in proportion as a man finds it easy to be virtuous so much the less is he to be morally admired for his good actions. The dilemma can be resolved only when we stop talking about difficulties standing in the way of virtuous action as if they were of only one kind. The fact is that some kinds of difficulties do indeed provide on occasion for much virtue, but that others rather show that virtue is incomplete.

To illustrate this point I shall first consider an example of honest action. We may suppose for instance that a man has an opportunity to steal, in circumstances where stealing is not morally permissible, but that he refrains. And now let us ask our old question. For one man it is hard to refrain from stealing and for another man it is not: which shows the greater virtue in acting as he should? It is not difficult to see in this case that it makes all the difference whether the difficulty comes from circumstances, as that a man is poor, or that his theft is unlikely to be detected, or whether it comes from something that belongs to his own character. The fact that a man is *tempted* to steal is something about him that shows a certain lack of honesty: of the thoroughly honest man we say that it "never entered his head," meaning that it was never a real possibility for him. But the fact that he is poor is something that makes the occasion more *tempting*, and difficulties of this kind make honest action all the more virtuous.

A similar distinction can be made between different obstacles standing in the way of charitable action. Some circumstances, as that great sacrifice is needed, or that the one to be helped is a rival, give an occasion on which a man's charity is severely tested. Yet in given circumstances of this kind it is the man who acts easily rather than the one who finds it hard who shows the most charity. Charity is a virtue of attachment, and that sympathy for others which makes it easier to help them is part of the virtue itself.

These are fairly simple cases, but I am not supposing that it is always easy to say where the relevant distinction is to be drawn. What, for instance, should we say about the emotion of fear as an obstacle to action? Is a man more courageous if he fears much and nevertheless acts, or if he is relatively fearless? Several things must be said about this. In the first place it seems that the emotion of fear is not a necessary condition for the display of courage; in face of a great evil such as death or injury a man may show courage even if he does not tremble. On the other hand even irrational fears may give an occasion for courage: if someone suffers from claustrophobia or a dread of heights he may require courage to do that which would not be a courageous action for others. But not all fears belong from this point of view to the circumstances rather than to a man's character. For while we do not think of claustrophobia or a dread of heights as features of character, a general timorousness may be. Thus, although pathological fears are not a result of a man's choices and values some fears may be. The fears that count against a man's courage are those that we think he could overcome, and among them, in a special class, those that reflect the fact that he values safety too much.

In spite of problems such as these, which have certainly not all been solved, both the distinction between different kinds of obstacles to virtuous action and the general idea that virtues are correctives will be useful in resolving a difficulty in Kant's moral philosophy closely related to the issues discussed in the preceding paragraphs. In a passage in the first section of the *Groundwork of the Metaphysics of Morals* Kant notoriously tied himself into a knot in trying to give an account of those actions which have as he put it "positive moral worth." Arguing that only actions done out of a sense of duty have this worth he contrasts a philanthropist who "takes pleasure in spreading happiness around him" with one who acts out of respect for duty, saying that the actions of the latter but not the former have moral worth. Much scorn has been poured on Kant for this curious doctrine, and indeed it does seem that something has gone wrong, but perhaps we are not in a position to scoff unless we can give our own account of the idea on which Kant is working. After all it does seem that he is right in saying that some actions are in accordance with duty, and even required by duty, without being the subjects of moral praise, like those of the honest trader who deals honestly in a situation in which it is in his interest to do so.

It was this kind of example that drove Kant to his strange conclusion. He added another example, however, in discussing acts of self-preservation; these he said, while they normally have no positive moral worth, may have it when a man preserves his life not from inclination but without inclination and from a sense of duty. Is he not right in saying that acts of self-preservation normally have no moral significance but that they may have it, and how do we ourselves explain this fact?

To anyone who approaches this topic from a consideration of the virtues the solution readily suggests itself. Some actions are in accordance with virtue without requiring virtue for their performance, whereas others are both in accordance with virtue and such as to show possession of a virtue. So Kant's trader was dealing honestly in a situation in which the virtue of honesty is not required for honest dealing, and it is for this reason that his action did not have "positive moral worth." Similarly, the care that one ordinarily takes for one's life, as for instance on some ordinary morning in eating one's breakfast and keeping out of the way of a car on the road, is something for which no virtue is required. As we said earlier, there is no general virtue of self-love as there is a virtue of benevolence or charity, because men are generally attached sufficiently to their own good. Nevertheless in special circumstances virtues such as temperance, courage, fortitude, and hope may be needed if someone is to preserve his life. Are these circumstances in which the preservation of one's own life is a duty? Sometimes it is so, for sometimes it is what is owed to others that should keep a man from destroying himself, and then he may act out of a sense of duty. But not all cases in which acts of self-preservation show virtue are like this. For a man may display each of the virtues just listed even where he does not do any harm to others if he kills himself or fails to preserve his life. And it is this that explains why there may be a moral aspect to suicide which does not depend on possible injury to other people. It is not that suicide is "always wrong," whatever that would mean, but that suicide is *sometimes* contrary to virtues such as courage and hope.

Let us now return to Kant's philanthropists, with the thought that it is action that is in accordance with virtue and also displays a virtue that has moral worth. We see at once that Kant's difficulties are avoided, and the happy philanthropist reinstated in the position which belongs to him. For charity is, as we said, a virtue of attachment as well as action, and the sympathy that makes it easier to act with charity is part of the virtue. The man who acts charitably out of a sense of duty is not to be undervalued, but it is the other who most shows virtue and therefore to the other that most moral worth is attributed. Only a detail of Kant's presentation of the case of the dutiful philanthropist tells on the other side. For what he actually said was that this man felt no sympathy and took no pleasure in the good of others because "his mind was clouded by some sorrow of his own," and this is the kind of circumstance that increases the virtue that is needed if a man is to act well.

III

It was suggested above that an action with "positive moral worth," or as we might say a positively good action, was to be seen as one which was in accordance with virtue, by which I mean contrary to no virtue, and moreover one for which a virtue was required. Nothing has so far been said about another case, excluded by the formula, in which it might seem that an act displaying one virtue was nevertheless contrary to another. In giving this last description I am thinking not of two virtues with competing claims, as if what were required by justice could nevertheless be demanded by charity, or something of that kind, but rather of the possibility that a virtue such as courage or temperance or industry which overcomes a special temptation, might be displayed in an act of folly or villainy. Is this something that we must allow for, or is it only good or innocent actions which can be acts of these virtues? Aquinas, in his definition of virtue, said that virtues can produce only good actions, and that they are dispositions "of which no one can make bad use,"[7] except when they are treated as objects, as in being the subject of hatred or pride. The common opinion nowadays is, however, quite different. With the notable exception of Peter Geach hardly anyone sees any difficulty in the thought that virtues may sometimes be displayed in bad actions. Von Wright, for instance, speaks of the courage of the villain as if this were a quite unproblematic idea, and most people take it for granted that the virtues of courage and temperance may aid a bad man in his evil work. It is also supposed that charity may lead a man to act badly, as when someone does what he has no right to do, but does it for the sake of a friend.

There are, however, reasons for thinking that the matter is not so simple as this. If a man who is willing to do an act of injustice to help a friend, or for the common good, is supposed to act out of charity, and he so acts where a just man will not, it should be said that the unjust man has more charity than the just man. But do we not think that someone not ready to act unjustly may yet be perfect in charity, the virtue having done its whole work in promoting him to do the acts that are permissible? And is there not more difficulty than might appear in the idea of an act of injustice which is nevertheless an act of courage? Suppose for instance that a sordid murder were in question, say a murder done for gain or to get an inconvenient person out of the way, but that this murder had to be done in alarming circumstances or in the face of real danger; should we be happy to say that such an action was an act of courage or a courageous act? Did the murderer, who certainly acted boldly, or with intrepidity, if he did the murder, also act courageously? Some people insist that they are ready to say this, but I have noticed that they like to move over to a murder for the sake of conscience, or to some other act done in the course of a villainous enterprise but whose immediate end is innocent or positively good. On their hypothesis, which is that bad acts can easily be seen as courageous acts or acts of courage, my original example should be just as good.

What are we to say about this difficult matter? There is no doubt that the murderer who murdered for gain was *not a coward:* he did not have a second moral defect which another villain might have had. There is no difficulty about this because it is clear that one defect may neutralize another. As Aquinas remarked, it is better for a blind horse if it is slow.[8] It does not follow, however, that an act of villainy can be courageous; we are inclined to say that it "took courage," and yet it seems wrong to think of courage as equally connected with good action and bad.

One way out of this difficulty might be to say that the man who is ready to pursue bad ends does indeed have courage, and shows courage in his action, but that in him courage is not a virtue. Later I shall consider some cases in which this might be the right thing to say, but in this instance it does not seem to be. For unless the murderer consistently pursues bad ends his courage will often result in good; it may enable him to do many innocent or positively good things for himself or for his family and friends. On the strength of an individual bad action we can hardly say that in him courage is not a virtue. Nevertheless there is something to be said even about the individual action to distinguish it from one that would readily be called an act of courage or a courageous act. Perhaps the following analogy may help us to see what it is. We might think of words such as "courage" as naming characteristics of human beings in respect of a certain power, as words such as "poison" and "solvent" and "corrosive" so name the properties of physical things. The power to which virtue-words are so related is the power of producing good action, and good desires. But just as poisons, solvents and corrosives do not always operate characteristically, so it could be with virtues. If P (say arsenic) is a poison it does not follow that P acts as a poison wherever it is found. It is quite natural to say on occasion "P does not act as a poison here" though P is a poison and it is P that is acting here. Similarly courage is not operating as a virtue when the murderer turns his courage, which is a virtue, to bad ends. Not surprisingly the resistance that some of us registered was not to the expression "the courage of the murderer" or to the assertion that what he did "took courage" but rather to the description of that action as an act of courage or a courageous act. It is not that the action *could* not be so described, but that the fact that courage does not here have its characteristic operation is a reason for finding the description strange.

In this example we were considering an action in which courage was not operating as a virtue, without suggesting that in that agent it generally failed to do so. But the latter is also a possibility. If someone is both wicked and fool-hardy this may be the case with courage, and it is even easier to find examples of a general connexion with evil rather than good in the case of some other virtues. Suppose, for instance, that we think of someone who is over-industrious, or too ready to refuse pleasure, and this is characteristic of him rather than something we find on one particular occasion. In this case the virtue of industry, or the virtue of temperance, has a systematic connexion with defective action rather than good action; and it might be said in either case that the virtue did not operate as a virtue in this man. Just as we might say in a certain setting "P is not a poison here" though P is a poison and P is here, so we might say that industriousness, or temperance, is not a virtue in some. Similarly in a man habitually given to wishful thinking, who clings to false hopes, hope does not operate as a virtue and we may say that it is not a virtue in him.

The thought developed in the last paragraph, to the effect that not every man who has a virtue has something that is a virtue in him, may help to explain a certain discomfort that one may feel when discussing the virtues. It is not easy to put one's finger on what is wrong, but it has something to do with a disparity between the moral ideals that may seem to be implied in our talk about the virtues, and the moral judgements that we actually make. Someone reading the foregoing pages might, for instance, think that the author of this paper always admired most those people who had all the virtues, being wise and temperate as well as courageous, charitable and just. And indeed it is sometimes so. There are some people who do possess all these virtues and who are loved and admired by all the world, as Pope John

XXIII was loved and admired. Yet the fact is that many of us look up to some people whose chaotic lives contain rather little of wisdom or temperance, rather than to some others who possess these virtues. And while it may be that this is just romantic nonsense I suspect that it is not. For while wisdom always operates as a virtue, its close relation prudence does not, and it is prudence rather than wisdom that inspires many a careful life. Prudence is not a virtue in everyone, any more than industriousness is, for in some it is rather an over-anxious concern for safety and propriety, and a determination to keep away from people or situations which are apt to bring trouble with them; and by such defensiveness much good is lost. It is the same with temperance. Intemperance can be an appalling thing, as it was with Henry VIII of whom Wolsey remarked that

> rather than he will either miss or want any part of his will or appetite, he will put the loss of one half of nis realm in danger.

Nevertheless in some people temperance is not a virtue, but is rather connected with timidity or with a grudging attitude to the acceptance of good things. Of course what is best is to live boldly yet without imprudence or intemperance, but the fact is that rather few can manage that.

Notes

1. Aquinas, *Summa Theologica*, 1a2ae Q.56 a.3.
2. Aristotle, *Nicomachean Ethics*, especially bk. VII.
3. von Wright op. cit. chapter VIII.
4. Aristotle op. cit. 1140 b 22–25. Aquinas op. cit. 1a2ae Q.57 a.4
5. Rightly or wrongly, Aquinas attributed this doctrine to Aristotle. See op. cit. 1a2ae Q.60 a.2.
6. Aquinas op. cit. 1a2ae Q.61 a.3.
7. Aquinas op. cit. 1a2ae Q.56 a.5
8. Aquinas op. cit. 1a2ae Q.58 a.4.

26

Why We Need the Virtues

Peter Geach is professor of logic at the University of Leeds. The section here, originally entitled "Why Men Need the Virtues," was the first of Geach's Stanton Lectures delivered in Cambridge in 1973-1974 and redelivered as the Hagerstrom Lectures at the University of Uppsala in 1975. It was subsequently published as part of his book, *The Virtues (1977)*.

Why We Need the Virtues

The definite article in my title is significant. I am concerned with why men need the seven virtues to which tradition gives pre-eminence: the theological virtues of faith, hope, and charity, and the cardinal virtues of prudence, temperance, justice, and courage. I commit myself to the thesis that all of these *are* virtues: and I shall argue that this thesis cannot rationally be doubted so far as the four cardinal virtues are concerned. . . .

We are familiar with the type of reasoning which starts from some aim or policy laid down as a premise and proceeds step by step to infer the means of securing the aim, carrying out the policy. The logical structure of such reasoning, and its relation to the structure of deductive propositional reasoning, is not yet fully a matter of agreement, but we may reasonably hope that the matter will be cleared up. Aristotle's doctrine of teleology is that if we speak as if Nature had aims or policies we may work out what happens in the world by constructing reasonings formally parallel to human practical deliberations. Because most of his examples, even in biology, can be faulted for inadequate natural knowledge, the Aristotelian doctrine has been much blown upon. All the same, I think, it can be strongly defended, and the common attacks upon it are quite worthless.

It should be clear from the way I have stated it that an Aristotelian teleological explanation does not ascribe either something like desire to inanimate natural agents, or a contrivance of means for ends to Almighty God. Hobbe's witticisms about how a pane of glass, if it knew what it would be at, would stay in the window and not fall into the street, may have hit at the doctrine of his contemporaries, but leave Aristotle untouched.

From Peter Geach, *The Virtues*, Reprinted with the permission of Cambridge University Press.

We may equally scout the idea that teleological explanation of this sort involves Divine adaptation of means to God's ends. By his free and unaccountable will, God produces a universe within which some teleological explanatory schemes actually work. But God has no need either of achieving the end formulated in the first premise of such a schema, since he is perfect and changeless, or of using means to the end; the reproduction of living things is manifestly teleological in its pattern, but God can get as many insects or elephants or oaks as he wants by merely dreaming them up, without any reproductive mechanism, since he is an Almighty Creator. The role of teleological explanation is not to add to the corpus of natural theology.

Nor are teleological explanations barren or scientifically useless. They often have heuristic value in biology: quite recently, J. Z. Young explained the present role of the human pineal gland by making the heuristic assumption that it wouldn't be there ("evolution" wouldn't have "let" it survive!) if it had no function.

Lastly, teleology is not straightforwardly incompatible with mechanism. An old-fashioned mechanical clock is a paradigm both of Newtonian explicability by efficient causes and of explicability in terms of what it is for—to tell the time—and of the way its parts subserve this end. This would of course still be true of a clock we unexpectedly found on arrival in the sandy desert of Mars; we need no information or conjecture about the existence and nature of Martians in order to satisfy ourselves that the clock is a complex mechanism *de facto* describable by elaborating a teleological analysis of its structure and movements. . . .

I maintain then that this teleological way of thinking, conducted on essentially Aristotelian principles but without his obsolete natural science, is intellectually respectable. And in that way of thinking it makes good sense to ask "What are men for?" We may not be so ready with an answer, even a partial answer, as when we ask "What are hearts for?" "What are teeth for?"; but Aristotle is right to my mind in desiderating an answer—the success in bringing men's partial organs and activities under a teleological account should encourage us to think that some answer may be found. But not as quickly as Aristotle thought: it does not show straight off what men are for if we know that men and men only are capable of theoretical discourse.

But in order to show that men need virtues to effect whatever men are for, it may turn out unnecessary to determine the end and the good of man. For people whose first practical premises, formulating their ultimate ends, are not only divergent but irreconcilable may nevertheless agree on bringing about some situation which is an indispensable condition of either end's being realized, or on avoiding some situation which would prevent the realization of either end. That is what compromise means, that is what diplomacy is in aid of.

Consider the fact that people of different religions or of no religion at all can agree to build and run a hospital, and agree broadly on what shall be done in the hospital. There will of course be marginal policy disagreements, e.g.

about abortion operations and the limits of experimentation on human beings. But there can be agreement on fighting disease, because disease impedes men's efforts towards most goals.

Of course such compromise agreement can be achieved only so long as there is not too violent disagreement about ultimate ends. A Christian Scientist would not agree about the hospital. But then, if a Christian Scientist takes his religion seriously, he must disagree about a great deal that the rest of us believe about how things are in the world. . . .

The thesis of the intractable nature of disputes about values, and of radical difference between these and disputes about facts, is often supported by a curiously circular argument; I believe Alan Gewirth was the first to notice this. When we say everybody agrees on some proposition of physics, we know very well, if we will clear our mind of cant, that "everybody" is a mere figure of speech; huge numbers of people on Earth will have heard of the matter, but among those who have only a minority are really competent to form an opinion, the rest accept it on authority. This holds good even for such notorious facts as that the Earth is round and the Sun a huge ball millions of miles away. But when it is a matter of practical judgment, then, some philosophers would have us think, anybody's and everybody's opinion must be fairly polled; we must consult the Christian Scientists, the Azande, the Trobriand Islanders, Herr Hitler, old Uncle Joe Stalin and all. It is not at all surprising that there is a very different result of the poll when a very different lot of people are being polled. . . .

I peremptorily exclude from discussion sufficiently crazy moral views, on the same footing as sufficiently crazy theoretical views. There is a sufficiency of theoretical and practical consensus between men, these exclusions once made, for people of diverse opinions to cooperate in building houses and roads and railways and hospitals, running universities, and so on. And on the basis of this consensus we can see the need of the four cardinal virtues to men: these virtues are needed for any large-scale worthy enterprise, just as health and sanity are needed. We need prudence or practical wisdom for any large-scale planning. We need justice to secure cooperation and mutual trust among men, without which our lives would be nasty, brutish, and short. We need temperance in order not to be deflected from our long-term and large-scale goals by seeking short-term satisfactions. And we need courage in order to persevere in face of setbacks, weariness, difficulties, and dangers. . . .

I have tried to expound men's need of the virtues in terms of what men are for, their inbuilt teleology. One reply to this might be "What of it? You have only described what by metaphor may be called Nature's intentions for man. But why should we care about these if they conflict with our intentions and our freely adopted values? Nature, as the Victorian radical Place put it, is a dirty old toad."

Of course a man is free to "know good and evil" in what I am told is the sense of Genesis; to lay down his own standards, regardless of his inbuilt teleologies. The trouble is that it will not work out. Nature is such that one living thing lives by destroying and consuming other life, and of course this is one of the things that make all men call Nature a dirty old toad or the like. But if someone decided to be a conscientious objector to this arrangement, he would soon have to choose whether to endure the pangs of conscience or of hunger. If this objection went so far as stopping the phagocytes in his blood from destroying alien life, he would die quickly and nastily. Other moral standards at odds with what by nature men are for would lead to disaster less quickly and less dramatically but no less surely. This, in Biblical language, is the wrath of God coming upon the children of disobedience: which is not a matter of an irascible Nobodaddy above the clouds, but of the daily experience that fools who persist in their folly are not spared the natural consequences, though by God's mercy the disaster may be delayed.

27

Ways of Wrongdoing:
A Theory of the Vices

Christine McKinnon is a member of the philosophy department at Trent University, Peterborough, Ontario, where she has taught since 1989. She received her B.A. from McGill University and her B.Phil. and D.Phil. from Oxford University. Interested in ethics and the philosophy of language, she is currently working on a study of the vices and a computer-aided multivariate analysis of some Wittgenstein texts.

There has recently been a modest renewal of interest in that approach to moral philosophy that stresses the study of virtue.[1] Sometimes old themes have been revived in various modern guises;[2] sometimes new ground has been forged against the background of a moral psychology;[3] and sometimes particular virtues have been subjected to close analytic scrutiny.[4] All these projects are, in their various ways, welcome. But they also all exhibit, in common with their antecedent studies, an almost total silence on the subject of vice.[5] It would appear that the presupposition is either that a study of vice is deemed to be unimportant for moral philosophy or that once one has a theory of the virtues one thereby has, by default, a theory of the vices, and that when one understands the nature of a particular virtue one thereby grasps the nature of its corresponding vice (or vices). And, more significantly, it is assumed that *all* kinds of bad behavior are to be explained by a theory-by-default of the vices. Brief reflection suggests that these thoughts are mistaken. There are interesting and important asymmetries between theoretical accounts of good characters and bad characters, and ones which seem to have remained unexplored.

Thinking systematically about the nature of virtue and about particular virtues can be uplifting, in that it reminds us of those persons we admire. Thinking about moral or intellectual failings or deficiencies or vices has no such inspirational value, but it might perhaps be seen as a necessary complement to any complete discussion of how reason and desire interact in moral agents. By being encouraged to see how immoral as well as moral

From Christine McKinnon, "Ways of Wrongdoing: A Theory of the Vices," *The Journal of Value Inquiry* 23, no. 4 (December 1989): 319–35. Copyright 1989, *The Journal of Value Inquiry*. Reprinted by permission of the publisher.

actions are motivated and structured, we might come to understand better human agency, and what counts as a worthy desire, and why. Much of what would be included in a successful account of wrong-doing will be parasitic upon the kinds of claims regarding desires, intention, motivation, choice, action, responsibility, and character which play so central a role in any discussion of virtue. The perceived need for a study of wrong-doing ought best to be interpreted as an invitation to look harder for an adequate theory of moral behavior that can accommodate the despicable along with the laudable. In thinking about the vices and about the kinds of errors that explain bad behavior, we have to confront the possibility that our underlying moral psychology might well have to be enriched or modified. The somewhat fond hope is that the successful search for a sufficiently rich moral psychology might serve to vindicate certain ways of doing moral philosophy, and perhaps to render other ways less attractive. In particular, the less direct gain might be an endorsement of that approach to moral philosophy that stresses the important roles played by the development of a moral sensibility (a willingness to imagine and a desire to consider the needs of others) in moral education and the assessment of character in moral judgement. To this end, the need for a thorough study of ways of wrong-doing is long overdue.

This paper cannot and will not try to answer that need. Instead, I shall, as a preliminary move, sketch the barest outline of what a theory of the vices would have to look like, noting how this theory would form just one part of an account of wrong-doing. . . . My hope is that even this programmatic sketch will be enough to indicate asymmetries of explanation regarding good and bad behavior which in turn suggest ways in which the relations between reason and desire ought to be explored. . . .

What would such a theory look like? If we allow that vices are character traits of a certain sort that are systematically related to types of vicious actions, then a likely candidate for such a theory would be one that exposed the motivational force of vicious dispositions and located the latter in a moral psychology or a theory of action in such a way as to make sense of the vicious behavior. For a study of vicious behavior surely obliges us to conclude that vicious behavior is neither necessarily nor obviously irrational behavior. Reasons are cited for vicious acts as much as they are for virtuous acts, and, given the desires and the dispositions of the agent, these reasons are taken to be compelling reasons. We need a conceptual account of the bad person's desires, of the ways they arise from certain character traits and of the ways they serve to motivate actions.

If we grant that virtues are settled states of character or dispositions to behave in certain beneficial ways, to have certain worthy desires, and to find certain sorts of reasons compelling, then we might think that vices are just these same sorts of things, except that they are associated with certain unworthy desires and they issue in generally harmful actions. There is some obvious truth to this: truly vicious behavior arises from certain settled dispositions, is deliberately chosen, and is generally harmful. The three aspects of this obvious truth deserve to be explored.

First, why do we insist on the requirement of settled dispositions? If, in assessing the moral worth of an agent, or of an action performed by that agent, we are to do more than simply evaluate the outcome of an action, then it is necessary to grasp correctly the agent's reasons for performing the action. These reasons will appeal to certain desires that the agent has. And why can these not be fleeting desires? Why do they have to be functions of some relatively permanent dispositions? An adequate answer to these questions would begin to reveal how very complex are the connections between reason and desire in the case of actions which are candidates for moral assessment. But perhaps the following minimal comment will suffice: those desires which are cited as providing reasons for behaving in ways which are deemed to be moral or immoral are desires which have already been objects of assessment, in some sense. That is, those desires which furnish reasons for those actions which are the object of moral judgement are precisely those desires which reflect how an individual has come to view the needs and wants of himself and of his fellow men. These needs and wants, both his own and others', are just the sorts of things that are taken to provide constraints on the legitimate desires and actions available to the agent. Whether these needs and wants are recognised or wilfully ignored or heeded reflects certain choices the agent has made. And these choices are what, at least in large part, constitute his character. For it is from these choices that desires flow. Furthermore, these choices, via the fulfillment of desires arising from them, determine what actions will give the agent pleasure and what will cause him pain.

Thus we require that moral dispositions arise from settled states of character *not* because we want to deny moral worth to cases of accidental or motivationally-isolated behaviors *because* they are done "out of character." Rather, precisely because they are done "out of character," they cannot express deepseated or reasoned convictions about how seriously the needs of others ought to be taken. Thus, while we might be able to cite cases of acts that we might concede were good acts, we might be less willing to allow that they were performed by a good man. Respecting the needs of others is not something like a preference which one can adopt on occasion. To view others' needs in this manner is to distort seriously both their needs and the manner in which these needs ought to confront other agents. Neither a whim nor a sudden awareness of another's needs can generate a morally good action done in the right spirit and for the right reasons. Only when an agent has a proper understanding of how it is that others' needs ought to be responded to do we want to say that his reason and his desires interact in such a way as to generate the right actions for the right reasons, and so as to cause him pleasure.

Just as we do not praise a man as a good man on the evidence of isolated good actions, neither, so one might think, should we condemn a man on the basis of isolated and perhaps aberrant behavior. Again, we want to ensure that the truly vicious person has a consistently wrong account of how the needs of others impinge upon him, this account generating in him desires which characterise the vicious person and which lead him to engage in vicious behavior.

But there seems to be another kind of way of being bad, and one which does not arise so obviously from pursuing those desires which, because of the faulty conception one has of others' needs and wants, strike one as legitimate. A person who errs in this way may just never have considered the manner in which his proposed actions affect other people. The fault seems to be one associated with failing to exercise his reason and imagination rather than one of drawing valid conclusions from mistaken premises about the needs of others. This person might better be described as lacking the kind of imaginative concern which characterises the most minimal of moral sensibilities and without which virtuous dispositions are impossible, rather than as possessing vicious traits. While lacking virtuous motives often accompanies excessive preoccupation with self, these two conditions are by no means the same. The latter discourages recognition and imaginative anticipation of others' needs, but it is consistent with being aware of and then ignoring those needs. For this reason, it is not quite correct to include as the limiting case of faulty conceptions of others as beings possessed of needs and wants the conception that can be imputed to one who has just failed to think of others. Both these agents are mistaken as regards what they ought to do, but the reasons they each have for arriving at their conclusions regarding what they ought to do are importantly different.

Thus it seems that one way of going wrong can receive an account in terms of perceived ends generating desires and reasons for acting that is, on the surface, quite symmetrical with that provided for virtuous activity. But we cannot ignore the other way of going wrong, that is, bad behavior that is to be explained by the agent's failure to consider others' needs. The thoughtless person need not have well-developed vicious character traits, but the lack of malicious intent may not suffice to render him blameless. Failure to think or anticipate outcomes is often taken to be morally blameworthy. Thus we have seen one way in which the relative multiplicity of ways of going wrong introduces variations which suggest that we cannot derive an account of wrongdoing from a theory of the virtues simply by default.

The second feature of a vicious action or agent which we noted was that deliberation must be present. This is obviously, but not clearly, related to the first set of points. The lack of perspicuity in the connection emerges when we ponder the two different ways in which deliberation can be deficient. We noted that we have to account both for those cases of vicious behavior which are inspired by a failure to recognise the needs of others and those cases where needs, even when recognised, are not taken to pose obstacles to the adherence to or satisfaction of some prior desire. Some are tempted to view the latter as the truly vicious and the former merely as manifesting a moral weakness. The agent who possesses a desire to cause harm is taken to be more vicious than the agent who lacks the desire to avoid causing harm. But we might wonder why we are not just as responsible for lacking those (good) desires that we do lack as for possessing those (bad) desires that we do possess. Why should this lack of imagination which blinds us to others' needs not be seen as blameworthy? Why should failure to foster a sensitivity to other persons' needs not be seen to be morally reprehensible?

Sometimes actions arising from thoughtlessness are excused as not evincing a bad motive, whereas they are all too frequently the product of a wilful disregard for the concerns of others. If this disregard can be seen to be due to deliberate and excessive attention to his own needs, we are inclined to view the agent as manifesting the trait of selfishness. But sometimes his lack of foresight regarding how his actions will affect others is accompanied by an equal disregard for his own well-being; so selfishness cannot always be the explanation. Perhaps, however, *some* sort of self-centredness or *some* form of the egocentric predicament is always the cause of such thoughtless behavior. An inability to anticipate the likely effects of his actions on other beings or to conjure up imaginative resolutions to dilemmas seems to be the thoughtless person's most ready excuse. But what kind of a failing is this? Such a person is clearly deficient as a person, but it is not obvious that he possesses a moral vice. Some are inclined to view this self-centred type as less bad than the agent who appears to possess what we might call a positive desire to do harm, or at least the knowledge that his actions are likely to cause harm. As long as the desire to act in such a way which is likely to cause harm is not present, harmful actions are often excused at least to the extent that they do not serve to paint the character of the agent as vicious. He is taken to possess flaws of character, not vices.

We want to salvage many of these intuitions about the relative badness of agents, without at the same time whitewashing the character of the thoughtless wrongdoer. This can be done if we can understand what role deliberation ought to play in actions which are the object of moral assessment. While we are morally culpable for developing vicious character traits, we should also be censured if we fail to develop virtuous dispositions, even if this failure is to be explained by a lack of awareness of the value of these dispositions. If we are to be responsible for our characters, we are surely as much responsible for their deficiencies as for what they comprise. If certain desires are taken by the agent to be legitimate or illegitimate depending on the manner in which reason has presented the needs of others to him, then the agent's pursuit of unworthy desires can be explained in terms of the faulty conception he has of other persons *as* persons, or because the cost to his selfish concerns of recognising their needs strikes him as too great, or because he lacks altogether a conception of other persons' needs. This last kind of person is certainly morally deficient, but he might be thought to err more along the dimension of reason than that of desire. Consequently, he may need only to be persuaded to come to exercise his reason; he does not have to undergo the business of exorcising bad desires.

The role of deliberation is thus something like this: we are responsible for our actions because we are responsible for having those desires which generate reasons for performing these actions. And we are responsible for our desires because we are responsible for our characters, from which these desires flow. We develop our characters by first being presented with reasons for acquiring certain traits, and subsequently acting on those desires to which the traits give rise. This can be done in the absence of an outrageously Aristotelian background, but it does seem to require some kind of picture of the good life, or at least of what one takes to count as a flourishing human life. One can display moral defects by deliberately cultivating vices or by wilfully failing to develop the kind of sensibility without which virtues are impossible.

It would seem, then, that a case can be made for holding people responsible and blameworthy, although perhaps less wicked, even in those cases where no identifiable motive to do ill or no awareness of the likelihood of causing harm is present. Thus, the requirement that deliberation be present has received some qualification. The third remark I made concerning the general nature of vicious actions, that is, that they usually issue in harmful behavior, deserves brief comment and also invites further qualification. In particular, we might wonder under what circumstances actions which do not in fact turn out to be harmful nonetheless provide evidence on which to condemn as bad the perpetrator of the action. Here the notions of agent-regret and of intention might be deployed to good purpose.

Without investigating every possible way in which intentions and outcomes can be mismatched, it seems necessary to modify the requirement that vicious actions result in harmful behavior. When nature confutes a man's intentions, we still condemn him if his aims were evil. If it is nature's fortuitous intervention that dictates that an agent's thoughtlessness not issue in a bad outcome, the degree of his regret can be used as a measure of his deficiencies. And if he displays no regret whatsoever, we are prepared to condemn him as a moral reprobate, even though we cannot cite a particular vicious trait which would account for his behavior.

The qualifications attending the requirement that vicious behavior be harmful suggest that the place to look for assistance is not in the actual outcomes of actions, but in the motives or desires that generate actions. To this end, we should turn now to develop somewhat the distinction introduced earlier: that between possessing a harmful motive that had positive force and lacking the requisite virtuous motive. The distinction is of interest for at least two reasons: first, it should allow us to begin to untangle the complexities of the relations between reason and desire in cases of bad behavior, and, second, it may enable us to see more clearly just what is wrong with the bad man. We will be reminded of the multiplicity of ways of going wrong, and of the variety of dimensions (including moral and intellectual) along which it is possible to err. This may in turn provide some help in the difficult task of ranking the vices.

As we saw, in cases of manifestations of virtue, we required both constancy of temperament or character and some kind of rational appreciation of the value of the particular motive to act that inspired the virtuous behavior. That is, the agent must have some understanding of the good for man which dictates that he acquire *this* disposition or set of desires. To be fair to the vicious person, we must likewise require a certain regularity: isolated vicious acts do not suffice to condemn one as a vicious person.

But there is an important difference between the two cases. We require of the truly virtuous person that he have a motive or a reason for his actions. They cannot be done involuntarily, accidentally, or even unthinkingly: he must possess a particular character trait which acts as a positive force in generating a certain type of action, or which presents that action as the right one out of a number of other would-be candidates. But we have seen that this requirement is not always met with regard to bad persons. Sometimes a bad action can be explained by citing a desire or disposition that serves to inspire it. But often there is no identifiable motive. We can do the right thing only if we have the right reasons for doing it and we choose to act upon these reasons. But we can fail to do the right thing by having desires which serve to make reasons for other actions more compelling or by not exercising our capacity to consider the needs of others.

No doubt it is sometimes the case that vicious behavior is characterised not so much by the presence of an identifiable motive, but by the lack of the appropriate virtuous motive. The clearest cases are probably those that could be classed as selfishly thoughtless actions. And perhaps one of the first steps in articulating a theory of wrong-doing, within which the vices could be ranked, would involve distinguishing those vices which have identifiable associated motives and those failings which seem to involve lack of the requisite virtuous motive.

Although Kant neither develops it nor uses it to serve the end of ranking the vices, he does give a formal account of something like this difference.[6] We are told that if virtue can be calculated as +a, then we have at 0 its logical contradictory, which is mere moral weakness (or lack of virtue), and at −a its logical contrary, which is vice proper. While there seems to be no room for this distinction between lacking the requisite virtuous motive and possessing a vicious motive within a theory of vice which is presumed to issue by default from a theory of virtue, Kant's little formal sketch captures a clear intuitive thought about the vices, and one which we should seek to incorporate into any adequate theory. This distinction is of prime importance, both in understanding the nature of vice, and in providing a structure within which the various vices can be ranked.

Another main area where what we might call a theory-by-default of the vices proves to be inadequate is where we try to understand how it is the vicious man comes to acquire the traits he possesses. What kinds of stories does he tell himself and those whom he is trying to educate about the relative merits of certain dispositions? It would seem that all the habits and desires he seeks to instil are of instrumental value. They are those traits which will allow him to pursue other extrinsic ends, and they will not likely make appeals to the perfectability of man.[7] It is not clear that an appeal to the proper end of man can play any part in the moral education of the bad man. Instead, he has to argue for the value of certain external goods, and then establish that certain character traits are better suited to the acquisition of these goods than are others.

There seems to be a significant difference in the kinds of reasons we give for valuing virtues and vices. While it is possible to explain the merits of acquiring a virtue or the merits of a particular action without regard to consequences, it is more compelling in the case of vices to appeal to consequences or to desired ends. There is one obvious reason for this: at least within the context of a very broadly Aristotelian account of virtue, we have the notion of the proper end for man, and it is with reference to this proper end that certain virtues are the ones to be acquired. The reasons we cite for the meritorious nature of certain character traits are that the possession of these traits enables man to fulfil his function, to attain his end, and not so that he can ameliorate the well-being of himself and others, except in so far as doing so constitutes part of the good life. It is just not plausible that there be a symmetric story which the vicious person could provide as a rationale for developing vicious character traits. The ends which the vicious person seeks are those extrinsic to his nature (wealth, power, status, . . .), and the vices he cultivates are not those which perfect his nature, but those which enable him to achieve his goals. The traits which it is good for the vicious man to possess have instrumental value; the traits valued by the virtuous man can plausibly be seen to possess intrinsic value: possessing them is constitutive of the good man.

A further difference between theoretical accounts of virtues and vices lies in theses regarding their unity. The claim that all the virtues stand or fall together acquires plausibility in so far as something like practical wisdom working in conjunction with desires informed by knowledge of the good for man can be seen to provide conditions for good behavior. Because, as we saw, there seems to be no analogue of the end for man in the case of the wilful bad man, there is no motivation to posit claims regarding the unity of the vices. Their instrumental nature attaches each vice more directly to its end, rather than to related vices. This is not, of course, to deny that some vices have greater affinities with one another than do others. Nor is it to suggest that certain dispositions do not spawn certain sets of vices. Excessive self-centered concern and cowardice are two examples of defects which give rise to a whole series of vicious traits. And what is required in order to provide a thorough ranking of the vices would be a clear account of the conceptual links between the various vices. . . .

Notes

1. See Gregory E. Pence, "Recent Work on Virtues," *American Philosophical Quarterly* 21.4 (1984). And see the bibliography in *The Virtues: Contemporary Essays on Moral Character* [ed. Robert B. Kruschwitz and Robert C. Roberts] (Belmont, CA: Wadsworth, 1987).
2. See, for example, Alasdair MacIntyre, *After Virtue* (London: Duckworth, 1981) or Peter Geach, *The Virtues* (Cambridge: Cambridge University Press, 1977) or G. H. von Wright *The Varieties of Goodness* (London: Routledge and Kegan Paul, 1963).

3. See, for example, Nicholas Dent, *The Moral Psychology of the Virtues* (Cambridge: Cambridge University Press, 1984) and John McDowell, "Virtue and Reason" in *The Monist* 62.3 (1979).
4. See, for example, Gabriele Taylor and Sybil Wolfram, "The Self-Regarding and Other-Regarding Virtues" in *The Philosophical Quarterly*, Vol. 18 (1968) and "Virtues and Passions" in *Analysis*, Vol. 31 (1971) or Bernard Williams, "Justice as a Virtue" in *Essays on Aristotle's Ethics*, ed. A. Rorty (Berkeley: University of California Press, 1981) or David Pears, "Courage as a Mean," ibid.
5. Exceptions to this claim are Theophrastus, with his illustrations of thirty different types of vicious men in *The Characters*, and Bishop Joseph Hall and La Bruyère, both of whom were representative of a minor revival in the seventeenth century of the tradition of providing descriptions of allegorical characters, the first with *Heaven upon Earth* (1606) and *Characters of Virtues and Vices* (1608), and the second with *Les Caractères* (1688). More recently, but in somewhat the same vein, Thackeray's *The Book of Snobs* appeared at the turn of this century.
     But, useful as these studies are in encouraging us to think about instances of vicious behavior and characters, none of them pretends to lay the groundwork for a theoretical account of vice. Likewise, where we do find prolonged and systematic study of virtue, as in Kant's *The Metaphysical Principles of Virtue* or Shaftesbury's *An Enquiry concerning Virtue, or Merit*, very much less is said about the vices. Two recent books, both entitled *Virtues and Vices*, and both with much to recommend them, one by Philippa Foot and the other by James D. Wallace, promise much in the way of overcoming this omission, but prove disappointing on the subject of vice (although Wallace's book has a very useful discussion of cowardice). And, again, books like Sisella Bok's *Lying* or Mary Midgely's *Wickedness* examine specific vices without attempting to view them against a theoretical backdrop. So, while there are several examples of systematic discussions of virtue and some instances of accounts of particular vices, we appear to lack a unified theory of vice.
6. Immanuel Kant, *The Metaphysical Principles of Virtue* (Indianapolis: Bobbs Merrill, 1964), p.41
7. Although, in bizarre and perverse circumstances, some have imagined that we could (cf. Nietzsche).

Questions for Discussion

1. What does Aristotle mean by saying that "happiness is an activity of the soul in accordance with virtue"?
2. Compare Aristotle's account of happiness with your own. In what ways are they different? In what ways the same?

3. According to St. Thomas Aquinas, faith, hope, and love need to be included on a list of the virtues because they are needed to achieve salvation with God. Would they also be virtues without a belief in God?

4. Aquinas counts love among the virtues humans should have. Are there times when humans would do well to hate some people rather than love them?

5. G. E. M. Anscombe argues that the notions of right, wrong, and duty are essentially legal ones. Do you agree? Can we make sense of these notions without appeal to a legislator?

6. Anscombe appeals to the notion of a fully developed or "flourishing" human being. What does she mean by this and what might such a human be like?

7. What does Alasdair MacIntyre mean by a "practice"?

8. Do you agree with MacIntyre that moral debates cannot be decided by rational argument and that they are therefore essentially indeterminable?

9. MacIntyre believes that our lives contain a narrative order, with a beginning, middle, and end, that links birth to death. Yet the objection has been raised that we have a disjointed, nonhistorical conception of ourselves. With which opinion do you agree and why?

10. Philippa Foot argues that it is by people's innermost desires and attitudes that their virtue is judged. Do you agree? How would you judge one who constantly desires to do good, has a morally respectable attitude, and yet always fails to do what is right?

11. What is Foot's "test" for distinguishing virtues from arts and skills? Discuss this test with reference to virtues not discussed by Foot.

12. Do you agree with Foot that virtue cannot be displayed in morally bad actions? Give reasons for your answer.

13. Foot seems to think that one who acts from a sense of duty shows less virtue than one to whom virtue comes naturally. For instance, one who is naturally generous shows more virtue than one who is stingy but performs generous acts out of a sense of duty. Do you agree with Foot? Do we not admire more the person who shows virtue despite an inclination to do otherwise? Discuss this in the light of the Talmudic saying: "On the ground where the repentant stand, even the righteous cannot walk."

14. Peter Geach believes that the question "What are people for?" can be answered in principle if not in fact. Against this view, consider the claim that the question "What is ___ for?" can be answered only where the blank is filled in with the name of a product of human invention.

15. Geach suggests that there is enough theoretical and practical consensus among people of diverse views to make cooperation possible in a social community. Do you agree? Why or why not?

16. Do you agree with Christine McKinnon that we need a theory of the vices to supplement a theory of the virtues, or do you think that a theory of the virtues is implicitly a theory of the vices as well?

17. Discuss some of the asymmetries McKinnon thinks exist between theoretical accounts of good and bad characters.

Selected Bibliography

Anscombe, G. E. M. "Modern Moral Philosophy." *Philosophy* 33 (1958): 1-19. Reprinted in *The Collected Papers of G. E. M. Anscombe, Volume I: Ethics, Religion and Politics*, 43-50. Minneapolis: University of Minnesota Press, 1981.

Aquinas, St. Thomas. *Treatise on the Virtues*. Translated by John A. Oesterle. Notre Dame, Ind.: University of Notre Dame Press, 1984.

Aristotle. *Nicomachean Ethics*. Translated by Terence Irwin. Indianapolis, Ind.: Hackett, 1985.

Baron, Marcia. "Varieties of Ethics of Virtue." *American Philosophical Quarterly* 22 (1985): 47-53.

Becker, Lawrence. "The Neglect of Virtue." *Ethics* 85 (1975): 110-22.

Dent, N. J. H. *The Moral Psychology of the Virtues*. Cambridge, England: Cambridge University Press, 1984.

___. "Ethical Theory: Character and Virtue." *Midwest Studies in Philosophy* 12 (1988): Special Issue.

Foot, Philippa. *Virtues and Vices*. Berkeley: University of California Press, 1978.

Geach, Peter. *The Virtues*. Cambridge, England: Cambridge University Press, 1977.

Guardini, Romano. *The Virtues: On Forms of Moral Life*. Translated by Stella Lange. Chicago: Henry Regnery, 1963.

Hauerwas, Stanley, and Alasdair MacIntyre, eds. *Revisions*. Notre Dame, Ind.: University of Notre Dame Press, 1983.

Hudson, Stephen D. "Taking Virtues Seriously." *Australian Journal of Philosophy* 59 (June 1981): 189-202.

Kruschwitz, Robert B., and Robert C. Roberts, eds. *The Virtues: Contemporary Ethics and Moral Character*. Belmont, Calif.: Wadsworth, 1987.

MacIntyre, Alasdair. *After Virtue*. 2nd ed. Notre Dame, Ind.: University of Notre Dame Press, 1984.

___. *Whose Justice? Which Rationality?* Notre Dame, Ind.: University of Notre Dame Press, 1988.

Pence, Gregory. "Recent Work on the Virtues." *American Philosophical Quarterly* 21 (1984): 281-96.

Slote, Michael. *Goods and Virtues*. Oxford, England: Oxford University Press, 1983.

Taylor, Richard. *Good and Evil: A New Direction*. New York: Macmillan, 1970.

Von Wright, George Henrik. *The Varieties of Goodness*. London: Routledge and Kegan Paul, 1963.

Wallace, James. *Virtues and Vices*. Ithaca, N.Y.: Cornell University Press, 1978.

Williams, Bernard. *Moral Luck*. Cambridge, England: Cambridge University Press, 1981.

B. APPLICATIONS

Virtue-Based Theories
and Their Applications

A virtue-based approach to moral philosophy has both a theoretical and a practical side to it. On the theoretical side, the task is to show how a study of the virtues contributes to the way we understand morality. The goal is to explain why the kind of persons we are is at least as important as the kind of actions we perform. But if the kind of persons we are is vital to our understanding of morality, then it is equally important to show what it is about us that makes us good or bad. This, in turn, leads to a concern with the practical side of virtue-theory; that is, with the analysis of particular virtues and vices and the way they impact the personal issues of everyday life.

It is hardly surprising, then, that in addition to the more theoretical treatments of virtue-ethics, there appear in the literature accounts of particular virtues such as autonomy, truthfulness, and wisdom. A cursory look at some recent philosophy journals shows articles with such titles as "The Possibility of Prudence," "Courage as a Mean," "On Mercy," "Gratitude," and so forth. (See the bibliography following this section.) Titles such as these give a good idea of the kind of work contemporary philosophers are doing on particular virtues and vices.

Of course, the moral life has as many facets to it as there are particular virtues, so an analysis of the virtues will only partly aid us in determining what traits make a person good. Nevertheless, when we investigate what such traits amount to, we get some idea of how a person's life becomes morally informed—how that life is shaped by the virtues and vices.

Take, for instance, the character of some outstandingly moral individuals. For the virtue-theorist, such persons are the starting point of moral philosophy. We need only to inquire what it is about these people that make them outstanding to know what it means to be moral. Having found our answer, our goal then is to be like them, to develop the traits that make those people special.

Take Socrates, for example. Among the many traits that made Socrates special were his courage and integrity. We should, then, cultivate these traits if we are to be special in the way that he was special. But this requires that we get a clear understanding of the nature and value of courage and integrity, and of what such traits entail, so that we may effectively cultivate them.

This strategy, however, is deceptively simple. Some virtues, such as forgiveness, are notoriously difficult to define. It is tempting, for instance, to say that forgiveness is the overcoming of resentment. But a moment's reflection will show that this will not do because we can overcome resentment without forgiving. We can, for instance, merely "forget" what we initially resented. Furthermore, even if we can clarify what forgiveness means, it will not do to simply say "Be forgiving!" We still need to know whether we ought always to be forgiving, whether there are some evils that we cannot forgive, whether we can forgive on behalf of others, and so forth.[1]

Our analysis of the virtues might lead to some surprising results. Depending on how we answer the foregoing questions, we may conclude that forgiveness lacks the value we thought it had. In "Forgiveness and Resentment" (pp. 389ff.), Jeffrie G. Murphy draws just this conclusion.

The study of individual virtues, therefore, is a fruitful and necessary component of an ethics of virtue. By investigating the nature and value of specific virtues as well as their interrelationships, we can hope to paint a comprehensive picture of what is required for being good and living a life in which we may flourish.

Summary of Readings

In the first reading in this section, "Cruelty and Compassion," Richard Taylor demonstrates the importance of virtue for moral philosophy by focusing on the virtue of compassion and the vice of cruelty. He begins by narrating two sets of stories, one concerning characters portraying the vice of cruelty, the other with characters portraying the virtue of compassion. He then asks what it is about these stories that stirs our moral sentiments. As Taylor sees it, the characters in these stories are good and evil apart from their actions. In the first set of stories what moves us to revulsion is that the characters are cruel; in the second set what moves us to delight is that the characters are compassionate. From this, Taylor concludes that the kind of persons we are is more important to morality then the actions we perform.

The next selection, "Generosity," by James D. Wallace, illustrates the kind of descriptive and analytical work that philosophers are doing on particular virtues. In this article, Wallace begins by observing that generosity is a virtue concerned with giving. However, he is quick to point out that not all giving is out of generosity. For Wallace, giving is generous if what is given is intended to benefit the recipient, and is above and beyond what is morally required. Wallace then distinguishes between economic generosity and generosity of heart or mind. In economic generosity, the object given has a distinct market value; in generosity of heart or mind, what is given is intangible, such as praise or encouragement.

"Trust and Antitrust" by Annette Baier is at once an analysis of trust, a critique of modern moral philosophy, and a defense of feminism. Baier begins by observing that trust is a neglected topic in moral philosophy. It is, however, a central one, and Baier is concerned to diagnose why philosophers have failed to give it the attention it deserves. Her answer is that moral philosophers too often presuppose moral agents to be mature, rational adults able to judge one another's actions and to exert some control over their own degree of vulnera-

---

[1] For these and other issues that pertain to forgiveness, see Joram Graf Haber, *Forgiveness* (Savage, Md.: Rowman & Littlefield, 1991).

bility. Using this model, the philosophers then assume that whatever needs to be explained about trust can be explained by reference to contracts among persons—contracts made by mature adults able to judge the performance of others.

Baier argues, however, that the contract model is inadequate to explain the trust expressed by persons in positions of relative inequality. Infants, for instance, trust their parents and nothing like a contract can be said to be between them. Thus, Baier argues that a satisfactory analysis of trust is most likely to be developed by those who, like women, have typically been in a position of relative inequality. She then offers a definition of trust that includes a reliance on the competence and willingness of others to look after and not harm things they care about and that are entrusted to their care. Because trust, so defined, may sometimes be a vice, she concludes with a test to decide when it is a virtue.

In the next selection, "Wickedness," S. I. Benn outlines the varieties of wickedness found in people who are typically thought wicked. First, there is the selfishly wicked person. This person pursues self-interest without reservation. He cares not for the constraints on moral behavior when they interfere with the pursuit of his good. Next, there is the conscientiously wicked person. This person is unconditionally loyal to a person or group. He differs from the selfishly wicked person in that he sees the principles he acts upon as universally binding, but he also sees the person or group to which he is loyal as manifesting a good that overrides all else. Third, there is the heteronomously wicked person. This person is unconditionally obedient to an external authority. By example, Benn mentions Adolph Eichmann. According to Benn, people who are wicked in the way Eichmann was hand over their conscience to others in authority and are indifferent to the values to which the authority lays claim.

As Benn sees it, none of the wickedness that characterizes these persons stems from sociopathology. Each understands the importance of morality and none pursues ends that are intrinsically bad. Their wickedness comes from their refusal to let morality interfere with their pursuits. However, there is a fourth type of wickedness that differs from these in important respects. This is malignant wickedness. The malignantly wicked person is one who does evil for its own sake. This, says Benn, is the worst form of wickedness because what motivates it is bad in itself.

It is hard to deny that generosity, compassion, and trust are all virtues just as cruelty and wickedness are both vices. The next three selections examine traits that arguably fall somewhere in between. In "Forgiveness and Resentment," Jeffrie G. Murphy argues that if forgiveness is a virtue, it is not an unequivocal one. He begins by defining forgiveness as the forswearing of resentment. But resentment, he says, is not always bad; often it is a sign of self-respect. But if resentment is linked to self-respect, then the overcoming of resentment that constitutes forgiveness may be as much a vice as a virtue. Consequently, Murphy concludes that forgiveness is not a virtue unless it is tendered for reasons that are consistent with a person's self-respect.

Like Murphy's analysis of forgiveness, Lawrence A. Blum's "Friendship" is an analysis of a virtue that is somewhat controversial. However, unlike Murphy, who argues that forgiveness may sometimes be a vice, Blum defends friendship against those who would see it as having moral disvalue. Here, however, an explanation is in order because many of us see friendship as unambiguously good.

Consider the value of friendship from the standpoint of utilitarianism. The utilitarian, as discussed in Part I, is committed to the view that we ought to bring about the greatest amount of happiness for the greatest number of people. Given this view, utilitarians would not endorse friendship because the special favors we accord our friends are not conducive to the greater good of humanity. Otherwise put, the time and resources spent on our friends can be put to better uses—uses that better promote the welfare of society. Still other philosophers, as Blum points out, consider the exaltation of friendship a distraction from the higher love of humankind. He mentions Kierkegaard, who argued that we, like God, should try to love everyone equally.

Against views such as these, Blum argues that friendship is a virtue, and what makes it a virtue is that friends act for the sake of one another. Such altruistic motives and behavior have moral value even if exhibited by persons of dubious character and even if directed to no one but one's friends. The only negative feature of friendship is the possibility that it might lead to negative feelings toward those not our friends.

Joshua Halberstam's "Fame" also considers a controversial virtue. Strictly speaking, it is not fame itself with which Halberstam is concerned, but the active pursuit of it. Why, asks Halberstam, do we value fame yet consider it a vice to pursue it? That we value it is evidenced by the custom of wishing our friends fame and good fortune; that we disvalue it is evidenced by our thinking poorly of those who actively and obviously seek it. As Halberstam sees it, the pursuit of fame is not blameworthy so long as it does not harm others. However, like the pursuit of power, it is often achieved at the cost of other values, such as integrity and friendship.

The next two selections show how virtue-theorists approach contemporary issues of social concern. In "Ideals of Human Excellence and Preserving Natural Environments," Thomas E. Hill Jr., seeks to explain the widespread view that it is wrong to treat nature as a resource to be used. After rejecting several arguments used to explain the plausibility of such a view, Hill concludes that it is the person, not her conduct, that accounts for this belief. More specifically, Hill argues that a person who views nature simply as a resource betrays a lack of humility.

In "Moral Character and Abortion," Janet E. Smith argues that the decision to have an abortion stems from and is productive of a morally bad character. She argues for this thesis by compiling a list of traits we all would agree are bad, and then demonstrating that women who undergo abortions have the traits that are on this list. In addition, Smith argues that women who undergo abortions typically do so despite their belief that abortion is wrong. In this regard, they fail to display the virtue of integrity.

In defending her thesis, Smith draws an interesting analogy to adultery. Like abortion, she says, adultery stems from and is productive of a morally bad character. Adulterers typically tend to be liars, untrustworthy, and unreliable; to this extent, they commit acts that proceed from morally bad characters. And because, "with each decision to commit adultery, he [the adulterer] commits adultery more easily" and is likely to commit other wrongful acts, acts of adultery breed vices.

The last two selections show how virtue-theorists analyze issues of professional ethics. In "The Virtuous Physician," Edmund D. Pellegrino endeavors to characterize the virtuous physician in terms of a certain conception of virtue as well as a theory of the ends of medicine. Following Aquinas, Pellegrino construes virtues to be dispositions that enable a person to act in accordance with right reason; that is, as character traits disposing individuals to habitually seek perfection. Pellegrino's theory of the ends of medicine identifies these ends with the good of the patient as expressed in a particular healing action. What follows from this is that the virtuous physician is one who is disposed to promote the patient's good through healing actions, and to place the patient's good above her own.

In the final selection, "The Good Lawyer," Susan Wolf is concerned with fashioning a moral ideal for the good lawyer. She begins by noting that "the good lawyer" is not the same thing as "the-person-who-is-good-as-a-lawyer." Rather, the good lawyer is one who takes on a role given by society and cultivates the virtues involved in performing it well. These, she says, are partly moral virtues, and so it will not do to say that the good lawyer is one who performs the role of lawyering well. Lawyers must perform their roles well within the confines of morality. Without this proviso, they would—like thieves—be good whenever they perform the tasks that characterize their roles.

28

Cruelty and Compassion

Richard Taylor, who sometimes publishes under the name of Diodoros Cronus, was professor of philosophy at the University of Rochester before he retired. He is the author of *Good and Evil* (1970), *Virtue Ethics: An Introduction* (1991), *Action and Purpose* (1966), and *Metaphysics* (1963). He is also a contributor to the *Encyclopedia of Philosophy*.

Malice: The First Class of Actions

Let us first, then, bring to our minds actions of the following sort, beginning with fairly insignificant ones so that we can see moral good and evil, whether small or great.

Story 1. A boy, strolling over the countryside on his way from Sunday school, came across a large beetle lumbering over the ground. Fascinated by its size and beauty, he took a pin from his pocket, stabbed the insect through the back, ran it up to the head of the pin, and impaled it on a nearby tree. Several days later, having forgotten this, while he was going about his daily play, the boy found himself again in the same place and curiosity led him again to the tree. There was the beetle, its legs still moving, although very slowly, against the empty air.

Story 2. A group of boys, wandering aimlessly about in search of amusement, found a dirty and emaciated old cat asleep in a barn. One of the boys was sent off with a tin can for some kerosene while the other tied the cat up in a bag and sat around waiting. The kerosene finally supplied, it was sprinkled liberally over the squirming animal, precautions being taken not to get any into its face and eyes, and then a match was applied to the tail. The effect was spectacular: a howling torch, streaking over the field, culminating in a series of wild gyrations and leaps, and finally into a twitching mass whose insides burst forth in wet sputters, the eyes bulging to the size and brilliance of agates.

Story 3. A trio of soldiers, ragged and bearded and evidently a long time away from home and hearth, was wending its way back to its encampment in recently conquered territory. The surroundings, as far as vision could see, bore the marks of recent incredible devastation by war. Coming upon the remains of a shack, they were surprised to see signs of life. They threw open what served as a door to find a bearded old man huddled in the corner, trembling from fear and cold. A Star of David inscribed on one of the walls was more than sufficient incitement for what followed. The old man was goaded outside with rifle butts, was made to scrape a crude hole in the ground, and was then bludgeoned into it with rocks and sticks. A bit of dirt was finally shoved over his still quaking body. When the soldiers had finished this work and resumed their trek a faint wail betrayed that there was an infant still in the shack. They found her at once, and soon managed to replace her crying with giggling by dangling bright objects in her face and tickling her toes. When her giggling and the laughter of the soldiers flowed freely, her skull was blown open with a single bullet, and what was left of her small body was added to the grave already dug.

Now, with the passing reminder that things of this sort happen, and with fair regularity, we must ask: What is it in stories like this that sickens and evokes revulsion?

Shall we say, with Protagoras, that man, after all, is the measure of all things, that the insensitivity or depravity that some might think they detect in these illustrations really exists only in the mind of the observer, and that modes of behavior simple differ from one group to another? Surely that is not insight, but blindness, and it adds no enlightenment to remark that some courses of conduct are *better*, in terms of their consequences. It is not the *consequences* of actions like this that appall, but what is in the hearts of the agents.

Shall we then, with Socrates, say of the soldiers, for example, that they have acted from ignorance, choosing the lesser in preference to the greater good? That is altogether too tepid, and only manages to assimilate such actions to those of the fool who fails to look before he leaps. It is not the mere folly of these men that produces horror, or their inability to distinguish better and worse. It is something of a different character altogether.

Shall we say then, with Plato, that the agents whose deeds we consider have evidently failed to preserve a harmony between the rational and the appetitive parts of their souls? This seems a bit better, but it still falls far short of explaining our revulsion, which cannot have very much to do with what we take to be the inner arrangements of someone's mind or soul.

Perhaps we should say, then, that the behavior of these agents is ill-calculated to advance the maximum of pleasure for the maximum number. It is, indeed, but what has that to do with moral revulsion?

Perhaps, then, they have all acted from their inclinations rather than from duty, and what they should have done was remind themselves of this maxim, clear to any rational being: So act, that you can will the maxim of your action to be a universal law, binding on all rational beings. Surely that is pedantic. What if they had so acted? Perhaps then they would have done the same things anyway, but with a bit more ceremony and rationalization. It is difficult to see, in any case, what is *irrational* about pinning an insect, or dispatching a stray cat or a starving old man and infant. Surely the words one wants here are not irrational or undutiful, but something like heartless or cruel.

Then maybe we should say that such agents evidently overlooked the theological consequences of what they do. Men may be lax in their laws and punishments, but the eye of God never sleeps. Men should remember that great happiness awaits those who conduct themselves properly, and great pain awaits those who forget. But this is only to say that they may be missing out on a good thing and taking a needless risk of going to Hell. Maybe so, but are they condemned in our eyes for *that*?

The recital of answers could go on, Aristotle perhaps noting that all these actions betray a disregard for that golden mean between excess and deficiency that honorable men prize; James observing that we should include in our accounting all of the interests and claims that are made (including, no doubt, the "claims" insisted on by the cat); and so on and on.

But clearly, all we *need* to say about these things is that they are wantonly *cruel*. That is the whole sum and substance of them all, and it is the perception of sheer cruelty or malice, of the intended infliction of injury and the delight derived from it, that fills us with that peculiar revulsion that is moral. Our perception does not stop at the irrationality of such agents, nor at their folly, imprudence, lack of wit, or intelligence. It hardly notices these things. We are not at all tempted to weigh interests against interests, to make summations of pleasures and pains, reserving our verdict until we are sure that none of these features has been overlooked. Even generally considered, it is not the consequences that gives them their moral significance. It is no disaster to the world that an insect should die, or a cat, or even an old man and baby who were destined to soon die of starvation anyway. That such things should result is doubtless an evil, but this is not what gives these actions the stamp of moral evil or distinguishes their authors as vicious. The moral perception goes straight to the heart, to the incentive that produced and was indeed aimed at producing those evils, and the one thing it sees, overriding everything else, is malice.

Compassion: The Second Class of Actions

We can now compare the foregoing with deeds of a very different kind.

Story 4. A boy, poking around in a lot where he had no business to be and looking for something to steal, came upon a cupola that had been screened off with chicken wire to prevent pigeons from roosting and nesting inside. Twenty or so of the birds were inside, however, having somehow gotten trapped there. They presented a lamentable appearance, some crawling about on the filth-encrusted floor, their wings half outstretched, and others lying about dead. They had evidently been there a long time. The boy resisted the temptation to tear off the screening and release them, for it had been put there by the owner; it would only be replaced eventually, and he might get himself into serious trouble by tampering. So he left things as they were. But that night he awakened with an image in his mind of the dumb birds up there in the dark loft, and particularly those too weakened to fly any more. He told his father about it the next day, but was firmly reproved for his trespassing and was given an unqualified order not to do it again, along with remarks about pigeons as a nuisance. He felt profoundly guilty, and the whole thing was put out of his mind until the next night, when his sleep was disturbed even more by the same images of suffering and death. Finally, on the third night, he slipped from the house before dawn armed with a flashlight and, although frightened to the bones of the darkness, he picked his way up to the high cupola. There, one by one he liberated each bird through a hole he tore in the screen, with many painful pecks to his hands and much flapping and commotion bringing constantly closer the possibility of attracting the attention of the owner or the police. He repaired the hole, and gathered the birds that were too weak to fly into a bag and carried them tenderly home. The next morning they betrayed the boy's disobedience to his father, and for this he was beaten, but with only a few deaths he nursed the sick pigeons back to strength and let them go.

Story 5. A man deeply conditioned by the traditions of his local culture was deputized as a sheriff, along with dozens more from the same community, in order to cope with the growing civil rights menace there. Like most of the others, this man thoroughly respected the law and the orderly traditions he swore to uphold. He had always respected, too, his fellow men, black or white, and his firm adherence to the conventions of separation could not fairly be ascribed to any hatred for anyone. Blacks had always worked for him and received decent wages, although he had never seen any reason to treat them as equals and had been taught from childhood not to. He was, therefore, appalled at the thought that they should vote and perhaps even hold elective office. The menace to his settled world came not, it seemed to him, from the local black community, which was peaceful enough, but from outsiders, black and white, who had for months been arousing people at mass meetings, hiring lawyers from outside, goading blacks into disregarding all the legally erected symbols of segregation and, it seemed to him, threatening to turn a peaceful community into a jungle. Matters became intensely critical with the scheduling of a massive parade onto the town hall, in defiance of the law, at which time, it was threatened, all the blacks willing to do so would register as voters. This man, together with a massive force of sheriffs and deputies, went forth heavily armed to repel that assault, and a scene of violence was quickly enacted, blacks falling bleeding by the road, but getting in a few wounds of their own with rocks and pop bottles and whatever came to their hands. Restraint on both sides disappeared entirely when one sheriff and two Negroes got killed. Our deputy then managed to seize at gunpoint one of the blacks who was obviously a leader, and a outsider. Throwing him into his own car, which was to serve as a paddy wagon, he drove for about half a mile and stopped. Red and sweating with fury and screaming "nigger," his gun in his victim's face, he began beating him about the head and face with his weapon. Then suddenly the deputy fell to the seat, tears streaming from his eyes. Sobbing like a child, and muttering epithets mingled with abject apology, he helped the beaten and astonished Negro from the car, wiped the blood and sweat from his brow, and gave him a drink of cold water and a clean handkerchief. The he drove home and got drunk.[1]

Story 6. Two soldiers found themselves marooned on a tiny island in the Pacific. One was an American marine, the other a Japanese, and for a day or so neither suspected the presence of the other. The Americans had, they thought, killed or captured every one of the enemy, who were not numerous to begin with. The marine had been left behind when he was knocked out and lost, but not otherwise seriously wounded, during the fighting. It was the American marine who first discovered the other, and discovered too, to his dismay, that his foe was armed with a rifle, luger, and knife, while he had only a large knife. From then on he lived only by stealth, hiding during the day, meagerly sustaining himself by silently picking about in the darkness and covering all his traces, for he knew he would be hunted as soon as his presence was known, and that he would die as soon as he was seen. He soon began to feel stalked, a naked and helpless animal for whom no concealment was safe, and he could sleep only in brief naps, when exhaustion forced sleep upon him, not knowing but that his enemy might at that moment be at his back. He knew that the bullet that was going to kill him would be in his skull before he would hear it, and he lived almost moment to moment expecting it. He began to contrive schemes for ambushing his hunter, who he knew must have learned of him by now, but the odds were so against him in all of these that he abandoned them as futile and lived furtively, certain that it could not go on indefinitely. Thirst, hunger, and exhaustion had after many days magnified his terror and hopelessness. He clutched his knife day and night, and his enemy became to his imagination a vast, omnipotent, and ineluctable spectre. But deliverance came suddenly one day when, in the early light of dawn, he stumbled upon the Japanese, lying in profound sleep, both guns at his side, and a huge knife laid out on his belly. His role as the hunted was ended, and with a single lunge he would abolish the source of his terror. His own knife raised high, he was ready to fall on his foe, when he began to shake and could find no strength in his limbs. Thus he remained for some seconds, until the knife fell from his hand. The other leaped awake, and each stood staring into the terrified face of the other. The Japanese reached slowly for his weapons, pushed them violently out of reach of both men, and then, hesitating, let his knife fall, harmless, beside the other.

The Significance of These Stories

There are no heroes in these stories. No one has earned any medal of honor, any citation from any society for the protection of animals, or any recognition from any council on civil liberties. Goodness of heart, tenderness toward things

---

[1] This story is suggested by, but is not intended as an account of, an episode described by Dick Gregory in *Nigger: An Autobiography* (New York: Pocket Books, 1968), pp. 171–172.

that can suffer, and the loving kindness that contradicts all reason and sense of duty and sometimes denies even the urge to life itself that governs us all are seldom heroic. But who can fail to see, in these mixtures of good and evil, the one thing that really does shine like a jewel, as if by its own light?

Are we apt to learn anything by reviewing these things in the light of the analysis moralists have provided? Who acted from a sense of duty, or recited to himself the imperative of treating rational nature as an end in itself, or of acting on no maxim that he could not will to be a law for rational beings, and so on? Nothing of this sort was even remotely involved in anyone's thinking. Nor can we talk about consequences very convincingly, or the maximization of pleasure, or of competing claims and interests, or of seeing the good and directing the will to its attainment, or of honoring a mean between extremes— in short, there is not much that is strictly *rational* in any of these actions. We are not at all struck by the philosophical acumen that somehow led these people to see what was "the right thing to do." Insofar as they thought at all about what they were doing, or consulted their duty, or weighed possible consequences, they were inclined to do precisely what they did not do. We have in all these cases a real war between the head and the heart, the reason and the will, and the one thing that redeems them all is the quality of the heart, which somehow withstands every solicitation of the intellect. It is the compassionate heart that can still somehow make itself felt that makes men's deeds sometimes noble and beautiful, and nothing else at all. This, surely, is what makes men akin to the angels and the powers of light, and snuffs out in them the real and ever present forces of darkness and evil.

If someone were to say, "This is a good and virtuous man—although, of course, he has a rather pronounced tendency to cruelty and is quite unfeeling of others," we would at once recognize an absurdity. It would be quite impossible to pick out any morally good man under a description like that. Similarly, if one were to say, "This is a truly vicious man, wholly bereft of human goodness—although he has a good heart, and is kind to all living things," the absurdity leaps up again. Virtue and vice are not evenly distributed among men; no doubt all men have some of both, and one or the other tends to prevail in everyone. Most men, however, seem to know just what human goodness is when they see it, whether they have read treatises on morality or not, or whether or not they have tried to fathom its metaphysical foundations. For the fact is, it seems to have no such foundations, and no treatises on morals or disquisitions on the nature of true justice make it stand forth with more clarity then it already has. It would be as odd to suppose that one must become a philosopher before he can hope to recognize genuine moral good and evil, as it would to suppose that no man can be overwhelmed by a sunset until he understands the physics of refraction.

The Scope of Compassion

It will, of course, appear that genuine morality is not, by this account, confined to our relations with men, but extends to absolutely everything that can feel. Why should it not? What but a narrow and exclusive regard for themselves and a slavish worship for rational nature would ever have led moralists to think otherwise? That men are the only beings who are capable of reason is perhaps true, but they are surely not the only things that suffer. It seems perfectly evident that morality is tied to the liability to suffer rather than to the strictly human capacity for science and metaphysics and similar expressions of reason.

It makes no essential difference to morality, but only a difference of degree, that in my stories it was an insect that was impaled, a cat that was burned, and common pigeons that were liberated. The incentives were quite plainly identical in my first three stories, and identical again in the latter three, and it is quite obviously this malice in the former and compassion in the latter that stirs the moral sentiment. Something very precious is lost when men die at the hands of others, but that is not the reason for its moral evil. It is perhaps far less bad that a cat should die, and almost insignificant that an insect should perish; yet, the quality of moral evil remains essentially the same in all these cases. Similarly, we can surely say of our marine in the last story, struggling to keep living and finding suddenly the threat to his life lying helpless before him, that he had a good heart. Do the words lose one bit of their force or meaning if said of the boy and his pigeons?

Most men have always recognized their kinship with the rest of creation and their responsibility to other living things, in spite of the fact that moralists in our tradition hardly so much as mention it. When the question comes up for wise men to consider, they more often than not relegate it to a footnote or an appendix, thinking it quite ancillary to any serious moral considerations, even though it has as much seriousness and urgency as any moral problem that can be raised. Enthralled by man's rational nature, and finding no sign of it among what men fondly refer to as the brutes, philosophers and moralists have tended to dismiss the latter as mere *things*. Descartes even went so far as to call them automata, implying that they do not even feel pain—an idea, one would think, that could never find lodgement in the mind of any man who had seen animals bleeding in traps. Nor has religion, in our culture, done much to offset such an error. The Christian religion, indeed, compares most unfavorably with others in this respect, and in not one of its creeds will one find the least consideration of animals generally. The theological emphasis, to be sure, is not on man's rational mind, but on his soul, which other animals are somewhat arbitrarily denied to possess. The result is the same as before, however; animals are thought of as mere things to be treated in any way that one pleases. One can hear a thousand sermons, or study the casuistic manuals of an entire theological library, without finding a word on the subject of kindness to animals. When, in fact, it was proposed to establish in Rome a society for the prevention of cruelty to animals, the effort was vetoed by Pope Pius IX on the ground that we have no duty to them.[2] His reason and theology were without doubt correct. It can be doubted, however, whether the abstract kind of duty he had in mind is owed to anything under the sun. Yet, it cannot be doubted that

---

[2] Edward Westermarck, *The Origin and Development of the Moral Ideas* (London: Macmillan, 1917), Vol. II, p. 508.

animals suffer exactly as men do, and they suffer unutterably because they cannot protest, cannot make their "claims," of which William James spoke, very articulate. The heart is no less evil that takes delight in the suffering of a cat, than one that extracts similar delight from the sufferings of men. The latter we may fear more, but the moral pronouncement is the same in each case.

Incentives and Consequences

Next it will be noted that on this account the consequences of one's deeds are of little relevance to pronouncing upon the moral significance of those deeds themselves. Here, again, this view is in perfect agreement with Kant, and in complete opposition to Mill. It is not, Kant said, what we happen to produce by our actions that counts, but why we perform those actions to begin with. But Kant, obsessed with rational nature, decided that the only acceptable moral incentive would have to be a rational one: namely, the rational apprehension of one's duty, according to the formula of the categorical imperative. My account, on the other hand, provides no such rational formula at all. Indeed, the impulse of compassion so far transcends reason that it can as easily as not contradict it. It is sometimes the very irrationality of compassion, the residual capacity to respond with tenderness and love when all one's reason counsels otherwise, that confers upon a compassionate act its sweetness, beauty, and nobility. In exactly the same way does the irrationality of malice, the *pointless* but deliberate infliction of suffering, produce its acute and revolting ugliness.

Still, Kant was surely right in directing perception straight to the incentive of action rather than to its results, and Mill quite wrong in wanting to consider only the latter. Thus, it is a great evil that men should suffer and die. Considering these effects by themselves, the evil is the same no matter what produces it. But it is not a *moral* evil. Whether a man dies from being struck by lightning, by an automobile, or by a bullet, the effect is exactly the same in each case; and, considering only the effect, its evil is the same. This, however, is no moral judgment at all. To note that a given man dies from a lightning bolt, and that this is an evil, is to make no moral judgment on the lightning, the man, or his death. It is only to make a pronouncement of good and evil, of the kind considered far back in this discussion. It is, in other words, to describe a fact and add to the description an indication of the reaction to that fact of some conative or purposeful being. This becomes all the more evident when we consider that *all* men suffer and die, simply because they are sentient and mortal beings. No one escapes this fate. Yet, no morality at all turns on it; it is simply a fact, against which men may recoil, but not one that gives rise to any moral praise or blame. Nor is the picture automatically altered when such evils are found to result from human actions. A thousand men die on American highways every week as a result of their own actions, those of others, or both, and although no one doubts that this is a great evil, it is only rarely that the question of moral evil even arises. It is a problem of good and evil not significantly different from the evil of cancer. It is an evil to cope with, to minimize, but not one that normally prompts moral condemnation. Even when we bring the matter down to particular actions that are deliberate and willed, the situation is not significantly changed. That an insect should be killed (by an entomologist, for example), or a cat (by a medical researcher), or even a man (by an enemy soldier) are in varying degrees evil, but it is not the moral sentiment that expresses itself here. What is expressed is a certain reverence for life, and also a fear and horror at its loss, as in wars; but the moral condemnation of a particular deed is far in the background, if not entirely absent. Indeed, if we recall my six stories, it is clear that most of the consequences of the actions described are quite insignificant. All are things that happen normally, all the time; and, yet, the moral judgment is identical, except for degree, in the first three examples and identical again in the rest. In one set of cases an insect dies, a cat dies, and an old man and an infant die, all things that happen pretty regularly. Now one might want, with good reason, to insist that the death of two human beings is hardly trivial, but the thing to note is that even if it were known that these two would have died soon of starvation, had they not been discovered, this would not in the least reduce the moral repugnance of their murders. The moral revulsion arises not from their deaths, but how they died and, in particular, from what was in the hearts of their murderers. And in the second set of stories we find that some pigeons live, to rejoin the millions of them already on earth, a man receives less of a beating than appeared imminent, and another, who had just narrowly escaped death in battle, does not die after all. These are hardly consequences that change the direction of man's destiny. From the standpoint of the good of the world as a whole, they are almost devoid of significance. Yet, one stands in a certain awe of them all, as soon as he sees what lies behind them: it is a compassionate heart that manages to overcome fear, hatred, and the sense of duty itself. However little it has won the praise of moralists and theologians, however little it may deck itself out with the ornamentation of intellect and reason, however strange and mysterious it may seem to the mind, it is still the fugitive and unpredictable thing that alone quickens moral esteem and stamps its possessor as a man who, although fallible and ignorant and capable of much evil, is nevertheless a man of deep goodness and virtue.

Compassion and Justice

It should be clear by now that the capacity for compassion provides not only the basis for moral approbation, but creates also the possibility of true justice. We are able now to fill in the lacuna left in my previous discussion of this. A philosophical system that, like that of Hobbes, recognizes only self-interest or egoism as a possible human incentive will not only fail to account for any uniquely human virtue or vice, but it will also, if consistent, fail to account for the possibility of justice. If we assume all men to act only from self-interest then we can, as we have seen, envisage how a peaceful society might be formed by such men. There are purely prudential incentives for refraining from injury to others and, beyond this, for cooperating with one's fellows.

Men can form themselves into a society in which the double principle of justice—not to hinder, but to help—can to some extent govern their conduct without any of them relinquishing his own ultimate interests or goals. This, however, is only a beginning, for the conception of the common good can take no deep root in such a society. The moment men begin to honor this idea a conflict is produced between it and their egoism. And it will by no means do to say that, after all, so long as a man is aiming at the common good, or the good of the society of which he is member, then he is to that extent promoting his own good, simply by virtue of his being a *part* of that society. This may serve as a slogan, but it does not express a philosophical truth. Service to the common good inevitably requires one to subordinate his interests, at times, to the interests of others, and *not* with any expectation or hope that this will even in the long run promote his own good.

If there is in a society a clear and natural distinction between two groups—between those who are black, for instance, and those who are white—and if one of those groups greatly exceeds the other in numbers and power, then there can, from self-interest alone, be no reason why the larger group should be solicitous of the needs of the other. Indeed, so long as we take account only of the incentive of self-interest, there is no reason at all why the larger group should not absolutely enslave the other, reducing its individuals to the status of mere things, to be used and disposed of as one pleases. For so long as the distinction is a natural and not a conventional one, as the distinction between black and white is, then there is no reason for any member of the larger group to fear that any man or law will abolish it, and that he might thus find himself in the very position that he has consigned to his slave. There may be, to be sure, *other* considerations of pure self-interest that might lead the larger group to reexamine such an institution—considerations of economics and the like—but we are on dangerous ground if we appeal entirely to these. There will always be the considerable likelihood that, when all the interests of the larger group are fully considered, the rational verdict will fall clearly on the side retaining such an institution as slavery. We shall get the same result if deprivations of lesser magnitude than slavery are considered. It is not at all clear that the larger group will somehow fail to serve its own interests by denying the smaller group the political right to vote, for example. And in general, it appears a truism that no reason can be given why I, even though my store of wealth may be great, should forfeit a single dime to another who is destitute, or why I should prefer a course of action that would add one dime to his empty purse, rather than one that would add two to my own account. If there is in fact no risk to myself in trivially augmenting my wealth at great deprivation to another—and very often there is no such risk—then an appeal to my self-interest will plainly carry no conviction at all, save the conviction that I should be selfish. It seems fairly clear, beyond this, that no *other* purely rational appeal will serve any better. One will search in vain for any *reason* why I should have more concern for a starving million than for a bit of jam to add to my bread.

The search for an incentive is not, however, so hopeless. For there remains the appeal to the heart, the hope that another man's needs can somehow be *felt* as my own, against the very clear knowledge that they are not. This is essential, for without it, the common good ceases to have any life.

The *common* good, by the very meaning of the expression, requires the maximum possible fulfillment of the interests of all, sacrificing the real and entirely legitimate interests of some to the more pressing and important interests of others. It can be increased in no other way than this giving and taking, for the totality of felt needs and purposes that men actually have do not automatically form a symphony, wherein nothing clashes with anything else. Why, then, should any rational man respect this common good? Why, indeed, if it means departing from his self-centered role and offers not the thinnest hope of fulfilling any of his own interests, but offers much threat of the opposite? I believe no real answer to this question exists. Kant's answer—that it is his duty as a rational being—is perhaps the bravest that has ever been tried, but it carries little conviction. If, on the other hand, we ask why men *do* in fact often behave in this way, and thereby do bring about some realization of the common good, then an answer is possible, and it has no great ring of the absurd. Men do this because to some extent they care about others: they have the capacity to feel sympathy for the woe of another that can even override their concern for themselves; they can sometimes respond with compassion. The kind of justice that supplants the Kingdom of Darkness, and then rises above simple trading of good for good and brings into existence a common good, would be impossible without this, and of course without it there would be not the slightest chance for anything remotely resembling a Kingdom of God.

29

Generosity

James D. Wallace is professor of philosophy at the University of Illinois in Urbana. He is the author of *Virtues and Vices* (1978).

1. Economic Generosity

Generosity is concerned with giving, and different kinds of generosity can be distinguished according to the kind of things given. Aristotle said that generosity (*eleutheriotēs*) has to do with giving and taking of things whose value is measured in money.[1] There is a virtue called generosity, the actions fully characteristic of which are meritorious, which has to do with freely giving things that have a *market value*—freely giving goods and services of a type that normally are exchanged on the open market. This sort of generosity I call "economic generosity" to distinguish it from other varieties. One can be generous in the judgments one makes about the merits and demerits of others, and one can be generous in forgiving those who trespass against one. "Generous-mindedness" and "generous-heartedness," as these other kinds of generosity might be called, do not involve being generous with things whose value is measured in money. These are like economic generosity in certain ways, but also differ in important respects, as I shall try subsequently to show. Unless otherwise indicated, however, by generosity I mean economic generosity.

A generous person is one who has a certain attitude toward his own things, the value of which is measured in money, and who also has a certain attitude toward other people. Generosity, like other forms of benevolence, in its primary occurrence, involves as one of its constituents a concern for the happiness and well-being of others. The actions fully characteristic of generosity have as their goal promoting someone else's well-being, comfort, happiness, or pleasure—someone else's good. In *primary generosity*, the agent is concerned directly about the good of another. Thus, an action fully

---

[1] *Nicomachean Ethics*, IV, 1, 1119b21–27.

---

characteristic of generosity might be done to please someone or to help someone, with no further end in view beyond pleasing or helping. "I just wanted to do something nice for them" or "I just wanted her to have it" are typical explanations of generous acts.

That an act fully characteristic of *the virtue*, generosity, is motivated in this way by a direct concern for the good of another is not immediately obvious, because we sometimes call giving "generous" and mean only that the giver is giving more than someone in his situation normally gives. Thus, the host is being generous with the mashed potatoes when he unthinkingly heaps unusually large portions on the plates. Or perhaps he does not do it unthinkingly. It might be that he is giving such generous portions because he wants to use up all the potatoes to prevent them from spoiling. Being generous in this way—giving a lot for reasons such as these—would not tend to show that the host is a *generous person*, even if he did so frequently. If we restrict ourselves to the kind of generous action that is fully characteristic of a generous person, then in every case, the agent's giving will be motivated by a direct concern for the good (in the broad sense) of another. I shall say in such cases that the agent intends to *benefit* the recipient.

There is a further complication. The virtue generosity, in its *primary occurrence*, I have said, involves a sort of direct concern for the good of others, as do other forms of benevolence. Someone who is deficient in such concern or who lacks it altogether might admire generous people for their generosity and want as far as he can to be like them. He might then want to do in certain situations what a generous person would do. Acting as a generous person would act because one regards generosity as a virtue and wants, therefore, to emulate the generous person is meritorious, and it reflects credit upon the agent. It is, however, a secondary sort of generosity. It depends, for its merit, upon the fact that primary generosity is a virtue and is thus a worthy ideal at which to aim. I will concentrate, therefore, upon primary generosity, which does involve a direct concern for the good of another. An account of why this is a virtue is easily extended to explain why a generous person is worthy of emulation.

A certain sort of attitude on the part of the agent toward what he gives is also a feature of actions fully characteristic of the virtue generosity. In acting generously, one must give something that one values—something that one, therefore, has some reason to keep rather than discard or abandon. If, for example, one is about to throw away an article of clothing, and on the way to the trash barrel one meets someone who would like to have it, it would not be *generous* of one to give it to him. What disqualifies such giving from being generous is neither the giver's motive nor the nature of what is given but rather the fact that the giver himself does not value the object enough. Similarly, when we do favors for one another, giving matches or coins for parking meters, often what is given is too insignificant for the giving of it to be generous. One may be being kind in giving things that one does not particularly value, but for the giving to be generous, one must value the thing given for some reason. I may have acquired a particularly repulsive piece of primitive art that I have no desire to keep. Still, I might generously give it to a museum if it were a valuable piece—one I could sell or exchange for something I really want. *How generous* one is being in giving something generally depends upon how much one values the thing given, how much one is giving up.

Usually, the giver must give in excess of what he is required to give by morality or custom, if his giving is to be generous. Where there exists a generally recognized moral obligation to give, or where giving is customary, then normally one's giving is not generous even though it is prompted by a direct concern for the good of the recipient. If one were certain of a more than ample and continuing supply of food, so that it would clearly be wrong not to give some food to a neighbor who would otherwise go hungry, giving the neighbor a portion of food would not be generous. Similarly, to give a person a gift when one is expected to do so, because it is customary to exchange gifts (for example birthdays, Christmas, weddings, etc.), is normally not a matter of generosity, even though one aims to please the recipient. If one gives *more* than what is expected in such cases, then the giving might be generous. A generous person is one who exceeds normal expectations in giving, and one who gives no more than what is generally expected in the circumstances is not apt to be cited for generosity.

A special problem arises in cases of the following sort. Although it would clearly be wrong for a certain person *not* to give, he does not see this. Nevertheless, he does give on a generous impulse. Suppose, for example, that a certain person is a social Darwinist, convinced that it is wrong to give the necessities of life to people in need, because this enables the weak to survive, thus weakening the species. She encounters a starving family, and, touched by their plight, she provides food for them, though not without a twinge of social Darwinist guilt. Assuming that what she gives is not insignificant to her, but that it is no more than what the family needs to keep them alive, is her giving generous? On the one hand, she is really doing no more than the minimum required of her by the duty to help people in distress, and this makes one hesitate to say that she is being generous. On the other hand, *she* does not recognize any moral obligation here, and it is the kind and generous side of her nature that overcomes her cruel principles and leads her to give. This seems to support the view that she is being generous.

An act fully characteristic of generosity will normally have the following features.

(1) The agent, because of his direct concern for the good of the recipient, gives something with the intention of benefiting the recipient.
(2) The agent gives up something of his that has a market value and that he has some reason to value and, therefore, to keep.
(3) The agent gives more than one is generally expected, because of moral requirements or custom, to give in such circumstances.

In normal cases, an act that meets these three conditions will be a generous act, and a generous act will have these three features. There are, however, abnormal cases—cases in which the agent has, concerning the circumstances mentioned in the three conditions, a false belief or an unusual or eccentric attitude. The case of the social Darwinist is such a case. She thinks she is morally required *not* to give, when in fact she is required to give. If one accepts *her* view of the situation, her act is generous. In fact, however, the third condition is not satisfied. In another sort of abnormal case, the agent values what he gives, but in fact the gift is utterly worthless—it is literally trash. Here it is not clear that the second condition is fulfilled, but from the agent's odd point of view, the act is generous. The very rich often give to charity sums of money that are large in comparison with what others give, and their gifts seem generous. These sums, however, which are substantial, may be relatively insignificant to the donors, and one may wonder whether condition (2) is satisfied in such a case. Does the donor, who has so much, in fact have reason to value and keep what he gives, or is his "gift" analogous to an ordinary person's giving away a book of matches? In a rather different sort of case, someone might be convinced that he is morally required to give away nearly all he has to the poor. For this reason, he divests himself of a substantial fortune. In such cases, it may be that condition (1) is not satisfied. The agent believes, in effect, that condition (3) is not satisfied, since he believes that he is required to do this. These circumstances will make one hesitate to call his giving generous, although other features of this case incline one toward the view that he is being generous.

In these cases involving unusual beliefs or attitudes, one is pulled simultaneously in two different directions. The way the agent sees the situation and the way one expects him to see the situation diverge. Crucial conditions are satisfied from one way of regarding the case and unsatisfied from the other. It is not surprising that one is reluctant to say simply that the act is (or is not) fully characteristic of the virtue generosity. Any such statement must be qualified, and the actual consequences of the qualification may or may not be important, depending upon the case. Normally, of course, the agent's beliefs about the features in (1)–(3) will not be grossly mistaken nor will his attitudes toward those things be unusual or eccentric. In such cases, if the three conditions are satisfied, the act is unqualifiedly generous, and vice versa.

A generous person is one who has a tendency to perform actions that meet these conditions. The stronger the tendency, the more generous the person.

2. Generous-Mindedness

The conditions in the preceding section are meant as an account of actions that are fully characteristic of *economic generosity*—generosity that involves giving things whose value is measured in money. Another kind of generosity, however, has to do with making judgments about the merits and failings of other people. This too is a virtue, which sometimes is called *generous-mindedness*.[2] I will try briefly to indicate some similarities and differences between this virtue and economic generosity.

---

[2] I am indebted to David Shwayder for bringing this topic to my attention.

Generous-mindedness is shown by seeing someone else's merit (technical, moral, etc.) in cases where it is difficult to see because the facts of the case admit of other, not unreasonable interpretations, or because the situation is complex and the merit is not immediately apparent. Generous-mindedness is also shown by seeing that a derogatory judgment is not called for in cases where the facts might not unreasonably be taken to indicate a derogatory judgment. Many of us actually dislike to find that others are as good or better than we are, so that we have some desire to find grounds for derogatory judgments. It is plausible to think that people of otherwise fair judgment are sometimes led to think less well of others than they should because they do not want to think well of them or because they want to think ill of them. They do not purposely close their eyes to merit; rather because they do not wish to find it, they do not try hard enough to find it. This may involve a certain amount of self-deception, but I suspect that in many cases the matter is more straightforward. If someone wants to find another inferior to himself in some respect, then where he sees some (prima facie) grounds for such a judgment, he is apt to be quick to seize upon it and regard the matter as settled. A generous-minded person is one who wants to think well of other people, so that in such cases he will look and find the merit that might otherwise go overlooked. Of course, it is possible to be too generous-minded—to overlook demerit because one does not want to find it.

If someone exhibits generous-mindedness in his judgment on a particular occasion, his act of judgment will not fulfill the conditions for an act of economic generosity. It will have features, however, that can be seen as analogous to the features characteristic of economic generosity. If an individual is well-disposed toward other people, then besides wanting to benefit them by giving them things, he will wish them well. He will tend to want their undertakings to succeed and to reflect well on them. If he wants to think well of others, he will be apt to look harder for merit, and he will, therefore, be more likely to find it. Generous-mindedness seems properly regarded as a manifestation of good will toward others that shows a direct concern for the well-being of others.

Economic generosity generally involves giving more than is required or customary, and there is a counterpart to this in generous-mindedness. The generous-minded person sees merit where a competent evaluator might miss it, where it would be reasonable (though incorrect) to find that there is no such merit. In this way, one might say that generous-mindedness leads a person to go beyond what is required of an evaluator. It is less clear whether there is with generous-mindedness a counterpart of the second condition for primary generosity—whether there is something of value to the agent that he gives up in being generous-minded. Two things suggest themselves for this role. One would expect that a generous-minded person will make a greater effort to find merit or to put a not unfavorable construction on facts that look bad, thus giving up time and effort. Secondly, in searching for the most favorable interpretation possible, a person, if he succeeds, must sometimes thereby forego the generally congenial thought that he is better than or as good as another. No doubt, a generous-minded person does not always expend more time and energy in making an assessment than he would if he were not generous-minded. Moreover, the generous-minded person is no doubt less likely than most to enjoy thinking himself better than others. It does seem that the parallels are not exact, and that "generosity" is used metaphorically in generous-mindedness.

For generous-mindedness not to distort one's judgment—for it not to lead one to incorrect evaluations—an individual must be a competent evaluator and be conscientious about reaching a correct judgment. Also, it does seem that if one has sufficiently good judgment and is sufficiently concerned to make the right judgment, then this by itself should lead one to see merit when it is present just as well as would the desire to *find merit*. The strong desire to make favorable judgments, moreover, *may* distort one's judgment. It may lead one to overlook defects and to find merit where it is not. A strong desire to make *the correct evaluation* cannot distort one's judgment in this way. Generous-mindedness should not be regarded as a primary virtue of evaluators. It can counteract an inclination to build oneself up by tearing others down, but so too can a strong desire to evaluate correctly. Generous-mindedness is a manifestation of the sort of concern for others that is characteristic of all forms of benevolence. It derives the greatest part of its merit from this concern.

30

*Trust and Antitrust**

Annette Baier is professor of philosophy at the University of Pittsburgh. She has published many articles in the philosophy of mind, ethics, and the history of philosophy, and is the author of *Postures of the Mind* (1985) and *A Progress of Sentiments: Reflections on Hume's Treatise* (1991). She has also served as president of the Eastern Division of the American Philosophical Association, 1990–1991.

Trust and Its Varieties

"Whatever matters to human beings, trust is the atmosphere in which it thrives." [Sissela Bok][1]

Whether or not everything which matters to us is the sort of thing that can thrive or languish (I may care most about my stamp collection) or even whether all the possibly thriving things we care about need trust in order to thrive (does my rubber tree?), there surely is something basically right about Bok's claim. Given that I cannot myself guard my stamp collection at all times, nor take my rubber tree with me on my travels, the custody of these things that matter to me must often be transferred to others, presumably to others I trust.

---

*I owe the second half of my title to the salutary reaction of Alexander Nehamas to an earlier and more sanguine version of this paper, read at Chapel Hill Colloquium in October 1984. I also owe many important points which I have tried to incorporate in this revised version to John Cooper, who commented helpfully on the paper on that occasion, to numerous constructive critics at later presentations of versions of it at CUNY Graduate Center, Brooklyn College, Columbia University, the University of Pennsylvania, and to readers for this journal. I received such a flood of helpful and enthusiastic advice that it became clear that, although few philosophers have written directly on this topic, very many have been thinking about it. It is only by ruthlessly putting finis to my potentially endless revisions and researches into hitherto unfamiliar legal, sociological, psychological, and economic literature that any paper emerged from my responses to these gratifying and generous responses.

[1]Sissela Bok, *Lying* (New York: Pantheon Books, 1978), p. 31n. Bok is one of the few philosophers to have addressed the ethics of trust fairly directly. The title of the chapter from which this quotation comes is "Truthfulness, Deceit and Trust."

From Annette Baier, "Trust and Antitrust," *Ethics* 96:2 (January 1986): 231–260. © 1986 by The University of Chicago. All rights reserved. Reprinted by permission of The University of Chicago.

Without trust, what matters to me would be unsafe, unless like the Stoic I attach myself only to what can thrive, or be safe from harm, *however* others act. The starry heavens above and the moral law within had better be about the only things that matter to me, if there is no one I can trust in any way. Even my own Stoic virtue will surely thrive better if it evokes some trust from others, inspires some trustworthiness in them, or is approved and imitated by them.

To Bok's statement, however, we should add another, that not all the things that thrive when there is trust between people, and which matter, are things that should be encouraged to thrive. Exploitation and conspiracy, as much as justice and fellowship, thrive better in an atmosphere of trust. There are immoral as well as moral trust relationships, and trust-busting can be a morally proper goal. If we are to tell when morality requires the preservation of trust, when it requires the destruction of trust, we obviously need to distinguish different forms of trust, and to look for some morally relevant features they may possess. In this paper I make a start on this large task.

It is a start, not a continuation, because there has been a strange silence on the topic in the tradition of moral philosophy with which I am familiar. Psychologists and sociologists have discussed it, lawyers have worked out the requirements of equity on legal trusts, political philosophers have discussed trust in governments, and there has been some discussion of trust when philosophers address the assurance problem in Prisoner's Dilemma contexts. But we, or at least I, search in vain for any general account of the morality of trust relationships. The question, Whom should I trust in what way, and why? has not been the central question in moral philosophy as we know it. Yet if I am right in claiming that morality, as anything more than a law within, itself requires trust in order to thrive, and that immorality too thrives on some forms of trust, it seems pretty obvious that we ought, as moral philosophers, to look into the question of what forms of trust are needed for the thriving of the version of morality we endorse, and into the morality of that and the other forms of trust. A minimal condition of adequacy for any version of the true morality, if truth has anything to do with reality, is that it not have to condemn the conditions needed for its own thriving. Yet we will be in no position to apply that test to the truth in which morality thrives until we have worked out, at least in a provisional way, how to judge true relationships from a moral point of view.

Moral philosophers have always been interested in cooperation between people, and so it is surprising that they have not said more than they have about trust. It seems fairly obvious that any form of cooperative activity, including the division of labor, requires the cooperators to trust one another to do their bit, or at the very least to trust the overseer with his whip to do his bit, where coercion is relied on. One would expect contractarians to investigate the forms of trust and distrust parties to a contract exhibit. Utilitarians too should be concerned with the contribution to the general happiness of various climates of trust, so be concerned to understand the nature, roots, and varieties of trust. One might also have expected those with a moral theory of the virtues to have looked at trustworthiness, or at willingness to give trust. But when we turn to the great moral philosophers, in our tradition, what we find can scarcely be said to be even a sketch of a moral theory of trust. At most we get a few hints of directions in which we might go.

Plato in the *Republic* presumably expects the majority of citizens to trust the philosopher kings to rule wisely and expects that elite to trust their underlings not to poison their wine, nor set fire to their libraries, but neither proper trust nor proper trustworthiness are among the virtues he dwells on as necessary in the cooperating parties in his good society. His version of justice and of the "friendship" supposed to exist between ruler and ruled seems to *imply* such virtues of trust, but he does not himself draw out the implications. In the *Laws* he mentions distrust as an evil produced by association with seafaring traders, but it is only a mention.[2] The same sort of claim can also be made about Aristotle—his virtuous person, like Plato's, must place his trust in that hypothetical wise person who will teach him just how much anger and pride and fear to feel with what reasons, when, and toward which objects. Such a wise man presumably also knows just how much trust in whom, on what matters, and how much trustworthiness, should be cultivated, as well as who should show trust toward whom, but such crucial wisdom and such central virtues are not discussed by Aristotle, as far as I am aware. (He does, in the *Politics*, condemn tyrants for sowing seeds of distrust, and his discussion of friendship might be cited as one place where he implicitly recognizes the importance of trust; could someone one distrusted be a second self to one? But that is implicit only, and in any case would cover only trust between friends.) Nor do later moral philosophers do much better on this count.[3]

There are some forms of trust to which the great philosophers *have* given explicit attention. Saint Thomas Aquinas, and other Christian moralists, have extolled the virtue of faith and, more relevantly, of hope, and so have said something about trust in God. And in the modern period some of the great moral and political philosophers, in particular John Locke, looked at trust in governments and officials, and some have shown what might be called an obsessive trust in contracts and contractors, even if not, after Hobbes's good example here, an equal obsession with the grounds for such trust. It is selective attention then, rather than total inattention, which is the philosophical phenomenon on which I wish to remark, tentatively to explain, and try to terminate or at least to interrupt.

---

[2] Plato, *Laws* 4.705a. I owe this reference to John Cooper, who found my charge that Plato and Aristotle had neglected the topic of trust ungenerous, given how much they fairly clearly took for granted about its value and importance. (But taking for granted is a form of neglect.)

[3] Besides Bok and Locke, whom I refer to, those who have said something about it include N. Hartmann, *Ethik* (Berlin: W. de Gruyter, 1962), pp. 468 ff.; Virginia Held, *Rights and Goods* (New York and London: Free Press, 1984), esp. chap. 5, "The Grounds for Social Trust"; D. O. Thomas, "The Duty to Trust," *Aristotelian Society Proceedings* (1970), pp. 89–101. It is invoked in passing by Aurel Kolnai in "Forgiveness," in *Ethics, Value and Reality*, ed. Bernard Williams and David Wiggins (Indianapolis: Macmillan Co., 1978): "Trust in the world, unless it is vitiated by hairbrained optimism and dangerous irresponsibility, may be looked upon not to be sure as the very starting point and very basis but perhaps as the epitome and culmination of morality" (p. 223); and by John R. S. Wilson in "In One Another's Power," *Ethics* 88 (1978): 303.

Trust, the phenomenon we are so familiar with that we scarcely notice its presence and its variety, is shown by us and responded to by us not only with intimates but with strangers, and even with declared enemies. We trust our enemies not to fire at us when we lay down our arms and put out a white flag. In Britain burglars and police used to trust each other not to carry deadly weapons. We often trust total strangers, such as those from whom we ask directions in foreign cities, to direct rather than misdirect us, or to tell us so if they do not know what we want to know; and we think we should do the same for those who ask the same help from us. Of course we are often disappointed, rebuffed, let down, or betrayed when we exhibit such trust in others, and we are often exploited when we show the wanted trustworthiness. We do in fact, wisely or stupidly, virtuously or viciously, show trust in a great variety of forms, and manifest a great variety of versions of trustworthiness, both with intimates and with strangers. We trust those we encounter in lonely library stacks to be searching for books, not victims. We sometimes let ourselves fall asleep on trains or planes, trusting neighboring strangers not to take advantage of our defenselessness. We put our bodily safety into the hands of pilots, drivers, doctors, with scarcely any sense of recklessness. We used not to suspect that the food we buy might be deliberately poisoned, and we used to trust our children to day-care centers.

We may still have no choice but to buy food and to leave our children in day-care centers, but now we do it with suspicion and anxiety. Trust is always an invitation not only to confidence tricksters but also to terrorists, who discern its most easily destroyed and socially vital forms. Criminals, not moral philosophers, have been experts at discerning different forms of trust. Most of us notice a given form of trust more easily after its sudden demise or severe injury. We inhabit a climate of trust as we inhabit an atmosphere and notice it as we notice air, only when it becomes scarce or polluted.

We may have no choice but to continue to rely on the local shop for food, even after some of the food on its shelves has been found to have been poisoned with intent. We can still rely where we no longer trust. What is the difference between trusting others and merely relying on them? It seems to be reliance on their good will toward one, as distinct from their dependable habits, or only on their dependably exhibited fear, anger, or other motives compatible with ill will toward one, or on motives not directed on one at all. We may rely on our fellows' fear of the newly appointed security guards in shops to deter them from injecting poison into the food on the shelves, once we have ceased to trust them. We may rely on the shopkeeper's concern for his profits to motivate him to take effective precautions against poisoners and also trust him to *want* his customers not to be harmed by his products, at least as long as this want can be satisfied without frustrating his wish to increase his profits. Trust is often mixed with other species of reliance on persons. Trust which is reliance on another's good will, perhaps minimal good will, contrasts with the forms of reliance on others' reactions and attitudes which are shown by the comedian, the advertiser, the blackmailer, the kidnapper-extortioner, and the terrorist, who all depend on particular attitudes and reactions of others for the success of their actions. We all depend on one anothers' psychology in countless ways, but this is not yet to trust them. The trusting can be betrayed, or at least let down, and not just disappointed. Kant's neighbors who counted on his regular habits as a clock for their own less automatically regular ones might be disappointed with him if he slept in one day, but not let down by him, let alone had their trust betrayed. When I trust another, I depend on her good will toward me. I need not either acknowledge this reliance nor believe that she has either invited or acknowledged such trust since there is such a thing as unconscious trust, as unwanted trust, as forced receipt of trust, and as trust which the trusted is unaware of. (Plausible conditions for proper trust will be that it survives consciousness, by both parties, and that the trusted has had some opportunity to signify acceptance or rejection, to warn the trusting if their trust is unacceptable.)

Where one depends on another's good will, one is necessarily vulnerable to the limits of that good will. One leaves others an opportunity to harm one when one trusts, and also shows one's confidence that they will not take it. Reasonable trust will require good grounds for such confidence in another's good will, or at least the absence of good grounds for expecting their ill will or indifference. Trust then, on this first approximation, is accepted vulnerability to another's possible but not expected ill will (or lack of good will) toward one.

What we now need to do, to get any sense of the variety of forms of trust, is to look both at varieties of vulnerability and at varieties of grounds for not expecting others to take advantage of it. One way to do the former, which I shall take, is to look at the variety of sorts of goods or things one values or cares about, which can be left or put within the striking power of others, and the variety of ways we can let or leave others "close" enough to what we value to be able to harm it. Then we can look at various reasons we might have for wanting or accepting such closeness of those with power to harm us, and for confidence that they will not use this power. In this way we can hope to explicate the vague terms "good will" and "ill will." If it be asked why the initial emphasis is put on trusting's vulnerability, on the risks rather than the benefits of trust, part of the answer has already been given—namely, that we come to realize what trust involves retrospectively and posthumously, once our vulnerability is brought home to us by actual wounds. The other part of the answer is that even when one does become aware of trust and intentionally continues a particular case of it, one need not intend to achieve any particular benefit from it—one need not trust a person in order to receive some gain, even when in fact one does gain. Trusting, as an intentional mental phenomenon, need not be purposive. But intentional trusting does require awareness of one's confidence that the trusted will not harm one, although they could harm one. It is not a Hobbesian obsession with strike force which dictates the form of analysis I have sketched but, rather, the natural order of consciousness and self-consciousness of trust, which progresses from initially unself-conscious trust to awareness of risk along with confidence that it is a good risk, on to some realization of why we are taking this particular risk, and eventually to some evaluation of what we may generally gain and what we may lose from the willingness to take such risks. The ultimate point of what we are doing when we trust may be the last thing that we come to realize.

The next thing to attend to is why we typically do leave things that we value close enough to others for them to harm them. The answer, simply, is that we need their help in creating, and then in not merely guarding but looking after the things we most value, so we have no choice but to allow some others to be in a position to harm them. The one in the best position to harm something is its creator or nurse-cum-caretaker. Since the things we typically do value include such things as we cannot singlehandedly either create or sustain (our own life, health, reputation, our offspring and their well-being, as well as intrinsically shared goods such as conversation, its written equivalent, theater and other forms of play, chamber music, market exchange, political life, and so on) we must allow many other people to get into positions where they can, if they choose, injure what we care about, since those are the same positions that they must be in in order to help us take care of what we care about. The simple Socratic truth that no person is self-sufficient gets elaborated, once we add the equally Socratic truth that the human soul's activity is *caring* for things into the richer truth that no one is able by herself to look after everything she wants to have looked after, nor even alone to look after her own "private" goods, such as health and bodily safety. If we try to distinguish different forms of trust by the different valued goods we confidently allow another to have some control over, we are following Locke in analyzing trusting on the model of *en*-trusting. Thus, there will be an answer not just to the question, Whom do you trust? but to the question, *What* do you trust to them?—what good is it that they are in a position to take from you, or to injure? Accepting such an analysis, taking trust to be a three-place predicate (A trusts B with valued thing C) will involve some distortion and regimentation of some cases, where we may have to strain to discern any definite candidate for C, but I think it will prove more of a help than a hindrance.

One way in which trusted persons can fail to act as they were trusted to is by taking on the care of more than they were entrusted with—the babysitter who decides that the nursery would be improved if painted purple and sets to work to transform it, will have acted, as a babysitter, in an untrustworthy way, however great his good will. When we are trusted, we are relied upon to realize *what* it is for whose care we have some discretionary responsibility, and normal people can pick up the cues that indicate the limits of what is entrusted. For example, if I confide my troubles to a friend, I trust her to listen, more or less sympathetically, and to preserve confidentiality, but usually not, or not without consulting me, to take steps to remove the source of my worry. That could be interfering impertinence, not trustworthiness as a confidante. She will, nevertheless, within the restricted scope of what is trusted to her (knowledge of my affairs, not their management) have some discretion both as to how to receive the confidence and, unless I swear her to absolute secrecy, as to when to share it. The relativization of trust to particular things cared about by the truster goes along with the discretion the trusted usually has in judging just what should be done to "look after" the particular good entrusted to her care. This discretionary power will of course be limited by the limits of what is entrusted and usually by some other constraints.

Is it plausible to construe all cases of being trusted not merely as cases of being trusted by someone else with access to what matters to the truster, but as some control over that, expected to be used to take care of it, and involving some discretionary powers in so doing?[4] Can we further elaborate the analysis of a relationship of trust as one where A has er.trusted B with some of the care of C and where B has some discretionary powers in caring for C? Admittedly there are many cases of trust where "caring for C" seems much more than A expects of B even when there is no problem in finding a fairly restricted value for C. Suppose I look quickly around me before proceeding into the dark street or library stacks where my business takes me, judge the few people I discern there to be nondangerous, and so go ahead. We can say that my bodily safety, and perhaps my pocketbook, are the goods I am allowing these people to be in a position to threaten. I trust them, it seems, merely to leave me alone. But this is not quite right, for should a piece of falling masonry or toppling books threaten to fall on my head, and one of these persons leap into action and shove me out of this danger, I would regard that as rather more than less than I had trusted these strangers to do—a case for gratitude, not for an assault charge, despite the sudden, unceremonious, possibly painful or even injurious nature of my close encounter with my rescuer. So *what* do I trust strangers in such circumstances to do? Certainly not anything whatever as long as it is done with good will, nor even anything whatever for my bodily safety and security of property as long as it is done with good will. Suppose someone I have judged nondangerous as I proceed into the stacks should seize me from behind, frightening but not harming me, and claim with apparent sincerity that she did it for my own good, so that I would learn a lesson and be more cautious in the future. I would not respond with gratitude but demand what business my long-term security of life was of hers, that she felt free to subject me to such unpleasant educational measures. In terms of my analysis, what I trusted her with was my peace and safety here and now, with "looking after" that, not with my long-term safety. We need some fairly positive and discretion-allowing term, such as "look after" or "show concern for," to let in the range of behavior which would not disappoint the library user's trust in fellow users. We also need some specification of what good was in question to see why the intrusive, presumptuous, and paternalistic moves disappoint rather than meet the trust one has in such circumstances. "Look after" and "take care of" will have to be given a very weak sense in some cases of trust; it

---

[4] A reader for this journal suggested that, when one trusts one's child to mail an important letter for one at the mailbox on the corner, no discretionary powers are given, although one is trusting him with the safe, speedy transfer of the letter to the box. But life is full of surprises—in Washington on Inauguration day mailboxes were sealed closed as a security precaution, and in some parts of Manhattan mailboxes are regularly sealed after dark. One trusts the child to do the sensible thing if such an unforeseen problem should arise—to bring the letter back, not leave it on the ledge of the sealed mailbox or go too far afield to find another.

will be better to do this than try to construe cases where more positive care is expected of the trusted as cases of trusting them to leave alone, or merely safeguard, some valued thing. Trusting strangers to leave us alone should be construed as trusting them with the "care" of our valued autonomy. When one trusts one's child to one's separated spouse, it is all aspects of the child's good as a developing person which are entrusted to the other parent's care. Trusting him or her with our children can hardly be construed as trusting them not to "interfere" with the child's satisfactory development. The most important things we entrust to others are things which take more than noninterference in order to thrive.

The more extensive the discretionary powers of the trusted, the less clear-cut will be the answer to the question of when trust is disappointed. The truster, who always needs good judgment to know whom to trust and how much discretion to give, will also have some scope for discretion in judging what should count as failing to meet trust, either through incompetence, negligence, or ill will. In any case of a questionable exercise of discretion there will be room both for forgiveness of unfortunate outcomes and for tact in treatment of the question of whether there is anything to forgive. One thing that can destroy a trust relationship fairly quickly is the combination of a rigoristic unforgiving attitude on the part of the truster and a touchy sensitivity to any criticism on the part of the trusted. If a trust relationship is to continue, some tact and willingness to forgive on the part of the truster and some willingness on the part of the trusted both to be forgiven and to forgive unfair criticisms, seem essential.[5] The need for this will be greater the more discretion the trusted has.

If part of what the truster entrusts to the trusted are discretionary powers, then the truster risks abuse of those and the successful disguise of such abuse. The special vulnerability which trust involves is vulnerability to not yet noticed harm, or to disguised ill will. What one forgives or tactfully averts one's eyes from may be not well-meant but ill-judged or incompetent attempts to care for what is entrusted but, rather, ill-meant and cleverly disguised abuses of discretionary power. To understand the moral risks of trust,

---

[5] This point I take from the fascinating sociological analysis of trust given by Niklas Luhmann (*Trust and Power* [Chichester, N.Y., 1979]) which I discovered while revising this paper. In many ways my analysis agrees with his, insofar as I understand the implications of his account of it as "reduction of complexity," in particular of complex future contingencies. He makes much of the difference between absence of trust and distrust, and distinguishes trust from what it presupposes, a mere "familiarity," or taking for granted. I have blurred these distinctions. He treats personal trust as a risky investment and looks at mechanisms for initiating and maintaining trust. Tact is said to play an important role in both. It enables trust-offering overtures to be rejected without hostility ensuing, and it enables those who make false moves in their attempts to maintain trust to recover their position without too much loss of face. "A social climate . . . institutionalizes tact and knows enough escape routes for self presentation in difficult situations" (p. 84). It is important, I think, to see that tact is a virtue which needs to be added to delicacy of discrimination in recognizing *what* one is trusted with, good judgment as to whom to trust with what, and a willingness to admit and forgive fault, as all functional virtues needed in those who would sustain trust.

it is important to see the special sort of vulnerability it introduces. Yet the discretionary element which introduces this special danger is essential to that which trust at its best makes possible. To elaborate Hume: "'Tis impossible to separate the chance of good from the risk of ill."[6]

It is fairly easy, once we look, to see how this special vulnerability is involved in many ordinary forms of trust. We trust the mailman to deliver and not tamper with the mail, and to some extent we trust his discretion in interpreting what "tampering" covers. Normally we do not expect him to read our mail but to deliver it unread, even when the message is open, on a postcard. But on occasion it may be proper, or at least not wrong, for him to read it. I have had friendly mailmen (in Greek villages and in small Austrian towns) who tell me what my mail announces as they hand it over: "Your relatives have recovered and can travel now, and are soon arriving!" Such interest in one's affairs is not part of the normal idea of the role of mailman and could provide opportunity for blackmail, but in virtue of that very interest they could give much more knowledgeable and intelligent service—in the above case by knowing our plans they knew when and where we had moved and delivered to the new address without instructions. What do we trust our mailmen to do or not to do? To use their discretion in getting our mail to us, to take enough interest in us and in the nature of our mail, (compatibly with their total responsibility) to make intelligent decisions about what to do with it when such decisions have to be made. Similarly with our surgeons and plumbers—*just* what they should do to put right what is wrong is something we must leave to them. Should they act incompetently, negligently, or deliberately against our interests, they may conceal these features of their activities from us by pretense that whatever happened occurred as a result of an honest and well-meaning exercise of the discretion given to them. This way they may retain our trust and so have opportunity to harm us yet further. In trusting them, we trust them to use their discretionary powers competently and non-maliciously, and the latter includes not misleading us about how they have used them.

Trust, on the analysis I have proposed, is letting other persons (natural or artificial, such as firms, nations, etc.) take care of something the truster cares about, where such "caring for" involves some exercise of discretionary powers. But not all the variables involved in trust are yet in view. One which the entrusting model obscures rather than highlights is the degree of explicitness. To entrust is intentionally and usually formally to hand over the care of something to someone, but trusting is rarely begun by making up one's mind to trust, and often it has no definite initiation of any sort but grows up slowly and imperceptibly. What I have tried to take from the notion of entrusting is not its voluntarist and formalist character but rather the possible specificity and restrictedness of *what* is entrusted, along with the discretion the trustee has in looking after that thing. Trust can come with no beginnings, with gradual as well as sudden beginnings, and with various degrees of self-consciousness, voluntariness, and expressness. My earlier discussion of the delicacy and tact needed by the truster in judging the performance of the trusted applied only to cases where the truster not merely realizes that she trusts but has some conscious control over the continuation of the trust relationship. The discussion of abuses of discretionary power applied only to cases where the trusted realizes that she is trusted and trusted with discretionary powers. But trust relationships need not be so express, and some important forms of them cannot be verbally acknowledged by the persons involved. Trust between infant and parent is such a case, and it is one which also reminds us of another crucial variable in trust relations to which so far I have only indirectly alluded. This is the relative power of the truster and the trusted, and the relative costs to each of a breakdown of their trust relationship. In emphasizing the toleration of vulnerability by the truster I have made attitudes to relative power and powerlessness the essence of trust and distrust; I have not yet looked at the varieties of trust we discern when we vary the power of the truster in relation to the power of the trusted, both while the trust endures and in its absence. Trust alters power positions, and both the position one is in without a given form of trust and the position one has within a relation of trust need to be considered before one can judge whether that form of trust is sensible and morally decent. Infant trust reminds us not just of inarticulate and uncritical or blind trust, but of trust by those who are maximally vulnerable, whether or not they give trust.

Trust and Relative Power

I have been apparently preoccupied up till now with dimensions of trust which show up most clearly in trust between articulate adults, in a position to judge one another's performance, and having some control over their degree of vulnerability to others. This approach typifies a myopia which, once noticed, explains the "regrettably sparse" attempts to understand trust as a phenomenon of moral importance.[7] For the more we ignore dependency relations between those grossly unequal in power and ignore what cannot be spelled out in an explicit acknowledgment, the more readily we will assume that everything that needs to be understood about trust and trustworthiness can be grasped by looking at the morality of contract. For it takes an adult to be able to make a contract, and it takes something like Hegel's civil society of

---

[7] Luhmann, p. 8, n. 1. It is interesting to note that, unlike Luhmann and myself, Bernard Barber begins his sociological treatment of trust in *The Logic and Limits of Trust* (New Brunswick, N.J.: Rutgers University Press, 1983) not by remarking on the neglect of the topic but rather, by saying, "Today nearly everyone seems to be talking about 'trust'" (p. 1). He lists "moral philosophers" along with "presidential candidates, political columnists, pollsters, social critics and the man in the street" as among those talking so much about it but cites only two moral philosophers, Bok and Rawls (who by his own account is *not* always talking about it). Between Luhmann's work on trust, first published in Germany in 1973, and Barber's, sociologists had ten years to get the talk about trust going, but it has scarcely spread yet to most of the moral philosophers I have encountered.

near equals to find a use for contracts. But one has to strain the contractarian model very considerably to see infant-parent relations as essentially contractual, both because of the nonexpressness of the infant's attitude and because of the infant's utter powerlessness. It takes inattention to cooperation between unequals, and between those without a common language, to keep one a contented contractarian. To do more, I must both show how infant trust, and other variations along the relative power dimension, can be covered and also indicate just where trust in contracts fits into the picture we then get.

Infant trust is like one form of non-contract-based trust to which some attention has been given in our philosophical tradition, namely, trust in God. Trust in God is total, in that whatever one cares about, it will not thrive if God wills that it not thrive. A young child too is totally dependent on the good will of the parent, totally incapable of looking after anything he cares about without parental help or against parental will. Such total dependence does not, in itself, necessarily elicit trust—some theists curse God, display futile distrust or despair rather than trust. Infants too can make suspicious, futile, self-protective moves against the powerful adults in their world or retreat into autism. But surviving infants will usually have shown some trust, enough to accept offered nourishment, enough not to attempt to prevent such close approach. The ultra-Hobbist child who fears or rejects the mother's breast, as if fearing poison from that source, can be taken as displaying innate distrust, and such newborns must be the exception in a surviving species. Hobbes tells us that, in the state of nature, "seeing the infant is in the power of the Mother, and is therefore obliged to obey her, so she may either nourish or expose it; if she nourish it, it oweth its life to the Mother and is therefore obliged to obey her rather than any other" (*Leviathan*, chap. 20). Even he, born a twin to fear, is apparently willing to take mother's milk on trust. Some degree of innate, if selective, trust seems a necessary element in any surviving creature whose first nourishment (if it is not exposed) comes from another, and this innate but fragile trust could serve as explanation both of the possibility of other forms of trust and of their fragility.

Infant trust that normally does not need to be won but is there unless and until it is destroyed is important for an understanding of the possibility of trust. Trust is much easier to maintain than it is to get started and is never hard to destroy. Unless some form of it were innate, and unless that form could pave the way for new forms, it would appear a miracle that trust ever occurs. The postponement of the onset of distrust is a lot more explicable than hypothetical Hobbesian conversions from total distrust to limited trust. The persistent human adult tendency to profess trust in a creator-God can also be seen as an infantile residue of this crucial innate readiness of infants to initially impute goodwill to the powerful persons on whom they depend. So we should perhaps welcome, or at least tolerate, religious trust, if we value any form of trust. Nevertheless the theological literature on trust in God is of very limited help to us if we want to understand trust in human persons, even that trust in parents of which it can be seen as a nostalgic fantasy-memory. For the child soon learns that the parent is not, like God, invulnerable, nor even, like some versions of God, subject to offense or insult but not injury. Infant trust, although extreme in the discrepancy of power between the truster and the trusted, is to some extent a matter of mutual trust and mutual if unequal vulnerability. The parents' enormous power to harm the child and disappoint the child's trust is the power of ones also vulnerable to the child's at first insignificant but ever-increasing power, including power as one trusted by the parent. So not very much can be milked from the theological literature on the virtues of trust, faith, and hope in God and returned to the human context, even to the case of infant and parent. Indeed we might cite the theological contamination of the concept of trust as part of the explanation for the general avoidance of the topic in modern moral philosophy. If trust is seen as a variant of the suspect virtue of faith in the competence of the powers that be, then readiness to trust will be seen not just as a virtue of the weak but itself as a moral weakness, better replaced by vigilance and self-assertion, by self-reliance or by cautious, minimal, and carefully monitored trust. The psychology of adolescents, not infants, then gets glorified as the moral ideal. Such a reaction against a religious version of the ethics of trust is as healthy, understandable, and, it is hoped, as passing a phenomenon as is adolescent self-assertive individualism in the life of a normal person.

The goods which a trustworthy parent takes care of for as long as the child is unable to take care of them alone, or continues to welcome the parent's help in caring for them, are such things as nutrition, shelter, clothing, health, education, privacy, and loving attachment to others. Why, once the child becomes at all self-conscious about trusting parents to look after such goods for her, should she have confidence that parents are dependable custodians of such goods? Presumably because many of them are also goods to the parent, through their being goods to the child, especially if the parent loves the child. They will be common goods, so that for the trusted to harm them would be self-harm as well as harm to the child. The best reason for confidence in another's good care of what one cares about is that it is a common good, and the best reason for thinking that one's own good is also a common good is being loved. This may not, usually will not, ensure agreement on what best should be done to take care of that good, but it rules out suspicion of ill will. However, even when a child does not feel as loved by a parent as she would like, or as she thinks her siblings or friends are, she may still have complete confidence that at least many of the goods she cares about can be entrusted to her parents' care. She can have plenty of evidence that, for reasons such as pride, desire to perpetuate their name, or whatever, they do care as she herself does about her health, her success, and her ties with them. She can have good reason to be confident of the continued trustworthiness of her parents in many regards, from what she knows of their own concerns.

As the child approaches adulthood, and as the parents draw nearer to the likely dependency of old age, the trust may approximate much more closely to mutual trust and mutual vulnerability between equals, and they may then make explicit or even formal agreements about what is to be done in return for what. But no such contractual or quasi-contractual agreement can convert the young child's trust and the parent's trustworthiness retrospectively into part of a contractual mutual exchange. At most it can transform what was a continuing relation of mutual trust into a contractual obligation to render some sort of service to one's parents. The previous parental care could become a moral *reason* for making a contract with parents, but not what one received as 'consideration' in such a contract. At best that could be a virtual 'consideration,' perhaps symbolized by the parents' formal cancelling of any until then outstanding 'debt' of gratitude, in return for the rights the contract gives them. But normally whatever grateful return one makes to another is not made in exchange for a 'receipt' which is proof against any outstanding 'debt.' Only those determined to see every proper moral transaction as an exchange will construe every gift as made in exchange for an IOU, and every return gift as made in exchange for a receipt. Only such trade fetishists will have any reason to try to construe the appropriate adult response to earlier parental care as part of a virtual contract, or as proper content for an actual contract. As Hume says, contract should not replace "the more generous and noble intercourse of friendship and good offices," which he construes as a matter of spontaneous service responded to by "return in the same manner."[8] We can resist this reduction of the more noble responses of gratitude to the fulfilling of contractual obligations if we focus our moral attention on other sorts of trust than trust in contracts. Looking at infant trust helps one do that. Not only has the child no concept of virtual contract when she trusts, but the parent's duty to the child seems in no way dependent on the expectation that the child will make a later return. The child or the parent may die before the reversal of dependency arrives. Furthermore, parent's knowledge either that the child, or that he himself, or both, will die within say ten years, in itself (and disability apart) makes no difference to the parent's responsibility while he lives, as that is usually understood. Parental and filial responsibility does not rest on deals, actual or virtual, between parent and child.

Trust and Voluntary Abilities

The child trusts as long as she is encouraged to trust and until the trust is unmistakably betrayed. It takes childhood innocence to be able to trust simply because of encouragement to trust. "Trust me!" is for most of us an invitation which we cannot accept at will—either we do already trust the one who says it, in which case it serves at best as reassurance,[9] or it is properly responded to with, "Why should and how can I, until I have cause to?"[10] The child, of

---

[8] Hume, p. 521.

[9] My thoughts about the role of the words "Trust me!" are influenced by an unpublished paper on promising by T. M. Scanlon. Indeed Scanlon's talk on this topic to the University of Pittsburgh philosophy department in April 1984 was what, along with Hume's few remarks about it, started me thinking about trust in and out of voluntary exchanges.

[10] Luhmann says, "It is not possible to demand trust of others; trust can only be offered and accepted" (p. 43). I am here claiming something stronger, namely, that one cannot offer it or accept it by an act of will: that one cannot demand it of oneself or others until some trust-securing social artifice invents something like promise that *can* be offered and accepted at will.

course, cannot trust at will any more than experienced adults can—encouragement is a condition of not lapsing into distrust, rather than of a move from distrust to trust. One constraint on an account of trust which postulates infant trust as its essential seed is that it not make essential to trusting the use of concepts or abilities which a child cannot be reasonably believed to possess. Acts of will of any sort are not plausibly attributed to infants; it would be unreasonable to suppose that they can do at will what adults cannot, namely, obey the instruction to trust, whether it comes from others or is a self-instruction.

To suppose that infants emerge from the womb already equipped with some ur-confidence in what supports them, so that no choice is needed to continue with that attitude, until something happens to shake or destroy such confidence, is plausible enough. My account of trust has been designed to allow for unconscious trust, for conscious but unchosen trust, as well as for conscious trust the truster has chosen to endorse and cultivate. Whereas it strains the concept of agreement to speak of unconscious agreements and unchosen agreements, and overstrains the concept of contract to speak of unconscious or unchosen contracts, there is no strain whatever in the concept of automatic and unconscious trust, and of unchosen but mutual trust. Trust between infant and parent, at its best, exhibits such primitive and basic trust. Once it is present, the story of how trust becomes self-conscious, controlled, monitored, critical, pretended, and eventually either cautious and distrustful of itself, or discriminatory and reflexive, so that we come to trust ourselves as trusters, is relatively easy to tell. What will need explanation will be the ceasings to trust, the transfers of trust, the restriction or enlargements in the fields of what is trusted, when, and to whom, rather than any abrupt switches from distrust to trust. Even if such occurrences do ever occur (when one suddenly falls in love or lust with a stranger or former enemy, or has a religious conversion), they take more than the mere invitation "Trust me."

In his famous account of what a promise (and a contract) involves, Hume strongly implies that it is an artificially contrived and secured case of mutual trust. The penalty to which a promisor subjects himself in promising, he says, is that of "never being trusted again in case of failure."[11] The problem which the artifice of promise solves is a generally disadvantageous "want of mutual confidence and security."[12] It is plausible to construe the offer whose acceptance counts as acceptance of a contract or a promise as at least implicitly including an invitation to trust. Part of what makes promises the special thing they are, and the philosophically intriguing thing they are, is that we *can* at will accept *this* sort of invitation to trust, whereas in general we cannot trust at will. Promises are puzzling because they seem to have the power, by verbal magic, to initiate real voluntary short-term trusting. They not merely create obligations apparently at the will of the obligated, but they create trust at the will of the truster. They present a very fascinating case of trust and trustworthiness, but one which, because of those very intriguing features, is ill suited

---

[11] Hume, p. 522.

[12] Ibid., p. 521.

to the role of paradigm. Yet in as far as modern moral philosophers have attended at all to the morality of trust, it is trust in parties to an agreement that they have concentrated on, and it is into this very special and artificial mold that they have tried to force other cases of trust, when they notice them at all.

Trust of any particular form is made more likely, in adults, if there is a climate of trust of that sort. Awareness of what is customary, as well as past experience of one's own, affects one's ability to trust. We take it for granted that people will perform their role-related duties and trust any individual worker to look after whatever her job requires her to. The very existence of that job, as a standard occupation, creates a climate of some trust in those with that job. Social artifices such as property, which allocate rights and duties as a standard job does, more generally also create a climate of trust, a presumption of a sort of trustworthiness. On the Humean account of promises and contracts which I find more or less correct,[13] their establishment as a customary procedure also reverses a presumption concerning trustworthiness, but only in limited conditions. Among these is a special voluntary act by the promisor, giving it to be understood that what he offers is a promise, and another voluntary act by the promisee, acceptance of that promise. Promises are "a bond or security,"[14] and "the sanction of the interested commerce of mankind."[15] To understand them is to see what sort of sanction is involved, what sort of security they provide, and the social preconditions of each. Then one understands how the presumption about the trustworthiness of self-interested strangers can be reversed, and how the ability to trust them (for a limited time, on a limited matter) can become a voluntary ability. To adapt Hume's words, "Hence I learn to count on a service from another, although he bears me no real kindness."[16] Promises are a most ingenious social invention, and trust in those who have given us promises is a complex and sophisticated moral achievement. Once the social conditions are right for it, once the requisite climate of trust in promisors is there, it is easy to take it for a simpler matter than it is and to ignore its background conditions. They include not merely the variable social conventions and punitive customs Hume emphasizes, but the prior existence of less artificial and less voluntary forms of trust, such as trust in friends and family, and enough trust in fellows to engage with them in agreed exchanges of a more or less simultaneous nature, exchanges such as barter or handshakes, which do not require one to rely on strangers over a period of time, as exchange of promises typically does.

Those who take advantage of this sophisticated social device will be, mainly, adults who are not intimate with one another, and who see one another more or less as equal in power to secure the enforcement of the rules of the contracting game (to extract damages for broken contracts, to set in

---

[13] I have discussed and defended Hume's account in "Promises, Promises, Promises," in my *Postures of the Mind: Essays on Mind and Morals* (Minneapolis: University of Minnesota Press, 1985).

[14] Hume, p. 541.

[15] Ibid., p. 522.

[16] Ibid., p. 521.

motion the accepted penalty for fraudulent promises, and so on). As Nietzsche emphasized, the right to make promises and the power to have one's promises accepted are not possessed by everyone in relation to everyone else. Not only can the right be forfeited, but it is all along an elite right, possessed only by those with a certain social status. Slaves, young children, the ill, and the mentally incompetent do not fully possess it. For those who do possess it, whose offer or acceptance of a promise has moral force, the extent to which use of it regulates their relations with others varies with their other social powers. Women whose property, work, and sexual services became their husbands' on marriage did not have much left to promise, and what was left could usually be taken from them without their consent and without the formality of exchange of promises. Their right to promise anything of significance was contracted into the right to make one vow of fixed and non-negotiable content, the marriage vow, and even that was often made under duress. The important relationships and trust relationships which structured women's lives for most of the known history of our species, relations to spouse, children, fellow workers, were not entered into by free choice, or by freely giving or receiving promises. They were, typically, relationships of which the more important were ones of intimacy, relationships to superiors or inferiors in power, relationships not in any strong sense freely chosen nor to chosen others. Like the infant, they found themselves faced with others to trust or distrust, found themselves trusted or not trusted by these given others. Their freely given and seriously taken promises were restricted in their content to trivialities. Contract is a device for traders, entrepreneurs, and capitalists, not for children, servants, indentured wives, and slaves. They were the traded, not the traders, and any participation they had in the promising game was mere play. It is appropriate, then, that Nietzsche, the moral philosopher who glorifies promise more even than contemporary contractarians, was also the one who advised his fellow male exchangers or givers of promises thus, "He must conceive of woman as a possession, as a property that can be locked, as something predestined for service and achieving her perfection in that."[17] Nietzsche faces squarely what Hume half faced, and what most moral philosophers have avoided facing, that the liberal morality which takes voluntary agreement as the paradigm source of moral obligation must either exclude the women they expect to continue in their traditional role from the class of moral subjects, or admit internal contradiction in their moral beliefs. Nor does the contradiction vanish once women have equal legal rights with men, as long as they are still expected to take responsibility for any child they conceive voluntarily or nonvoluntarily, either to abort or to bear and either care for or arrange for others to care for. Since a liberal morality both *must* let this responsibility rest with women, and yet cannot conceive of it as self-assumed, then the centrality of voluntary agreement to the liberal and contractarian morality must

---

[17] Nietzsche, *Beyond Good and Evil*, pt. 7, §238, trans. Walter Kaufmann, *Basic Writings of Nietzsche* (New York, 1968), p. 357.

be challenged once women are treated as full moral fellows. Voluntary agreement, and trust in others to keep their agreements, must be moved from the center to the moral periphery, once servants, ex-slaves, and women are taken seriously as moral subjects and agents.

The Male Fixation on Contract

The great moral theorists in our tradition not only are all men, they are mostly men who had minimal adult dealings with (and so were then minimally influenced by) women. With a few significant exceptions (Hume, Hegel, J. S. Mill, Sidgwick, maybe Bradley) they are a collection of gays, clerics, misogynists, and puritan bachelors. It should not surprise us, then, that particularly in the modern period they managed to relegate to the mental background the web of trust tying most moral agents to one another, and to focus their philosophical attention so single-mindedly on cool, distanced relations between more or less free and equal adult strangers, say, the members of an all male club, with membership rules and rules for dealing with rule breakers and where the form of cooperation was restricted to ensuring that each member could read his *Times* in peace and have no one step on his gouty toes. Explicitly assumed or recognized obligations toward others with the same obligations and the same power to see justice done to rule breakers then are seen as the moral norm.

Relations between equals and nonintimates will *be* the moral norm for male adults whose dealings with others are mainly business or restrained social dealings with similarly placed males. But for lovers, husbands, fathers, the ill, the very young, and the elderly, other relationships with their moral potential and perils will loom larger. For Hume, who had several strong-willed and manipulative women to cooperate or contend with in his adult life, for Mill, who had Harriet Taylor on his hands, for Hegel, whose domestic life was of normal complication, the rights and duties of equals to equals in a civil society which recognized only a male electorate could only be *part* of the moral story. They could not ignore the virtues and vices of family relationships, male-female relationships, master-slave, and employer-employee relationships as easily as could Hobbes, Butler, Bentham, or Kant. Nor could they as easily adopt the usual compensatory strategies of the moral philosophers who confine their attention to the rights and duties of free and equal adults to one another—the strategy of claiming, if pressed, that these rights are the *core* of all moral relationships and maybe also claiming that any other relationships, engendering additional or different rights and duties, come about only by an exercise of one of the core rights, the right to promise. Philosophers who remember what it was like to be a dependent child, or know what it is like to be a parent, or to have a dependent parent, an old or handicapped relative, friend, or neighbor will find it implausible to treat such relations as simply cases of co-membership in a kingdom of ends, in the given temporary conditions of one-sided dependence.

To the extent that these claims are correct (and I am aware that they need more defense than I have given them here)[18] it becomes fairly easy to see one likely explanation of the neglect in Western moral philosophy of the full range of sorts of trust. Both before the rise of a society which needed contract as a commercial device, and after it, women were counted on to serve their men, to raise their children to fill the roles they were expected to fill and not deceive their men about the paternity of these children. What men counted on one another for, in work and war, presupposed this background domestic trust, trust in women not merely not to poison their men (Nietzsche derides them for learning less than they might have in the kitchen), but to turn out sons who could trust and be trusted in traditional men's roles and daughters who would reduplicate their own capacities for trust and trustworthiness. Since the women's role did not include the writing of moral treatises, any thoughts they had about trust, based on their experience of it, did not get into our tradition (or did Diotima teach Socrates something about trust as well as love?). And the more powerful men, including those who did write the moral treatises, were in the morally awkward position of being, collectively, oppressors of women, exploiters of women's capacity for trustworthiness in unequal, non-voluntary, and non-contract-based relationships. Understandably, they did not focus their attention on forms of trust and demands for trustworthiness which it takes a Nietzsche to recognize without shame. Humankind can bear only so much reality.

The recent research of Carol Gilligan has shown us how intelligent and reflective twentieth-century women see morality, and how different their picture of it is from that of men, particularly the men who eagerly assent to the claims of currently orthodox contractarian-Kantian moral theories.[19] Women cannot now, any more than they could when oppressed, ignore that part of morality and those forms of trust which cannot easily be forced into the liberal and particularly the contractarian mold. Men may but women cannot see morality as essentially a matter of keeping to the minimal moral traffic rules, designed to restrict close encounters between autonomous persons to self-chosen ones. Such a conception presupposes both an equality of power and a natural separateness from others, which is alien to women's experience of life and morality. For those most of whose daily dealings are with the less powerful or the more powerful, a moral code designed for those equal in power will be at best nonfunctional, at worst an offensive pretense of equality as a substitute for its actuality. But equality is not even a desirable ideal in all relationships—children not only are not but should not be equal in power to adults, and we need a morality to guide us in our dealings with those who either cannot or should not achieve equality of power (animals, the ill, the dying, children while still young) with those with whom they have unavoidable and often intimate relationships.

---

[18] I defend them a little more in "What Do Women Want in a Moral Theory?" *Nous* 19 (March 1985): 53–64.

[19] Carol Gilligan, *In a Different Voice* (Cambridge, Mass.: Harvard University Press, 1982).

Modern moral philosophy has concentrated on the morality of fairly cool relationships between those who are deemed to be roughly equal in power to determine the rules and to instigate sanctions against rule breakers. It is not surprising, then, that the main form of trust that any attention has been given to is trust in governments, and in parties to voluntary agreements to do what they have agreed to do. As much as possible is absorbed into the latter category, so that we suppose that paying for what one takes from a shop, doing what one is employed to do, returning what one has borrowed, supporting one's spouse, are all cases of being faithful to binding voluntary agreements, to contracts of some sort. (For Hume, none of these would count as duties arising from contract or promise.) Yet if I think of the trust I show, say in the plumber who comes from the municipal drainage authority when I report that my drains are clogged, it is not plausibly seen as trust that he will fulfill his contractual obligations to me or to his employer. When I trust him to do whatever is necessary and safe to clear my drains, I take his expertise and his lack of ill will for granted. Should he plant explosives to satisfy some unsuspected private or social grudge against me, what I might try to sue him for (if I escaped alive) would not be damages for breach of contract. His wrong, if wrong it were, is not breach of contract, and the trust he would have disappointed would not have been that particular form of trust.

Contract enables us to make explicit just what we count on another person to do, in return for what, and should they not do just that, what damages can be extracted from them. The beauty of promise and contract is its explicitness.[20] But we can only make explicit provisions for such contingencies as we imagine arising. Until I become a victim of a terrorist plumber I am unlikely, even if I should insist on a contract before giving plumbers access to my drains, to extract a solemn agreement that they not blow me up. Nor am I likely to specify the alternative means they *may* use to clear my drains, since if I knew enough to compile such a list I would myself have to be a competent plumber. Any such detailed instructions must come from their plumbing superiors; I know nothing or little about it when I confidently welcome the plumber into the bowels of my basement. I trust him to do a nonsubversive plumbing job, as he counts on me to do a nonsubversive teaching job, should he send his son to my course in the history of ethics. Neither of us relies on a contract with the other, and neither of us need know of any contract (or much about its contents) the other may have with a third coordinating party.

---

[20] Norbert Hornstein has drawn my attention to an unpublished paper by economist Peter Murrell, "Commitment and Cooperation: A Theory of Contract Applied to Franchising." Murrell emphasizes the nonstandard nature of franchise contracts, in that they typically are vague about what is expected of the franchisee. The consequent infrequency of contract termination by the franchisor is linked by him to the long duration of the contracts and to the advantage, to the more powerful proprietor of the trademark, of keeping the trust of the less powerful scattered franchises and maintaining quality control by means other than punitive contract terminations. This, I persuade myself, is a case where the exception proves the rule, where the nonstandardness of such inexplicit and trusting contracts points up to the explicitness and minimal trustingness of standard contracts.

It does not, then, seem at all plausible, once we think about actual moral relations in all their sad or splendid variety, to model all of them on one rather special one, the relation between promisor to promisee. We count on all sorts of people for all sorts of vital things, without any contracts, explicit or implicit, with them or with any third coordinating party. For these cases of trust in people to do their job conscientiously and not to take the opportunity to do us harm once we put things we value into their hands are different from trust in people to keep their promises in part because of the very indefiniteness of what we are counting on them to do or not to do. The subtlety and point of promising is to declare precisely *what* we count on another to do, and as the case of Shylock and Bassanio shows, that very definiteness is a limitation as well as a functional excellence of an explicit agreement.

Another functional excellence of contracts, which is closely connected with the expressness that makes breach easily established and damages or penalty decidable with a show of reasonable justice, is the *security* they offer the trusting party. They make it possible not merely for us to trust at will but to trust with minimal vulnerability. They are a device for trusting others enough for mutually profitable future-involving exchanges, without taking the risks trusters usually do take. They are designed for cooperation between mutually suspicious risk-averse strangers, and the vulnerability they involve is at the other extreme from that incurred by trusting infants. Contracts distribute and redistribute risk so as to minimize it for both parties, but trusting those more powerful persons who purport to love one increases one's risks while increasing the good one can hope to secure. Trust in fellow contracters is a limit case of trust, in which fewer risks are taken, for the sake of lesser goods.

Promises do, nevertheless, involve some real trust in the other party's good will and proper use of discretionary powers. Hume said that "to perform promises is requisite to beget trust and confidence in the common offices of life."[21] But performing promises is not the only performance requisite for that. Shylock did not welsh on an agreement, but he was nevertheless not a trustworthy party to an agreement. For to insist on the letter of an agreement, ignoring the vague but generally understood unwritten background conditions and exceptions, is to fail to show that discretion and goodwill which a trustworthy person has. To be someone to be trusted with a promise, as well as to be trusted as a promisor, one must be able to use discretion not as to when the promise has been kept but, rather, as to when to insist that the promise be kept, or to instigate penalty for breach of promise, when to keep and when not to keep one's promise. I would feel morally let down if someone who had promised to help me move house arrived announcing, "I had to leave my mother, suddenly taken ill, to look after herself in order to be here, but I couldn't break my promise to you." From such persons I would accept no further promises, since they would have shown themselves untrustworthy in the always crucial respect of judgment and

---

[21] Hume, p. 544.

willingness to use their discretionary powers. Promises *are* morally interesting, and one's performance as party to a promise is a good indicator of one's moral character, but not for the reasons contractarians suppose.

The domination of contemporary moral philosophy by the so-called Prisoner's Dilemma problem displays most clearly this obsession with moral relations between minimally trusting, minimally trustworthy adults who are equally powerful. Just as the only trust Hobbist man shows is trust in promises, provided there is assurance of punishment for promise breakers, so is this the only sort of trust nontheological modern moral philosophers have given much attention at all to, as if once we have weaned ourselves from the degenerate form of absolute and unreciprocated trust in God, all our capacity for trust is to be channelled into the equally degenerate form of formal voluntary and reciprocated trust restricted to equals. But we collectively cannot bring off such a limitation of trust to minimal and secured trust, and we can deceive ourselves that we do only if we avert our philosophical gaze from the ordinary forms of trust I have been pointing to. It was not really that, after Hobbes, people *did* barricade their bodies as well as their possessions against all others before daring to sleep. Some continued to doze off on stagecoaches, to go abroad unarmed, to give credit in business deals, to count on others turning up on time for appointments, to trust parents, children, friends, and lovers not to rob or assault them when welcomed into intimacy with them. And the usual array of vicious forms of such trust, trustworthiness, and demands for them, continued to flourish. Slaves continued to be trusted to cook for slaveowners; women, with or without marriage vows, continued to be trusted with the property of their men, trusted not to deceive them about the paternity of their children, and trusted to bring up their sons as patriarchs, their daughters as suitable wives or mistresses for patriarchs. Life went on, but the moral philosophers, or at least those we regard as the great ones, chose to attend only to a few of the moral relations normal life exhibited. Once Filmer was disposed of, they concentrated primarily *not* on any of the relations between those of unequal power—parent to child, husband to wife, adult to aged parent, slaveowner to slave, official to citizen, employer to employee—but on relations between roughly equal parties or between people in those respects in which they could be seen as equals.

Such relationships of mutual respect are, of course, of great moral importance. Hobbes, Locke, Rousseau, Hume, Kant, Sidgwick, Rawls, all have helped us to see more clearly how we stand in relation to anonymous others, like ourselves in need, in power, and in capacity. One need not minimize the importance of such work in moral philosophy in order to question its completeness. But a complete moral philosophy would tell us how and why we should act and feel toward others in relationships of shifting and varying power asymmetry and shifting and varying intimacy. It seems to me that we philosophers have left that task largely to priests and revolutionaries, the self-proclaimed experts on the proper attitude of the powerless to the powerful. But these relationships of inequality—some of them, such as parent-child, of unavoidable inequality—make up much of our lives, and they, as much as our relations to our equals, determine the state of moral health or corruption in which we are content to live. I think it is high time we look at the morality and immorality of relations between the powerful and the less powerful, especially at those in which there is trust between them.

A Moral Test for Trust

The few discussions of trust that I have found in the literature of moral philosophy assume that trust is a good and that disappointing known trust is always prima facie wrong, meeting it always prima facie right. But what is a trust-tied community without justice but a group of mutual blackmailers and exploiters? When the trust relationship itself is corrupt and perpetuates brutality, tyranny, or injustice, trusting may be silly self-exposure, and disappointing and betraying trust, including encouraged trust, may be not merely morally permissible but morally praiseworthy. Women, proletarians, and ex-slaves cannot ignore the virtues of watchful distrust, and of judicious untrustworthiness. Only if we had reason to believe that most familiar types of trust relationship were morally sound would breaking trust be any more prima facie wrong than breaking silence. I now turn to the question of when a given form of trust is morally decent, so properly preserved by trustfulness and trustworthiness, and when it fails in moral decency. What I say about this will be sketchy and oversimplified. I shall take as the form of trust to test for moral decency the trust which one spouse has in the other, in particular as concerns their children's care.

Earlier in discussing infant trust I said that the child has reason to trust the parents when both the child and parents care about the same good—the child's happiness, although the child may not see eye to eye with those trusted parents about how that is best taken care of. When one parent, say the old-style father, entrusts the main care of his young child's needs to the old-style mother, there, too, there can be agreement on the good they both want cared for but disagreement about how best it is cared for. The lord and master who entrusts such care to his good wife, the mother, and so gives her discretionary power in making moment-by-moment decisions about what is to be done, will have done so sensibly if these disagreements are not major ones, or if he has reason to think that she knows better than he does about such matters. He should defer to her judgment, as the child is encouraged to do to the parents', and as I do to my plumber's. He sensibly trusts if he has good reason to think that the discretionary powers given, even when used in ways he does not fully understand or approve of, are still used to care for the goods he wants cared for. He would be foolish to trust if he had evidence that she had other ends in view in her treatment of the child, or had a radically different version of what, say, the child's healthy development and proper relation to his father consisted in. Once he suspects that she, the trusted nurse of his sons and daughters, is deliberately rearing the daughters to be patriarch-toppling Amazons, the sons to be subverters of the father's values, he will sensibly withdraw his trust and dispatch his children to suitably chosen female relatives or boarding schools. What would properly undermine his trust would be beliefs he came to hold about the formerly trusted person's motives and purposes in her care of what he entrusted to her. The disturbing and trust-undermining suspicion is not necessarily that she doesn't care about the children's good, or cares only about her own—it is the suspicion that what she cares about conflicts with rather than harmonizes with what he cares about and that she is willing to sacrifice his concerns to what she sees as the children's and her own. Trusting is rational, then, in the absence of any reason to suspect in the trusted strong and operative motives which conflict with the demands of trustworthiness as the truster sees them.

But trusting can continue to be rational, even when there are such unwelcome suspicions, as long as the truster is confident that in the conflict of motives within the trusted the subversive motives will lose to the conformist motives. Should the wife face economic hardship and loss of her children if she fails to meet the husband's trust, or incurs too much of his suspicion, then she will sensibly continue as the dutiful wife, until her power position alters—sensibly, that is, given what she cares about. The husband in a position to be sure that the costs to the wife of discovered untrustworthiness are a sufficient deterrent will sensibly continue in trusting her while increasing his vigilance. Nor is he relying only on her fear, since, by hypothesis, her motives are conflicting and so she is not without some good will and some sympathy for his goals. Should he conclude that *only* fear of sanctions keeps her at her wifely duties, then the situation will have deteriorated from trust to mere reliance on his threat advantage. In such a case he will, if he has any sense, shrink the scope of her discretionary powers to virtually zero, since it is under cover of those that she could not merely thwart his purposes for his children but work to change the power relations in her own favor. As long as he gives her any discretion in looking after what is entrusted to her, he must trust her, and not rely solely on her fear of threatened penalties for disappointing his expectations.

The trusted wife (who usually, of course, also trusts her husband with many things that matter to her) is sensible to try to keep his trust, as long as she judges that the goods which would be endangered should she fail to meet his trust matter more to her than those she could best look after only by breaking or abusing trust. The goods for the sake of whose thriving she sensibly remains trustworthy might include the loving relation between them, their mutual trust for its own sake, as well as their agreed version of their children's good; or it might be some vestiges of these plus her own economic support or even physical safety, which are vulnerable to his punitive rage should she be found guilty of breach of trust. She will sensibly continue to meet trust, even when the goods with whose case she is trusted are no longer clearly common goods, as long as she cares a lot about anything his punitive wrath can and is likely to harm.

Sensible trust could persist, then, in conditions where truster and trusted suspect each other of willingness to harm the other if they could get away with it, the one by breach of trust, the other by vengeful response to that. The stability of the relationship will depend on the trusted's skill in cover-up activities, or on the truster's evident threat advantage, or a combination of these. Should the untrustworthy trusted person not merely have skill in concealment of her breaches of trust but skill in directing them toward increasing her own power and increasing her ability to evade or protect herself against the truster's attempted vengeance, then that will destabilize the relation, as also would frequent recourse by the truster to punitive measures against the trusted.

Where the truster relies on his threat advantage to keep the trust relation going, or where the trusted relies on concealment, something is morally rotten in the trust relationship. The truster who in part relies on his whip or his control of the purse is sensible but not necessarily within his moral rights in continuing to expect trustworthiness; and the trusted who sensibly relies on concealment to escape the penalty for untrustworthiness, may or may not be within her moral rights. I tentatively propose a test for the moral decency of a trust relationship, namely, that its continuation need not rely on successful threats held over the trusted, or on her successful cover-up of breaches of trust. We could develop and generalize this test into a version of an expressibility test, if we note that knowledge of what the other party is relying on for the continuance of the trust relationship would, in the above cases of concealment and of threat advantage, itself destabilize the relation. Knowledge of the other's reliance on concealment does so fairly automatically, and knowledge of the other person's partial reliance on one's fear of his revenge would tend, in a person of normal pride and self-assertiveness, to prompt her to look for ways of exploiting her discretionary powers so as to minimize her vulnerability to that threat. More generally, to the extent that what the truster relies on for the continuance of the trust relation is something which, once realized by the truster, is likely to lead to (increased) abuse of trust, and eventually to destabilization and destruction of that relation, the trust is morally corrupt. Should the wife come to realize that the husband relies on her fear of his revenge, or on her stupidity in not realizing her exploitation, or on her servile devotion to him, to keep her more or less trustworthy, that knowledge should be enough to begin to cure these weaknesses and to motivate untrustworthiness. Similarly, should the truster come to realize that the trusted relies on her skill at covering up or on her ability to charm him into forgiveness for breaches of trust, that is, relies on *his* blindness or gullibility, that realization will help cure that blindness and gullibility. A trust relationship is morally bad to the extent that either party relies on qualities in the other which would be weakened by the knowledge that the other relies on them. Where each relies on the other's love, or concern for some common good, or professional pride in competent discharge of responsibility, knowledge of what the other is relying on in one need not undermine but will more likely strengthen those relied-on features. They survive exposure as what others rely on in one, in a way that some forms of stupidity, fear, blindness, ignorance, and gullibility normally do not. There are other mental states whose sensitivity to exposure as relied on by others seems more variable: good nature, detachment, inattention, generosity, forgiveness, sexual bondage to the other party to the trust may not be weakened by knowledge that others count on their presence in one to sustain some wanted relationship, especially if they are found equally in both parties. But the knowledge that others are counting on one's nonreciprocated generosity or good nature or forgiveness can have the power of the negative, can destroy trust.

I assume that in some forms of trust the healthy and desired state will be mere self-maintenance, while in others it will be change and growth. Alteration of the trust relationship need not take the form of destruction of the old form and its replacement by a new form, but of continuous growth, of slight shifts in scope of discretionary powers, additions or alterations in scope of goods entrusted, and so on. Of course some excitement-addicted persons may cultivate a form of trust in part for the opportunity it provides for dramatic disruption. Trust is the atmosphere necessary for exhilarating disruptions of trust, and satisfyingly spectacular transfers of trust, as well as for goods we value. For persons with such tastes, immoral forms of trust may be preferable to what, according to my test, are moral forms of trust.

It should be noted that my proposed test of moral decency of trust is quite noncommittal as to what cases of reliance on another's psychology will be acceptable to the other. I have assumed that most people in most trust situations will not be content to have others rely on their fear, their ignorance, and their spinelessness. In some cases, however, such as trusting police to play their role effectively, and trusting one's fellows to refrain from open crime, some element of fear must play a role, and it is its absence not its presence which would destabilize trust in such contexts. In others, such as trust in national intelligence and security officers to look after national security, some ignorance in the trusting is proper, and awareness that such persons may be relying on one's not knowing what they know will not destabilize any trust one has in them to do what they are entrusted to do. What will be offensive forms of reliance on one's psychological state will vary from context to context, depending on the nature of the goods entrusted and on other relationships between the trusting and the trusted. Variations in individual psychology will also make a difference. Some are much more tolerant than others of having their good nature or preoccupation taken advantage of—not merely in that they take longer to recognize that they are victims of this, but they are less stirred to anger or resentment by the awareness that they are being deceived, blackmailed, or exploited in a given trust relation. I have used the phrase "tend to destroy" in the test for moral decency in the assumption that there is a normal psychology to be discerned and that it does include a strong enough element of Platonic *thumos*. Should that be false, then all sorts of horrendous forms of trust may pass my test. I do not, in any case, claim that it is the only test, merely an appropriate one. It is a test which amounts to a check on the will and good will of the truster and trusted, a look to see how good their will to one another is, knowing what they do about each other's psychology.

It may be objected that the expressibility test I have proposed amounts to a reversion, on my part, to the contractarian attitude which I have deplored.[22] Have I not finally admitted that we must treat trust relationships

---

[22] Objections of this sort were raised by a reader for this journal.

as hypothetical contracts, with all the terms fully spelled out in order to determine their moral status? The short answer is that contractualists do not have a monopoly on expressibility tests. In any case, I have applied it at a place no contractualist would, and *not* applied it where he does. Where he assumes self-interest as a motive and makes explicit what goods or services each self-interested party is to receive from the other, I have left it open what motives the trusting and trusted have for maintaining the relation, requiring only that these motives, insofar as they rely on responses from the other, survive the other's knowledge of that reliance, and I have not required that relied-on services be made explicit. What the contractualist makes explicit is a voluntary mutual commitment, and what services each is committed to provide. I have claimed that such explicitness is not only rare in trust relationships, but that many of them must begin inexplicitly and nonvoluntarily and would not do the moral and social work they do if they covered only what contract does—services that could be pretty exactly spelled out. My moral test does not require that these nonexplicit elements in trust should be made explicit but, rather, that something else survive being made explicit, one's reliance on facts about others' psychological states relevant to their willingness to continue serving or being served, states such as love, fear, ignorance, sense of powerlessness, good nature, inattention, which one can use for one's secret purposes. It is not part of contracts or social contracts to specify what assumptions each party needs to make about the other in respect of such psychological factors. Perhaps constraints regarding duress and fraud can be linked with the general offensiveness of having others rely on one's ignorance, fear, or sense of powerlessness, especially when these are contrived by the one who relies on them; but contracts themselves do not make express what it is in the state of mind of the other that each party relies on to get what he wants from the deal. What I have proposed as a general moral test of trust is indeed a generalization of one aspect of the contractarian morality, namely, of the assumptions implicit in the restrictions of valid contracts to those not involving fraud or duress. Whereas contracts make explicit the services (or service equivalent) exchanged, trust, when made express, amounts to a sort of exchange of responses to the motives and state of mind of the other, responses, in the form of confident reliance. Contractualists and other exchange fetishists can see this as a spiritual exchange, if it pleases them to do so, but it is not voluntary in the way contracts are, nor does it presuppose any equality of need or of power in the parties to this "exchange." The relation of my account of the morality of trust to standard contractarian morality seems to me as close as it should be, and at roughly the right places, if, as I have claimed, trust in fellow contracters is a limit case of trust.

Nevertheless, there are two aspects of my test which worry me, which may indicate it is not sufficiently liberated from contractarian prejudices. One difficulty is that it ignores the *network* of trust, and treats only two-party trust relationships. This is unrealistic, since any person's attitude to another in a given trust relationship is constrained by all the other trust and distrust relationships in which she is involved. Although I have alluded to such society-wide phenomena as climates of trust affecting the possibilities for individual trust relationships, my test is not well designed for application to the whole network but has to be applied piecemeal. That is a defect, showing the same individualist limitations which I find in contractarianism. The second thing that worries me is that the test seems barely applicable to brief trusting encounters, such as those with fellow library frequenters. As the contractarian takes as his moral paradigm a relationship which has some but not a very complex temporal depth, assimilating simultaneous exchange to the delayed delivery which makes a contract useful, and treats lifelong mutual trust as iterated mutual delayed deliveries, so I have shown a bias toward the medium-length trust relationship, thereby failing to say or imply anything very helpful either about brief encounters or about cross-generational trust. Probably these two faults are connected. If one got a test for the whole network of trust, with all the dependencies between the intimate and the more impersonal forms properly noted, and had the right temporal dimensions in that, both the morality of brief trusting encounters and the morality of trust between generations who do not encounter each other would fall into place.

Since I have thus oversimplified the problem of morally evaluating trust relationships by confining my attention to relationships one by one, my account of trusting as acceptance of having as it were entrusted and my consequent expansion of trusting from a two-place into a three-place predicate will seem forced and wrong. For there are some people whom one would not trust with anything, and that is not because one has considered each good one might entrust to that one and rejected that possibility. We want then to say that unless we first trust them we will not trust them *with anything*. I think that there is some truth in this, which my account has not captured. For some kinds of enemy (perhaps class enemies?) one will not trust even with one's bodily safety as one raises a white flag, but one will find it 'safer' to fight to the death. With some sorts of enemies, a contract may be too intimate a relation. If the network of relationships is systematically unjust or systematically coercive, then it may be that one's status within that network will make it unwise of one to entrust anything to those persons whose interests, given their status, are systematically opposed to one's own. In most such corrupt systems there will be limited opportunity for such beleaguered persons to "rescue" their goods from the power of their enemies—they usually will have no choice but to leave them exposed and so to act as if they trusted, although they feel proper distrust. In such conditions it may take fortitude to display distrust and heroism to disappoint the trust of the powerful. Courageous (if unwise) untrustworthiness and stoic withdrawal of trust may then be morally laudable. But since it usually will take such heroic disruptions of inherited trust relationships for persons to distance themselves from those the system makes their enemies, my test will at least be usable to justify such disruptions. In an earlier version of this paper I said that the ghost of plain trust and plain distrust haunted my account of goods-relativized or 'fancy' trust. I think that I now see that ghost for what it is and see why it ought to continue to haunt. Still, such total oppositions of interest are rare, and one satisfactory thing about my account is that it enables us to see how we can salvage some respects in which we may trust even those whose interests are to some extent opposed to our own.

Meanwhile, my account of what it is to trust, and my partial account of when it is immoral to expect or meet trust, will have to be treated as merely a beginning (or, for some, a resumption, since there doubtless are other attempts at this topic which have escaped my notice). Trust, I have claimed, is reliance on others' competence and willingness to look after, rather than harm, things one cares about which are entrusted to their care. The moral test of such trust relationships which I have proposed is that they be able to survive awareness by each party to the relationship of *what* the other relies on in the first to ensure their continued trustworthiness or trustingness. This test elevates to a special place one form of trust, namely, trusting others with knowledge of what it is about them which enables one to trust them as one does, or expect them to be trustworthy. The test could be restated this way: trust is morally decent only if, in addition to whatever else is entrusted, knowledge of each party's reasons for confident reliance on the other to continue the relationship could in principle also be entrusted—since such mutual knowledge would be itself a good, not a threat to other goods. To the extent that mutual reliance can be accompanied by mutual knowledge of the conditions for that reliance, trust is above suspicion, and trustworthiness a nonsuspect virtue. "Rara temporum felicitas . . . quae sentias dicere licet."[23]

This paper has an antiphonal title and a final counterpoint may not be out of order. Although I think this test is an appropriate moral test, it is another matter to decide whether and when it should be applied to actual cases of trust. Clearly in some cases, such as infant trust and parental trustworthiness, which could in principle pass it, it cannot actually be applied by both parties to the relationship. That need not unduly worry us. But in other cases it may well be that the attempt to apply it will ensure its failing the test. Trust is a fragile plant, which may not endure inspection of its roots, even when they were, before the inspection, quite healthy. So, although some forms of trust would survive a suddenly achieved mutual awareness of them, they may not survive the gradual and possibly painful process by which such awareness actually comes about. It may then be the better part of wisdom, even when we have an acceptable test for trust, not to use it except where some distrust already exists, better to take nonsuspect trust on trust. Luhmann says that "it is a characteristic mark of civilizing trust that it incorporates an element of reflexivity."[24] But to trust one's trust and one's distrust enough to refrain from applying moral tests until prompted by some distrust is to take a very risky bet on the justice, if not the "civilization," of the system of trust one inhabits. We may have to trade off civilization for justice, unless we can trust not only our trust but, even more vitally, our distrust.

---

[23]Hume placed on the title page of his *A Treatise of Human Nature* these words of Tacitus: "Rara Temporum felicitas, ubi sentire, quae velis, and quae sentias, dicere licet."

[24]Luhmann, p. 69.

31

Wickedness

S. I. Benn was professorial fellow in philosophy in the Research School of
Social Sciences of the Australian National University, Canberra. He was joint
author, with R. S. Peters, of *Social Principles and the Democratic State* (also
issued as *Principles of Political Thought*) (1959), and joint editor with
G. F. Gaus, of *Public and Private in Social Life* (1983).

Evils in Nature and Evils in Persons

When philosophers talk of the problem of evil, they generally mean a problem
in theodicy. Anyone who believes in a morally perfect, omniscient, and
omnipotent God needs to explain and justify the existence of evils in the
world. Unbelievers have no such problem. Nevertheless there are still uses to
which the concept of evil can be put. Diseases, deformities, earthquakes and
floods that destroy crops and wreck cities—these are, for anyone, too intelligibly evils, instances of what I shall term "evils in nature." I do not confine that
term, however, to what we commonly call "natural disasters" but use it to
denote any object, property, or happening about which it is both intelligible
and correct to say that it would be a better state of affairs if that object et cetera
did not exist or occur.

I take evil in nature to be a simple fact. It is a feature of the world that
animals and human beings alike suffer pain, that there is ugliness as well as
beauty, that there are bereavements and grievous disappointments. These
things simply happen and are no less natural evils for their happening to conscious and rational beings. I do not mean, of course, that consciousness of the
evil is never a necessary constituent: clearly this must be so in the case of a

From S. I. Benn, "Wickedness," *Ethics*, 95 (July 1985: 795–810). © 1985 by The University of
Chicago. All rights reserved. Reprinted by permission of The University of Chicago. An earlier
version of this article was presented to a seminar in Sydney sponsored by the Australian Society
for Legal Philosophy and the Department of Jurisprudence of the University of Sydney. I wish to
acknowledge the help I received from John Kleinig, who commented on the paper, from other
members of the seminar, from Jerry Gaus, who made valuable suggestions for the analysis of
malignity, from Sam Goldberg, and from Miriam Benn, whose criticism was, as always, penetrat-
ing, even though she found this topic rather lowering.

bereavement or a disappointment, though it is more problematic in cases of evils of ugliness. But bereavements and disappointments, while evils for human beings, are not evils in human beings. I shall make no attempt to say why such things are accounted evil; on the contrary, evil in nature I take for present purposes to be unproblematic, so that I shall not consider that I am begging any questions if I use that concept in explicating evil in human beings.

One kind of evil in human beings is "wickedness"—a word that has fallen undeservedly on bad times with the secularization of moral discourse. Wickedness in human beings is still a new kind of evil in nature, but one which raises special problems because, having in general a capacity for rational action and judgment, wicked people not merely are evil but also do evil, with evil intent. My purpose in this article is to inquire into forms of human wickedness, their relation with other evils in human beings, and their relation to freedom of choice and motivation to evil.

By "wickedness" I mean whatever it is about someone that warrants our calling him a wicked person. It is therefore a different notion from what makes an action an evil deed, for an evil deed may be done by someone who is not wicked but only weak or misguided. Neither is every wrongdoer evil, for one may do wrong with good intentions or even (some would say) because in some situations whatever one did would be wrong. And conversely, someone who was fully conscious and rational but also completely paralyzed and aphasic, who spent his life hating everyone about him, rejoicing in their misfortune, wishing them ill, and reveling in malignant fantasies, would be a wicked person who did no wrong at all. Indispensable, however, to the notion of a wicked person is a cognitive capacity, or at least a capacity to envisage states of affairs in the imagination, conjoined with a set of attitudes toward such states of affairs. G. E. Moore, whose account of evil is in terms not of persons but of "states of things," nevertheless describes the "great positive evils" as "organic unities" constituted by "cognitions of some object, accompanied by some emotion," where "emotion" is roughly equivalent to what I mean by "attitude."[1]

Common, however, to both wickedness in action and wickedness in attitude is an evil maxim, in something like Kant's sense. A person perceives situations, real or imagined, under certain descriptions and has attitudes in respect of them in accordance with general maxims. If I recognize someone as virtuous and hate him just for being virtuous, I have the maxim, Virtuous people are to be hated. Vandals act on the maxim, Beautiful objects are to be destroyed, racists on the maxim, Blacks are to be despised or hurt, egoists on the maxim, No one's interests but my own are to count. In each case the gerundival form of the maxim specifies a kind of action or attitudinal response, in accordance with what that person takes as a rule of life.

A person may be wicked because the maxims that order his life are, by and large, evil maxims, that is, maxims that no one ought to act on at all. Sometimes this may be seen as a kind of mistake on his part; he may believe to

---

[1] G. E. Moore, *Principia Ethica* (Cambridge: Cambridge University Press, 1903), p. 208.

be good what is really evil, and vice versa. And then we may need some way of distinguishing culpable and nonculpable mistakes. But in other instances there is no mistake: a person may act on an evil maxim, knowing it to be so. That is the nature of malignant or Satanic wickedness. These are both problematic issues to which I return.

It is possible, however, for a person to be wicked not because the first-order maxims of his actions are inherently wicked but because they are regulated by some higher-order maxim which systematically excludes consideration of any good which might circumscribe his first-order maxims. An example of such a restrictive higher-order maxim might be, No maxim is to be entertained as a rule of conduct that would circumscribe the duty to obey the orders of superior officers. Selfish wickedness and conscientious wickedness, which I shall consider a little later, are restrictive in much the same way, for whether or not, in either case, the maxims of action are inherently evil, the regulating principle will be found to be excluding in the required sense. These forms of wickedness I shall term "wickednesses of exclusion."

By contrast with those who act on evil first-order maxims, or who so order their first-order maxims as to exclude what ought nevertheless to be taken account of, the merely weak willed and the morally indolent and the people who cannot control their passions are not wicked people, for the maxims they really do acknowledge and on which they would wish to act are good ones. Such people are morally defective, and therefore bad, precisely because their actions fall short of their good intentions. That very incoherence is a mitigating condition, though not, of course, an excusing one.

I shall outline, in most of the remainder of this article, a typology of wickedness, which will shed some light on the difficult moral and philosophical questions of responsibility and culpability and on the possibility of evil actions knowingly performed. The primary distinctions are between self-centered, conscientious, and malignant forms of wickedness. In each case I shall ask how far ignorance, error, or incapacity is necessarily or possibly a feature of the actions and maxims of action under discussion and what difference it could make to the judgment of wickedness.

Self-Centered Forms of Wickedness

The least problematic kind of self-centered wicked person is the selfish one, but the category includes as well any person whose maxims are regulated by a higher-order maxim restricting consideration to goods and evils respecting only subjects and groups defined by reference to the agent himself. So a person who devoted himself exclusively to promoting the interests of his family or of his firm or to the aggrandizement of his nation might be wicked in this way if he did so with a ruthless unconcern for whether other people might be entitled or required to act on corresponding maxims of their own. The cruder kind of chauvinist or jingoist—My country, right or wrong—acts on just such a self-centered principle, providing he does not universalize it for citizens of others countries too.

The merely selfish person recognizes his own well-being as a good and acts for the sake of it. That is to say, in being selfish he does not embrace evil as such, under that description. Self-interest is not merely an intelligible motive but also one that many philosophers have thought to be a paradigm of a motive, the motive of self-love. Selfishness is wicked not on account of its end but for what is excludes, for it consists in closing one's eyes and one's heart to any good but a self-centered good. In Kant's view, this is the most characteristic form of human wickedness.

According to Kant, the moral law, as the law of reason, is not merely accessible to any rational being but also, for human beings at least, always one spring of action, necessarily motivating in some degree. So it is not that the selfishly wicked person is motivated by a perverse antagonism to the moral law. Rather, self-love, which is for any rational person a genuine spring, assumes an irrational precedence over the moral law. Accordingly, a wicked person is not one whom the law cannot motivate but rather someone who "reverses the moral order of the springs in adopting them into his maxims: he adopts, indeed, the moral law along with that of self-love; but. . . . he makes the spring of self-love and its inclinations the condition of obedience to the moral law; whereas, on the contrary, the latter ought to be adopted. . . . as the sole spring, being the *supreme condition* of the satisfaction of the former."[2]

The selfish person may, however, be mistaken in his belief that what he intends is really good, even from his own narrow perspective; it may in reality be damaging, even to himself. Someone altogether committed to increasing his own wealth or power—a miser or a megalomaniac—may be wrong to value such things, at any rate as ends instead of as means to other goods. That error is not, however, an excuse for his wickedness since his specific wickedness as a selfish person derives from what is excluded rather than from the end he actually seeks. That, of course, can add to his wickedness. Sadistic wickedness is more shocking, perhaps, than miserliness because the suffering of others, to which the miser or the vain person may be merely indifferent and inattentive, is for the sadist itself the source of the pleasure which makes it seem a good. In taking it to be so, however, the sadist may still be mistaken, even in his own terms, if, for instance, the pleasure is part of a self-destructive rake's progress of personal degradation. There would be no inconsistency, however, in deeming the sadist wicked on account both of the intrinsic evil and of the exclusiveness of his maxim while yet feeling compassion for someone who is destroying himself so worthlessly.

Psychopathy

In contrast to selfish wickedness, the form of self-centered evil in persons manifested in a psychopathic personality may not count as wickedness at all. This takes the form of a kind of moral imbecility. The psychopath, like the

---

[2] I. Kant, "Of the Indwelling of the Bad Principle along with the Good, or On the Radical Evil in Human Nature," in *Kant's Theory of Ethics*, trans. T. K. Abbot (London: Longman, Green & Co., 1927), p. 343.

selfishly wicked person, acts from self-love. His is capable, at least within limits, of instrumental deliberation, though he may be prone to discount future satisfactions heavily in favor of immediate gratification. So he may be liable to do evil impulsively to satisfy a whim. But the more significant point is that he does not see it as evil, except, perhaps, in a conventional sense: This is something that I know most people do not like being done, so I had better conceal the body. But the kind of considerations that might justify and rationalize conventional disapproval can get no purchase on his understanding. To the extent that the psychopath has, and perceives in himself, the capacity to make decisions which can make a difference to the way things turn out—to the extent that he is capable of forming beliefs taking account of evidence and argument and of acting on those beliefs—he satisfies the minimal conditions for being a rational chooser or, one may say, a natural person.[3] Full rationality does not, however, consist only in the capacity to take account of relevant considerations advanced by others. It includes also the capacity to decenter: to conceive of ways of looking at the world, and at oneself, from someone else's standpoint or from no particular standpoint at all—from the standpoint of anyone. It is this capacity that the psychopath lacks. Whereas the selfish person understands well enough how the well-being of other persons can be a reason for someone's action or forbearance but disregards such reasons, the psychopath is simply unable to see how that could be a reason for him at all. To be asked to take account of such a reason would be, to him, like being asked to have regard to sensibilities of a stone or, perhaps, to the relevance of the color of someone's hair when deciding whether to make off with his wallet. While it would be wrong to say that the psychopath has no view of good and evil (for he knows what he would enjoy and what he would prefer not to suffer), he is incapable of understanding that distinction in any but a self-centered way. So though his maxims never take account of others' interests, it is not because a higher-order maxim excludes them; it is that first-order maxims embodying them are simply unintelligible to him. Such a person does not act on an evil maxim, knowing it to be evil, nor does he act on a self-centered second-order maxim that excludes relevant first-order maxims since he can hardly be said to have any second-order maxims at all. Such a person cannot be wicked. Nevertheless, he may be both an evil in nature and an instance of evil in a person.

Moral imbecility may well fill us with horror; certainly it is frightening. As much might be said, however, of other evils in nature, such as cancers or leprosy. But there may be something besides to account for our special hostility toward the moral imbecile. It is hard to see him simply as an evil but amoral force, like a man-eating tiger in a Bengal village, for he is defective in a capacity without which people in society could not live together. He seems at once to claim consideration as a fellow person and to disqualify himself from that

---

[3] For a fuller statement of the theory of natural and moral personality on which this article relies, see S. I. Benn, "Freedom, Autonomy, and the Concept of a Person," *Aristotelian Society Proceedings* (1975–76) 76 (1976): 109–30

consideration. Because he satisfies the minimal conditions for a rational chooser, he qualifies for the respect due to a person and is a bearer of rights, but as a moral defective, he is incompetent to bear the corresponding obligations and responsibilities. In assessing his moral status, it is hard not to judge him by the standards appropriate to a person of normal capacities, of which he is a monstrously deformed travesty. Nevertheless, though qualified as a person, he is disqualified from counting as a wicked one. And precisely because he is a person, we are subject to moral constraints in dealing with this evil that do not apply to our dealings with man-eating tigers.

Conscientious Wickedness

The conscientiously wicked person is distinguished from the self-centered one in that the maxims of his actions are seen by him as universally valid and applicable. Unlike the crude chauvinist's complete indifference to other nations' claims, the conscientiously wicked nationalist might hold that his nation's supremacy would be universally valid and overriding good, perhaps because it would be good for all humanity, perhaps because it had some excellence which any rational being would have to recognize as generating an overriding claim. The higher-order maxim by which the conscientiously wicked person lives is not self-centered; rather, it rules that all considerations not directly validated by his primary ideal goal or principle are necessarily subordinate when they conflict with it. So a conscientious Nazi need not always be indifferent to the claims of humanity instantiated in the plight of Jews. Were they anywhere but in Germany, or perhaps anywhere but in Europe, and were they not (as the Nazis claimed) an international conspiracy against the German nation, there would be a case for not exterminating them, perhaps even for manifesting concern for their well-being; but any such considerations were necessarily and totally overridden by the Herrenvolk ideal, which thus, in a Nazi's view, legitimated the Final Solution. Of course, the conscientious Nazi was himself one of the Herrenvolk, but it was not for that self-centered reason that he maintained its exclusive moral priority.

As with self-centered wickedness, conscientious wickedness can arise when the putative ideal is genuinely a good but is pursued with a ruthlessness that excludes other goods which ought to be taken account of. But it is also possible that the putative ideal is itself a monstrous error. In both cases it is alike necessary to build into the analysis criteria of culpability for the misjudgment of values. Suppose, for instance, that Aztec priests truly believed that human sacrifice gave pleasure to the god and that to please the god was good not because that way the harvests would be good (an acceptably valuable if not always an acceptably overriding end) but just as a good in itself and, further, that individual human beings as such were of subordinate concern. But suppose, also, that there was nothing in their moral consciousness with which such beliefs would not cohere. It is hard to see how they could then be called wicked. It is that reservation, however, that their moral consciousness be coherent, that makes their case problematic, where the case of Adolf Hitler is not. We must deplore murderous behavior as evil since slaying human beings is evil in nature, and if it is the result of intentional action, it must count as an evil in persons that they could act like that. But for it to count as a wickedness in persons, they must have within their repertoire some humane principles that the Aztecs (at least the Aztecs of my hypothesis) did not have. That exoneration cannot be extended, however, to tyrants and fanatics nearer home— Adolf Hitler, for instance. The resources of the European moral tradition afforded him ample reasons for treating the sufferings of Jews as of some account even set against the objective of racial purity, itself an end which that tradition provided ample grounds for questioning

Conscientious wickedness is rarely a case of pursuing an end unaware of attendant consequences as evils; it is more often a case of a single-minded pursuit of an objective which (unlike racial purity) can reasonably be seen as good, but at the cost of a callous insensitivity to evil done by the way. It is not that the person believes the incidental evil to be itself good but rather that, having reason to think it evil, he nevertheless systematically disregards it. It is not that one cannot honestly believe with Robespierre and Saint-Just, that out of a Terror can emerge a Republic of virtue or, with the IRA, that only through indiscriminate violence can a united Ireland arise but that to go through with it one must almost certainly stifle sensibility to the horrors through which one must wade to bring it about. That sensibility, too, is a part of one's moral consciousness, no less than the perceived ideal. For a person whose conception of the moral law has developed within a moral tradition that recognizes indiscriminate murder as evil, such single-mindedness may be possible only if he has a sense of mission so great or an arrogance so overwhelming that he can desensitize himself, school himself to a callous disregard for considerations to which he nevertheless can and ought to attend.

Doing evil that good may come of it, or a greater evil be avoided, is not, however, a sufficient condition for wickedness in a person. Everyone responsible for major political decisions is likely to have been confronted with such difficult and painful choices. The history of atomic warfare is a record of one such dilemma after another. The mark of the wicked person is that such choices are for him neither difficult nor painful since the considerations that would make them so are systematically neutralized. It may, indeed, be a causally necessary condition for making such choices that one make of oneself a wicked person in this sense; in an evil world, perhaps only the wicked are callous enough to do the evil that needs to be done. "Whoever wants to engage in politics at all," wrote Max Weber, ". . . . must know that he is responsible for what may become of himself under the impact of these paradoxes. . . . He lets himself in for the diabolical forces lurking in all violence. . . . Everything that is striven for through political action operating with violent means and following an ethic of responsibility endangers the 'salvation of the soul.' "[4]

---

[4] Max Weber, "Politics as a Vocation," in *From Max Weber*, ed. H. H. Gerth and C. Wright Mills (London: Kegan Paul, Trench, Trubner & Co., 1948), pp. 125–26.

Conscientious wickedness is not so radically different, then, from selfish wickedness. In both cases it is the refusal to acknowledge the moral significance of evils which one nevertheless knows or could reasonably be expected to know as evils that constitutes the person's wickedness.

Heteronomous Wickedness

The kinds of wickedness identified so far are manifested in people whose responses to situations, whether active or merely contemplative, are their own; theirs is the judgment, theirs the act, theirs the wickedness. But if the Nuremberg defendants were arguably like that, Eichmann in Jerusalem pleaded that he simply obeyed orders and could not therefore be responsible for the evils in which he had participated. He had not, he said, felt any hatred of the Jews or any pleasure from their sufferings and destruction. He had committed himself conscientiously to a line of duty, but unlike Hitler and his leading henchmen, he could plausibly disclaim responsibility for having adopted the aims to which his official duties directed him. His defense amounted to the claim that what he did must be seen under the global description of doing his duty, not of pursuing evil, and the former is not itself a description of wickedness, not in any of the terms that I have set out so far. If, then, wickedness in a person requires that he adopt an evil maxim, how was Eichmann wicked? In a perceptive discussion of Hannah Arendt's report of the Eichmann Trial, Barry Clarke has created the category of "heteronomous evil" to cover such a case, and I shall follow him in this, though I shall call it "heteronomous wickedness."[5]

Clarke's argument depends on a distinction between acting spontaneously and acting autonomously. Eichmann not only relied utterly on his superiors for directions for acting in all relevant regards but in joining the Nazi Party and the bureaucracy also opted out of critical judgment in all matters affecting his official duties. He had chosen heteronomy, and the evil that he did followed from that decision.[6] Could he be said, then, to have possessed the capacity for free choice that is the mark of a person, the condition for responsibility for oneself, and therefore a necessary condition for one's being a wicked person?

A correct perspective on such an argument must distinguish between the ordinary practical capacity of a normal minimally rational chooser to make decisions (which I have elsewhere called "autarchy"—a self-directing condition) and the capacity to make autonomous judgments.[7] The salient conditions for autarchy were outlined above, in discussing the moral status of the

---

[5] Barry Clarke, "Beyond 'The Banality of Evil,'" *British Journal of Political Science* 10 (1980): 417–39 (on Hannah Arendt, *Eichmann in Jerusalem: A Report on the Banality of Evil* [London: Faber & Faber, 1963]).

[6] "Eichmann made two exceptions in his merciless anti-Semitic programme, once when he helped a half-Jewish cousin, and another time when at his uncle's request he helped a Viennese Jewish couple: but his conscience bothered him so much afterwards that he 'confessed his sins' (Eichmann's phrase) to his superiors" (John Kleinig, "Always Let Your Conscience Be Your Guide?" *Interchange* 1 [1967]: 107, referring to the account in Arendt, p. 131).

[7] See my analysis of autarchy and autonomy, heterarchy and heteronomy, set out at greater length in Benn.

psychopath, who in my view satisfies them while yet lacking moral responsibility. In some people, however, autarchy is impaired, in various degrees ranging from catatonia through autism to compulsions of various kinds. Under hypnosis, a person loses autarchy to a considerable degree; a person acting under posthypnotic suggestion less so. Such people are programmed—and by other people—and are therefore heterarchic. To the extent that one is autistic, compulsive, or heterarchic, one lacks the capacity to decide for oneself, which is the condition for free, responsible action, and to just that extent one lacks the capacity for wickedness. But Eichmann was heteronomous, not heterarchic, and heteronomy is not merely consistent with autarchy—it requires it.

By autonomy I understand a character trait amounting to a capacity to act on principles (i.e., in accordance with a *nomos*) that are one's own because one has made them so by a process of rational reflection on the complex of principles and values that one has assimilated from one's social environment. It is a process in which one confronts the incoherences and conflicts within that complex and works to resolve them into something like a coherent set of moral attitudes. We do not invent our morality ex nihilo; we make it our own by creatively testing it for consistency. Now Eichmann certainly did nothing like that. On the contrary, he handed over his conscience to the care of the party, the state, and the Fuehrer, thereby imposing on his power of autarchic decision (which remained all the same quite unimpaired) constraints which he thereafter would not look at critically. But, of course, nothing made it impossible for him to do so. He had, as Clarke puts it, elected for heteronomy, and though as time went on it no doubt became increasingly difficult, psychologically speaking, to challenge the system to which he had put himself in thrall, still he had made it so himself; he had willfully made himself the compliant and unreflecting tool of wickedness, which is a perversion of the moral nature of persons as choosers.

I do not mean that one may never accept moral leadership from others or commit oneself to a role in a movement or an organization, nor do I mean that in the performance of the duties of an office one must always do precisely what one would have chosen to do irrespective of the requirements of the office. Social practices and institutions would lose their point if that were the case; they are, after all, ways of coordinating the acts of many people toward common goals and will work as such only if people can rely on one another to do what is expected of them. But this does not entail a duty to suspend all judgment. In accepting the guidance of an authority, we are responsible for satisfying ourselves that the principles for which it stands are ones which in general we can endorse; though its particular injunctions may sometimes puzzle us, we must be prepared to monitor its performance over all.

We have to distinguish, therefore, between a conditional and an absolute heteronomy. A person who chooses a conditional heteronomy may reasonably submit to the guidance of the party or the church, providing he does not surrender the power to judge whether it remains true to the principles that led him to choose just that one as the good one. We resign ourselves absolutely to heteronomy at the risk of becoming, like Eichmann, people of evil will, with a capacity in no way impaired to grasp the evil that we do in obeying wicked orders but willfully disregarding it as evil. As with the conscientiously and the selfishly wicked persons, the heteronomously wicked has become insensitive to certain morally significant states of affairs just because the maxim of his actions and attitudes leaves no place for them in his moral constitution.

Wickedness and Moral Luck

Of course, not every absolutely heteronomous person in necessarily wicked. Someone who submits in this total fashion to the guidance of a saint may be less than admirable as a person; but it would be both perverse and wildly censorious to call him wicked. For that one must be disposed to act, or respond, in accordance with evil maxims or in disregard of good ones. The saint's disciple will do neither. But a person who does evil by reason of having elected to put his moral judgment into the keeping of evil persons or institutions has taken a gamble that, as a morally responsible person, he is not entitled to take—and has lost.

This qualification suggests a more general and far-reaching one, affecting all the categories of wickedness discussed so far. Selfish people, people dedicated solely to their families or to the interests of their firms or their countries, and fanatics conscientiously pursuing a blinkered ideal all have it in them to be wicked people. But if the actions picked out for them by their restrictive second-order maxims happened never to be evil actions, it would be harsh to call such people wicked, even if their first-order maxims were always self-centered or narrowly principled. For, as I suggested earlier, such maxims are not always intrinsically bad. Imagine someone who acted single-mindedly on a maxim of self-interest but whose actions were, by social circumstances, under such close scrutiny that any action that damaged someone else, or any denial of help to someone in need, would invite the penalties of public censure. He would have reasons for taking account of appropriate other-regarding maxims, though they would be reasons encapsulated in a self-interested strategy. Such a person would be morally unworthy, but his social institutions would save him from actualizing the wickedness which was latent in him. The Puritan communities of the seventeenth century maintained strict moral surveillance over their members because they were more concerned with saving people from doing wickedness of which they were capable than with moral worth, which, they believed, few, if any, people possessed, and then only by divine election. But we do not have to accept the doctrine of predestination to believe that what preserves many quite ordinary people from wickedness is the good fortune of their circumstances and that in a Belsen or an Auschwitz they might be capable not merely of the desperate meanness of so many of the inmates but also of the wickedness of very nearly all the guards.

Malignity

In all the forms of wickedness treated so far, the regulative maxim has been directed to something understood by the agent, however perversely, as a good. For some philosophers, as we shall see, this has been held to be a necessary condition for any rational action at all. The kind of wickedness, however, which Coleridge saw instantiated in Iago as "motiveless malignity," and which Milton's Satan epitomizes in "Evil be thou my good," throws doubt on this supposition.

Iago and Satan are, of course, the paradigm instances in literature of the unalloyed wickedness of malignity, of pursuing evil under the aspect of evil. According to Kant, "In order to call a man bad, it should be possible to argue a priori from some actions, or from a single consciously bad action to a bad maxim as its foundation, and from this to a general source in the actor of all particular morally bad maxims, this source again being itself a maxim."[8] But Kant denies that human beings can adopt as a fundamental maxim, informing all rational choices as a kind of perverse moral law, the maxim, Do evil for evil's sake. A "malignant reason," a "bad Rational Will," would require that "antagonism to the law would itself be made a spring of action . . . so that the subject would be made a *devilish* being."[9] Kant believes that human beings cannot be like this yet it is not easy to see why since he believes that devils who are presumably also rational, can be. Perhaps to be a devil is to be irrational in the special way that, while apprehending the moral law, one responds to it, like Satan, antagonistically, finding in it not a spring of action but a spring of counteraction. I shall consider in a moment whether it is logically possible to make evil one's end, but if it is not, then it must be impossible for devils too. And if the impossibility is not of this kind, I cannot see why human beings may not also be Satanic.

I suggested earlier that the attitudes and actions of a selfishly wicked person are governed by a conception of the good, albeit the good of the agent himself; his wickedness consists in his indifference to other values. A malignant person, by contrast, should take account of the suffering of someone else as a reason for action, irrespective of self-love, just as much as would a benevolent person. But unlike the latter, he would promote it. It is as evil that he rejoices in the suffering and not because he sees it, in some partial or distorted way, as a good, even for himself. He does not think himself better off for it; he is no less disinterested in rejoicing in it than is a benevolent person who rejoices in someone else's good fortune. Just as the prospect of satisfying one's own sexual desire is pleasurable to contemplate, as a good, so, for the malignant person, someone else's suffering is a pleasure to contemplate, but as an evil, apprehended as such. Correspondingly, it is unalloyed wickedness to hate the good, apprehended as good, and because it is good, and to seek its destruction on that account.

---

[8] Kant, p. 327.

[9] Ibid., p. 342.

The unalloyed wickedness of malignity presents a logical or a psychological problem, not a moral one. The difficulty is not to decide what attitude to adopt toward it; if it exists at all, it is to be totally abhorred. The problem is rather to understand its motivation or, indeed, to decide whether the very description of it is coherent. Is it perhaps that we perceive something as unalloyed wickedness only because we haven't fully understood it?

According to Socrates, a man who knows the good cannot choose to do evil; no one intentionally chooses evil knowing it to be so.[10] Since my account of unalloyed wickedness implicitly denies this claim, it is necessary to consider why Socrates may have made it. But more than that, what account can we give of motivation to evil if the one given by Socrates turns out not to be true?

Socrates' paradox can be made plausible given a certain view of the motives of action. If we suppose that all intentional or voluntary action is undertaken with some aim, it must be supposed that what is aimed at must be desired; and if someone desires it, he must see it as a good thing to bring it about.[11] Accordingly, for Socrates, whoever aims at evil does so in ignorance of its true nature, under the misapprehension of it as good.

The trouble with Socrates' story is that it distorts the nature of true malignity. I said earlier that a malignant person recognizes the suffering of someone else as an evil and rejoices in it just because it is evil and that he would not rejoice in it were it not that he saw it as such. Even more perplexing, on Socrates' account, is the case of self-destructive action prompted by self-hatred. One must go a long and devious way round to find a good that such a person might believe that he was promoting in spiting himself. Clearly if one aims at an outcome then, in a rather weak sense, one must desire it; but it is not, even for the person desiring it, necessarily desirable on that account. For what is desirable is what it is appropriate to desire, and the malignant person desires things very often precisely because they are not appropriate. Consider the case of Claggart, the master-at-arms, in Herman Melville's story *Billy Budd*. Claggart conceives a hatred of "the Handsome Sailor," "who in Claggart's own phrase was 'the sweet and pleasant young fellow,'" and falsely charges him with sedition in order to destroy him.[12] Claggart has no reason to hate Billy if by "reason" we mean reason of interest. There is no apparent good that can come

---

[10] See Plato, *Protagoras* 352a—358d. In the *Laws*, Plato asserts: "No wrongdoer is so of deliberation. For no man will ever deliberately admit supreme evil, and least of all in his most precious possessions. But every man's most precious possession, as we said, is his soul; no man, then, we may be sure, will of set purpose receive the supreme evil into this most precious thing and live with it there all his life through" (731c).

[11] Michael Stocker has examined the claim that it is not possible to desire the bad in "Desiring the Bad: An Essay in Moral Psychology," *Journal of Philosophy* 76 (1979): 738–53

[12] Herman Melville, *Billy Budd and Other Tales* (New York: New American Library of World Literature, Inc., 1961), chap. 11, p. 35.

to him, or to anyone else, from the evil that will come about. So far from moving him to act for the sake of something he sees as a good, his hatred moves him to spite and to destroy it.[13]

Claggert's reason for hating Billy is precisely his goodness. He can appreciate it only as a reproach, as something that diminishes him, that he must therefore hate and destroy.[14] There is a passage in Schopenhauer that expresses this state of mind most eloquently: "Very bad men bear the stamp of inward suffering in the very expression of the countenance. . . . From this inward torment, which is absolutely and directly essential to them, there finally proceeds that delight in the suffering of others which does not spring from mere egoism, but is disinterested, and which constitutes wickedness proper, rising to the pitch of cruelty. For this the suffering of others is not a means for the attainment of the ends of its own will, but an end in itself."[15] Schopenhauer's explanation is that such wicked persons suffer "an intensity of will" that nothing could assuage. "Every privation" (every frustration of desire) "is infinitely increased by the enjoyment of others, and relieved by the knowledge that others suffer the same privation." Moreover, an "attained end never fulfills the promise of the desired object." From "a manifestation of will reaching the point of extraordinary wickedness, there necessarily springs an excessive inward misery, an eternal unrest, an incurable pain; he seeks indirectly the alleviation which directly is denied him,—seeks to mitigate his own suffering by the sight of the suffering of others, which at the same time he recognises as an expression of his power. The suffering of others now becomes for him an end in itself, and is a spectacle in which he delights; and thus arises the phenomenon of pure cruelty, blood thirstiness, which history exhibits so often in the Neros and Domitians, in the African Deis, in Robespierre, and the like."[16]

Of course, one might say that Coleridge was mistaken and that the malignity of Iago and Claggart, with which Schopenhauer's story accords so well, was not "motiveless" but was motivated by envy or resentment. But these motives are not motives of interest, prompted by a good to be brought about by action. They explain the action only by filling out further the description of what is done by giving us a better grasp of the organic relation between the state of affairs, the beliefs of the agent, and the attitude that binds us together. Envious and resentful people are not aiming to bring about a good; nor does the good that they recognize appeal to them. On the contrary, it inflames and enrages them.

---

[13] See Peter Kivy, "Melville's *Billy* and the Secular Problem of Evil: The Worm in the Bud," *Monist* 63 (1980): 480–93, for a stimulating discussion of the problem of malignity in general and Claggart in particular.

[14] Compare Iago, of Cassio: "He hath a daily beauty in his life that makes me ugly" (Othello, 5.1.19–20).

[15] A. Schopenhauer, *The World as Will and Idea*, in *The Philosophy of Schopenhauer*, ed. Irwin Edman (New York: Modern Library, 1928), p. 293.

[16] Ibid., p. 294.

I have interpreted the Socratic position up to this point as a psychological theory about how an end must be perceived for it to be a motivating cause, and I have tried to rebut this theory by showing that one can grasp the motives of Iago and Claggart without having to convert them into perceived goods, whether goods for the agents themselves or goods that the agents themselves perceived as appropriately desired.[17] Suppose, however, that we take the Socratic claim to be logical rather that psychological. On this interpretation, seeing something as good is to acknowledge that there is the strongest possible practical reason for seeking it, however one may fail in practice through weakness of will. Conversely, to see something as evil would be to recognize that there is a reason not to seek it. So it would be incoherent to adopt Satan's policy of pursuing evil for its own sake since this would be to have as one's reason for action what was logically a reason against action.

Schopenhauer's account of malignity is too plausible, however, for the logical objection to clinch the matter. That objection depends on an assumed nexus between recognizing that there is a reason for action, having that reason as one's own, and being motivated to act on it. There seems to be two ways, though, in which one could recognize the good (or the desirable) and the evil (the undesirable). Paradigmatically, it is true, to see a state of affairs as desirable is to acknowledge that, by criteria of value and appropriateness that one can acknowledge as one's own, there is a reason for desiring things so. But we can envisage a person imagining very well what it would be like to have such a moral experience, to make the appraisals that most people make, and to see why, indeed, they found desirable the things that they did, given the kind of people that they were. And he could envy them for being as they are while being filled, like Claggart, with resentment and hate for them and the things they love and value just because he knows that there is no possibility that he could be like them, think like them, feel like them, or care like them. Precisely because the good that he sees cannot motivate him, he hates it for its very inaccessibility. He grasps the attraction of the good and knows its opposite as evil, but in an encapsulated way that prevents its being also—for him—a reason for action in the way that it is for them. His acknowledging it as good amounts to seeing that it is a reason, but it is not a reason that he can have or that could be his motive.

---

[17] Iago makes some pretense that his animosity toward Othello is prompted by a report that the latter had seduced his wife. Supposing him really to have believed that, it is interesting to see how that could change our judgment of Iago. It would still be the case that he knowingly wished an evil on Othello, but not now simply for evil's sake. Revenge, responding to an injury, represents a primitive kind of justice; the maxim of his action would then have been not to do evil for evil's sake but to exact just recompense. And this, presumably, is where a retributivist's defense of punishment must begin since he defends the inflicting of evil not, like the malignant, for evil's sake but in the name of justice. To satisfy one's claim to vengeance is thus not merely an intelligible motive but also one that in some measure redeems malignity, as envy does not. Resentment straddles these two possibilities. Like Claggart and Iago, one can resent being diminished by goodness, which is no injury, but one can also resent a real injury, and someone who wished another ill on that account, though falling short of charity, would be a wicked person only to the extent that his justified grievance made him insensitive to counterconsiderations.

The way in which the malignant subject experiences such a rancorous motivation to evil may be set out schematically as follows:

1. Properties $C_1 \ldots C_n$ in a person are virtues (V).
2. Anyone is a good person (G) if and only if he has properties V.
3. For any G, X is a reason for action (e.g., the principle that one should turn the other cheek).
4. I value someone's being a G if and only if I believe I could myself succeed in being a G.
5. I value V if and only if I can be a G.
6. I do not believe I can have X as my reason for action.
7. Therefore I do not believe I could succeed in being a G.
8'. Any properties that I would value if I had them (P), but which I believe I cannot succeed in having, are to be despised (maxim 1).
8''. Any person (S) who succeeds in having P is to be made to suffer for having them (maxim 2).
8'''. Any action that only an S would have a reason for doing is to be avoided, and the contrary action is to be done (maxim 3).
9. To despise virtue, to cause good people to suffer, and to do wrong, that is, to act on maxims 1, 2, and 3, is evil.
10. So evil is to be done (maxim 4).

It might be objected that anyone adopting maxims 1–4 would do so only in order to assuage a sense of his own inadequacy and that this amounts to embracing evil only for the sake of a perceived good. But of course, if one knew that this was what one was doing—crying "sour grapes"—the strategy would be ineffective. The malignant could assuage a sense of inadequacy only if he was really unaware of this aspect of his motivation; otherwise he would know when he said that he detested virtue that he really admired it. The explanatory methods of depth psychology consist precisely in constructing scenarios such that the end of every action is an intelligible good or the relief of an intelligible unease. But the putative unconscious strategies are by no means always successful—the malignant's rancor is not assuaged, nor does he feel any the less inadequate when his rival is laid low; for if it is indeed his own moral failing in comparison with his rival's virtue that dismays him, acting viciously as a reprisal can only aggravate the sense of inferiority. The method of depth psychology must explain, therefore, why the good that is the imputed objective is so ineffectually pursued. Meanwhile, whatever the psychiatric explanation, there can be little doubt that the malignant subject really is hating good and delighting in evil under precisely these descriptions, without feeling that there is anything logically incoherent in doing so. And while the phenomenology of rancor may not apply in precisely the same way to every instance of malignancy, it is enough to suggest that the nexus between recognition of a reason, having it as one's own, and being motivated to act on it can be broken.

32

Forgiveness and Resentment

Jeffrie G. Murphy teaches law and philosophy at Arizona State University. He is the author of many books and articles on moral, political, and legal philosophy, including *The Philosophy of Law: An Introduction to Jurisprudence* (coauthored with Jules L. Coleman) and *Forgiveness and Mercy* (coauthored with Jean Hampton).

> Understand, and forgive, my mother said, and the effort has quite exhausted me. I could do with some anger to energize me, and bring me back to life again. But where can I find that anger? Who is to help me? My friends? I have been understanding and forgiving my friends, my female friends, for as long as I can remember. . . . Understand and forgive. . . . Understand husbands, wives, fathers, mothers. Understand dog fights above and the charity box below, understand fur-coated women and children without shoes. Understand school—Jonah, Job and the nature of the Deity; understand Hitler and the Bank of England and the behavior of Cinderella's sisters. Preach acceptance to wives and tolerance to husbands; patience to parents and compromise to the young. Nothing in this world is perfect; to protest takes the strength needed for survival. Grit your teeth, endure. Understand, forgive, accept, in the light of your own death, your own inevitable corruption. . . .
>
> Oh mother, what you taught me! And what a miserable, crawling, sniveling way to go, the worn-out slippers neatly placed beneath the bed, careful not to give offense.
>
> Fay Weldon
Female Friends

I have opened with this passage from Fay Weldon's marvelous novel *Female Friends* in order to set a certain tone for the following ruminations on the topic of forgiveness.[1] For the passage conveys the rather Nietzchean thought that forgiveness might actually be harmful and wrong—a weakness or *vice*, in short, instead of the virtue which conventional Christian wisdom takes it to

From Jeffrie G. Murphy, "Forgiveness and Resentment," *Midwest Studies in Philosophy* 7 (1982): 503–16. Copyright 1982. University of Minnesota Press. Reprinted by permission of the University of Minnesota Press.

be. I shall ultimately argue that there is much to be said in favor of forgiveness; but it is also important to stress that there is much to be said against it—that it is not unambiguously a virtue in all contexts. Forgiveness, like love, is a topic that tends to elicit respectful piety rather than serious thought from those who consider it. I want none of this.

Why am I interested in the topic of forgiveness? Is it simply to atone for all the years I have spent writing in defense of a retributive theory of punishment? Psychologically, this may be part of the story; but I would also argue that the topic of forgiveness is both socially important and intrinsically interesting. It is intrinsically interesting because it is part of a set of concerns —too long neglected by moral philosophers—centering upon the role of *feelings* in the moral life. I shall later argue (following Bishop Butler) that forgiveness is the forswearing of *resentment*—where resentment is a negative feeling (anger, hatred) directed toward another who has done one moral injury or harm (e.g. violated one's rights). And thus forgiveness, if it is a virtue at all, is primarily concerned with overcoming resentment, i.e., primarily concerned with how one feels instead of how one acts.

But why do feelings matter? They may matter for at least two different reasons. First, they may matter in this sense: It is simply unacceptable in the mental life of a rational person to have feelings that are inappropriate or unfitting to their objects—e.g., irrational fears (phobias) or instances of neurotic guilt.[2] One may fairly be charged with a rational failing (regardless of one's actions) if one has these feelings where they are inappropriate—much as one may be so charged if one has beliefs that are not true (or at least reasonable) even if these beliefs have no public consequences in one's actions.

A second reason that feelings matter is that, of course, they sometimes do have social or public consequences in action—e.g., resentment or hatred toward criminals may have something to do with our willingness to let prisons remain the inhuman pestholes they now tend to be. This might be permissible if the level of resentment involved is justified, but very likely it is not—at least in the vast majority of cases. Resentment is an obstacle to the restoration of equal moral relations among persons, and thus it cannot always be the final "bottom line" as the response we take to those who have wronged us. For this reason, the attractive or virtuous side of forgiveness is quite easy to see. Forgiveness heals and restores; and, without it, resentment would remain as an obstacle to many human relationships we value. This can be seen most clearly in such intimate relationships as love and friendship. The people with whom we are most intimate are those who can harm us the most, for they are persons to whom we have let down our guard and have exposed our vulnerabilities. (Recall that Aristotle claimed that friendship requires the virtue of courage. He saw that it is a risky business.) Because of the nature of intimacy, moral injuries here tend to be not just ordinary injustices but also *betrayals*. Thus resentment here can be deep and nearly intractable—as revealed in Francis Bacon's quotation from Cosmus, Duke of Florence: "You shall read that we are commanded to forgive our enemies; but you never read that we are commanded to forgive our friends."[3] However, deep as these hurts of intimacy may be, what would be the consequences of never forgiving any of them? Surely it would be this: the impossibility of ever having the kind of intimate relationships that are one of the crowning delights of human existence. The person who cannot forgive is the person who cannot have friends or lovers.

But, given this, where is the bad side of forgiveness—the side which, as I suggested at the outset, may make forgiveness at least sometimes a vice instead of a virtue? The bad side is found here: that a too ready tendency to forgive may be a sign that one lacks *self-respect*. Not to have what Peter Strawson calls the "reactive attitude" of resentment when our rights are violated is to convey—emotionally—either that we do not think we have rights or that we do not take our own rights very seriously.[4] Forgiveness may restore relationships, but to seek restoration at all costs—even at the cost of one's self-respect—can hardly be a virtue. And, in intimate relationships, it can hardly be true love or friendship either (the kind of love and friendship that Aristotle claimed is an essential part of the virtuous life). When we are willing to be doormats for others, we have—not love or friendship—but rather what the psychiatrist Karen Horney called "morbid dependency."[5] If I count morally as much as anyone else (as surely I do), a failure to resent moral injuries done to me is a failure to care about moral value incarnate in my own moral personality (that I am, in Kantian language, an end-in-myself) and a failure to care about the very rules of morality. To put the point yet another way: If it is proper (perhaps even sometimes mandatory) to feel *indignation* when I see third parties morally wronged, must it not be equally proper (perhaps even sometimes mandatory) to feel *resentment* when I experience moral wrong done to myself? Just as the psychopath who feels no guilt, shame, or remorse for the wrong he does can be said to lack a true appreciation of morality, so too can the person who feels no indignation or resentment be said to lack a true appreciation of morality. Morality, in short, is not simply something to be believed; it is something to be *cared* about. This caring includes concern about those persons (including oneself) who are the proper objects of moral judgment.[6]

Interestingly enough, a hasty readiness to forgive—or even a refusal to display resentment initially—may reveal a lack of respect, not just for oneself, but for others as well. The Nietzschean view, for example, is rather like this: There is no need for forgiveness because a truly strong person will never feel resentment. Why? Because other people—those who harm us—simply do not matter enough. We do not resent the insect that stings us (we simply brush it off and perhaps crush it), and neither should we resent the human who wrongs us. This saves our self-respect, of course, but what a terrible view to have about all other persons.[7] Thus, if forgiveness is acceptable, it must be of a kind that is consistent with self-respect, respect for others as moral agents, and allegiance to the rules of morality (i.e., forgiveness must not involve any complicity or acquiescence in wrongdoing).[8]

Enough by way of introduction. Let me now move to a consideration of the two basic philosophical questions concerning forgiveness: (1) What is forgiveness, i.e., how is the concept to be analyzed? and (2) When, if at all, is forgiveness justified? (If it is sometimes unjustified, then—at least in those cases—it clearly cannot be a virtue.)

First the question of meaning—what is it to forgive? As a way into this question, it will be helpful to begin by noting three things that forgiveness is *not*: it is not *excuse*, it is not *justification*, and it is not *mercy*.[9] (There are countless other things which forgiveness is also not, of course, but I select these three because they represent concepts with which forgiveness is easily and often confused.) To excuse is to say this: What was done was morally wrong; but, because of certain factors about the agent (e.g., insanity), it would be unfair to hold the wrongdoer responsible or blame him for the wrong action. To justify is to say this: What was done was prima facie wrong; but, because of other morally relevant factors (e.g., the need to save a life), the action was—all morally relevant factors considered—the right thing to do. And why are neither of these forgiveness? Because we may forgive only that which it is initially proper to resent; and, if a person has done nothing wrong or was not responsible for what he did, there is *nothing to resent* (though perhaps much to be sad about). Resentment—and thus forgiveness—is directed toward *responsible wrongdoing*; and thus, if resentment and forgiveness are to have an arena, it must be where such wrongdoing remains intact—i.e., neither excused nor justified. ("Father forgive them for they know not what they do" would go better as "Father *excuse* them for they know not what they do.")

Forgiveness is also not mercy. To be merciful is to treat a person less harshly than, given certain rules, one has a right to treat that person. For example: The rules of chivalry give me the right to kill you under certain circumstances of combat.[10] If you beg for mercy, you are begging that I do something less severe than kill you. When Portia advises Shylock to show mercy, she is asking that he accept a payment less harsh than the one which, given the terms of his bargain, he has a right to demand. Three things are present in such cases: some notion of just or rightful authority, some notion of the supplicant having fallen afoul of certain public rules, and the consideration of a certain external action (a killing, a payment of a "pound of flesh"). None of these are necessarily involved in forgiveness. Forgiveness is primarily a matter of how I feel about you (not how I treat you), and thus I may forgive you in my heart of hearts or even after you are dead. (I cannot show you mercy in my heart of hearts or after you are dead, however.) I may think I have forgiven you; but, when old resentments rise up again, I may say "I was wrong—I really have not forgiven you after all." But if I have shown you mercy, this has been done—once and for all. Also, with respect to mercy, it is not necessary that I—in showing it—must be the one wronged or injured by your wrongful conduct. (It is not even necessary that anyone be wronged.) All that is required is that you stand under certain rules and that I have authority to treat you in a certain harsh way because of those rules. But the matter is different with forgiveness. To use a legal term, I do not have *standing* to resent or forgive you unless I have myself been the victim of your wrongdoing.[11] I may forgive you for embezzling my funds; but it would be ludicrous for me, for example, to claim that I had decided to forgive Hitler for what he did to the Jews. I lack the proper standing for this.[12] Thus: I may legitimately resent (and thus consider forgiving) wrong done to me. If I forgive, this will primarily be a matter of my forswearing my resentment toward the person who has wronged me—a change of attitude quite compatible with still demanding certain harsh public consequences for the wrongdoer. My forgiving you for embezzling my funds is not, for example, inconsistent with a demand that you return my funds to me or even with a demand that you suffer just legal punishment for what you have done. Neither does my forgiveness entail that I must trust you with my money again in the future. Forgiveness restores moral equality but not necessarily equality in every respect—e.g., equality of trust.

This brief discussion of what forgiveness is not has already begun to make it apparent what I think forgiveness is. Like Bishop Butler, I regard forgiveness as at least involving the *overcoming of resentment*.[13] Butler's puzzle was this: How could a loving God who commanded that we love our neighbor implant in us so unloving a passion as resentment? Is not this attitude unambiguously bad and any actions or practices based on it (retributive punishment perhaps) also bad? In answering *no* to this question, Butler suggests that resentment understandably arouses suspicion because it is often inappropriate (i.e., directed toward trivial affronts instead of real moral injury) and sometimes provokes excessive behavior (e.g., personal revenge or vigilante activity). As Butler sees, however, it would be a mistake to condemn a passion simply because it admits of pathological or irrational extensions. (What passion does not?) Resentment expresses our respect for self, for others, and for morality; and it is thus—when so described—consistent, in Butler's view, with any reasonable interpretation of a gospel of love. (Butler has no patience with attempts to view the Christian ethic as irrational sentimentality.) What is not consistent with a gospel of love is being dominated by the passion of resentment or acting unjustly on the basis of that passion; and thus Butler sees forgiveness as a virtue that functions to check resentment and keep it within proper bounds.

Is forgiveness then nothing but the overcoming of resentment? Is every instance where resentment is overcome a case of the virtue or forgiveness? I think not; and two sorts of cases will aid in establishing this negative answer. First, consider the case of *forgetting*. Sometimes we lose a vivid memory of old wrongs, become bored with our resentments, and simply forget. But this just *happens* to us, i.e., it is totally nonvoluntary. As such, how could it be a virtue at all and thus the virtue of forgiveness? We tend to use the phrase "forgive and forget," and I do not believe the phrase is redundant.

Or consider this second case: You have wronged me deeply, and I deeply resent you for it. The resentment eats away at my peace of mind, e.g., I lose sleep, snap at my friends, become less effective at my work, and so on. In short, my resentment so dominates my mental life that I am being made miserable. In order to regain my peace of mind, I go to a behavior-modification therapist to have my resentment extinguished. (Let us suppose there are such techniques.) Have I forgiven you? Surely not—at least not in any sense where forgiveness is supposed to be a moral virtue. For my motivation here was not moral at all; it was purely *selfish*, i.e., the desire to promote my own mental health.

What is starting to emerge from this discussion is this: The question "What is forgiveness?" cannot after all be sharply distinguished from the question "How is forgiveness justified?" As the cases above show, not all cases of ceasing to resent will be cases of forgiveness, e.g., forgetting is not. We cannot define forgiveness and *then* ask what moral reasons make it appropriate; because, I suggest, my ceasing to resent you will not constitute forgiveness unless it is *done for a moral reason*. Forgiveness is not the overcoming of resentment *simpliciter*; it is rather this: to foreswear resentment on moral grounds.[14]

What, then, are the moral grounds, i.e. what sorts of reasons justify or at least render appropriate an act of forgiveness? Let me start to answer this question simply by listing five reasons that are, in ordinary life and discourse, those most often given as grounds for forgiveness. We will then consider if this is just a laundry list or if some rational principle unites them or some set of them. The reasons are these:

I will forgive the person who has willfully wronged me because

(1) He repented or had a change of heart *or*
(2) He meant well (his motives were good)[15] *or*
(3) He has suffered enough *or*
(4) He has undergone humiliation (perhaps some ritual humiliation, e.g., the apology ritual of "I beg forgiveness") *or*
(5) Of old time's sake (e.g., "He has been a good and loyal friend to me in the past").

Let me say something about what these reasons tend to have in common and then say something in detail about each one. But first recall the background here: acceptable grounds for forgiveness must be compatible with self-respect, respect for others as moral agents, and respect for the moral order (i.e., the rules of morality). And we can clearly salvage this final goal (respect for the moral order) if we can draw some distinction between the immoral *act* and the *agent*; for then we can follow St. Augustine's counsel and "hate the sin but not the sinner." It is, of course, impossible to hate the sin but not the sinner if the sinner is intimately identified with his sin (better talk: if the wrongdoer is intimately identified with his wrongdoing). But, to the extent that the agent separates himself from his act, then to that extent forgiveness *of him* is possible without a tacit approval of his evil act. A similar divorce of act from agent will also help to square forgiveness with personal respect. One reason we so deeply resent moral injuries done to us is not simply that they hurt us in some tangible or sensible way; it is because such injuries are also *messages*, i.e., symbolic communications. They are ways a wrongdoer has of saying to us "I count and you do not," "I can use you for my purposes," or " I am here up high and you are there down below." Intentional wrongdoing *degrades* us—or at least represents an attempt to degrade us—and thus it involves a kind of injury that is not merely tangible and sensible. It is moral injury. (As Justice Holmes observed, even a dog notices and cares about the difference between being tripped over accidentally and being kicked intentionally.) Nietzsche to the contrary, we tend to care about what others (*some* others, some significant group whose good opinion we value) think about us—how much they think we matter. And we are thus *insulted* when they chose to express their contempt for us by violating our rights intentionally. We resent them and want to separate ourselves from them. But what if they come to separate themselves from their own evil act? (True repentance is a clear way of doing this.) Then the insulting message is no longer present, i.e., no longer endorsed by the wrongdoer. We can then join the wrongdoer in condemning the very act from which he now stands emotionally separated.[16] Thus, to a degree that the items on the list above represent ways in which the agent can be divorced or severed from his evil act, they represent ways in which forgiveness of an agent is possible without lack of self-respect or respect for the rules of moral order. To explore this idea of "divorce of agent from act," let us now look a bit more closely at each of the five listed reasons.

(1) *Repentance.* This is the clearest way in which a wrongdoer can sever himself from his past wrong act. In having a sincere change of heart, he is withdrawing his endorsement from his own immoral past behavior; he is saying "I no longer stand behind this wrongdoing and want to be separated from it; I stand with you in condemning it." Of such a person it certainly cannot be said that he is *now* conveying the message that he holds one in contempt— even though it may be true that he did in the past. Thus I can relate to him now, through forgiveness, without fearing my own acquiescence in immorality or in judgments that I lack worth. I forgive him for what he *now* is.

(2) *Good Motives.* Sometimes people wrong us without meaning to convey that they hold us in contempt or think we are of less worth than they are. Paternalism is a good example to illustrate this point. A person who interferes with my liberty for what he thinks is my own good is, in my judgment, acting wrongly, i.e., he is interfering in my "moral space" in a way he has no right to. His grounds for interfering, however, are well-meaning (i.e., he seeks to do me good) even if his actions are misguided and morally insensitive. (Perhaps he is overly sensitive to utilitarian considerations at the expense of a concern for rights and justice.) It is hard to view the friend who locks up my liquor cabinet because he knows I drink too much as on the same moral level as the person who embezzles my funds for his own benefit; and thus the case for forgiving the former may have some merit. (Repeat and warned offenders in such matters are another story entirely, however.)

(3) *Enough Suffering.* The claim "he has suffered enough" as a ground for forgiveness may understandably be viewed with suspicion, e.g., we may think it was involved in such unsavory events as Gerald Ford's pardon of Richard Nixon on the grounds that Nixon, disgraced as president, had suffered enough. But two cautions are relevant here. First, Nixon was not simply forgiven; he was treated with mercy. To pardon someone is not simply to change the way one feels about him but is to let him avoid what may well be his just

deserts. Second, just because some suffering may be relevant to forgiveness, it does not follow that any suffering is. The suffering occasioned by falling from a position that (as one's wrongful actions demonstrate) one had no right to occupy in the first place hardly seems relevant from the moral point of view.[17]

But what would relevant suffering be? I am not sure, actually, and some part of me wants to throw this consideration out entirely as simply confusion or even superstition. And yet some other part of me cannot quite do this. There is the thought, widespread in our cultural history, that *suffering is redemptive*. (One thinks, for example, of the old Oedipus of *Oedipus at Colonus*.) This connection between suffering and redemption could, of course, simply be a kind of empirical claim, e.g., the claim that suffering tends to provoke repentance. If so, then the intelligible content of "he has suffered enough" is redundant, i.e., it collapses into my point (1) above. So too if the suffering is simply guilt or other pangs of conscience. But this does not seem quite all there is here. (Old Oedipus, for example, did not feel guilt and did not repent.) Perhaps there is something in this thought: Wrongdoers degrade us; they bring us low—lower than themselves. We cannot forgive and restore relations with them in this posture without acquiescing in our own lowered status—something which no honorable person could do. But suffering tends to bring people low, to reduce them, to humble them. If so, then enough equality may be restored in order to forgive consistent with self-respect.[18]

(4) *Humiliation.* What I want to say about humiliation continues the above thought about suffering and involves the role of *ritual* in our moral life. We tend to think that rituals are practices that primitive savages have, and that we civilized folks have outgrown this sort of thing. But we are obviously mistaken when we think this. Philosophers have not, I think, paid sufficient attention to the role of ritual in moral relations—a role which illuminates certain aspects of forgiveness. As I mentioned before, wrongdoers degrade or insult us; they bring us low; they say "I am up here on high while you are down there below." As a result, we in a real sense *lose face* when done moral injury—one reason why easy forgiveness tends to compromise our self-esteem. But our moral relations provide for a ritual whereby the wrongdoer can symbolically bring himself low (or raise us up—I am not sure which metaphor best captures the point I want to make)—i.e., the humbling ritual of *apology*, the language of which is often that of *begging* forgiveness. The posture of begging is not very exalted, of course, and thus some symbolic equality—necessary if forgiveness is to proceed consistently with self-respect—is now present. Sometimes, of course, the apology is more than ritual—indeed, in the best of cases it is likely to be (if sincere) a way of manifesting repentance. Here it will collapse into (1) above. At other times we will settle simply for the ritual—so long as it is not transparently insincere.[19]

(5) *Old Time's Sake.* As with repentance, we have here a clear case of divorce of act from agent. When you are repentant, I forgive you for what you *now are*. When I forgive you for old time's sake, I forgive you for what you *once were*. Much of our forgiveness of old friends and parents, for example, is of this sort.

The upshot of what I have argued thus far is this: Forgiveness of a wrong-doer on the basis of any of the above grounds (grounds which in various ways divorce act from agent) may be consistent with self-respect, respect for others, and respect for the rules of the moral order. This does not mean that forgiveness is obligatory (no one has a right to be forgiven) but simply that, in these cases, forgiveness will not be inappropriate. At the very least, these grounds remove important moral obstacles to forgiveness and thus open the door for it.

But, once the door is open, should we walk through it? Is forgiveness sometimes a gift that we *ought* to bestow, or is it something that is merely permissible and optional? If the grounds previously discussed simply make forgiveness permissible (i.e., not wrong or vicious), we could always refuse to forgive (as we can always refuse to do anything that is merely permissible) without being open to moral criticism. But then forgiveness would not be a virtue; for its being a virtue entails that at least sometimes we ought to forgive and are subject to moral criticism if we never forgive. Thus the question: Is forgiveness a virtue?

To answer this question it is important to note that the grounds cited above have involved more than the mere removal of obstacles to forgiveness. These grounds have also been ways of suggesting that resentment would be inappropriate if directed to a certain class of agents (e.g., the genuinely repentant). And surely if I have reasons for thinking that my resentment is inappropriate, I also have—to that same degree—reasons for thinking that I should foreswear and attempt to overcome my resentment. There is a sense in which it is not permissible (because not reasonable) to continue holding attitudes when I have come to believe that they are inappropriate.[20] This does not mean that persons have a right to be forgiven, i.e., I am not obligated in some strong sense to forgive (even the genuinely repentant) in the same sense that I am obligated to keep my promises. But simply because forgiveness is not obligatory in this strong sense (i.e., is not a perfect duty) it does not follow that forgiveness is totally optional—any more than the imperfect duty of benevolence is totally optional. Christians often like to speak of forgiveness as a free gift or act of grace. Insofar as they are making the point that no one has a right to be forgiven, they are making a sound point. But if they are attempting to argue that no reasons can be given in favor of forgiveness, they are mistaken. Even with respect to literal gifts, we can have good reasons for bestowing them ("It is your birthday") and so too can we have good reasons for bestowing forgiveness in certain cases. To have a good moral reason for doing something is not the same as having a perfect duty (resting on respect for rights) to do it; but it is not morally arbitrary either. Forgiveness might, like benevolence, be thought of in the camp of imperfect duties—duties which, as Kant said, admit of some latitude in the time and place of their fulfillment.[21] Just as I have a right to choose within limits to whom I will be benevolent (e.g., to support cancer research instead of giving to the heart fund), so too do I have a right to choose which of all "deserving" persons I shall forgive. I have a right to refuse to forgive even a sincerely repentant wrongdoer. (Perhaps he did me an injury so deep that I regard it and him as unforgivable.) That latitude I am allowed.[22]

But if I never forgave anyone and continued to resent (for example) all members of the class of the repentant, then I would surely reveal a moral defect. As a moral person I must have some tendency to respond to those good reasons that make resentment inappropriate and thus forgiveness appropriate. If I have this tendency I manifest a virtue—not simply the absence of a vice.

Before closing this rather rambling free-association on the topics of forgiveness and resentment, let me now consider two grounds often given for forgiveness which do not involve at all the "divorce between act and agent" feature I discussed above. These are religious—perhaps particularly Christian—grounds for forgiveness:

(1) We should forgive in order to reform the wrongdoer, i.e., we forgive, not because the wrongdoer has repented, but as a step toward bringing his repentance about, making it at least easier for him.

(2) We should forgive because we ourselves need to be forgiven. (This, I take it, is the point of the parable of the unforgiving servant at *Matthew* 18, 21–35.)

These grounds for forgiveness may be what has prompted Feuerbach and others to suggest that forgiveness cannot be accounted for in ordinary moral terms—that it takes us beyond morality and into a religious dimension that transcends or suspends the ordinarily ethical.[23] I know that some people value obscurity and mystery for its own sake, but I am myself inclined to resist these leaps into special realms. Sometimes we can mine these religious traditions for nuggets of secular value, i.e., values which we can recognize independently of the metaphysical theory in which they were originally embedded. Thus we can sometimes avoid leaps into the mysterious and edifying simply if we will think about the matter a bit more. Point (1) above, for example, could be a kind of empirical prediction—almost therapeutic in nature—about what is likely to produce reform. As such this ground for forgiveness is surely compatible with one's own self-respect. Less clear, however, is the extent to which it is compatible with the self-respect of the wrongdoer. (Suppose you have wronged someone. How would you like it if that person assumed that you could not come to repentance? Might you not feel patronized—condescended to? Turning the other cheek can be an act of weakness, or course. But it can also, as Nietzsche noted, be an act of arrogance. Seeing it in this way, the wrongdoer might well resent the forgiveness! "Who do you think you are to forgive me?!")

But what about (2)—the need of all of us to be forgiven? It might be helpful here to quote the entire parable.

> Then came Peter to him and said, Lord, how oft shall my brother sin against me, and I forgive him? till seven times? Jesus saith unto him, I say not unto thee, Until seven times; but, Until seventy times seven. Therefore is the kingdom of heaven likened unto a certain king, which would take account of his servants. And when he had begun to reckon, one was brought unto him, which owed him

ten thousand talents. But forasmuch as he had not to pay, his lord commanded him to be sold, and his wife, and children, and all that he had, and payment to be made. The servant therefore fell down, and worshipped him, saying, Lord, have patience with me, and I will pay thee all. Then the lord of that servant was moved with compassion, and loosed him and forgave him the debt. But the same servant went out, and found one of his fellow-servants, which owed him an hundred pence: and he laid hands on him, and took him by the throat, saying, Pay me that thou owest. And his fellow-servant fell down at his feet, and besought him, saying, Have patience with me, and I will pay thee all. And he would not: but went and cast him into prison, till he should pay the debt. So when his fellow-servants saw what was done, they were very sorry, and came and told unto their lord all that was done. Then his lord, after that he had called him, said unto him, O thou wicked servant, I forgave thee all that debt, because thou desiredst me: Shouldest not thou also have compassion on thy fellow-servant, even as I had pity on thee? And his lord was wroth, and delivered him to the tormentors, till he should pay all that was due unto him. So likewise shall my heavenly Father do also unto you, if ye from your hearts forgive not every one his brother their trespasses.

Matthew, 18, 21–35

This parable makes a very strong plea for forgiveness. (But not an unlimited plea, you will notice. Jesus does give a *finite number* as his answer to the question of how many times we must forgive those who wrong us.) But what are the grounds for the forgiveness? Are they metaphysically respectable? Are they morally respectable? On one interpretation, the whole appeal looks pretty dreadful—of the kind that Nietzsche liked to note when arguing that Christianity is nothing but sublimated *ressentiment*. What we have at one level here is simply an appeal to base self-interest: if you do not forgive others, God will not forgive you. One might reject this appeal either because one does not believe in God or because one will try to resist, on grounds of moral integrity, being influenced by appeals to one's lesser nature. How, in short, can an act of forgiveness be a moral virtue if it is motivated by a fear of what some supernatural sorehead will do if one fails to forgive?

But such a rejection would, I think, be too quick. As is often the case with Christian parables, there is moral insight waiting to be discovered if one will simply clear away some of the surrounding mythology. And the insight in the present parable (which can surely be granted by the most secular or even atheistic reader) is to be seen in its character as a parable on *moral humility*. Each one of us, if honest, must admit two things about ourselves: (1) We will within the course of our lives wrong others—even others about whom we care deeply; and (2) Because we care so deeply about these others and our relationships with them, we shall want to be forgiven by them for our wrongdoings. In this sense we do all need and desire forgiveness, would not want to live in a world where the disposition to forgive was not present and regarded as a healing and restoring virtue. Given that this is the sort of moral world we all need and want, is it not then incumbent upon each of us to cultivate the disposition to forgive—not the flabby sentimentality of forgiving any wrong, no matter how deep or unrepented, but at least the willingness to be open to the possibility of forgiveness with hope and some trust? Only a person so arrogant as to believe that he will never wrong others or need to be forgiven by them could (in Kantian language) consistently will membership in a world without forgiveness.[24] To see that none of us is such a person is a lesson in moral humility and is, at least in part, the message of the parable.

This closes my discussion of forgiveness; but, before closing the essay, let me attempt to answer a question I perhaps should have attempted to answer at the outset: Why am I placing an essay on the moral virtue of forgiveness in a volume supposedly devoted to essays in social and political philosophy? The answer is in part autobiographical and in part substantive. Punishment is an acceptable (i.e., traditional) topic under the heading of social and political philosophy, and one who thinks about the topic of punishment—the *hard* response—will at some point naturally think about such *softer* responses as excuse, mercy, and forgiveness. As I started to think about forgiveness, however, I found that I was becoming more and more interested in it as a moral virtue—and stopped caring directly about its social, political, and legal ramifications. I thus gave the editor of this series the opportunity to withdraw his invitation—an offer which he kindly if not wisely refused. And so now here it is, sitting here in the company of essays that are clearly about social and political philosophy.

Does it belong? My current inclination is to think that it does belong—at least that it belongs more than I thought when I offered to withdraw it. Many important social practices are direct outgrowths—in institutional form—of deep human feelings or passions. Punishment, for example, may be regarded as in part the institutionalization of such feelings as resentment and indignation. (The institutionalization of these feelings was the home that Athena gave to the Furies in *Eumenides*.) Insofar as our social and legal practices reflect our feelings, the examination of those feelings is not, I think, out of place as a part of the body of social and political philosophy. It is a limitation of the liberal tradition to think that social and political matters are limited to concerns with how we act—how we treat others. In this tradition, the concern with social and political philosophy simply is a concern with just our rightful rules of conduct. This concern is important, of course; but, in focusing upon it exclusively, the liberal tradition leaves out something of social and political importance, something stressed by such otherwise diverse writers as Plato, Aristotle, Rousseau, Marx, and Marcuse. It is this: that one legitimate concern of politics and social life is a concern with the moral quality of the lives of citizens, i.e., with the question of what kind of people will grow up and flourish.

The liberal tradition tends to take passions or desires at face value, and sees politics to be concerned with the promotion of freedom where freedom is understood as the ability to obtain objects of desire without external impediment. But there is a kind of slavery—slavery of the mind or personality—which no "Bill of Rights," no guarantees of external freedom, can correct. If we are in bondage to pointless or irrational passions, we lack what Spinoza thought of as freedom of the mind—perhaps the most important kind of freedom for an autonomous human being.

We are all, to a very great degree, products of whatever system of socialization is operative in our culture. If this socialization process cultivates certain damaging or self-demeaning or irrational feelings within us, we will become prisoners to those feelings—no matter how free we may think ourselves in acting without impediment upon them. Thus it must be regarded as a relevant project within social and political philosophy to examine the passions or feelings (such as resentment) in order to at least attempt to deal with the question of the degree to which, if at all, these passions or feelings should be reinforced, channeled in certain directions, or even eliminated.

Even liberal Mill came to see the importance of this issue when he wrote his *The Subjection of Women*; for he saw that women were as much enslaved by their feelings of subservience as by any external legal obstacles to their actions. And when Marx claimed that religion is the opiate of the masses, he surely meant in part to suggest that Christianity has encouraged the development of meek and forgiving dispositions which will tolerate oppression, and which will call that tolerance virtue. And when Fay Weldon cries out against forgiveness, her point is in part a feminist one: that women have been taught to forgive and accept where they should have been taught to resent and resist. Thus political and social philosophy must concern itself with the passions—their nature, their justification, their proper scope and social influence, their possible control. The present essay can be viewed as a part of social and political philosophy so conceived.

> Marat
> these cells of the inner self
> are worse than the deepest stone dungeon
> and as long as they are locked
> all your revolution remains
> only a prison mutiny
> to be put down
> by corrupted fellow prisoners
>
> *Marat/Sade*
> Peter Weiss

Notes

1. Fay Weldon, *Female Friends* (London, 1975).
2. See my "Rationality and the Fear of Death" in my collection of essays *Retribution, Justice, and Therapy* (Boston and Dordrecht, 1979).
3. Francis Bacon, "Of Revenge" (1597).
4. P. F. Strawson, "Freedom and Resentment," *Proceedings of the British Academy* (1962).
5. Karen Horney, *Neurosis and Human Growth* (New York, 1950).
6. See Thomas E. Hill, Jr., "Servility and Self-Respect," *The Monist* (January 1973).

7. See *Genealogy of Morals*, I, 10.
8. See Aurel Kolnai, "Forgiveness," *Proceedings of the Aristotelian Society* (1973–74).
9. In ordinary discourse we tend to be careless with these terms and sometimes use them interchangeably. I am here concerned with forgiveness as a distinct moral virtue.
10. See P. Twambley, "Mercy and Forgiveness," *Analysis* (January 1976).
11. I will be psychically identified with some persons, of course, and will see them as a part of myself and injuries to them as in some sense injuries to me. I may feel this way, for example, about my children. Here resentment does have a life.
12. In "Rebellion" (Dostoevski, *The Brothers Karamozov*) Ivan considers the suffering of innocents—especially children—and he is outraged at the thought that anyone except the child (or perhaps the mother) could forgive the injuries suffered.
13. Sermon 8 "Upon Resentment" and Sermon 9 "Upon Forgiveness of Injuries."
14. This does not mean that all forgiveness is justified; for one can base the forgiveness on faulty or incorrect or inapplicable moral judgments.
15. This point is stressed by Elizabeth Beardsley in her "Understanding and Forgiveness" in *The Philosophy of Brand Blanshard*, e. P. A. Schilpp (La Salle, Ill., 1981).
16. He is not separated in every sense, or course, for even repented acts leave traces, e.g., liability for damages or punishment.
17. See *U.S. v Bergman*, United States District Court, S.D.N.Y., 1976, 416 F. Supp. 496. Rabbi Bergman was convicted of criminal fraud in connection with the operation of some of his nursing homes. He tried to avoid a prison sentence by arguing that he had now been disgraced and had thus suffered enough. Judge Frankel was underwhelmed by this argument and suggested that, as Bergman's crimes demonstrated, he was "suffering from loss of public esteem . . . that had been, at least in some measure, wrongly bestowed and enjoyed."
18. Suffering does not exactly divorce the act from the agent; but it certainly can—if severe enough—focus our *attention* from the act to the agent.
19. On the role of humiliation ("humbling the will") see Herbert Fingarette, "Punishment and Suffering," *Proceedings of the American Philosophical Association* (1977).
20. Feelings often have a cognitive (belief) component. For example, if I am angry at you for stealing my car, how can I rationally remain angry at you if I come to believe that you are not, in fact, the one who stole my car?
21. Second Section, *Foundations of the Metaphysics of Morals*.
22. I am not totally happy with this. If I see you bleeding to death in the road and easily saved by me, can I say to you: "Sorry. I am a benevolent person, but you happen not to be the one I choose to help or assist. This duty admits of latitude, after all, and I will help others some other time." This response seems morally unacceptable—which means either that the

imperfect duty of benevolence admits of less "latitude" than Kant thought or that the duty to help people in distress is not the same as a duty of benevolence. Similar problems could be developed for the imperfect duty model for forgiveness, e.g., can I really choose not to forgive an abjectly repentant person who has done me only a little wrong? The matter requires more thought. Of course forgiveness is not always in my power. I can resolve and try the best I can to overcome resentment, but I will sometimes fail.

23. For a discussion of Feuerbach and others on this matter, see chapter 6 of Allen Wood's *Kant's Moral Religion* (Ithaca, 1970).

24. See note 21.

33

Friendship

Lawrence A. Blum is professor of philosophy at the University of Massa-
chusetts, Boston. He is the author of *Friendship, Altruism and Morality* (1980);
co-author of *A Truer Liberty: Simone Weil and Marxism* (1989); and has written
several articles in the fields of moral theory, moral development, and multi-
cultural education.

I

. . . Friendship is a largely unfamiliar territory for modern moral philosophy,
dominated as it has been by Kantian concerns or with utilitarianism, neither of
which is hospitable to particular relationships which are both personally and
morally significant. For example, contemporary emphasis on conduct which is
morally required of us, or on considerations which we are required to take
into account, does not easily allow for a focus on friendship as an arena for
morally good, yet not morally obligatory, behavior and sentiments.

Let me begin with two central claims. The first is that, other things being
equal, acts of friendship are morally good insofar as they involve acting from
regard for another person for his own sake. This does not mean that every
altruistic act within a friendship is morally admirable or praiseworthy. Some
forms of considerateness towards one's friend, or willingness to help, are such
that their absence would constitute a moral failure, and their presence merely
something which is to be expected of a friend. So acts can be morally significant though not morally praiseworthy, and this is what I mean by saying that
any action done out of regard for the friend for his own sake is morally good.
It is analogous to saying that every dutiful act is morally good although some
are such that performing them is only what is to be expected, whereas failure
to perform them is blameworthy.

Second, the deeper and stronger the concern for the friend—the stronger
the desire and willingness to act on behalf of the friend's good—the greater

the degree of moral worth (again, other things being equal). Thus a friendship which involves a very deep and genuine regard for the friend's good is a morally excellent relationship.

The argument that friendship is, or can be, a source of moral excellence begins best with an example of what such a friendship might look like. Kate and Sue are friends. Both are clerical workers in the same large insurance firm. Sue is a quiet, thoughtful and somewhat moody person; Kate is cheery and outgoing.

Sue and Kate enjoy each other's company. They enjoy talking about people they know and events that take place in the office. They appreciate and value qualities they see in each other. Kate feels she learns a lot from Sue.

Kate cares very much for Sue. Sue has a tendency to get depressed quite often. Kate has learned how to make Sue feel better when she is in such moods. Sue is not naturally or readily open about what is bothering her; but Kate has learned how to draw her out when she feels that Sue wants to talk. Sometimes she pushes Sue too hard and is rebuffed by her, in a not especially sensitive way. Kate is hurt by such rebuffs. But more often Sue is glad to have such a good friend to talk to, and is grateful for Kate's concern for her, and for Kate's initiative in getting her to talk. Sometimes Kate can cheer Sue up just by being cheerful herself (as she naturally is anyway), but she often senses when such a mood would not be appropriate.

Kate and Sue are comfortable with each other. They feel able to "be themselves" with each other, more so than with most other people. They trust each other and do not feel that they need to "keep up a good front" with one another. The women trust each other with personal matters which they do not usually discuss with their husbands. They know that the other will treat the matter seriously, and will not breach the confidence involved. They know each other well and know how to be helpful to the other in discussing intimate personal matters. They care deeply for each other, and they know this about each other, though they do not express it to each other explicitly. Each one appreciates the care and concern which she knows the other has for her. This is part of what enables them to be so open with each other—the knowledge that the response will be a caring one, even when it is not directly helpful in a practical sense.

Kate and Sue are willing to go to great lengths to help each other out. They readily do favors for each other—helping shop, picking up something at the cleaners, making excuses and covering for each other at work, taking care of each other's children.

When Kate is troubled about something Sue is concerned too; and vice versa. Sue thinks about how to help Kate out. For example, she helps her to think about how to deal with her horrible boss.

The relationship between Sue and Kate was not always so close. They came to know each other gradually. Their different temperaments kept them from taking to each other immediately. In addition, Kate often felt, and still sometimes feels, shut out by Sue's reserve, and her rebuffs. She was anxious to please Sue, to have Sue like her, and this often made her forget her own desires and needs. In her insecurities in the relationship she would also not be able to focus attention on Sue's own needs, feelings, and situation. In struggling with Sue, and with herself, to reach a deeper level of commitment, she worked through these insecurities. She was thereby enabled to distinguish more clearly Sue's needs and feelings from her own, to overcome tendencies to distort.

I have attempted here to describe a friendship which is both realistic (i.e., not involving saints) and yet which has reached a high degree of moral excellence. I mean to have brought out the following features: the concern, care, sympathy, and the willingness to give of oneself to the friend which goes far beyond what is characteristic and expected of people generally. The caring within a friendship is built up on a basis of knowledge, trust, and intimacy. One understands one's friend's good through knowing him well, much better than one knows non-friends, hence much better and more deeply than one knows their good. One is more sensitive to one's friend's needs and wants than one is to non-friends. In genuine friendship one comes to have a close identification with the good of the other person, an occurrence which is generally much rarer and at a much shallower level with other people.

In addition one gives much of oneself, unselfishly, to one's friend, as part of caring for him. One takes this for granted and does not typically regard it as a sacrifice; this is because one does care about the friend, and not because one is motivated by self-interest. The level of self-giving is generally much greater, though also of a different nature, than with non-friends. All these aspects of friendship are of great moral worth and significance. I will refer to these aspects generally as "deep caring and identification with the good of the other."

The caring in such a friendship ranges over a period of time and involves a commitment into the future. Kate and Sue know that neither one will simply drift away from the other. They will stick by each other. Their caring means that if trouble arises between them, they will try to work it through. Of course they know that, human existence being what it is, there is always a possibility of some kind of breach that would drive them apart. But this possibility is not translated into any actual distancing of themselves from one another, or into self-protection through "lowering one's expectations." In fact, each expects the other's care, concern, and commitment to extend into the foreseeable future; this is a source of deep comfort and joy to both of them, though they are seldom aware of it explicitly.

It is not the willing self-giving which is by itself the ground of the moral excellence of friendship, but only the self-giving which takes place within a relationship in which one genuinely understands and knows the other person, and understands one's separateness from him. For under the influence of a romantic passion one might be willing to do all sorts of things for the other person, to sacrifice for him. But this passion, and its associated disposition to act for the sake of the other, might be superficial, though very intense. It is not grounded in a real knowledge and understanding of the other, and of one's relationship to the other, such as exists in the example of Kate and Sue. In such a passion one not only gives of oneself—which is morally meritorious—but one, as it were, gives oneself away. And, as many writers have pointed out, this giving oneself away—failing to retain a clear sense of the other's otherness and of one's own separateness and integrity as a person—can stem not only from romantic passion or infatuation, but can be an integral part of long-standing and stable relationships, and can be a settled tendency within an individual's way of relating to others.[1]

We can say, in summary, that the moral excellence of friendship involves a high level of development and expression of the altruistic emotions of sympathy, concern, and care—a deep caring for and identification with the good of another from whom one knows oneself clearly to be other.

II

Let us consider some conceptions of friendship which would deny its moral significance.

On the first conception, friendship is pictured as a sort of natural process, as something which merely happens to one. In one's life one runs across certain people whom one likes and is drawn to, and some of these people become one's friends. This happens to virtually everyone. There is nothing special about it, rather it is simply a natural part of human life, not a particular achievement or a matter of something which one works at.

Moreover, the course of friendship is largely a matter of the vagaries of our emotions. It is thus not really something over which we have control.

> Personal relations cannot be controlled by morality because they cannot be controlled at all. . . . they are not the sort of thing of which it makes sense to speak of making them different. They exist or occur; they are lived, experienced, and they change; but they are not controlled.[2]

Thus friendship cannot be a moral excellence, because it is not the sort of thing on which we exercise moral control and agency.

There are several things deeply wrong with this picture of friendship and of personal relationships generally. Most fundamentally, not everyone does have friends in the same way. People have very different relationships to their friends and treat their friends differently, and some of these differences are morally significant. In particular the levels of caring for and giving of oneself to one's friends are very different among different people (and within the same person's friendships).

I might have a genuine friend, someone whom I genuinely like to be with and to do certain kinds of things with, yet I might not care for and about him very deeply. I wish him well, hope for good things for him, and am willing to do some things for him, even if they inconvenience me to some extent. But I do not give much of myself to him. Perhaps I do not even know him very well, and do not make an effort to do so. I do not in any very significant way identify with his goals and aspirations, nor substantially desire his good for its own sake.

There is not necessarily anything wrong with this friendship. Perhaps, even if I could care more about my friend, I do not wish to do so. We understand each other's feelings and neither would want the relationship to be more than it is. There is nothing blameworthy here.

Nevertheless, this friendship is evidently not at the personal and moral level of Kate and Sue's friendship. It involves much less in the way of caring, of the giving of oneself to the other; of the transcendence of self involved in the deep identification with the other's good; of the level of considerateness, sympathy, and concern involved in Kate and Sue's friendship.

We all, I would think, can recognize that we have friendships at differing levels of commitment, care, and concern. Though all genuine human caring has moral worth and significance, is it not evident that a deeper level of caring involves greater moral worth? Such caring, far from being a natural process, is difficult to achieve, and is not really so common. It involves getting outside oneself, being able to focus clearly on and to know another person. It involves being willing to give of oneself, and in a way which is not simply experienced as self-sacrifice or self-denial. It involves overcoming within oneself obstacles, defenses, or distortions which prevent the deep caring for the other. (And this will generally involve some kind of shared process with the other person.)

Not only are there variations of moral level within one's own friendships; but it is also true that people may vary greatly among themselves in this regard. Some people are generally more caring, giving, helpful, and considerate towards their friends than are others.

III

Thus some people may have no friendships of a high level of moral excellence. And, as Aristotle recognized, some people may actually be incapable of such friendships. A truly selfish person could not have friends in the fullest sense. If he were genuinely able to care for another person for his own sake, if he were able to give much of himself to the other freely and for his own sake, based on a genuine understanding of him, then he would not be selfish.

It is true that selfish people can be very attached to one or another person, e.g., a spouse or friend. But it seems that such a friendship could not be a friendship of the most morally excellent kind. The attachment or friendship would be too grounded in self-centered considerations. Thus a selfish man could be very attached to his wife, dote on her, and in some ways do a lot for her. But this does not mean that he really cares for her for her own sake. His behavior would be compatible with his caring for her, so to speak, for her willingness to serve him, to be at his command, to flatter his ego. His giving could be either a minor concession for her serving him or even a further expression or assertion of his power over her and of her dependence on him. If he were truly selfish then something like this would be the most likely explanation of his "beneficent" behavior. That a person should care very genuinely and fully for only one person while basically being very selfish seems an impossibility.[3]

Nevertheless, it would be wrong to say that a selfish person cannot really have friends at all, in any sense of the term. For first of all there are important aspects of friendship besides caring for the other, i.e., enjoying being with the other person or sharing certain kinds of activities with him, liking the other person. So a selfish man can have friends, in that there are people whom he likes and enjoys sharing certain activities with. Second, even a selfish person can wish another well, be well-disposed towards another. (Here we have to keep in mind the difference between a humanly selfish person and a sociopath.) It is only caring in the full sense which is incompatible with selfishness.[4]

Thus there are very different levels of friendship, levels which are understood in moral terms, in terms of how fully one cares for the other. If this is so then there is something wrong with the conception that friendships happen, so to speak, naturally, without our moral intervention, and that friendships are of a uniform moral type. Friendship always involves a giving of self to the other and a valuing of the other for his own sake. Friendship thus involves an orientation of our (moral) selves towards another person, rather than a process which merely happens to us and which (in Mayo's word) cannot be "controlled." On a more general level, personal relations are not merely "lived" and "experienced," nor is their "change" a merely natural process unrelated to moral aspects of ourselves, as Mayo implies. Rather friendship is an expression of moral activity on our part—of a type of regard for another person, a giving of oneself, and a caring for another for his own sake.

IV

In the case of Kate and Sue, the "moral activity" involved in the friendship is especially evident. For I have described the deep level of caring between the women as an outcome of effort and struggle, and hence as a kind of moral achievement. Certainly, attaining a deep level of friendship, in which the parties mean a great deal to one another and care deeply for one another, often involves obstacles and difficulties, the overcoming of which requires effort. One friend disappoints the other, or feels let down by him; they misunderstand each other; they quarrel and feel that there are insuperable barriers between them. Such happenings within the history of a friendship can lead to a distancing and weakening of the bonds between the friends. Or they can constitute tests of the relationship, which ultimately strengthen the ties and deepen the meaning of the friendship. The friends can make the effort to rectify or to correct a misunderstanding, to struggle to achieve the greater mutual understanding which will prevent such disappointments and misunderstandings in the future.

It is difficult to conceive of a deep friendship which does not involve some such effort and struggle. Nevertheless, it is not such effort and struggle in its own right which grounds the moral significance of friendship. For one thing, friendships which involve something like the same level of caring do differ in the amount of effort and struggle which has gone into them, and, I would argue, it is not the effort and struggle but the level of caring itself which primarily determines the level of moral value in the friendship. It is the genuine care for another person which constitutes a moral activity of the self, not primarily the exertion of will or effort which might have gone into the development of that caring. In caring we as it were go out from ourselves to another person; we give of ourselves; we affirm the friend in his own right. These processes cannot be portrayed as something which merely happens to us, or which we simply experience, as is, e.g., finding ourselves attracted to someone. And so effort and will are not required for the activity essential to morality.[5] This is not to exclude the possibility, however, that effort and will could be a further source of moral value in a friendship beyond (though also requiring as a condition of this moral value) the caring involved.

Thus in a friendship in which the parties care deeply for each other but in which the relationship has developed without much pain, difficulty, effort, and struggle, there is still great moral merit in the caring.[6]

V

Another conception of friendship which conduces to failing to see its moral significance pictures friendship, or rather doing good for one's friends, as a kind of extension of the self, so that when one acts for the other one is simply promoting what is in a sense one's own good. This self-centeredness would exclude friendship from being a moral good, much less a moral excellence.

Our discussion can help us to see what is wrong with this conception as a general characterization of friendship. For a genuine friend truly cares for the other for his own sake. He is willing to give of himself to promote the other's good; he understands the other in his own being and interests, and can distinguish the other's interests from his own, even while he is able to care deeply for their realization and in that sense identify with the friend and his good. He grieves for the friend's sorrows. He is happy for him at his good fortune or successes in valued endeavors; he is sad for him at his losses and disappointments. It is his human growth and happiness which he desires—and for the friend's own sake, not his own.[7]

Thus the sense of identification involved in genuine friendship is not a matter of self-interest at all, and caring for the friend is not simply an extension of caring for oneself. This mistaken conception of friendship trades on an ambiguity within the notion of "identification," which can have either an egoistic or a non-egoistic sense. Even in the non-egoistic sense described above, the one who identifies gets pleasure from the good accruing to the one with whom he identifies. But this pleasure is not the motive of his beneficent action; in fact it is a sign of the degree to which he cares for the other as other than himself and in his own right.

The conception of friendship as extended self-interest is more appropriate to a kind of symbiotic attachment to another person (in which one has no clear sense of a self separate from the other, and in which one lives through the other so that, in that sense, his pleasures are one's own). Such an attachment can be of great importance to the person, of great emotional intensity, and can take on some of the forms of friendship—but is not at all friendship in the fullest sense.[8]

In arguing that Kate cares for her friend Sue for Sue's sake and not for Kate's own, that Kate is aware of Sue in her otherness from herself, and that Kate gives of herself to Sue, I am not arguing that Kate sacrifices herself for Sue. Nor am I arguing that when she acts for Kate's good, she acts in a manner unconnected with her own interests. She acts altruistically in the sense that her actions are motivated by genuine concern for her friend's weal and woe for its own sake; but not in the (more familiar) sense in which it implies acting in disregard of or contrary to one's own interests. . . . But this is, partly, to say that the terms "egoism" and "altruism" as usually understood serve us ill in describing acting from friendship. Let us explore this further.

Friendship involves persons being bound up with one another. The different sorts of emotions and feelings which the friends have towards one another get their meaning and significance from the entire relationship of which they are a part. In caring about the weal and woe of my friend Dave it is integral to the nature of this caring that it be for someone whom I like, whom I know likes me, who cares about my weal and woe, whom I trust, who is personally important to me, who cares about our friendship, etc. In acting from friendship towards Dave I express my acknowledgment of a relationship which includes all these feelings and attitudes. This is why the caring and the acts of beneficence in friendship are not separate from my own interests, from what is personally a good to me; it is not, in that sense, "disinterested." In fact friendship is a context in which the division between self-interest and other-interest is often not applicable. The friendship itself defines what is of importance to me, and in that sense what is in my interest. In that sense I do not generally sacrifice my own interest in acting for the good of my friend. I act with a sense of the friendship's importance to me, even though it is the friend whose benefit I directly aim at (i.e., which is my motive for acting), and not my own.

It is not that in acting for the friend's good I am acting from a combination of altruistic and egoistic motives, e.g., that I am both disinterestedly concerned with my friend's good, yet I also enjoy acting to help him. Nor am I acting from the former motive in combination with acting in order to preserve the friendship (which I am conceiving to be of benefit to me), nor in combination with the thought that my friend will be led to be more likely to benefit me in the future. These latter three portrayals involve possible motivations, which can be seen as a combination of an egoistic and an altruistic motive; but they are not accurate portrayals of our typical beneficent acts of friendship.

The way in which the value to me of my friendship with Dave figures into my acting for his good is not as a consideration for the sake of which I act. Nor is my liking of Dave a liking to do or enjoy doing every action which promotes his good. Rather, these figure in as a context of meaning of my action. They are background conditions of my being motivated to act for the sake of Dave's good. I am not doing less than acting fully for the sake of his good, and in that sense altruistically.

The notion of sacrifice implies an interest which the agent forgoes in order to promote something which is not an interest of his. It implies a clear separation between the interest he forgoes and the one for the sake of which he acts. It is the absence of such a separation in the case of friendship which means that it is not true as a general characterization of acting from friendship that in acting for the good of one's friend one is sacrificing for him. (Nevertheless in some particular actions it would be true to say that we sacrificed something of what we wanted in order to help our friend.)[9]

VI

Even if the notion that friendship is a kind of extended self-interest is abandoned, the previous discussion indicates what might be thought to be a moral deficiency in the kind of concern involved in friendship, namely that one would not have the concern if the other were not one's friend. The friendship, with all it involves, is a necessary condition for the concern, even if the concern is granted to be directed genuinely towards the friend for his own sake. Let us call this "conditional altruism."

Conditional altruism might be thought to be deficient precisely because it is not a universal form of concern. It is not directed towards the friend simply in virtue of his humanity but rather only in virtue of some relationship in which he stands towards oneself. This line of thinking, which I will call "universalist," is given a particularly stringent expression in Kierkegaard's *Works of Love*. He says that love of one's friend (one's beloved) has no moral value except insofar as it stems from a love which one would have for "one's neighbor," i.e., for any human being; and so, for example, if one saves a drowning person because he is one's friend—i.e., one would not do so if he were not one's friend—one's act would not have moral significance. Kierkegaard does not say there is anything wrong with loving one's friend and acting out of love for him; he says only that such love has no moral significance.[10]

A weaker view would be that love or concern for one's friend, though not without moral significance altogether, is yet in important ways deficient as a moral attitude towards another person. Though Kant himself does not say this in his own discussions of friendship (which are generally sensitive and sensible),[11] it can be seen as an extension of some themes within the Kantian outlook, in particular the focus on universality and impartiality in the moral attitudes we take towards others. On this view conditional altruism would be, though not without value, yet without the full moral value that a universalistic altruism would have.

The consequences of this challenge to conditional altruism go far beyond the moral significance of friendship itself. For there are many sorts of special attachments, connections, and relationships between people—such as family member, neighbor (in the non-Christian sense), fellow worker, comrade, fellow member (of various organizations), member of same ethnic group of community, regular frequenter of the same pub, fellow citizen or countryman—which can be sources of a stronger sympathy, concern, and willingness to help one another than might exist in their absence.[12] The special connection or relationship is a condition of the altruism, which is therefore not purely universalistic.

Thus the issue here is at the core of the moral significance of the altruistic emotions themselves. For these special connections give rise to sympathy, compassion, and concern, and on the view which I am putting forth here these are morally good, independent of how they have arisen and whether they would exist towards the person in question in the absence of those special circumstances or relationships.

VII

Let us then examine the universalist challenge to all conditional altruism, or altruism based on special relationships. On my view, such conditional altruism does involve concern for the other for his own sake. The fact that if he were not our friend we would not have this concern for him does not mean that it is not for his own sake that we care about him. What detracts from such concern is only if the regard to the other's good stems primarily from self-concern. One could be concerned about one's friend Joe primarily because how Joe is doing reflects on oneself in the eyes of others. One could be involved in helping poor persons who are members of one's ethnic group primarily because one feels that the existence of such persons reflects badly on the group as a whole, and therefore on oneself. These examples would be excluded by my own formulation, of caring for the good of the other for his own sake, for they involve a primary concern with oneself rather than with the other.

On the other hand, if an Italian is dedicated to helping poor Italians, and is genuinely concerned for their welfare, then, even if he would not be so concerned if the persons were not Italians, he is still concerned genuinely for them for their own sakes; and, on my view, that attitude (and the actions stemming from it) have moral value.

Conditional altruism might be thought to be defective because concern with those in special relationships to oneself often takes the form primarily of hating, being opposed to, or denying the legitimacy of the interests of those outside the relationship in question. These are the familiar phenomena of chauvinism and provincialism. (It is less clear how this would work in regard to friendship; perhaps jealousy is an analogous phenomenon in that one's energies are directed against someone outside the relationship rather than towards one's friend or towards strengthening or enriching the relationship itself.)

There are two negative aspects of this chauvinism, which can exist independently of one another. The first is the opposition to those outside the relationship, an attitude bad in itself. The second is that the outside focus may mean a deficiency in one's concern for those within the relationship; one may be not so much genuinely concerned with their good as with hating or opposing those outside it. (Yet this connection is not an invariable one. It is quite possible for someone to be genuinely concerned with a group to which he is attached—to really care about their well-being—and yet also to have despicable attitudes towards those outside of his group.)

These are deficiencies within conditional altruism. But my view allows for the condemning of the despicable attitude towards those outside the special relationship, and also accords no moral value to the attitude towards those within it which does not consist in a genuine regard for the weal and woe of the persons in question. My view does, however, say that if the concern is genuine then it is *ceteris paribus* morally good; and if it is accompanied by a despicable attitude towards those outside then it is this accompanying attitude which is condemned and not the conditional altruism itself.

There may be some tendency on the part of a universalist outlook to think that conditional altruism always involves a negative attitude towards those who do not satisfy the condition. If this were true it would be a reason for regarding conditional altruism as a whole as fundamentally defective. But it clearly is not true. A person may be deeply devoted to the welfare of the Italian community without being suspicious of, or wishing the harm of, non-Italians. He may even wish well for non-Italian communities and recognize the worthiness of their aspirations, though he does not have the actual concern for them which he has for his own community. Sympathy for the interests of other groups could fairly naturally grow from concern for the interests of one group. Conditional altruism merely implies not being as concerned about the good of those who do not satisfy the condition as one is about those who do. It does not necessarily involve having an attitude towards those who do not which is in itself morally deficient.

It is important to recognize that genuine devotion to a particular group—family, neighborhood, ethnic community, ethnic group, club—is in itself morally good, and becomes morally suspect only when it involves a deficient stance towards others. It is morally good in that it involves (among other things) an admirable degree of sympathy, compassion, and concern for others. Moral philosophy ought to be able to give expression to the moral value of such an attitude, and an exclusively universalist perspective cannot do so.

On the other hand, the pitfalls of such conditional altruism should not be ignored. The connection between concern for those who satisfy the condition and opposition to those who do not is often no mere coincidence. For example, in a situation of scarce resources, devotion to one group competing for those resources can well mean opposition to others, and this can easily involve blameworthy attitudes towards these other people. (It should be noted, however, that merely competing against other groups for resources which one desires for one's own is not in itself reprehensible. It becomes so only if one either competes in an unfair or despicable way, or if, as is unfortunately too natural, one comes to develop unjustified and negative attitudes towards the other group.) Moreover, in some situations alleged devotion to the welfare of one group can, as things stand, mean little more than hatred or opposition to groups outside. Devotion to the welfare of whites as whites in America would be an example of this; there is virtually no room for this to be a genuinely altruistic attitude, or for it really to be other than opposition to non-whites.

Notes

1. On this issue see Anna Freud, "A Form of Altruism," in *The Ego and the Mechanisms of Defense*; Max Scheler, *The Nature of Sympathy*, pp. 42–3 and *passim*, and Blum, Homiak, Housman, and Scheman, "Altruism and Women's Oppression."
2. Bernard Mayo, *Ethics and the Moral Life*, p. 198.
3. This line of thought should make one suspicious of an interesting argument put forward by Bernard Williams in *Morality*, chapter 1, that a person who is generally selfish but who cares for just one person could be led to extend his caring to others, the transition from one to many being a fairly natural one (a matter of quantity rather than quality), and the gap between one and many being much smaller than that between none and one. If my own argument is right, then the kind of caring which a selfish person has for only one person is likely to be minimal and deficient, and not such as could be readily extended to a genuine caring for others.

    I am not denying here that a person could care genuinely and deeply about only one person, but only that such a person could be a fundamentally selfish person, essentially unresponsive to the weal and woe of others.
4. A selfish person will have many relationships which are not friendships at all, but which are sustained solely by his deriving some pleasure or advantage from them. If he does not wish the other well at all, nor really like him or enjoy being with him, then there is no friendship. But if these elements do exist, then even if the man's primary concern with the other is the advantage he derives from him there is still some sort of friendship. And so the basically selfish person can have friendships of a minimal sort. (I follow Aristotle's account of friendship here: *Nichomachean Ethics*, books 8 and 9, and in particular John Cooper's reconstruction of that account in "Aristotle on the Forms of Friendship.")
5. Part of the problem here is that the language and antitheses of "activity/passivity," "doing something/something happening to one," are ill-suited to express how our friendship is a reflection of ourselves morally.
6. The previous and following sections owe their existence to some well-taken criticisms by Jennifer Radden of a previous draft. I fear, however, that I have inadequately addressed the issues raised in those criticisms.
7. This conception of caring is powerfully spelled out by M. Mayeroff in *On Caring*.
8. This unhealthy form of pseudo-friendship is described by Scheler, *op. cit.*, p. 42.
9. The general inapplicability of the notion of self-sacrifice and the limitations of the concepts of egoism and altruism in the context of friendship have wider implications for moral and social philosophy. For it can be argued that such concepts are misleading in the context of any genuinely cooperative endeavor, i.e., one in which there is a shared goal among the participants, a goal regarded by them as a good, and thus a good which is

in essence shared rather than being merely an aggregate of individual and private goods. Such a cooperative enterprise, even if it can be seen also as fostering the individual and private interests of its participants, becomes a context of meaning which is essential to understanding the significance of actions which individuals take within that common endeavor. Acting for the sake of the good-of-cooperation is here analogous to acting out of friendship. (In fact friendship can be seen as a type of cooperative relationship, on this definition.) It cannot typically be seen as involving self-sacrifice; nor, on the usual understanding, can concepts of egoism and altruism be usefully applied. For a discussion of this perspective on the concepts of egoism and altruism see Alasdair MacIntyre, "Egoism and Altruism." In "Community," chapter 5 of *The Poverty of Liberalism*, R. P. Wolff makes an important beginning to defining concepts necessary for conceptualizing cooperative relationships and endeavors.

10. Soren Kierkegaard, *Works of Love*, part 1, chapter 2B.
11. Kant, *The Doctrine of Virtue*, pp. 140-6:468-73, and *Lectures on Ethics*, pp. 200-9.
12. John Cooper, "Aristotle on the Forms of Friendship," p. 620, has argued that Aristotle uses the concept of friendship (*philia*) to refer to many different forms of social connection between people ("civic friendship"), all of which are different ways in which, or contexts in which, we come to care about another for his own sake.

34

Fame

Joshua Halberstam taught philosophy at C. W. Post College of Long Island University and now teaches ethics at NYU. He is editor of *Virtues and Values: An Introduction to Ethics* (1988).

> For as long as a man is possessed by any desire, he is necessarily at the same time possessed by this [ambition]. 'Every noble man is led by glory,' says Cicero, 'and even the philosophers who write books despising glory place their names on the title page.'[1]
>
> —Spinoza

I

"Fame is so sweet that we love anything with which we connect it, even death," Pascal observes in the Pensées.[2] Indeed, fame does seem to hold a peculiar fascination for many of us. The young dream of their future fame half expecting it to be their destiny only to experience the disappointment of finding themselves older but just one of the crowd, anonymous and unacknowledged. This attraction to fame is not only self-regarding but extends to others who have achieved it. Biographies and magazine articles devoted to the famous abound and the passing thoughts of celebrities are avidly recorded and quoted. This should not be thought of as some sort of foolishness peculiar to the mindless masses—anecdotes and gossip concerning the famous are the conversational stock of the literati, though these tales be of little inherent interest and hardly worth repeating did they involve ordinary unillustrious persons. There are few who would not be at least mildly titillated at the prospect of dining with Woody Allen or Sophia Loren and the attraction, surely, cannot be wholly attributable to the satisfaction of intellectual or aesthetic curiosity.

There are few who are born rich, fewer still who are born famous, and rarer still are those, who like John F. Kennedy's children, are born both rich and famous. All others who desire fame and fortune, excluding the unusually

From Joshua Halberstam, "Fame," *American Philosophical Quarterly* 21 (January 1984): 93–99. Copyright 1984, *American Philosophical Quarterly*. Reprinted by permission of the publisher.

lucky, must actively pursue these goals if they are to attain them. Becoming famous is like becoming rich, too, in that neither is considered a bad thing to happen to someone—both fame and fortune are the traditional blessings of well-wishes—yet the *pursuit* of either is generally deemed objectionable. But if being famous isn't harmful to those who are, if devoid of any apparent harm to others, and if, to the contrary, it is a status one might enjoy, then just what is the objection to trying to achieve it?

It is this question I consider here. Although fame and wealth (and their close relatives, ambition and avarice) are usually coupled in the "wisdom literature" of the sages, the relative inattention which philosophers have paid to fame as compared to money and its pursuit is glaring. With few exceptions, they have limited themselves to passing remarks dismissing the desire for fame as being either hopelessly unreasonable and irrational or as exhibiting a moral defect of some sort. Both responses do seem plausible, at least initially—the striving for fame often does appear foolhardy and we do wonder about the hierarchy of values of those who dedicate themselves to fame at the expense of other goals we deem more central—but we still need to show just why this is so. The fact is that the pursuit of fame can be skillfully managed—and is by no means always foolhardy, and designating the character-flaw of those who pursue fame, explaining just what the flaw is, turns out to be a more complicated task than one might suppose. There is an important philosophical interest in examining this problem: any complete moral theory must attend not only to the analysis and determination of the moral worth of acts and rules but to the moral character and values of agents, and insofar as the attainment of fame is so important to so many, is valued by so many, it ought not escape our consideration.[3]

We cannot undertake this challenge, however, without first considering why anyone would want to be famous, and even before doing that, we must, if only briefly, examine the notion of fame itself, focusing on those aspects of fame which will be of relevance to these other concerns.

II

Who is famous? Posing the question in this way is somewhat misleading, for it excludes vast numbers of potential candidates for fame. After all, not just people are famous: Lassie is a famous animal, Everest a famous natural object and the Mona Lisa a famous man-made one. Indeed, there is no reason to restrict the class of famous things to physical objects: we have famous mythological creatures, fictional characters, physical theories, famous stories and famous jokes. (Query: Is God famous?)

As the concern here is with the desire for fame, and inasmuch as no person can intelligibly desire to become a famous Greek god, a famous waterfall or famous musical composition, our discussion will center on the conditions necessary for human fame.

What these examples do indicate, however, is that fame, in its widest sense, amounts to being well known, widely recognized, an object of public interest. Someone can, of course, be famous within a restricted domain, within a given profession say, but this should not be confused with professional success, esteem or distinction. In some fields, such as politics, success does as a rule ensure fame, and in other careers fame may be a criterion of success—the notion of "stardom" in film acting comes to mind. In general, however, success does not entail fame, nor, for that matter, does fame entail success: Leroy Nieman may be a famous artist but few art critics would consider him successful in his art: notice too that an artist can become famous posthumously but one cannot become a successful artist posthumously. In noting that fame within certain professions (particularly those that enjoy access to the media) provides more total fame than does fame within other endeavors, I am keeping within this strictly quantitative reading of fame which is determined independently of the quality of fame involved. Thus we can say that Jackie Onassis is more famous than my parent's grocer, Herman Klotzker, and that Willard Van Orman Quine is somewhere in between the two. It is this purely quantitative sense which we readily presume when asked to name the most famous person we ever met.

While one can hardly be famous yet obscure, widespread recognition is only a necessary condition for fame; it isn't sufficient. That more is required can be shown by the following considerations: a) the square root of 81 is well known yet it would be most odd to deem the number nine a famous number (compare, on the other hand, the fame of Fermat's last theorem); b) imagine a community in which everyone is known by everyone else—should we say of all these residents that each is famous? It is conceivable that everyone alive be famous for some period of time and then lose their fame—recall Andy Warhol's prediction that in the future everyone will be famous for fifteen minutes—but what seems less intelligible is for everyone to be famous at the same time; here the quality of being distinct required for fame would be absent. Moreover, to be famous requires being recognized by more people than one has actual contact with. You cannot claim to be famous with your family and friends, and even if through personal interactions you were known to thousands, we would still be reluctant to consider you famous if you were not also known to others with whom you'd had no such contact.

In explicating fame in these descriptive, quantitative terms I am deliberately disregarding the more limited use of the word fame as a positive evaluation. It is only in this latter sense that fame contrasts with infamy: both are members of the larger class of the famous, the opposite of which is anonymity, not infamy.

The nature of the fame a person possesses is determined by that aspect by which he or she is recognized: in the case of models it may be their faces but not their names, and with writers their names but not their faces. In all cases, however, one cannot just be famous, *simpliciter*—one must be famous *for* some reason or other, for some quality, position, accomplishment, talent or skill. The statement, "S is famous" always invites the question, "Famous for what?" (Even if we recognize that with the advent of the current media, fame, like wealth can be self-perpetuating, making some famous *as* celebrities, famous for being famous, as it were, still, these celebrities are now famous for something, i.e., for being famous).

The qualities that can make one famous need not reflect some personal quality but can be derivative, feeding off various kinds of associations with other established famous persons or institutions. Whoever is married to the President of the United States will be famous, as will be whoever occupies the position of Pope. One can become famous by luck too—imagine a heavenly voice booming across the globe instructing us to pay attention to Herman Klotzker the grocer from Brooklyn. Moreover, one can be genuinely famous without knowing that one is. This occurs in cases of posthumous fame but it can happen to someone alive as well; imagine some shipwreck survivor who has won five million in the lottery and has become the object of a country-wide search, the subject of countless newspaper articles, and perhaps even something of a legend—all unbeknownst to the shipwreck survivor.

Although being famous entails being famous for some quality, it need not be the case that this fame is deserved. A plagiarist or one who has his novels ghost-written may be famous, and indeed famous *as* a great novelist, though in fact he is not one. The fact that being famous in this way is unacceptable to most of us, that even those who yearn to be famous would balk at the invitation to become famous for qualities they do not actually possess or for having done what they did not in fact do, indicates that what is truly desired is not fame itself but "deserved" fame (though surely there are those who have no such inhibitions in their quest for fame). This qualification is of special significance in evaluating the motivations for becoming famous.

III

Why do people want to become famous? Fame has many facets and its gifts are various, so we ought not to expect to find one single explanation for its pursuit. We can, however, distinguish broadly between two kinds of motivations or reason for pursuing fame: a) fame sought as a source of pleasure, and b) fame sought as a satisfaction of interests.

Those who desire fame as a source of pleasure believe that being famous will somehow or other improve their present lives, that its achievement will lavish immediate rewards and advantages. The others see the benefit of fame as the fulfillment of those interests which go beyond what affects one's life in an immediate way. Interests of this sort are generally viewed as ends in themselves, e.g., the interest in achieving honor, maintaining a respected reputation, or the long-term interest in having the memory of oneself survive one's death—the interest which underlies the desire for posthumous fame. Since both the rationality and value of the pursuit of fame turns on which motive propels the pursuit, it would be helpful to make this distinction sharper.

Fame provides pleasures of various kinds. Lyndon Johnson is said to have said that the nicest thing about being famous is that you get to meet so many interesting people. For others, the allure of fame is its potential as an entrée to career opportunities, money, travel, power, sex, or perhaps, just more exciting parties.

There are still others for whom the pleasure of fame does not derive from its consequences, from what it can procure for those who possess it, but for whom the very belief that one is famous, widely recognized and of interest to others, is a direct source of pleasure. Surely, there are many who enjoy, and not a few crave, seeing their name in print, their face in newspapers and on television, and who delight in the knowledge that they are the topic of others' conversations. The etiology of the psychological need for attention is, thankfully, beyond the scope of the present discussion, but as this need is latent in many different appeals to fame, it deserves special notice.

It is not, however, mere recognition that most wish for but the positive affirmation that usually goes along with such recognition. In his discussion "Of the Love of Fame," David Hume suggests that it is this need to be praised that is at the root of the longing for fame. This explains, Hume observes, why, in seeking fame, we seek to be praised for qualities we ourselves respect and have little interest in being famous or praised for qualities we do not ourselves esteem: "a mere soldier little values the character of eloquence: a gownsman of courage: a bishop of humour: or a merchant of learning . . ."[4] In addition to the requirement that we ourselves esteem the qualities for which we are praised, Hume notes too that we must admire the source of this praise: "though fame in general be agreeable, . . . we receive a much greater satisfaction from the approbation of those whom we ourselves esteem and approve of than of those whom we hate and despise."[5] And if we nonetheless appreciate the accolades of the masses it is only in recognition of their "added weight and authority."

For Hume then, the desire for fame is really the desire to be praised, and insofar as praise is only pleasurable if its recipient both values what he is praised for and who is doing the praising, so fame will only be pleasurable to one who both values the trait for which he is famed and those among whom he is famed. In tying the notion of fame to that of praise, Hume calls our attention to what is for most the central attraction of fame. Fame is an attestation of worth, and it provides the assurance that one's abilities, status or work is recognized and admired. It is the sweet sound of public applause. According to this Humean explication, it is nonetheless the *pleasure* that praise affords that is the attraction of fame and, as such, praise must be included along with those other motivations which look to fame as a source of pleasure and immediate benefit.

But one can *value* being praised or being famous as a value in itself, without regard to the pleasures or benefits it brings, as an intrinsic rather than an instrumental good. According to this view, the impetus for fame is the need many feel to have made a mark in the world. We do not abide by the idea that we may come into this world and go unheralded as if we never existed at all. In becoming famous, we can be assured that at least our existence has been noticed. This wish for fame has, as we might expect, been tied to the wish for immortality. Thus Socrates in his address in the *Symposium* remarks "that all men do all things, and the better they are the more they do them, in hope of the glorious fame of immortal virtue, for they desire the immortal." The interest here is not in leaving just any trace in the world—that much our bodies will do in any case—nor is it the interest in leaving the world a better place: the artist may appreciate the creation of great works of art but he would not be content to have been the patron of other artists, for what he really aspires to is *his* being the creator of these great works of art. And while there may be those who are satisfied by the mere knowledge that they will be remembered, this isn't enough for most of us: wherein is the pride in the belief that one will be remembered as the first person to be hit by a falling satellite? Rather, the trace that one hopes to leave is one that, as Nozick points out, "people know of in particular and that they know is due to you, one due (people know) to some action, choice, plan of yours, that expresses something you take to be important about the kind of person you are, such that people respect or positively evaluate both the trace and that aspect of yourself."[6] In wanting to be famous we want to be credited for having qualities we truly have and for contributions we have truly made. Unlike the first set of reasons for wanting to be famous which looked to the coterminous pleasures which fame brings in its wake, here fame is sought for the benefits it provides as a measure and testimony of having lived a worthwhile, or at least noteworthy, life.

IV

Is there something wrong with wanting to be famous? Admittedly, being famous may have its annoyances, but these impositions need not, and for many clearly do not, outweigh the advantages of fame. It is rather the pursuit of fame that is usually found wanting.

One line of criticism focuses on the presumed irrationality of the undertaking. Consider first how this objection is directed to those who seek fame during their lifetime.

A. It is often suggested that the pursuit of fame is foolhardy because there is no guarantee of success: one can neither be sure that he will succeed at his endeavors nor that his activities will in fact receive the recognition coveted. Moreover, given the vicissitudes of mass opinion, there is little security even for those who have achieved fame, for as Spinoza cautions, "those who glory in the good opinion of the multitude anxiously and with daily care strive, labor and struggle to preserve this fame. For the multitude is changeable and fickle, so that fame, if it is not preserved, soon passes away."[7]

While these observations indicate the inherent riskiness of pursuing fame, they do not demonstrate that it must always be an irrational quest. The uncertainty of success does not show this, for after all, success is not assured in many of our endeavors; true, one cannot be certain of becoming a famous sculptor, but then one cannot be certain of becoming a good sculptor either, yet this is hardly a good enough reason for not trying to become one. In actuality fame is attainable, and with the awesome powers of present-day electronic media and communication networks, coupled with the endemic interest in the lives of celebrities, fame is more easily attained and more easily sustained than ever before.

B. The charge of irrationality is also aimed at those who wish for posthumous fame. Montaigne, for example, ridicules those who engage in military battles in the hope of attaining everlasting glory, noting that the vast majority of those who have done so have disappeared into oblivion along with their deeds of bravery.[8] It is also often remarked that the fickleness of history is on par with the whims of contemporary popularity and tomorrow's hero might be forgotten the day after tomorrow. Nevertheless, as with the pursuit of immediate fame, these observations only indicate the risk in pursuing fame, not its impossibility; the galaxy of famous names that have managed to endure illustrates that long-lasting fame is a genuine possibility. To be sure, the achievement of either present or posthumous fame depends on many variables beyond one's control but we cannot on that account alone prejudge its pursuit as a hopeless miscalculation.

There are, however, other problems which relate specifically to the rationality of seeking posthumous fame. If, as some think, the desire for posthumous fame stems from the desire to be immortal, then anything less than eternal fame should not suffice.[9] But this expectation does seem wildly unrealistic. And if one settles for something less than eternal fame why should it matter if one's fame is limited to one year or a thousand? And why some year in the future rather than some year during one's life? Indeed, just what is the interest in becoming famous after you are no longer around? Certainly, people do care about what will transpire after they are gone as many are nourished by the idea that they will be famous to those not yet born. But while we understand and even admire the desire to contribute to the welfare of future lives, inasmuch as the supposed beneficiary of posthumous fame will not be around when that fame finally arrives, the rationality of this interest seems suspect.

We can, perhaps, make some sense of this interest if, following Aristotle, we accept the notion that a person's interests continue beyond the grave. More recently, Joel Feinberg has defended this view, concluding that "the area of a person's good or harm is necessarily wider than his subjective experience and longer than his biological life"; that one's contracts and promises are honored and contributions properly credited are the sorts of interests that are thought to endure after death, as would be, we might suppose, the interest in posthumous fame.[10] However, the notion that there are genuine interests of the deceased which are affected by later events is questionable, to say the least. The fact that we ought to honor a dead person's promises and contracts and accurately credit his achievements does not support the claim, as sometimes argued, for these obligations can be accounted for by straightforward utilitarian or deontological considerations which are directed to the living.[11]

The notion that there is an ongoing posthumous interest in being famous is even more problematic than these other posthumous interests. Inasmuch as fame involves more than just deserved credit, not only is there no obvious obligation on anyone to make someone famous, with the beneficiary not being present, one wonders how that interest can be satisfied. So the interest in posthumous fame can only be understood as the present interest of the living to be thought of by others in the future, but then it is not easy to see just what that interest consists of, or why anyone should have it.

V

Whether or not the pursuit of either posthumous or contemporary fame can be judged as irrational, both pursuits can and have been attacked on axiological grounds. What disturbs these critics is not the foolhardiness of the aspiration but the flawed values it manifests; the deficiency is not one of strategy but of character. These objections tend to revolve around what is viewed as an improper attitude and lack of dedication that the seeker of fame has toward his work. These criticisms will have different force depending upon which form of fame is sought.

A. Concerning those who seek immediate fame, one prevalent worry is that because others will need to be accommodated, standards will be lowered: in his aim to please, the ambitious artist will forgo his superior ideas and ideals. The problem with this objection, however, is that more often than not, the very opposite occurs—the desire for fame spurs one on to do his very best. The medical researcher who becomes famous is usually the one who actually discovers the cure and Nobel prizes most often do reward genuine talent.

Another objection, deontological in flavor, looks not to the consequences of work undertaken for self-aggrandizement, but to the attitude itself: as acts acquire moral worth only if they are committed in the performance of duty, so too work should be done for its own sake. But this parallel is misconstrued: for one thing, a good symphony is a good symphony no matter what motivated its composition, and more importantly, why should we assume that there is some proper, morally proper, attitude that we ought to have toward our labors? Why insist that there is a greater virtue in playing baseball for the sake of baseball rather than for the enjoyment, financial security or fame that it provides?

Still another objection points to the lack of self-worth that is exhibited by those who wish for fame. Those with self-respect will respect themselves and their labor without depending on the judgments of others. For this reason, Aristotle rejects honor as the ultimate source of happiness arguing that it is "too superficial to be what we are looking for, since it is thought to depend on those who bestow it rather than him who receives it, but the good we define as something proper to a man and not easily taken from him."[12] But this observation hardly shows that there is something wrong with valuing honor or fame. Commendable though it otherwise be, self-esteem totally unattended by the judgments of others is seriously wanting, and indeed according to some contemporary social psychologists, such total independence is not even possible.[13] In any case, even if we allow that honor and fame ought not be anyone's ultimate goals, we can still maintain that they are good things for one to possess.

B. With regard to posthumous fame, these objections fare even less well. Since it is generally assumed (though perhaps incorrectly) that superior work will sooner or later "out" and receive the appreciation it is due, those whose look toward the more discerning audience of posterity can be expected to hold to even higher standards than most. And while they too desire the favorable judgments of others, inasmuch as they eschew immediate glory, we can assume that this group possesses considerable self-respect and self-assurance. Nonetheless, precisely because they do seem able to do without evident appreciation of their work, as well as without the other immediate advantages of fame, the value placed on becoming famous is the more easily challenged: a true devotion to excellence should be enough. But this criticism seems too harsh—the desire for fame, be it contemporaneous or posthumous, does not preclude a genuine devotion to one's endeavors but may be an addition to it. So it is not at all clear why we ought not value fame, and what characterological fault is exhibited by those who do.

VI

Still, the feeling lingers that there is something amiss with those who consciously and conscientiously pursue fame. We sense, and sense correctly I think, that this pursuit manifests a confused hierarchy of priorities.

Again, the analogy with wealth is opportune. Many dream of having great riches and such idle fantasies bespeak no serious flaw of moral character. Only the saintly few find the prospect of vast wealth unattractive. And so with fame: at different times and with varying intensity most of us have enjoyed imagining ourselves the object of widespread public adoration and we are no less morally worthy for having such passing dreams.

It is, rather, the active pursuit of fame (or wealth) that gives rise to our reservations. For in pursuing fame one indicates not only his valuation of fame but its valuation over other competing values. The active pursuit of fame requires real expenditures of time, effort and determination—all resources we have in limited supply. In choosing to channel one's energies toward the attainment of fame, other, more important values must be abandoned.

This misjudgment of priorities is more commonly recognized with regard to those who dedicate their lives to amassing huge fortunes. Even if we value being rich and admit its real benefits, we recognize, nonetheless, that on deeper level it is just not *that* beneficial to one's life and certainly not worth pursuing to the exclusion of other more central goods and values. Similarly, insofar as fame does bring its benefits and satisfies various interests, its pursuit would be unobjectionable but for the fact that one can only actively pursue fame at a high cost to other values. Here we might recall some of the objections noted and dismissed earlier. Singly, each criticism may be insufficient but conjoined they add up significantly. The pursuit of fame does usually entail the devaluation of one's work for its own sake and one's self-respect; it does require that one constantly attend to the vicissitudes of the marketplace and public opinion, and it can easily promote sycophancy, dishonesty and undue competitiveness. To be sure, it need not involve all of these things, but it rarely avoids at least some of them.

What too often has characterized discussions of the pursuit of fame and other valued goals is the implicit assumption that if there is something wrong with this pursuit the defect must be traced to a defect in the goal itself. It is important to see that this need not be the case; the pursuit of fame is a case in point. A comprehensive analysis of the hierarchy of values must include an examination not only of how one orders one's values but must also address the choice of which value one actually pursues. And we must be prepared to fault these choices even when the target itself is of value and morally acceptable.

Notes

1. Spinoza, *Ethics*, Pt. III. "General Definition of the Emotions," Prop. XLIV.
2. Pascal, *Pensées*, Sect. II, No. 158.
3. The question of who achieves fame in a society ought to be of special concern to social and political philosophers. (Again, compare this with the attention given to the role of wealth in society.) The fact that in our own society, baseball players are so much more famous than composers or scientist says much about the values of our society. But, as important as they are, these issues are not the present concern.
4. David Hume, *Treatise of Human Nature*, ed. Selby-Bigge (Oxford, 1967), Bk. II, Pt. I, p. 322.
5. *Ibid.*, p. 32. Aristotle makes much the same observation: "But those who desire to be honored by the good and the wise are really seeking to be confirmed in the favorable opinion they have of themselves. Thus their pleasure comes from their confidence in the judgment of those who tell them they are fine fellows." *Nichomachean Ethics*, Bk. 8, Ch. 8.
6. Robert Nozick, *Philosophical Explanations* (Cambridge MA, 1981), p. 584. Douglas Lackey raises the interesting problem of having one's name so closely tied to some act or discovery that the name itself is remembered and not the person to whom it refers. People might be able to name Darwin as the discoverer of evolution but the name 'Darwin,' for them, might be seen as an abbreviation for "discoverer of evolution." In what sense is the "personhood" of Darwin being recalled? "Fame as a Value Concept," unpublished manuscript.
7. Spinoza, *Ethics*, Part IV, Prop. LVIII.
8. Montaigne, "Of Glory," reprinted in *Essays of Michel de Montaigne*, tr. Charles Cotton (New York, 1892), pp. 110–117.
9. In Godard's "Breathless," a director says his greatest wish is "to become immortal, and then die."
10. Joel Feinberg, "Harm and Self-Interest," in *Law, Morality and Society: Essays in Honor of H. L. A. Hart*, eds. P. M. S. Hacker and J. Raz (Oxford, 1977), pp. 289–300. Reprinted in *Rights, Justice and Bounds of Liberty* (Princeton, 1980), Ch. 3.

11. Ernest Partridge, in "Posthumous Interests and Posthumous Respect," *Ethics*, Vol. 91 (1981), pp. 243–264, presents a convincing criticism of Feinberg's position.
12. Aristotle, *Nichomachean Ethics*, Bk. 1, Ch. 5.
13. In particular, I have in mind the work of Erving Goffman. Helpful too is the investigation of the inter-relatedness of self and public image in Rom Harré's *Social Being* (Totowa, 1980).

35

Ideals of Human Excellence and Preserving Natural Environments

Thomas E. Hill, Jr., is professor of philosophy at the University of North Carolina, Chapel Hill. His research interests include Kant's moral philosophy and current moral issues, on which he has published numerous articles.

The moral significance of preserving natural environments is not entirely an issue of rights and social utility, for a person's attitude toward nature may be importantly connected with virtues or human excellences. The question is, "What sort of person would destroy the natural environment—or even see its value solely in cost/benefit terms?" In what follows I suggest that willingness to do so may well reveal the absence of traits which are a natural basis for a proper humility, self-acceptance, gratitude, and appreciation of the good in others.

I

A wealthy eccentric bought a house in a neighborhood I know. The house was surrounded by a beautiful display of grass, plants, and flowers, and it was shaded by a huge old avocado tree. But the grass required cutting, the flowers needed tending, and the man wanted more sun. So he cut the whole lot down and covered the yard with asphalt. After all it was his property and he was not fond of plants.

It was a small operation, but it reminded me of the strip mining of large sections of the Appalachians. In both cases, of course, there were reasons for the destruction, and property rights could be cited as justification. But I could not help but wonder, "What sort of person would do a thing like that?"

Many Californians had a similar reaction when a recent governor defended the leveling of ancient redwood groves, reportedly saying, "If you have seen one redwood, you have seen them all."

From Thomas E. Hill, Jr., "Ideals of Human Excellence and Preserving Natural Environments," *Environmental Ethics* 5 (1983): 211–24. Copyright 1983, Thomas E. Hill, Jr. Reprinted by permission of the author and the publisher. The author thanks Gregory Kavka, Catherine Harlow, the participants at a colloquium at the University of Utah, and the referees for *Environmental Ethics*, Dale Jamieson and Donald Scherer, for helpful comments on earlier drafts of this paper.

Incidents like these arouse the indignation of ardent environmentalists and leave even apolitical observers with some degree of moral discomfort. The reasons for these reactions are mostly obvious. Uprooting the natural environment robs both present and future generations of much potential use and enjoyment. Animals too depend on the environment; and even if one does not value animals for their own sakes, their potential utility for us is incalculable. Plants are needed, of course, to replenish the atmosphere quite aside from their aesthetic value. These reasons for hesitating to destroy forests and gardens are not only the most obvious ones, but also the most persuasive for practical purposes. But, one wonders, is there nothing more behind our discomfort? Are we concerned solely about the potential use and enjoyment of the forests, etc., for ourselves, later generations, and perhaps animals? Is there not something else which disturbs us when we witness the destruction or even listen to those who would defend it in terms of cost/benefit analysis?

Imagine that in each of our examples those who would destroy the environment argue elaborately that, even considering future generations of human beings and animals, there are benefits in "replacing" the natural environment which outweigh the negative utilities which environmentalists cite.[1] No doubt we could press the argument on the facts, trying to show that the destruction is shortsighted and that its defenders have underestimated its potential harm or ignored some pertinent rights or interests. But is this all we could say? Suppose we grant, for a moment, that the utility of destroying the redwoods, forests, and gardens is equal to their potential for use and enjoyment by nature lovers and animals. Suppose, further, that we even grant that the pertinent human rights and animal rights, if any, are evenly divided for and against destruction. Imagine that we also concede, for argument's sake, that the forests contain no potentially useful endangered species of animals and plants. Must we then conclude that there is no further cause for moral concern? Should we then feel morally indifferent when we see the natural environment uprooted?

II

Suppose we feel that the answer to these questions should be negative. Suppose, in other words, we feel that our moral discomfort when we confront the destroyers of nature is not fully explained by our belief that they have miscalculated the best use of natural resources or violated rights in exploiting

---

[1] When I use the expression "the natural environment," I have in mind the sort of examples with which I began. For some purposes it is important to distinguish cultivated gardens from forest, virgin forests from replenished ones, irreplaceable natural phenomena from the replaceable, and so on; but these distinctions, I think, do not affect my main points here. There is also a broad sense, as Hume and Mill noted, in which all that occurs, miracles aside, is "natural." In this sense, of course, strip mining is as natural as a beaver cutting trees for his dam, and, as parts of nature, we cannot destroy the "natural" environment but only alter it. As will be evident, I shall use *natural* in a narrower, more familiar sense.

them. Suppose, in particular, we sense that part of the problem is that the natural environment is being viewed exclusively as a natural *resource*. What could be the ground of such a feeling? That is, what is there in our system of normative principles and values that could account for our remaining moral dissatisfaction?[2]

Some may be tempted to seek an explanation by appeal to the interests, or even the rights, of plants. After all, they may argue, we only gradually came to acknowledge the moral importance of all human beings, and it is even more recently that consciences have been aroused to give full weight to the welfare (and rights?) of animals. The next logical step, it may be argued, is to acknowledge a moral requirement to take into account the interests (and rights?) of plants. The problem with the strip miners, redwood cutters, and the like, on this view, is not just that they ignore the welfare and rights of people and animals; they also fail to give due weight to the survival and health of the plants themselves.

The temptation to make such a reply is understandable if one assumes that all moral questions are exclusively concerned with whether *acts* are right or wrong, and that this, in turn, is determined entirely by how the acts impinge on the rights and interests of those directly affected. On this assumption, if there is cause for moral concern, some right or interest has been neglected; and if the rights and interests of human beings and animals have already been taken into account, then there must be some other pertinent interests, for example, those of plants. A little reflection will show that the assumption is mistaken; but, in any case, the conclusion that plants have rights or morally relevant interests is surely untenable. We do speak of what is "good for" plants, and they can "thrive" and also be "killed." But this does not imply that they have "interests" in any morally relevant sense. Some people apparently believe that plants grow better if we talk to them, but the idea that the plants suffer and enjoy, desire and dislike, etc., is clearly outside the range of both common sense and scientific belief. The notion that the forests should be preserved to avoid *hurting* the trees or because they have a *right* to life is not part of a widely shared moral consciousness, and for good reason.[3]

---

[2] This paper is intended as a preliminary discussion in *normative* ethical theory (as opposed to *metaethics*). The task, accordingly, is the limited, though still difficult, one of articulating the possible basis in our beliefs and values of certain particular moral judgments. Questions of ultimate justification are set aside. What makes the task difficult and challenging is not that conclusive proofs from the foundation of morality are attempted; it is rather that the particular judgments to be explained seem at first not to fall under the most familiar moral principles (e.g., utilitarianism, respect for rights).

[3] I assume here that having a right presupposes having interests in a sense which in turn presupposes a capacity to desire, suffer, etc. Since my main concern lies in another direction, I do not argue the point, but merely note that some regard it as debatable. See, for example, W. Murray Hunt, "Are *Mere Things* Morally Considerable?" *Environmental Ethics* 2 (1980): 59–65; Kenneth E. Goodpaster, "On Stopping at Everything," *Environmental Ethics* 2 (1980): 288–94; Joel Feinberg, "The Rights of Animals and Unborn Generations," in William Blackstone, ed., *Philosophy and Environmental Crisis* (Athens: University of Georgia Press, 1974), pp. 43–68; Tom Regan, "Feinberg

Another way of trying to explain our moral discomfort is to appeal to certain religious beliefs. If one believes that all living things were created by a God who cares for them and entrusted us with the use of plants and animals only for limited purposes, then one has a reason to avoid careless destruction of the forests, etc., quite aside from their future utility. Again, if one believes that a divine force is immanent in all nature, then too one might have reason to care for more than sentient things. But such arguments require strong and controversial premises, and, I suspect, they will always have a restricted audience.

Early in this century, due largely to the influence of G. E. Moore another point of view developed which some may find promising.[4] Moore introduced, or at least made popular, the idea that certain states of affairs are intrinsically valuable—not just valued, but valuable, and not necessarily because of their effects on sentient beings. Admittedly Moore came to believe that in fact the only intrinsically valuable things were conscious experiences of various sorts,[5] but this restriction was not inherent in the idea of intrinsic value. The intrinsic goodness of something, he thought, was an objective, nonrelational property of the thing, like its texture or color, but not a property perceivable by sense perception or detectable by scientific instruments. In theory at least, a single tree thriving alone in a universe without sentient beings, and even without God, could be intrinsically valuable. Since, according to Moore, our duty is to maximize intrinsic value, his theory could obviously be used to argue that we have reason not to destroy natural environments independently of how they affect human beings and animals. The survival of a forest might have worth beyond its worth *to* sentient beings.

This approach, like the religious one, may appeal to some but is infested with problems. There are, first, the familiar objections to intuitionism, on which the theory depends. Metaphysical and epistemological doubts about nonnatural, intuited properties are hard to suppress, and many have argued that the theory rests on a misunderstanding of the words *good, valuable,* and the like.[6] Second, even if we try to set aside these objections and think in Moore's terms, it is far from obvious that everyone would agree that the existence of forests, etc., is intrinsically valuable. The test, says Moore, is what we would say when we imagine a universe with just the thing in question, without any effects or accompaniments, and then we ask, "Would its existence be better than its nonexistence?" Be careful, Moore would remind us, not to construe this question as, "Would you *prefer* the existence of that universe to its nonexistence?" The question is, "Would its existence have the objective, nonrelational property, intrinsic goodness?"

---

on What Sorts of Beings Can Have Rights," *Southern Journal of Philosophy* (1976): 485–98; Robert Elliot, "Regan on the Sort of Beings that Can Have Rights," *Southern Journal of Philosophy* (1978): 701–05; Scott Lehmann, "Do Wildernesses Have Rights?" *Environmental Ethics* 2 (1981): 129–46.

[4] G. E. Moore, *Principia Ethica* (Cambridge: Cambridge University Press, 1903); *Ethics* (London: H. Holt, 1912).

[5] G. E. Moore, "Is Goodness a Quality?" *Philosophical Papers* (London: George Allen and Unwin, 1959), pp. 95–97.

[6] See, for example, P. H. Nowell-Smith, *Ethics* (New York: Penguin Books, 1954).

Now even among those who have no worries about whether this really makes sense, we might well get a diversity of answers. Those prone to destroy natural environments will doubtless give one answer, and nature lovers will likely give another. When an issue is as controversial as the one at hand, intuition is a poor arbiter.

The problem, then, is this. We want to understand what underlies our moral uneasiness at the destruction of the redwoods, forests, etc., even apart from the loss of these as resources for human beings and animals. But I find no adequate answer by pursuing the questions, "Are rights or interests of plants neglected?" "What is God's will on the matter?" and "What is the intrinsic value of the existence of a tree or forest?" My suggestion, which is in fact the main point of this paper, is that we look at the problem from a different perspective. That is, let us turn for a while from the effort to find reasons why certain *acts* destructive of natural environments are morally wrong to the ancient task of articulating our ideals of human excellence. Rather than argue directly with destroyers of the environment who say, "Show me why what I am doing is *immoral*," I want to ask, "What sort of person would want to do what they propose?" The point is not to skirt the issue with an *ad hominem*, but to raise a different moral question, for even if there is no convincing way to show that the destructive acts are wrong (independently of human and animal use and enjoyment), we may find that the willingness to indulge in them reflects the absence of human traits that we admire and regard morally important.

This strategy of shifting questions may seem more promising if one reflects on certain analogous situations. Consider, for example, the Nazi who asks, in all seriousness, "Why is it wrong for me to make lampshades out of human skin—provided, of course, I did not myself kill the victims to get the skins?" We would react more with shock and disgust than with indignation, I suspect, because it is even more evident that the question reveals a defect in the questioner than that the proposed act is itself immoral. Sometimes we may not regard an act wrong at all though we see it as reflecting something objectionable about the person who does it. Imagine, for example, one who laughs spontaneously to himself when he reads a newspaper account of a plane crash that kills hundreds. Or, again, consider an obsequious grandson who, having waited for his grandmother's inheritance with mock devotion, then secretly spits on her grave when at last she dies. Spitting on the grave may have no adverse consequences and perhaps it violates no rights. The moral uneasiness which it arouses is explained more by our view of the agent than by any conviction that what he did was immoral. Had he hesitated and asked, "Why shouldn't I spit on her grave?" it seems more fitting to ask him to reflect on the sort of person he is than to try to offer reasons why he should refrain from spitting.

III

What sort of person, then, would cover his garden with asphalt, strip mine a wooded mountain, or level an irreplaceable redwood grove? Two sorts of answers, though initially appealing, must be ruled out. The first is that persons who would destroy the environment in these ways are either shortsighted, underestimating the harm they do, or else are too little concerned for the well-being for other people. Perhaps too they have insufficient regard for animal life. But these considerations have been set aside in order to refine the controversy. Another tempting response might be that we count it a moral virtue, or at least a human ideal, to love nature. Those who value the environment only for its utility must not really love nature and so in this way fall short of an ideal. But such an answer is hardly satisfying in the present context, for what is at issue is *why* we feel moral discomfort at the activities of those who admittedly value nature only for its utility. That it is ideal to care for nonsentient nature beyond its possible use is really just another way of expressing the general point which is under controversy.

What is needed is some way of showing that this ideal is connected with other virtues, or human excellences, not in question. To do so is difficult and my suggestions, accordingly, will be tentative and subject to qualification. The main idea is that, though indifference to nonsentient nature does not *necessarily* reflect the absence of virtues, it often signals the absence of certain traits which we want to encourage because they are, in most cases, a natural basis for the development of certain virtues. It is often thought, for example, that those who would destroy the natural environment must lack a proper appreciation of their place in the natural order, and so must either be ignorant or have too little humility. Though I would argue that this is not necessarily so, I suggest that, given certain plausible empirical assumptions, their attitude may well be rooted in ignorance, a narrow perspective, inability to see things as important apart from themselves and the limited groups they associate with, or reluctance to accept themselves as natural beings. Overcoming these deficiencies will not guarantee a proper moral humility, but for most of us it is probably an important psychological preliminary. Later I suggest, more briefly, that indifference to nonsentient nature typically reveals absence of either aesthetic sensibility or a disposition to cherish what has enriched one's life and that these, though not themselves moral virtues, are a natural basis for appreciation of the good in others and gratitude.[7]

Consider first the suggestion that destroyers of the environment lack an appreciation of their place in the universe.[8] Their attention, it seems, must be focused on parochial matters, on what is, relatively speaking, close in space

---

[7] The issues I raise here, though perhaps not the details of my remarks, are in line with Aristotle's view of moral philosophy, a view revitalized recently by Philippa Foot's *Virtue and Vice* (Berkeley: University of California Press, 1979), Alasdair MacIntyre's *After Virtue* (Notre Dame: Notre Dame Press, 1981), and James Wallace's *Virtues and Vices* (Ithaca and London: Cornell University Press, 1978), and other works. For other reflections on relationships between character and natural environments, see John Rodman, "The Liberation of Nature," *Inquiry* (1976): 83–131 and L. Reinhardt, "Some Gaps in Moral Space: Reflection on Forests and Feelings," in Mannison, McRobbie, and Routley, eds., *Environmental Philosophy* (Canberra: Australian National University Research School of Social Sciences, 1980).

[8] Though for simplicity I focus upon those who do strip mining, etc., the argument is also applicable to those whose utilitarian calculations lead them to preserve the redwoods, mountains, etc., but who care for only sentient nature for its own sake. Similarly the phrase "indifferent to nature" is meant to encompass those who are indifferent *except* when considering its benefits to people and animals.

and time. They seem not to understand that we are a speck on the cosmic scene, a brief stage in the evolutionary process, only one among millions of species on Earth, and an episode in the course of human history. Of course, they know that there are stars, fossils, insects, and ancient ruins; but do they have any idea of the complexity of the processes that led to the natural world as we find it? Are they aware how much the forces at work within their own bodies are like those which govern all living things and even how much they have in common with inanimate bodies? Admittedly scientific knowledge is limited and no one can master it all; but could one who had a broad and deep understanding of his place in nature really be indifferent to the destruction of the natural environment?

This first suggestion, however, may well provoke a protest from a sophisticated anti-environmentalist.[9] "Perhaps *some* may be indifferent to nature from ignorance," the critic may object, "but *I* have studied astronomy, geology, biology, and biochemistry, and I still unashamedly regard the nonsentient environment as simply a resource for our use. It should not be wasted, of course, but what should be preserved is decidable by weighing long-term costs and benefits." "Besides," our critic may continue, "as philosophers you should know the old Humean formula, 'You cannot derive an *ought* from an *is.*' All the facts of biology, biochemistry, etc., do not entail that I ought to love nature or want to preserve it. What one understands is one thing; what one values is something else. Just as nature lovers are not necessarily scientists, those indifferent to nature are not necessarily ignorant."

Although the environmentalist may concede the critic's logical point, he may well argue that, as a matter of fact, increased understanding of nature tends to heighten people's concern for its preservation. If so, despite the objection, the suspicion that the destroyers of the environment lack deep understanding of nature is not, in most cases, unwarranted, but the argument need not rest here.

The environmentalist might amplify his original idea as follows: "When I said that the destroyers of nature do not appreciate their place in the universe, I was not speaking of intellectual understanding alone, for, after all, a person can *know* a catalog of facts without ever putting them together and seeing vividly the whole picture which they form. To see oneself as just one part of nature is to look at oneself and the world from a certain perspective which is quite different from being able to recite detailed information from the natural sciences. What the destroyers of nature lack is this perspective, not particular information."

---

[9] For convenience I use the labels *environmentalist* and *anti-environmentalist* (or *critic*) for the opposing sides in the rather special controversy I have raised. Thus, for example, my "environmentalist" not only favors conserving the forests, etc., but finds something objectionable in wanting to destroy them even aside from the costs to human beings and animals. My "anti-environmentalist" is not simply one who wants to destroy the environment; he is a person who has no qualms about doing so independent of the adverse effects on human beings and animals.

Again our critic may object, though only after making some concessions: "All right," he may say, "*some* who are indifferent to nature may lack the cosmic perspective of which you speak, but again there is no *necessary* connection between this failing, if it is one, and any particular evaluative attitude toward nature. In fact, different people respond quite differently when they move to a wider perspective. When *I* try to picture myself vividly as a brief, transitory episode in the course of nature, I simply get depressed. Far from inspiring me with a love of nature, the exercise makes me sad and hostile. You romantics think only of poets like Wordsworth and artists like Turner, but you should consider how differently Omar Khayyam responded when he took your wider perspective. His reaction, when looking at his life from a cosmic viewpoint, was 'Drink up, for tomorrow we die.' Others respond in an almost opposite manner with a joyless Stoic resignation, exemplified by the poet who pictures the wise man, at the height of personal triumph, being served a magnificent banquet, and then consummating his marriage to his beloved, all the while reminding himself, 'Even this shall pass away.'"[10] In sum, the critic may object, "Even if one should try to see oneself as one small transitory part of nature, doing so does not dictate any particular normative attitude. Some may come to love nature, but others are moved to live for the moment; some sink into sad resignation; others get depressed or angry. So indifference to nature is not necessarily a sign that a person fails to look at himself from the larger perspective."

The environmentalist might respond to this objection in several ways. He might, for example, argue that even though some people who see themselves as part of the natural order remain indifferent to nonsentient nature, this is not a common reaction. Typically, it may be argued, as we become more and more aware that we are parts of the larger whole we come to value the whole independently of its effect on ourselves. Thus, despite the possibilities the critic raises, indifference to nonsentient nature is still in most cases a sign that a person fails to see himself as part of the natural order.

If someone challenges the empirical assumption here, the environmentalist might develop the argument along a quite different line. The initial idea, he may remind us, was that those who would destroy the natural environment fail to *appreciate* their place in the natural order. "Appreciating one's place" is not simply an intellectual appreciation. It is also an attitude, reflecting what one values as well as what one knows. When we say, for example, that both the servile and the arrogant person fail to *appreciate* their place in a society of equals, we do not mean simply that they are ignorant of certain empirical facts, but rather that they have certain objectionable attitudes about their importance relative to other people. Similarly, to fail to appreciate one's place in nature is not merely to lack knowledge or breadth of perspective, but to take a certain attitude about what matters. A person who *understands* his place

---

[10] "Even this shall pass away," by Theodore Tildon, in *The Best Loved Poems of the American People*, ed. Hazel Felleman (Garden City, N.Y.: Doubleday & Co., 1936).

in nature but still views nonsentient nature merely as a resource takes the attitude that nothing is *important* but human beings and animals. Despite first appearances, he is not so much like the pre-Copernican astronomers who made the intellectual error of treating the Earth as the "center of the universe" when they made their calculations. He is more like the racist who though well aware of other races, treats all races but his own as insignificant.

So construed, the argument appeals to the common idea that awareness of nature typically has, and should have, a humbling effect. The Alps, a storm at sea, the Grand Canyon, towering redwoods, and "the starry heavens above" move many a person to remark on the comparative insignificance of our daily concerns and even of our species, and this is generally taken to be a quite fitting response.[11] What seems to be missing, then, in those who understand nature but remain unmoved is a proper humility.[12] Absence of proper humility is not the same as selfishness or egoism, for one can be devoted to self-interest while still viewing one's own pleasures and projects as trivial and unimportant.[13] And one can have an exaggerated view of one's own importance while grandly sacrificing for those one views as inferior. Nor is the lack of humility identical with belief that one has power and influence, for a person can be quite puffed up about himself while believing that the foolish world will never acknowledge him. The humility we miss seems not so much a belief about one's relative effectiveness and recognition as an attitude which measures the importance of things independently of their relation to oneself or to some narrow group with which one identifies. A paradigm of a person who lacks humility is the self-important emperor who grants status to his family because it is *his*, to his subordinates because *he* appointed them, and to his country because *he* chooses to glorify it. Less extreme but still lacking proper humility is the elitist who counts events significant solely in proportion to how they affect his class. The suspicion about those who would destroy the environment, then, is that what they count important is too narrowly confined insofar as it encompasses only what affects beings who, like us, are capable of feeling.

This idea that proper humility requires recognition of the importance of nonsentient nature is similar to the thought of those who charge meat eaters with "species-ism." In both cases it is felt that people too narrowly confine their concerns to the sorts of beings that are most like them. But, however intuitively appealing, the idea will surely arouse objections from our non-environmentalist critic. "Why," he will ask, "do you suppose that the sort of

---

[11] An exception, apparently, was Kant, who thought "the starry heavens" sublime and compared them with "the moral law within," but did not for all that see our species as comparatively insignificant.

[12] By *"proper* humility" I mean that sort and degree of humility that is a morally admirable character trait. How precisely to define this is, of course, a controversial matter; but the point for present purposes is just to set aside obsequiousness, false modesty, underestimation of one's abilities, and the like.

[13] I take this point from some of Philippa Foot's remarks.

humility I *should* have requires me to acknowledge the importance of nonsentient nature aside from its utility? You cannot, by your own admission, argue that nonsentient nature *is* important, appealing to religious or intuitionist grounds. And simply to assert, without further argument, that an ideal humility requires us to view nonsentient nature as important for its own sake begs the question at issue. If proper humility is acknowledging the relative importance of things as one should, then to show that I must lack this you must first establish that one *should* acknowledge the importance of nonsentient nature."

Though some may wish to accept this challenge, there are other ways to pursue the connection between humility and response to nonsentient nature. For example, suppose we grant that proper humility requires only acknowledging a due status to sentient beings. We must admit, then, that it is logically possible for a person to be properly humble even though he viewed all nonsentient nature simply as a resource. But this logical possibility may be a psychological rarity. It may be that, given the sort of beings we are, we would never learn humility before persons without developing the general capacity to cherish, and regard important, many things for their own sakes. The major obstacle to humility before persons is self-importance, a tendency to measure the significance of everything by its relation to oneself and those with whom one identifies. The processes by which we overcome self-importance are doubtless many and complex, but it seems unlikely that they are exclusively concerned with how we relate to other people and animals. Learning humility requires learning to feel that something matters besides what will affect oneself and one's circle of associates. What leads a child to care about what happens to a lost hamster or a stray dog he will not see again is likely also to generate concern for a lost toy or a favorite tree where he used to live.[14] Learning to value things for their own sake, and to count what affects them important aside from their utility, is not the same as judging them to have some intuited objective property, but it is necessary to the development of humility and it seems likely to take place in experiences with nonsentient nature as well as with people and animals. If a person views all nonsentient nature merely as a resource, then it seems unlikely that he has developed the capacity needed to overcome self-importance.

IV

This last argument, unfortunately, has its limits. It presupposes an empirical connection between experiencing nature and overcoming self-importance, and this may be challenged. Even if experiencing nature promotes humility before others, there may be other ways people can develop such humility in a world of concrete, glass, and plastic. If not, perhaps all that is needed is limited experience of nature in one's early, developing years; mature adults, having

---

[14] The causal history of this concern may well depend upon the object (tree, toy) having given the child pleasure, but this does not mean that the object is then valued only for further pleasure it may bring.

overcome youthful self-importance, may live well enough in artificial surroundings. More importantly, the argument does not fully capture the spirit
of the intuition that an ideal person stands humbly before nature. That idea is
not simply that experiencing nature tends to foster proper humility before
other people; it is, in part, that natural surroundings encourage and are appropriate to an ideal sense of oneself as part of the natural world. Standing alone
in the forest, after months in the city, is not merely good as a means of curbing
one's arrogance before others; it reinforces and fittingly expresses one's acceptance of oneself as a natural being.

Previously we considered only one aspect of proper humility, namely, a
sense of one's relative importance with respect to other human beings.
Another aspect, I think, is a kind of *self-acceptance*. This involves acknowledging, in more than a merely intellectual way, that we are the sort of creatures
that we are. Whether one is self-accepting is not so much a matter of how one
attributes *importance* comparatively to oneself, other people, animals, plants,
and other things as it is a matter of understanding, facing squarely, and
responding appropriately to who and what one is, e.g., one's powers and limits, one's affinities with other beings and differences from them, one's unalter-
able nature and one's freedom to change. Self-acceptance is not merely
intellectual awareness, for one can be intellectually aware that one is growing
old and will eventually die while nevertheless behaving in a thousand foolish
ways that reflect a refusal to acknowledge these facts. On the other hand, self-
acceptance is not passive resignation, for refusal to pursue what one truly
wants within one's limits is a failure to accept the freedom and power one has.
Particular behaviors, like dying one's gray hair and dressing like those twenty
years younger, do not *necessarily* imply lack of self-acceptance, for there could
be reasons for acting in these ways other than the wish to hide from oneself
what one really is. One fails to accept oneself when the patterns of behavior
and emotion are rooted in a desire to disown and deny features of oneself, to
pretend to oneself that they are not there. This is not to say that a self-accepting person makes no value judgments about himself, that he likes all facts
about himself, wants equally to develop and display them; he can, and should
feel remorse for his past misdeeds and strive to change his current vices. The
point is that he does not disown them, pretend that they do not exist or are
facts about something other than himself. Such pretense is incompatible with
proper humility because it is seeing oneself as better than one is.

Self-acceptance of this sort has long been considered a human excellence,
under various names, but what has it to do with preserving nature? There is, I
think, the following connection. As human beings we are part of nature, living, growing, declining, and dying by natural laws similar to those governing
other living beings; despite our awesomely distinctive human powers, we
share many of the needs, limits, and liabilities of animals and plants. These
facts are neither good nor bad in themselves, aside from personal preference
and varying conventional values. To say this is to utter a truism which few
will deny, but to accept these facts, as facts about oneself, is not so easy—or so
common. Much of what naturalists deplore about our increasingly artificial

world reflects, and encourages, a denial of these facts; an unwillingness to avow them with equanimity.

Like the Victorian lady who refuses to look at her own nude body, some would like to create a world of less transitory stuff, reminding us only of our intellectual and social nature, never calling to mind our affinities with "lower" living creatures. The "denial of death," to which psychiatrists call attention,[15] reveals an attitude incompatible with the sort of self-acceptance which philosophers, from the ancients to Spinoza and on, have admired as a human excellence. My suggestion is not merely that experiencing nature causally promotes such self-acceptance, but also that those who fully accept themselves as part of the natural world lack the common drive to disassociate themselves from nature by replacing natural environments with artificial ones. A storm in the wilds helps us to appreciate our animal vulnerability, but, equally important, the reluctance to experience it may *reflect* an unwillingness to accept this aspect of ourselves. The person who is too ready to destroy the ancient redwoods may lack humility, not so much in the sense that he exaggerates his importance relative to others, but rather in the sense that he tries to avoid seeing himself as one among many natural creatures.

V

My suggestion so far has been that, though indifference to nonsentient nature is not itself a moral vice, it is likely to reflect either ignorance, a self-importance, or a lack of self-acceptance which we must overcome to have proper humility. A similar idea might be developed connecting attitudes toward nonsentient nature with other human excellences. For example, one might argue that indifference to nature reveals a lack of either an aesthetic sense or some of the natural roots of gratitude.

When we see a hillside that has been gutted by strip miners or the garden replaced by asphalt, our first reaction is probably, "How ugly!" The scenes assault our aesthetic sensibilities. We suspect that no one with a keen sense of beauty could have left such a sight. Admittedly not everything in nature strikes us as beautiful, or even aesthetically interesting, and sometimes a natural scene is replaced with a more impressive architectural masterpiece. But this is not usually the situation in the problem cases which environmentalists are most concerned about. More often beauty is replaced with ugliness.

At this point our critic may well object that, even if he does lack a sense of beauty, this is no moral vice. His cost/benefit calculations take into account the pleasure others may derive from seeing the forests, etc., and so why should he be faulted?

Some might reply that, despite contrary philosophical traditions, aesthetics and morality are not so distinct as commonly supposed. Appreciation of beauty, they may argue, is a human excellence which morally ideal persons

---

[15] See, for example, Ernest Becker, *The Denial of Death* (New York: Free Press, 1973).

should try to develop. But, setting aside this controversial position, there still may be cause for moral concern about those who have no aesthetic response to nature. Even if aesthetic sensibility is not itself a moral virtue, many of the capacities of mind and heart which it presupposes may be ones which are also needed for an appreciation of other people. Consider, for example, curiosity, a mind open to novelty, the ability to look at things from unfamiliar perspectives, empathetic imagination, interest in details, variety, and order, and emotional freedom from the immediate and the practical. All these, and more, seem necessary to aesthetic sensibility, but they are also traits which a person needs to be fully sensitive to people of all sorts. The point is not that a moral person must be able to distinguish beautiful from ugly people; the point is rather that unresponsiveness to what is beautiful, awesome, dainty, dumpy, and otherwise aesthetically interesting in nature probably reflects a lack of the openness of mind and spirit necessary to appreciate the best in human beings.

The anti-environmentalist, however, may refuse to accept the charge that he lacks aesthetic sensibility. If he claims to appreciate seventeenth-century miniature portraits, but to abhor natural wildernesses, he will hardly be convincing. Tastes vary, but aesthetic sense is not *that* selective. He may, instead, insist that he *does* appreciate natural beauty. He spends his vacations, let us suppose, hiking in the Sierras, photographing wildflowers, and so on. He might press his argument as follows: "I enjoy natural beauty as much as anyone, but I fail to see what this has to do with preserving the environment independently of human enjoyment and use. Nonsentient nature is a resource, but one of its best uses is to give us pleasure. I take this into account when I calculate the costs and benefits of preserving a park, planting a garden, and so on. But the problem you raised explicitly set aside the desire to preserve nature as a means to enjoyment. I say, let us enjoy nature fully while we can, but if all sentient beings were to die tomorrow, we might as well blow up all plant life as well. A redwood grove that no one can use or enjoy is utterly worthless."

The attitude expressed here, I suspect, is not a common one, but it represents a philosophical challenge. The beginnings of a reply may be found in the following. When a person takes joy in something, it is a common (and perhaps natural) response to come to cherish it. To cherish something is not simply to be happy with it at the moment, but to care for it for its own sake. This is not to say that one necessarily sees it as having feelings and so wants it to feel good; nor does it imply that one judges the thing to have Moore's intrinsic value. One simply wants the thing to survive and (when appropriate) to thrive, and not simply for its utility. We see this attitude repeatedly regarding mementos. They are not simply valued as a means to remind us of happy occasions; they come to be valued for their own sake. Thus, if someone really took joy in the natural environment, but was prepared to blow it up as soon as sentient life ended, he would lack this common human tendency to cherish what enriches our lives. While this response is not itself a moral virtue, it may be a natural basis of the virtue we call "gratitude." People who have no tendency to cherish things that give them pleasure may be poorly disposed to respond gratefully to persons who are good to them. Again the connection is not one of logical necessity, but it may nevertheless be important. A nonreligious person unable to "thank" anyone for the beauties of nature may nevertheless feel "grateful" in a sense; and I suspect that the person who feels no such "gratitude" toward nature is unlikely to show proper gratitude toward people.

Suppose these conjectures prove to be true. One may wonder what is the point of considering them. Is it to disparage all those who view nature merely as a resource? To do so, it seems, would be unfair, for, even if this attitude typically stems from deficiencies which affect one's attitudes toward sentient beings, there may be exceptions and we have not shown that their view of nonsentient nature is itself blameworthy. But when we set aside questions of blame and inquire what sorts of human traits we want to encourage, our reflections become relevant in a more positive way. The point is not to insinuate that all anti-environmentalists are defective, but to see that those who value such traits as humility, gratitude, and sensitivity to others have reason to promote the love of nature.

36

Moral Character and Abortion

Janet E. Smith received her Ph.D. in classical languages from the University of Toronto and presently teaches in the philosophy department at the University of Dallas. She has published articles in *International Philosophical Quarterly*, *The Thomist*, and the *New Scholasticism*, and is the author of *Humanae Vitae: A Generation Later* (1991). She frequently lectures on abortion and on the Catholic Church's teaching on marital ethics.

Much ethical theory has recognized that the very importance of the attempt to live an ethical life lies in the fact that in acting the individual forms herself or himself either for the better or for the worse. That is, each and every human act, each act stemming from the deliberate choice of the human agent determines the type of human being an individual is, or in other words, the kind of moral character that an individual has. Then, in turn, the moral character that one has influences what decisions one makes. For those who share this perspective, one of the foremost questions to be asked by the moral agent in the decision to do an action is: What kind of person will I become if I do this act?

Ethical reasoning of this sort is distinguished from other kinds of ethical inquiry because it focuses on the agent; it is variously known as ethics of the agent, ethics of virtue, or ethics of character. This is not to say that those who are concerned with an ethics of character are not also concerned with other means of determining the rightness or wrongness of an act. An ethics of character can be combined with nearly any means of evaluating an action. Yet, for an ethics of character the question of the effect of an act upon the character of the agent is one of the primary considerations taken into account in evaluating whether or not an action is moral.

Socrates was one of the first to make the effect of an action upon moral character an essential feature of his ethical thought. In the *Gorgias* he argues that "it is better to have harm done to you, than to harm another." He argued that it is better to have another do injustice to you than to do injustice to another because one harms one's own soul through doing injustice; this is a worse harm than any suffering that one may experience at the hands of another. Aristotle, in his *Nicomachean Ethics*, stated the basic premise of an ethics of virtue in these precise terms: "For a given kind of activity produces a corresponding character. This is shown by the way in which people train themselves for any kind of contest or performance: they keep on practicing for it. Thus, only a man who is utterly insensitive can be ignorant of the fact that moral characteristics are formed by actively engaging in particular actions" (1114a).[1] In this view, an individual should avoid telling lies, for instance, not only because it harms the truth, because it harms another who deserves the truth, because it creates distrust in society, but also because in lying, the individual does harm to her or his moral character; lying serves to mold one's character in the direction of being an untrustworthy person. Aristotle also draws upon the analogy of health to explain how one can eventually develop characteristics that may not please one but for which one may be responsible. He notes that much in the same way that one who enjoys good health might gradually become ill through dissolute living, so, too, one might through a series of unjust or selfish acts gradually become an unjust and selfish person (1114a10ff).

While few who have worked in the area of an ethics of virtue have applied this way of reasoning to specific actions, such a way of reasoning may indeed help us understand more fully why some actions are wrong. Here I shall first apply an ethics of virtue to evaluating adultery, a relatively uncontroversial action, and then I will turn to considering abortion and to evaluating its likely affects on the moral character of women.

An ethics of character assumes that there are some qualities or virtues that are beneficial for most men and women to have. Aristotle, in his study of ethics, relied enormously upon the views of the common man in drawing up the virtues or characteristics that a good person must have. Let us explore the possibility that even in our pluralistic and fragmented and politicized age a list of characteristics that most would laud as appropriate to a good human being could be compiled.

The first task must be the careful choice of words to designate the qualities or characteristics that constitute the goodness of a human being. What qualities would most agree that they would like to possess? Would not at least kindness, generosity, self-reliance, loyalty, commitment, responsibility, reliability, supportiveness, self-determination, sincerity, honesty, good-naturedness, trustworthiness, and self-discipline appear on the list of most people? Do we not also admire those who have reflected upon morality and show a concern for acting morally? We tend to admire those who can articulate and justify their reasons for their behavior and who act in accord with the moral principles they have accepted for themselves. We may observe that not many possess these qualities but we would agree that it would be good to have them. And to the question why people would want to possess these and other beneficial qualities, would not most of us say that having such qualities would enable us to function as we wish to function? That is, if we had these qualities, we would be able to accomplish what we wish to accomplish (given necessary external goods) and to have the relationships we would like to have—that is, we would be good co-workers, good friends, good spouses, and good parents. Do we not think that such individuals will make good moral decisions? We rely upon a just woman to do what is just, a generous man to do what is generous.

How do we judge who possesses these qualities? A common way of doing so is by observing how individuals act. That is, we deem some actions as generous and tend to think that those who consistently perform such actions are generous individuals. Yet, certainly it is not necessarily true that every individual who performs a certain kind of action will acquire the characteristics generally associated with the action, for character is very dependent upon the reasons given for the choice made. We may hold that individuals who perform certain actions tend to do so for typical reasons and before making a judgment we would need to determine if the individual being judged is acting for the typical reasons. The best that we can say is that *it is likely* that individuals who perform certain actions have certain characteristics. (Nonetheless, those who perform bad actions even for good reasons, may suffer some ill effect in their characters; lying for good purposes may still assist one in becoming an adept liar for bad reasons as well.) If we can determine an individual's true reasons for making his or her choice, our evaluation would, of course, have greater accuracy. This is important, for it is easy to over-absolutize statements such as "adulterers are untrustworthy"; it is likely that it is so, but not certainly the case that it is so. Nor, of course, does the claim that adulterers are generally certain sorts of individuals entail that those who do not commit adultery are therefore individuals of admirable character. The reasons individuals have for not committing adultery may not be admirable ones (one may fear that one's rich spouse would cancel one's credit cards, for instance). Again, the reasons that one gives for one's action are of decisive importance.

It must also be noted that individuals are not always fully responsible for the moral character that they have. Aristotle repeatedly stresses the importance of a good upbringing for helping one form a good moral character (e.g., 1095b). For instance, individuals who as children have been raised to act responsibly and fairly are much more likely to be responsible and fair adults. Conversely, those who have been spoiled and indulged may grow up to be self-centered and greedy adults; their parents may be greatly responsible for their moral character, but the children are the ones who suffer the effects of being selfish and greedy. Society may be responsible, for instance, for a propensity of its members to be adulterers if there are no disincentives to adultery, approval of it and abundant opportunity for it.

Let us now consider how the choice to commit adultery might reveal and affect one's moral character. While there is a kind of assumption here that adultery is wrong, our foremost concern is not with proving the wrongness of adultery. Rather, our concern is to determine what are the moral characters of those who commit adultery and to answer the question if it is likely or usual for those with admirable moral characters to engage in adultery. If it is true, however, that adulterers can be said to have undesirable moral characteristics and/or that they are forming undesirable moral characters through their choice to commit adultery, this would be taken as an indication at least—though hardly a proof—that adultery is a morally bad action.

For an analysis in accord with an ethics of virtue, answers to the following questions would be useful: What sort of people generally commit adultery? Are they, for instance, honest, temperate, kind, etc.? What sorts of reasons do they give for the actions that they choose? How do they assess their action? Do they understand themselves to be doing something moral or immoral with their choice? Why do adulterers choose to have sex with people other than their spouses? Are their reasons selfish or unselfish ones? Do they seem to speak of their reasons for their choice honestly or do they seem to be rationalizing? What sort of lives have they been leading prior to the action that they choose; are they the sorts of lives that exhibit the characteristics we admire?

Let us suppose that the ethicist might be able to make some generalizations about adulterers. He or she might observe that most who commit adultery are experiencing some difficulties in their marriages. Probably few enter marriage with the intention of committing adultery. They would find such an intention contrary to their commitment to their spouse. Most acts of adultery are most likely the result of a series of dissatisfactions, a series of choices, a series of "separations" from the marital relationship. Yet, given two individuals, both equally dissatisfied with their marriages, one who refuses to engage in adultery and the other who so chooses, the act of adultery by one signifies that he is a different "sort" of person than the other. Thus the individual's response to an opportunity for infidelity would suggest much about the person's character prior to the choice for or against adultery, and, perhaps, also gives some indication of the direction of the person's life after the choice.

It would also be valuable to know how adultery has affected the marriage of the adulterer, his or her relation to his or her children and other family members, his or her relations with co-workers, etc. We would be interested to learn if adulterers drank more, cheated on the job more, were estranged from their families. If we discovered that their lives showed such disarray, we might be able to conclude that these difficulties were connected with and grew out of certain qualities and were reinforced by the decision to commit adultery.

Even those who think it is a moral choice on occasion may well agree that adulterers usually are not the finest of individuals. Indeed, those who think that adultery is a moral choice in some circumstances—unless they are complete nihilists—would still observe that suitable reasons must be given to justify committing adultery. Thus, although some might not feel comfortable saying that all adulterers are liars and unkind and unreliable, most may agree that some true generalizations could be made about adulterers that would lead us to think that in general adultery is not compatible with the moral virtues that we admire. The reaction of the American public to the extra-marital affairs of Jim Bakker and Gary Hart reveal well the wide-spread view that lying predictably accompanies the act of adultery and that adulterers are not to be trusted. Certainly, if someone told us that he or she wanted to be an honest, trustworthy, stable and kind individual with good family relationships, and wanted to know if an adulterous affair would conflict with this goal, we would have little hesitation in advising against adultery.

The judgments that we make about an adulterer's character are made without scientific studies about adulterous individuals. We come to these conclusions, it seems, from the moral lessons of our youth, from novels we have read, from experience with the adulterers we have known. Certainly, we may encounter those who think adulterers are fun-loving, life-embracing, and generous. With those who do not share our analysis of the character of adulterers, we would be interested in comparing the reasons for the differing judgements. But an ethics of character depends upon such judgments. It requires us to draw upon whatever information we have that will help us to judge human character and the effect of human actions upon human character.

There is quite a remarkable amount of information available about women who have had abortions;[2] perhaps no other moral action is as well documented from the perspective of the experience of the agent. The value of reading this material for one who wishes to get an idea of what enters into the abortion decision and the abortion experience is inestimable. Nearly all of this material has been compiled and evaluated by those who find abortion to be morally permissible, and thus, if it is biased in any way, it is biased in the direction of portraying abortion as a good action.[3] Let me acknowledge my position on abortion, for admittedly this may introduce some bias into my interpretation. I consider abortion to be an intrinsically wrong action. Because there is no need to develop a complete argument here, suffice it to say that it is my judgment that abortion involves the taking of an innocent human life. But what I wish to demonstrate here is that abortion does serious harm not only to the unborn child, but to the woman herself, in her formation of her moral character.

One does not need to hold that abortion is intrinsically wrong to see that it may harm a woman's moral character. It is the judgment of this author that by and large many, even those who find abortion morally permissible, upon reading these interviews, would be disturbed by the quality of the moral character of the women having abortions and by the moral reasoning that informs the abortion decision. More precisely, I wish to show that the reasons that many women give for their abortion decisions are not reasons that most would find admirable or acceptable, again, even those who consider abortion morally permissible. The following discussion hopes to show that the choice for abortion is not often, if ever, compatible with the list given above of those qualities that most of us admire and would like to have. Finally, I would also like to note that it is not only women who suffer harm to their moral characters through abortion. If the analysis given here is correct, the men involved, the doctors and medical staff involved, those advising the women all risk great damage to their moral character.[4] And indeed, the community itself may be most responsible for the harm done for it permits abortion and has had a role in forming the character of the individuals who perform such actions, and it may suffer through being a community that does not provide for women in need, through not fostering a proper respect for life.[5] The focus here, though, is on the woman for she is most directly involved.

What are the features of the lives of women who have abortions that may be revealing of their moral character? What kinds of reasons do they give for their abortions? The studies referred to above give some indication of how some women view their decision to abort. Interviews with women who have had abortions provide a fairly full picture of the lives of women who have abortions and the quality of their abortion decision. They show that women who have abortions are involved in relationships that are not prepared for the eventuality of a child; they show that many, if not most, of the women who abort were pregnant not by "accident," but by some kind of calculated choice; and they also show that many of the women believe that they are taking a human life when they abort. Let us look at some of the evidence that supports these claims.

Upon reading the testimonies of many women who had abortions, Stanley Hauerwas observed,

> . . . I am impressed that in spite of the hundreds of articles published defending or opposed to abortion, the way people decide to have or not to have an abortion rarely seems to involve the issues discussed in those articles. People contemplating abortion do not ask if the fetus has a right to life, or when does life begin, or even if abortion is right or wrong. Rather, the decision seems to turn primarily on the quality of the relationship (or lack of relationship) between the couple.[6]

The quality of the relationship that exists between the couple is, as Hauerwas notes, frequently the key to the abortion decision. The one characteristic that is nearly universal among women deciding to have abortions is that they are engaged in relationships that are not conducive to raising a child. Perhaps it is obvious that most of the women who have abortions are unwed, some of the married women are pregnant by men other than their husbands, and many who are married regularly speak of troubled marriages that they fear cannot sustain a child or another child. Those who are unwed have quite clearly been involved in relationships that, although sexual, were not strong enough to accommodate a child conceived by the sexual union. Since the women having abortions have usually been involved in relationships not designed to accommodate all the responsibilities it may engender, perhaps it is fair to say that they display a significant amount of irresponsibility.

Nor do the relationships in which the women are involved seem to offer them much support as they face their pregnancies. Some women never inform the father of the child of the pregnancy. Those who do tell the male involved do not seem really to involve him and his wishes in the decision-making process, they simply inform him of their decision.[7] That most of the women make their decisions without giving full weight to the view of the male supports the observation that these were not stable and satisfying relationships—for the sense of mutually sharing one's life and decisions seems not to have been present in these relationships.

Moreover, the fact that over half acted without the agreement of the men involved indicates troubled relationships. One researcher, Linda Bird Francke, tells us that in her research almost every relationship between single people broke up either before or after the abortion.[8] Although Francke mentions one study which showed that in marital relationships the abortion was a positive act, this study was done only six months after the abortion.[9] Most of the statements taken from married women speak of resentment towards the husband. Thus, the relationships of women who have abortions seem characterized by instability, poor communication, and lack of true mutuality. Again, those involved in such relationships seem to be characterized by irresponsibility, and confusion about what they really want—which results in them being dishonest both with themselves and with their partners.

This charge of "irresponsibility" finds support in the contraceptive practices of these women (and the men with whom they are involved), for not only do the women engage in acts that have possible consequences for which they are not prepared but they also do not seem to be willing to take the steps necessary to prevent the occurrence of a situation for which they are not prepared to be responsible. Studies show that the women having abortions are not ignorant of birth control methods; the great majority are experienced contraceptors but, as Zimmerman observed, they display carelessness and indifference in their use of contraception.[10]

Moreover, the failure to use birth control indicates some other characteristics of the women having abortions. There are, of course, many subtle psychological reasons for failing to use contraceptives. Zimmerman reports on the many different reasons that women give: these include such reasons as a break-up in the relationship that seemed to signal that contraceptives would not be needed, a dislike for the physical exam required for the pill, a dislike of the side effects, inconvenience or difficulty in getting the pills. Zimmerman observes that many unmarried women do not like to think of themselves as sexually active and that using contraceptives conflicts with their preferred self-image.[11] The failure to use birth control is a sign that many women are not comfortable with being sexually active. That is, many of the women are engaged in an activity that, for some reason, they do not wish to admit to themselves. These women seem not to have much self-knowledge, nor do they seem to be self-determining—they seem to be "letting things happen" that, were they reflective and responsible individuals, they might not accept as actions for themselves.

Kristin Luker in an earlier book *Taking Chances: Abortion and the Decision Not to Contracept* attempted to discover why, with contraceptives so widely available, so many women, virtually all knowledgeable about contraception, had unwanted pregnancies and abortions. The conclusions of Luker's studies suggest that it is not simple "carelessness" or "irresponsibility" that lead women to have abortions, but that frequently the pregnancies that are aborted are planned or the result of a calculated risk. She begins by dismissing some of the commonly held views about why women get abortions; she denies that they are usually had by panic-stricken youngsters or that they are had by unmarried women who would otherwise have had illegitimate births. She also maintains that statistics do not show that abortion is a last ditch effort used by poor women and "welfare mothers" or that abortion is often sought by women who have more children than they can handle. What she attempts to discern is what *reason* women had for not using contraception although they were contraceptively experienced and knew the risks involved in not using contraception.[12] Luker seeks to substantiate in her study that "unwanted pregnancy is the end result of an informed decision-making process; and more important, that this process is a rational one, in which women use means appropriate to their goals. That pregnancy occurred anyway, for the women in this study, is because most of them were attempting to achieve more diffuse goals than simply preventing pregnancy."[13]

Luker argues that for these women (women who are having non-contraceptive sex, but who are not intending to have babies), using contraceptives has certain "costs" and getting pregnant has certain "benefits." The women make a calculation that the benefits of not using contraception and the benefits of a pregnancy outweigh the risks of getting pregnant and the need to have an abortion. Luker's analysis of the "costs" of using contraception parallels closely that of Zimmerman. She concurs that many women prefer "spontaneous sex" and do not like thinking of themselves as "sexually active." She notes that some wondered whether or not they were fertile and thus did not take contraceptives.[14] The "benefits" of a pregnancy for many women were many; pregnancy "proved that one is a woman,"[15] or that one is fertile;[16] it provides an excuse for "forcing a definition in the relationship";[17] it "forces her parents to deal with her";[18] it is used as a "psychological organizing technique." . . .

As noted, Luker argues that these women are rational in their risk-taking, in their not using contraception although they did not intend a pregnancy. She maintains that though it is not often an explicit or articulated calculation, that the women weighed the costs of using contraception against the costs and benefits of a pregnancy. . . .

It seems fair to call Luker's evaluation into question. First let it be noted that Luker was not attempting to evaluate the moral character of these women or to assess the morality of their decision to have an abortion. Luker's primary concern was to show that women had *reasons* for not using contraception, reasons that, evaluated in terms of the risks involved, were justifiable. On the basis of this claim, she undertook to argue that more and better access to contraception would not stem unwanted pregnancies; she advised greater access to abortion. Luker, though, stretches to the point of unrecognizability the word "rational." "Rational" more properly refers to behavior that is reflective, based upon clearly articulated judgments in accord with the facts of a situation, and one well-designed to achieve one's end. Luker, in spite of her intentions, depicts these women as taking risks on the basis of ill-defined and unarticulated reasons and pressures, risks that seemed ill-suited to achieve the desired ends. Luker makes no attempt to discern if the women explored other means to the ends that they desired. She never questions, for instance, if it is an intelligent decision for a young woman to get pregnant and have an abortion for the sake of having her family take notice of her, or for the sake of proving her fertility to herself, or for the sake of learning if her boyfriend cares about her.

Furthermore, a usual criterion for a good and rational moral decision (or any decision, for that matter) is that the decision be a fully informed one. Few of the interviews of women having abortions give any indication that the women were fully aware of the size and development of the fetus they were carrying, that they knew the risks to their reproductive capacities or to their emotional health.[19] Many knew little enough about the procedure of abortion itself.

Luker does not write with the purpose of explaining why women have abortions but her study is most revealing of the reasons why women have abortions. Her study leads this interpreter to judge that these women were not adept at determining how to solve the problems that their lives presented them and that they did not realistically evaluate their relationships and their own expectations for these relationships. Despite Luker's claim to the contrary, I believe that Luker's study supports the claim that many if not most of the women who choose abortion are irresponsible, and to some extent irrational.[20]

Women may get pregnant for a variety of reasons, but the most common reason for having an abortion is that the women are not prepared for the responsibilities of a baby. Again, most are not prepared because they are not married to and not intending to marry the man who impregnated them. It must also be noted that although these women were not prepared to have a child, many reluctantly have abortions. Many state that they felt pressured into having the abortion either because they feared or knew that their parents would reject them, that their boyfriends or husbands would leave them, or because their friends and co-workers thought abortion was the responsible choice for them. This indicates that for many women the decision to abort was only weakly self-determined; they were very much pressured by their situation and their "advisors" to have the abortion. Gilligan, who studied the abortion from the perspective of moral development, maintains that women have been socialized not to make choices for themselves, not to take responsibility for their choices.[21] Again, women may not be responsible for the moral characters that they have, but the evidence seems to suggest that the decision to abort is one that women often wish to attribute not to their own values, but to the pressure that others have put upon them. Insofar as making choices in accord with one's own values is indicative of a good moral character, many women who abort seem devoid of this power—whatever the reason for their lacking this power.

One notable recurrent feature found in the interviews of women who have had abortions is the acknowledgment by the women of their belief that they are taking a human life when they have an abortion.[22] Certainly, some claim that they are not taking a life; for instance, a young woman named Chris felt this way: ". . . I was talking to the pastor who helped me to get here and he asked me what my conception of life was. And I said, well, I suppose you know just right off the bat the baby is born, you pat it on the back, and it starts breathing. That's life to me. But before then it's nothing. Kind of like a growth."[23] But many others think differently. Consider these statements taken from different sources; seventeen-year-old Dawn, who decided to have an abortion because she was not emotionally ready to have a baby, admitted, "Well, it's abortion killing all the way through but—um—I'm all mixed up about this. I think it's just killing all the way through."[24] Maria speaks of her second abortion, "This time I hoped the baby was a boy and that I could keep it. My husband and I discussed it and discussed it. We had to convince ourselves to have the abortion. It makes it much harder when you already have a child. You realize it's a wonderful thing to go through a pregnancy and then have a baby dependent on you. This time I couldn't help thinking it was a human being, living being."[25] Sandra asserts, "I have always thought abortion was a fancy word for murder."[26] Sandra commented on her abortion: "I am saying that abortion is morally wrong, but the situation is right, and I am going to do it."[27] One interviewer, Zimmerman, found that most women who had abortions, prior to their abortion did not approve of abortion except for specific situations—and these situations did not include the situation in which they found themselves; on the basis of her research she observed,

> In summary, the prior abortion attitudes of the women studied here indicate that abortion is considered acceptable only under specific circumstances. The majority of the women would be likely to disapprove an abortion unless the woman had been raped, or unless she had health problems relating to her pregnancy, or unless she were financially unable to take care of a baby. Interestingly, their own abortions did not always fall within these circumstances. . . . Many of the women claimed that they had approved of abortion but then later qualified that statement by saying, "But I never thought I would have one myself" or "It's the lesser of two evils." None of the women stated their approval without some qualifying remark. The fact that most of these women did not appear to enter into their abortion experience with complete and unqualified approval of abortion is certainly noteworthy.[28]

Zimmerman maintained that the women themselves evaluated their own choice as a form of deviance.[29] Their feeling that they were "treading on thin moral ice" led women to be secretive about their abortions so they would not risk being morally challenged about their abortions.[30]

A pattern seems to emerge here. These testimonies suggest that women who are having abortions are not living in accord with some of the most important values they hold. They themselves frequently, if not usually, characterize abortion and indeed their own decision as taking a human life. Although the women do not generally approve of abortion, they make exceptions for themselves. It seems that the reasons that many women give for their abortion decisions are not reasons that most would find admirable or acceptable, even those who consider abortion morally permissible, even those who are having abortions. If, then, it is a virtue to act in accord with one's principles, many of the women having abortions seem not to have this virtue and are acting in a way that will not advance their possession of it.

The analysis here has been based upon a reading of the testimonies of women who have had abortions, testimony gathered almost exclusively by those who themselves believe abortion to be morally permissible. Most if not all of the interviewers would consider themselves to be feminists. Most believe that through exercising control over their fertility, women who have abortions are acquiring virtues or characteristics once associated only with men. Most of those who subscribe to the values of feminism tend to judge the women who choose abortion to be acquiring some admirable characteristics such as self-assertiveness, rational control over their lives, independence. Still, Sidney Callahan, who considers herself a "pro-life feminist," argues that abortion violates the deeper values of feminism, that it fosters characteristics that are desirable neither for men nor women.

Callahan's argument has many parts. She states that feminists are dedicated to fighting for the rights of the oppressed; that they are interested in equality and due process and fairness; she maintains that it is inconsistent for feminists, then, to deny the unborn child the right to life, to use the power of technology to kill the innocent and defenseless. She argues that feminists should not adopt the value of individual autonomy with its emphasis on complete control over one's life; a control and autonomy that rejects the responsibilities that come with an unplanned pregnancy. She maintains that being a part of the human family, being a woman, brings with it certain responsibilities that ought to be accepted whether or not freely chosen, whether or not convenient. But what is most important to the thesis here is her observation that there is a general chaos in the lives of many, if not most, of the women who have abortions and a real confusion about the place of sexuality in their lives, about the connection between characteristics that are valuable in one's professional life and in one's personal life. She states:

> . . . many pro-choice feminists preach their own double standard. In the world of work and career, women are urged to grow up, to display mature self-discipline and self-control; they are told to persevere in long-term commitments, to cope with unexpected obstacles by learning to tough out the inevitable sufferings and setbacks entailed in life and work. But this mature ethics of commitment and self-discipline, recommended as the only way to progress in the world of work and personal achievement, is discounted in the domain of sexuality. . . . Responsibly choosing an abortion supposedly ensures that a young woman will take charge of her own life, make her own decisions, and carefully practice contraception. But the social dynamics of a permissive erotic model of sexuality, coupled with permissive laws, work toward repeat abortions. Instead of being empowered by their abortion choices, young women having abortions are confronting the debilitating reality of *not* bringing a baby into the world; not being able to count on a committed male partner; *not* accounting oneself strong enough, or the master of enough resources, to avoid killing the fetus. Young women are hardly going to develop the self-esteem, self-discipline, and self-confidence necessary to confront a male-dominated society through abortion.[31]

In terms used here, these women do not exhibit much virtue, much moral strength, nor does their choice to abort appear to be an act that will further their virtue or moral strength. A list of moral characteristics was tentatively offered earlier in this paper to provide a base upon that an analysis of action in terms of virtue could proceed. The claim was made that we all would want to have these characteristics and we would want those we associate with to have them, too. The list included kindness, generosity, self-reliance, loyalty, commitment, responsibility, reliability, supportiveness, self-determination, sincerity, honesty, good-naturedness, trustworthiness, and self-discipline. The interviews of women who choose to have abortions indicate that they could not be described in these terms.

Finally let us note that though there is not a great deal of documentation on how women fare after their abortion, what little evidence there is suggests that it is not an overwhelmingly positive experience.[32] Indeed, yearly nearly one third of abortions are repeat abortions. It would seem that many of these women, at least, return to much the same life that they were leading prior to their abortions. By their own testimony many of the women who were not promiscuous before the abortion become so afterwards; most have difficulty sustaining long-term relationships with a male. Most women maintain that relief is the immediate outcome of an abortion though most speak of some depression and confusion afterwards. The conclusions of the psychological studies of those who have had abortions are remarkably mixed. Before the legalization of abortion several studies showed that abortion was traumatic for women. After the legalization of abortion, most studies show that few women suffer little long-term psychological consequences. The validity of these studies has been called into question in terms of the scientific reliability. Certainly the conclusions may also be affected by a bias produced by an ideological commitment to abortion rights.

It is well documented that some women come to regret their abortions and suffer severe trauma after the abortion. They regularly speak of feeling that they were pressured into the abortion. They speak of their confusion at the time of the abortion, their troubled relationships with family and boyfriend; they tell of their suicidal desires, their alienation and loneliness after the abortion. Several groups have been formed to assist women who have come to regret their abortions; Women Exploited by Abortion and Victims of Abortion are both such groups. One author describing women who have had abortions tells that even those who have come to terms with their regret ". . . will tell you that their decision-making skills are damaged, that self-doubt has become the common denominator of their personalities. After all, they made one terrible mistake. When will they stumble into the next?"[33] Women who regret their abortions believe that there are millions of women "out there" who are "broken" and agonizing inside about their abortions, that they are in a state of deep denial about their feelings about their abortions.

Information about the psychological aftermath of abortion should assist us in determining the moral character of women after the abortion. Certainly, some psychological weaknesses or strengths are closely connected with moral character. High self-esteem may assist one in having the confidence and presence of mind to take into account all factors in a situation and to make a good decision. It may enable one to resist undue pressure from others and it may keep one free from debilitating fears that could lead one to act out of cowardice. Indeed, high self-esteem may be connected with how one assesses one's own moral character; those who believe themselves to be morally good may have greater self-esteem. Depression could lead one to be unable to meet one's commitments and obligations and lead to moral failure as a reliable and dependable person. But until the studies done on the psychological aftermath of abortion are standardized and attain a higher degree of reliability, most judgments will continue to be made on the basis of more randomly acquired testimony. This testimony, I submit, suggests that many women exhibit characteristics after their abortion experience that make it difficult for them to advance in moral strength.

An ethics of virtue assesses actions by the type of character that produces and chooses these actions. Abortion, in the eyes of this interpreter, does not fare well as a moral action, according to this analysis. Those seeking to assess the morality of abortion, those seeking to find some ground for discussion and understanding about the morality of abortion other than the question of a conflict of rights, would do well to ponder what kind of moral judgment goes into choosing an abortion, what kind of moral character results from an abortion.

Notes

1. Aristotle, *Nicomachean Ethics*, trans. by Martin Ostwald (Indianapolis: 1962) 66.
2. See, Magda Denes, *In Necessity and Sorrow* (New York: 1976); Linda Bird Francke, *The Ambivalence of Abortion* (New York: 1978); Carol Gilligan, *In a Different Voice* (Cambridge, Mass.: 1982); Nona Lyons, "Two Perspectives: On Self, Relationships, and Morality," *Harvard Educational Review* 53:2 (1983): 125-145; Judith G. Smetana, *Concepts of Self and Morality* (New York: 1982); and Mary K. Zimmerman, *Passage Through Abortion* (New York: 1977). Some "reinterpreting" of several of these texts cited has been done by James Tunstead Burtchaell, *Rachel Weeping and Other Essays on Abortion* (Kansas City: 1982) 1-60. For a full and up-to-date accounting of the consequences of the decision to abort by one who is opposed to abortion, see the extensive study done by David C. Reardon, *Aborted Women: Silent No More* (Westchester, Illinois: 1987). He interviews only those who regret their abortions, but his findings do not diverge significantly from studies done by those who believe abortion to be moral.
3. I have done a fairly extensive critique of Carol Gilligan's studies of women who have had abortions. This critique attempted to show that her proabortion views skewed her interpretation of interviews of women who had abortions; *International Philosophical Quarterly* 28:1 (March 1988): 31-51.
4. See particularly Magda Denes' work.
5. This a point powerfully made by Stanley Hauerwas, "Why Abortion Is a Religious Issue," and "Abortion: Why the Arguments Fail," chapters 11 and 12 in his *A Community of Character* (Notre Dame: 1981).
6. Hauerwas, 199.

7. Zimmerman, 136.
8. Francke, 47.
9. Francke, 93.
10. Kristin Luker, *Taking Chances: Abortion and the Decision Not To Contracept* (Berkeley: 1975); cf. Reardon, 8, and see Zimmerman, 77.
11. Zimmerman, 81.
12. Luker, 16.
13. Luker, 32.
14. Luker, 62–63.
15. Luker, 65.
16. Luker, 68.
17. Luker, 70.
18. Luker, 71.
19. Reardon, 14 and 16.
20. James Burtchaell has done a comprehensive analysis of a substantial number of interviews of women who have had abortions. He summarizes his conclusions by labeling the aborters "estranged, submissive, and incoherent" (p. 44). He speaks of the estrangement that women having abortions have from their family, of their submission to others and their blaming of others for their decisions, of a conflict or incoherence between the values they purport to hold and those upon which they act. He speaks of these women as "ricochetting through life" (p. 45). His truly is not an unsympathetic portrayal of these women and their decisions; the evidence quite manifestly supports his assessment.
21. Gilligan, 67.
22. Indeed, I believe that there is good evidence that women having abortions generally concede that they are taking a human life, however sorrowfully so. Stanley Hauerwas in his comments on Linda Bird Francke's *The Ambivalence of Abortion* observes that few of the women "claim to have aborted a fetus—they abort a 'child' or a 'baby.'" (*A Community of Character*, p. 199). Mary K. Zimmerman calls the issue of "wanting or not wanting a baby" to be the central orienting point for the woman's decision process (p. 110). Burtchaell observes in regard to his reading of Francke's book and Katrina Maxtone-Graham's *Pregnant by Mistake* (1973): "No one among the nearly one hundred persons interviewed addresses the morality of abortion as a serious intellectual issue, or offers a moral defense of having chosen it on grounds other than her or his own feelings. Feelings are invariably the determinant factor, not principles or evidence or facts or even ideas" (p. 28).
23. Denes, 121.
24. Smetana, 75.
25. Francke, 99.
26. Gilligan, 85.
27. Gilligan, 86.
28. Zimmerman, 70.
29. Zimmerman, 72; see also, Reardon, 13.
30. Zimmerman,

31. Sidney Callahan, "Abortion and the Sexual Agenda," *Commonweal* (25 April 1986): 236.
32. For a description of the psychological aftermath of abortion, see Reardon, 115ff.
33. Paula Ervin, *Women Exploited: The Other Victims of Abortion* (Huntington, Indiana; Our Sunday Visitor, Inc.), 16.

37

The Virtuous Physician

Edmund D. Pellegrino is director of the Kennedy Institute of Ethics, and John Carroll Professor of Medicine and Medical Humanities, Georgetown University, Washington, D.C. He is the author of *The Human and the Physical* (1979), and the joint editor of *Catholic Perspectives on Foundational Medical Issues* (1989).

> Consider from what noble seed you spring: You were created not to live like beasts, but for pursuit of virtue and of knowledge.
>
> Dante, *Inferno* 26, 118–120

Introduction

In the opening pages of his *Dominations and Powers*, Santayana asserts that "Human society owes all its warmth and vitality to the intrinsic virtue of its members" and that the virtues therefore are always "hovering silently" over his pages ([32], p. 3). And, indeed, the virtues have always hovered over any theory of morals. They give credibility to the moral life; they assure that it will be something more than a catalogue of rights, duties, and rules. Virtue adds that extra 'cubit' that lifts ethics out of its legalisms to the higher reaches of moral sensitivity.

Yet, as MacIntyre's brilliant treatise so ably attests, virtue-ethics since the Enlightenment has become a dubious enterprise [19]. We have lost consensus on a definition of virtue, and without moral consensus there is no vantage point from which to judge what is right and good. Virtue becomes confused with conformity to the conventions of social and institutional life. The accolades go to those who get along and get ahead. Without agreeing on the nature of the good, moreover, we can hardly know what a 'disposition' to do the right and good may mean.

These uncertainties force us to rely on ethical systems built upon specific rights, duties, and the application of rules and principles. Their concreteness seems to promise protection against capricious and antithetical interpretations of vice and virtue. But that concreteness turns to illusion once we try to agree on what is the right and good thing to do, in a given circumstance.

Despite the erosion of the concept of virtue, it remains an inescapable reality in moral transactions. We know there are people we can trust to temper self-interest, to be honest, truthful, faithful, or just, even in the face of the omnipresence of evil. Sadly, we also know that there are others who cannot be trusted habitually to act well. We may not be virtuous ourselves, we may even sneer at the folly of the virtuous man in our age, yet we can recognize him nonetheless. It is as Marcus Aurelius said, ". . . no thing delights as much as the examples of the virtues when they are exhibited in the morals of those who live with us and present themselves in abundance as far as possible. Wherefore we must keep these before us" [23].

And, in fact, the virtues are again being brought before us in the resurgence, among moral philosophers, of an interest in virtue-based ethics [9, 11, 13, 17, 21, 29, 33, 34, 35, 38, 39]. For the most part the resurgence is based in a re-examination, clarification, and refurbishment of the classical-medieval concept of virtue. On the whole, the contemporary reappraisal is not an abnegation of rights or duty-based ethics, but a recognition that rights and duties notwithstanding, their moral effectiveness still turns on the disposition and character traits of our fellow men and women.

This is preeminently true in medical ethics where the vulnerability and dependence of the sick person forces him to trust not just in his rights but in the kind of person the physician *is*. The variability with which this trust is honored, and at times its outright violation, account for the current decline in the moral credibility of the profession. It accounts, too, for the trend toward asserting patients' rights more forcefully in contract as opposed to covenantal models of the physician-patient relationship. In illness, when we are most exploitable, we are most dependent upon the kind of person who will intend, and do, the right and the good thing, because he cannot really do otherwise.

MacIntyre has expressed his pessimism about the possibilities of an ethic of virtue in our times. He ends his tightly reasoned treatise with a surprisingly romantic hope for ". . . a local form of community within which civility and the intellectual and moral life can be sustained in the rough new dark ages which are already upon us" ([19], p. 245). One can accept MacIntyre's astute historical diagnoses without waiting too quietistically for the appearance of his new and 'doubtless very different' St. Benedict to lead us into some new moral consensus. Even in this 'dark age', it may be possible to incorporate the remnants of the classical-medieval idea of virtue into a more satisfactory moral structure that also includes rights and duties.

This essay examines that possibility in the limited domain of professional medical ethics. Using the classical-medieval concept of virtue, it attempts to define the virtuous physician, to relate his virtue to the ends of medicine and to the usual principles applied in medical ethics, as well as to the prevailing rights and duty-based systems of professional ethics.

This essay is part of a larger effort to link a theory of the patient-physician relationship, a theory of patient good, and theory of virtue in a unified conceptual substructure for the professional ethics of medicine [24, 25].

The Virtuous Person, The Virtuous Physician

Through multitudinous definitions of virtue a set of common themes seems discernible. Virtue implies a character trait, an internal disposition, habitually to seek moral perfection, to live one's life in accord with the moral law, and to attain a balance between noble intention and just action. Perhaps C. S. Lewis has captured the idea best by likening the virtuous man to the good tennis player: "What you mean by a good player is the man whose eye and muscles and nerves have been so trained by making innumerable good shots that they can now be relied upon. . . . They have a certain tone or quality which is there even when he is not playing. . . . In the same way a man who perseveres in doing just actions gets in the end a certain quality of character. Now it is that quality rather than the particular actions that we mean when we talk of virtue" [18].

On almost any view, the virtuous person is someone we can trust to act habitually in a 'good' way—courageously, honestly, justly, wisely, and temperately. He is committed to *being* a good person and to the pursuit of perfection in his private, professional and communal life. He is someone who will act well even when there is no one to applaud, simply because to act otherwise is a violation of what it is to be a good person. No civilized society could endure without a significant number of citizens committed to this concept of virtue. Without such persons no system of general ethics could succeed, and no system of professional ethics could transcend the dangers of self interest. That is why, even while rights, duties, obligations may be emphasized, the concept of virtue has 'hovered' so persistently over every system of ethics.

Is the virtuous physician simply the virtuous person practicing medicine? Are there virtues peculiar to medicine as a practice? Are certain of the individual virtues more applicable to medicine than elsewhere in human activities? Is virtue more important in some branches of medicine than others? How do professional skills differ from virtue? These are pertinent questions propaedeutic to the later questions of the place of virtue in professional medical ethics.

I believe these questions are best answered by drawing on the Aristotelian–Thomist notion of virtues and its relationship to the ends and purposes of human life. The virtuous physician on this view is defined in terms of the ends of medicine. To be sure, the physician, before he is anything else, must be a virtuous person. To be a virtuous physician he must also be the kind of person we can confidently expect will be disposed to the right and good intrinsic to the practice he professes. What are those dispositions?

To answer this question requires some exposition of what we mean by the good in medicine, or more specifically the good of the patient—for that is the end the patient and the physician ostensibly seek. Any theory of virtue must be linked with a theory of the good because virtue is a disposition habitually to do the good. Must we therefore know the nature of the good the virtuous man is disposed to do? As with the definition of virtue we are caught here in another perennial philosophical question—what is the nature of the Good? Is the good whatever we make it to be or does it have validity independent of our desires or interest? Is the good one, or many? Is it reducible to riches, honors, pleasures, glory, happiness, or something else?

I make no pretense to a discussion of a general theory of the good. But any attempt to define the virtuous physician or a virtue-based ethic for medicine must offer some definition of the good of the patient. The patient's good is the end of medicine, that which shapes the particular virtues required for its attainment. That end is central to any notion of the virtues peculiar to medicine as a practice.

I have argued elsewhere that the architectonic principle of medicine is the good of the patient as expressed in a particular right and good healing action [26]. This is the immediate good end of the clinical encounter. Health, healing, caring, coping are all good ends dependent upon the more immediate end of a right and good decision. On this view, the virtuous physician is one so habitually disposed to act in the patient's good, to place that good in ordinary instances above his own, that he can reliably be expected to do so.

But we must face the fact that the 'patient's good' is itself a compound notion. Elsewhere I have examined four components of the patient's good: (1) clinical or biomedical good; (2) the good as perceived by the patient; (3) the good of the patient as a human person; and (4) the Good, or ultimate good. Each of these components of patient good must be served. They must also be placed in some hierarchical order when they conflict within the same person, or between persons involved in clinical decisions [27].

Some would consider patient good, so far as the physician is concerned, as limited to what applied medical knowledge can achieve in *this* patient. On this view the virtues specific to medicine would be objectivity, scientific probity, and conscientiousness with regard to professional skill. One could perform the technical tasks of medicine well, be faithful to the skills of good technical medicine per se, but without being a virtuous person. Would one then be a virtuous physician? One would have to answer affirmatively if technical skill were all there is to medicine.

Some of the more expansionist models of medicine—like Engel's biopsychosocial model, or that of the World Health Organization (total well-being) would require compassion, empathy, advocacy, benevolence, and beneficence, i.e., an expanded sense of the affective responses to patient need [8]. Some might argue that what is required, therefore, is not virtue, but simply greater skill in the social and behavioral sciences applied to particular patients. On this view the physician's habitual dispositions might be incidental to his skills in communication or his empathy. He could achieve the ends of medicine without necessarily being a virtuous person in the generic sense.

It is important at this juncture to distinguish the virtues from technical or professional skills, as MacIntyre and, more clearly, Von Wright do. The latter defines a skill as 'technical goodness'—excellence in some particular activity—

while virtues are not tied to any one activity but are necessary for "the good of man" ([38], pp. 139–140). The virtues are not "characterized in terms of their results" ([38], p. 141). On this view, the technical skills of medicine are not virtues and could be practiced by a non-virtuous person. Aristotle held *techne* (technical skills) to be one of the five intellectual virtues but not one of the moral virtues.

The virtues enable the physician to act with regard to things that are good for man, when man is in the specific existential state of illness. They are dispositions always to seek the good intent inherent in healing. Within medicine, the virtues do become in MacIntyre's sense acquired human qualities ". . . the possession and exercise of which tends to enable us to achieve those goods which are internal to practices and the lack of which effectively prevents us from achieving any such goods" ([19], p. 178).

We can come closer to the relationships of virtue to clinical actions if we look to the more immediate ends of medical encounters, to those moments of clinical truth when specific decisions and actions are chosen and carried out. The good the patient seeks is to be healed—to be restored to his prior, or to a better, state of function, to be made 'whole' again. If this is not possible, the patient expects to be helped, to be assisted in coping with the pain, disability or dying that illness may entail. The immediate end of medicine is not simply a technically proficient performance but the use of that performance to attain a good end—the good of the patient—his medical or biomedical good to the extent possible but also his good as he the patient perceives it, his good as a human person who can make his own life plan, and his good as a person with a spiritual destiny if this is his belief [24, 25]. It is the sensitive balancing of these senses of the patient's good which the virtuous physician pursues to perfection.

To achieve the end of medicine thus conceived, to practice medicine virtuously, requires certain dispositions: conscientious attention to technical knowledge and skill to be sure, but also compassion—a capacity to feel something of the patient's experience of illness and his perceptions of what is worthwhile; beneficence and benevolence—doing and wishing to do good for the patient; honesty, fidelity to promises, perhaps at times courage as well—the whole list of virtues spelled out by Aristotle: ". . . justice, courage, temperance, magnificence, magnanimity, liberality, placability, prudence, wisdom" (*Rhetoric*, 1, c, 13666, 1–3). Not every one of these virtues is required in every decision. What we expect of the virtuous physician is that he will exhibit them when they are required and that he will be so habitually disposed to do so that we can depend upon it. He will place the good of the patient above his own and to seek that good unless its pursuit imposes an injustice upon him, or his family, or requires a violation of his own conscience.

While the virtues are necessary to attain the good internal to medicine as a practice, they exist independently of medicine. They are necessary for the practice of a good life, no matter in what activities that life may express itself. Certain of the virtues may become duties in the Stoic sense, duties because of the nature of medicine as a practice. Medicine calls forth benevolence, beneficence, truth telling, honesty, fidelity, and justice more than physical courage, for example. Yet even physical courage may be necessary when caring for the wounded on battlefields, in plagues, earthquakes, or other disasters. On a more ordinary scale courage is necessary in treating contagious diseases, violent patients, or battlefield casualties. Doing the right and good thing in medicine calls for a more regular, intensive, and selective practice of the virtues than many other callings.

A person who is a virtuous person can cultivate the technical skills of medicine for reasons other than the good of the patient—his own pride, profit, prestige, power. Such a physician can make technically right decisions and perform skillfully. He could not be depended upon, however, to act against his own self-interest for the good of his patient.

In the virtuous physician, explicit fulfillment of rights and duties is an outward expression of an inner disposition to do the right and the good. He is virtuous not because he has conformed to the letter of the law, or his moral duties, but because that is what a good person does. He starts always with his commitment to be a certain kind of person, and he approaches clinical quandaries, conflicts of values, and his patient's interests as a good person should.

Some branches of medicine would seem to demand a stricter and broader adherence to virtue than others. Generalists, for example, who deal with the more sensitive facets and nuances of a patient's life and humanity must exercise the virtues more diligently than technique-oriented specialists. The narrower the specialty the more easily the patient's good can be safeguarded by rules, regulations rights and duties; the broader the specialty the more significant are the physician's character traits. No branch of medicine, however, can be practiced without some dedication to some of the virtues. [21]

Unfortunately, physicians can compartmentalize their lives. Some practice medicine virtuously, yet are guilty of vice in their private lives. Examples are common of physicians who appear sincerely to seek the good of their patients and neglect obligations to family or friends. Some boast of being 'married' to medicine and use this excuse to justify all sorts of failures in their own human relationships. We could not call such a person virtuous. Nor could we be secure in, or trust, his disposition to act in a right and good way even in medicine. After all, one of the essential virtues is balancing conflicting obligations judiciously.

As Socrates pointed out to Meno, one cannot really be virtuous in part:

> Why did not I ask you to tell me the nature of virtue as a whole? And you are very far from telling me this; but declare every action to be virtue which is done with a part of virtue; as though you had told me and I must already know the whole of virtue, and this too when frittered away into little pieces. And therefore my dear Meno, I fear that I must begin again, and repeat the same question: what is virtue? For otherwise, I can only say that every action done with a part of virtue is virtue; what else is the meaning of saying that every action done with justice is virtue? Ought I not to ask the question over again; for can any one who does not know virtue know a part of virtue? (*Meno*, 79)

Virtues, Rights and Duties in Medical Ethics

Frankena has neatly summarized the distinctions between virtue-based and rights- and duty-based ethics as follows:

> In an ED (ethics of duty) then, the basic concept is that a certain kind of external act (or doing) ought to be done in certain circumstances; and that of a certain disposition being a virtue is a dependent one. In an EV (ethics of virtue) the basic concept is that of a disposition or way of being—something one has, or is not does—as a virtue, as morally good; and that of an action's being virtuous or good or even right, is a dependent one. [10]

There are some logical difficulties with a virtue-based ethic. For one thing, there must be some consensus on a definition of virtue. For another there is a circularity in the assertion that virtue is what the good man habitually does, and that at the same time one becomes virtuous by doing good. Virtue and good are defined in terms of each other and the definitions of both may vary among sincere people in actual practice when there is no consensus. A virtue-based ethic is difficult to defend as the sole basis for normative judgments.

But there is a deficiency in rights- and duty-ethics as well. They too must be linked to a theory of the good. In contemporary ethics, theories of good are rarely explicitly linked to theories of the right and good. Von Wright, commendably, is one of the few contemporary authorities who explicitly connects his theory of good with his theory of virtue. This essay, together with three previous ones, is part of the author's effort in that direction [25–27].

In most professional ethical codes, virtue and duty-based ethics are intermingled. The Hippocratic Oath, for example, imposes certain duties like protection of confidentiality, avoiding abortion, not harming the patient. But the Hippocratic physician also pledges: ". . . in purity and holiness I will guard my life and my art." This is an exhortation to be a good person and a virtuous physician, in order to serve patients in an ethically responsible way.

Likewise, in one of the most humanistic statements in medical literature, the first century A. D. writer, Scribonius Largus, made *humanitas* (compassion) an essential virtue. It is thus really a role-specific duty. In doing so he was applying the Stoic doctrine of virtue to medicine [3, 28].

The latest version (1980) of the AMA 'Principles of Medical Ethics' similarly intermingles duties, rights, and exhortations to virtue. It speaks of 'standards of behavior', 'essentials of honorable behavior', dealing 'honestly' with patients and colleagues and exposing colleagues 'deficient in character'. The *Declaration of Geneva*, which must meet the challenge of the widest array of value systems, nonetheless calls for practice 'with conscience and dignity' in keeping with 'the honor and noble traditions of the profession'. Though their first allegiance must be to the Communist ethos, even the Soviet physician is urged to preserve 'the high title of physician', 'to keep and develop the beneficial traditions of medicine' and to 'dedicate' all his 'knowledge and strength to the care of the sick'.

Those who are cynical of any protestation of virtue on the part of physicians will interpret these excerpts as the last remnants of a dying tradition of altruistic benevolence. But at the very least, they attest to the recognition that the good of the patient cannot be fully protected by rights and duties alone. Some degree of supererogation is built into the nature of the relationship of those who are ill and those who profess to help them.

This too may be why many graduating classes, still idealistic about their calling, choose the Prayer of Maimonides (not by Maimonides at all) over the more deontological Oath of Hippocrates. In that 'prayer' the physician asks: ". . . may neither avarice nor miserliness, nor thirst for glory or for a great reputation engage my mind; for the enemies of truth and philanthropy may easily deceive me and make me forgetful of my lofty aim of doing good to thy children." This is an unequivocal call to virtue and it is hard to imagine even the most cynical graduate failing to comprehend its message.

All professional medical codes, then, are built of a three-tiered system of obligations related to the special roles of physicians in society. In the ascending order of ethical sensitivity they are: observance of the laws of the land, then observance of rights and fulfillment of duties, and finally the practice of virtue.

A legally based ethic concentrates on the minimum requirements—the duties imposed by human laws which protect against the grosser aberrations of personal rights. Licensure, the laws of torts and contracts, prohibitions against discrimination, good Samaritan laws, definitions of death, and the protection of human subjects of experimentation are elements of a legalistic ethic.

At the next level is the ethics of rights and duties which spells out obligations beyond what law defines. Here, benevolence and beneficence take on more than their legal meaning. The ideal of service, of responsiveness to the special needs of those who are ill, some degree of compassion, kindliness, promise-keeping, truth-telling, and non-maleficence and specific obligations like confidentiality and autonomy, are included. How these principles are applied, and conflicts among them resolved in the patient's best interests, are subjects of widely varying interpretation. How sensitively these issues are confronted depends more on the physician's character than his capability at ethical discourse or moral casuistry.

Virtue-based ethics goes beyond these first two levels. We expect the virtuous person to do the right and the good even at the expense of personal sacrifice and legitimate self-interest. Virtue ethics expands the notions of benevolence, beneficence, conscientiousness, compassion, and fidelity well beyond what strict duty might require. It makes some degree of supererogation mandatory because it calls for standards of ethical performance that exceed those prevalent in the rest of society [30].

At each of these three levels there are certain dangers from over-zealous or misguided observance. Legalistic ethical systems tend toward a justification for minimalistic ethics, a narrow definition of benevolence or beneficence, and a contract-minded physician–patient relationship. Duty- and rights-based ethics may be distorted by too strict adherence to the letter of ethical principles without the modulations and nuances the spirit of those principles implies. Virtue-based ethics, being the least specific, can more easily lapse into self-righteous paternalism or an unwelcome over-involvement in the personal life of the patient. Misapplication of any moral system even with good intent converts benevolence into maleficence. The virtuous person might be expected to be more sensitive to these aberrations than someone whose ethics is more deontologically or legally flavored.

The more we yearn for ethical sensitivity the less we lean on rights, duties, rules, and principles, and the more we lean on the character traits of the moral agent. Paradoxically, without rules, rights, and duties specifically spelled out, we cannot predict what form a particular person's expression of virtue will take. In a pluralistic society, we need laws, rules, and principles to assure a dependable minimum level of moral conduct. But that minimal level is insufficient in the complex and often unpredictable circumstances of decision-making, where technical and value desiderata intersect so inextricably.

The virtuous physician does not act from unreasoned, uncritical intuitions about what feels good. His dispositions are ordered in accord with that 'right reason' which both Aristotle and Aquinas considered essential to virtue. Medicine is itself ultimately an exercise of practical wisdom—a right way of acting in difficult and uncertain circumstances for a specific end, i.e., the good of a particular person who is ill. It is when the choice of a right and good action becomes more difficult, when the temptations to self interest are most insistent, when unexpected nuances of good and evil arise and no one is looking, that the differences between an ethics based in virtue and an ethics based in law and/or duty can most clearly be distinguished.

Virtue-based professional ethics distinguishes itself, therefore, less in the avoidance of overtly immoral practices than in avoidance of those at the margin of moral responsibility. Physicians are confronted, in today's morally relaxed climate, with an increasing number of new practices that pit altruism against self interest. Most are not illegal, or, strictly speaking, immoral in a rights- or duty-based ethic. But they are not consistent with the higher levels of moral sensitivity that a virtue-ethics demands. These practices usually involve opportunities for profit from the illness of others, narrowing the concept of service for personal convenience, taking a proprietary attitude with respect to medical knowledge, and placing loyalty to the profession above loyalty to patients.

Under the first heading, we might include such things as investment in and ownership of for-profit hospitals, hospital chains, nursing homes, dialysis units, tie-in arrangements with radiological or laboratory services, escalation of fees for repetitive, high-volume procedures, and lax indications for their use, especially when third party payers 'allow' such charges.

The second heading might include the ever decreasing availability and accessibility of physicians, the diffusion of individual patient responsibility in group practice so that the patient never knows whom he will see or who is on call, the itinerant emergency room physician who works two days and skips three with little commitment to hospital or community, and the growing over-indulgence of physicians in vacations, recreation, and 'self-development.'

The third category might include such things as 'selling one's services' for whatever the market will bear, providing what the market demands and not necessarily what the community needs, patenting new procedures or keeping them secret from potential competitor-colleagues, looking at the investment of time, effort, and capital in a medical education as justification for 'making it back'; or forgetting that medical knowledge is drawn from the cumulative experience of a multitude of patients, clinicians, and investigators.

Under the last category might be included referrals on the basis of friendship and reciprocity rather than skill, resisting consultations and second opinions as affronts to one's competence, placing the interest of the referring physician above those of the patients, looking the other way in the face of incompetence or even dishonesty in one's professional colleagues.

These and many other practices are defended today by sincere physicians and even encouraged in this era of competition, legalism, and self-indulgence. Some can be rationalized even in a deontological ethic. But it would be impossible to envision the physician committed to the virtues assenting to these practices. A virtue-based ethics simply does not fluctuate with what the dominant social mores will tolerate. It must interpret benevolence, beneficence, and responsibility in a way that reduces self interest and enhances altruism. It is the only convincing answer the profession can give to the growing perception clearly manifest in the legal commentaries in the FTC ruling that medicine is nothing more than business and should be regulated as such.

A virtue-based ethic is inherently elitist, in the best sense, because its adherents demand more of themselves than the prevailing morality. It calls forth that extra measure of dedication that has made the best physicians in every era exemplars of what the human spirit can achieve. No matter to what depths a society may fall, virtuous persons will always be the beacons that light the way back to moral sensitivity; virtuous physicians are the beacons that show the way back to moral credibility for the whole profession.

Albert Jonsen, rightly I believe, diagnoses the central paradox in medicine as the tension between self-interest and altruism [15]. No amount of deft juggling of rights, duties, or principles will suffice to resolve that tension. We are all too good at rationalizing what we want to do so that personal gain can be converted from vice to virtue. Only a character formed by the virtues can feel the nausea of such intellectual hypocrisy.

To be sure, the twin themes of self-interest and altruism have been inextricably joined in the history of medicine. There have always been physicians who reject the virtues or, more often, claim them falsely. But, in addition, there have been physicians, more often than the critics of medicine would allow, who have been truly virtuous both in intent and act. They have been, and remain, the leaven of the profession and the hope of all who are ill. They form the seawall that will not be eroded even by the powerful forces of commercialization, bureaucratization, and mechanization inevitable in modern medicine.

We cannot, need not, and indeed must not, wait for a medical analogue of MacIntyre's 'new St. Benedict' to show us the way. There is no new concept of virtue waiting to be discovered that is peculiarly suited to the dilemmas of our own dark age. We must recapture the courage to speak of character, virtue, and perfection in living a good life. We must encourage those who are willing to dedicate themselves to a "higher standard of self effacement" [6].

We need the courage, too, to accept the obvious split in the profession between those who see and feel the altruistic imperatives in medicine, and those who do not. Those who at heart believe that the pursuit of private self-interest serves the public good are very different from those who believe in the restraint of self-interest. We forget that physicians since the beginnings of the profession have subscribed to different values and virtues. We need only recall that the Hippocratic Oath was the Oath of physicians of the Pythagorean school at a time when most Greek physicians followed essentially a craft ethic [7]. A perusal of the Hippocratic Corpus itself, which intersperses ethics and etiquette, will show how differently its treatises deal with fees, the care of incurable patients, and the business aspects of the craft.

The illusion that all physicians share a common devotion to a high-flown set of ethical principles has done damage to medicine by raising expectations some members of the profession could not, or will not, fulfill. Today, we must be more forthright about the differences in values commitment among physicians. Professional codes must be more explicit about the relationships between duties, rights, and virtues. Such explicitness encourages a more honest relationship between physicians and patients and removes the hypocrisy of verbal assent to a general code, to which an individual physician may not really subscribe. Explicitness enables patients to choose among physicians on the basis of their ethical commitments as well as their reputations for technical expertise.

Conceptual clarity will not assure virtuous behavior. Indeed, virtues are usually distorted if they are the subject of too conscious a design. But conceptual clarity will distinguish between motives and provide criteria for judging the moral commitment one can expect from the profession and from its individual members. It can also inspire those whose virtuous inclinations need re-enforcement in the current climate of commercialization of the healing relationship.

To this end the current resurgence of interest in virtue-based ethics is altogether salubrious. Linked to a theory of patient good and a theory of rights and duties, it could provide the needed groundwork for a reconstruction of professional medical ethics as that work matures. Perhaps even more progress can be made if we take Shakespeare's advice in *Hamlet*: "Assume the virtue if you have it not. . . . For use almost can change the stamp of nature."

Bibliography

1. Aquinas, T.: 1875, 'De Virtutibus in Communi', in S. Fretté (ed.), *Opera Omnia*, Louis Virés, Paris, Vol. 14, pp. 178–229.
2. Aquinas, T.: 1964, *Summa Theologica*, Blackfriars, Cambridge, England, Vol. 23.
3. Cicero: 1967, *Moral Obligations*, J. Higginbotham (trans.), University of California Press, Berkeley and Los Angeles.

4. Copleston, F.: 1959, *Aquinas*, Penguin Books, New York.
5. Cornford, F.: 1932, *Before and After Socrates*, Cambridge University Press, Cambridge, England.
6. Cushing, H.: 1929, *Consecratio Medici and Other Papers*, Little, Brown and Co., Boston.
7. Edelstein, L.: 1967, 'The Professional Ethics of the Greek Physician', in O. Temkin (ed.), *Ancient Medicine: Selected Papers of Ludwig Edelstein*, Johns Hopkins University Press, Baltimore.
8. Engel, G.: 1980, 'The Clinical Application of the Biopsychosocial Model', *American Journal of Psychiatry* 137: 2, 535–544.
9. Foot, P.: 1978, *Virtues and Vices*, University of California Press, Berkeley and Los Angeles.
10. Frankena, W.: 1982, 'Beneficence in an Ethics of Virtue', in E. Shelp (ed.), *Beneficence and Health Care*, D. Reidel, Dordrecht, Holland, pp. 63–81.
11. Geach, P.: 1977, *The Virtues*, Cambridge University Press, Cambridge, England.
12. Gould, J.: 1972, *The Development of Plato's Ethics*, Russell and Russell, New York.
13. Guthrie, W.: 1971, *Socrates*, Cambridge University Press, Cambridge, England.
14. Hauerwas, S.: 1981, *A Community of Character*, University of Notre Dame Press, Notre Dame, Indiana.
15. Jonsen, A.: 1983, 'Watching the Doctor', *New England Journal of Medicine* 308: 25, 1531–1535.
16. Jowett, B.: 1953, *The Dialogues of Plato*, Random House, New York.
17. Kenny, A.: 1978, *The Aristotelian Ethics*, Clarendon Press, Oxford, England.
18. Lewis, C.: 1952, *Mere Christianity*, Macmillan Co., New York.
19. MacIntyre, A.: 1981, *After Virtue*, University of Notre Dame Press, Notre Dame, Indiana.
20. Maritain, J.: 1962, *Art and Scholasticism With Other Essays*, Charles Scribner and Sons, New York.
21. May, W.: Personal communication, 'Virtues in a Professional Setting', unpublished.
22. McKeon, R. (ed.): 1968, *The Basic Works of Aristotle*, Random House, New York.
23. Oates, W. (ed.): 1957, *The Stoic and Epicurean Philosophers*, Modern Library, New York.
24. Pellegrino, E.: 1979, 'The Anatomy of Clinical Judgments: Some Notes on Right Reason and Right Action', in H. T. Engelhardt, Jr. *et al.* (eds.), *Clinical Judgment: A Critical Appraisal*, D. Reidel, Dordrecht, Holland, pp. 169–194.
25. Pellegrino, E.: 1979, 'Toward a Reconstruction of Medical Morality: The Primacy of the Act of Profession and the Fact of Illness', *Journal of Medicine and Philosophy*, 4: 1, 32–56.
26. Pellegrino, E.: 1983, 'The Healing Relationship: The Architectonics of Clinical Medicine', in E. Shelp (ed.), *The Clinical Encounter*, D. Reidel,

Dordrecht, Holland, pp. 153–172.

27. Pellegrino, E.: 1983, 'Moral Choice, The Good of the Patient and the Patient Good', in J. Moskop and L. Kopelman (eds.), *Moral Choice and Medical Crisis*, D. Reidel, Dordrecht, Holland.

28. Pellegrino, E.: 1983, '*Scribonius Largus* and the Origins of Medical Humanism', address to the American Osler Society.

29. Pieper, J.: 1966, *The Four Cardinal Virtues*, University of Notre Dame Press, Notre Dame, Indiana.

30. Reader, J.: 1982, 'Beneficence, Supererogation, and Role Duty', in E. Shelp (ed.), *Beneficence and Health Care*, D. Reidel, Dordrecht, Holland, pp. 83–108.

31. Ross, W.: 1959, *Aristotle: A Complete Exposition of His Works and Thoughts*, Meridian Books, New York.

32. Santayana, G.: 1951, *Dominations and Powers: Reflections on Liberty, Society and Government*, Charles Scribner and Sons, New York.

33. Shelp, E. (ed.): 1982, *Beneficence and Health Care*, D. Reidel, Dordrecht, Holland.

34. Shelp, E. (ed.): 1981, *Justice and Health Care*, D. Reidel, Dordrecht, Holland.

35. Sokolowski, R.: 1982, *The Good Faith and Reason*, University of Notre Dame Press, Notre Dame, Indiana.

36. Taylor, A.: 1953, *Socrates: The Man and His Thought*, Doubleday and Co., New York.

37. Versanyi, L.: 1963, *Socratic Humanism*, Yale University Press, New Haven, Connecticut.

38. Von Wright, G.: 1965, *The Varieties of Goodness*, The Humanities Press, New York.

39. Wallace, J.: 1978, *Virtues and Vices*, University of California Press, Berkeley and Los Angeles.

38

The Good Lawyer

Susan Wolf is professor of philosophy at Johns Hopkins University. She is the author of several papers on ethics and metaphysics and has recently completed a book on free will entitled *Freedom Within Reason* (1990). Her essay "Moral Saints" is widely anthologized.

I

Why do the vast majority of practicing lawyers and law students groan when the subject of legal ethics comes up? A few may be expressing an aversion to ethics in general, but I suspect that their number is small. In their nonprofessional lives, lawyers are no less willing to apply ethical considerations to practical decisions than other people; as a group, they may even have a higher than average interest in theoretical discussions of ethics. Others may be indicating their expectation of a quarrel in which they will be put on the defensive. They predict, in other words, that they will be accused of systematically immoral activity, probably by some naive and high-minded philosopher who doesn't understand the realities of law. Members of this group who still hear the speaker out will then be pleasantly surprised in those instances when the typical lawyer is defended as a paragon of virtue and nobility. But I suspect that for many, the normative position of the legal ethicist is truly irrelevant to the disgust they feel. Their objection is not to the answers that the legal ethicist is apt to give to the moral questions he or she raises, but rather to the idea that it is particularly appropriate to raise moral questions in this context at all.

This objection may be expressed more fully once we recognize that the questions legal ethicists seem generally concerned to answer are "How, if at all, can a lawyer be a good person?" and "What, if a lawyer is to be a good

From Susan Wolf, "Ethics, Legal Ethics, and the Ethics of Law" in *The Good Lawyer*, 38–59, ed. David Luban. Copyright 1983, Rowman and Littlefield Publishers. Reprinted by permission of the publisher. *The Good Lawyer* was originally published by Rowman and Allenheld.

person, ought the lawyer to do?" Though some lawyers may "believe that they should conform to 'higher' ethical standards than laypersons"[1] and may therefore find these questions fully in order, it would not be unreasonable for others to wonder why moral scrutiny should be directed so especially at them. We do not ordinarily expect or require people to justify either their choice of career or their conduct within it in specifically moral terms. Excluding professions like slavetrader or concentration camp director, the very existences of which are morally suspect, we allow people to choose their jobs and professions according to their tastes. Once they have chosen their professions, we regard conduct within them to be adequately justified, for the most part, by considerations to the effect that such conduct is necessary in order to do their jobs well.

Thus, practicing lawyers who wince at the suggestion that they should always be considering the morally distasteful consequences that zealous advocacy of clients might entail might be equally repelled by the suggestion that they should regard such advocacy as a sacred trust of the highest moral order. Why isn't it enough that lawyers, like most people, be able to justify their activities by pointing out that these activities are necessary for doing their jobs well? From the point of view of the law student, the source of annoyance may be differently cast. If the central question of legal ethics is "How, if at all, can a lawyer be a good person?" the law student may reply, "I didn't come to law school to learn how to be a good person. I came to learn how to be a good lawyer."

Many considerations might at this point be advanced in an attempt to urge lawyers to develop a higher moral consciousness. But before too readily mounting a high horse, it would be useful to reflect on a fact that contemporary moral philosophy fails generally to appreciate—namely, that the role distinctively moral thought plays in most of our lives is quite small and that much of what we most deeply value in ourselves and those around us has nothing to do with morality at all. We do not typically pass our contemplated actions through a moral filter in developing and maintaining the relationships, interests, and personal commitments that are central to the meaning of most of our lives. If we were to make a habit of applying a moral filter, it is highly questionable whether our abilities to develop and maintain these relationships, interests, and commitments would remain. In other words, there are limits to the degree to which the average person consciously tries to be a good person, and we have reason to question the assumption that we would all be better off if the average person tried more.[2] Thus, it seems permissible for a lawyer or law student, before submitting to the requirement that he or she learn how to be a better person, to demand to be given a reason why being a better person is something he or she must want to learn how to do.

I shall not in this essay provide such a reason, though I leave open the possibility that one may eventually be provided. It is to be hoped, moreover, that many people, and many lawyers among them, do not *require* a reason in order for the question of how they are to be better persons to be of practical as well as theoretical interest, and this is sufficient to justify the continuing pursuit of answers to it. Nonetheless, if legal ethics is to be understood as a subject with which lawyers *as lawyers* are obliged to be concerned, it cannot without further argument be conceived as a subject that is centrally defined by these questions. In this paper I shall offer a different conception of the subject of legal ethics, one that substantially concedes the point of those who object to the aggressive infiltration of moral reasoning into the practice of law. It does not, however, admit what may seem to be a natural corollary to this objection—namely, that no consideration of ethical principles and virtues has any special relevance or any special force to the members of the legal profession.

II

I propose that legal ethics be conceived as a subject that takes as its central focus the study of what ethical principles and virtues are essential, not to being a good person, but rather to being a good lawyer. Though the subject, on this conception, would remain a study of ethical principles and virtues, it will be less natural to see it as a subset of ethics than it will be to construe it as a branch of legal education. It is expected that insofar as anyone is motivated to pursue the field of inquiry and/or to put it to practical use, the chief motivation will be connected to an interest in understanding what it is to become a good lawyer. I assume that this is an interest most law students and practicing lawyers have.

That legal ethics as understood above is a bona fide subject at all remains to be shown, and my attempt to do so will involve some arguments that have substantive, normative conclusions. But my proposal is chiefly a classificatory one, and what can be said in its favor is, at least to some extent, independent of the attractiveness of the normative claims I support. Many of the questions with which legal ethicists are currently most occupied will, on my conception of the subject, be excluded from it. I believe that a good portion of these questions form a more or less coherent subject in their own right, which we may call the ethics of law.

But now my project may seem either trivial or practically sterile. The categorization of ethical questions may appear to be an intellectual distraction, or worse, an evasion of the more difficult and more pressing need actively to grapple with these questions. Why waste time thinking and arguing about how to classify ethical questions when it can be devoted to the more serious task of finding answers to them?

Part of the answer lies in the hope that success in the former task will facilitate the latter. For a classification of questions inevitably presents those questions in a particular light. A good classification may suggest fruitful analogies and may dispel temptations to make unfruitful ones. It may also reveal the possibility of making progress in one isolable area of a subject despite inveterate difficulties that hold up solutions in another.

Acknowledging the instrumental value of a classificatory project, however, should not distract us from recognizing more direct justifications of it. Although it is undoubtedly true that the project of answering the ethical questions is in some sense a more serious task, it seems to me useful and, indeed, only fair to reflect on whose task it is—or rather, to reflect on the fact that the answering of ethical questions is not a single, unified task at all, but a collection of tasks that different people may have different degrees and kinds of obligations to perform. A second, but not a secondary, motive for proposing the classification of questions that I do is that it provides what seems to me to be a fair and reasonable way of allocating responsibility for asking these various questions and subsequently acting on the answers to them.

Finally, if my proposal is accepted, it may be hoped that the two possible benefits just cited may give rise as a corollary to a third. In particular, it may be hoped that by means of this proposal we can achieve a degree of reconciliation between the currently polarized groups who respectively advocate and oppose the project of bringing morality to bear on the profession of law.

III

The proposal itself is, to repeat, that legal ethics be understood as a subject defined by the central question, "What ethical principles and virtues are essential to being a good lawyer?" The very framing of the question appeals to a shared understanding of phrases of the form "a good X." It will be helpful in approaching the question at hand to make some elements of this shared understanding explicit.

It is of fundamental importance to recognize that when one calls an individual "a good X," one is not making a claim equivalent to "that individual is good and it is an X." Rather, one is saying that it is good *as* an X. The "good" is, as it were, logically glued to the "X."[3] Thus, the same object may be both a good clock and a bad paperweight, and the same person may be both a good driver and a bad cook.

At one time, it was common to elaborate on this by suggesting that "good" has a "functional" use—that is, that when one says of something that it is a good X, one is saying that it performs the function of an X well. But aside from the fact that only a very broad interpretation of "function" would allow us to make use of this suggestion in understanding what it is for something to be a good work of art or for someone to be a good marathon runner, this suggestion neglects the fact that the qualities that make an object a good object of its kind may not be restricted to those qualities that are relevant to the performance of the object's function. It is unquestionable, for example, that the function of a clock is to keep time. But one may well hesitate before calling even the most accurate timepiece a good clock if, for example, it is inordinately ugly or expensive or it ticks too loudly. In addition to the primary function or purpose for which objects of a certain kind or roles in a society are designed, there may be a context of other interests and concerns into which these objects and roles must be fit. The ability to cohere with or even to contribute to the satisfaction of these background interests and concerns may be relevant to whether an object is a good object of its kind despite the fact that these interests and concerns do not constitute any part of the object's raison d'etre.

The criteria and standards we use to determine whether an object is a good object of its kind may also vary with the context in which the question arises. Depending on the comparison class, the degree of excellence necessary to qualify say, as a good writer will vary considerably. The criteria of excellence may vary, moreover, according to the purpose for which the question of evaluation is raised. In one conversation we may unhesitantly admit that John McEnroe is a very good athlete, while in another we recommend the tennis coach who teaches his or her charges that a good athlete must be a good sport. While the meaning of "a good X" may thus be said to vary with the context in which the phrase is being used, however, it would be wrong to attribute any variation in criteria or standards to a difference in the meaning of that phrase. A debate about whether a good father is one who brings up his children strictly is not a discussion about the meaning of the phrase "a good father"—it is a substantive disagreement about how and to whom a shared concept should properly be applied.

For our purposes, it is of a particular interest to focus on those expressions in which "good" is used to qualify a distinctively human role and to note especially how widely the moral connotations of such expressions vary. The qualities involved in being a good cook, a good gardener, or a good violinist seem virtually independent of any qualities of significant moral import, whereas the characteristics that determine whether a person is a good citizen, a good neighbor, or a good friend overlap extensively with the qualities that figure into a moral evaluation of the person as a whole. A similarly wide spectrum of moral connotations is covered by the range of professional ideals. An inquiry into whether someone is a good artist, chemist or typist will typically reveal nothing about a person's moral character or his or her obedience to moral principles. The examination of traits necessary for determining whether a person is a good rabbi, teacher, or politician, on the other hand, is apt to reveal quite a lot.

Sharp lines cannot be drawn between those professional ideals that essentially involve moral qualities and those ideals that do not. Moreover, sharp lines cannot be drawn between those qualities that *are* moral qualities and those that are not. But implicit in my proposal for a conception of legal ethics is an expression of my conviction that the professional ideal of a lawyer most naturally is and, in any case, ought to be understood as an ideal with substantial moral content. In other words, in this respect, being a good lawyer is more like being a good teacher than it is like being a good artist.

It is natural to expect that the moral content of a professional ideal will increase in accordance with the degree to which the profession involves interaction with other people and that it will become more explicit as the opportunities and temptations to engage in immoral activities in one's professional life expand. This in turn will be related to such considerations as whether the profession involves relationships with clients, customers, and the like, and whether these client-type relationships, when they exist, substantially define the scope of the professional's (intraprofessional) responsibility. Thus, the range of professions whose professional ideals have little or no moral content will include not only those professions that can be carried on with little or no human interaction but also those professions in which the primary forms of interaction provide self-interested reasons for treating people in morally acceptable ways.

A plumber or a shoemaker, for example, whose success depends on the satisfaction of his or her customers will be naturally motivated to treat customers fairly by honoring commitments to them and charging reasonable prices. Since his or her professional activities have an insignificant effect on people outside of these customer relationships and since the customers can competently evaluate the quality of the services provided, moral questions simply need not arise in determining which plumbers are good plumbers or which shoemakers are good shoemakers. But it is not so clear that the test of a good teacher rests solely on the opinions of his or her students or that the test of a good politician consists in the ability to get reelected. In part, this is because the people most directly served in these cases may not themselves be able to evaluate the quality of the service. More interestingly, it may be thought that members of these professions take on professional responsibilities that extend beyond the scope of the interests held by the people most directly served. The social roles of the members of the professions are more complex than the roles of the members of the professions earlier mentioned. The social roles of lawyers are also complex. In order to form a conception of what a good lawyer would be, we must begin with some shared understanding of what these social roles are.

IV

It is important to distinguish between the social roles of the individual lawyer and the social roles of the law or of the legal system as a whole. The law is set up to resolve disputes, to protect the rights and interests of persons and groups against unjust manipulation and interference by others, and to foster substantive social goals. Since ours is an adversary system, however, it would be wrong to identify the purposes of the law with the purposes of the lawyer. The lawyer must rather direct the use of his or her professional expertise to the narrower goals of promoting and protecting the interests of the individuals and groups whom he or she is contracted or otherwise assigned to help and protect. The categories of ways in which lawyers as lawyers carry out their roles include advising and informing clients of the scope and limits of the law, preventing and defending clients against unlawful interference or harm imposed by others, acting as the client's agent in negotiations, and enabling clients to gain whatever benefits might be acquired by straightforward appeal to existing law. These methods in turn require the lawyer to engage in more concrete specialized activities: filing suits, examining witnesses, researching, drafting documents.

This portrayal of the lawyer's roles and functions is undoubtedly somewhat simplistic and incomplete. But it is concrete and accurate enough in its broad outlines to provide us with a rough basis on which to begin to develop a conception of what it is to be a good lawyer. As in other cases, where understanding what it is to be a good X falls out rather naturally from a full understanding of what it is to be an X, understanding what it is to be a good lawyer is in large part a matter of understanding what a lawyer is. A good lawyer is simply someone who is good *as* a lawyer—who does whatever a lawyer is supposed to do *well*. In light of the above portrayal of the lawyer, then, much of our answer to the question "What virtues, talents, and skills are essential to being a good lawyer?" will be relatively straightforward. A good lawyer is one who is knowledgeable in the law, creative and thorough in his or her ability to apply it, good at dealing with clients and understanding their interests and situations, and skillful in negotiating with other parties and in speaking before judges and juries. A good lawyer is careful and efficient in researching the law, in drawing up patents, wills, and contracts.

The question that most interests us, of course, is "What, if any, *moral* virtues, talents and skills are involved in being a good lawyer?" It should be acknowledged at the outset that in asking this question we find ourselves in an area neither of pure fact nor of pure value, but rather in that murky conceptual space where the distinction between fact and value cannot be clearly maintained. As a result, the process of trying to answer this question will be neither pure discovery, for which we can appeal to empirical research and to the logical analysis of the meanings of our terms, nor pure practical choice, for which we can tally the normative pros and cons and simply decide what answer to adopt.

Insofar as the structure of our legal system is an established fact and not in our immediate power to change, the development of a conception of a good lawyer will be substantially constrained by the roles to which, according to this system, the lawyer is assigned. It would be incoherent to offer a conception of the good lawyer whose realization would either undermine the legal system or ensure the lawyer's professional demise. On the other hand, accepting the basic structure of our present legal system still leaves us with some room to move. There is some range to the kinds of models we can choose to make ideals and which it is in our power, as writers and teachers, as lawyers and philosophers, to encourage or condemn.

The conception of the good lawyer that I will defend is a familiar and relatively conservative one. It is a conception that I think is supported by both factual and normative considerations. That is, it seems to me that this conception is the most natural and straightforward conception to form. In addition, it seems to me to be a morally better conception than any existing alternative.

This conception of the good lawyer can most easily be characterized as the conjunction of two ordered claims, which jointly rely on seeing the practice of law as consisting fundamentally of the provision of a specifiable set of *means* for the protection and advancement of the ends and interests of particular persons and groups. In this context, I suggest that:

(i) The intraprofessional moral requirements of a good lawyer consist in ensuring the full utilization of these means on behalf of the client subject to the moral constraints that attach directly to these means, and

(ii) The moral constraints that attach directly to these means are simply the ordinary moral constraints that are generally recognized to attach directly to any activity in the absence of special exception.

The first claim aims at once to establish the lawyer's positive professional responsibility to the client and to delineate a range within which moral considerations may qualify how far this responsibility extends. The second claim explains, in general terms, what these moral considerations in fact require—in other words, it states what the intraprofessional moral qualifications on a lawyer's responsibility to a client are.

Implicit in this conception of the good lawyer is a commitment to taking seriously the distinction between how the law is used and what it is used for. For, according to (i), a lawyer is professionally responsible for using the law in morally acceptable ways but not responsible for using the law to promote morally acceptable ends.[4] Except in special circumstances, a good lawyer has no professional obligation, on the one hand, to take on or retain a client with legal interests of which he or she cannot morally approve, but on the other hand, there is no professional obligation to refuse or dismiss a client under these conditions.[5] While retaining a client, a lawyer is obliged to make whatever legal claims the law explicitly and straightforwardly permits that can be expected to foster that client's legal interests. But (i) allows, and (ii) insists, that this obligation is qualified not only by legal but by certain moral constraints as well. Thus it is to be understood as following from (ii) that the lawyer cannot make claims on behalf of a client that involve a perversion or distortion of the law. Moreover, the lawyer must treat all persons with whom he or she professionally interacts justly and honestly, with dignity and respect.

This means that a good lawyer must, for example, invoke the statute of limitations when it applies in a way that promotes the achievement of a client's goals,[6] but must refrain from filing frivolous claims to harass a client's foes and from initiating proceedings as a diversionary tactic to forestall legal action to which the client is (legitimately) subject. A good lawyer must discredit hostile witnesses who are clearly discreditable by, for example, calling attention to legally accessible information about the witness's history, but cannot ridicule or humiliate someone on the witness stand in ways that would be generally recognized as morally unacceptable. A good lawyer cannot take unfair advantage of the ignorance or vulnerability either of the client or of parties hostile to the client. But what counts as "unfair advantage" is a difficult matter to determine and one that is to some extent relative to what is generally understood and expected as common legal practice.

These suggestions are admittedly and intentionally vague and leave room within their bounds for considerable controversy. If this conception of the lawyer's professional ideal is to be effective in shaping and evaluating lawyers' actual behavior, many issues will have to be resolved and many phrases clarified. What counts, for example, as "straightforward appeal" to the law as opposed to a distortion or perversion of it? When is a witness "clearly discreditable"? Investigation of such questions can best be carried on in conjunction with and by reference to detailed study of concrete examples. But even in this vague form, the conception just sketched can be meaningfully contrasted and compared with other possible conceptions of the lawyer's professional ideal. In particular, it is clear that with respect to moral content, this conception falls between the vision of a good lawyer as one who makes the promotion of truth and justice the direct overriding aim of his or her professional endeavors and the alternative of one who uses moral blinders to screen out all commitments and constraints other than devotion to fostering a client's self-declared interests.

Whether this conception of the good lawyer is, as I believe, the most natural and straightforward conception is presumably a largely empirical matter. But it is a consideration in support of this claim that this conception makes the lawyer's professional ideal analogous to the professional ideals we associate with professions that, like the legal profession, involve client-like relationships in a context of competition. Let me make this point clearer by a brief discussion of two other professions, teaching and advertising.

While it is to be hoped that a good teacher will emphasize those aspects of the subjects that he or she takes to be of greatest educational value, the teacher is also responsible for fostering the more concrete education-related goals that students are likely to have. Thus, for example, a good high school teacher may, in a certain context, be expected to train students in ways that will help them do well on the SATs and to write recommendations that will increase their chances of getting into the colleges of their choice. But clearly, the goals that it is a teacher's responsibility to help students achieve must be relative to the students' own abilities and efforts. A teacher who managed to help students achieve all their educational goals by supplying them with advance stolen copies of the aptitude tests or by lying in his or her evaluation of their intellectual talents would not be a good teacher.

Similarly, an advertiser, with a job of presenting the attractions of a client's product, has a responsibility to promote a client's goals (increasing sales, enhancing public image) within certain limits. A good advertiser is one who is creative and effective in discovering and presenting the attractions of the product. But the advertiser's responsibilities to the client, like those of a teacher to students, are constrained by ordinary responsibilities to the larger community whom these activities affect. In other words, a good advertiser cannot make false claims attributing virtues to a product that the product does not have and cannot appeal to racist or sexist sentiments in creating a context that makes the product seem attractive.

A good teacher or a good advertiser is one who does the best (teaching or advertising) job possible *with the material he or she has to work with*. A person who does a "better" job than this, if doing so involves behavior that in non-professional contexts would be generally recognized as immoral, is not better at his or her profession, just more unscrupulous. In the absence of special arguments to the contrary, it seems natural to interpret the lawyer's responsibilities in the same way.

The analogy between lawyers, on the one hand, and teachers or advertisers, on the other, brings out the distinctness of the goals and responsibilities of the professional from the goals and responsibilities of the client whom the professional is assigned or contracted to serve. The good lawyer, like the good teacher or advertiser, gives the client the best professional care possible subject to the constraints of ordinary morality that apply inside, as well as outside, the context of the job. The professional excellence of the professional is to be judged by the quality of the professional care given the client, and not by the quality of the client to whom it is given.

In light of this, we can better see why the conception of the good lawyer that takes the lawyer's professional ideal to be analogous to the ideals of teaching and advertising seems to fall between the alternative conceptions of a good lawyer that I earlier mentioned. For, like the conception of the good lawyer as an Arm of Society, solely, and directly dedicated to the promotion of truth and justice, this conception assigns responsibilities to the lawyer that extend beyond the interests of the client to the larger range of individuals whom his or her professional activities necessarily affect. But, like the conception of the good lawyer as the Arm of the Client, unconditionally devoted to promoting and protecting the client's interests, this conception denied that the lawyer is professionally responsible for the moral quality of the interests that the lawyer, in contracting with a client, takes on the explicit and special responsibility to promote.

A good teacher is no worse a teacher for teaching stupid, lazy students; a good advertiser no worse an advertiser for promoting inferior products. Similarly, a good lawyer is no worse a lawyer for representing clients who are legally culpable or for defending clients who are morally but not legally guilty of performing any wrong. Like the good teacher and the good advertiser, the good lawyer must do the best he or she can for whatever client he or she has. But "the best he or she can" will be limited by the legitimacy of the client's interests. In other words, the good lawyer must say what there *is* to be said in favor of the client and bring out what there *is* to be brought out on the client's behalf, but he or she cannot make claims on behalf of the client that do not correspond to the facts or suppress or thwart opponents' efforts to discover and reveal what there is to be said on the other side.

By now my image of the kind of person most aptly called "a good lawyer" may seem all too clearly drawn, and it may even be granted that this image is the most natural and intuitive one to associate with that phrase. But the naturalness of a conception is not a sufficient justification for encouraging it. If we have moral reasons to prefer an alternative conception of a good lawyer, we must consider departing from our linguistic intuitions and try to revise our conception in the direction of what is morally more favorable.

The alternative conceptions of the good lawyer that I have already suggested, however, do not seem to me morally favorable. Or rather, the conception of the good lawyer as the Arm of Society does not seem to be a fully coherent alternative at all, while the conception of the good lawyer as the Arm of the Client seems to be a morally worse conception. These alternative conceptions are admittedly extremes between which more moderate and more plausible conceptions may lie. But the detailed examination and comparison of these other alternatives will be more easily undertaken after some shared understanding of the general methods and types of arguments appropriate to these tasks has been reached. A comparison between the ideal I am advocating and the two simple but extreme alternatives I have named will most clearly and concisely illustrate these general methods and types of argument.

The conception of the good lawyer as an Arm of Society seems less than fully coherent because it is incompatible with the fact that the legal profession essentially involves clients. A client is a person whose interests the professional is obliged specifically to serve, and to serve in virtue of the fact that he or she *is* the professional's client. If lawyers were to model their professional selves according to an ideal that consistently made the promotion of truth and justice the direct, overriding aim, it would make no sense for persons to contract the services of a lawyer. If the person in question had truth and justice on his or her side, the lawyer would, according to this model, be obliged to help even without being contracted to do so, and if the person did not have truth and justice on his or her side, no contract could oblige the lawyer to act on the person's behalf.

This is not to say that an occasional individual lawyer cannot make truth and justice his or her sole, direct, and overriding aims and survive in this profession. A commitment to the ruthless defense of an appropriately selected group of clients and/or a willingness to subtly undermine the legal interests of clients with less noble legal goals may allow an individual lawyer to achieve this ideal. But in doing so, he or she would not be achieving a professional ideal, an ideal of the lawyer *as* lawyer. On the contrary, this lawyer would be achieving an ideal that, were it generally adopted by other members of the profession, would undermine the profession itself.[7]

Of course, it is a contingent fact that our legal system assigns lawyers a role that essentially involves client relationships. A radically different legal system could be constructed whose practitioners would operate very differently. Similarly, it is a contingent fact that shoemakers are expected to make and repair shoes according to the wishes of the customer. In a different society, shoemakers could be expected to make shoes that, independent of customers' tastes and preferences, most effectively protected people's feet. But as things stand now, a shoemaker who returned a customer's sling-backed, high-heeled sandals with lowered heels and strengthened arch supports, on the grounds that they will be better for her feet, would not thereby be established as a good shoemaker. And as things stand now, a lawyer who ignored which member of a given dispute happened to be paying him, and instead promoted whichever party was most morally deserving, would not thereby prove to be a good lawyer.

The conception of the good lawyer as an Arm of the Client, whose advocacy is so zealous as to ignore normal moral requirements to all other parties, is not similarly incoherent. That is, the adoption of this conception is logically compatible with the structure of our present legal system. From a moral point of view, however, it seems that we have every reason to prefer the conception of the good lawyer that I have been advocating to this alternative. For the difference between these conceptions lies solely in the fact that the latter conception of the lawyer's professional responsibility requires the good lawyer to ignore prima facie moral requirements that the former conception does not. In the absence of special argument, this just means that a good lawyer is more likely to be immoral on the latter conception than on the former. For the decision to exclude a moral constraint from a professional ideal does not constitute an exemption from that constraint. The moral constraint still applies to the person who *is* a lawyer; it simply has no bearing on our evaluation of this person's quality *as* a lawyer. If being a good lawyer requires a person to ignore a prima facie moral constraint, what follows, in the absence of special argument, is that being a good lawyer requires immorality.

Of course, it is sometimes suggested that there *is* a special argument, which mitigates this conclusion and gives us a moral reason to adopt the Arm of the Client conception. More specifically, it is suggested that our legal system may better accomplish its goals if lawyers act according to this conception than if lawyers emulate the model that I earlier elaborated. Since the goals of the legal system are important moral goals, this would provide an important moral reason to favor the Arm of the Client conception. But it is important to note that even if this suggestion were convincingly supported, the moral reason it would provide would not necessarily be definitive. For whether the gain in moral consequences that would result from adopting the Arm of the Client conception of the good lawyer is sufficient to outweigh or, differently, remove the loss in obedience to ordinary moral requirements is a matter of considerable controversy. In other words, if this suggestion were convincingly supported, what conception of the good lawyer to adopt would become a real moral dilemma. However, I have never seen convincing support for this suggestion and have no reason to believe that the suggested claims are true.[8]

As ethicists, our search for the best conception of the good lawyer is a search for a conception that best meets two objectives. First, it must offer a model for lawyers that allows them to fulfill the role to which the present legal system assigns them in a way that maximally contributes to the achievement of the goals for which that system is designed. Second, it must minimize the tensions between the virtues and principles lawyers must strive to achieve in their aspiration for professional excellence and the virtues and principles they must try to achieve to be morally admirable members of the human community. The conception of the good lawyer that I have been advocating better meets these joint objectives than the two alternatives I have discussed. In the absence of other alternatives, this seems to be the best conception of the good lawyer that we have.

V

Reaching a moral consensus about the best conception of the good lawyer, however, is not sufficient to put all ethical questions about the legal profession to rest. We can most suggestively even if obscurely characterize the questions that remain as those that give rise to doubts as to whether the best conception of the good lawyer we have—or even the best conception of the good lawyer we *can* have—is really good enough.

In Sections I and II, I stressed the distinction between a professional ideal and a personal one, or, to put it another way, the distinction between a conception of a person who is good at his or her profession and a conception of a good person who is a member of a specific profession. This distinction not only allows us to speak of professional ideals whose realizations are totally independent of the realizations of personal ideals with any moral content; it also allows us to speak of professional ideals that are explicitly incompatible with any morally acceptable personal ideal. Thus, for example, we can coherently discuss what it would be for someone to be a good thief—we can discuss, that is, what it would be to be good *as* a thief, what would constitute stealing *well*. Being a good thief, however, may be incompatible with being a good person.

That a professional ideal contains explicitly moral features provides no guarantee that a person who achieves this ideal lives a morally praiseworthy or even a morally acceptable life. Perhaps this is obvious since one's professional life is, after all, only a part of one's whole life, and a person who admirably fulfills his or her role as a member of even the noblest of professions may nonetheless fail to meet minimal moral standards as a parent or a neighbor or a friend. But that a professional ideal contains explicitly moral features does not even guarantee that the realization of that ideal is compatible with living a morally acceptable life. We can even imagine including explicitly moral features in a conception of a good thief. We might, for example, take it to be a feature of a good thief that he or she is able, with no loss of profit or safety, to minimize the incidental harms to the victims that result from stealing property he or she can use.

That the conception of a good lawyer I have been advocating has substantial moral content, then, provides no guarantee that a good lawyer will be or even can be a good person. It is possible that a lawyer who wants to be a good person may on occasion feel called upon to act in explicit defiance of professional ideals. There do not seem to be any conceptual tensions, as there are in the case of the good thief, between the conception of the good lawyer that has been advocated above and ordinary conceptions of what is required in order to be a good person. But empirical considerations suggest that there may be practical tensions. It is well known that lawyers are often called upon to represent clients whose goals and purposes in contracting with a lawyer are morally suspect. Although it is no part of the lawyer's intraprofessional moral responsibilities to refrain from zealously defending such clients—indeed, intraprofessional responsibilities require that if a lawyer does take them as clients, he or she must zealously defend them—the lawyer who becomes a zealous advocate of such clients inevitably becomes morally tainted. Although a zealous defense of immoral clients who want to use the law to achieve immoral (but legal) goals requires no compromise of the lawyer's professional principles, it may force the lawyer to compromise his or her personal moral integrity.

It would be unrealistic, moreover, not to consider the effects on one's character that, while in no way required by the realization of the lawyer's professional ideal, are likely to result from the process of aspiring to achieve that ideal. The environment in which lawyers or would-be-lawyers must place themselves and the training they must undergo may encourage them habitually to block out certain kinds of moral considerations or to develop certain patterns of reasoning that are likely to diminish their sensitivity to moral issues or their ability to recognize their full moral force.[9] Thus, even if it is possible for someone to be both a good lawyer and a good person, there may be identifiable risks of specific ways in which someone may fail to achieve or be diverted from the aspirations to achieve these goals.

These considerations raise difficult questions about the morality of being a lawyer, even about the morality of being or trying to be a good lawyer with all the moral as well as nonmoral virtues and commitments to moral principles that being a good lawyer entails. But it is important to notice who are most likely to be interested in these questions, and in what contexts and for what reasons these questions are most likely to be brought to bear.

Most obviously and most urgently, some of these questions will arise for the practicing lawyer who, faced with a recognizably morally difficult situation, must make a more or less immediate decision about what to do. For example, the goals of a client that a lawyer is already representing may come to seem morally abhorrent in circumstances in which withdrawal from the case would seriously compromise the client's ability to secure adequate legal counsel or defense. Alternatively, the client's goals may be unobjectionable in themselves, but the best legal argument for advancing these goals might require the lawyer to urge an interpretation or change in the law that would have bad social consequences. A host of situations can be imagined in which the dictates of a lawyer's professional responsibilities are clear, but with respect to which the question remains whether it is morally good or even morally permissible for the lawyer to follow these dictates. In such situations, a lawyer must simply (or, more often, not so simply) take stock of his or her commitments to the profession and to nonprofessional values and principles, and decide.

The expectation of such situations and retrospective reflection on them will in addition raise questions about the moral desirability of being a (good) lawyer for well-meaning persons who are wondering whether to become lawyers and to those who already are lawyers and are wondering whether to remain so. After all, these are situations of painful conflict that anyone might have reason to want to minimize or avoid. But the prospect of becoming insensitive to or dismissive of moral dilemmas may be at least as disturbing as the prospect of painfully experiencing them. Thus members of these groups will also have reason to be concerned about the risks to their character and values that the legal professional environment inherently contains. Furthermore, some persons may want their profession not only to be compatible with their deepest commitments and values, but also partially to express them. For these persons, that the ends lawyers promote are often determined not by themselves but by their clients may be a reason to prefer some other profession to the practice of law.

The preceding paragraphs highlight a few of the issues that raise difficult ethical questions for persons who at once want to live morally acceptable or admirable lives and want to enter into or maintain a commitment to the profession of law. These questions are undeniably important ones—more specifically they are undeniably important *to* lawyers and would-be lawyers insofar as they care about living morally decent or praiseworthy lives. But it would be a mistake to think that these questions are to be asked or answered by lawyers *as lawyers*, that these questions arise from within, so to speak, the lawyer's point of view. On the contrary, the forcefulness and indeed the very intelligibility of these questions rely on an appreciation of the fact that persons who are lawyers are not *just* lawyers, but human beings with a range of moral and personal commitments and values into which their professional commitments and values must be made, as comfortably as possible, to fit. In other words, these questions are not intraprofessional questions, but personal ones of a straightforwardly ethical sort. They are questions that persons who are lawyers may have to confront, but they are not questions of legal ethics as I have proposed to define it.

In addition to and in part because of the interest that persons who are or would be lawyers might have in answering these questions, socially concerned members of society at large will have reason to care about them. For insofar as our society allows and makes use of the existence of a legal system, we condone and rely on the existence of practicing lawyers. If the legal system is structured in ways that discourage morally upright people from entering the profession of law and that tend to corrupt the people who do choose to enter it, then we have reason to try to alter that system in ways that alleviate these defects.

Perhaps the tendency for members of the legal profession to develop morally unattractive traits of character may be lessened by departing from the adversary system in certain areas of legal practice. Perhaps a different method of assigning lawyers to clients may reduce the intrapersonal conflicts that lawyers are likely to face, either by further distinguishing the goals of the lawyer from the goals of the client or by increasing the lawyer's opportunity to choose cases or withdraw from them on the basis of moral scruples. The establishment of nonlegal methods for resolving certain kinds of disputes or for negotiating certain kinds of agreements, or a revision in the ways in which legal fees are set, may alleviate some of the moral discomfort that makes people reluctant to identify themselves with the legal profession. Of course, in contemplating these changes, the personal moral protection of lawyers will have to be recognized as one among several goals. Our interest in the overall effectiveness of the legal system and our interest in the social consequences for nonlegal sectors of society will also have to be weighed in the balance.

The ethical assessment of our present legal system and the comparison in ethical terms between that system and other possible systems will again undoubtedly be of special interest to some lawyers, in part because they *are* lawyers. Moreover, because there is a kind of familiarity with the workings of the present legal system that only lawyers can have, the contribution of lawyers to this project will be uniquely and especially valuable. But again, this project ought not to be conceived as an intraprofessional project, but rather as a social one. For it is as citizens with an interest in maintaining or improving the moral quality of society that we have reason to engage in this project, and it is only by conscientious attention to the benefits and harms that various legal systems might have to all sectors of society that this project can successfully be completed.

VI

The preceding two sections will, I hope, make it easier to understand and evaluate the suggestion with which this paper began—the suggestion, that is, that we distinguish one set of questions, which may be understood to comprise the subject of legal ethics, from other questions, which also concern relationships between ethics and the law. Legal ethics, I suggested, should focus on the development of the best conception of a good lawyer. That is, it should aim to clarify and encourage the most morally desirable conception of the lawyer's professional responsibilities that is compatible with the social roles and functions that, according to our present legal system, the lawyer is required or expected to fulfill. But I pointed out that even the best conception of a good lawyer may not be morally good enough. On the one hand, it may not be good enough for an individual lawyer or would-be lawyer as a model with which to identify or as an ideal to which one can and wants to aspire. On the other hand, it may not be good enough for our society as an embodiment of values that will promote and preserve the moral quality of the relationships and lives of its citizens. Thus, even if we solve the problems of legal ethics, a variety of ethical questions would remain. Those that confront individuals who must choose whether to commit themselves or maintain a commitment to the values of the legal profession fall into the domain of personal ethics proper. Those that confront the society that must choose whether and, if so, how to revise its legal system comprise a topic within social ethics that we might call the ethics of law.

Obviously, the relationships among these three categories and among individual questions within them will be numerous. If the roughly sketched conception of the good lawyer advocated in Section IV seems as obviously correct to others as it does to me, then the subject of legal ethics, which the discussion of Section IV was intended to exemplify, may prove the least philosophically difficult or interesting category of the three. In any case, answers to questions in one category will inform and be informed by answers to questions in the others. These categories need not be exclusive, and the proper classification of some questions and issues may be either indeterminate or pointless to determine. In light of the considerable interdependence among the three categories, the usefulness of my classificatory proposal may seem particularly dubious. As a final task, let me recall and slightly elaborate on what can be said on its behalf.

First, it is always in the interest of intellectual clarity to explicitly distinguish two questions that are otherwise frequently confused. And it seems to me that the two questions that my proposal is at pains to distinguish *are* frequently confused—namely, "What does it take for a person to be a good lawyer?" and "What does it take for a lawyer to be a good person?" Distinguishing these questions is not meant to imply that their answers are totally unrelated, nor should it suggest that these questions taken separately are non-controversial or easy to answer. Nonetheless, some controversies result from misunderstanding what question is being debated, and in some cases, finding a clear characterization of one's problem is a large step toward solving it.

Some readers may have already noticed a similarity between the conception of a good lawyer advocated in Section IV and the professional ideal that seems to underlie a noncynical reading of the ABA's Code of Professional Responsibility.[10] A plausible hypothesis that explains this coincidence is that the developers of the code took their task to be just the task that I have suggested for legal ethics. That is, their concern was to answer the question "What ethical responsibilities and virtues are relevant to determining one's quality as a *lawyer*?" or "What ethical features should be included in a lawyer's *professional* ideal?"

Critics of the code, however, often raise objections that suggest that they understand the point of the code differently. Thinking that the code is to be regarded as an answer to the question, "What is ethically required for a lawyer to be a good (or a morally acceptable) person?" some people object that the developers of the code have accepted a project for which they have no authority. Others who support the idea of this project are unhappy with the way it has been carried out. That is, they believe that the code's substantive moral conclusions are either too weak or completely misdirected. Distinguishing the purposes for which the code is designed from the goals at which it may be mistakenly thought to aim may allow us to partially reinterpret what appeared to be a controversy as instead a comment on the code's limited scope and implications, which the code's defenders as well as its critics may be willing to accept. The controversial and divisive issues that remain will then be given a new formulation that, if it does not directly aid the solution, will at least clarify the problems in need of being solved.

In addition to the advancement of intellectual clarity, separating the moral questions that concern the legal profession into the categories I have suggested may lead to a kind of moral clarity. That is, it may help us understand who is responsible for asking and acting on the answers to these moral questions, and this would enable us to form fairer judgments of who is to be praised or blamed for giving or failing to give these questions consideration. Intraprofessional responsibilities are responsibilities a person takes on in identifying his or herself as a member of a given profession. This professional status justifies us in expecting a person to fulfill those responsibilities and in criticizing any professional who does not. We can justly require a member of any given profession to be aware of these intraprofessional responsibilities and to take whatever steps are necessary to fulfill them.

Insofar as we can reasonably include the adherence to certain moral principles and the cultivation of certain moral virtues in our conception of a lawyer's intraprofessional responsibilities, then the lawyer's professional status justifies us in expecting lawyers to engage in certain kinds of moral behavior. It seems, moreover, that we can expect the institutions that are importantly connected to the legal profession, such as law schools and bar associations, to make explicit efforts to develop an adequate conception of lawyers' intraprofessional responsibilities and to do what they can to make sure that the members of the legal profession fulfill them. In other words, because, in the case of lawyers, some moral responsibilities are intraprofessional responsibilities, we have special reason to expect lawyers *as lawyers* to live up to certain kinds of moral standards.

The classificatory proposal I am making, however, suggests that not all moral questions *about* a profession are intraprofessional questions. In particular, questions concerning the compatibility of being a good person with being a lawyer, or with being a good lawyer, are not questions one asks as a lawyer, but rather as a person who must confront the problems of integrating one's professional life with one's personal ideals. Insofar as a lawyer has a moral obligation to grapple with these problems—to make sure, for example, that personal ideals meet morally acceptable standards and that the actions comprising professional life are sufficiently constrained by these ideals—it is an obligation that each of us has in deciding whether and how much to identify ourselves with a profession and its associated ideals. Questions concerning the moral evaluation of the legal system as a whole and of the need, if need there be, of altering that system are likewise, according to my proposal, not intraprofessional questions but social ones. They are among the questions that we as citizens must ask if we are to make and maintain our society as one in which the principles of justice are satisfied and morally important goals are achieved.

It may be that we as individuals all have rather stringent obligations to try to be good persons, and that those of us who have chosen to become lawyers must, by the nature of that profession, face more difficult challenges in the fulfillment of these obligations than others. It may be, moreover, that we as citizens all have obligations to devote some attention and energy toward maintaining and/or improving the moral quality of our society's life. If so, then the widespread concern about the social effects of our present legal system gives us reason to hope, perhaps even to insist, that some lawyers direct their share of obligatory attention and energy to the specific issues about which they have special expertise and authority. But whatever such obligations lawyers have, they have them not because they are lawyers but for reasons more general than that. If we conclude that lawyers do have significant obligations of these kinds, we must be prepared to acknowledge corresponding obligations that fall upon nonlawyers as well.

If the responsibilities for evaluating and, if need be, reforming our legal system are shared by lawyers and nonlawyers alike, then so are the responsibilities for condoning that system and the institutions associated with it. Insofar as we choose to allow the present system to continue without basic structural changes and insofar as we utilize, directly and indirectly, the services with which that system provides us, we implicitly condone the present legal system. If we do condone it, then it seems to me unfair to condemn individuals for taking on the professional role that is essential to the system's continued existence. That is, it seems unfair to condemn lawyers for being lawyers, with all the moral tensions that the legal profession, if not inevitably, at least predictably, entails. If we allow people to become lawyers, we must allow them to become good lawyers—that is, we cannot condemn them for acting in ways that the ideals of the profession must encourage.

The division of ethical questions concerning the law that my proposed classification suggests thus encourages a corresponding division of moral labor. It encourages us to allocate responsibility for answering and acting on the answers to these questions in a particular way. We can expect lawyers *as lawyers* to try to develop the best intraprofessional ethical standards that can plausibly be attributed to their profession, and we can blame the individual lawyers *as individual lawyers* if they fail to live up to these standards. Moreover, since it is perhaps inevitable that even the best intraprofessional legal standards will on rare occasions conflict with fundamental moral requirements, we can expect individuals who are lawyers *as persons* to keep their professional standards in moral perspective—that is, we can expect them to do this to the extent that we expect analogous behavior on the part of others as well. But if we are unhappy with the intraprofessional standards themselves, once they are admitted to be the best standards that the profession can have, then our problem is not an intraprofessional or a personal one but a metaprofessional and social one. We must blame, not the individual lawyers, but the system that assigns them their role and the society that allows or even promotes the continued existence of that system.

It seems that we do have reason to be unhappy with the lawyer's intraprofessional standards. There are significant moral tensions between the values a person must uphold if he or she wants to excel as a lawyer and the values a person with any of a variety of morally praiseworthy ideals may want his or her life to reflect. These tensions discourage some people from entering and remaining in the legal profession; they deflect others who do become lawyers from the pursuit of some morally desirable goals; and they form a basis for a public image that portrays lawyers generally as morally suspect. If one takes seriously the classificatory proposal of this paper, however, one will be inclined to see this less as a problem of professional ethics and more as a social problem about which we all have equal reason to be concerned and equal responsibility to try to alleviate.

Thus my proposal suggests that there are several different kinds of ethical tensions inextricably connected to the legal profession and that, associated with these different kinds of tensions, are different kinds of responsibility and culpability. As a third and final reason for adopting this proposal, it is hoped that the recognition of these differences will reduce the current polarization of parties who do and parties who do not want to participate in discussions of what is currently called legal ethics. Those who object to the idea of singling out lawyers and would-be lawyers for special moral scrutiny may yet acknowledge that the professional scrutiny to which they are more appropriately subject might contain some distinctively moral elements. With this sphere delimited, the remaining moral problems about law have to do, not with the moral evaluation of individuals *within* the legal profession, but with the uncomfortable moral status *of* that profession. These problems, however, need not be viewed as expressing a conflict between an immoral group of lawyers and the rest of a victimized society. Rather, they are problems that people inside and out of the legal profession may attempt to resolve, not as adversaries, but as cooperative individuals with mutual interests in the moral quality of their common society and its institutions.

Notes

1. Gerald J. Postema, "Moral Responsibility in Professional Ethics," *New York University Law Review* 55 (April 1980): 63.
2. I have argued this at length in "Moral Saints," *The Journal of Philosophy* 79 (August 1982): 419–39.
3. This point is often made and discussed by moral philosophers, particularly in connection with Aristotle's moral philosophy. See, e.g., Bernard Williams, *Morality: An Introduction to Ethics* (New York: Harper & Row, 1972), pp. 40–58; and J. L. Mackie, *Ethics: Inventing Right and Wrong* (Harmondsworth, England: Penguin, 1977), pp. 50–59.
4. In this respect, the intraprofessional norms that I advocate seem to me very close to the norms simpliciter that are advocated by Charles Fried in "The Lawyer as Friend: The Moral Foundations of the Lawyer-Client Relation," *Yale Law Journal* 85 (1976): 1060–89. It is curious, however, that the theoretical background that Fried thinks justifies his conclusions is not merely different from but even, in a way, opposed to the one that I am offering. Both Fried and I want to distinguish between moral scruples having to do with using the law in immoral ways as a means of attaining a (moral or immoral) goal and those having to do with using the law in morally acceptable ways for the purpose of attaining an immoral goal. Fried thinks that the lawyer is personally accountable for attending to scruples of the first kind and not accountable at all for attending to scruples of the second kind. I think that the lawyer is intraprofessionally accountable for the first and not intraprofessionally accountable for the second. But my account leaves open the degree to which the lawyer is personally accountable—or, simply, accountable—in the second kind of case.

   Indeed it is hard to understand Fried's position in light of his view that the lawyer is to be regarded on the model of a friend who "adopts (the client's) interests as his own." If one adopts some interests as one's own, it would seem one becomes to that extent personally accountable for them. Thus, if the interests are immoral, one can be personally blamed for having them. If, on the other hand, the lawyer is not to be blamed for the immorality of the client's goals, this would have to be because these goals are *not* identified with the lawyer's goals.
5. For two excellent and provocative discussions about the special circumstances under which a lawyer may be obliged to take on or refuse a client, see Murray L. Schwartz, "The Zeal of the Civil Advocate," and Charles W. Wolfram, "A Lawyer's Duty to Represent Clients, Repugnant and

Otherwise," both in this volume. These discussions do not, however, distinguish between the professional obligations of a lawyer and the moral obligations of a person who is a lawyer.

6. As in the case of *Zabella* v. *Pakel,* 242 F.2d 452 (7th Cir. 1957), much discussed by legal ethicists.

7. An exception must be made for the special role of public prosecutor, which is generally recognized to require the adoption of truth and justice as sole, overriding aims.

8. Reasons to believe that the suggested claims cannot be convincingly defended are offered by David Luban in "The Adversary System Excuse," this volume, and by Alan Goldman in chap. 3 of *The Moral Foundations of Professional Ethics* (Totowa, N.J.: Rowman and Littlefield, 1980).

9. This problem is discussed by Andreas Eshete in "Does a Lawyer's Character Matter?" this volume.

10. It must be admitted that among experts there seems to be tacit understanding that the code is to be read cynically—that is, in a way that exploits all loopholes and ambiguities in the phrasing of the code so as to make a lawyer's failure to accord with a robust interpretation of the code virtually unenforceable.

Questions for Discussion

1. According to Philippa Foot ("Virtues and Vices," p. 297f.), the distinguishing features of virtues are that they engage the will, are beneficial to the possessor and recipient, and correct a temptation to be resisted or a deficiency of motivation. Discuss whether generosity as considered by James D. Wallace meets these three criteria.

2. In "Famine, Affluence, and Morality" (pp. 113f.), Peter Singer argues that we are morally obligated to feed the hungry and that giving charity to the poor is not an act that is above and beyond the call of duty. Given that Singer acts upon the principles he champions, would he be considered generous from Wallace's point of view? Discuss.

3. Do you agree with Richard Taylor that the quality of moral evil is essentially the same in his tales of cruelty? Why or why not?

4. According to Taylor, most people simply know what goodness is when they see it, quite apart from any theory they may have concerning what makes right actions right. Do you agree with this claim? Discuss also his claim that we do not need a theory of morality to recognize goodness any more than we need a theory of physics to appreciate a sunset.

5. Why, according to Annette Baier, can trust sometimes be a vice and not a virtue?

6. Discuss the importance of trust in the light of Aristotle's claim that "if people are friends, they have no need of justice" (*Nicomachean Ethics,* 1155a10).

7. S. I. Benn cites Adolph Eichmann as exemplifying the vice of heteronomous wickedness. Discuss this claim in the light of Eichmann's saying he would go to his death laughing, knowing that he had the murder of millions of Jews on his conscience.

8. Benn seems to think that malignant wickedness is diabolic because the malignantly wicked person desires evil for its own sake. However, a case could be made that the malignantly evil person is not diabolic but desires goodness above all else. He may genuinely want virtue without having to admit that he lacks it, therefore hate virtue for reminding him of the kind of person he is not, and act accordingly. Discuss this claim in the light of Benn's thesis.

9. Jeffrie G. Murphy is sympathetic to the view that forgiveness may, in certain circumstances, be a vice rather than a virtue. Given that forgiveness entails forswearing resentment, does this imply that resentment can be a virtue?

10. According to Murphy, forgiveness is consistent with self-respect if the forgiver can separate the wrongdoer from the wrongdoing. Do you agree? Might forgiveness be inconsistent with self-respect unless the *wrongdoer* can separate herself from her wrong? Discuss.

11. Why does Joshua Halberstam believe that the desire for fame is reasonable but the pursuit of it is not? Do you agree?

12. It has been said that the pursuit of happiness is self-defeating because happiness is achieved when we pursue other activities and accompanies success in them. Might the same be said for the pursuit of fame? Discuss.

13. Lawrence A. Blum believes that friendship is a virtue because friends act for the sake of one another. Suppose, however, that your friend acts immorally. Would friendship still be a virtue under these conditions?

14. Discuss Aristotle's claim that the best kind of friendship is between virtuous people.

15. Thomas E. Hill, Jr., argues that people insensitive to nature betray a lack of humility in that they are unable to overcome their own self-importance. Discuss the plausibility of this claim if one does not believe in God.

16. Hill suggests that one who would ask, "Why *shouldn't* I cover my garden with asphalt?" is not unlike the Nazi who asks, "Why *shouldn't* I make lampshades out of human skin?" since asking the question reveals a defect in the questioner. Do you agree with Hill?

17. According to the studies which Janet Smith cites, the typical aborter has misgivings about having an abortion and this is indicative of a lack of integrity. Might this not equally be indicative of moral ambivalence incidental to moral growth and development? Discuss.

18. Smith deduces that abortion is wrong if the decision to abort is contrary to one's belief that abortion is wrong. Assuming that one believes an act is

wrong and yet performs the act, does it follow that the act *is* wrong or is the morality of an act logically distinguishable from the morality of the agent?

19. Smith seems to think that it is always bad to act against one's moral principles. Michael Stocker ("The Schizophrenia of Modern Ethical Theories," pp. 180f.) suggests the same thought when he says: "Not to be moved by what one values. . . bespeaks a malady of the spirit." Do you agree that it is always bad to violate one's principles or might it depend on the principles one has? In discussing this question, consider the case of Huckleberry Finn whose principles suggested he turn his slave friend in but whose sentiments steered him in the opposite direction.

20. Edmund D. Pellegrino argues that the virtuous physician is one who is habitually disposed to promoting the patient's own good through acts of healing, and who can be relied upon to place the patient's own good above her own. But consider the patient whose own conception of the good includes therapies that are medically suspect or scientifically questionable. Does the physician show virtue in administering such treatments?

21. Given Pellegrino's conception of the virtuous physician, does a physician show virtue when she performs a procedure that violates her moral code? Does she show virtue, for instance, when at the patient's request she performs an abortion or euthanasia even though she believes these acts are wrong?

22. Susan Wolf suggests that a good lawyer is one who fully avails himself of legal means on behalf of a client subject to the moral constraints that attach to these means. And the constraints she thinks attach to these means are the ones that attach to any activity. Do you agree? Is this the lawyer people have in mind when they say, "I need a good lawyer"?

23. It is sometimes said that the traits required by a lawyer's role—guile, aggression, zealousness—are virtues in a lawyer but vices in someone else. If this is true, can a good lawyer be a good person?

24. Is it possible for a lawyer to lose all of her cases and still be considered a good lawyer? Is it possible for a physician to lose all her patients and still be considered a good physician? What do the answers to these questions tell us about the roles of the lawyer and physician?

Selected Bibliography

Adams, Robert M. "The Virtue of Faith." *Faith and Philosophy* 1 (January 1984): 3–15.

Benson, John. "Who Is the Autonomous Man?" *Philosophy* 58 (1983): 5–17.

Berger, Fred. "Gratitude." *Ethics* 85 (July 1975): 298–309.

Boxill, Bernard. "Self-Respect and Protest." *Philosophy and Public Affairs* 6 (Fall 1976): 58–69.

Eshete, Andreas. "Does a Lawyer's Character Matter?" In *The Good Lawyer: Lawyers' Roles and Lawyers' Ethics*, edited by David Luban, 270–85. Savage, Md.: Rowman and Littlefield, 1984.

Farber, Leslie. "On Jealousy." *Commentary* 56 (October 1973): 50–58.

Fingarette, Herbert. *Self-Deception.* New York: Humanities Press, 1969.

Garside, Christine. "Can a Woman Be Good in the Same Way as a Man?" *Dialogue* (Canada) 10 (September 1971): 534–44.

Green, Ronald. "Jewish Ethics and the Virtue of Humility." *Journal of Religious Ethics* 1 (Fall 1973): 53–64.

Haber, Joram Graf. *Forgiveness.* Savage, Md.: Rowman and Littlefield, 1991.

Haber, Joram Graf, and Bernard H. Baumrin. "The Moral Obligations of Lawyers." *The Canadian Journal of Law and Jurisprudence* 1 (January 1988): 105–17.

Halfon, Mark. *Integrity: A Philosophical Inquiry.* Philadephia: Temple University Press, 1989.

Hill, Thomas E., Jr. "Servility and Self-Respect." *The Monist* 62 (January 1979): 87–104.

Horsbrugh, H. J. N. "Prudence." *Proceedings of the Aristotelian Society, Supplementary Volume* 36 (1962): 65–76.

Jefferson, Mark. "What Is Wrong with Sentimentality?" *Mind* 92 (October 1983); 519–29.

Kekes, John. "Wisdom." *American Philosophical Quarterly* 20 (July 1983): 277–86.

May, William F. "The Virtues in a Professional Setting." *Soundings* 67 (Fall 1984): 245–66.

Muyskens, James. "What Is Virtuous about Faith? *Faith and Philosophy* 2 (January 1985): 43–52.

Pincoffs, Edmond. "Virtue, the Quality of Life, and Punishment." *The Monist* 63 (April 1980): 38–50.

Shelp, Earl E. "Courage and Tragedy in Clinical Medicine." *Social Science and Medicine* 18 (1984): 351–60.

Shklar, Judith N. *Ordinary Vices.* Cambridge, Mass.: Harvard University Press, 1984.

Szabodos, Bela. "Hypocrisy." *Canadian Journal of Philosophy* 9 (June 1979): 195–210.

Williams, Bernard. "Justice as a Virtue." In *Essays on Aristotle's Ethics*, edited by Amelie Oksenberg Rorty, 189–200. Berkeley: University of California Press, 1980.

Wren, Thomas E. "Whistle Blowing and Loyalty to One's Friends." In *Police Ethics*, edited by W. Heffernan and T. Stroup. New York: John Jay Press, 1985.

Young, Robert. "The Value of Autonomy." *Philosophical Quarterly* 32 (January 1982): 35–44.

DATE DUE

7/20/08			

DEMCO 38-296